GREEK ISLANDS

1st Edition

Where to Stay and Eat
for All Budgets

Must-See Sights
and Local Secrets

Ratings You Can Trust

Fodor's Travel Publications   New York, Toronto, London, Sydney, Auckland
www.fodors.com

FODOR'S GREEK ISLANDS

Editors: Robert I.C. Fisher, lead editor; Carissa Bluestone, Diana Varvara

Editorial Production: Tom Holton, Astrid deRidder
Editorial Contributors: Alexia Amvrazi, Stephen Brewer, Elizabeth Carson, Jeffrey Carson, Angelike Contis, Natasha Giannousi, Joanna Kakissis, Diane Shugart, Adrian Vrettos
Maps & Illustrations: Mark Stroud, Henry Colomb, Ed Jacobus, David Lindroth, William Wu, *Cartographers*; Robert Blake and Rebecca Baer, *map editors*
Design: Fabrizio LaRocca, *creative director*; Guido Caroti, Siobhan O'Hare, *art directors*; Tina Malaney, Chie Ushio, Ann McBride, *designers*; Melanie Marin, *senior picture editor*; Moon Sun Kim, *cover designer*
Cover Photo: (Santorini Church on the Caldera at Ia, the Cyclades): San Rostro/age fotostock
Production/Manufacturing: Matthew Struble

1st Edition

ISBN 978–1–4000–1936–6

ISSN 1940–3291

SPECIAL SALES

This book is available at special discounts for bulk purchases for sales promotions or premiums. Special editions, including personalized covers, excerpts of existing books, and corporate imprints, can be created in large quantities for special needs. For more information, write to Special Markets/Premium Sales, 1745 Broadway, MD 6-2, New York, New York 10019, or e-mail specialmarkets@randomhouse.com.

AN IMPORTANT TIP & AN INVITATION

Although all prices, opening times, and other details in this book are based on information supplied to us at press time, changes occur all the time in the travel world, and Fodor's cannot accept responsibility for facts that become outdated or for inadvertent errors or omissions. So **always confirm information when it matters**, especially if you're making a detour to visit a specific place. Your experiences—positive and negative— matter to us. If we have missed or misstated something, **please write to us.** We follow up on all suggestions. Contact the Greek Islands editor at editors@fodors.com or c/o Fodor's at 1745 Broadway, New York, NY 10019.

PRINTED IN THE UNITED STATES OF AMERICA
10 9 8 7 6 5 4 3 2

Be a Fodor's Correspondent

Your opinion matters. It matters to us. It matters to your fellow Fodor's travelers, too. And we'd like to hear it. In fact, we need to hear it.

When you share your experiences and opinions, you become an active member of the Fodor's community. That means we'll not only use your feedback to make our books better, but we'll publish your names and comments whenever possible. Throughout our guides, look for "Word of Mouth," excerpts of your unvarnished feedback.

Here's how you can help improve Fodor's for all of us.

Tell us when we're right. We rely on local writers to give you an insider's perspective. But our writers and staff editors—who are the best in the business—depend on you. Your positive feedback is a vote to renew our recommendations for the next edition.

Tell us when we're wrong. We're proud that we update most of our guides every year. But we're not perfect. Things change. Hotels cut services. Museums change hours. Charming cafés lose charm. If our writer didn't quite capture the essence of a place, tell us how you'd do it differently. If any of our descriptions are inaccurate or inadequate, we'll incorporate your changes in the next edition and will correct factual errors at fodors.com immediately.

Tell us what to include. You probably have had fantastic travel experiences that aren't yet in Fodor's. Why not share them with a community of like-minded travelers? Maybe you chanced upon a beach or bistro or B&B that you don't want to keep to yourself. Tell us why we should include it. And share your discoveries and experiences with everyone directly at fodors.com. Your input may lead us to add a new listing or highlight a place we cover with a "Highly Recommended" star or with our highest rating, "Fodor's Choice."

Give us your opinion instantly at our feedback center at www.fodors.com/feedback. You may also e-mail editors@fodors.com with the subject line "Greek Islands Editor." Or send your nominations, comments, and complaints by mail to Greek Islands Editor, Fodor's, 1745 Broadway, New York, NY 10019.

You and travelers like you are the heart of the Fodor's community. Make our community richer by sharing your experiences. Be a Fodor's correspondent.

Kaló taxídi! (Or simply: Happy traveling!)

Tim Jarrell, Publisher

CONTENTS

GREEK ISLANDS IN FOCUS

MAPS

ABOUT THIS BOOK

Our Ratings

Sometimes you find terrific travel experiences and sometimes they just find you. But usually the burden is on you to select the right combination of experiences. That's where our ratings come in.

As travelers we've all discovered a place so wonderful that its worthiness is obvious. And sometimes that place is so unique that superlatives don't do it justice: you just have to be there to know. These sights, properties, and experiences get our highest rating, **Fodor's Choice**, indicated by orange stars throughout this book.

Black stars highlight sights and properties we deem **Highly Recommended**, places that our writers, editors, and readers praise again and again for consistency and excellence.

By default, there's another category: any place we include in this book is by definition worth your time, unless we say otherwise. And we will.

Disagree with any of our choices? Care to nominate a place or suggest that we rate one more highly? Visit our feedback center at www.fodors.com/feedback.

Budget Well

Hotel and restaurant price categories from ¢ to $$$$ are defined in the opening pages of each chapter. For attractions, we always give standard adult admission fees; reductions are usually available for children, students, and senior citizens. Want to pay with plastic? **AE, D, DC, MC, V** following restaurant and hotel listings indicate whether American Express, Discover, Diner's Club, MasterCard, and Visa are accepted.

Restaurants

Unless we state otherwise, restaurants are open for lunch and dinner daily. We mention dress only when there's a specific requirement and reservations only when they're essential or not accepted.

Hotels

Hotels have private bath, phone, TV, and air-conditioning (unless noted otherwise) and operate on the European Plan (aka EP, meaning without meals), unless specified they use the Continental Plan (CP, with a Continental breakfast), Breakfast Plan (BP, with a full breakfast), or Modified American Plan (MAP, with breakfast and dinner), or are all-inclusive (AI, including all meals

and most activities). We always list facilities but not whether you'll be charged an extra fee to use them, so inquire when booking.

Many Listings

★	Fodor's Choice
★	Highly recommended
⊠	Physical address
⊹	Directions
⬧	Mailing address
☎	Telephone
🖶	Fax
⊕	On the Web
✍	E-mail
🖃	Admission fee
☉	Open/closed times
Ⓜ	Metro stations
▭	Credit cards

Hotels & Restaurants

🛏	Hotel
➾	Number of rooms
⌂	Facilities
⦿	Meal plans
✕	Restaurant
⌂	Reservations
⟍	Smoking
🍷	BYOB
✕🛏	Hotel with restaurant that warrants a visit

Outdoors

🏌	Golf
⛺	Camping

Other

☾	Family-friendly
⇨	See also
⊠	Branch address
☞	Take note

Experience Greece

Caryatids of the Erechtheion, Acropolis, Athens.

WORD OF MOUTH

"Hello to the Fodorites who patiently helped and answered my questions about Santorini and Mykonos (travelerjan, Heimdall, Brotherlee love). Well, my husband and I got back two weeks ago and we loved Greece! What a great country! The people were friendly, the country was beautiful and clean, and the food delicious. We spent one week on the islands and another week on the mainland. We will most definitely return!!"

—nilady

WHAT'S NEW

Arriving in a taxi (sorry, no chariots), today's traveler may be surprised to find Athenians garbed by Armani and driving the latest sports car. Shouldn't they look like truncated marble statues in the Acropolis Museum and have brows habitually crowned with wild olive? Incongruous as it may seem, most natives have two arms attached to the torso in the normal place. And if visitors still arrive nurtured on the truth and beauty of Keats' Grecian Urn, they shouldn't be puzzled by the locals talking about the latest hipsterious nightspot.

After all, only the most scholarly bookworm still believes that Greece is a dusty museum. The country is now alive with vibrant trends and styles, especially after the mammoth 2004 Olympic Games were held in Athens. Everything old—even 25 centuries old—is new again. While still an agelessly beautiful land, the post-Olympic "European" Greece is burgeoning with boutique hotels, hot restaurants, and sophisticated nightlife that challenges the Zorba-era conceptions of the spartan Aegean. To get you acquainted with the "new" Greece, here's a rundown of the topics the natives are busy discussing in neighborhood tavernas or, as the case may be, the latest nouvelle restaurants.

Burning Issues

Scorched earth throughout Greece is a grim reminder of the summer of 2007, when massive fires killed at least 63 people, destroyed up to 100 villages, and burned as many as 6 million acres. You don't have to venture far into the countryside to see the evidence—most of the forests on the slopes of Mt. Parnitha, visible from the Acropolis, went up in flames, as did the pine groves that surround ancient Olympia. The fires have fueled outrage in Greece about the lack of a government fire-prevention strategy and launched endless speculation about what caused the fires.

Some of the hottest temperatures on record following a winter drought certainly contributed, but many Greeks suspect arson, pointing their fingers at developers who take advantage of legal maneuvering to build on forest land that has been cleared by fire and reclassified as abandoned farmland. Changes to close the loopholes are afoot, but real and lasting reform might be as slow to come to fruition as the new trees that are being planted in the fire-ravaged regions.

Pride & Hubris at the Acropolis

The new Acropolis Museum, opening in stages in mid-to-late 2008, has awakened a sense of pride in Greeks, happy to see many of their country's greatest treasures housed in appropriately stunning quarters (designed by cutting-edge Swiss architect Bernard Tschumi).

As with many events in Greece, though, the good news is laced with a liberal dose of controversy. One concerns what's *not* on display: the Parthenon Marbles. The opening of the museum is rekindling interest in demands for return of the marble sculptures that British diplomat Lord Elgin had removed from the Acropolis in 1803 and which now enjoy pride of place at the British Museum. For the time being, the Acropolis Museum has installed copies of the friezes and strikingly covered them with transparent veils to symbolize the absence of the originals. Many Athenians are also outraged at the museum's plans to destroy two 1930s-era buildings that block the view of the Acropolis from the café and lower-floor galleries—critics

see this as a heedless act of hubris on the part of museum officials, a serious offense in ancient Athens that clearly still rankles the Greek spirit.

What Are They Going to Take Away Next, My Worry Beads?

Greece has imposed some antismoking measures, but in general these have been as wan as a menthol light—you'll probably find it hard to believe this nation of smokers has ever made an honest attempt to quit. After all, how do you take prohibitions that ban smoking in most public places (and also on the job for municipal employees) seriously when it's common to see everyone from bus drivers to postal workers with cigarettes dangling out of their mouths?

Overall, Greece has the highest prevalence of smoking in the European Union—an estimated 40% of Greeks puff away regularly, and some estimates put the number as lofty as 60%. Stakes are getting tragically high as smoking takes an increasing and costly toll on national health, and efforts to help Greeks kick the habit are stepping up. One deterrent that's worked well in Ireland, England, and other northern climes—making smokers step outside if they want to light up—will probably not work in Greece, where socializing is an outdoor affair for most of the year anyway.

Can Slow Food Get Any Slower?

It seems that Greek cooking might have already set the gold standard for the Slow Food movement (first founded in Italy back in the 1980s and now a worldwide fashion), part of whose credo is to use local produce, grains, meats, and fish. After all, even the simplest taverna will use only fresh ingredients and the chef is often a grandma who's following her grandma's recipes.

Isn't *magirefta*, the Greek way of cooking a casserole in the morning and letting it warm and steep all day, the very essence of "slow"? Yet, perhaps to uproot the albeit rather shallowly planted presence of fastfoudadika, the Slow Food movement has many practitioners in Greece. The not-for-profit Zante's Feast organization (⊕www.zante-feast.org), for instance, lures foodies to the Ionian island of Zakynthos for sessions in healthful cooking. Elsewhere, an increasing number of restaurants are making a big show of using fresh local ingredients in traditional dishes, and others just do so without fanfare, as they have for years—either way, enjoying a "slow" meal full of tasty fresh ingredients is still something you can count on in Greece.

The Shock of the New

A country where the spotlight shines most brightly on ancient art got a sometimes shocking glimpse of what contemporary artists are up to when the First Athens Biennial opened at Technopolis in the Gazi district in the fall of 2007. The show was called "Destroy Athens," but given public reaction to many of the provocatively violent and sexually explicit pieces, "Annoy Athens" or "Confuse Athens" might have been more apt. No one seems to have been able to determine exactly what the work had to do with the title or with the exhibition's stated mission to "deny the precondition of collectivity and abolish any connection or relationship." Hmmmm. Well, until the Second Biennial brings more work to town in 2009, how about a visit to the new IKEA megastore near the airport? Now, there's a surefire hit.

WHAT'S WHERE

3 Athens. The capital has greeted the new millennium with new swaths of parkland, a sleek subway, and other spiffy and long-overdue municipal makeovers. But for 5 million Athenians and their 15 million annual visitors, it's still the tried-and-true pleasures that put the spin on urban life here: sitting in an endless parade of cafés, strolling the streets of the Plaka and other old neighborhoods, and, most of all, admiring the glorious remnants of one of the greatest civilizations the West ever produced, such as the Acropolis, the Agora, and the Theater of Herodes Atticus.

4 The Saronic Gulf Islands. When Athenians want a break, they often make a quick crossing to the idyllic islands of the Saronic Gulf. You're well advised to follow suit, and all the better if your island of choice is Hydra, where what's here (stone houses set above a gorgeously festive harbor) and what's not (cars) provide a relaxing retreat. Aegina is noted for its medieval Palaia-chora (Old Town) and ancient Temple of Aphaia; while Spetses has a time-burnished town hiding treasures like Bouboulina's House.

5 The Sporades. Island-hopping the northern Sporades, strung from Mt. Pelion to the center of the Aegean, delivers quintessential Greek-island pleasures: boat journeys, pretty harbors, villages spilling down hillsides like giant sugar cubes, Byzantine monasteries, and silent paths, cobbled in the last millennium, where the tinkle of goat bells may be the only sound for miles. Weekenders don't make it far beyond Skiathos, but Skopelos has great beaches, and Skyros is washed by some of the clearest waters in Greece.

6 Corfu. Temperate, multithued Corfu—of emerald mountains; turquoise waters lapping rocky coves; ocher and pink buildings; shimmering silver olive leaves; puffed red, yellow, and orange parasails; scarlet roses, bougainvillea, lavender wisteria, and jacaranda spread over cottages—could have inspired impressionism. The island has a history equally as colorful, reflecting the commingling of Corinthians, Romans, Goths, Normans, Venetians, French, Russians, and British. First stop, of course, is Corfu town—looking for all the world like a stage set for a Verdi opera.

WHAT'S WHERE

7 The Cyclades. The ultimate Mediterranean archipelago, the Cyclades easily conjure up the magical words of "Greek islands." If you long for azure skies, warm seas, and whitewashed peasant architecture, these are isles of quintessential plenty. Santorini, with its ravishing caldera, is the most picturesque; Mykonos, with its sexy jet-set lifestyle, takes the prize for hedonism. Mountainous Folegandros, verdant Naxos, bustling Syros, idyllic Sifnos, church-studded Tinos, and Brad Pitt–discovered Antiparos have their own distinct charms, and all center around ancient Delos, birthplace of Apollo.

8 Crete. Crete is the southernmost and largest island, and the claims to superlatives don't stop there. Here, too, are some of Greece's tallest mountains, its deepest gorge, many of its best beaches, and a wealth of man-made wonders—the copious remains of Minoans, Romans, Byzantines, Turks, and Venetians. The Palace of Knossos is the incomparable monument of ancient Minoan culture. If these charms don't cast a spell, the island's upland plateaus, remote seaside hamlets, and quiet mountain villages will.

9 Rhodes & the Dodecanese. Wrapped enticingly around the shores of Turkey, the Dodecanese ("Twelve Islands") are the easternmost holdings of Greece. Their key position in the sea lanes of Asia Minor have attracted some notable visitors. St. John the Divine received his Revelations on Patmos, Hippocrates established a healing center on Kos, and the Crusader Knights of St. John lavished their wealth on palaces in Rhodes. The recent legacy of legions of vacationers on Rhodes and Kos is glitzy resort life, but on Symi, and some of the other isles, life seems to be unfazed by outsiders.

10 Northern Islands. Each of these green and gold islands is distinct: Though ravaged by fire, Chios retains an eerie beauty and fortified villages, old mansions, Byzantine monasteries, and stenciled-wall houses; Lesbos, Greece's third-largest island and birthplace of legendary artists and writers, is dense with gnarled olive groves and dappled with mineral springs; and lush, mountainous Samos, land of wine and honey, whispers of the classical wonders of antiquity.

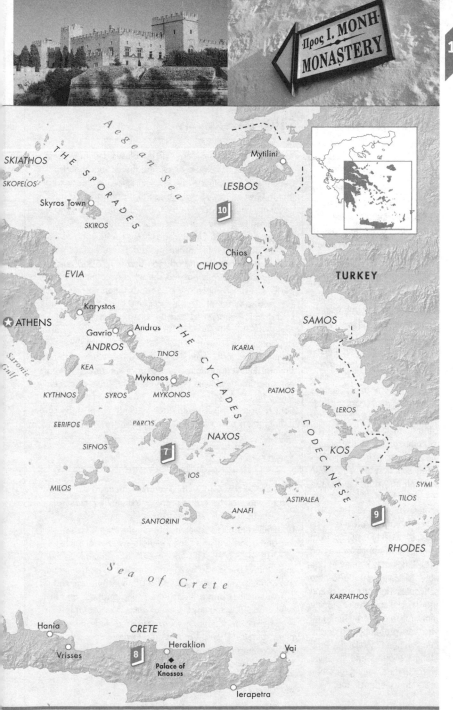

GREEK ISLANDS PLANNER

Don't Miss the Boat

Greece's extensive ferry system (see map on p. 65) provides the best way to get from island to island, an experience that can make getting around one of the highlights of a trip. Boats from Piraeus and other mainland ports serve virtually every island; boat travel between islands is also frequent; and more and more high-speed hydrofoils are taking over routes, cutting travel times in half. On the downside, it's not necessarily easy to plan boat travel. Individual lines have Web sites (⇨ Boat & Ferry travel sections in each regional chapter of this guide), but in the absence of centralized listings it's difficult to compare alternative schedules and prices. Travel agencies often sell tickets for just one line and may not be willing to tell you about a competitor's routes. What to do? The GNTO office in Athens provides listings of weekly sailings from Piraeus, and tourist offices on the islands may or may not be able to give you up-to-date schedules. Harbor masters and tourist police often provide more-reliable information, and you can probably gather the info you need by taking a stroll along the docks and speaking with vendors selling tickets—that's an experience, too.

Drive Defensively

You've probably considered all the pluses. Driving makes it easier to reach remote ruins, find the perfect slip of a beach, see the countryside. Car-rental fees are not exorbitant in Greece, on par with those in North America, and gasoline, while expensive by U.S. standards, is a bargain compared to prices in Western Europe. But, are you really ready to tackle Greek roads? Greece has one of the highest accident rates in Europe, a dubious distinction shared with Ireland and Portugal, and after a few minutes on the road it's pretty easy to see why. Accounting for the perils, not surprisingly, are bad roads (often narrow, poorly surfaced, and full of hairpin turns and blind corners) and bad drivers (who speed and are often reckless and aggressive behind the wheel). In some places you can add stubborn, won't-get-out-of-the-road livestock and slowpoke farm vehicles to the watch-out-fors. So, hone your defensive driving skills—approach any crossroads carefully, keep in mind that many drivers pass on the right, drive at or below speed limits, slow down at curves. You'll have more cautions to add to this list with each passing milepost. Be sure to heed them.

Gear

Outside Athens, Greek dress tends to be middle of the road—you won't see torn jeans or extremely expensive suits, though locals tend to dress up for nightclubs and bouzoukia joints. In summer bring lightweight, casual clothing and good walking shoes. A light sweater or jacket, or a shawl, is a must for cool evenings, especially in the mountains. There's no need for rain gear in high summer, but don't forget sunglasses and a sun hat. Be prepared for cooler weather and some rain in spring and fall, and in winter add a warm coat. Casual attire is acceptable everywhere except in the most expensive restaurants in large cities, but you should be prepared to dress conservatively when visiting churches or monasteries. It's not appropriate to show a lot of bare arm and leg; anyone wearing shorts must cover up, as must women in pants, in some stricter monasteries.

Rooms to Spare

Unless you're visiting Athens or a resort at the height of the tourist season, you'll probably not have a hard time finding a room in Greece. The issue is finding a place you'll enjoy. Chances are you won't want to stay in one of the banal hotels geared to package tourism that have marred many a Greek shoreline, and you will want certain amenities—not necessarily luxuries, mind you, but a terrace, a view of the sea or the mountains, a fridge to keep water and snacks cool. By and large, prices for high-quality accommodations nationwide have reached an almost equal standard—one that doesn't differ that significantly from prices for same-level accommodations in Athens.

When it comes to making reservations, it is probably wise to book at least one month in advance for the months of June, July, and September, and ideally even two to three months in advance for the high season, from late July to the end of August, especially when booking top-end hotels in high-profile destinations like Santorini and Hydra. Sometimes during off-season you can bargain down the official prices (rumor has it to as much as a quarter of the price). The most advisable method is to politely propose a price that's preferable to you, and persevere. The response you get will depend largely on the length of your stay, the hotel's policy, and on the season in question. When booking, it's worth asking whether the hotel provides transportation from the airport/port as part of their services. If you're not certain about directions, ask a travel agent at the port/airport for detailed directions. For low-cost accommodation, consider Greece's ubiquitous "rooms to rent," bed-and-breakfasts without the breakfast. You can count on a clean room, often with such amenities as a terrace and a private bath, at a *very* reasonable price, in the range of €40–€50 for two. Look for signs in any Greek town or village; or, let the proprietors find you—they have a knack for spotting strangers who look like they might need a bed for the night. When renting a room, take a good look first and be sure to check the bathroom before you commit. If there are extra beds in the room, clarify in advance that the amount agreed on is for the entire room—owners occasionally try to put another person in the same room. When approached by one of the touts who meet the island ferries, make sure he or she tells you the location of the rooms being pushed, and look before you commit. Avoid places on main roads or near all-night discos. Rates vary tremendously from month to month; in the off-season, rooms may cost half of what they do in August.

When Less is Not More...

Though Greece is becoming more liberal socially, old standards still prevail, especially among the middle-aged and elderly. Some Western habits can cause offense, and the big no-no's include:

Showing public displays of attention. Greeks hug, stroll arm and arm, kiss each cheek in greeting, but an amorous smooch or wandering hand will raise eyebrows.

Baring it all. Nudity is common on Greek beaches, but it's a question of where you decide to drop trou this is usually appropriate only at the far ends of a strand, away from the areas where Greek families congregate. Topless sunbathing is permissible, but again, discretion is advised.

Showing legs and arms. Appendages, especially female, should be well covered when entering monasteries and churches. An attendant will usually be waiting near the entrance to drape the under-clad in cloaks or skirtlike garments. Women might want to bring along a wrap or large scarf for such occasions.

To help you decipher the complexity of Greek culture, read the excellent *Exploring the Greek Mosaic*, by Benjamin Broome (Intercultural Press, 1996), which thoughtfully analyzes Greece's social landscape and provides insights that are still valuable today.

GREECE TODAY

Being Part of the European Union (E.U.)

It wasn't too long ago that a Greek village was, well, Greek. If there were any outsiders, they were transplants from the other side of the island. But now that E.U. membership has made it easier for residents of other countries to buy property in Greece, properties that have been in Greek families for generations are suddenly vacation getaways for Klaus and Gudrun and Colin and Priscilla. It's common to hear grumblings that the foreigners are snapping up property that's the birthright of Greeks, but no one seems to be complaining about the new influx of cash the newcomers are pouring into local economies. In a case of good things coming to those who wait, Greek women are coming out ahead in many land deals. By tradition, sons inherited flat, farmable land, while daughters received unusable parcels on hillsides—that is, the "view property" that's now going for top euro.

With membership in the E.U., English, the language of tourism, has grown in popularity. That noted, you should still carry a phrase book, because your hosts will appreciate a greeting, thank you, or other occasional kind word in Greek. Also have on hand a list (such as the one at the back of this book) that transliterates the Greek alphabet—this will be helpful in deciphering street names and road signs that are only in Greek (and many signs on country roads still are).

Government & Politics

Greece, it's worth remembering, has only been a bona-fide democracy since the mid-1970s (not forgetting the fact that it invented the concept back in 5th century BC Athens). After years of civil war and military dictatorship, many Greeks aren't so much interested in the politicians who come and go—currently the moderate New Democrats are holding on by their fingernails—as they are in some ages-old issues, most of them having to do with the country's uneasy relationships with its neighbors.

Names not to mention unless you have a couple of hours to listen include: Albania, homeland of more than a million immigrants who have flooded into Greece in recent years; Turkey, which for much of the 20th century seemed about to pounce and invade Greece and did indeed persecute Greeks in Turkey on more than one occasion; Cyprus, still uneasily divided between the Greeks and Turks; and the Former Yugoslavian Republic of Macedonia, which Greeks think has no right to use the name of one of their country's most historic regions, birthplace of Alexander the Great.

The Economy

It's a good thing Greeks are optimistic by nature, because the economic news is not particularly sunny. Greece has a huge deficit; unemployment is high; shipping—the mainstay of Greek wealth for centuries—is flat; and that leaves tourism and agriculture, both of which are volatile. The average Greek is likely to gripe about increases in the cost of living, being in debt (credit cards and mortgages were unheard of in Greece until about a decade ago), and how hard it is to find a decent job. At the same time, many Greeks are enjoying cars, second homes, and other bourgeois perks they've never had before.

As a traveler to Greece, you'll find that the country is a lot more expensive than it was even a decade ago, but it's still a bar-

gain compared to other places in Europe. You can, of course, spend a lot of money if you choose to live in the lap of luxury, but you can find comfortable lodgings for less than €100 a night for a double and dinner for two needn't clock in at more than €30. The savings will be welcome, because you'll spend a lot of money to get to Greece—as much as $1,500 or $2,000 from New York's J.F.K. airport at the height of the summer season. A lot of travelers take advantage of airline frequent-flyer programs for this trip, but if you want to use miles, make your plans as much as a year in advance—the free seats fly out the door at supersonic speed.

People

You don't have to be a sociologist to note some pretty stellar qualities of the Greek character. For one thing, Greeks are generous, even to the tourists who besiege them—they will often offer a plate of cookies or a bottle of home-brewed *raki* to a traveler, just to create a bond and establish a level of comfort. They are family oriented, to say the least—it's still common for men and women to live with their parents until they marry, and actually, marriage is not necessarily a reason to move out, with extended families living together all their lives. Which brings us to the relationships between men and women, which is, like many aspects of Greek life, somewhat complex. While Greek men might swagger around in what outwardly can seem to be a male-dominated society, women run the home, often take a partnership role in family businesses, and—now that the Greek birthrate is one of the lowest in the E.U., freeing women to pursue careers—are an increasing presence in the white-collar workplace.

Greeks pamper their children, and they'll extend the same affection to yours and probably spoil them rotten. Among other privileges, kids can wander freely around restaurants as you linger over a meal, play safely in many squares and other car-free zones, and stay up late (it's not unusual to see a family enjoying a round of ice cream around midnight on a hot summer evening). Many beaches are family oriented, with shallow waters and concessions that rent floats and other water toys. Young travelers will enjoy wandering around ruins, in limited doses, and will probably be intrigued by stories of gods and goddesses—introducing them to mythology before the trip will enhance their visits to Mt. Olympus, Delphi, and other godly realms.

Culture & Other Pursuits

The father in *My Big Fat Greek Wedding* (who is so quick to point out the Greek roots of any English word) is not really Hollywood hyperbole. Proud of their language and its precision in capturing the complexities of emotion and nuance, Greeks often discuss etymology—as well as the Peloponnesian Wars, Homeric descriptions, and other aspects of their illustrious heritage. They are eager audiences at the many performances of ancient dramas throughout the country, proud of such recent literary lions as Odysseus Elytis and Nikos Kazantzakis, and put a high value on education—the culture that gave rise to the schools of Socrates and Aristotle offers a free university education. At the same time, Greeks are many-time champs in European basketball, and the enthusiasm for football has led to spurts of violence that put fans firmly in league with other European soccer hooligans.

TOP GREECE ATTRACTIONS

The Acropolis

(C) The great emblem of classical Greece has loomed above Athens (whose harbor of Piraeus is gateway to all the Greek islands) for 2,500 years. Even from afar, the sight of the Parthenon—the great marble temple that the 5th century BC statesmen Pericles conceived to crown the site—stirs strong feelings about the achievements and failings of Western Civilization.

Corfu

(B) More than a million visitors a year answer the call of the island that inspired the landscapes of Shakespeare's *The Tempest*. Historically, these admirers are in good company—Normans, Venetians, Turks, Napoléon Bonaparte, and the British have all occupied Corfu, leaving fortresses, seaside villas, and an unforgettable patina of cosmopolitan elegance.

Hydra

This barren island, just a hop and skip away from Athens, is home to one of Greece's most picturesque ports, immortalized in all its Hollywoodian splendor when Sophia Loren emerged from its waters in the 1960 film *Boy on a Dolphin*. Today, sophisticated travelers head here to enjoy the 19th-century merchant's mansions and the white-and-periwinkle cafés.

Knossos

(F) Crete will introduce you to the marvels of the Minoans, the first great European civilization that flourished around 1500 BC. First stop is Knossos, the massive palace complex of King Minos, then it's on to the nearby archaeological museum in Heraklion, where the playful frescoes that once lined the royal chambers show just how urbane these early forbearers were.

Mykonos

(A) Backpackers and jet-setters alike share the beautiful beaches and the Dionysian nightlife—this island is not called the St-Tropez of the Aegean without reason—but the old ways of life continue undisturbed in fishing ports and along mazelike town streets. Not only are the hotels and cafés picture-perfect, the famous windmills actually seem to be posing for your camera.

Old Rhodes Town

(E) The famed Colossus of Rhodes may have toppled, but the sturdy walls and palaces the Knights of St. John built in the wake of the Crusades have fared better. Protected as a UNESCO World Heritage Site, this remarkable medieval assemblage bespeaks of the vast wealth of the knights, who for all their might lost their fiefdom to the 300 Ottoman ships of Süleyman the Magnificent in 1522.

Patmos

The relics, ornate icons, silver artifacts, and rich vestments on view at the medieval monastery of St. John the Theologian are among the great cultural treasures of the Orthodox church. The well-educated monks had the buildings decorated with fine sculptures and other artwork. Unfortunately, only men are allowed to visit.

Santorini

(D) One of the world's most picturesque islands cradles the sunken caldera of a volcano that last erupted around 1600 BC. To merely link the phenomenon to the Atlantis myth and the Minoan collapse misses the point—what matters is the ravishing sight of the multicolor cliffs rising 1,100 feet out of sparkling blue waters, a visual treat that makes the heart skip a beat or two.

QUINTESSENTIAL GREECE

If you want to get a sense of Greek culture and indulge in some of its pleasures, start by familiarizing yourself with the rituals of daily life. These are a few highlights—things you can take part in with relative ease.

The Greek Spirit

"Come back tomorrow night. We're always here at this time," is the gracious invitation that usually terminates the first meeting with your outgoing Greek hosts. The Greeks are open, generous, and above all, full of a frank, probing curiosity about you, the foreigner. They do not have a word for standoffishness, and their approach is direct: American? British? Where are you staying? Are you married or single? How much do you make? Thus, with the subtlety of an atomic icebreaker, the Greeks get to know you, and you, perforce, get to know them.

In many villages there seems to always be at least one English-speaking person for whom it is a matter of national pride and honor to welcome you and, perhaps, insist on lending you his only mule to scale a particular mountain, then offer a tasty dinner meal. This is the typically Greek, deeply moving hospitality which money cannot buy and for which, of course, no money could be offered in payment.

Worry Beads

Chances are that your host—no doubt, luxuriantly moustached—will greet you as he counts the beads of what appears to be amber rosaries. They are *komboloia* or "worry beads," a legacy from the Turks, and Greeks click them on land, on the sea, in the air to ward off that insupportable silence that threatens to reign whenever conversation lags. Shepherds do it, cops do it, merchants in their shops do it. More aesthetic than thumb-twiddling, less

expensive than smoking, this Queeg-like obsession indicates a tactile sensuousness, characteristic of a people who have produced some of the Western world's greatest sculpture.

Siestas

When does Greece slow down? In Athens, it seems never. But head out to the countryside villages and you'll find another tradition, the siesta—the only time Greeks stop talking and really sleep it seems. Usually after lunch and until 4 PM, barmen drowse over their bars, waiters fall asleep in chairs, and all good Greeks drift off into slumber wherever they are, like the enchanted courtiers of Sleeping Beauty. Then, with a yawn, a sip of coffee, and a large glass of ice water, Greece goes back to the business of the day.

Folk Music & Dance

It's a rare traveler to Greece who does not encounter Greek song and folk dancing, sure to be vigorous, colorful, spontaneous, and authentic. The dances are often rooted in history or religion, or both: the *zeimbekiko,* a man's solo dance, is performed with a pantherlike grace and an air of mystical awe, the dancer, with eyes riveted to the floor, repeatedly bending down to run his hand piously across the ground. The music, played by bouzoukis, large mandolins, is weighted with melancholy. The most-popular, however, are the *kalamatianos* and *tsamikos.* The former is performed in a circle, the male leader waving a handkerchief, swirling and lunging acrobatically. The latter, more martial in spirit, represents men going to battle, all to the sound of cries of *opa!* Remember, plate-smashing is now verboten. Today, a more-loving tribute is paid—many places have flower vendors, whose blooms are purchased to be thrown upon the dancers as they perform.

IF YOU LIKE

Ancient Splendors

The sight greets you time and again in Greece—a line of solid, sun-bleached masonry silhouetted against a clear blue sky. If you're lucky, a cypress waves gently to one side. What makes the scene all the more fulfilling is the realization that a kindred spirit looked up and saw the same temple or theater some 2,000 or more years ago. Temples, theaters, statues, a stray Doric column or two, the fragment of a Corinthian capital: these traces of the ancients are thick on the ground in Greece, from the more than 3,000-year-old **Minoan Palace of Knossos** on the island of Crete to such relatively "new" monuments as the **Parthenon.** You can prepare yourself by reading up on mythology, history, and Greek architecture, but get used to the fact that coming upon these magnificent remnants of ancient civilizations is likely to send a chill up your spine every time you see them.

Palace of Phaistos, near Ayii Deka, Crete. The ancients knew where to build: the evocative ruins of one of the greatest Minoan palaces sit on a hill with the sea on one side and mountains on the other.

Delos, off Mykonos, the Cyclades. Birthplace of Apollo, Delos is the sacred center around which the 29 Cyclades islands form a rough circle (*kyklos* in Greek). Extensive ruins include the famous Avenue of the Lions, where five archaic beasts (Naxian work of the 7th century) are symbolical guardians of the sanctuary.

Temple of Hera in Heraion, Samos, Northeast Aegean. The tyrant Polycrates built this temple where the Samians worshipped their patron goddess, Hera. Pythagoras, Aesop, and Anthony and Cleopatra all visited.

Majestic Monasteries

A legacy of the great Byzantine era, and often aligned with great historic churches of the Greek Orthodox church, the monasteries of Greece seem as spiritual and as peaceful as when the land was strode by St. John. A religious mystique hangs over many of these island retreats, infusing them with a sense of calm that you will appreciate even more when escaping from party-central towns like Mykonos or overcrowded beaches. The natural beauty and calm of many of these places, many visitors find, heal your body and soul, revitalizing you for the rest of your trip.

Monastery of St. John the Theologian, Patmos. On the hill overlooking Hora is this retreat built to commemorate St. John in the 11th century—not far away is the cave where he wrote the text of *Revelation,* near the Monastery of the Apocalypse.

Chrysopigi, Sifnos, the Cyclades. The island of Sifnos has an array of stunningly perched monasteries, including this one, set on its own rocky promontory; residents call it Paradise and you can actually overnight here in guest rooms.

Profitis Ilias, Sifnos, the Cyclades. Also on Sifnos is this Byzantine extravaganza that sits atop the island's highest mountain. After touring the interior with a monk, take in the panoramic views which stop all conversation.

Evangelistria, Skiathos, the Sporades. Sitting on Skiathos's highest point, not far from the town of Lalaria, is this late-18th-century jewel, looming above a gorge and set with a magnificent church with three domes.

Natural Wonders

Some countries have serene pastures and unobtrusive lakes, environments beautiful in a subtle way. Not Greece. Its landscapes seem put on Earth to astound outright, and often the intertwined history and spiritual culture are equally powerful. This vibrant modern nation is a land of majestic mountains whose slopes housed the ancient gods long before they nestled Byzantine monasteries or ski resorts. The country's sapphire-rimmed islands served as a cradle of great civilizations before they became playgrounds for sailors and beach lovers. If there are no temples to the ancient gods on many of the mountains on the Greek islands, the looming summits that seem to reach into the heavens, impressive from any perspective, inspired the Greeks to worship natural forces. Many islands have ancient goat and donkey trails that are sublime hikes; prime walking months are April and May, when temperatures are reasonable, wildflowers seem to cover every surface, and birds are on their migratory wing.

Samaria Gorge, Hania, Crete. From Omalos a zigzag path descends steeply 2,500 feet into the tremendous Samaria gorge that splits the cliffs here for 13 km (8 mi) down to Ayia Roumeli on the Libyan Sea. Catch views of the Cretan *kri-kri* goat near the famous "Iron Gates" stone passageway.

The flooded caldera, Santorini, the Cyclades. What may be the most beautiful settlements in the Cyclades straddle the wondrous crescent of cliffs, striated in black, pink, brown, white, and pale green, rising 1,100 feet over the haunting, wine-color Aegean Sea.

The Most Beautiful Towns & Villages

Historic, simple, famous, nondescript, or perfectly preserved: almost any Greek village seems to possess that certain balance of charm and mystique that takes your breath away. The sight of miragelike, white clusters of houses appearing alongside blue waters or tumbling down cliffs and hillsides is one of the top allures of any trip here. Villages are awash in cubical, whitewashed houses—often built atop another along mazelike streets (designed to confound invaders). Add in distinctive architectural landmarks—a Byzantine cathedral, a Venetian 16th-century kastro (or fortress), and monasteries that seem sculpted of zabaglione custard—and these villages and towns often look like unframed paintings that belong in anyone's National Gallery.

Rethymnon, Crete. A Venetian *fortessa* rests on a hill above this city, where cobblestone alleyways squirm their way through Turkish and Italianate houses. Bypass the newer parts of town to stroll through the Venetian harbor, packed solid with atmospheric cafés and shops.

Ia, Santorini, the Cyclades. Here is where you will find the cubical white houses you've dreamed of, and a sunset that is unsurpassed.

Hydra, the Saronic Gulf Islands. The chicoscenti steal away to this harbor beauty, set with crumbling 19th-century merchant's mansions, joyously festive waterside cafés, and some Hollywood pixie dust (Sophia Loren filmed *Boy on a Dolphin* here).

SUNBELIEVABLE!: GREECE'S TOP BEACHES

Greece is ringed by 15,000 km (9,000 mi) of shoreline, a geographic blessing for sunseekers who pay homage to Helios and Poseidon and bask on seemingly endless expanses of sand. Call it hedonism if you will—after all, that's a Greek term.

Greeks are very accepting of *xéni* (foreigners) and tend to overlook our strange beach-going habit of seeking out patches of sand as far from the crowds as possible. For Greeks, the beach is an extension of the *platia* (square) or the *kafenio* (café)—it's another place to gather, gossip, catch up on local news, argue about politics, play a game of *tavli*, keep an eye on the neighbors, or enjoy a meal in a beachside taverna. Socializing isn't confined to the sand, either—don't be surprised to hear animated chatter emanating from a sea full of bobbing heads.

The sea is sometimes full of other things, including entire ancient sites—who can forget Roger Moore's and Carole Bouchet's underwater swim through a Greek temple in *For Your Eyes Only*? That should remind you that snorkeling gear is handy on almost any Greek beach and a necessity to see the sunken ancient city of Olous off the shores of Crete's Elounda peninsula. If you venture to Skantzoura, a tiny islet off Alonissos in the Sporades, you'll want to have a pair of binoculars as well—the ruins of the ancient city of Skandyle lie submerged just offshore, and rare falcons and black-headed Aegean seagulls roost in the pines.

But when night falls, the scuba gear gets put away and the Versace sandals come out. Dionysus comes on duty when the sun goes down, presiding over Aegean-style nightlife for which a string of Greek islands are justly popular. Whether the setting is Mykonos, Rhodes, or Corfu, the ingredients are the same—a view of the sea, an international crowd, and the promise that dawn will bring another flawless day.

Life's a Beach

Choosing the best Greek beach is a task of almost mythic proportions—think of Sisyphus rolling his stone up the hill on his never-to-be-completed task: you will continually come upon a stretch of sand that enchants you, then find an even better spot a little farther down the way. No one is going to disagree, though, that these get pretty high scores in the idyllic category.

- **Super Paradise, Mykonos, the Cyclades.** Partly gay, partly nude, almost totally "beautiful peopled" by day, and a party scene by night, this golden strand of international fame is aptly named for beachgoers looking for more than sand and surf.

- **Mavra Volia, Chios, Northern Islands.** A "wine-dark sea" washes the black volcanic shores of a cove nestled between sheltering cliffs—little wonder the strangely appealing place is aptly called "Black Pebbles."

- **Plaka, Naxos, the Cyclades.** The most beautiful beach of all on an island of beautiful beaches is backed by sand dunes and bamboo groves, an exotic setting enhanced by a predictably spectacular sunset almost every evening.

- **Vai and Falasarna, Crete.** Here is where you will find the cubical white houses you've dreamed of, and a sunset that is unsurpassed.

LIVING LIKE THE GODS: TOP HOTELS

The new, post-Olympic, E.U. Greece with its boutique hotels, luxury villas, sybaritic spas, and sophisticated nightlife overturns most of the Zorba-era conceptions of "Spartan" Greece. The days of the bare cottage, the creaky apartment, and the shabby motel have come and gone. Of course, many travelers still want hotels that deliver on the simple—or rather, simpler—life. These chosen Greek getaways may lack worldly amenities but compensate with other luxuries—an abundance of sand and sea, perhaps, or stunning mountain views and other natural enhancements. At these places, the greatest luxury is knowing you don't have to do anything except maybe notice how the water in the pool color-coordinates the sky. But, today, Greece has also a much more stylish side, and not only in Mykonos and Santorini.

Some new Greek resort xanadus would not only please the gods but might even make them blush a bit. Several such temples of hedonism, including the Elounda Mare and the Elounda Beach are nestled on the Elounda peninsula on the coast of Crete. Others, such as the Princess on Skiathos, are set amid a flurry of resort action and nightlife. At their skyward rates, you expect world-class service and accommodation, but the vibe also comes with an easygoing elegance that is distinctly Greek, plus amenities that set the gold standard. Satellite TV, Wi-Fi, gyms, bars, restaurants, lounges—all these are to be taken for granted at top resorts. Some of the other amenities to expect include: your own villa or bungalow, swimming pool, and slip of beach or waterside terrace; a sumptuous marble bathroom with whirlpool, steam room, and/or sauna; a spa with treatment pools and a full range of services; tennis courts and golf courses; a full array of water sports like windsurfing, parasailing, snorkeling, and boating; and a helipad for those harried, overworked CEOs. Although accommodations in Greece can vary from grand hotel to country house, all happily provide the quintessentially Greek quality of *filoxenia,* or welcome—easygoing, heartfelt hospitality.

Greek Chic

- **Aigialos, Santorini, the Cyclades.** No need to venture out to view the jaw-dropping sunset over Santorini's caldera—a cluster of sumptuously restored 18th- to 19th-century village houses in Fira are the perfect perch.

- **Semeli, Mykonos.** Traditional furnishings and elegant surroundings evoke the high Mykoniot style.

- **Marco Polo Mansion, Rhodes, the Dodecanese.** Live like a pasha in a 15th-century Ottoman mansion fitted out with all the trappings—plush carpets, cushioned divans, and canopied beds.

- **Elounda Mare, Elounda, Eastern Crete.** The first of the super-luxe Greek resorts, this is Relais-&-Chateaux fabulous.

- **Tsitouras Hotel, Santorini, the Cyclades.** Like stepping into the pages of Architectural Digest, this Firostefani redoubt has welcomed the likes of Nana Mouskouri and Jean-Paul Gaultier.

- **Corfu Palace, Corfu, Ionian Islands.** Lush gardens, a sprawling pool, and a sea view from every room complement huge marble baths and elegant furnishings.

ISLAND-HOPPING: CYCLADES TO CRETE

There is no bad itinerary for the Greek islands. Whether you choose the Sporades, the Dodecanese, or any of those other getaways floating in the Aegean, the leading isles in Greece differ remarkably, and they are all beautiful. But when the needle flies off the beauty-measuring gauge when it comes to the Cyclades. It might be possible to "see" any of these famous islands in a day: the "must-see" sights—monasteries or ancient temples—are often few. Still, it is best to take a slower pace and enjoy a sumptuous, idyllic, 14-day tour. Planning the details of this trip depends on your sense of inclusiveness, your restlessness, your energy, and your ability to accommodate changing boat schedules. Just be warned: the danger of sailing through the Cyclades is that you will never want to leave them. From these suggested landfalls, some of the most justly famous, you can set off to find other idyllic retreats on your own.

Days 1–2: Mykonos
Jewel of the Cyclades, this very discovered island manages to retain its seductive charm. Spend the first day and evening enjoying appealing Mykonos town, where a maze of beautiful streets are lined with shops, bars, restaurants, and discos; spend time on one of the splendid beaches; and, if you want to indulge in some hedonism, partake of the wild nightlife. The next morning take the local boat to nearby Delos for one of the great classical sites in the Aegean. Mykonos is one of the main transport hubs of the Greek islands, with many ferries, boats, and planes connecting to Athens and its port of Piraeus. ⇨ *Mykonos in Chapter 7.*

Days 3–4: Naxos
Sail south to Naxos—easily done in summer, harder in other seasons. Plan on arriving from Mykonos in the late afternoon or evening, and begin with a predinner stroll around Naxos town, visiting the Portara (an ancient landmark), the castle, and other sights in the old quarter. The next morning, visit the Archaeological Museum; then drive through the island's mountainous center for spectacular views. Along the way, visit such sights as the Panayia Drosiani, a church near Moni noted for 7th-century frescoes; the marble-paved village of Apeiranthos; and the Temple of Demeter. If you have time, stop for a swim at one of the beaches facing Paros, say Mikri Vigla. ⇨ *Naxos in Chapter 7.*

Days 5–7: Paros
Go west, young man, to Paros, where the large spaces provide peace and quiet. Paros town has delights profane—buzzing bars—and sacred, such as the legendary Hundred Doors Church. But the highlight will be a meal in the impossibly pretty little fishing harbor of Naousa or, on a morning drive around the island, a visit to the lovely mountain village of Lefkes. Then spend an extra night of magic on the neighboring isle of Antiparos, where off-duty Hollywood celebs bliss out with all the white sands, pink bougainvillea, and blue seas. ⇨ *Paros in Chapter 7.*

Gulf of Corinth

Aegean Sea

Athens

TURKEY

Syros
Ermoupoli○

Mykonos

Paros &
Antiparos

Naxos

CYCLADES

Folegandros

Oia○
Santorini ○Fira

DODECANESE

Sea of Crete

Hania○

Rethymnon○

Heraklion
Mallia
Siteia

Ionian Sea

Knossos
Phaistos

Ayios Nikolaos
Ierapetra

Crete

Days 8–9: Folegandros

This smaller isle is not only beautiful but, rarer in these parts, authentic. It boasts one of the most stunning Chora towns; deliberately downplayed touristic development; several good beaches; quiet evenings; traditional local food; and respectful visitors. The high point, literally and figuratively, is the siting of the main town—set on a towering cliff over the sea, its perch almost rivals that of Santorini. ⇨ *Folegandros in Chapter 7*.

Days 10–12: Santorini

Take a ferry from Folegandros south to the spectacle of all spectacles. Yes, in summer the crowds will remind you of the running of the bulls in Pamplona but even they won't stop from you gasping at the vistas, the seaside cliffs, and stunning Cycladic cubist architecture. Once you've settled in, have a sunset drink on a terrace overlooking the volcanic caldera but you'll also find many view-providing watering holes in Fira, the capital, or Ia, Greece's most-photographed village. The next day, visit the Museum of Prehistoric Thera; then enjoy a third just swimming one of the black-sand beaches at Kamari or Perissa. ⇨ *Santorini in Chapter 7*.

Days 13–14: Crete

Despite the attractions of sea and mountains, it is still the mystery surrounding Europe's first civilization and empire that draws many travelers to Crete. Like them, you'll discover stunning testimony to the island's mysterious Minoan civilization, particularly at the legendary Palace of Knossos. Along these shores are blissful beaches as well as the enchanting Venetian-Turkish city of Hania. From Heraklion, Crete's main port, there are frequent flights and ferries back to Piraeus, Athens, and reality. ⇨ *Crete in Chapter 8*.

BY PUBLIC TRANSPORTATION

■ High-speed catamarans have halved travel time between Piraeus and Santorini.

■ In summer, when ferries and boats run frequently, you should have little trouble moving from any of these islands to another.

■ All islands are served by air as well as by boat.

WHEN TO GO

The best time to visit Greece is late spring and early fall. In May and June the days are warm, even hot, but dry, and the seawater has been warmed by the sun. For sightseeing or hitting the beach, this is the time. Greece is relatively tourist free in spring, so if the beach and swimming aren't critical, April and early May are good; the local wildflowers are at their loveliest, too. Carnival, usually in February just before Lent, and Greek Easter are seasonal highlights. July and August (most locals vacation in August) are always busy—especially on the islands. If you visit during this peak, plan ahead and be prepared to fight the crowds. September and October are a good alternative to spring and early summer, especially in the cities where bars and cultural institutions reopen. Elsewhere, things begin to shut down in November. Transportation to the islands is limited in winter, and many hotels outside large cities are closed until April.

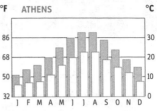

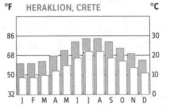

Climate

Greece has a typical Mediterranean climate: hot, dry summers and cool, wet winters. Chilliness and rain begin in November, the start of Greece's deceptive winters. Any given day may not be very cold—except in the mountains, snow is uncommon in Athens and to the south. But the cold is persistent, and many places are not well heated. Spring and fall are perfect, with warm days and balmy evenings. In the south a hot wind may blow across the Mediterranean from Africa. The average high and low temperatures for Athens and Heraklion and the average temperature for Thessaloniki are presented below.

Forecasts National Observatory of Athens ⊕www.noa.gr. **Weather Channel Connection** [900/932–8437 95¢ per minute from a touch-tone phone ⊕www.weather.com.

GREEK BY DESIGN

Shopping is now considered an Olympic sport in Greece—get the urge to splurge in the chic shops of Athens's Kolonaki district or head to Rhodes, Mykonos, and Crete, the islands that launched a thousand gifts. For the best in Greek style, here's where to get the goods.

The Greeks had a word for it: *tropos*. Style. You would expect nothing less from the folks who gave us the Venus de Milo, the Doric column, and the lyre-back chair. To say that they have had a long tradition as artisans and craftsmen is, of course, an understatement. Even back in ancient Rome, Greece was the word. The Romans may have engineered the stone vault and perfected the toilet, but when it came to style and culture, they were perfectly content to knock off Grecian dress, sculpture, décor, and architecture, then considered the height of fashion. Fast forward 2,500 years and little has changed. Many works of modern art were conceived as an Aegean paean, including the statues of Brancusi and Le Corbusier's minimalistic skyscrapers—both artists were deeply influenced by ancient Cycladic art. Today, the goddess dress struts the runways of Michael Kors and Valentino while Homer has made the leap to Hollywood in such recent box-office blockbusters as *300* and *Troy*.

Speaking of which, those ancient Trojans may have once tut-tutted about Greeks bearing gifts but would have second thoughts these days. Aunt Ethel has now traded in those plastic souvenir models of the Parthenon for a new Athenian bounty: pieces of Byzantine-style gold jewelry; hand-woven bedspreads from Hydra; strands of amber *komboloi* worry beads; and reproductions of red-figure ceramic vases. These are gifts you cannot resist and will be forever be glad you didn't.

BEARING GIFTS?

Seeing some of the glories of Aegean craftsmanship is probably one of the reasons you've come to Greece. The eggshell-thin pottery Minoans were fashioning more than 3,500 years ago, Byzantine jewelry and icons, colorful rugs that were woven in front of the fire as part of a dowry, not to mention all those bits of ancient masonry—these comprise a magnificent legacy of arts and crafts.

LEATHER SANDALS

Ancient Greek women with means and a sense of style wore sandals with straps that wrapped around the ankles—what today's fashion mags call "strappy sandals," proof that some classics are always in vogue. The most legendary maker is Athens's very own Stavros Melissinos, whose creations were once sported by the Beatles and Sophia Loren. He has been crafting sandals for more than 50 years.

TAVLÍ BOARDS

No matter where you are in Greece, follow the sound of clinking die and you'll probably find yourself in a kafenion. There, enthusiasts will be huddled over Greece's favorite game, a close cousin to backgammon. Tavlí boards are sold everywhere in Greece, but the most magnificent board you'll ever see is not for sale—a marble square inlaid with gold and ivory, crafted sometime before 1500 bc for the amusement of Minoan kings and now on display at the archaeological museum in Heraklion, Crete.

WORRY BEADS

Feeling fidgety? Partake of a Greek custom and fiddle with your worry beads, or komboloi. The amber or coral beads are loosely strung on a long strand and look like prayer beads, yet they have no religious significance. Even so, on a stressful day the relaxing effect can seem like divine intervention. Particularly potent are beads painted with the "evil eye."

ICONS

Icon painting flourished in Greece as the Renaissance took hold of Western Europe, and panels of saints and other heavenly creatures are among the country's greatest artistic treasures. Some, like many of those in the 799 churches on the island of Tinos, are said to possess miraculous healing powers, attracting thousands of cure-seeking believers each year. Icons attract art buyers too, but if you can easily afford one, it's almost certainly a modern reproduction.

JEWELRY

Greece's long gold- and silver-smithing tradition thrives in workshops on Rhodes and Corfu and in such mainland towns and villages as Ioannina and Stemnitsa. Many artisans turn to the past for inspiration—Bronze Age cruciform figures, gold necklaces from the Hellenistic period dangling with pomegranates, Byzantine-style pendants—while others tap out distinctly modern creations using age-old techniques.

CERAMICS

Ancient Greek pottery was a black-and-red medium: the Spartans and Corinthians painted glossy black figures on a reddish-orange background; later ceramicists switched the effect with stunning results, reddish-hued figures on a black background. Artisans still create both, and potters on Crete and elsewhere in Greece throw huge terracotta storage jars, pithoi, that are appealing, if no longer practical, additions to any household.

WEAVING

Even goddesses spent their idle hours weaving (remember Arachne, so proud of her skills at the loom that Athena turned her into a spider?). From the mountains of Arcadia to such worldly enclaves as Mykonos, mortals sit behind handlooms to clack out folkloric rugs, bedspreads, and tablecloths.

BARGAINING FOR BEGINNERS:

In Greece there is often the "first price" and the "last price." Bargaining is still par for the course (except in the fanciest stores). And if you're planning a shopping day, leave those Versace shoes at home—shopkeepers often decide on a price after sizing up the prospective buyer's income bracket.

ATHENS: PASSPORT TO STYLE

If you want to find the best in Greek craftsmanship, head to the shops of Athens. Greece may not have always been a land of great artists, but these top offerings will remind you that it has always been a place for great artistry.

Baba (Ifestou 30, Monastiraki) is Backgammon Central—get a great tavlí board here.

Center of Hellenic Tradition (Mitropoleous 59, Monastiraki) is a mecca for old Greek folk crafts, with regional ceramics, weavings, and antique sheep bells all making for evocative room accents.

Kombologadiko (6 Koumbari, Kolonaki) was praised by *Vogue* a few years ago for its chic take on old traditional komboloi worry beads, having remade this previously for-men-only item into high-fashion necklaces.

Lalaounis (Panepistimiou 6, Syntagma Square), Athens's most famous jeweler, allows jet-setters and collectors to "go for the gold" with necklaces, bracelets, headpieces, and rings inspired by ancient pieces.

Lykeio Ellinidon (Dimokritou 7a, Kolonaki) is famed for its resident weavers who copy folkloric motifs at two on-site looms.

Stavros Melissinos (Ayias Theklas 2, Monastiraki), Athens's most famous sandal-maker, boasts a clientele that has included Jackie Onassis and Gary Cooper.

A. Patnkiadou (58 Pandroussou, Plaka) has fashionistas raving about jewelry that incorporates ancient coins and Byzantine jewels.

Pylarinos (Panepistimious 18, Syntagma Square) is known for its selection of ancient coins and vintage engravings—pick up a 19th-century view of the Acropolis here.

Riza (Voukourestiou 35, Kolonaki) is tops for Greek Island accents like traditional brass candlesticks.

Tanagrea (Voulis 26 and Mitropoleous 15, Syntagma Square) is one of Athens's oldest gift shops and is famed for its hand-painted ceramic pomegranates, symbol of good fortune.

Thiamis (Asklipiou 71, Syntagma Square) gives a new take on an old art form with hand-painted icons.

Cruising the Greek Islands

THE BEST SHIPS & ITINERARIES

Thira, Santorini

WORD OF MOUTH

"How can anyone pass up a cruise to Greece? Santorini, Mykonos, Crete, and Rhodes: these are the islands that launched a thousand trips! Even Poseidon, god of the waters, would have been jealous of the beautiful cruise ships now sailing the Aegean seas."

—WiseOwl

By Linda
Coffman

TRAVELERS HAVE BEEN SAILING
Greek waters ever since 3,500
B.C.C. (before Chris-Crafts). The
good news is that today's visitor
will have a much, much easier time
of it than Odysseus, the world's first
tourist and hero of Homer's *Odyssey*. Back in his day, exploring the
Greek islands—1,425 geological
jewels thickly scattered over the
Aegean Sea like stepping stones
between East and West—was a
fairly daunting assignment. Zeus
would often set the schedule (dur-

> **SHIP, SHIP, HURRAY!**
>
> Did you know that the Mediterranean cruise ship industry, which is based in Greece, is second only in popularity in number of cruises to the Caribbean region? Nearly 2.2 million passengers a year set sail, with Greece holding the number one spot for the highest embarkation rate of all European Union countries.

ing the idyllic days in midwinter the master of Mt. Olympus forbade
the winds to blow during the mating season of the halcyon or kingfishers); waterlogged wooden craft could be tossed about in summer, when
the meltemi, the north wind, would be a regular visitor to these waters;
and pine-prow triremes often embarked with a scramble of 170 oarsmen, not all of them pulling in the right direction.

Now, in 2008, travelers can sail those same blue highways in effortless fashion. A flotilla of—often—spectacularly outfitted cruise liners
helps banish many typical landlubbers' irritations: ferry schedules,
hotel reservations, luggage porterage, to name a few. When you add in
21st-century allurements—pulling into Santorini after a deck-side luncheon created by the gastronomic wizard of Nobu; a game of golf in
Mykonos via your onboard 18-hole miniature-golf course; a renowned
archaeologist illuminating the fascinating history of Rhodes, your next
stop—you can see why a vacation aboard one of these gleaming white
islands has become one of the most popular travel choices available.

Cruises have always had a magical quality, even without dramatic
views of whitewashed Cycladic villages and ancient ruins anchored
for eternity above a sheer drop (for a rundown of the ABC's, see the
Cruise-Taker's Primer in the second half of this chapter). Sailing into
harbor has a grand ceremonial feel lacking in air travel arrivals and
Greece, the eastern Mediterranean's showcase, is an ideal cruise destination for travelers with limited time who wish to combine sightseeing
with relaxation. This is especially true in the spring and autumn seasons, when milder Aegean and Ionian climates are better suited than
the sweltering summer months to, for example, exploring those hilltop
ancient ruins.

Although cruises have historically attracted an older group of travelers, more and more young people and family groups are setting sail in
Europe. With the peak season conveniently falling during schools' summer hiatus, cruise lines have responded to multigenerational travel with
expanded children's programs and discounted shore excursions for
youngsters under age 12. Shore excursions have become more varied,
too, often incorporating activities that families can enjoy together, such
as bicycling and hiking. Cruise lines now offer more programs than ever

before for adults as well, including pre- or post-cruise land tours as options, plus extensive onboard entertainment and learning programs. Some lines increasingly hire expert speakers to lead discussions based on local cultures.

Cruise ships may idyllically appear to be floating resorts, but keep in mind that if you should decide you don't like your ship, you can't check out and move somewhere else. Whichever one you choose will be your home for seven days, or more in some cases. The chosen ship will determine the type of accommodations you'll enjoy, the kind of food you'll eat, the entertainment program, and even the destinations you'll visit. That is why the most important endeavor you can undertake when planning a cruise is evaluating the proposed itinerary, the cruise line, and the particular ship.

> ### THE MED FROM STEM TO STERN
>
> Many of today's most popular Greek Island cruises are actually part and parcel of larger itineraries that cover wider swaths of the Mediterranean, extending from Rome to Alexandria, but this has been the Greek way of seafaring for more than 3,000 years. In ancient time, the Aegean and the Mediterranean were propitious for coastal trade, and it was by sea that the Greek way was spread. Greek ships colonized the whole Mediterranean coast to such an extent that for a thousand years the Mediterranean was known as a veritable Greek lake.

CHOOSING YOUR CRUISE

Which cruise is right for you depends on a number of factors, notably the size and style of ship you opt for, the itinerary you choose, and how much you're willing to spend. Prices quoted here are subject to change.

DREAM ITINERARIES

Cruise ships typically follow one of two itinerary types in the eastern Mediterranean: round-trip loops starting and finishing in the same port city; and one-way cruises that pick you up in one port and drop you off at another for the flight home. Itineraries are usually 7 to 10 days, though some lines offer longer sailings covering a larger geographic span. Some cruises concentrate on covering an area that includes the Greek islands, Turkish coast, Cyprus, Israel, and Egypt, while others reach from Gibraltar to the Ionian isles, the western Peloponnese, and Athens.

For an overview of Greece's top sights, choose an itinerary that includes port calls in Piraeus for a shore excursion to the Acropolis and other sights in Athens; Mykonos, a sparkling Cycladic isle with a warren of whitewashed passages, followed by neighboring Delos, with its Pompeii-like ruins; Santorini, a stunning harbor that's actually a partially submerged volcano; Rhodes, where the Knights of St. John built their first walled city before being forced to retreat to Malta; and Heraklion, Crete, where you'll be whisked through a medieval harbor to the reconstructed Bronze Age palace at Knossos. Port calls at Katakolon and Itea mean excursions to Olympia and the Temple of Apollo at Delphi. Some cruises call at Epidauros and Nafplion, offering an opportunity for visits to the ancient theater and the citadel of Mycenae, or at Monemvassia or Patmos, the island where St. John wrote the book of Revelations.

If you'd rather relax by the pool than trek through temples, opt for a cruise with more time at sea and fewer or shorter port calls. If you'd like time to explore each island destination, you'll want to choose a cruise where the ship spends the entire day in port and travels at night. Alternately, if the number of places you visit is more important than the time you spend in each one, book a cruise with a full itinerary and one or two port calls a day.

A cruise spares the planning headaches of solitary island-hopping and the inconvenience of carting luggage from one destination to the next, and, for budget-conscious travelers, cruises offer the advantage of controlled expenses. However, because one disadvantage is that port calls may be long enough only to allow time for a quick visit to one or two main attractions, cruises may be best for an overview, useful for planning a return trip to the more-appealing island stops.

WHEN TO GO

When to go is as important as where to go. In July or August, the islands are crowded with Greek and foreign vacationers, so expect sights, beaches, and shops to be crowded. High temperatures could also limit time spent on deck. May, June, September, and October are the best months—warm enough for sunbathing and swimming, yet not so uncomfortably hot as to make you regret the trek up Lindos. Cruising in the low seasons provides plenty of advantages besides discounted fares. Availability of ships and particular cabins is greater in the low and shoulder seasons, and the ports are almost completely free of tourists.

THE MAIN CRUISE LINES: AZAMARA TO WINDSTAR

Posh or penny-pinching? Two weeks or seven days? EasyCruise burgers or SeaDream Yacht Club's champagne-and-caviar beach barbecues? Large ships or small? There are any number of questions you have to ask yourself when lining up your dream Greek islands cruise but deciding to opt for either a large or small ship may be the most important. Large cruise lines account for the vast majority of passengers sailing in Europe. These typically have both larger cruise ships and megaships in their fleets. Cruise ships have plentiful outdoor deck space, and most have a wraparound outdoor promenade deck that allows you to stroll or jog the ship's perimeter. In the newest vessels, traditional meets trendy, but for all their resort-style innovations, they still feature cruise-

10 Questions to Answer Before Visiting a Travel Agent

If you've decided to use a travel agent, ask yourself these 10 simple questions, and you'll be better prepared to help the agent do his or her job:

1. Who will be going on the cruise?

2. What can you afford to spend for the entire trip?

3. Where would you like to go?

4. How much vacation time do you have?

5. When can you get away?

6. What are your interests?

7. Do you prefer a casual or structured vacation?

8. What kind of accommodations do you want?

9. What are your dining preferences?

10. How will you get to the embarkation port?

ship classics—afternoon tea, complimentary room service, and lavish pampering. The smallest cruise ships carry 500 or fewer passengers, while larger vessels accommodate 1,500 passengers and offer a wide variety of diversions. Megaships boast even more amenities and amusements, and carry between 1,500 and 3,000 passengers—enough people to outnumber the residents of many Greek port towns.

Megaships are a good choice if you're looking for nonstop activity and lots of options; they're especially appealing for groups traveling together and families with older kids. Experiences on these ships range from basic, comfortable vacations to white-glove luxury; from traditional cruises with formal nights, afternoon tea, and assigned dining places, to lively ships bustling with activity. All of them allow you the flexibility of seeing a variety of ports while still enjoying such cruise amenities as spas, nightly entertainment, and fine dining. These ships tend to follow conventional itineraries and stop at the best-known, larger ports of call; because of their size they can't venture too close to shore, thus you won't see much scenery from the deck. If you prefer a gentler pace and a chance to get to know your shipmates, consider a smaller ship.

Classic or midsize ships, which are more popular with Europeans than with Americans, offer a range of amenities and comfortable accommodations but are not as flashy as the new megaships. Luxury ships are generally small to midsize and are distinguished by high staff-to-guest ratios, superior cuisine, few onboard charges, and much more space per passenger than you'll find on the mainstream lines' vessels.

SMALL SHIPS

Compact vessels bring you right up to the shoreline where big ships don't fit. Destinations, not casinos or spa treatments, are the focus of these cruises. You'll call into smaller ports, as well as the larger, better-known cities. Port lectures and cultural talks are the norm. But in comparison with those on traditional cruise ships, cabins on these ships can be quite tiny, often with no phone or TV, and some bathrooms are no bigger than cubbyholes. Often, the dining room and the lounge are the only common public areas on these vessels. Some small ships, however, are luxurious yachtlike vessels with cushy cabins, comfy lounges and libraries, and hot tubs on deck. You won't find discos or movie theaters aboard, but what you trade for space and onboard diversions is a unique and detailed glimpse of ports that you're unlikely to forget.

Small-ship cruising can be pricey as costs are spread over a few dozen, rather than hundreds of, passengers. Fares tend to be quite inclusive (except for airfare), with few onboard charges, and, given the size of ship and style of cruise, fewer opportunities to spend money on board. Small ships typically offer the same kinds of early-booking and other discounts as the major cruise lines.

AZAMARA CRUISES

"The adventuresome (yet pampered) soul has met its match" is the catchy new slogan for this fledgling outfit newly launched by parent company Royal Caribbean in 2007. Named partly in honor of the star Acamar—the most-southerly bright star that can be viewed from the latitude of Greece—the firm has two vessels, built for now-defunct Renaissance Cruises, and refitted for the deluxe-cruise crowd. Designed to offer exotic destination-driven itineraries, Azamara offers a more-intimate onboard experience, while allowing access to the less-traveled ports of call experienced travelers want to visit. And the enrichment programs are some of the best on offer.

Itineraries and Ships. *Azamara Quest* (694 passengers) has multiple sailings of its exciting 14-night "Ancient Empires" itinerary, which begins in Rome, then sails to such ports as Sorrento and Greece's Athens, Chios, Heraklion (Crete), with a number of stops in Turkey, including Bodrum and Istanbul, and one in Alexandria, Egypt. Rates begin at $2,499 (note that all itineraries and rates quoted in this chapter are as of fall 2007). *Azamara Journey* (694 passengers) kicks off its "Holyland" 14-day cruise in Athens, then includes such destinations as Greece's Chios, Santorini, Cyprus's Limassol, Israel's Haifa, Egypt's Port Said, Italy's Sorrento and Rome, and Spain's Barcelona. Rates begin at $2,799. The two ships also feature longer "Black Sea" and "Classical Mediterranean" tours.

Your Shipmates. Azamara is designed to appeal to discerning travelers, primarily American couples of any age who appreciate a high level of service in an unstructured atmosphere. The ships are not family oriented and do not have facilities or programs for children.

Food. Expect all the classic dinner favorites but with an upscale twist, such as gulf shrimp with cognac and garlic, or a filet mignon with black truffle sauce. Each ship offers two specialty restaurants: the Mediterranean-influenced Aqualina and the stylish steak-and-seafood restaurant Prime C. Guests in suites receive two nights of complimentary dining in the two restaurants, while guests in staterooms receive one. Daily in-cabin afternoon tea service and delivery of canapés are available to all passengers.

Fitness and Recreation. In addition to a well-equipped gym and an outdoor jogging track, Azamara's fitness program includes yoga at sunset, Pilates, and access to an onboard wellness consultant. Both ships offer a full menu of spa treatments, an outdoor spa relaxation lounge, and an aesthetics suite featuring acupuncture, laser hair removal, and micro-dermabrasion.

> **HOW TO EARN YOUR SEA MAJOR**
>
> A distinguishing aspect of Azamara is a wide range of enrichment programs to accompany the destination-rich itineraries. Programs include guest speakers and experts on a wide variety of topics, including technology, cultural explorations, art, music, and design.

Contact. ✆1050 Caribbean Way, Miami, FL 33132 ☎877/222–2526 or 877/999–9553 🌐www.azamaracruises.com.

CELEBRITY CRUISES

Founded in 1989, Celebrity has gained a reputation for fine food and professional service. The cruise line has built premium, sophisticated ships and developed signature amenities, including a specialty coffee shop, martini bar, large standard staterooms with generous storage, spas, and butler service for passengers booking the top suites. Although spacious accommodations in every category are a Celebrity standard, the addition of Concierge Class makes certain premium ocean-view and balcony staterooms almost the equivalent of suites in terms of amenities and service.

Itineraries and Ship. *Galaxy* (1,890 passengers) is the European flagship of this popular American line and has some winning cruises. The 10-day "Eastern Mediterranean" kicks off in Rome, then heads to Sicily, Ephesus (Turkey), and winds up back in Naples/Capri but has a sizable chunk in Greece, with stops in Athens, Mykonos, Rhodes, and Santorini; the itinerary, which has multiple sailings from May to November, bumps up to 14 nights and other stops like the Bosphorus Straits in its "Exotic Mediterranean and Black Sea" version. Rates start at $1,029. *Galaxy* is a traditional and quietly elegant ship; the double-height dining room is nothing short of gorgeous with its soaring columns and window walls; there are three pools, with the Oasis pool replete with its own set of palm trees.

Your Shipmates. Celebrity caters to American cruise passengers, primarily couples from their mid-thirties to mid-fifties. Many families enjoy cruising on Celebrity's fleet during summer months and holiday periods. Each vessel has a dedicated playroom and offers a five-tiered program of activities designed for children and teens aged 3 to 17, plus Toddler Time for parents and their children under age 3.

Food. In early 2007, Celebrity announced plans to advance its fleet-wide culinary program to the next level. Every ship in the fleet has a highly experienced team headed by executive chefs and food and beverage managers who now work in concert with the line's new cuisine consultants, Las Vegas–based Blau & Associates, a strategic restaurant planning and development firm.

Fitness and Recreation. Celebrity's fitness centers and AquaSpa by Elemis are some of the most tranquil and nicely equipped at sea. State-of-the-art exercise equipment, a jogging track, and some fitness classes are available at no charge. Spa treatments include a variety of massages, body wraps, and facials. The *Galaxy* has an Acupuncture at Sea program administered by a specialist in Asian medicine. Hair and nail services are offered in the salons.

Contact. ✉ *1050 Caribbean Way, Miami, FL33132* ☎ *305/539–6000 or 800/437–3111* ⊕ *www.celebrity.com.*

COSTA CRUISES

Europe's number one cruise line combines a Continental experience, enticing itineraries, and the classical design and style of Italy with romantic nights at sea. Genoa-based Costa Crociere, parent company of Costa Cruise Lines, had been in the passenger business for almost 50 years when Carnival Corporation completed a buyout of the line in 2000 and began expanding the fleet with larger and more-dynamic ships. "Italian-style" cruising is a mixture of Mediterranean flair and American comfort. Beginning with a *buon viaggio* (bon voyage) celebration, the supercharged social staff works overtime to get everyone in the mood and encourages everyone to be a part of the action.

Itineraries and Ships. *CostaEuropa* (1,488 passengers) was built in 1986, "stretched" in 1990, and in 2002 had her decor brightened up, yet she retains classic touches of elegance such as the teak wraparound promenade deck lined with wooden steamer chairs. As on other ships of her vintage, she has few balconies. Think she looks vaguely familiar? It could be because she starred in *Out to Sea* with Walter Matthau and Jack Lemmon. One sample 11-day cruise leaves from northern Italy's Savona then steams south to Alexandria, Cyprus, and Naples, and stops in Greece at Rhodes, Athens, and Katakolon (Olympia); rates begin at $1,399. *CostaClassica* (1,308 passengers) was designed to bring the Costa fleet up to speed with other cruise lines in the 1990s, and the effort has paid off. Public areas clustered on four upper decks are filled with marble and furnished with sleek, contemporary furnishings and modern Italian artwork. The effect is vibrant, chic, and surprisingly restful. Lounges and bars are sweeping and grand; however, the areas set aside for children are pretty skimpy by today's family-friendly standards. There is no promenade deck, but the Lido areas for sunning and swimming are expansive. One sample 7-day cruise (rates begin at $799) leaves from Trieste in northern Italy, then heads down to Corfu, Athens, Santorini, and Mykonos, and returns to Trieste. *Costa Atlantica* (2,114 passengers) has a Venice vibe, with tons of Murano glass, the Tiziano restaurant as big as an art nouveau football stadium, and an atrium with elevators that soar 12 passenger decks (named after Fellini movies); the knockout is the reproduction of Venice's Caffe Florian. *Costa Romantica* (1,344 passengers) has a 7-day cruise, leaving from Rome, heading to Sicily and Turkey (Izmir), with stops in Greece including Patmos, Santorini, and Mykonos. Every month of the year has cruises scheduled.

Your Shipmates. An international air prevails on board and announcements are often made in a variety of languages. On Mediterranean itineraries approximately 80% of passengers are Europeans, including many from Italy. Youth programs provide daily age-appropriate activities for children ages 3 to 17. Special counselors supervise activities and specific rooms are designed for children and teens, depending on the ship.

> ### SHIP SHAPE
>
> Taking a cue from the ancient Romans, Costa places continuing emphasis on wellness and sybaritic pleasures. Spa treatments include a variety of massages, body wraps, and facials that can be scheduled à la carte or combined in packages to encompass an afternoon or the entire cruise. State-of-the-art exercise equipment in the terraced gym, a jogging track, and basic fitness classes for all levels of ability are available.

Food. Dining features regional Italian cuisines, a variety of pastas, chicken, beef, and seafood dishes, as well as authentic pizza. European chefs and culinary school graduates who are members of Chaîne des Rôtisseurs provide a dining experience that's notable for a delicious, properly prepared pasta course. Vegetarian and healthful diet choices are also offered. Alternative dining is by reservation only in the upscale supper clubs, which serve choice steaks and seafood from a Tuscan Steakhouse menu as well as traditional Italian specialties. Costa chefs celebrate the tradition of lavish nightly midnight buffets.

Contact. ⌂*200 S. Park Rd., Suite 200, Hollywood, FL33021-8541* ☎*954/266–5600 or 800/462–6782* ⊕*www.costacruise.com.*

CRYSTAL CRUISES

Winner of accolades and hospitality-industry awards, Crystal Cruises offers the grandeur of the past with all the modern touches discerning passengers demand. Founded in 1990 and owned by Nippon Yusen Kaisha (NYK) in Japan, Crystal ships, unlike other luxury vessels, are large—carrying upward of 900 passengers. Superior service, a variety of dining options, spacious accommodations, and some of the highest ratios of space per passenger of any cruise ships make them distinctive. Beginning with ship designs based on the principles of feng shui, not even the smallest detail is overlooked to provide passengers with the best-imaginable experience. Crystal stands out in their variety of enrichment and educational programs.

Itineraries and Ship. *Crystal Serenity* (1,080 passengers) is stylish, uncrowded, and uncluttered, with clubby drawing rooms done in muted colors and warm woods, creating a refined environment. A West Coast lifestyle laid-back vibe prevails, with sensational restaurants (the alternative choices are yours to enjoy at the cost of a nominal gratuity). Design of smallish standard cabins for this level of luxury ship are disappointing, while public spaces are design-award worthy. Design of even smaller cabins are soigné, while public spaces are design-award worthy. One sample itinerary is the 11-day "Temples of Gods and Pharoahs," which begins in Istanbul, includes Kusadasi and Alexandria/Cairo, and stops in Greece's Rhodes/Lindos, Santorini, and Athens; rates start at $4,345. The 7-day "Greek Gods and Gondolas" kicks off in Athens, then heads to Kusadasi, Santorini, Split (Croatia), and Albania, and ends up in Venice; rates begin at $3,440. Sailings of the many various cruises extend from April to October.

Your Shipmates. Affluent, well-traveled couples, from their late-thirties to retirees, are attracted by Crystal Cruises' destination-rich itineraries, onboard enrichment programs, and the ship's elegant ambience. Children are welcome aboard, but Crystal Cruises reserves the right to restrict the number of children under age three traveling with their parents and is unable to accommodate children younger than six months of age without a signed waiver of parental consent.

Food. The food is a good enough reason to book a cruise on Crystal ships. Dining in the main restaurants is an event starring Continental-inspired cuisine served by trained European waiters. Off-menu item requests are honored when possible. Casual poolside dining from the grills is offered on some evenings in a relaxed, no-reservations-required option. A variety of hot and cold hors d'oeuvres are served in bars and lounges every evening before dinner and again during the wee hours. Where service and the dishes really shine are in the specialty restaurants; the Serenity has Asian-inspired and Italian specialty restaurants.

Fitness and Recreation. Large spas offer innovative pampering therapies, body wraps, and exotic Asian-inspired treatments. Fitness centers feature a range of exercise and weight-training equipment and workout areas for aerobics classes, plus complimentary yoga and Pilates instruction. In addition, golfers enjoy extensive shipboard facilities, including a driving range, practice cage, and putting green.

Contact. *⌖2049 Century Park E, Suite 1400, Los Angeles, CA90067 ☎310/785–9300 or 888/799–4625 ⊕www.crystalcruises.com.*

CUNARD LINE

One of the world's most-distinguished names in ocean travel since 1840, Cunard Line's history of transatlantic crossings and worldwide cruising is legendary for its comfortable British style. After a series of owners tried with little success to revive the company's flagging passenger shipping business in the era of jet travel, Carnival Corporation saved the day in 1998 with an infusion of ready cash and the know-

2

how to turn the cruise line around. There is a decidedly British vibe to salons and pubs, while a wide variety of musical styles can be found for dancing and listening in the bars and lounges. Quality enrichment programs are presented by expert guest lecturers in their fields.

Itinerary and Ship. *Queen Victoria* (1,080 passengers) is premiered in 2008 as the third "queen" in Cunard's fleet, with its maiden cruise long sold out. Victoria herself would feel quite at home in the

> ## SEA & CRUMPETS
>
> Not surprisingly, entertainment and authentic pubs have a decidedly English flavor aboard Cunard, as do some of the grand salons, including the Queen Victoria's double-height Queens Room, a loggia-style venue designed in the manner of the grand ballrooms found in large English country houses, such as Her Majesty's own Osborne House.

triple-height grand lobby. On board is an extensive Cunardia museum exhibit, a two-deck library connected by a spiral staircase, posh entertainment venues, and shops inspired by London's Burlington and Royal Arcades. More contemporary than traditional, however, is the glass-domed Hemispheres nightclub. Other eye-knocking features include the giant Royal Court Theatre, which touts the first-at-sea private boxes with unobstructed views; the luxe Royal Spa & Fitness Centre; 10,000 square feet of promenade-worthy open deck; wine-tasting classrooms; and staterooms, two-thirds of which boast private balconies to catch the sea winds.

Yours truly, Shipmates. Discerning, well-traveled British and American couples from their late-thirties to retirees are drawn to Cunard's traditional style. The availability of spacious accommodations and complimentary self-service laundry facilities make Cunard liners a good option for families, although there may be fewer children on board than you might expect. Kid-friendly features include a dedicated play area for children ages one to six. Separate programs are reserved for older children ages 7–12 and teens. Toddlers are supervised by English nannies. Children ages one to two sail free (except for government fees).

Food. In the tradition of multiple-class ocean liners, dining room assignments are made according to the accommodation category booked: you get the luxury you pay for. Passengers in junior suites are assigned to single-seating Princess Grill, while the posh Queen's Grill serves passengers booked in the most lavish suites. All other passengers are assigned to one of two seatings in the dramatic Britannia Restaurant. Specialty restaurants require reservations and there is an additional charge.

Fitness and Recreation. Swimming pools, golf driving ranges, table tennis, a paddle tennis court, shuffleboard, and jogging tracks barely scratch the surface of onboard facilities dedicated to recreation. Top-quality fitness centers offer high-tech workout equipment, a separate weight room, and classes ranging from aerobics to healthful living workshops. The spas are top rate with a long menu of treatments and salon services for women and men.

Contact. *24303 Town Center Dr., Valencia, CA91355* *661/753–1000 or 800/728–6273* *www.cunard.com.*

EASYCRUISE

Introduced with great fanfare in 2005 by Stelios (the guiding force behind budget air carrier easyJet), easyCruise is easily the quirkiest endeavor to hit the cruise industry—and it is one option with a calendar heavily slated for Greek cruises. Aimed at youthful travelers interested in island-hopping and sampling local nightlife, itineraries are scheduled to arrive in port mid-morning, stay until the partying winds down, and then move on to the next destination, somewhat like a cross between a traditional cruise ship and a ferry. Passengers have the flexibility to book as few as three nights, embarking and departing in any port along the way; however, fares are now available in more-traditional 3- to 7-night packages. Rock-bottom prices eliminate all onboard frills and nearly all necessities. Meals aren't included and you'll pay extra for cabin services, including cleaning, fresh towels, and bed linens.

Itineraries and Ships. *EasyCruise 1* (170 passengers) is the more spartan of the two easyCruise ships sailing the Aegean. Although the bright neon-orange hull emblazoned with "easycruise.com" acted in the past as a beacon to late-night revelers returning from shoreside restaurants and clubs, the garish look has undergone a transformation: a new graphite-gray paint job with discreet orange trim gives the ship a more refined appearance but shouldn't hamper the party spirit of its passengers. Even in its new livery, *easyCruise1* is easy to spot late at night—it's likely to be the only ship at the pier. The ship's public spaces have also been redecorated and now have more of the look of a boutique hotel. An ambitious itinerary offered on this ship is the 11-night "Around the Ionian Sea," which kicks off in Piraeus (Athens), then sails to Itea (Delphi), Ithaca, Paxos, Albania, Corfu, Preveza, Kefalonia, Zakynthos, Corinth, Aegina, and back to Athens; rates start at €198. Even though the prices still start as low as €70 per person for a 7-day trip, *easyCruise Life* has ramped up the space (500 passengers) and added amenities like the FusionOn6 bar and restaurant, the Apivita spa, and a range of cabins that even extend to suitelike accommodations. One popular itinerary is the 7-day "Greek Islands and Turkey" cruise, which begins in Piraeus, then goes to Ermoupoli on Syros, then Kalymnos, and on to Turkey's Bodrum, then back to Greece's Kos, Samos, Mykonos, and Paros; rates begin at €140.

Your Shipmates. The plan was to appeal to active adults in their twenties and thirties. In reality, depending on the season and itinerary, passenger ages might lean toward the fortysomething and older set. Most passengers hail from Great Britain or North America, with Brits usually in the majority. There are no provisions made for children's facilities or entertainment. You are unlikely to encounter kids on board.

Food. An upgraded restaurant supplements the diner-quality snacks, sandwiches, and dessert items that have always been available. However, the quality of the food is more like Starbucks or Ruby Tuesday. The best offerings are often found at breakfast. You pay for all food on board; there are no meal plans and individual items are on the pricey side for what you get. You will also pay in euros, which is even more painful for Americans. The best dining is still found ashore when in port.

Fitness and Recreation. A small gym has exercise equipment, but you will be more likely to burn off calories walking in ports and swimming when you head for the beach. There's no pool, but there is a popular hot tub.

Contact. ⌂ *The Rotunda, 42/43 Gloucester Crescent, London, UKNW1 7DL* ☎ *30211/211–6211* ⊕ *www.easycruise.com.*

HOLLAND AMERICA LINE

Holland America Line has enjoyed a distinguished record of traditional cruises, world exploration, and transatlantic crossings since 1873—all facets of its history that are reflected in the fleet's multimillion dollar shipboard art and antiques collections. Noted for focusing on passenger comfort, Holland America Line cruises are classic in design and style. Although they may never be considered cutting edge, even with an infusion of younger adults and families on board, they remain refined without being stuffy or stodgy.

Itineraries and Ships. The *Prinsendam* (794 passengers) was launched in 1998 and refurbished with an array of goodies, including a selection of oil paintings of Holland America ships by Captain Stephen Card, an exhilarating Crow's Nest observation lounge, and a tall cylinder of Bolae glass in the atrium area, which is lighted from within by fiber optics so that etched dolphins and sea turtles seem to swim up the center. Unfortunately, a mere 38% of outside cabins and suites have private balconies and some cabins near the bow have portholes instead of large windows—for these reasons, cabin selection must be made carefully. A sample itinerary on the *Prinsendam* is the 14-day "Ancient Mysteries" cruise, which kicks off in Piraeus, and also pulls into Greece's Rhodes, Santorini, and Katakolon (Olympia), with other stops including Alexandria, Jerusalem, Haifa, Kusadasi, Malta, Sicily, and Rome; rates begin at $3,281. The *Noordam* (1,848 passengers) is a more youthful and family-friendly ship, where an exquisite Waterford Crystal sculpture adorns the triple-deck atrium and reflects keep-your-sunglasses-on color schemes throughout; nearly 80% of rooms have a private balcony, although those next to the panoramic elevator are not as "private" as they seem. This ship often sails on extensive 20-day cruises like the "Mediterranean Mosaic," which begins in Rome (Civitavecchia) and stops in Greece's Corfu, Katakolon (Olympia), and Santorini, while ranging from Monte Carlo, Barcelona, Mallorca, Carthage, Palermo, Dubrovnik, Sicily, and Malta; rates begin at $3,768.

Your Shipmates. No longer your grandparents' cruise line, today's Holland America attracts families and discerning couples, mostly from their late thirties on up. Comfortable retirees are often still in the majority, particularly on longer cruises; however, holidays and summer months are peak periods when you'll find more children in the mix. Group activities are planned for children ages 3 to 7 and 8 to

12 in Club HAL, Holland America Line's professionally staffed youth program. Club HAL After Hours offers late-night activities from 10 PM until midnight for an hourly fee. Teens aged 13 to 17 have their own lounge with activities.

Food. You have your choice of two assigned seatings or open seating for evening meals in the formal dining room. In the reservations-required, $20-per-person Pinnacle Grill alternative restaurant, fresh seafood and premium cuts of Sterling Silver beef are used to prepare creative specialty dishes. Delicious onboard traditions are afternoon tea, a Dutch Chocolate Extravaganza, and Holland America Line's signature bread pudding.

Fitness and Recreation. Well-equipped and fully staffed fitness facilities contain state-of-the-art exercise equipment; basic fitness classes are available at no charge. There's a fee for personal training, and specialized classes such as yoga and Pilates. The Greenhouse Spa offers a variety of treatments. Both ships have a jogging track, multiple swimming pools, and sports courts.

Contact. ✉ *300 Elliott Ave. W, Seattle, WA 98119* ☎ *206/281–3535 or 800/577–1728* ⊕ *www.hollandamerica.com.*

MSC CRUISES

Since it began introducing graceful new designs to large-size ships in 2003, MSC (Mediterranean Shipping Cruises) has grown to be a formidable presence in European cruising. The extensive use of marble, brass, and wood in ships' interiors reflect the best of Italian styling and design. Clean lines and bold colors often set the modern sophisticated tone—no glitz, no clutter—elegant simplicity is the standard of MSC's decor.

Itineraries and Ships. Often sailing with a Greece-heavy itinerary, the MSC *Musica* (2,550 passengers) is an extravaganza of curves and seductive colors, crowned by a vast red-and-gold La Scala theater. A highlight is a three-deck waterfall in the central foyer, where a piano is suspended on a transparent floor above a pool of water. Interiors are a blend of art deco and art nouveau themes, with some restaurants saddled with rather cartoony murals. Elsewhere, the elegant Cigar Bar and Giardino restaurant bring things down to earth. A whopping 80% of staterooms have an ocean view and 65% have balconies. Decorated in jewel-tone colors, all are comfortable yet somewhat smaller than the average new-ship cabin. A typical cruise is the 7-night journey that starts in Venice, then calls on Greece's Katakolon (Olympia), Santorini, Mykonos, Piraeus/Athens, and Corfu, plus Dubrovnik. The MSC *Orchestra* (2,550 passengers) is a design beauty, ranging from a three-deck lobby to a Star Trek–like Internet café to a sophisticated Shaker Lounge to a bevy of restaurants that are suave and understated; the main Covent Garden theater is vast, festive, and fun. One of the many cruises sailing to Greece includes an 11-night itinerary that begins in Genoa, and stops at Greece's Katakolon (Olympia), Piraeus/Athens, Rhodes, and Heraklion, with other ports including Alexandria, Cyprus, and Naples. Rates for MSC cruises were not set at press time.

Your Shipmates. On Mediterranean itineraries you will find a majority of Europeans, including Italians, and announcements are made in a number of languages. Most American passengers are couples in the 35- to 55-year-old range and family groups who prefer the international atmosphere prevalent on board. Children from ages 3 to 17 are welcome to participate in age-appropriate youth programs in groups for ages 3–8 and 9–12. The Teenage Club is for youths 13 years and older.

> ### THE FACE THAT LAUNCHED A THOUSAND TRIPS
>
> Garnering plenty of headlines, the MSC *Musica* was launched in 2006 by silver-screen diva Sophia Loren and commentators noted that this curvaceous, sexy vessel was one Sophia of a ship.

Food. Dinner on MSC ships is a traditional seven-course event centered around authentic Italian fare. Menus list Mediterranean regional specialties and classic favorites prepared from scratch the old-fashioned way. "Healthy Choice" and vegetarian items are offered as well as tempting sugar-free desserts. A highlight is the bread-of-the-day, freshly baked on board. The nightly midnight buffet is a retro food feature missing from most of today's cruises.

Fitness and Recreation. Up-to-date exercise equipment, a jogging track, and basic fitness classes for all levels are available. Treatments include a variety of massages, body wraps, and facials that can be scheduled à la carte or combined in packages to encompass an afternoon or the entire cruise.

Contact. 6750 N. Andrews Ave., Fort Lauderdale, FL33309 954/662–6262 or 800/666–9333 www.msccruises.com.

NORWEGIAN CRUISE LINE

A cruise industry innovator since its founding in 1996, Norwegian Cruise Line's "Freestyle" cruising was born when Asian shipping giant Star Cruises acquired the Miami-based line. Confounded that Americans meekly conformed to rigid dining schedules and dress codes, the new owners set out to change the traditional formula by introducing a variety of dining options in a casual, free-flowing atmosphere. Noted for top-quality, high-energy entertainment and emphasis on fitness facilities and programs, NCL combines action, activities, and a resort-casual atmosphere.

Itinerary and Ship. Purpose-built for NCL's revolutionary Freestyle cruising concept (eat when you want and where you want—or almost), the *Norwegian Jewel* (2,224 passengers) has more than a dozen dining options. Decor showstoppers include the theater reminiscent of a European opera house, with lavish production shows and a full proscenium stage. Reflecting perhaps the somewhat gaudy painting of jewels on the exterior of the ship's hull, the Azura main restaurant and a bevy of other public spaces (including the aptly-named Fyzz Lounge & Bar) have some over-the-top jewel-tone carpets; other settings, including Cagney's Steakhouse, the Library, and the Star Bar, are lush, elegant, and elegantly decorated. A popular itinerary is featured on the 12-day "Egypt and Greek Isles" cruise, which sets off from Istanbul, and stops at Greece's Mykonos, Santorini, Heraklion/Crete, Corfu, Katakolon (Olympia), and Piraeus/Athens, and also includes Egypt's Alexandria and Turkey's Ephesus; prices were not available at press time.

Your Shipmates. NCL's mostly American cruise passengers are active couples ranging from their mid-thirties to mid-fifties. Longer cruises and more exotic itineraries attract passengers in the over-55 age group. Many families enjoy cruising on NCL ships during summer months. For children and teens, each NCL vessel offers the "Kid's Crew" program of supervised entertainment for young cruisers ages 2 to 17. Younger children are split into three groups from age 2 to 5, 6 to 9, and 10 to 12. For 13- to 17-year-olds there are clubs where they can hang out in adult-free zones.

Food. Main dining rooms serve what is traditionally deemed Continental fare, although it's about what you would expect at a really good hotel banquet. Where NCL stands above the ordinary is in their specialty restaurants, especially the French-Mediterranean Le Bistro (on all ships), the Pan-Asian restaurants, and steak houses (on the newer ships). In addition, you may find a Spanish tapas bar and an Italian trattoria. Some, but not all, restaurants carry a cover charge or are priced à la carte and require reservations. An NCL staple, the late-night Chocoholic Buffet continues to be a favorite event.

Fitness and Recreation. Mandara Spa offers a long list of unique and exotic spa treatments fleet wide on NCL. State-of-the-art exercise equipment, jogging tracks, and basic fitness classes are available at no charge. There's a nominal fee for personal training, and specialized classes such as yoga and Pilates.

Contact. ⊠ *7665 Corporate Center Dr., Miami, FL 33126* ☎ *305/436–4000 or 800/327–7030* ⊕ *www.ncl.com.*

OCEANIA CRUISES

This distinctive cruise line was founded by Frank Del Rio and Joe Watters, cruise industry veterans with the know-how to satisfy the wants of inquisitive passengers by offering itineraries to interesting ports of call and upscale touches—all for fares much lower than you would expect. Oceania Cruises set sail in 2003 to carve a unique, almost "boutique" niche in the cruise industry by obtaining midsize "R-class" ships that formerly made up the popular Renaissance Cruises fleet. Intimate and cozy public room spaces reflect the importance of socializing on Oceania ships while varied, destination-rich itineraries are an important characteristic of the line.

Itineraries and Ships. *Nautica* and *Insignia* (684 passengers each) strike some of the most sumptuous, elegant decor notes of any ships sailing—lobbies and public salons are dazzling with old-world gilt-famed paintings, glittery banisters, tapestried rugs, and enough wood paneling to line a hundred libraries—the effect is like a Vanderbilt yacht but magnified to the nth degree. A popular itinerary offered on the *Nautica* is the 12-day "Enchanted Escapade," which embarks in Athens and continues with Greece's Delos, Mykonos, Rhodes, and Santorini, then continues on to such far-flung spots as Malta, Sicily, Capri, Positano, Florence, Monte Carlo, Portofino, and Rome; rates begin at $3,599. A sample itinerary aboard the *Insignia* (684 passengers) is the 10-day "Path of the Phoenicians," which kicks off in Athens, then takes in Greece's Delos, Mykonos, Santorini, and Crete, with other stops in Kusadasi, Albania, Dubrovnik, and Venice; rates begin at $3,699.

Your Shipmates. Oceania Cruises appeal to singles and couples from their late-thirties to well-traveled retirees who have the time for and prefer longer cruises. Most are attracted to the casually sophisticated atmosphere, creative cuisine, and European service. Oceania Cruises are adult oriented and not a good choice for most families, particularly those traveling with infants and toddlers. Teenagers with sophisticated tastes (and who don't mind the absence of a video arcade) would enjoy the emphasis on intriguing ports of call.

Food. Top cruise industry chefs ensure that the artistry of world-renowned master chef Jacques Pépin, who crafted 5-Star menus for Oceania, is carried out. The results are sure to please the most discriminating palate. Oceania simply serves some of the best food at sea, particularly impressive for a cruise line that charges far less than luxury rates. The main open-seating restaurant offers trendy French-Continental cuisine with an always-on-the menu steak, seafood, or poultry choice and vegetarian option. Intimate specialty restaurants require reservations, but there is no additional charge.

Fitness and Recreation. While small, the spa, salon, and well-equipped fitness center are adequate for the number of passengers on board. In addition to individual body-toning machines and complimentary exercise classes, there is a walking/jogging track circling the top of the ship. Spa menus list massages, body wraps, and facials. Forward of the locker rooms you will find a large therapy pool and quiet deck for relaxation and sunning on padded wooden steamer chaises.

Contact. *8300 N.W. 33rd St., Suite 308, Miami, FL 33122* 305/514–2300 or 800/531–5658 *www.oceaniacruises.com.*

OCEAN VILLAGE

This small division of Carnival Corporation is just about as hip as a cruise line can get and still be considered a cruise line. Headquartered and marketed in the United Kingdom, the line's motto promises "the cruise for people who don't do cruises." Quite simply, Ocean Village cruises are flexible and relatively unstructured, although the company follows the typical British holiday scheme of being a total package deal (including airfare to the embarkation port), if that's what you desire.

Although the vessels in the current fleet aren't brand new, they have been extensively refurbished and have many of the amenities typical of much newer ships. They're also family-friendly. Upbeat and trendy, Ocean Village places stress on informal island-hopping and itineraries that include sunny, beach-centric destinations along with major city ports of call.

Itineraries and Ship. *Ocean Village One* (1,578 passengers) was redesigned a few years back to appeal to the young, trendy British market, which tends to be a bit unconventional. Interiors are bright and cheerful, with tons of teak and warm woods, and there's no stuffiness in the decor of the public spaces or the cabins. This ship has some of the nicest Greece-based itineraries around. A popular cruise is the 7-night "Olives and Ouzo" Mediterranean cruise that begins in Heraklion, Crete, sets sail for Rhodes, Santorini, and Mykonos, and also puts in at Ephesus, Turkey, and Limassol, Cyprus; rates begin at €1,388. Another typical itinerary is the 7-night "Temples and Tavernas" Mediterranean cruise, which kicks off in Heraklion, Crete, then moves on to Dubrovnik, Corfu, Kefalonia (of Captain Corelli fame), Katakolon (Olympia), and Athens. Rates begin at €1,169.

> **COME AND HEAR THOSE DANCING FEET**
>
> The pool area on the *Ocean Village One* is particularly interesting, with structures devoted to contemporary circus performances. Yes, that's right—the over-the-top "Moonshow" at night is right out of Barnum & Bailey, with acrobats and half-naked dancers tapping up a storm in echt-Riverdance style.

Your Shipmates. Ocean Village cruises draw mostly active British singles and couples from their thirties to fifties. Many consider themselves unconventional in a don't-tell-us-what-we-want-to-do manner. This relaxed cruising style is ideal for families and particularly for multigenerational family groups. Age-appropriate group programs are offered for children and teens from 2 to 17 years of age.

Food. Dining is buffet style for the most part, and dishes lean heavily toward British favorites with a sprinkling of Mediterranean- and Asian-influenced items for variety. Alternative dining spots with waiter service include menus inspired by British celebrity chef James Martin; these restaurants carry an extra charge. A popular children's tea is served every afternoon.

Fitness and Recreation. The ship has swimming pools, a well-equipped gym, exercise classes—some complimentary, others for a small fee—as well as deck spaces designated for joggers. Spas offer a typical menu of massages, facials, and exotic treatments. There is a fee for the use of saunas and steam rooms. In a unique twist on activities, you can learn to juggle or fly on a trapeze in circus workshops.

Contact. ⌂ *Richmond House, Terminus Terr., Southampton, UK SO14 3PN* ☎ *0845/358–5000* ⊕ *www.oceanvillageholidays.co.uk.*

P&O CRUISES

P&O Cruises (originally, Peninsular & Oriental Steam Navigation Company), boasts an illustrious history in passenger shipping since 1837. Although the company's suggestion that they "invented" cruising may not be entirely accurate, P&O is assuredly an industry pioneer. Having set aside such throwbacks as passenger classes, the company remains Britain's leading cruise line, sailing the United Kingdom's largest and most modern fleet. Ships are equipped with every facility you could think of, from swimming pools to stylish restaurants, spas, bars, casinos, theaters, and showrooms. Abundant balcony and outside cabins ensure that a view to the sea is never far away.

Itineraries and Ships. *Artemis* (1,188 passengers) was launched as the *Royal Princess* in 1984 by no less than Diana, Princess of Wales, who added an air of style during her christening that remains undiminished. The ship was a trailblazer—the first mainstream ship to feature only outside cabins. One of the most drastic changes the ship has undergone since joining the P&O fleet is that it is now an adults only vessel. A popular voyage is the 25-night "Glories of the Mediterranean" cruise, which leaves from Southampton, and takes in Greece's Nafplion, Athens, Heraklion, and Rhodes, while also calling at Ibiza, Cyprus, Cairo, Tripoli, Malta, and Lisbon; rates for the *Artemis* were not available at press time but a good sign is that the October 2007 voyage was "sold out." The *Arcadia* (1,948 passengers) was envisioned adults only, and her sophisticated and fresh elegance is highlighted by an extensive art collection that showcases modern British artists. P&O's first new ship in a decade, it sports a lively British Victorian-style pub; Arcadian Rhodes, the extra-charge specialty restaurant, is the creation of Gary Rhodes, one of Britain's most popular contemporary chefs. A typical cruise is the 17-night "Splendours of the Mediterranean," which sails from Southampton, and puts in at Greece's Corfu and Naxos, along with an extended range visiting Cadiz, Rome, Naples, Dubrovnik, and Malta; rates begin at €1,452.

Your Shipmates. Count on fellow passengers to be predominantly British singles, couples, and families, although you may find Scandinavians, Americans, and Australians aboard for some sailings. *Arcadia* and *Artemis* are adults-only ships; passengers must be 18 or older to sail aboard them.

Food. P&O has jumped on the choice bandwagon in dining and offers a somewhat dizzying number of options, although actual menu offerings vary quite a bit across the fleet. Club Dining, with assigned seating, is available on all ships; Select Dining in specialty restaurants requires reservations and carries a small charge; Freedom Dining is an open-seating dinner offered in certain restaurants on *Arcadia*. Meals are tailored to British tastes, so you will see a lot of curries on the menu. Afternoon tea is served daily.

Fitness and Recreation. Spa and salon facilities for men and women list an extensive range of therapeutic and rejuvenating treatments, from massages to facials, manicures, and body wraps. Each ship has a well-equipped gym and exercise classes. Deck quoits, an informal shipboard form of ring toss (rope rings are thrown alternately by players at round targets on the deck), is popular with passengers, and areas are set aside for the game.

> **AT SEE LEVEL**
>
> Aboard the *Artemis*, a sea view is never far from sight; not only do all cabins have a large window or balcony, there are windows in all public spaces.

Contact. ⌂ *Richmond House, Terminus Terr., Southampton, UK SO15 2BF* ☎ *0845/678–0014* ⊕ *www.pocruises.com.*

PRINCESS CRUISES

Princess Cruises may be best known for introducing cruise travel to millions of television viewers when its flagship became the setting for *The Love Boat* TV series in 1977. Since that heady time of small-screen stardom, the Princess fleet has grown both in the number and the size of ships. Although most are large in scale, Princess vessels manage to create the illusion of intimacy in understated, yet lovely public rooms graced by impressive art collections. In today's changing times, Princess has introduced more flexibility; Personal Choice Cruising offers alternatives for open-seating dining and entertainment options as diverse as those found in resorts ashore. Welcome additions to Princess's roster of adult activities are ScholarShip@Sea Enrichment programs featuring guest lecturers, cooking classes, wine-tasting seminars, pottery workshops, and computer and digital photography classes.

Itineraries and Ships. *Star Princess* (2,600 passengers) was built in 2002 and is one of the largest megaships prowling the Mediterranean. These Grand-class Princess ships feature soothing pastel tones with splashy glamour in the sweeping staircases and marble-floor atriums. Four pools, the Skywalker's Disco, and Times Square–style LED screens draw the crowds, while you can escape to your own seaside aerie: 80% of outside staterooms have balconies (although many are stepped, with a resultant loss in total privacy). A typical itinerary is the 12-day "Greek Isles–Venice to Rome" cruise, which embarks in Venice, then calls on Greece's Corfu, Katakolon (Olympia), Mykonos, Athens, Rhodes, and Santorini, along with other ports including Naples and Turkey's Kusadasi; rates are from $1,699; a slightly larger sister ship, *Emerald Princess* (3,100 passengers) offers the same cruise along with the popular 12-day "Greek Isles and Mediterranean," which departs from Rome, stops at Greece's Santorini, Mykonos, Athens, Corfu, and Katakolon (Olympia), with stops in Venice, Naples, Monte Carlo, and Florence; rates start at $2,240. Similar cruises are also offered on sister ship *Grand Princess,* as well as fleetmates *Sea Princess, Pacific Princess,* and *Royal Princess.* Smaller than the larger Grand-class ships, the refined and graceful *Sea Princess* (1,950 passengers) offers the onboard choices attributed to the fleet's larger vessels without sacrificing the smaller-ship atmosphere for which it's noted. A four-story atrium with a circular marble floor, stained-glass dome, and magnificent floating staircase strikes an ideal setting for relaxation, people-watching, and making a grand entrance. *Pacific Princess* (670 passengers) and *Royal Princess* (710 passengers) appear positively tiny beside their megaship fleetmates. In reality, they are medium-size ships that offer real choice to Princess loyalists—a true alternative for passengers who prefer the clubby atmosphere of a smaller "boutique"-style ship, yet one that has big-ship features galore.

Your Shipmates. Princess Cruises attract mostly American passengers ranging from their mid-thirties to mid-fifties. Longer cruises

> ### CROWD PLEASERS
>
> On Princess ships, personal choices regarding where and what to eat abound, but there's no getting around the fact that most are large and carry a great many passengers. Unless you opt for traditional assigned seating, you could experience a brief wait for a table in one of the open-seating dining rooms. Alternative restaurants are a staple. With a few breaks in service, Lido buffets on all ships are almost always open, and a pizzeria and grill offer casual daytime snack choices.

appeal to well-traveled retirees and couples who have the time. Families enjoy cruising together on the Princess fleet, particularly during summer months, when many children are on board. For young passengers aged 3 to 17, each Princess vessel has a playroom, teen center, and programs of supervised activities designed for different age groups. To afford parents independent time ashore, youth centers operate as usual during port days.

Food. Menus are varied and extensive in the main dining rooms, and the results are good to excellent considering how much work is going on in the galleys. Vegetarian and healthy lifestyle options are always on the menu, as well as steak, fish, or chicken. A special menu is offered for children. Possible options run from round-the-clock Lido buffets to Ultimate Balcony Dining, where a server is on duty and a photographer stops by to capture the romantic evening.

Fitness and Recreation. Spa and salon rituals include massages, body wraps, facials, and numerous hair and nail services, as well as a menu of special pampering treatments designed specifically for men, teens, and couples. Modern exercise equipment, a jogging track, and basic fitness classes are available at no charge. Grand-class ships have a resistance pool so you can get your "laps" in.

Contact. ✉*24305 Town Center Dr., Santa Clarita, CA91355-4999* ☎*661/753–0000 or 800/774–6237* ⊕*www.princess.com.*

REGENT SEVEN SEAS CRUISES

Regent Seven Seas Cruises (formerly Radisson Seven Seas Cruises) sails an elegant fleet of vessels that offer a nearly all-inclusive cruise experience in sumptuous, contemporary surroundings. The line's tried-and-true formula works; delightful ships feature exquisite service, generous staterooms with abundant amenities, a variety of dining options, and superior enrichment programs. Cruises are destination focused, and most sailings host guest lecturers—historians, anthropologists, naturalists, and diplomats.

Itineraries and Ships. The world's second all-suite, all-balcony ship, the *Seven Seas Voyager* (700 passengers) is a jewel of the fleet, with a high-tech Constellation Theater and four soigné restaurants keeping the beat going. For pure pampering, the Carita Spa—which received the "Best Cruise Line Spa" in *Condé Nast Traveler*'s 2006 Readers Poll—can't be beat. A typical itinerary is featured on the 8-day "Piraeus (Athens) to Venice" voyage, which starts in Piraeus, then sails for Greece's Mykonos, Nafplion, and Corfu, plus Dubrovnik and Venice; rates begin at $5,395. The much smaller *Seven Seas Navigator* (490 passengers) offers a more-intimate experience, and everything is downscaled, with only two restaurants and a large lounge for entertainment. The luxe is upped by some of the highest space and service ratios at sea and all-marble bathrooms. A popular itinerary is the 11-night "Monte Carlo to Piraeus" option, which kicks off in Monte Carlo and then sails to Rome, Sorrento, Sicily, Mytilini (Lesvos) as the first stop in Greece, then on to Istanbul and Kusadasi, then back to Greece for Mykonos, Nafplion, and Piraeus.

Your Shipmates. Regent Seven Seas Cruises are inviting to active, affluent, well-traveled couples ranging from their late thirties to retirees who enjoy the ships' elegance and destination-rich itineraries. Longer cruises attract veteran passengers in the over-60 age group. Regent vessels are adult oriented and do not have dedicated children's facilities. However, a "Club Mariner" youth program for children ages 5 to 9, 10 to 13, and 14 to 17 is offered on selected sailings.

Food. Menus may appear to include the usual cruise ship staples, but in the hands of Regent Seven Seas chefs, the results are some of the most-outstanding meals at sea. Specialty dining varies within the fleet, but the newest ships have the edge with the sophisticated Signatures, which features the cuisine of Le Cordon Bleu of Paris, and Latitudes, offering menus either inspired by regional American favorites or nouveau international cuisine. In addition, Mediterranean-inspired bistro dinners are served in the venues that are the daytime casual Lido buffet restaurants. Wines chosen to complement dinner menus are freely poured each evening.

Fitness and Recreation. Although gyms and exercise areas are well equipped, these are not large ships, so the facilities tend to be on the small side. Each ship has a jogging track, and the larger ones feature a variety of sports courts. Exclusive to Regent Seven Seas, the spa and salon are operated by high-end Carita of Paris.

Contact. ✉ *1000 Corporate Dr., Suite 500, Fort Lauderdale, FL 33334* ☎ *954/776–6123 or 877/505–5370* ⊕ *www.rssc.com.*

ROYAL CARIBBEAN INTERNATIONAL

Big, bigger, biggest! More than a decade ago, Royal Caribbean launched the first of the modern megacruise liners for passengers who enjoy traditional cruising with a touch of daring and whimsy tossed in. Expansive multideck atriums and the generous use of floor-to-ceiling glass windows give each RCI vessel a sense of spaciousness and style. A variety of lounges and high-energy stage shows draws passengers of all ages out to mingle and dance the night away. Production extravaganzas showcase singers and dancers in lavish costumes. The action is nonstop in casinos and dance clubs after dark, although daytime hours are filled with games and traditional cruise activities. Port "talks" tend to lean heavily on shopping recommendations and the sale of shore excursions. And then there are those famous rock-climbing walls.

> ### WHAT, NO FERRIS WHEEL?
>
> Royal Caribbean has pioneered such new and unheard-of features as rock-climbing walls, ice-skating rinks, bungee trampolines, and even the first self-leveling pool tables on a cruise ship. Exercise facilities vary by ship class but all Royal Caribbean ships have state-of-the-art exercise equipment and jogging tracks, and passengers can work out independently or participate in a variety of basic exercise classes. Spas are top-notch.

Itineraries and Ships. *Splendour of the Seas* (1,800 passengers) is one of the Royals that are noted for their acres of glass skylights that allow sunlight to flood in and windows that offer wide sea vistas. A double-height dining room with sweeping staircase is a showstopper but has to be, as there are no real specialty restaurants on board. Smaller cabins can be a tight squeeze for more than two people. A popular itinerary, with a good helping of Greece, is the 7-night "Greek Isles" cruise, which sails from Venice, then calls at Mykonos, Piraeus, Katakolon (Olympia), and Corfu, before returning to Venice via Split in Croatia; rates start at $649. *Legend of the Seas* (1,800 passengers) is a sister ship with lots and lots of wide-open space everywhere; the color schemes are both joyous and tranquil in hue, with lots of restful aquas, blues, and whites. A typical itinerary is the 12-night "Greece and the Eastern Mediterranean" tour, which sails from Rome, then mixes up Greece, Turkey, Egypt, and Italy, as it heads to Mykonos, Kusadasi, Rhodes, Cyprus, Alexandria, Piraeus, Naples, and back to Rome; rates start at $1,559.

Your Shipmates. Royal Caribbean cruises have a broad appeal for active couples and singles, mostly in their thirties to fifties. Families are partial to the newer vessels that have larger staterooms, huge facilities for children and teens, and seemingly endless choices of activities and dining options. Supervised age-appropriate activities are designed for children ages 3 through 17. Children are assigned to the Adventure Ocean youth program by age. For infants and toddlers 6 to 36 months of age, interactive playgroup sessions are planned, while a teen center with a disco is an adult-free gathering spot that will satisfy even the pickiest teenagers. Pluses are "family-size" staterooms on most newer ships, but a drawback is the lack of self-service laundry facilities.

Food. Dining is an international experience with nightly changing themes and cuisines from around the world. Passenger preference for casual attire and a resortlike atmosphere has prompted the cruise line to add laid-back alternatives to the formal dining rooms in the Windjammer Café.

Fitness and Recreation. Can a bowling alley be next? Fabled for its range of top-of-the-line recreations, Royal Caribbean also delivers on the basics: most exercise classes, aimed at sweating off those extra calories, are included in the fare (although there's a fee for specialized spinning, yoga, and Pilates classes, as well as the services of a personal trainer). Spas have full spa-style menus and full services for pampering for adults and teens.

Contact. ✉ *1050 Royal Caribbean Way, Miami, FL 33132–2096* ☎ *305/539–6000 or 800/327–6700* ⊕ *www.royalcaribbean.com.*

SAGA CRUISES

Saga Holidays, the U.K.-based tour company designed to offer vacation packages to mature travelers, started its cruise program in 1975. After building a 20-year reputation for comfortable cruise travel, Saga purchased its first ship in 1996 and a sister ship was acquired in 2004. Saga Cruises takes care of the details that discerning passengers don't wish to leave to chance—from providing insurance and arranging visas to placing fruit and water in every cabin. Activities and entertainment on board range from dance lessons to presentations of West End–style productions, computer software lessons, and lectures on wide-ranging topics. Both ships have card rooms, but you won't find casinos. With numerous accommodations designed for solo cruisers, Saga Cruises are particularly friendly for senior singles.

Itinerary and Ship. *Saga Ruby* (587 passengers) was originally christened the *Vistafjord* in 1973, but its interiors were fine-tuned in 2005, and the ship is now replete with modern furnishings, a spa, and a top-deck fitness center. She also has a ballroom and cinema, a card room, and a library, where DVDs and computers with Internet access can be found in addition to books. One of her top itineraries is the 16-night "Ancient Mediterranean Treasures" cruise, which sails from Marseilles, then heads to Rome, Katakolon (Olympia) as the first stop in Greece, then onward to Rhodes, Cyprus, Israel's Haifa, Egypt's Alexandria, back to Greece for Piraeus, then on to Malta and Marseilles; rates begin at €2,474.

Your Shipmates. Saga Cruises are exclusively for passengers age 50 and older; the minimum age for traveling companions is 40. The overwhelming majority of passengers are from Great Britain, with a sprinkling of North Americans in the mix. Saga Cruises are adults only—children are strictly not allowed.

Food. In addition to offering a wide selection of dishes to appeal to a variety of discriminating tastes, many British favorites find their way onto menus in the main restaurants. Ingredients are high in quality, well prepared, and served in a single leisurely seating. Traditional English tea is served every afternoon and midnight buffets are set up in the Lido restaurants.

Fitness and Recreation. Gentle exercise classes, tailored to different levels of ability, and fully equipped gyms are available for active seniors, and each ship has two swimming pools, one outdoors and one indoors. Passengers can work on their golf swing at the practice nets, jog on deck, or book a fitness session with a personal trainer. Each ship has a full-service spa tailored especially for mature cruisers.

Contact. ✍ *The Saga Bldg., Folkstone, Kent, UK CT20 3SE* ☎ *1303/771–111* ⊕ *www.sagacruises.com.*

SEABOURN CRUISE LINE

Seabourn was founded on the principle that dedication to personal service in elegant surroundings would appeal to sophisticated, independent-minded passengers whose lifestyles demand the best. Lovingly maintained since their introduction in 1987, the megayachts remain favorites with people who can take care of themselves, but would rather do so aboard a ship that caters to their individual preferences. Recognized as a leader in small-ship, luxury cruising, you can expect complimentary wines and spirits, elegant amenities, and even the pleasure of mini-massages while lounging poolside. Guest appearances by luminaries in the arts and world affairs highlight the enrichment program. Wine tasting, trivia, and other quiet pursuits might be scheduled, but most passengers prefer to simply do what pleases them.

Itinerary and Ship. *Seabourn Spirit* (208 passengers) had its maiden voyage in 1989 but was scheduled to receive a multimillion dollar makeover in January 2008. The ship's intimate scale is a nice plus although decor will never be featured on the cover of *Architectural Digest:* public spaces are beige-on-beige, with little glamour given to white wall treatments (other than paintings). Exotic colors, warm woods, stupendous fabrics, and conversation-piece rooms have been traded in for a restaurant and entertainment lounge that would not upset a staid banker; vast overhead lighting in public areas does not do wonders for a woman's complexion. But if you're looking for tranquillity and oh-so-subtle decor, this ship delivers. It often sails the eastern Mediterranean, and one of its popular itineraries is the 11-day "Glories of Greece" cruise, which kicks off in Alexandria, then sails to Greece's Rhodes, then Turkey's Bodrum, then back to Greece for Santorini, Chania (Crete), Gythion, Pylon, Itea (Delphi), Corinth Canal, Nafplion, and finally Piraeus; rates begin at $6,598. Another typical cruise-tour for Seabourn is the 11-day "Sail and Stay" option of "Greek Isles and Turkey," which allows days to tour Athens and Istanbul with voyages to Mykonos, Patmos, Tethiye and Kusadasi (Turkey), and the Dardanelles; rates start at $5,798.

Your Shipmates. Seabourn's yachtlike vessels appeal to affluent couples of all ages who enjoy destination-rich itineraries, a subdued atmosphere, and exclusive service. Passengers tend to be 50-plus and retired couples who are accustomed to the formality. Seabourn is adult oriented and unable to accommodate children under one year of age.

Food. Exceptional cuisine created by celebrity chef-restaurateur Charlie Palmer is prepared "à la minute" and served in open-seating dining rooms. Creative menu offerings include foie gras, quail, and fresh seafood. Vegetarian dishes and meals low in cholesterol, salt, and fat are prepared with the same care and artful presentation. Wines are chosen to complement each day's luncheon and dinner menus and caviar is always available.

Fitness and Recreation. A full array of exercise equipment, free weights, and basic fitness classes are available in the small gym, while some specialized fitness sessions are offered for a fee. The water-sports marina is popular with active passengers who want to jet ski, windsurf, kayak, or swim in the integrated saltwater "pool" while anchored in calm waters.

Contact. ⌂6100 Blue Lagoon Dr., Suite 400, Miami, FL33126 ☎305/463–3000 or 800/929–9391 ⊕www.seabourn.com.

SEADREAM YACHT CLUB

SeaDream yachts began sailing in 1984 and, after a couple of changes of ownership and total renovation in 2002, they have evolved into the ultimate boutique ships—as they put it, "it's yachting, not cruising." Passengers enjoy an unstructured holiday at sea doing what pleases them, making it easy to imagine the diminutive vessels are really private yachts. The ambience is refined and elegantly casual. Fine dining and socializing with fellow passengers and the ships' captains and officers are preferred pastimes. Other than a tiny piano bar, a small casino, and movies in the main lounge, there is no roster of activities. A well-stocked library has books and movies for those who prefer quiet pursuits in the privacy of their staterooms.

Itineraries and Ships. *SeaDream I* and *SeaDream II* (each 110 passengers) are known for their gorgeously soigné decor, flawless service, and one-of-a-kind delights, such as the Balinese sun beds (so comfortable that passengers sometimes choose to forsake their own quarters to spend the night on them) and beach-barbecue "splashes" replete with champagne and caviar. Although not huge ships, the public areas on board are quite spacious; the chic ambience conjures up a rich man's yacht, with tons of warm woods, brass accents, laid-back rattan chairs, and high-style deck awnings to shade you from the sun. Add in a richly-hued entertainment lounge, an extensive library, and perfect-taste cabins with sleep-inducing mattresses, ultra-deluxe bedding, and a shower big enough for two, and even Onassis would have approved. A popular cruise on *SeaDream I* is a 10-day voyage from Piraeus (Athens) to Venice, with stops in Hydra, Corinth Canal, Itea, Fiskardho, Corfu, and Dubrovnik; rates start at $5,299. A typical itinerary on *SeaDream II* is the 10-day Piraeus (Athens)–to–Dubrovnik cruise, with stops in Mykonos, Santorini, Hydra, Corinth Canal, Zakynthos, Corfu, and Croatia; rates begin at $5,799.

Your Shipmates. SeaDream yachts appeal to energetic, affluent travelers of all ages, as well as groups. Passengers tend to be couples from 45-year-olds and up to retirees who enjoy the unstructured informality, subdued ambience, and exclusive service. No children's facilities or organized activities are available.

> ### ROW, ROW, ROW YOUR BOAT
>
> The SeaDream water-sports marina is well used by active passengers who want to water-ski, kayak, windsurf, or take a Jet Ski for a whirl while anchored in calm waters.

Food. Every meal is prepared to order using the freshest seafood and prime cuts of beef. Menus include vegetarian alternatives and Asian wellness cuisine for the health-conscious. Cheeses, petits fours, and chocolate truffles are offered with after-dinner coffee, and desserts are to die for. All meals are open seating, either in the main restaurant or, weather permitting, alfresco in the canopied Topsider Restaurant daily for breakfast, lunch, and special dinners. Complimentary wines accompany each meal.

Fitness and Recreation. Small gyms on each ship are equipped with treadmills, elliptical machines, recumbent bikes, and free weights. A personal trainer is available. SeaDream's unique Asian Spa facilities are also on the small size, yet offer a full menu of individualized gentle pampering treatments including massages, facials, and body wraps utilizing Eastern techniques. Mountain bikes are available for use ashore.

Contact. ⌖2601 S. Bayshore Dr., Penthouse 1B, Coconut Grove, FL 33133 ☎305/856 5622 or 800/707–1911 ⓦ www.seadreamyacht-club.com.

SILVERSEA CRUISES

Intimate ships, paired with exclusive amenities and unparalleled hospitality, are the hallmarks of Silversea luxury cruises. Personalization is a Silversea maxim. Their ships offer more activities than other comparably sized luxury vessels, although you can also opt for quiet pursuits. Guest lecturers are featured on nearly every cruise; language, dance, and culinary lessons and excellent wine-appreciation sessions are always on the schedule of events. A multitiered show lounge is the setting for classical concerts, big-screen movies, and folkloric entertainers from ashore.

Itineraries and Ships. *Silver Whisper* (382 passengers) cuts a beautiful picture, large enough for ocean grandeur, small enough for smaller-port charm. Clean, modern decor that defines public areas and lounges verges on stark but it showcases large expanses of glass for sunshine and sea views, and that's a huge plus. Other signature touches include extremely wide passageways roomy enough for display cabinets featuring destination arts and crafts, a Davidoff Humidor, and totally free laundry rooms. A popular itinerary is the 7-day "Rome to Athens" cruise, with ports of call including Sorrento, Dubrovnik, and Greece's Corfu, Kythira, and Mykonos; rates start at $5,180. *Silver Cloud* (296 passengers), a yachtlike gem is all about style, understatement, and personal choice. While simply not large enough for huge public spaces, room on board is more than adequate and functions as well as on her larger fleetmate. A typical itinerary is the "Istanbul to Athens" cruise, with stops at Turkey's Kusadasi, Greece's Patmos, Rhodes, Mykonos, and Santorini; rates begin at $4,548.

Your Shipmates. Silversea Cruises appeals to sophisticated, affluent couples who enjoy the country clublike atmosphere, exquisite cuisine, and polished service. Although Silversea Cruises is adult oriented and unable to accommodate children less than one year of age, occasionally there's a sprinkling of children on board. There are no dedicated children's facilities available.

Food. Dishes from the galleys of Silversea's master chefs are complemented by those of La Collection du Monde, created by Silversea's culinary partner, the world-class chefs of Relais & Châteaux. Special off-menu orders are prepared whenever possible, provided that the ingredients are available. Nightly alternative theme dinners in La Terrazza (by day, the Terrace Café) feature regional specialties from the Mediterranean.

Fitness & Recreation. The rather small gyms are well equipped with cardiovascular and weight-training equipment, and fitness classes are held in the mirror-lined, but somewhat confining, exercise room. South Pacific–inspired Mandara Spa offers numerous treatments including exotic-sounding massages, facials, and body wraps.

Contact. ✉ *110 E. Broward Blvd., Fort Lauderdale, FL33301* ☎ *954/522–4477 or 800/722–9955* ⊕ *www.silversea.com.*

STAR CLIPPERS

Satisfy your inner pirate on Star Clippers' four- and five-masted sailing beauties—the world's largest barkentine and full-rigged sailing ships—which come filled with modern high-tech equipment as well as the amenities of private yachts. They were launched in 1991 as a new, spectacularly lovely tall-ship alternative for sophisticated travelers whose wants included adventure at sea, but not on board a conventional cruise ship. One of their most appealing attractions is that Star Clippers are not cruise ships in the ordinary sense with strict schedules and pages of activities. You are free to do what you please day and night, but many passengers enjoy socializing on deck.

Itineraries and Ship. *Star Clipper* (170 passengers) is a gorgeous four-master with brass fixtures, teak-and-mahogany paneling and rails, and antique prints and paintings of famous sailing vessels—the decor is a homage to the days of grand sailing ships. The library is vaguely Edwardian in style, replete with a belle-epoque fireplace, while the main restaurant has surprisingly vast dimensions but is made cozy by warm red hues, panel detailing, and elegant French Provençal–style chairs. Guest cabins are yachtlike and can be compact, with stepladders to beds. A popular cruise is the 10-night "Mediterranean Sailing," which starts in Venice, then heads to Dubrovnik and two other Croatian ports, before calling on Montenegro and Greece's Corfu, Yithion, Santorini, Mykonos, and ending up in Athens (Piraeus); rates begin at $1,995. A longer version lasts for 12 nights and includes stops at Sorrento and Stromboli. There are also many other idyllic itineraries that chart the northern and southern halves of the eastern Mediterranean.

> **LOVE FOR SAIL**
>
> The Star Clippers ships rely on sail power while at sea unless conditions require the assistance of the engines; you can't help but appreciate the silence and harmony with the sea when the engines are turned off and the ship is under sail.

Your Shipmates. Star Clippers cruises appeal to active, upscale American and European couples from their thirties on up who enjoy sailing, but in a casually sophisticated atmosphere with modern conveniences. Many sailings are about 50-50 from North American and Europe and announcements are made in several languages accordingly. This is not a cruise line for the physically challenged; there are no elevators, ramps, or staterooms/bathrooms with wheelchair accessibility. Star Clippers is adult oriented and there are no dedicated youth facilities.

Food. Not noted for gourmet fare, the international cuisine is what you would expect from a trendy shoreside bistro, albeit an elegant one. Fresh fruits and fish are among the best choices from Star Clippers' galleys. Lunch buffets are quite a spread of seafood, salads, and grilled items.

Fitness and Recreation. Formal exercise sessions take a backseat to water sports, although aerobics classes and swimming are featured on all ships.

Contact. 7200 N.W. 19th St., Suite 206, Miami, FL 33126 305/442–0550 or 800/442–0551 www.starclippers.com.

WINDSTAR CRUISES

Are they cruise ships with sails or sailing ships designed for cruises? Since 1986, the Windstar vessels have presented a conundrum. In actuality they are masted sailing yachts, pioneers in the upscale sailing niche. Often found in ports of call inaccessible to large traditional ships, Windstar ships seldom depend on wind alone to sail—their motors are necessary in order to maintain their schedules.

Itineraries and Ships. *Wind Spirit* (148 passengers) is a blue-and-cream-hue essay in Windstar style, with proportionately small public spaces replete with yachtlike touches of polished wood, columns wrapped in rope, and nautical artwork. Lots of time is spent on deck, which can get crowded; you can always escape to your cabin and watch DVDs with room-service popcorn. With its large windows and skylight, the main lounge is flooded with natural light. A popular itinerary is the 7-day "Rome to Athens" sailing, which includes Capri, Sicily, and Greece's Gythion, Nafplion, and Ermoupoli, city capital of the Cyclades; rates begin at $2,399. *Wind Star* (148 passengers) is a sister ship that also offers many voyages through the eastern Mediterranean, including the 7-day "Athens to Venice" cruise, which begins in Athens, then sails to Monemvassia, Katakolon (Olympia), Corfu, Albania, Dubrovnik, and Venice; rates begin at $3,999.

Your Shipmates. Windstar Cruises appeals to upscale professional couples in their late thirties to sixties and on up to retirees who enjoy the unpretentious, yet casually sophisticated atmosphere, creative cuisine, and refined service. The unregimented atmosphere is adult oriented; children, especially toddlers, are not encouraged. No dedicated children's facilities are available.

Food. Since 1994, Windstar menus have featured dishes originated by trendy West Coast chef and restaurateur Joachim Splichal and his Patina Group of bistro-style restaurants. In a nod to healthful dining, low-calorie and low-fat Sail Lite spa cuisine created by chef and cookbook author Jeanne Jones is available. A mid-cruise deck barbecue featuring grilled seafood and other favorites is fine dining in an elegantly casual alfresco setting. With afternoon tea and hot and cold hors d'oeuvres served several times during the afternoon and evening, no one goes hungry.

Fitness and Recreation. Windstar's massage and exercise facilities are quite small on *Wind Star* and *Wind Spirit* as would be expected on ships that carry fewer than 150 passengers. Stern-mounted watersports marinas are popular with active passengers who want to kayak, windsurf, and water-ski.

Contact. ⌂ *2101 4th Ave., Suite 1150, Seattle, WA98121* ☎ *206/292–9606 or 800/258–7245* ⊕ *www.windstarcruises.com.*

CRUISE BASICS

BOOKING YOUR CRUISE

According to the Cruise Line International Association (CLIA), cruisers plan their trips anytime from a year to a month in advance, with the majority planning four to six months ahead of time. It follows then that a four- to six-month window should give you the pick of sailing dates, ships, itineraries, cabins, and flights to the port city. You'll need more time if you're planning to sail on a small adventure vessel as some of their more-popular itineraries can be fully booked six to eight months ahead of time. If you're looking for a standard itinerary and aren't choosy about the vessel or dates, you could wait for a last-minute discount, but industry experts warn that these are harder to find than they used to be, now that cruising is so popular in Europe.

If you cruise regularly with the same line, it may be easiest to book directly with them, by phone or Web. Most cruises (90% according to CLIA) are, however, booked through a travel agent. Your best bet is a larger agency that specializes in cruises. They'll be able to sort through the myriad options for you, and often have the buying clout to purchase blocks of cabins at a discount. Cruise Lines International Association ⊕ *www. cruising.org* lists recognized agents throughout the United States.

> ### A SHORE THING
>
> If a particular shore excursion is important to you, consider booking it when you book your cruise to avoid disappointment later. You can even book your spa services pre-cruise on some cruise lines' Web sites so you can have your pick of popular times, such as sea days or the afternoon before a formal night.

CRUISE COSTS

The average daily price for a cruise varies dramatically depending on when you sail, which ship and grade of cabin you choose, and when you book. At the bargain end, cruising remains one of the best travel deals around: a weeklong cruise on an older ship, for example, with an interior stateroom, in the off-season, can still be had at a basic fare of less than $100 per day (before airfare, taxes, and other costs); or about $150 per day in the high season. At the other end of the scale, a voyage on a luxury line such as Silversea Cruises or a small luxury yacht may cost more than four times as much as a cruise on a mainstream line such as Carnival. Cruises on smaller vessels tend to be pricier than trips on mainstream lines because there are fewer passengers to cover the fixed costs of the cruise.

When you sail will also affect your costs: published brochure rates are highest in July and August; you'll pay less, and have more space on ship and ashore, if you sail in May, June, or September.

Whenever you choose to sail, remember that the brochure price is the highest fare the line can charge for a given cruise. Most lines offer early-booking discounts. Although these vary tremendously, many lines will offer at least some discount if you book several months ahead of time, usually by the end of January for a summer cruise; this may require early payment as well. You may also find a discounted last-minute cruise if a ship hasn't filled all its cabins, but you won't get your pick of cabins or sailing dates, and you may find airfare is sky-high or unavailable. However, since most cruise lines will, if asked, refund the difference in fare if it drops after you've booked and before the final payment date, there's little advantage in last-minute booking. Some other deals to watch for are "kids sail free" specials, where children under 12 sail free in the same cabin as their parents; free upgrades rather than discounts; or discounted fares offered to frequent cruisers from their preferred cruise lines.

SOLO TRAVELERS

Solo travelers should be aware that single cabins are extremely rare or nonexistent on most ships; taking a double cabin for yourself can cost as much as twice the advertised per-person rates (which are based on two people sharing a room). Exceptions are found on some older ships belonging to European-based cruise lines. A few cruise lines will find roommates of the same sex for singles so that each can travel at the regular per-person, double-occupancy rate.

> ### AND ONE LAST TIP
>
> Although most other kinds of travel are booked over the Internet nowadays, for cruises, booking with a travel agent who specializes in cruises is still your best bet. Agents have built strong relationships with the lines, and have a much better chance of getting you the cabin you want, and possibly even a free upgrade.

EXTRAS

Your cruise fare typically includes accommodation, onboard meals and snacks, and most onboard activities. It does not normally include airfare to the port city, shore excursions, tips, soft drinks, alcoholic drinks, or spa treatments. You may also be levied fees for port handling, security and fuel surcharges, as well as sales taxes, which will be added to your cruise fare when you book.

Athens

Greek soldiers "evzones", after the flag rise, Sunday morning in Acropolis ancient temple, Athens

WORD OF MOUTH

"As we climb the Parthenon's hill at my very slow pace, stopping for photographs every minute, I feel the weight of all who have climbed before us. It brings tears to my eyes. Even now."

—nikk

"Athenians love their Byzantine churches, so you will find modern buildings over and next to these churches. This is what gives Athens some of its charm."

—TJS

WELCOME TO ATHENS

TOP REASONS TO GO

★ **The Acropolis:** An ancient beacon of by-gone glory rising above Athens's smog, this iconic citadel represents everything the Athenians were and still aspire to be.

★ **Evzones on Syntagma Square:** Unmistakable in tasseled hats and pom-pommed shoes, they act out a traditional changing of the guard that falls somewhere between discipline and comedy.

★ **The Ancient Agora & Monastiraki:** Socrates and Plato once discoursed—and scored excellent deals on figs—at the Agora, and today you can do the same at the nearby Monastiraki marketplace.

★ **Opa!:** Whether jamming to post-grunge in Gazi—Athens's Greenwich Village—or dirty dancing on the tables at live bouzouki clubs, the Athenians party like no one else.

★ **Benaki Bounty:** Housed in a neoclassic mansion, the Benaki Museum—Greece's oldest private collection—has everything from ancient sculpture to 19th-century gowns.

1 Acropolis. A survivor of war, time, and smog, this massive citadel and its magnificent buildings epitomize the glories of classical Greek civilization.

2 Plaka/Anafiotika. This pretty neighborhood remains the last corner of 19th-century Athens, a quiet maze of streets dotted by Byzantine churches. Anafiotika, built on winding lanes climbing up the slope of the Acropolis, looks like a whitewashed Cycladic village.

3 Monastiraki. This area—adjacent to the ancient Agora—once housed the Turkish bazaar and it retains that Near East feel. Go to the flea market here to revel in the bustle of a chaotic, energizing marketplace.

4 Central Athens. Ranging from ancient Athens's majestic Kerameikos cemetery to top people-watching cafés, this is a chaotic mix of 16th-century Byzantine churches and 1970s apartments. Not for the fainthearted is Central Market, where you'll find everything from fresh

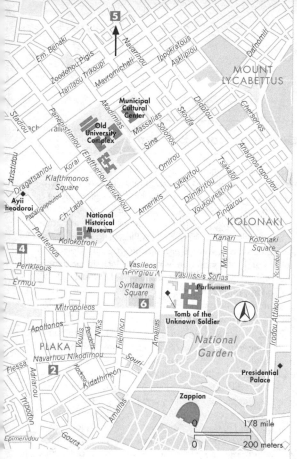

GETTING ORIENTED

3

Ancient glory may still define Athens internationally but it also has a modern cachet as a chaotic, exhilarating, spontaneous metropolis. In the midst of a mass of concrete apartment blocks, Athens's Greek, Roman, and Byzantine landmarks are mercifully concentrated around the city center—walk from the Parthenon to many other sites and still find time to sip an icy frappé in a café. The hub stretches from the Acropolis in the southwest to Mt. Lycabettus in the northeast. The main grid consists of three parallel streets—Stadiou, Eleftheriou Venizelou, and Akadimias—that link two main squares, Syntagma and Omonia. But be sure to detour to the Central Market, the shops in Monastiraki and Psirri, and Gazi, the emerging arts district.

cheeses to suspended carcasses. West lies Psirri, once the decrepit home to knife-wielding "manges" (tough guys) but today a district that beats to the hedonistic pulse of young Athenian clubbers.

5 Exarchia. In the northern reaches of the city, this somewhat run-down neighborhood is Student Central—filled with old-fashioned bars and rembetika clubs—and home to that must-see, the National Archaeological Museum, with its great ancient art.

6 Syntagma Square. The heart of modern Athens, the streets radiating out from Syntagma Square are lined with government agencies, neoclassic mansions, Queen Amalia's National Garden, and the Temple of Olympian Zeus. Here, too, is the museum district, where star attractions include the Goulandris Collection of ancient art and the Benaki Museum. To the east, at the foot of Mt. Lycabettus, lies Kolonaki—a fashionable residential area loaded with see-and-be-seen restaurants.

ATHENS PLANNER

Those Touristy, Kitschy, Wonderful Guided Bus Tours

Don't be a snob. Leave those three-piece suits at your hotel and enjoy one of the most festive ways to get acquainted with any big city: the basic multi-hour guided bus tour. In Athens, most tours include a visit to the Acropolis and National Archaeological Museum, plus other sites and lunch in a Plaka taverna. There are also "Athens by Night" bus tours. Morning tours begin around 8:45. Reserve through most hotels or travel agencies (many of which are clustered around Filellinon and Nikis streets off Syntagma Square). Tours run daily, year-round, and cost around €50. Book at least a day in advance and ask if you'll be picked up at your hotel or if you have to meet the bus. Two top tour bus companies are CHAT Tours (4 Stadiou, 210/322–3137, *www.chatours.gr*) and Key Tours (4 Kallirois, 210/923–3166, *www.keytours.gr*). Or opt for the "Athens Sightseeing Public Bus Line," or Bus 400, which stops at all the city's main sights. Those buses run every 30 minutes, from 7:30 am to 9 pm and tickets cost €5. The full tour takes 90 minutes, but you can hop on and off as you please. Bus 400 stops are marked by bright-blue waist-high pillars.

Getting Around by Metro

The best magic carpet ride in town is the metro. Cars are not worth the stress and road rage and, happily, the metro is fast, cheap, and convenient; its three lines go to all the major spots in Athens. Line 1, or the Green Line, of the city's metro (subway) system, is often called the *elektrikos*, or the electrical train and runs from Piraeus to the northern suburb of Kifissia, with several downtown stops. Downtown stations on Line 1 most handy to tourists include Victorias Square, near the National Archaeological Museum; Omonia Square; Monastiraki, in the old Turkish bazaar; and Thission, near the ancient Agora and the nightlife districts of Psirri and Thission.

In 2000, the city opened Lines 2 and 3 of the metro, many of whose gleaming stations function as mini-museums, displaying ancient artifacts found on-site. These lines are safe and fast but cover limited territory, mostly downtown. Line 2, or the Red Line, cuts northwest across the city, starting from Syntagma Square station and passing through such useful stops as Panepistimiou (near the Old University complex and the Numismatic Museum); Omonia Square; the Stathmos Larissis stop next to Athens's train stations, and Acropolis, at the foot of the famous site. Line 3, or the Blue Line, runs from the suburb of Aegaleo through Kerameikos (the stop for Gazi) and Monastiraki; some trains on this line go all the way to the airport, but they only pass about every half hour. The stops of most interest for visitors are Evangelismos, near the Byzantine and Christian Museum, Hilton Hotel, and National Gallery of Art, and Megaron Mousikis, next to the U.S. Embassy and concert hall. Work on extending the metro network continues.

The fare is €0.70 if you stay only on Line 1; otherwise, it's €0.80 A daily travel pass, valid for use on all forms of public transportation, is €3; it's good for 24 hours after you validate it. You must validate all tickets at the machines in metro stations before you board. Trains run between 5:30 AM and 11:30 PM. Maps of the metro, including planned extensions, are available in stations. There is no phone number for information about the system, so check the Web site (⊕*www.ametro.gr*), which has updates on planned extensions.

Getting Around by Bus & Tram

Athens and its suburbs are covered by a good network of buses, with express buses running between central Athens and major neighborhoods, including nearby beaches. During the day, buses tend to run every 15–30 minutes, with reduced service at night and on weekends. Buses run from about 5 AM to midnight. Main bus stations are at Akadimias and Sina and at Kaningos Square. Bus and trolley tickets cost €0.45. No transfers are issued; you validate a new ticket every time you change vehicles.

If you're making several short stops, a 90-minute ticket (€1 for all modes of public transport and €0.70 for bus, trolley, and tram only) may be cheaper. Day passes for €3, weekly passes for €10, and monthly passes for €38 (€35 for metro, trolleys, and buses only and €17.50 for buses only) are sold at special booths at the main terminals. (Passes are not valid for travel to the airport or on the E22 Saronida Express.) Purchase individual tickets at terminal booths or at kiosks.

Maps of bus routes (in Greek) are available at terminal booths or from EOT. KTEL (Greece's regional bus system, made up of local operators) has an English-language Web site. The Web site of the Organization for Urban Public Transportation has an excellent English-language section. You can type in your starting point and destination and get a list of public transportation options for making the journey.

Orange-and-white KTEL buses provide efficient service throughout the Attica basin. Most buses to the east Attica coast, including those for Sounion (€3.70 for inland route and €4.10 on coastal road) and Marathon (€2.40), leave from the KTEL terminal. A tram link between downtown Athens and the coastal suburbs features two main lines.

Line A runs from Syntagma to Glyfada; Line B traces the shoreline from Glyfada to the Peace & Friendship Stadium on the outskirts of Piraeus. Single tickets cost €0.60 or €0.40 for five stops and are sold at machines on the tram platforms.

City trams (⊕ *www.tramsa.gr*). **KTEL Buses** (⊠ *Aigyptou Sq. at corner of Mavromateon and Leoforos Alexandras near Pedion Areos park, Pedion Areos* ☎ *210/821–0872, 210/821–3203 for Sounion, 210/821–0872 for Marathon* ⊕ *www.ktel.org*). **Organization for Urban Public Transportation** (⊠ *Metsovou 15, Exarchia* ⊕ *www.oasa.gr*).

How's the Weather?

Athens often feels like a furnace in summer, due to the capital's lack of parks and millions of circulating cars. Mornings between 7 AM and 9 AM or evenings after 5 PM are often pleasant but temperatures can still hover in the 90s during heat waves. The capital is far more pleasant in spring and fall. The sunlight is bright but bearable, the air feels crisp and invigorating, and even the famously surly Athenians are friendlier. Winters are mild here, just as they are in all of Greece: it rains but rarely snows, so a light coat is all that is needed.

Multi-Trip Passes

If you are planning to take the bus, trolley, and metro several times in one day during your stay, buy a 24-hour ticket for all the urban network (€3) or a single ticket (€1) valid for all travel completed within 90 minutes. You must use a new ticket (€0.50–€0.70) for each leg of the journey for each method of transportation. A pass also saves you the hassle of validating tickets numerous times. Or opt for a weekly pass or a monthly pass, available at the beginning of the month from terminal kiosks and metro stations (€17.50 for unlimited bus and trolley travel; €35 with metro included). You need a passport-size photograph of yourself for the pass.

Updated
by Joanna
Kakissis

IT'S NO WONDER THAT ALL roads lead to the fascinating and maddening metropolis of Athens. Lift your eyes 200 feet above the city to the Parthenon, its honey-color marble columns rising from a massive limestone base, and you behold architectural perfection that has not been surpassed in 2,500 years. But, today, this shrine of classical form, this symbol of Western civilization and political thought, dominates a 21st-century boomtown. Athens is now home to 4.4 million souls, many of whom spend the day discussing the city's faults: the murky pollution cloud known as the *nefos,* the overcrowding, the traffic jams with their hellish din, and the characterless cement apartment blocks. Romantic travelers, nurtured on the truth and beauty of Keats's Grecian Urn, are dismayed to find that much of Athens has succumbed to that red tubular glare that owes only its name, neon, to the Greeks.

DISCOUNTS & DEALS

Athens's best deal is the €12 ticket that allows one week's admission to all the sites and corresponding museums along the Unification of Archaeological Sites walkway. You can buy the ticket at any of the sites, which include the Acropolis, ancient Agora, Roman Agora, Temple of Olympian Zeus, Kerameikos, and Theater of Dionysus. Admission to almost all museums and archaeological sites is free on Sunday from mid-November through March. Entrance is usually free every day for European Union students, half off for students from other countries, and about a third off for senior citizens.

To experience Athens—Athìna in Greek—fully is to understand the essence of Greece: ancient monuments surviving in a sea of cement, startling beauty amid the squalor, tradition juxtaposed with modernity—a smartly dressed lawyer chatting on her cell phone as she maneuvers around a priest in flowing robes heading for the ultramodern metro. Locals depend upon humor and flexibility to deal with the chaos; you should do the same. The rewards are immense if you take the time to catch the purple glow of sundown on Mt. Hymettus, light a candle in a Byzantine church beside black-shrouded grandmas while teens outside argue vociferously about soccer, or breathe in the tangy sea air while sipping a Greek coffee after a night at the coastal clubs.

Wander into less-touristy areas and you will often discover pockets of incomparable charm, in refreshing contrast to the dreary repetition of the modern facades. In lovely Athenian neighborhoods you can still delight in the pleasures of strolling. *Peripato,* the Athenians call it, and it's as old as Aristotle, whose students learned as they roamed about in his Peripatetic school. This ancient practice survives in the modern custom of the evening *volta,* or stroll, taken along the pedestrianized Dionyssiou Areopagitou street skirting the base of the Acropolis. Along your way, be sure to stop in a taverna to observe Athenians in their element. They are lively and expressive, their hands fiddling with worry beads or gesturing excitedly. Although often expansively friendly, they are aggressive and stubborn when they feel threatened, and they're also insatiably curious.

Amid the ancient treasures and the 19th-century delights of neighborhoods such as Anafiotika and Plaka, the pickax, pneumatic drill, and cement mixer have given birth to countless office buildings and modern apartments. Hardly a monument of importance attests to the city's history between the completion of the Temple of Olympian Zeus 19 centuries ago and the present day. That is the tragedy of Athens: the long vacuum in its history, the centuries of decay, neglect, and even oblivion. But within the last 150 years the Greeks have created a modern capital out of a village centered on a group of ruined marble columns. And since the late 1990s, inspired by the 2004 Olympics, they have gone far in transforming Athens into a sparkling modern metropolis that the ancients would strain to recognize but would heartily endorse.

> ## COLD RELIEF
>
> The center of modern Athens is small, stretching from the Acropolis in the southwest to Mt. Lycabettus in the northeast, crowned by the small white chapel of Ayios Georgios. The layout is simple: three parallel streets—Stadiou, Eleftheriou Venizelou (familiarly known as Panepistimiou), and Akadimias—link two main squares, Syntagma (Constitution) and Omonia (Concord). Try to detour off this beaten tourist track: seeing the Athenian butchers in the Central Market sleeping on their cold marble slabs during the heat of the afternoon siesta may give you more of a feel for the city than seeing scores of toppled columns.

EXPLORING ATHENS

Although Athens covers a huge area, the major landmarks of the ancient Greek, Roman, and Byzantine periods are close to the modern city center. You can easily walk from the Acropolis to many other key sites, taking time to browse in shops and relax in cafés and tavernas along the way. From many quarters of the city you can glimpse "the glory that was Greece" in the form of the Acropolis looming above the horizon, but only by actually climbing that rocky precipice can you feel the impact of the ancient settlement. The Acropolis and Filopappou, two craggy hills sitting side by side; the ancient Agora (marketplace); and Kerameikos, the first cemetery, form the core of ancient and Roman Athens. Preparations for the 2004 Olympics made these more accessible: along the Unification of Archaeological Sites promenade, you can follow stone-paved, tree-lined walkways from site to site, undisturbed by traffic. Cars have also been banned or reduced in other streets in the historical center. In the National Archaeological Museum, vast numbers of artifacts illustrate the many millennia of Greek civilization; smaller museums such as the Goulandris Cycladic and Greek Ancient Art Museum and the Byzantine and Christian Museum illuminate the history of particular regions or periods.

Athens may seem like one huge city, but it is really a conglomeration of neighborhoods with distinctive characters. The Eastern influences that prevailed during the 400-year rule of the Ottoman Empire are still evident in Monastiraki, the bazaar area near the foot of the Acropolis. On the northern slope of the Acropolis, stroll through Plaka (if possible by moonlight), an area of tranquil streets lined with renovated mansions, to get the flavor of the 19th-century's gracious lifestyle. The narrow lanes of Anafiotika, a section of Plaka, thread past tiny churches and small, color-washed houses with wooden upper stories, recalling a Cycladic island village. In this maze of winding streets, vestiges of the older city are everywhere: crumbling stairways lined with festive tavernas; dank cellars filled with wine vats; occasionally a court or diminutive garden, enclosed within high walls and filled with magnolia trees and the flaming trumpet-shape flowers of hibiscus bushes.

Formerly run-down old quarters, such as Thission and Psirri, popular nightlife areas filled with bars and *mezedopoleia* (similar to tapas bars), are now in the process of gentrification, although they still retain much of their original charm, as does the colorful produce and meat market on Athinas. The area around Syntagma Square, the tourist hub, and Omonia Square, the commercial heart of the city about 1 km (½ mi) northwest, is distinctly European, having been designed by the court architects of King Othos, a Bavarian, in the 19th century. The chic shops and bistros of ritzy Kolonaki nestle at the foot of Mt. Lycabettus, Athens's highest hill (909 feet). Each of Athens's outlying suburbs has a distinctive character: in the north is wealthy, tree-lined Kifissia, once a summer resort for aristocratic Athenians, and in the south and southeast lie Kalamaki, Glyfada, and Vouliagmeni, with their sandy beaches, seaside bars, and lively summer nightlife. Just beyond the city's southern fringes is Piraeus, a bustling port city of waterside fish tavernas and Saronic Gulf views.

THE ACROPOLIS & ENVIRONS ΑΚΡΟΠΟΛΗ & ΠΕΡΙΧΩΡΑ

Although Athens, together with its suburbs and port, sprawls across the plain for more than 150 square miles, most of its ancient monuments cluster around the Acropolis, which rises like a massive sentinel, white and beautiful, out of the center of the city. In mountainous Greece, most ancient towns were backed up by an acropolis, an easily defensible upper town (which is what the word means), but when spelled with a capital "A" it can only refer to antiquity's most splendid group of buildings—the Acropolis of Athens.

Towering over the modern metropolis of 4 million as it once stood over the ancient capital of 50,000, it has remained Athens's most spectacular attraction ever since its first settlement around 5000 BC. It had been a religious center long before Athens became a major city-state in the 6th century BC. It has been associated with Athena ever since the city's mythical founding, but virtually all of the city's other religious cults had temples or shrines here as well. As Athens became the dominant city-state in the 5th century BC, Pericles led the city in making the Acropolis the crowning symbol of Athenian power and successful democracy.

After the Acropolis all will at first seem to be an anticlimax. But there is still much that is well worth seeing on the citadel's periphery, including the neoclassic buildings lining its main street, Dionyssiou Areopagitou; the centuries-old Odeon of Herodes Atticus; the Dionysus theater; and the Ilias Lalaounis Jewelry Museum. Nearby is Filopappou, a pine-clad summit that has the city's best view of the Acropolis; the Pnyx where the Athenian assembly met; and the tiny, rustic church of Ayios Dimitrios Loumbardiaris.

Wear a hat for protection from the sun and low-heel, rubber-sole shoes, as the marble on the Acropolis steps and near the other monuments is quite slippery. Bring plenty of water—you'll need it, and there are usually long lines at the on-site cantinas.

Numbers in the text correspond to numbers in the margin and on the Athens: Acropolis, Plaka, Anafiotika, and Central Athens map.

WHAT TO SEE: THE MAIN ATTRACTIONS

❶ **Acropolis.** Towering over a modern city of 12 million much as it stood over the ancient capital of 50,000, the Acropolis (literally "high city") continues to be Athens's most spectacular, photogenic, and visited attraction despite hundreds of years of renovations, bombings, and artistic lootings. The buildings, constructed under the direction of Pericles during the city's Golden Age in the 5th century BC, were designed to be as visually harmonious as they were enormous, and they stand today in a perfect balance of stubborn immortality and elegant fragmentation. For an in-depth look at this emblem of the glories of classical Greek civilization, and the adjacent, headline-making New Acropolis Museum, see our photo-feature, "The Acropolis: Ascent to Glory" in this chapter.

Fodor'sChoice
★

❷ **Filopappou.** This summit includes **Lofos Mousson** (Hill of the Muses), whose peak offers the city's best view of the Parthenon, which appears almost at eye level. Also there is the **Monument of Filopappus,** depicting a Syrian prince who was such a generous benefactor that the people accepted him as a distinguished Athenian. The marble monument is a tomb decorated by a frieze showing Filopappus driving his chariot. In 294 BC a fort strategic to Athens's defense was built here, overlooking the road to the sea. On the hill of the **Pnyx** (meaning "crowded"), the all-male general assembly (Ecclesia) met during the time of Pericles. Originally, citizens of the Ecclesia faced the Acropolis while listening to speeches, but they tended to lose their concentration as they gazed upon the monuments, so the positions of the speaker and the audience were reversed. The speaker's platform is still visible on the semicircular terrace; from here, Themistocles persuaded Athenians to fortify the city and Pericles argued for the construction of the Parthenon. Farther north is the **Hill of the Nymphs,** with a 19th-century observatory designed by Theophilos Hansen, responsible for many of the capital's grander edifices. He was so satisfied with his work, he had *servare intaminatum* ("to remain intact") inscribed over the entrance. ✉ *Enter from Dionyssiou Areopagitou or Vasileos Pavlou, Acropolis* Ⓜ *Acropolis.*

Continued on page 87

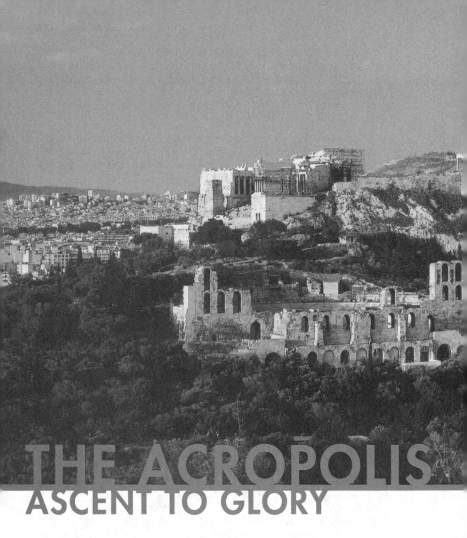

THE ACROPOLIS
ASCENT TO GLORY

One of the wonders of the world, the Acropolis symbolizes Greece's Golden Age. Its stunning centerpiece, the Parthenon, was commissioned in the 5th century BC by the great Athenian leader Pericles as part of an elaborate building program designed to epitomize the apex of an iconic culture. Thousands of years later, the Acropolis pulls the patriotic heartstrings of modern Greeks and lulls millions of annual visitors back to an ancient time.

You don't have to look far in Athens to encounter perfection. Towering above all—both physically and spiritually—is the Acropolis, the ancient city of upper Athens and womb of Western civilization. Raising your eyes to the crest of this *ieros vrachos* (sacred rock), the sight of the Parthenon will stop you in your tracks. The term Akropolis (to use the Greek spelling) means "High City" and today's traveler who climbs this table-like hill is paying tribute to the prime source of civilization as we know it.

A TITANIC TEMPLE

Described by the 19th-century French poet Alphonse de Lamartine as "the most perfect poem in stone," the Acropolis is a true testament to the Golden Age of Greece. While archaeological evidence has shown that the flat-top limestone outcrop, 512 feet high, attracted settlers as early as Neolithic times, most of its most imposing structures were built from 461 to 429 BC, when the intellectual and artistic life of Athens flowered under the influence of the Athenian statesman, Pericles. Even in its bleached and silent state, the Parthenon—the Panathenaic temple that crowns the rise—has the power to stir the heart as few other ancient relics do.

PERICLES TO POLLUTION

Since the Periclean Age, the buildings of the Acropolis have been inflicted with the damages of war, as well as unscrupulous transformations into, at various times, a Florentine palace, an Islamic mosque, a Turkish harem, and a World War II sentry. Since then, a more insidious enemy—pollution—has emerged. The site is presently undergoing conservation measures as part of an ambitious rescue plan. Today, the Erechtheion temple has been completely restored, and work on the Parthenon, Temple of Athena Nike, and the Propylaea is due for completion by the end of 2010. A final phase, involving massive landscaping works, will last through 2020. Despite the ongoing restoration work, a visit to the Acropolis today can evoke the spirit of the ancient heroes and gods who were once worshiped here.

THE PARTHENON
PINNACLE OF THE PERICLEAN AGE

DEDICATED TO ATHENA

At the loftiest point of the Acropolis stands the Parthenon, the architectural masterpiece conceived by Pericles and executed between 447 and 438 BC by the brilliant sculptor Pheidias, who supervised the architects Iktinos and Kallikrates in its construction. It not only raised the bar in terms of sheer size, but also in the perfection of its proportions.

Dedicated to the goddess Athena (the name Parthenon comes from the Athena Parthenos, or the virgin Athena) and inaugurated at the Panathenaic Festival of 438 BC, the Parthenon served primarily as the treasury of the Delian League, an ancient alliance of cities formed to defeat the Persian incursion.In fact, the Parthenon was built as much to honor the city's power as to venerate Athena. Its foundations, laid after the victory at Marathon in 490 BC, were destroyed by the Persian army in 480–79 BC. In turn, the city-state of Athens banded together with Sparta to rout the Persians by 449 BC.

To proclaim its hegemony over all Greece, Athens envisioned a grand new Acropolis. After a 30-year building moratorium, the titanic-scale project of reconstructing the temple was initiated by Pericles around 448 BC.

490 BC
Foundation for Acropolis laid

447-438 BC
The Parthenon is constructed

420 BC
Temple of Athena Nike is complete

TIMELINE

EDIFICE REX: PERICLES

His name means "surrounded by glory." Some scholars consider this extraordinary, enigmatic Athenian general to be the architect of the destiny of Greece at its height, while others consider him a megalomaniac who bankrupted the coffers of an empire, and an elitist who catered to the privileged few at the expense of the masses.

Indeed, Pericles (460–429 BC) plundered the treasury of the Athenian alliance for the Acropolis building program. One academic has even called the Periclean building program the largest embezzlement in human history.

MYTH IN MARBLE

But Pericles' masterstroke becomes more comprehensible when studied against the conundrum that was Athenian democracy. In truth an aristocracy that was the watchdog of private property and public order, this political system financed athletic games and drama festivals; it constructed exquisite buildings. Its motto was not only to live, but to live well. Surrounded by barbarians, the Age of Pericles was the more striking for its high level of civilization, its qualities of proportion, reason, clarity, and harmony, all of which are epitomized nowhere else as beautifully as in the Parthenon. To their credit, the Athenians rallied around Pericles' vision: the respect for the individualistic character of men and women could be revealed through art and architecture.

Even jaded Athenians, when overwhelmed by the city, feel renewed when they lift their eyes to this great monument.

TRICK OF THE TRADE

One of the Parthenon's features, or "refinements," is the way it uses meiosis (tapering of columns) and entasis (a slight swelling so that the column can hold the weight of the entablature), deviations from strict mathematics that breathed movement into the rigid marble. Architects knew that a straight line looks curved, and vice versa, so they cleverly built the temple with all the horizontal lines somewhat curved. The columns, it has been calculated, lean toward the center of the temple; if they were to continue into space, they would eventually converge to create a huge pyramid.

1456
Converted to mosque by occupying Turks

September 26, 1687
The Parthenon, used for gunpowder storage, explodes after being hit by a mortar shell

THE MISSING MARBLES

In Pericles' day, the Parthenon was most famous for two colossal (now vanished) statues fashioned by Pheidias: a tall bronze statue of Athena inside the temple, and one of Athena the Champion (Promachos), which faced anyone approaching the great hill. Neither of these works survive today but a second-century guidebook by the early travel writer Pausanias remembered how a seafarer approaching the harbor Piraeus could see the sun's rays glinting on Athena the Champion's spear and armor.

Today, however the Parthenon is notorious for its "missing" marbles—the legendary statues from the temple frieze and pediments that were shipped to England by Lord Elgin between 1801 and 1805. One of the most evocative sculpted friezes, the Procession of the Panathenaia was 524 feet long, depict-

ing an extraordinary parade of 400 people, including maidens, magistrates, horsemen, and musicians, plus 200 animals. To show ordinary mortals, at a time when almost all sculpture featured mythological or battle scenes, was lively and daring. About 50 of the best-preserved pieces of this panel, called the Parthenon Marbles by Greeks but known as the Elgin Marbles by almost everyone else, are in the British Museum; a few others can be seen in the New Acropolis Museum, while a few—showing scenes of battle: Athenians versus Amazons, and gods and goddesses against giants—remain on the temple itself.

In the first decade of the 19th century, during the time of the Ottoman Empire, Lord Elgin, the British ambassador in Constantinople, was given permission by the Sultan Selim III to remove stones with inscriptions from the Acropolis; he took this as permission to dismantle

Dull is the eye that will not weep to see / Thy walls defaced, thy mouldering shrines removed / By British hands, which it had best behoved / To guard those relics ne'er to be restored.

—From the poem "Childe Harolde's Pilgrimage" by the philhellene Lord Byron, published between 1812–18.

IN THIS CORNER: LORD ELGIN

The British nobleman and future diplomat Thomas Bruce, the seventh Earl of Elgin, became Britain's ambassador to the Ottoman Empire in 1799. His years in Constantinople were not happy: he suffered from what was very likely syphilis (the disease ate away his nose), and his wife soon took off with her personal escort. But Lord Elgin found purpose in "saving" priceless antiquities ignored by the ruling Turks and shipping them to Britain at enormous personal expense. Today, some consider him "a prince among thieves."

IN THIS CORNER: MELINA MERCOURI

She was so beloved as an actress and singer that people called her only by her first name. But behind the smoky eyes and husky voice that lit up the film *Never On Sunday* (1960) lay the heart of a fierce activist. As the country's first female culture minister, Melina led the fight to reclaim the Parthenon Marbles from Britain—"In the world over, the very name of our country is immediately associated with the Parthenon," she proclaimed. After she passed away, in 1994, a bust of her likeness was placed in the Dionysiou Areopagitou pedestrian walkway, in the shadow of the Acropolis.

shiploads of sculptures. Some historians say Elgin was neither ethical nor delicate in removing two-thirds of the famous Parthenon friezes and half of the marbles, causing irreparable damage to both the marbles and the Parthenon. On the other side, many argue that the marbles would have been destroyed if left on site. Today, a spirited long-term campaign aims to have them returned to Greece, to be appreciated in their original context. The New Acropolis Museum is being built with a special room for the marbles, in which they would be laid out in their original order; it will be constructed with glass walls, through which the temple the marbles originally adorned will be clearly visible.

(Above): Scenes from the so-called Elgin marbles (c 447- 432 BC) preserved at the British Museum in London; reconstruction of Parthenon interior, showing statue of Athena.

The Acropolis in Pericles' Time

RAISING A HUE

"Just by color—beige!" So proclaimed Elsie de Wolfe, celebrated decorator to J. Pierpont Morgan, when she first saw the Parthenon. As it turns out, the original Parthenon was anything but beige. Especially ornate, it had been covered with a tile roof, decorated with statuary and marble friezes, adorned with gilded wooden doors and ceilings, and walls and columns so brightly hued that the people protested, "We are adorning our city like a wanton woman" (Plutarch). The finishing touch was provided by the legendary sculptor Pheidias, who created some of the sculpted friezes—these were also brightly hued.

THE ERECHTHEION

PARTHENON

ATHENA PROMACHOS
Pheidias's colossal bronze statue of Athena Promachos, one of the largest of antiquity at 30' (9m) high, could be seen from the sea. It was destroyed after being moved to Constantinople in 1203.

THE PROPYLAEA

TOURING THE ACROPOLIS

Most people take the metro to the Acropolis station, where the New Acropolis Museum is to open in 2008. They then follow the pedestrianized street Dionyssiou Aerogapitou, which traces the foothill of the Acropolis to its entrance at the Beulé Gate. Another entrance is along the rock's northern face via the Peripatos, a paved path from the Plaka district.

THE BEULÉ GATE

You enter the Acropolis complex through this late-Roman structure named for the French archaeologist Ernest Beulé, who discovered the gate in 1852. Made of marble fragments from the destroyed monument of Nikias on the south slope of the Acropolis, it has an inscription above the lintel dated 320 BC, dedicated by "Nikias son of Nikodemos of Xypete." Before Roman times, the entrance to the Acropolis was a steep processional ramp below the Temple of Athena Nike. This Sacred Way was used every fourth year for the Panathenaic procession, a spectacle that honored Athena's remarkable birth (she sprang from the head of her father, Zeus).

THE PROPYLAEA

This imposing structure was designed to instill the proper reverence in worshipers as they crossed from the temporal world into the spiritual world of the sanctuary, for this was the main function of the Acropolis. Conceived by Pericles, the Propylaea was the masterwork of the architect Mnesicles. Conceived to be the same size as the Parthenon, it was to have been the grandest secular building in Greece. Construction was suspended during the Peloponnesian War, and it was never finished. The structure shows the first use of both Doric and Ionic columns together, a style that can be called Attic. Six of the sturdier fluted Doric columns, made from Pendelic marble, correspond with the gateways of the portal. Processions with priests, chariots, and sacrificial animals entered via a marble ramp in the center (now protected by a wooden stairway), while ordinary visitors on foot entered via the side doors. The slender Ionic columns had elegant capitals, some of which have been restored along with a section of the famed paneled ceiling, originally decorated with gold eight-pointed stars on a blue background. Adjacent to the Pinakotheke, or art gallery (with paintings of scenes from Homer's epics and mythological tableaux), the south wing is a decorative portico. The view from the inner porch of the Propylaea is stunning: the Parthenon is suddenly revealed in its full glory, framed by the columns.

THE TEMPLE OF ATHENA NIKE

The 2nd-century traveler Pausanias referred to this fabled temple as the Temple of Nike Apteros, or Wingless Victory, for "in Athens they believe Victory will stay forever because she has no wings." Designed by Kallikrates, the mini-temple was built in 427–424 BC to celebrate peace with Persia. The bas-reliefs on the surrounding parapet depicting the Victories leading heifers to be sacrificed must have been of exceptional quality, judging from the section called "Nike Unfastening Her Sandal" in the Acropolis Museum. In 1998, Greek archaeologists began dismantling the entire temple for conservation. After laser-cleaning the marble, to remove generations of soot, the team will reconstruct the temple on its original site.

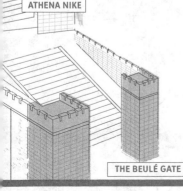

TEMPLE OF ATHENA NIKE

THE BEULÉ GATE

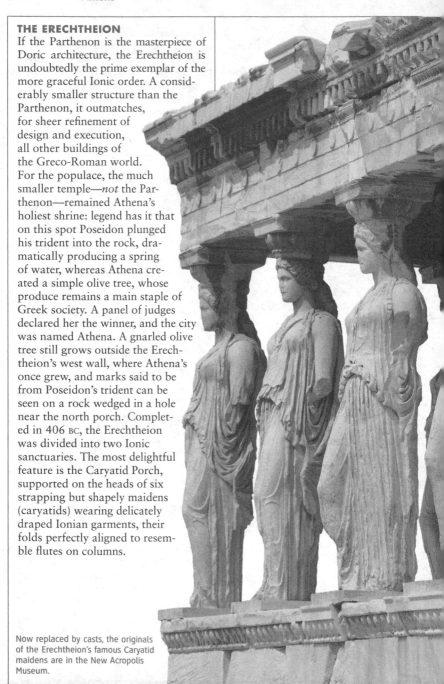

THE ERECHTHEION

If the Parthenon is the masterpiece of Doric architecture, the Erechtheion is undoubtedly the prime exemplar of the more graceful Ionic order. A considerably smaller structure than the Parthenon, it outmatches, for sheer refinement of design and execution, all other buildings of the Greco-Roman world. For the populace, the much smaller temple—*not* the Parthenon—remained Athena's holiest shrine: legend has it that on this spot Poseidon plunged his trident into the rock, dramatically producing a spring of water, whereas Athena created a simple olive tree, whose produce remains a main staple of Greek society. A panel of judges declared her the winner, and the city was named Athena. A gnarled olive tree still grows outside the Erechtheion's west wall, where Athena's once grew, and marks said to be from Poseidon's trident can be seen on a rock wedged in a hole near the north porch. Completed in 406 BC, the Erechtheion was divided into two Ionic sanctuaries. The most delightful feature is the Caryatid Porch, supported on the heads of six strapping but shapely maidens (caryatids) wearing delicately draped Ionian garments, their folds perfectly aligned to resemble flutes on columns.

Now replaced by casts, the originals of the Erechtheion's famous Caryatid maidens are in the New Acropolis Museum.

PLANNING YOUR VISIT

Dionysiou Areopagitou, Acropolis

☎ 210/321–4172 or 210/321–0219

✎ www.culture.gr

🎟 Joint ticket for all Unification of Archaeological Sites €12. Good for five days—and for free admission to the Ancient Agora, Theatre of Dionysus, Kerameikos cemetery, Temple of Olympian Zeus, and the Roman Forum.

🕐 Apr.–Oct., daily 8–sunset; Nov.–Mar., daily 8–2:30

Sooner or later, you will climb the Acropolis hill to witness, close up, its mighty marble monuments whose beauty and grace have not been surpassed in two millennia. When you do, keep these pointers in mind.

What Are the Best Times to Go? Such is the beauty of the Acropolis and the grandeur of the setting that a visit in all seasons and at all hours is rewarding. In general, the earlier you start out the better. In summer, by noon the heat is blistering and the reflection of the light thrown back by the rock and the marble ruins is almost blinding. An alternative, in summer, is to visit after 5 PM, when the light is best for taking photographs. In any season the ideal time might be the two hours before sunset, when occasionally the fabled violet light spreads from the crest of Mt. Hymettus (which the ancients called "violet-crowned") and gradually embraces the Acropolis. After dark the hill is spectacularly floodlighted, creating a scene visible from many parts of the capital. A moonlight visit—sometimes scheduled by the authorities during full moons in summer—is highly evocative. In winter, if there are clouds trailing across the mountains, and shafts of sun lighting up the marble columns, the setting takes on an even more dramatic quality.

How Long Does a Visit Usually Run? Depending on the crowds, the walk takes about four hours, including one spent in the Acropolis Museum.

Are Tour Guides Available? The Union of Official Guides (Apollonos 9A, Syntagma, 210/322-9705, 210/322-0090) offers licensed guides for tours of archaeological sites within Athens. Another option is Amphitrion Holidays (Syngrou 7, Koukaki, 210/900-6000), which offers walking tours of the Acropolis. Guides will also help kids understand the site better.

What's the Handiest Place to Refuel? The Tourist Pavilion (Filoppapou Hill, 210/923-1665), a landscaped, tree-shaded spot soundtracked by chirping birds. It serves drinks, snacks, and a few hot dishes.

DON'T FORGET:

■ If it's hot, remember to bring water, sunscreen, and a hat to protect yourself from the sun.

■ Get a free bilingual pamphlet guide (in English and Greek) at the entrance gate. It is packed with information, but staffers usually don't bother to give it out unless asked.

■ An elevator now ascends to the summit of the Acropolis, once inaccessible to people with disabilities.

■ All large bags, backpacks, and shopping bags will have to be checked in the site cloakroom.

THE NEW ACROPOLIS MUSEUM

Designed by the celebrated New York-based Franco-Swiss architect, Bernard Tschumi, the New Acropolis Museum (✉ *Dionyssiou Areopagitou 15, Makriyianni* ☎ *210/900–0900* ✉ *€5* ⊕ *www.theacropolismuseum.gr* ⊗ *Tues.–Sun., 8–8* Ⓜ *Acropolis*) opened to great acclaim in June 2009. It not only represents the latest in cutting-edge museum design but is seen as the perfect opportunity to showcase the Parthenon Marbles from London's British Museum, which the government of Greece has long been fighting to repatriate to their homeland. Set at the southern foot of the Acropolis hill (in the Makriyanni district), the new museum is a subtle, light-embued blend of high-tech glass and timeless stone.

In the five-level museum, every shade of marble is on display and bathed in abundant, UV-safe natural light. Visitors pass into the museum through a broad entrance and move ever upwards. The second floor contains a restaurant and shop, while the first floor exhibits ancient art works from the Acropolis and surrounding areas.

CAN YOU DIG IT?

Linking the floors is a spectacular ramp, presided over by the fabled Caryatid statues from the Erechtheion; its floor is studded with cutaway glass panels to reveal an ongoing excavation of an ancient Athenian village (discovered as the museum was being constructed). The third floor centerpiece is a glassed-in rooftop room, built to the exact proportions of the Parthenon, with grand views of the temple itself. There, the Parthenon sculptures that Greece still owns are arranged in their original order; pointedly, the museum avoids replicas of the British Museum pieces, thereby drawing attention to the missing treasures.

ART'S FOSSILS

Other than the *Caryatid figures* and the *Parthenon Marbles*, the most notable displays of the museum include, in Room IV, the *Rampin Horseman* and the compelling *Hound*, both by the sculptor Phaidimos; the noted pediment sculpted into a calf being devoured by a lioness—a 6th century BC treasure that brings to mind Picasso's *Guernica*; the charismatic *Calf-Bearer*, or Moschophoros, an early Archaic work showing a man carrying on his shoulders a calf intended to be sacrificed; a porous-stone pediment of the Archaic temple of Athena shows *Heracles fighting against Triton*—on its right side, note the rather scholarly looking "three-headed demon," bearing traces of the original color striking pedimental figures from the Old Temple of Athena (525 BC), depicting the battle between Athena and the Giants; and the great *Nike Unfastening Her Sandal*, taken from the parapet of the Temple of Athena Nike.

NEED A BREAK?

The little Tourist Pavilion (⊠ *Filo-pappou hill, Filopappou* ☎ *210/923–1665*) is a blissful hideaway far from the bustle of the archaeological sites and the streets. It is landscaped and shaded by overhanging pines, with chirping birds. Drinks, snacks, and a few hot dishes are served.

❸ **Odeon of Herodes Atticus.** Hauntingly beautiful, this ancient theater was built in AD 160 by the affluent Herodes Atticus in memory of his wife, Regilla. Known as the Irodion by Athenians, it is nestled Greek-style into the hillside, but with typi-

---

THE SCARLET TATTOO

On the hill of the Pnyx (meaning "crowded"), the all-male general assembly (Ecclesia) met during the time of Pericles. Gathering the quorum of 5,000 citizens necessary to take a vote was not always easy, as Aristophanes hilariously points out in his comedy *Ecclesiazusae* (Women of the Assembly). Archers armed with red paint were sent out to dab it on vote dodgers; the offenders were then fined.

---

cally Roman arches in its three story stage building and barrel-vaulted entrances. The circular orchestra has now become a semicircle, and the long-vanished cedar roof probably covered only the stage and dressing rooms, not the 34 rows of seats. The theater, which holds 5,000, was restored and reopened in 1955 for the Elliniko Festival, or Hellenic Festival (formerly known as the Athens Festival). To enter you must hold a ticket to one of the summer performances, which range from the Royal Ballet to ancient tragedies and Attic comedies usually performed in modern Greek. Contact the Elliniko Festival (Hellenic Festival) box office for ticket information. ⊠ *Dionyssiou Areopagitou near intersection with Propylaion, Acropolis* ☎ *210/323–2771* ⊙ *Open only during performances* Ⓜ *Acropolis.*

❹ **Theater of Dionysus.** It was on this spot in the 6th century BC that the Dionyssia festivals took place; a century later, dramas such as Sophocles's *Oedipus Rex* and Euripides's *Medea* were performed for the entire population of the city. Visible are foundations of a stage dating from about 330 BC, when it was built for 15,000 spectators as well as the assemblies formerly held on Pnyx. In the middle of the orchestra stood the altar to Dionysus. Most of the upper rows of seats have been destroyed, but the lower levels, with labeled chairs for priests and dignitaries, remain. The fantastic throne in the center was reserved for the priest of Dionysus: regal lions' paws adorn it, and the back is carved with reliefs of satyrs and griffins. On the hillside above the theater stand two columns, vestiges of the little temple erected in the 4th century BC by Thrasyllus the Choragus (the ancient counterpart of a modern impresario). ⊠ *Dionyssiou Areopagitou across from Mitsaion, Acropolis* ☎ *210/322–4625, 210/323–4482 box office* ☎€2; €12 joint ticket for all Unification of Archaeological Sites ⊙ *May–Oct., daily 8–7; Nov.–Apr., daily 8:30–2:30* Ⓜ *Acropolis.*

ALSO WORTH SEEING

⑤ Ilias Lalaounis Jewelry Museum. Housing the creations of the internationally renowned artist Ilias Lalaounis, this private foundation also operates as a study center. The 45 collections include 3,000 pieces inspired by subjects as diverse as the Treasure of Priam to the wildflowers of Greece; many of the works are eye-catching, especially the massive necklaces evoking the Minoan and Byzantine periods. Besides the well-made videos that explain jewelry making, craftspeople in the workshop demonstrate ancient and modern techniques, such as chain weaving and hammering. During the academic year the museum can arrange educational programs in English for groups of children. The founder also has several stores in Athens. ⊠*Kallisperi 12, at Karyatidon, Acropolis* ☎*210/922–1044* ⊕*www.lalaounis-jewelrymuseum.gr* ⊠*€4, free Wed. after 3 and Sat. 9–11* ⊙*Sept.–mid-Aug., Mon. and Thurs.–Sat. 9–4, Wed. 9–9, Sun. 11–4* Ⓜ*Acropolis.*

PLAKA & ANAFIOTIKA ΠΛΑΚΑ & ΑΝΑΦΙΩΤΙΚΑ

Fanning north from the slopes of the Acropolis, the relentlessly picturesque Plaka is the last corner of 19th-century Athens. Set with Byzantine accents provided by churches, the "Old Town" district extends north to Ermou street and eastward to the Leofóros Amalias. During the 1950s and '60s, the area became garish with neon as nightclubs moved in and residents moved out, but locals, architects, and academicians joined forces in the early 1980s to transform a decaying neighborhood. Noisy discos and tacky pensions were closed, streets were changed into pedestrian zones, and old buildings were well restored. At night merrymakers crowd the old tavernas, which feature traditional music and dancing; many have rooftops facing the Acropolis. If you keep off the main tourist shopping streets of Kidathineon and Adrianou, you will be amazed at how peaceful the area can be, even in summer.

Above Plaka is Anafiotika, built on winding lanes that climb up the slopes of the Acropolis, its upper reaches resembling a tranquil village. In classical times it was abandoned because the Delphic Oracle claimed it as sacred ground. The buildings here were constructed by masons from Anafi island, who came to find work in the rapidly expanding Athens of the 1830s and 1840s. They took over this area, whose rocky terrain was similar to Anafi's, hastily erecting homes overnight and taking advantage of an Ottoman law that decreed that if you could put up a structure between sunset and sunrise, the property was yours. Ethiopians, imported as slaves by the Turks during the Ottoman period, stayed on after independence and lived higher up, in caves, on the northern slopes of the Acropolis.

WHAT TO SEE: THE MAIN ATTRACTIONS

⑨ Anafiotika. Set in the shadow of the Acropolis, this is the closest thing you'll find in Athens to the whitewashed villages of the Cycladic islands featured on travel posters of Greece. It is populated by many descendants of the Anafi stonemasons who arrived from that small island in

STEP-BY-STEP: A WALK THROUGH PLAKA

Take time to explore the side streets graced by old mansions under renovation by the Ministry of Culture. Begin your stroll at the ancient, jewel-like **Monument of Lysikrates**, one of the few remaining supports (334 BC) for tripods (vessels that served as prizes) awarded to the producer of the best play in the ancient Dionyssia festival. Take Herefondos to Plaka's central square, Filomoussou Eterias (or Kidathineon Square), a great place to people-watch.

Up Kidathineon Square is the small but worthy **Greek Folk Art Museum**, with a rich collection ranging from 1650 to the present, including works by the beloved naive artist Theophilos Hatzimichalis. Across from the museum is the 11th- to 12th-century church of Sotira Tou Kottaki, in a tidy garden with a fountain that was the main source of water for the neighborhood until sometime after Turkish rule. Down the block and around the corner on Hatzimichali Aggelou is the **Center of Folk Art and Tradition**. Continue west to the end of that street, crossing Adrianou to Hill, then right on Epimarchou to the striking Church House (on the corner of Scholeiou), once a Turkish police post and home to Richard Church, who led Greek forces in the War of Independence.

At the top of Epimarchou is Ayios Nikolaos Rangavas, an 11th-century church built with fragments of ancient columns. The church marks the edge of the **Anafiotika** quarter, a village smack dab in the middle of the metropolis: its main street, Stratonos, is lined with cottages, occasional murals painted on the stones, and a few shops. Wind your way through the narrow lanes off Stratonos, visiting the churches Ayios Georgios tou Vrachou, Ayios Simeon, and Metamorphosis Sotiros. Another interesting church is 8th-century Ayioi Anargyroi, at the top of Erechtheos. From the church, make your way to Theorias, which parallels the ancient *peripatos* (public roadway) that ran around the Acropolis. The collection at the **Kanellopoulos Museum** spans Athens's history; nearby on Panos you'll pass the Athens University Museum (Old University), the city's first higher-learning institution. Walk down Panos to the **Roman Agora**, which includes the Tower of the Winds and the Fethiye Mosque. Nearby visit the engaging **Museum of Greek Popular Musical Instruments**, where recordings will take you back to the age of *rembetika* (Greek blues). Also next to the Agora is Athens's only remaining Turkish Bathhouse, providing a glimpse into a daily social ritual of Ottoman times. On your way back to Syntagma Square, cut across Mitropolis Square to the impressive 12th-century church of **Little Mitropolis**.

the 19th century to work in the expanding capital. Anafiotika is an enchanting area of simple stone houses, many nestled right into the bedrock, most little changed over the years, others stunningly restored. Cascades of bougainvillea and pots of geraniums and marigolds enliven the balconies and rooftops, and the prevailing serenity is in blissful contrast to the cacophony of modern Athens. You seldom see the residents—only a line of washing hung out to dry, the lace curtains on the tiny houses, or the curl of smoke from a wood-burning fireplace

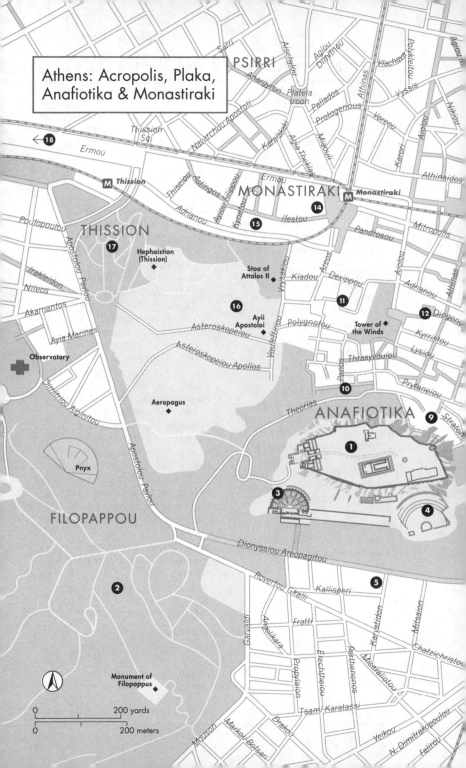

Athens: Acropolis, Plaka, Anafiotika & Monastiraki

3

indicate human presence. Perched on the bedrock of the Acropolis is **Ayios Georgios tou Vrachou** (St. George of the Rock), which marks the southeast edge of the district. One of the most beautiful churches of Athens, it is still in use today. **Ayios Simeon,** a neoclassic church built in 1847 by the settlers, marks the western boundary and contains a copy of a famous miracle-working icon from Anafi, Our Lady of the Reeds. The **Church of the Metamorphosis Sotiros** (Transfiguration), a high-dome 14th-century stone chapel, has a rear grotto carved right into the Acropolis. For those with children, there is a small playground at Stratonos and Vironos. ⊠*On northeast slope of Acropolis rock, Plaka* Ⓜ*Acropolis.*

❼ **Greek Folk Art Museum.** Run by the Ministry of Culture, the museum focuses on folk art from 1650 to the present, with especially interesting embroideries, stone and wood carvings, Carnival costumes, and *Karaghiozis* (shadow player figures). Everyday tools—stamps for communion bread, spinning shuttles, raki flasks—attest to the imagination with which Greeks have traditionally embellished the most utilitarian objects. Don't miss the room of uniquely fanciful landscapes and historical portraits by beloved Greek naive painter Theophilos Hatzimichalis, from Mytilini. ⊠*Kidathineon 17, Plaka* ☎*210/321–3018* ⊕*www.culture.gr* ☜€3 ⊙*Tues.–Sun. 10–2.*

❿ **Kanellopoulos Museum.** The stately Michaleas Mansion, built in 1884, now showcases the Kanellopoulos family collection. It spans Athens's history from the 3rd century BC to the 19th century, with an emphasis on Byzantine icons, jewelry, and Mycenaean and Geometric vases and bronzes. Note the painted ceiling gracing the first floor. ⊠*Theorias and Panos, Plaka* ☎*210/321–2313* ⊕*www.culture.gr* ☜€2 ⊙*Tues.– Sun. 8:30–3.*

NEED A BREAK?
Stop for an ice-cold frappé (Nescafé frothed with sugar and condensed milk) and a game of backgammon at Ionos (⊠*Geronta 7, Plaka* ☎*210/322– 3139*). If you're craving a good dessert, go to the lovely nearby café Tristrato (⊠*Geronta & Dedalou 34, Plaka* ☎*210/324–4472*) for some fresh baklava, *galaktoboureko* (custard-filled phyllo), or cheesecake.

⓭ **Little Mitropolis.** This church snuggles up to the pompous **Mitropolis** (on
★ the northern edge of Plaka), the ornate Cathedral of Athens. Also called Panayia Gorgoepikoos ("the virgin who answers prayers quickly"), the chapel dates to the 12th century; its most interesting features are its outer walls, covered with reliefs of animals and allegorical figures dating from the classical to the Byzantine period. Look for the ancient frieze with zodiac signs and a calendar of festivals in Attica. Most of the paintings inside were destroyed, but the famous 13th- to 14th-century Virgin, said to perform miracles, remains. If you would like to follow Greek custom and light an amber beeswax candle for yourself and someone you love, drop the price of the candle in the slot. ⊠*Mitropolis Sq., Plaka* ☜*Free* ⊙*Hrs depend on services, but usually daily 8–1* Ⓜ*Syntagma.*

❻ **Monument of Lysikrates.** Located on one of the ancient city's grandest
★ avenues (which once linked the Theater of Dionysus with the Agora),

this tempietto-like monument is a delightfully elegant jewel of the Corinthian style. It was originally built (335–334 BC) by a *choregos* (theatrical producer) as the support for the tripod (a three-footed vessel used as a prize) he won for sponsoring the best play at the nearby Theater of Dionysus. Six of the earliest Corinthian columns are arranged in a circle on a square base, topped by a marble dome from which rise acanthus leaves. In the 17th century the exceedingly picturesque monument was incorporated into a Capuchin monastery where Byron stayed while writing part of *Childe Harold*. The monument was once known as the Lantern of Demosthenes because it was incorrectly believed to be where the famous orator practiced speaking with pebbles in his mouth in an effort to overcome his stutter. A fresh-looking dirt track at the monument's base is a section of the ancient street of the Tripods (now called Tripodou), where sponsors installed prizes awarded for various athletic or artistic competitions. ⊠ *Lysikratous and Herefondos, Plaka* Ⓜ *Acropolis*.

🔟 **Museum of Greek Popular Musical Instruments.** An entertaining crash course in the development of Greek music, from regional *dimotika* (folk) to rembetika (blues), this museum has three floors of instruments. Headphones are available so you can appreciate the sounds made by such unusual delights as goatskin bagpipes and discern the differences in tone between the Pontian lyra and Cretan lyra, string instruments often featured on World Music compilations. The museum, which has a pretty shaded courtyard, is home to the Fivos Anoyiannakis Center of Ethnomusicology. ⊠ *Diogenous 1–3, Plaka* ☎ *210/325-0198* ⊕ *www.culture.gr* ⊠ *Free* ۞ *Tues. and Thurs.–Sun. 10–2, Wed. noon– 6* Ⓜ *Monastiraki.*

🔟 **Roman Agora.** The city's commercial center from the 1st century BC to the 4th century AD, the Roman Market was a large rectangular courtyard with a peristyle that provided shade for the arcades of shops. Its most notable feature is the west entrance's Bazaar Gate, or **Gate of Athena Archegetis,** completed around AD 2; the inscription records that it was erected with funds from Julius Caesar and Augustus. Halfway up one solitary square pillar behind the gate's north side, an edict inscribed by Hadrian regulates the sale of oil, a reminder that this was the site of the annual bazaar where wheat, salt, and oil were sold. On the north side of the Roman Agora stands one of the few remains of the Turkish occupation, the **Fethiye (Victory) Mosque.** The eerily beautiful mosque was built in the late 15th century on the site of a Christian church to celebrate the Turkish conquest of Athens and to honor Mehmet II (the Conqueror). During the few months of Venetian rule in the 17th century, the mosque was converted to a Roman Catholic church; now used as a storehouse, it is closed to the public. Three steps in the right-hand corner of the porch lead to the base of the minaret, the rest of which no longer exists.

Fodor'sChoice ★ Surrounded by a cluster of old houses on the western slope of the Acropolis, the world-famous **Tower of the Winds (Aerides)** is the most appealing and well preserved of the Roman monuments of Athens, keeping time since the 1st century BC. It was originally a sundial, water clock, and weather vane topped by a bronze Triton with a metal rod in his hand, which followed the direction of the wind. Its eight sides face the direction of the eight winds into which the compass was divided; expressive reliefs around the tower personify these eight winds, called *I Aerides* (the Windy Ones) by Athenians. Note the north wind, Boreas, blowing on a conch, and the beneficent west wind, Zephyros, scattering blossoms. ⊠*Pelopidas and Aiolou, Plaka* ☎*210/324–5220* ⊕*www. culture.gr* ⊠*€2; €12 joint ticket for all Unification of Archaeological Sites* ☉*May–Oct., daily 8–7; Nov.– Apr., daily 8–3* Ⓜ*Monastiraki.*

WATER GAMES

During Ottoman times, every neighborhood in Athens had a *hammam*, or public bathhouse, where men and women met to socialize among the steam rooms and take massages on marble platforms. If you want to see Athens's last remaining example, head to Kyrrestou 8. Sunlight streaming through holes cut on the domed roofs and playing on the colorful tiled floors created a languorous atmosphere here. The pretty 15th-century building now functions as a museum. Admission is free and hours are Wednesday and Sunday 10 to 2.

ALSO WORTH SEEING

⑧ Center of Folk Art and Tradition. Exhibits in the comfortable family mansion of folklorist Angeliki Hatzimichali include detailed costumes, ceramic plates from Skyros, handwoven fabrics and embroideries, and family portraits. ⊠*Hatzimichali Aggelikis 6, Plaka* ☎*210/324–3987* ⊠*Free* ☉*Sept.–July, Tues.– Fri. 9–1 and 5–9, weekends 9–1.*

NEED A BREAK? Vyzantino (⊠*Kidathineon 18, Plaka* ☎ *210/322–7368*) is directly on Plaka's main square—great for people-watching and a good, reasonably priced bite to eat. Try the fish soup, roast potatoes, or baked chicken. Glikis (⊠*Aggelou Geronta 2, Plaka* ☎ *210/322–3925*) and its shady courtyard are perfect for a Greek coffee or ouzo and a *mikri pikilia* (a small plate of appetizers, including cheese, sausage, olives, and dips).

THE ANCIENT AGORA, MONASTIRAKI & THISSION
ΑΡΧΑΙΑ ΑΓΟΡΑ, ΜΟΝΑΣΤΗΡΑΚΙ & ΘΗΣΕΙΟ

The Times Square, Piccadilly Circus, and St. Basil's Square of ancient Athens, the Agora was once the focal point of urban life. All the principal urban roads and country highways traversed it; the procession of the great Panthenaea Festival, composed of chariots, magistrates, virgins, priests, and sacrificial animals, crossed it on the way to the Acropolis; the Assembly met here first, before moving to the Pnyx; it was where merchants squabbled over the price of olive oil; the forum where Socrates met with his students; and centuries later, where St. Paul went about his missionary task. Lying just under the citadel of the Acropolis, it was indeed the heart of the ancient city and a general meeting place, where news was exchanged and bargains transacted, alive with all the rumors and gossip of the marketplace. The Agora became important under Solon (6th century BC), founder of Athenian democracy; construction continued for almost a millennium. Today, the site's sprawling confusion of stones, slabs, and foundations is dominated by the best-preserved Doric temple in Greece, the Hephaestion, built during the 5th century BC, and the impressive reconstructed Stoa of Attalos II, which houses the Museum of the Agora Excavations.

You can still experience the sights and sounds of the marketplace in Monastiraki, the former Turkish bazaar area, which retains vestiges of the 400-year period when Greece was subject to the Ottoman Empire. On the opposite side of the Agora is another meeting place of sorts: Thission, a former red-light district. Although it has been one of the most sought-after residential neighborhoods since about 1990, Thission remains a vibrant nightlife district.

TIMING Monastiraki is at its best on Sunday mornings, when the flea market is in full swing; Ermou street, on the other hand, is most interesting Saturday mornings, when it's also most crowded. The ancient Agora has little shade, so in summer it's better to visit the site in early morning or, better, in late afternoon, so you can check out Thission's café scene afterward.

WHAT TO SEE: THE MAIN ATTRACTIONS

16 **Ancient Agora.** The commercial hub of ancient Athens, the Agora was
Fodor's Choice once lined with statues and expensive shops, the favorite strolling
★ ground of fashionable Athenians as well as a mecca for merchants and students. The long colonnades offered shade in summer and protection from rain in winter to the throng of people who transacted the day-to-day business of the city, and, under their arches Socrates discussed matters with Plato and Zeno expounded the philosophy of the Stoics (whose name comes from the six *stoa,* or colonnades of the Agora). Besides administrative buildings, it was surrounded by the schools, theaters, workshops, houses, stores, and market stalls of a thriving town. The foundations of some of the main buildings which may be most easily distinguished include the circular Tholos, the principal seat of executive power in the city; the Mitroon, shrine to Rhea, the mother of gods, which included the vast state archives and registry office (*mitroon* is still used today to mean registry); the Bouleterion, where the council met; the Monument of Eponymous Heroes, the Agora's information center, where announcements such as the list of military recruits were hung; and the Sanctuary of the Twelve Gods, a shelter for refugees and the point from which all distances were measured.

The Agora's showpiece was the **Stoa of Attalos II,** where Socrates once lectured and incited the youth of Athens to adopt his progressive ideas on mortality and morality. Today, the Museum of Agora Excavations, this two-story building was first designed as a retail complex and erected in the 2nd century BC by Attalos, a king of Pergamum. The reconstruction in 1953–56 used Pendelic marble and creamy limestone from the original structure. The colonnade, designed for promenades, is protected from the blistering sun and cooled by breezes. The most notable sculptures, of historical and mythological figures from the 3rd and 4th centuries BC, are at ground level outside the museum. In the exhibition hall, chronological displays of pottery and objects from everyday life (note the child's terra-cotta potty) illustrate the settlement of the area from Neolithic times, including fascinating ancient toys and masks.

Take a walk around the site and speculate on the location of Simon the Cobbler's house and shop, which was a meeting place for Socrates and his pupils. The carefully landscaped grounds display a number of plants known in antiquity, such as almond, myrtle, and pomegranate. By standing in the center, you have a glorious view up to the Acropolis. **Ayii Apostoloi** is the only one of the Agora's nine churches to survive, saved because of its location and beauty. Inside, the dome and the altar sit on ancient capitals. Plans displayed in the narthex give an idea of the church's thousand-year-old history.

On the low hill called Kolonos Agoraios in the Agora's northwest corner stands the best-preserved Doric temple in all Greece, the **Hephaestion**, sometimes called the Thission because of its friezes showing the exploits of Theseus. Like the other monuments, it is roped off, but you can walk around it to admire its preservation. A little older than the Parthenon, it is surrounded by 34 columns and is 104 feet in length, and was once filled with sculptures (the only remnant of which is the mutilated frieze, once brightly colored). It never quite makes the impact of the Parthenon, in large part due to the fact that it lacks a noble site and can never be seen from below, its sun-matured columns towering heavenward. The Hephaestion was originally dedicated to Hephaistos, god of metalworkers, and it is interesting to note that metal workshops still exist in this area near Ifestou. Behind the temple, paths cross the northwest slope past archaeological ruins half hidden in deep undergrowth. Here you can sit on a bench and contemplate the same scene that Englishman Edward Dodwell saw in the early 19th century, when he came to sketch antiquities. ⊠ *3 entrances: from Monastiraki on Adrianou; from Thission on Apostolou Pavlou; and descending from Acropolis on Ayios Apostoloi, Monastiraki* ☎ *210/321–0185* ⊕ *www. culture.gr* ⊠ *€4; €12 joint ticket for all Unification of Archaeological Sites* ⊙ *May–Oct., daily 8–7; Nov.–Apr., daily 8–5; museum closes ½ hr before site* Ⓜ *Thiseio.*

⑱ Melina Mercouri Cultural Center. Named in honor of the famous *Never on Sunday* Greek actress who became a political figure in the 1980s, this center is installed in the former Poulopoulos hat factory built in 1886. Delightfully, the center gives a rare glimpse of Athens during the 19th century. You can walk through a reconstructed Athens street with facades of neoclassic homes that evoke the civilized elegance of the past, a pharmacy, printing press, dry goods store, *kafeneio* (coffeehouse), and dress shop, all painstakingly fitted out with authentic objects collected by the Greek Literary and Historical Archives. Throughout the year the center showcases temporary exhibitions, usually featuring contemporary Greek art. ⊠ *Iraklidon 66a, at Thessalonikis, Thission* ☎ *210/345–2150* ⊠ *Free* ⊙ *Tues.–Sat. 9–1 and 5–9, Sun. 9–1* Ⓜ *Petralona.*

17 Thission. This neighborhood, easily accessible by metro and offering a lovely view of the Acropolis, has become one of the liveliest café and restaurant districts in Athens. The area has excellent *rakadika* and *ouzeri*—publike eateries that offer plates of appetizers to go with *raki*, a fiery spirit made from grape must, and the ever-appealing ouzo, as well as barrels of homemade wine. The main strip is the Nileos pedestrian zone across from the ancient Agora entrance, lined with cafés that are cozy in winter and have outdoor tables in summer. The rest of the neighborhood is quiet, an odd mix of mom-and-pop stores and dilapidated houses that are slowly being renovated; take a brief stroll along Akamantos (which becomes Galatias) around the intersections of Dimofontos or Aginoros, or down Iraklidon, to get a feel for the quarter's past. ⊠ *West of ancient Agora, Apostolou Pavlou, and Akamantos, Thission* Ⓜ *Thiseio.*

IN & AROUND THE AGORA

After browsing through the market stalls, enter the Ancient Agora at the corner of Kinetou and Adrianou (the latter runs parallel to Ifestou). Be sure to visit the site's Museum of Agora Excavations, which offers a fascinating glimpse of everyday life in the ancient city. Exit at the site's opposite end onto Dionyssiou Areopagitou, crossing the boulevard to the Thission quarter, a lively area with neoclassical homes overlooking trendy cafés and home to the noted Melina Mercouri Cultural Center, where exhibits re-create the streets of Athens during different epochs.

NEED A BREAK? For a fancy coffee (think espresso mixed with sambuca) and sweet crepes (banana and chocolate hazelnut), stop at Athinaion Politeia (⊠ *Akamantos 1 and Apostolou Pavlou, Thission* ☎ *210/341–3795*), a restored mansion where you can watch the crowds on Apostolou Pavlou. Thirtysomething hipsters hold court here, telling raucous stories that spill into laughter, making you feel like you're in the middle of the best party in town.

ALSO WORTH SEEING

15 Flea Market. Here is where the chaos, spirit, and charm of Athens turn into a feast for the senses. The Sunday morning market has combined sight, sound, and scent into a strangely alluring little world where everything is for sale: 1950s-era scuba masks, old tea sets, antique sewing machines, old tobacco tins, gramophone needles, old matchboxes, and lacquered eggs. Haggle, no matter how low the price. ⊠ *Along Ifestou, Kynetou, and Adrianou, Monastiraki* Ⓜ *Monastiraki.*

14 Monastiraki Square. The square takes its name from the small **Panagia Pantanassa Church,** commonly called Monastiraki (Little Monastery). It once flourished as an extensive convent, perhaps dating to the 10th century, which stretched from Athinas to Aiolou. The nuns took in poor people, who earned their keep weaving the thick textiles known as *abas.* The buildings were destroyed during excavations and the train (and later metro) line construction that started in 1896. The convent's basic basilica form, now recessed a few steps below street level, was altered through a poor restoration in 1911, when the bell tower was added. The square's focal point, the 18th-century **Tzistarakis Mosque** (✉*Areos 1, Monastiraki* ☎*210/324–2066* ✆*€2* ⊙*Wed.–Mon. 9– 2:30*), houses a ceramics collection that is beautifully designed, with the exhibits handsomely lighted and labeled. The mosque's creator, a newly appointed Turkish civil governor, knocked down a column from the Temple of Olympian Zeus to make lime for the mosque. Punished by the sultan for his audacity, he was also blamed by Athenians for an ensuing plague; it was believed the toppling of a column released epidemics and disasters from below Earth. ✉*South of Ermou and Athinas junction, Monastiraki.*

NEED A BREAK?

On Mitropoleos off Monastiraki Square are a handful of counter-front places selling souvlaki—grilled meat rolled in a pita with onions, *tzatziki* (yogurt-garlic dip), and tomatoes—the best bargain in Athens. Make sure you specify either a souvlaki sandwich or a "souvlaki plate," an entire meal. Hands down the best kebab in town is Thanassis (✉*Mitropoleos 69, Monastiraki* ☎*210/324–4705*), which is always crowded with Greeks who crave the specially spiced ground meat.

FROM CENTRAL ATHENS TO NATIONAL ARCHAEOLOGICAL MUSEUM ΑΘΗΝΑ (ΚΕΝΤΡΟ) ΤΟ ΕΘΝΙΚΟ ΑΡΧΑΙΟΛΟΓΙΚΟ ΜΟΥΣΕΙΟ

Numbers in the text correspond to numbers in the margin and on the Syntagma Square, Kolonaki, and Exarchia map.

Downtown Athens is an unlikely combination of the squalid and the grand: the cavernous, chaotic Central Market, which replaced the bazaar in Monastiraki when it burned down in 1885, is 10 minutes from the elegant, neoclassic Old University complex. The surrounding area is filled with the remains of the 19th-century mansions that once made Athens world renowned as a charming city. Some of these are crumbling into the streets; others, like the exquisite mansion that has been converted into the Numismatic Museum (once the grand abode of Heinrich Schliemann, discoverer of Troy) have regained their lost loveliness. Such buildings rub shoulders with incense-scented, 12th-century Byzantine churches as well as some of the city's most hideous 1970s apartment blocks, many of which are occupied by Greece's growing migrant population. The mix has become more heady as artists and fashionistas move to the neighborhoods of Psirri and Gazi and transform long-neglected warehouses into galleries, nightclubs, and ultra-chic restaurants.

At the western edge of all this is the wide, green expanse of Kerameikos, the main cemetery in ancient Athens until Sulla destroyed the city in 86 BC. The name is associated with the modern word "ceramic": in the 12th century BC the district was populated by potters who used the abundant clay from the languid Iridanos River to make funerary urns and grave decorations. Kerameikos contains the foundations of two ancient monuments: the Dipylon Gate, where visitors entered the city, and the Sacred Gate, used for both the pilgrimage to the Eleusinian rites and for the Panathenaic procession in which the tunic for the statue of Athena was carted to the Acropolis.

Heading back east, a good 10 blocks directly north of the Old University complex, the glory that was Athens continues at the city's legendary National Archaeological Museum. One of the most exciting collections of Greek antiquities in the world, this is a must-do for any travelers to Athens, nay, Greece. Here are the sensational finds made by Heinrich Schliemann, discoverer of Troy and father of modern archaeology, in the course of his excavations of the royal tombs on the Homeric site of Mycenae in the 1870s. Here, too, are world-famous bronzes such as the *Jockey of Artemision* and a bronze of Poseidon throwing a trident (or is it Zeus hurling a thunderbolt?). An added treat is the neighborhood the museum presides over: Exarchia, a bohemian district that is mentioned in hundreds of Greek folk songs and novels. The area evokes strong feelings in every Athenian for here, in 1973, the students of Athens Polytechnic rose up in protest against Greece's hated military dictatorship. The colonels crushed the uprising and tanks killed many students, but the protests led to the junta's fall the following year. Today, the neighborhood still bubbles with rebellious energy; students, intellectuals, and anarchists often fill its many cafés and tavernas, debating the latest in domestic and global affairs.

WHAT TO SEE: THE MAIN ATTRACTIONS

㉒ Central Market. The market runs along Athinas: on one side are open-air stalls selling fruit and vegetables at the best prices in town, although wily merchants may slip overripe items into your bag. At the corner of Armodiou, shops stock live poultry and rabbits. Across the street, in the huge covered market built in 1870, the surrealistic composition of suspended carcasses and shimmering fish on marble counters emits a pungent odor that is overwhelming on hot days. The shops at the north end of the market, to the right on Sofokleous, sell the best cheese, olives, halvah, bread, and cold cuts, including *pastourma* (spicy cured beef), available in Athens. Small restaurants serving *patsa*, or tripe soup, dot the market; these stay open until almost dawn and are popular stops with weary clubbers trying to ease their hangovers. ⊠ *Athinas, Central Market* ⊘ *Weekdays and Sat. morning* Ⓜ *Monastiraki.*

NEED A BREAK? For a true taste of bygone Athens, don't miss Krinos (⊠ *Aiolou 87, Central Market* ☎ *210/321-6852*), an endearingly old-timey café that serves Athens's best *loukoumades*—irresistible, doughnutlike fritters sprinkled with cinnamon and drizzled with a honeyed syrup based on a Smyrna recipe. Krinos has been serving the treat since it opened its doors in the 1920s and also makes excellent *boughatsa* (cream pies), *rizogalo* (rice pudding), and sandwiches; it is closed Sunday. Squeeze into one of the many tables and enjoy your treat with the old gents and ladies who have been regulars for decades.

⓴ Kerameikos Cemetery. From the 7th century BC onward, Kerameikos was the smart cemetery of ancient Athens. During succeeding ages cemeteries were superimposed on the ancient one until the latter was

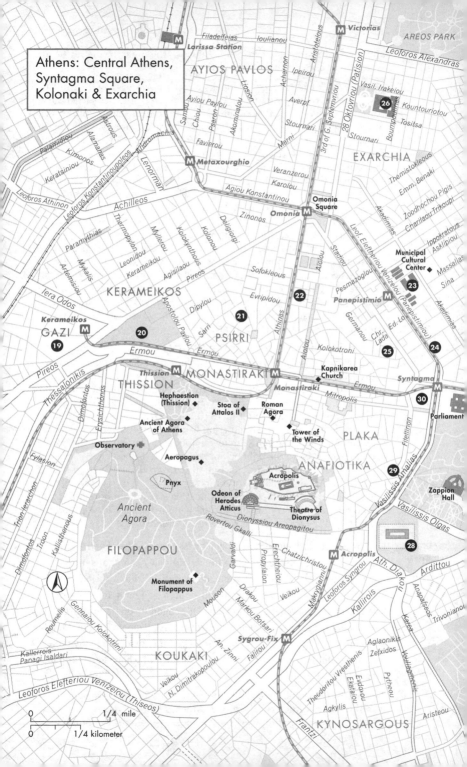

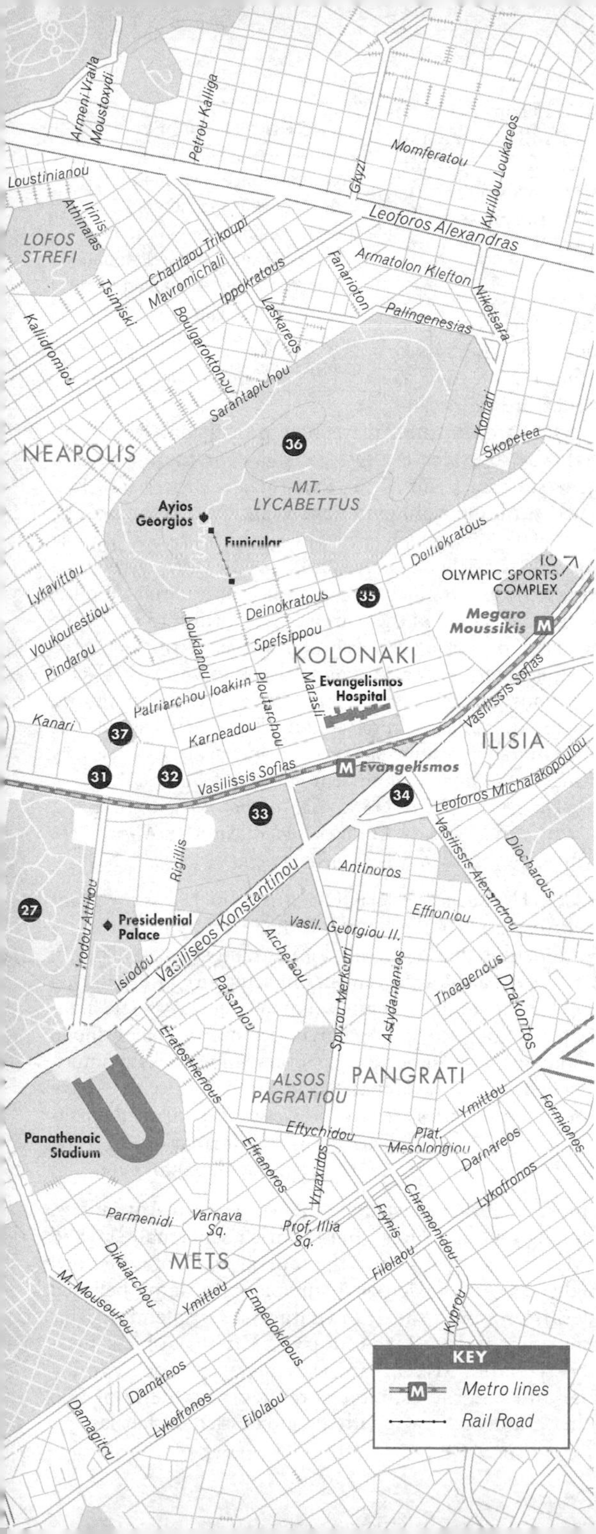

3

Map labels

Armeni Vralla
Moustoxydi
Petrou Kalliga
Momferatou
Gkizi
Kyrillou Loukareos
Loustinianou
Leoforos Alexandras
Irinis
Athinaias
LOFOS
STREFI
Charilaou Trikoupi
Mavromichali
Armatolon Klefton
Nikosara
Tsimiski
Ippokratous
Fanariotou
Palingenesias
Kallidromiou
Boulgarokioriou
Iaskareos
Sarantapichou
Koniari
Skopetea
NEAPOLIS
36
MT.
LYCABETTUS
Ayios
Georgios
Deinokratous
Lykavittou
Funicular
TO
OLYMPIC SPORTS
COMPLEX
Voukourestiou
Deinokratous
35
Pindarou
Spefsippou
Megaro
Moussikis **M**
Loukianou
KOLONAKI
Kanari
Patriarchou Ioakirn
Ploutarchou
Evangelismos
Hospital
Marasli
37
Karneadou
ILISIA
31
32
Vasilissis Sofias
M Evangelismos
Vasilissis Sofias
33
34
Leoforos Michalakopoulou
Rigillis
Antinoros
Vasilissis Alexandrou
Diocharous
27
Trodou Attihou
Presidential
Palace
Vasil. Georgiou II.
Effroniou
Isiodou
Vasiliseos Konstantinou
Archelaou
Spyrou Merkouri
Astydamantos
Theagenous
Drakontos
Pasirion
Eratosthenous
ALSOS
PAGRATIOU
PANGRATI
Ymittou
Panathenaic
Stadium
Eftychidou
Plat.
Mesilongiou
Damareos
Formionos
Parmenidi
Varnava
Sq.
Prof. Ilia
Sq.
Iraxidou
Frynis
Lykofronos
Dikaiarchou
METS
Filolaou
Kiprou
M. Mousourou
Ymittou
Empedokleous
Damatreos
Lykofronos
Filolaou
Damagitou

KEY

M Metro lines
Rail Road

discovered in 1861. From the main entrance, you can still see remains of the **Makra Teixoi** (Long Walls of Themistocles), which ran to Piraeus, and the largest gate in the ancient world, the **Dipylon Gate,** where visitors entered Athens. The walls rise to 10 feet, a fraction of their original height (up to 45 feet). Here was also the **Sacred Gate,** used by pilgrims headed to the mysterious rites in Eleusis and

> ## ROUSED TO RALLY
>
> From the terrace near the tombs, Pericles gave his celebrated speech honoring those who died in the early years of the Peloponnesian War, thus persuading many to sign up for a campaign that ultimately wiped out thousands of Athenians.

by those who participated in the Panathenaic procession, which followed the Sacred Way. Between the two gates are the foundations of the **Pompeion,** the starting point of the Panathenaic procession. It is said the courtyard was large enough to fit the ship used in the procession. On the **Street of Tombs,** which branches off the Sacred Way, plots were reserved for affluent Athenians. A number of the distinctive *stelae* (funerary monuments) remain, including a replica of the marble relief of Dexilios, a knight who died in the war against Corinth (394 BC); he is shown on horseback preparing to spear a fallen foe. To the left of the site's entrance is the **Oberlaender Museum,** also known as the Kerameikos Museum, whose displays include sculpture, terra-cotta figures, and some striking red-and-black-figured pottery. The extensive grounds of Kerameikos are marshy in some spots; in spring, frogs exuberantly croak their mating songs near magnificent stands of lilies. ⊠ *Ermou 148, Kerameikos/Gazi* ☎ *210/346–3552* 🖾 *Site and museum €2; €12 joint ticket for all Unification of Archaeological Sites* ☉ *May–Oct., daily 7:30–7; Nov.–Apr., daily 8:30–3* Ⓜ *Kerameikos.*

㉖ **National Archaeological Museum.** The classic culture which was the grandeur of the Greek world no longer exists. It died, for civilizations are mortal, but it left indelible markers in all domains, most particularly in art—and many of its greatest achievements in sculpture and painting are housed here in the most important museum in Greece. Artistic highlights from every period of ancient Greek civilization, from Neolithic to Roman times, make this a treasure trove beyond compare. With a massive renovation scheduled to be completed in 2008, works that have languished in storage for decades are now on view, reorganized displays are accompanied by enriched English-language information, and the panoply of ancient Greek art appears more spectacular than ever.

Fodor's Choice
★

The museum's most celebrated display is the **Mycenaean Antiquities.** Here are the stunning gold treasures from Heinrich Schliemann's 1876 excavations of Mycenae's royal tombs: the funeral mask of a bearded king, once thought to be the image of Agamemnon but now believed to be much older, from about the 15th century BC; a splendid silver bull's-head libation cup; and the 15th-century BC Vaphio Goblets, masterworks in embossed gold. Mycenaeans were famed for their carving in miniature, and an exquisite example is the ivory statuette of two curvaceous mother goddesses, each with a child nestled on her lap.

Withheld from the public since they were damaged in the 1999 earthquakes, but not to be missed, are the beautifully restored **frescoes from Santorini,** delightful murals depicting daily life in Minoan Santorini. Along with the treasures from Mycenae, these wall paintings are part of the museum's Prehistoric Collection.

Other stars of the museum include the works of Geometric and Archaic art (10th to 6th century BC), and kouroi and funerary stelae (8th to 5th century BC), among them the stelae of the warrior Aristion signed by Aristokles, and the unusual *Running Hoplite* (a hoplite was a Greek infantry soldier). The collection of classical art (5th to 3rd century BC) contains some of the most renowned surviving ancient statues: the bareback *Jockey of Artemision,* a 2nd-century BC Hellenistic bronze salvaged from the sea; from the same excavation, the bronze *Artemision Poseidon* (some say Zeus), poised and ready to fling a trident (or thunderbolt?); and the *Varvakios Athena,* a half-size marble version of the gigantic gold-and-ivory cult statue that Pheidias erected in the Parthenon.

SHOELESS IN ATHENS

Some of the museum's most moving displays are those of funerary architecture: the spirited 2nd-century relief of a rearing stallion held by a black groom, which exemplifies the transition from classical to Hellenistic style, the latest period in the museum's holdings. Among the most famous sculptures in this collection is the humorous marble group of a nude *Aphrodite* getting ready to slap an advancing Pan with a sandal, while Eros floats overhead and grasps one of Pan's horns.

Light refreshments are served in a lower ground-floor café, which opens out to a patio and sculpture garden. ⊠*28 Oktovriou (Patission) 44, Exarchia* ☏*210/821–7717* ⊕*www.culture.gr* ⊠*€6* ☉*Apr. 15–Oct. 15, Mon. 1–7:30, Tues.–Sun. 8–7:30; Oct. 16–Apr. 14, Mon. 1–7:30, Tues.–Fri. 8:30–7:30, weekends 8:30–3. Closed Jan. 1, Mar. 25, May 1, Easter Sun., Dec. 25–26; open reduced hrs other holidays* Ⓜ*Victorias, then 10-min walk.*

㉕ **National Historical Museum.** After making the rounds of the ancient sites, you might think that Greek history ground to a halt when the Byzantine empire collapsed. A visit to this gem of a museum will fill in the gaps, often vividly, as with Lazaros Koyevina's copy of Eugene Delacroix's *Massacre of Chios.* Paintings, costumes, and assorted artifacts from small arms to flags and ships' figureheads are arranged in a chronological display tracing Greek history from the mid-16th century and the Battle of Lepanto through World War II and the Battle of Crete. A small gift shop near the entrance has unusual souvenirs, like a deck of cards featuring Greece's revolutionary heroes. ⊠*Stadiou 13, Syntagma Sq.* ☏*210/323–7617* ⊠*€3, free Sun.* ☉*Tues.–Sun. 9–2* Ⓜ*Syntagma.*

㉔ **Numismatic Museum Iliou Melathron.** Even those uninterested in coins
FodorsChoice might want to visit this museum for a glimpse of the former home of
★ Heinrich Schliemann, who excavated Troy and Mycenae in the 19th century. In this exquisite neoclassical mansion, seemingly haunted by

Continued on page 113

When Greece Worshipped Beauty

As visitors to the many treasure-filled galleries of the National Archaeological Museum will discover, Greek art did not spring in a blinding flash like Athena fully modeled from the brain of Zeus. The earliest ceramic cup in a Greek museum, said by legend to have been molded after the breast of Helen of Troy, is a libel on that siren's reputation: it is coarse, clumsy, and rough. But fast-forward a millennium or so and you arrive at the Golden Age, when Greek art forevermore set the standard for ideals of beauty, grace, and realism in Western art, when the Parthenon gave proof of an architectural genius unique in history. The time was the 5th century BC, about 2,000 years before the Italian Renaissance. Just as that glorious age flourished, thanks to Italian city-states, so did ancient Greece reach its apogee in its cities. And it was in Athens that Greek citizens realized they could reveal the free blossoming of the human being and respect the individualistic character of men and women through art and architecture. This affirmation was largely the work of one man, Pericles, the famous Athenian general and builder of the Parthenon. During his day, Greek artistic genius fed on a physical ideal—spectacularly represented in the culture with its hero worship of athletes—as it did on religion, and religion itself, far from being an abstraction, was an anthropomorphic reflection of a passion for physical beauty.

The inspiration, however, would not have sufficed to ensure the grandeur of Greek art had it not been served by a perfection of technique. Whoever created any object had to know to perfection every element of his model, whether it was a man or woman or god or goddess. Witness the marvels of the sculpture of the age, such as the *Delphi Charioteer*, the Parthenon frieze figures, or the *Venus de Milo*. Basically the cult of the god was the cult of beauty. The women of Sparta, desirous of having handsome children, adorned their bedchambers with statues of male and female beauties. Beauty contests are not an invention of modern times. The Greeks organized them as early as the 7th century BC, until Christianity came to frown on such practices.

In like form, architecture was also the reflection of the personality of this Greek world. Thus, when we note the buildings of the Acropolis, we note the Doric order is all mathematics; the Ionian, all poetry. The first expresses proud reserve, massive strength, and severe simplicity; the second, suppleness, sensitivity, and elegance. No matter what the order, the column was the binding force—the absolute incarnation of reason in form. Study the columns of the Parthenon and you quickly realize that the Greeks did not propose to represent reality with its clutter of details; their aim was to seize the essence of things and let its light shine forth.

But it would be false to conclude, as certain romantic spirits have done, that the Greeks were mere aesthetes, lost in ecstasy before abstract beauty and subordinating their lives to it. Quite the reverse: it was the art of living which, for the Greeks, was the supreme art. A healthy utilitarian inclination combined with their worship of beauty to such an extent that art within their homes was not an idle ornament, but had a functional quality related to everyday life.

Still from Warner Brother's movie *300*

THE MARCH OF GREEK HISTORY

The 21st-century Greek is one of the oldest men on the face of the earth: he has seen everything. While Greeks are now subjected to an annual full-scale invasion by an army of camera-toting legions, their ancestors were conquered by numberless encroachers for the past four millennia. During this epic time-span, Greece was forged, torn asunder, and remade into the vital nation it is today.

Paradox is a Greek word and highly applicable to Greek history. Since the rehabilitation of Homer by Hermann Schliemann's excavations, Agamemnon, Great King of Mycenae, and the earliest heroes of ancient Greece have moved from legend into history. Today, the remote 13th century BC sometimes appears more familiar than most Greek events in better documented later periods. Not that subsequent ages were any duller—the one epithet that is utterly unsuitable in Greece—but they lacked the master touch of the great epic poet.

However, while ancient temples still evoke Homer, Sophocles, Plato, and the rest, today's Greeks are not just the watered-down descendants of a noble people living in the ruined halls of their ancestors. From time immemorial the Greeks have been piling the present on top of the past, blithely building, layering, and overlapping their more than 30 centuries of history to create the amazing fabric that is modern Greece.

(top) Gerald Butler as King Leonidas in the 2006 film *300*

(top left) Cycladic female figure; (top right) Bull fresco from Minoan ruins on Crete; (bottom) Fresco of ladies from Minoan ruins on Crete

3000–1900 BC

CYCLADIC ORIGINS

Greece is far older than the glory days of the Classical age—the 5th-century BC—which gave us the Parthenon. It has been inhabited almost continuously for the past 13,000 years. Tools made on the island of Milos around 11,000 BC have been found in a cave in the Peloponnese, suggesting that even in those long-ago reaches of history Greeks were sailing across the sparkling Aegean between islands and mainland shores. Around 3000 BC, about the time cultures were flourishing in Egypt and Mesopotamia, small cities were springing up throughout the Cycladic

islands—the first major Greek settlements, today known as the Keros-Syros culture. These early Cycladic people lived by sea and, as the need for protection from invaders intensified, in fortified towns in the uplands. Objects found in mass graves tell us they made tools, crockery, and jewelry. The most remarkable remnants of Cycladic civilization are flat, two-dimensional female idols, strikingly modern in appearance.

■ Museum of Cycladic Art (Goulandris Foundation), Athens

2000–1150 BC

MINOAN BRONZE AGE

By 2000 BC, a great culture—Europe's oldest state (as opposed to mere tribal groupings)—had taken root on the island of Crete. What these inhabitants of Greece's southernmost island actually called themselves is not known; archaeologist Sir Arthur Evans named the civilization Minoan after Minos, the legendary king of the famous labyrinth who probably ruled from the magnificent palace of Knossos. Their warehouses were filled with spices traded throughout the Mediterranean, and royal chambers were decorated with sophisticated art—statuary, delicate rythons, and,

(top) Replica of Trojan Horse; (top, right) Lion Gate at Mycenae; (bottom) Mycenaen gold funeral mask

1500–1100 BC

THE MYCENAEANS

most evocative of all, alluring frescoes depicting fanciful secular scenes as well as the goddesses who dominated the matriarchal Minoan religion. A system of writing, known as Linear A and Linear B script, appears on seal stones. The cause of the downfall of the Minoans remains a mystery—political unrest, invasions from the mainland, a volcano on nearby Santorini and subsequent earthquakes? Enter the mainland Mycenaeans.

■ Palace of Knossos, Crete

■ Archaeological Museum, Heraklion

By the 14th century BC, the Mycenaeans wielded power throughout main-land Greece and much of the rest of the known world, from Sicily to Asia Minor. Their capital, Mycenae (in the Peloponnese), was one of several great cities they built around palaces filled with art and stories of the new Olympian gods and fortified heavily. As civilized as the Mycenaeans were, they were also warlike. Their exploits inspired the *Iliad* and *Odyssey*, and Agamemnon, legendary hero of the 12th-century Trojan Wars—the starting point in the endless ping-pong match between

Europe and Asia—is said to have ruled from Mycenae. For all their might, the Mycenaeans fell into decline sometime around 1100 BC. Soon the Dorians, from northern Greece, moved south, pushing the Mycenaeans into a dark age during which art and writing were lost. But Greeks who sailed across the Aegean to flee the Dorians established Ephesus, Smyrna, and other so-called Ionian cities in Asia Minor, where a rich culture soon flourished.

■ Lion Gate, Mycenae, the Argolid

■ Cyclopean Walls, Tiryns, the Argolid

■ Nestor's Palace, Messinia

(top) Ancient vase depicting Olympic athletes; (left) Bust of Homer; (right) Statue of King Leonidas

1100–800 BC

THE AGE OF HOMER

By the 8th century BC, Greeks were living in hundreds of *poleis*, city-states that usually comprised a walled city that governed the surrounding countryside. Most poleis were built around a raised acropolis and an agora (a marketplace), as well temples and often a gymnasium; limited power lay with a group of elite citizens—the first inklings of democracy. As the need for resources grew, Greeks began to establish colonies in Sicily and Gaul and on the Black Sea, and with this expansion came contact with the written word that laid the foundations of the Greek alphabet. Two essential elements of Greek culture led the new Greek renaissance that forged a nation's identity: Homeric legends began circulating, recounting the deeds of heroes and gods, and athletes showed off their strength and valor at the Olympic Games, first staged in 776 BC.—Participation in these games meant support of Hellenism—the concept of a united Greece.

- Greek colonies set up in Asia Minor, Sicily, and southern Italy
- Persian Invasions
- Marathon Tomb, Marathon, Attica
- Archaeological Museum, Marathon, Attica

499–449 BC

PERSIAN INVASIONS

The most powerful poleis, Athens and Sparta, would soon become two of history's most famous rivals—but for a brief time in the fifth century, they were allies united against a common foe, the Persians, who, in 490 BC, launched an attack against Athens. Though far outnumbered, the Athenians dealt the Persians a crippling blow on the Marathon plain. Ten years later, the Persians attacked again, this time with a massive army and navy commanded by King Xerxes. The Spartan King Leonidas and his "300"—the men of his royal guard (along with an unknown number of

(top) Still from Warner Brothers movie *300*; (top right) Bust of Pericles; (right) Relief sculpture fragment depicting the King of Persia; (bottom) Greek helmet

slaves, or Helots) —sacrificed their lives to hold the Persians off at Thermopylae, allowing the Athenians time to muster ships and sink much of the Persian fleet. Xerxes returned the following year, in the summer of 479 bc, to sack Athens, but an army drawn from city-states throughout Greece and under the command of Pausanias, a Spartan general, defeated the Persians and brought the Persian Wars to an end.

■ Marathon Tomb, Marathon, Attica

PERICLES' GOLDEN AGE

460–431 BC

Athens thrived for much of the fifth century BC under the leadership of the enlightened statesman Pericles. The city became the center of the Hellenic world—and the cradle of Western civilization—due to a series of revolutionary events. The Parthenon was built; Socrates engaged in the dialogues that, recorded by Plato, became the basis of European thought; Aeschylus, Aristophanes, Euripides, and Sophocles wrote dramas; Praxiteles sculpted his masterpieces; and Herodotus became the "father of history."

■ The Parthenon, Athens
■ Sanctuary of Apollo, Delphi

PELOPON- NESIAN WAR

431–404 BC

Athens was leader of the Delian League, a confederation of 140 Greek city-states, and Sparta headed the Peloponnesian League, a formidable alliance of city-states of southern and central Greece. From 431 to 404 bc these two powers engaged in battles that plunged much of Greece into bloodshed. Sparta emerged the victor after Athens suffered two devastating defeats: the destruction of a massive force sent to attack Syracuse, a Spartan ally in Sicily, and the sinking of the Athenian fleet.

■ Archaeological Museum, Sparta, Laconia

(top) Alexander the Great listening to his tutor Aristotle; (top right) Byzantine basilica; (bottom) Alexander the Great on horseback

338 BC-323 AD

ALEXANDER THE GREAT

In the years following the Peloponnesian War, Sparta, Athens, and an emerging power, Thebes, battled for control of Greece. Eventually, the victors came from the north: Macedonians led by Philip II defeated Athens in the Battle of Chaeronea in 338 bc. Philip's son, Alexander the Great, who had been tutored by Aristotle, quickly unified Greece and conquered Persia, most of the rest of the Middle East, and Egypt. In the ensuing 11 years of unparalleled triumphs he spread Greek culture from the Nile to the Indus. Alexander died in Babylon of a mysterious illness in 323 bc and the great empire he amassed soon fell asunder. Roman armies began moving toward Athens, Greece became the Roman province of Achaia in 27 bc, and for the next 300 years of peace Rome readily adapted Greek art, architecture, and thought. This cultural influence during the Pax Romana compensated for the loss of a much abused independence.

- Birthplace, Pella, Central Macedonia
- Royal Tombs, Vergina, Central Macedonia
- Roman Agora, Athens Archaeological Museum, Marathon, Attica

324-1204 AD

BYZANTINE GREECE

With the division of the Roman Empire into East and West, Greece came under the control of the Eastern Empire, administered from the Greek city of Byzantium (later Constantinople) where Emperor Constantine moved the capital, in 324. The Empire had embraced Christianity as its official religion and Byzantium became the seat of the Eastern Orthodox Church, which led to the Great Christian Schism of 1094. Byzantium's Greek culture evolved into a distinct architectural style and religious art forms best represented by mosaics and icon paintings. For centuries Byzantine Greece fended off invasions from Vi-

(top) Gold leaf mosaics; (left) Palace of the Grand Masters, Rhodes; (right) Portrait of Mehmet II

sigoths, Vandals, Slavs, Muslims, Bulgars and Normans. As an ally of the empire, the Republic of Venice developed trading strongholds in Greece in the 11th century. Interested in the control of maritime routes, the Venetians built a network of fortresses and fortified towns along the Ionian coast of Greece. Venice later extended its possessions over several Aegean islands and Crete, which it held until 1669.

- Monastery of Daphni, Attica
- Mt. Athos, Central Macedonia
- Meteora Monasteries, Thessaly

1204–1453 AD
CRUSADERS AND FEUDAL GREECE

The Byzantine Empire and Greece with it, finally succumbed to Crusaders who pillaged Constantinople in 1204. Frankish knights create vassal feudal states in Thessalonica, the Peloponnese, and Rhodes, while other short-lived kingdoms in Epirus and on the shores of the Black Sea became the refuge of Byzantine Greek populations. Soon, however, a new threat loomed as Ottoman Turks under Sultan Mehmet II began marching into Byzantine lands, occupying most of Asia Minor, Macedonia, and Thessaly.

- Churches of Thessaloniki, Central Macedonia

1453–1821
OTTOMAN AGE

Constantinople fell to the Ottomans in 1453, and by the 16th century Sultan Suleyman the Magnificent had expanded his Empire from Vienna through the Middle East. Greece was the stage of many battles between East and West. In 1687, Athens was besieged and the Parthenon heavily damaged by Venetian bombardments. Only in 1718 all of Greece was conceded to the Ottoman Empire, just in time for a resurgence of Hellenist culture in Europe, Neoclassicism in the arts, and a brand-new interest in Greek archaeology.

- Aslan Mosque, Ioannina, Epirus

1522 Knights of St. John surrender Rhodes to the Ottomans	Lord Elgin removes marbles	Athens's Olympic Games
	Greeks drive Turks out	

1600   1800   2000

(top) 2004 Olympic Greek stadium; (far left) Portrait of Lord Byron; (left) Portrait of Eleftherios Venizelos

1821–1935 AD

A GREEK NATION

Ottoman rulers allowed a degree of autonomy to Greece yet uprisings became increasingly fierce. In 1821, the bloody War of Independence, which started as a successful rebellion in the Peloponnese, spread across the land. Western Europeans, including the Romantic poet Lord Byron, rushed to the Greek cause. After years of setbacks and civil wars, Britain, France, and Russia mediated with the Ottomans to establish Greece as an autonomous region. Otto of Bavaria, only 17, was named sovereign of Greece in 1831, the first of the often-unpopular monarchs who reigned intermittently until 1974. Public favor soon rested with prime ministers like Eleftherios Venizelos, who colonized Crete in 1908. In 1919 Venizelos, a proponent of a "Greater Greece," sought to conquer ethnic Greek regions of the new Turkish nation, but his forces were defeated and hundreds of thousands, on both sides, were massacred. The subsequent peace decreed the massive population exchange of two million people between the two countries, resulting in the complete expulsion of Greeks from Asia Minor, after 3,000 years of history.

■ Achilleion Palace, Corfu

■ National Garden, Athens

1936–PRESENT

WAR AND THE NEW REPUBLIC

Greece emerged from the savagery of Axis occupation during World War II in the grip of civil war, with the Communist party battling right-wing forces. The right controlled the Greek government until 1963, when Georgios Papandreou became prime minister and proposed democratic reforms that were soon put down by a repressive colonels' junta led by Georgios Papadopoulos. A new republic was proclaimed in 1973, and a new constitution replaced the monarchy with an elective government—democratic ideals born in Greece more than 2,000 years earlier.

■ 2004 Olympic Stadium, Athens

the spirit of the great historian, you can see more than 600,000 coins; displays range from the archaeologist's own coin collection to 4th-century BC measures employed against forgers to coins grouped according to what they depict—animals, plants, myths, and famous buildings like the Lighthouse of Alexandria. Instead of trying to absorb everything, concentrate on a few cases—perhaps a pile of coins dug up on a Greek road, believed to be used by Alexander the Great to pay off local mercenaries. There is also a superb 4th-century BC

> ## POETRY 101 CLASSROOM
>
> Hermann Schliemann called his magnificent neoclassical house, designed for him by Ernst Ziller, the "Palace of Troy." Note the Pompeiian aesthetic in the ocher, terra-cotta, and blue touches; the mosaic floors inspired by Mycenae; and the dining-room ceiling painted with food scenes, under which Schliemann would recite the *Iliad* to guests.

decadrachm (a denomination of coin) with a lissome water goddess frolicking among dolphins (the designer signed the deity's headband). A silver *didrachm* (another denomination of coin) issued by the powerful Amphictyonic League after Philip II's death shows Demeter on one side and, on the other, a thoughtful Apollo sitting on the navel of the world. ✉*Panepistimiou 12, Syntagma Sq.* ☎*210/361–2190 or 210/364–3774* ⊕*www.nma.gr* 🖃*€3* ⊙*Tues.–Sun., 8:30* AM–*3* PM Ⓜ*Syntagma or Panepistimiou.*

ALSO WORTH SEEING

❷ **Old University complex.** In the sea of concrete that is central Athens, this imposing group of marble buildings conjures up an illusion of classical antiquity. The three dramatic buildings belonging to the University of Athens were designed by the Hansen brothers in the period after independence in the 19th century and are built of white Pendelic marble, with tall columns and decorative friezes. In the center is the **Senate House** of the university. To the right is the **Academy,** flanked by two slim columns topped by statues of Athena and Apollo; paid for by the Austro-Greek Baron Sina, it is a copy of the Parliament in Vienna. Frescoes in the reception hall depict the myth of Prometheus. At the left end of the complex is a griffin-flanked staircase leading to the **National Library,** containing more than 2 million Greek and foreign-language volumes and now undergoing the daunting task of modernization. ✉*Panepistimiou between Ippokratous and Sina, Central Athens* ☎*210/361–4301 Senate, 210/360–0209 Academy, 210/361–4413 Library* ⊙*Senate and Academy weekdays 9–2; library Sept.–July, Mon.–Thurs. 9–8, Fri. 9–2* Ⓜ*Panepistimiou.*

NEED A BREAK? One of the toniest pedestrian malls in Athens is Voukourestiou, where you will find the hippest cafés in the city, Clemente VIII (✉*Voukourestiou 3, City LinkKolonaki* ☎*210/321–9340*). With the best espresso and cappuccino (both hot and iced) in town and a fresh daily platter of sandwiches and sweets, this café, which opened in October 2006, can bask in its quality alone. But surrounded by the luxury jewelry stores and the Armani-clad lunch crowd, it's become the place to see and be seen in the city. This was once the site of one of Athens's most beloved cafés, Brazilian.

㉑ **Psirri.** Similar to New York City's Tribeca, this district has been targeted by developers who have spurred a wave of renovations and a bevy of new nightspots. At dusk, this quiet quarter becomes a whirl of theaters, clubs, and restaurants, dotted with dramatically lighted churches and lively squares. Defined by Ermou, Kerameikou, Athinas, Evripidou, Epikourou, and Pireos streets, Psirri has many buildings older than those in picturesque Plaka. If you're coming from Omonia Square, walk down Aiolou, a pedestrian zone with cafés and old shops as well as an interesting view of the Acropolis. Peek over the wrought-iron gates of the old houses on the narrow side streets between Ermou and Kerameikou to see the pretty courtyards bordered by long, low buildings, whose many small rooms were rented out to different families. In the Square of the Heroes, revolutionary fighters once met to plot against the Ottoman occupation. Linger on into the evening if you want to dance on tabletops to live Greek music, sing along with a soulful accordion player, hear salsa in a Cuban club, or watch the hoi polloi go by as you snack on updated or traditional *mezedes* (appetizers). ⊠ *Off Ermou, centered on Iroon and Ayion Anargiron Sqs., Psirri* ⊕ *www.psiri.gr* Ⓜ *Monastiraki.*

⑲ **Technopolis.** Gazi, the neighborhood surrounding this former 19th-century-foundry–turned–arts complex, takes its name from the toxic gas fumes that used to spew from the factory's smokestacks. Today Gazi is synonymous with the hippest restaurants, edgiest galleries, and trendiest nightclubs in town. The smokestacks now glow crimson with colored lights, anchoring a burgeoning stretch that runs from the central neighborhood of Kerameikos to the once-decrepit neighborhood of Rouf. The city of Athens bought the disused foundry in the late 1990s and helped convert it into Technopolis. The transformation preserved all the original architecture and stonework, and includes six exhibition spaces and a large courtyard open to the public. The spaces regularly host shows on a range of topics—war photography, open-air jazz, comic-book art, rock and theater performances, rave nights, and parties. ⊠ *Pireos 100, Gazi* ☎ *210/346–0981* ⊠ *Free* ⊘ *9* AM*–9* PM *during exhibitions* Ⓜ *Thiseio.*

> ### IT'S CALLASTROPHIC!
>
> Hidden within jazzy Technopolis is the small Maria Callas Museum (Andreas Embirikos Hall, Pireos 100, Gazi, open 10 AM–3 PM, Monday through Friday), where you can study the opera diva's personal photo albums, letters, and clothes. To get the real poop on La Divina, however, you'll have to read Nicholas Gage's *Greek Fire*, an in-depth book on her torrid and tragic love affair with Aristotle Onassis. One of the many secrets revealed: Ari was more interested in wooing Jacqueline Kennedy's sister until Lee Radziwill told him that her sister would be a better match. Admission is free to the museum.

SYNTAGMA SQUARE TO KOLONAKI
ΠΛΑΤΕΙΑ ΣΥΝΤΑΓΜΑΤΟΣ & ΚΟΛΩΝΑΚΙ

Dressed in their *foustanelles* (pleated skirts), the Evzone guards standing on duty at the Tomb of the Unknown Soldier; Queen Amalia's National Garden, built as an oasis of green in a desert of marble; a temple to Zeus and an arch built by Emperor Hadrian; and a funicular ride to the top of Mt. Lycabettus, three times the height of the Acropolis. The view from its top—pollution permitting—reveals that this center-city sector is packed with marvels and wonders. Sooner or later, everyone passes through its heart, the spacious Syntagma Square (Constitution Square), which is surrounded by sights that span Athens's history from the days of the Roman emperors to King Othos's reign after the 1821 War of Independence. Some may have likened his palace (now the Parliament) to a barracks but they shouldn't complain: it was paid for by Othos's father, King Ludwig I of Bavaria, who luckily vetoed the plans for a royal residence atop the Acropolis itself, using one end of the Parthenon as the entrance and blowing up the rest. The palace was finished just in time for Othos to grant the constitution of 1843, which gave the name to the square. Neighboring Kolonaki—the chic shopping district and one of the most fashionable residential areas—occupies the lower slopes of Mt. Lycabettus. Besides visiting its several museums, you can spend time window-shopping and people-watching, since cafés are busy from early morning to dawn.

WHAT TO SEE: THE MAIN ATTRACTIONS

③① **Benaki Museum.** Greece's oldest private museum, established in 1926 by
Fodor'sChoice an illustrious Athenian family, the Benaki was one of the first to place
★ emphasis on Greece's later heritage at a time when many archaeologists were destroying Byzantine artifacts to access ancient objects. The collection (more than 20,000 items are on display in 36 rooms, and that's only a sample of the holdings) moves chronologically from the ground floor upward, from prehistory to the formation of the modern Greek state. You might see anything from a 5,000-year-old hammered gold bowl to an austere Byzantine icon of the Virgin Mary to Lord Byron's pistols to the Nobel medals awarded to poets George Seferis and Odysseus Elytis. Some exhibits are just plain fun—the re-creation of a Kozani (Macedonian town) living room; a tableau of costumed mannequins; a Karaghiozi shadow puppet piloting a toy plane—all contrasted against the marble and crystal-chandelier grandeur of the Benaki home. The mansion was designed by Anastassios Metaxas, the architect who helped restore the Panathenaic Stadium. The Benaki's gift shop, a destination in itself, tempts with exquisitely reproduced ceramics and jewelry. The second-floor café serves coffee and snacks, with a few daily specials, on a veranda overlooking the National Garden. ✉*Koumbari 1, Kolonaki* ☎*210/367–1000* ⊕*www.benaki.gr* 💶*€6, free Thurs.* ⊗*Mon., Wed., Fri., and Sat. 9–5; Thurs. 9 AM–midnight; Sun. 9–3* Ⓜ*Syntagma or Evangelismos.*

③② **Museum of Cycladic Art.** Also known as the Nicholas P. Goulandris Foundation, and funded by one of Greece's richest families, this museum
Fodor'sChoice has an outstanding collection of 350 Cycladic artifacts dating from the
★

Bronze Age, including many of the enigmatic marble figurines whose slender shapes fascinated such artists as Picasso, Modigliani, and Brancusi. Other collections focus on Greek art from the Bronze Age through the 6th century AD. A glass corridor connects the main building to the gorgeous adjacent Stathatos Mansion, where temporary exhibits are mounted. There's also a lovely café in a courtyard centered around a Cycladic-inspired fountain. ⊠*Neofitou Douka 4, Kolonaki* ☎*210/722–8321 through 210/722–8323* ⊕*www.cycladic.gr* 🎫*€3.50* ◷*Mon. and Wed.–Fri. 10–4, Sat. 10–3* Ⓜ*Evangelismos.*

> **INFORMATION, PLEASE?**
>
> The main office of the Greek National Tourism Organization (GNTO; EOT in Greece) is at Tsocha 7, in the Ambelokipi district, just by the National Gardens, not far from Syntagma Square, the heart of Athens. Their offices generally close around 2 PM. The Web site of the city of Athens (⊕*www.cityofathens.gr*) has a small but growing section in English.

㉙ **Hadrian's Arch.** This marble gateway, built in AD 131 with Corinthian details, was intended both to honor the Hellenophile emperor Hadrian and to separate the ancient and imperial sections of Athens. On the side facing the Acropolis an inscription reads THIS IS ATHENS, THE ANCIENT CITY OF THESEUS, but the side facing the Temple of Olympian Zeus proclaims THIS IS THE CITY OF HADRIAN AND NOT OF THESEUS. ⊠*Vasilissis Amalias at Dionyssiou Areopagitou, National Garden* ⊕*www.culture.gr* 🎫*Free* ◷*Daily* Ⓜ*Acropolis.*

㊱ **Mt. Lycabettus.** Myth claims that Athens's highest hill came into exis-
Ⓒ tence when Athena removed a piece of Mt. Pendeli, intending to boost
★ the height of her temple on the Acropolis. While she was en route, a crone brought her bad tidings, and the flustered goddess dropped the rock in the middle of the city. Kids love the ride up the steeply inclined *teleferique* (funicular) to the summit, crowned by whitewashed **Ayios Georgios** chapel with a bell tower donated by Queen Olga. On a clear day, you can see Aegina island, with or without the aid of coin-operated telescopes. Built into a cave on the side of the hill, near the I Prasini Tenta café, is a small shrine to **Ayios Isidoros.** In 1859 students prayed here for those fighting against the Austrians, French, and Sardinians with whom King Othos had allied. From Mt. Lycabettus you can watch the sun set and then turn about to watch the moon rise over "violet-crowned" Hymettus as the lights of Athens blink on all over the city. ⊠*Base: 15-min walk northeast of Syntagma Sq.; funicular every 10 mins from corner of Ploutarchou and Aristippou (take Minibus 060 from Kanari or Kolonaki Sq., except Sun.), Kolonaki* ☎*210/722–7065* 🎫*Funicular €4* ◷*Funicular daily 9 AM–3 AM.*

㉞ **National Gallery of Art.** The permanent collections of Greek painting and sculpture of the 19th and 20th centuries (including the work of naive artist Theophilos) are still on display, but popular traveling exhibitions enliven the gallery. The exhibitions are usually major loan shows from around the world, such as an El Greco retrospective, Dutch 17th-century art, and an exhibit tracing the influence of Greece on works of the Italian Renaissance. ✉ *Vasileos Konstantinou 50, Ilisia* ☎*210/723–5857 or 210/723–5937* 💶*€6.50* 🕙*Mon. and Wed. 9–3 and 6–9, Thurs.– Sat. 9–3, Sun. 10–2* Ⓜ*Evangelismos.*

㉗ National Garden. When you can't take the city noise anymore, step into this oasis completed in 1860 as part of King Othos and Queen Amalia's royal holdings. Here old men on the benches argue politics, police officers take their coffee breaks, and animal lovers feed the stray cats that roam among the more than 500 species of trees and plants, many labeled. At the east end is the neoclassic **Zappion hall,** built in 1888 and used for major political and cultural events: it was here that Greece signed its accession to what was then the European Community. Children appreciate the playgrounds, duck pond, and small zoo (✉*East end of park, National Garden*). Ⓜ*Syntagma.*

NEED A BREAK? Visit the elegant Aiglí (✉*National Garden*), an excellent spot for a classic Greek coffee. Nestled among fountains and flowering trees next to the Zappion Exhibition Hall in the National Garden, it's an ideal spot to sample a fresh dessert or some haute cuisine.

㉚ Syntagma (Constitution) Square. At the top of the city's main square stands **★ Parliament,** formerly King Othos's royal palace, completed in 1838 for the new monarchy. It seems a bit austere and heavy for a southern landscape, but it was proof of progress, the symbol of the new ruling power. The building's saving grace is the stone's magical change of color from off-white to gold to rosy mauve as the day progresses. Here you can watch the **changing of the Evzone guards** at the **Tomb of the Unknown Soldier**—in front of Parliament on a lower level—which takes place at intervals throughout the day. On a wall behind the Tomb of the Unknown Soldier, the bas-relief of a dying soldier is modeled after a sculpture on the Temple of Aphaia in Aegina; the text is from the funeral oration said to have been given by Pericles. Pop into the gleaming **Syntagma metro station** (✉*Upper end of Syntagma Sq.* 🕙*Daily 5 AM–midnight*) to examine artfully displayed artifacts uncovered during subway excavations. A floor-to-ceiling cross section of earth behind glass shows finds in chronological layers, ranging from a skeleton in its ancient grave to traces of the 4th-century BC road to Mesogeia to an Ottoman cistern. ✉*Vasilissis Amalias and Vasilissis Sofias, Syntagma Sq.* Ⓜ*Syntagma.*

NEED A BREAK? Lovely cafés like Ethnikon (✉*Syntagma Sq.* ☎*210/331–0676*) have opened as a result of the city's 2004 Olympics remodeling. This café is shady, atmospheric, and has an excellent selection of desserts, including chocolate cake and homemade spoon sweets, or *glyka koutaliou.*

㉘ Temple of Olympian Zeus. Begun in the 6th century BC, the temple was completed in AD 132 by Hadrian, who also commissioned a huge gold-and-ivory statue of Zeus for the inner chamber and another, only slightly smaller, of himself. Only 15 of the original Corinthian columns remain, but standing next to them may inspire a sense of awe at their bulk, which is softened by the graceful carving on the acanthus-leaf capitals. The clearly defined segments of a column blown down in 1852 give you an idea of the method used in its construction. The site is floodlighted on summer evenings, creating a majestic scene when you round the bend from Syngrou. On the outskirts of the site to the north are remains of Roman houses, the city walls, and a Roman bath. Hellenic "neopagans" also use the site for ceremonies. ⊠ *Vasilissis Olgas 1, National Garden* ☎*210/922–6330* ☜*€2; €12 joint ticket for all Unification of Archaeological Sites* ⊙ *Tues.–Sun. 8:30–3* Ⓜ *Acropolis.*

ALSO WORTH SEEING

③③ ★ Byzantine and Christian Museum. One of the few museums in Europe concentrating exclusively on Byzantine art displays an outstanding collection of icons, mosaics, and tapestries. Sculptural fragments provide an excellent introduction to Byzantine architecture. When the museum finishes a massive renovation and extension in late 2008, it will include never-before-seen exhibits such as magnificent illuminated manuscripts. Fans of classical Greece will be happy to know you can explore the onsite archaeological dig of Aristotle's Lyceum. ⊠ *Vasilissis Sofias 22, Kolonaki* ☎*210/721–1027, 210/723–2178, or 210/723–1570* ⊕ *www.culture.gr* ☜*€4* ⊙ *Tues.–Sun. 8:30–3; call for periodic closings* Ⓜ *Evangelismos.*

③⑤ Gennadius Library. Book lovers who ascend the grand staircase into the hallowed aura of the Reading Room may have difficulty tearing themselves away from this superb collection of material on Greek subjects, from first editions of Greek classics to the papers of Nobel Laureate poets George Seferis and Odysseus Elytis. The heart of the collection consists of thousands of books donated in the 1920s by Greek diplomat John Gennadius, who haunted London's rare-book shops for volumes connected to Greece, thus amassing the most comprehensive collection of Greek books held by one man. He died bankrupt, leaving his wife to pay off his debts, mostly to booksellers. The library's collection includes Lord Byron's memorabilia (including a lock of his hair); Heinrich Schliemann's diaries, notebooks, and letters; and impressionistic watercolors of Greece by Edward Lear. Pride of place is given to the first edition printed in Greek of Homer (The *Iliad* and The *Odyssey*). The Gennadius, which is under the custody of the American School of Classical Studies, is not a lending library. ⊠ *Souidias 61, Kolonaki* ☎*210/721–0536* ⊕ *www.ascsa.edu.gr* ⊙ *Mid-Sept.–mid-Aug., Mon.–Wed. and Fri. 9:30–5, Thurs. 9:30–8, Sat. 9:30–2* Ⓜ *Evangelismos.*

FULL FRONTAL FASHION

Near the Parliament, you can watch the **changing of the Evzone guards** at the Tomb of the Unknown Soldier—in front of Parliament on a lower level—which takes place at intervals throughout the day. On Sunday the honor guard of tall young men don a dress costume—a short white *foustanella* (kilt) with 400 neat pleats, one for each year of the Ottoman occupation, and red shoes with pompons—and still manage to look brawny rather than silly. A band accompanies them: they all arrive by 11:15 AM in front of Parliament.

③⑦ Kolonaki Square. To see and be seen, Athenians gather not on the square, hub of the chic Kolonaki district, but at the cafés on its periphery and along the Tsakalof and Milioni pedestrian zone. Clothespin-thin models, slick talk show hosts, middle-aged executives, elegant pensioners, and expatriate teen queens all congregate on the square (officially known as Filikis Eterias) for a coffee before work, a lunchtime gossip session, a drink after a hard day of shopping, or for an afternoon of sipping iced cappuccinos while reading a stack of foreign newspapers and magazines purchased from the all-night kiosk. On the lower side of the square is the **British Council Library** (⊠ *Kolonaki Sq. 17, Kolonaki* ☎ *210/364–5768* ⊙ *Mon. and Thurs. 3–8; Tues., Wed., and Fri. 9:30–2:30; closed 3 wks in Aug.*), which has some children's videos and a screening facility. ⊠ *Intersection of Patriarchou Ioakeim and Kanari, Kolonaki* Ⓜ *Metro Evangelismos, then 15-min walk.*

> ### RULES OF THE GAME
>
> If you can't understand the menu, just go to the kitchen and point at what looks most appealing, especially in tavernas. In most cases, you don't need to ask—just walk to the kitchen (some places have food displayed in a glass case right at the kitchen's doorway), or point to your eye and then the kitchen; the truly ambitious can ask a question (Bo-ro na dtho tee *eh-he-teh* steen koo-*zee*-na?, or "May I see what's in the kitchen?"). When ordering fish, which is priced by the kilo, you often go to the kitchen to pick out your fish, which is then weighed and billed accordingly.

NEED A BREAK? Enjoy a cappuccino and an Italian sweet standing at Da Capo (⊠ *Tsakalof 1, Kolonaki* ☎ *210/360–2497*). This place is frequented by young trendsetters, especially on Saturday afternoons; people-watching is part of the pleasure.

WHERE TO EAT

Whether you sample octopus and ouzo near the sea, roasted goat in a 100-year-old taverna, or cutting-edge cuisine in a trendy restaurant, dining in the city is just as relaxing as it is elsewhere in Greece. Athens's dining scene is experiencing a renaissance, with a particular focus on the intense flavors of regional Greek cooking. International options such as classic Italian and French still abound—and a recent Greek fascination with all things Japanese means that sushi is served in every happening bar in town—but today, traditional and nouvelle Greek are the leading contenders for the Athenian palate. The most exciting new, upscale restaurants are contemporary playgrounds for innovative chefs offering a sophisticated mélange of dishes that pay homage to Greek cooking fused with other cuisines. Some of these have also incorporated sleek design, late-night hours, DJs, and adjoining lounges full of beautiful people, forming all-in-one bar-restaurants, renowned for both star Greek chefs and glitterati customers.

Traditional restaurants serve cuisine a little closer to what a Greek grandmother would make, but more formal, and with a wider selection than the neighborhood tavernas. Truly authentic tavernas have wicker chairs that inevitably pinch your bottom, checkered tablecloths covered with butcher paper, wobbly tables that need coins under one leg, and wine drawn from the barrel and served in small metal carafes. The popular hybrid—the modern taverna—serves traditional fare in more-stylish surrounds; most are in the up-and-coming industrial-cum-artsy districts. If a place looks inviting and is filled with Greeks, give it a try. Mezedopoleia serve plates of appetizers—basically Levantine tapas—to feast on while sipping ouzo, though many now serve barrel and bottled wine as well.

In the last three weeks of August, when the city empties out and most residents head for the seaside, many restaurants and tavernas popular among the locals close, though bar-restaurants may reopen in different summer locations by the sea. Hotel restaurants, seafood restaurants in Piraeus, and tavernas in Plaka usually remain open. Most places serve lunch from about noon to 4 (and sometimes as late as 6) and dinner from about 9 to at least midnight.

As in most other cosmopolitan cities, dress varies from casual to fancy, according to the establishment. Although Athens is informal and none of the restaurants listed here requires a jacket or tie, you may feel more comfortable dressing up a bit in the most expensive places. Conservative casual attire (not shorts) is acceptable at most establishments.

WHAT IT COSTS IN EUROS				
	¢	$	$$	$$$	$$$$
AT DINNER	under €8	€8–€16	€16–€22	€22–€30	over €30

Prices are for one main course at dinner, or for two mezedes (small dishes) at restaurants that serve only mezedes.

ACROPOLIS & SOUTH ΑΚΡΟΠΟΛΗ & ΠΡΟΣ ΤΑ ΝΟΤΙΑ

In the shadow of Greece's most famous landmark, arty-chic neighborhoods such as Koukaki and Philopappou offer both historic views and classical-meets-urban ambience.

$$$$ ✕ **Edodi.** Bajazzo—the restaurant that introduced Athenians to haute cuisine—is no more, but when it closed in 1999, several top staffers decided to open an intimate, candlelit dining room (with fewer than 10 tables) in a neoclassic house. Nearly 10 years on, the menu still pays homage to the gastronomic splendor of Bajazzo but in a decidedly new theatrical way: instead of a menu, raw seasonal ingredients are brought to your table, chosen by you, then cooked to order according to your mood and tastes, which the waitstaff are quite skilled at gauging. Offerings are always changing, but the lobster with spicy Parmesan sauce is a perennial favorite. ⊠ *Veikou 80, Koukaki* ☎ *210/921–3013* ⊕ *www. edodi.gr* ⌁ *Reservations essential* ⊟ *AE, DC, MC, V* ⊘ *Closed Sun. and 2 wks in Aug. No lunch.*

3

$-$$ ✕**Strofi.** Walls lined with autographed photos of actors from the nearby Odeon of Herodes Atticus attest to Strofi's success with the after-theater crowd. Despite the many tourists, the dramatic rooftop garden views of the Acropolis still attract locals who have been coming here for decades. Start with a tangy *taramosalata* (fish roe dip) or velvety tzatziki, which perfectly complements the thinly sliced fried zucchini. Another good appetizer is *fava*, a puree of yellow split peas. For the main coarse, choose roast lamb with *hilopites* (thin egg noodles cut into small squares), rabbit *stifado* (a stew of meat, white wine, garlic, cinnamon, and spices), veal with eggplant, or kid goat prepared with oil and oregano. ⊠*Rovertou Galli 25, Makriyianni* ☎*210/921–4130 or 210/922–3787* ▤*DC, MC, V* ⊗*Closed Sun. No lunch.*

PLAKA ΠΛΑΚΑ

Just northeast of the Acropolis, Plaka and Anafiotika delight in their traditional homes, winding alleys, and bustle of cafés and shops.

$$-$$$ ✕**I Palia Taverna tou Psarra.** Founded way back in 1898, this is one of the few remaining Plaka tavernas serving reliably good food as well as having the obligatory mulberry-shaded terrace. The owners claim to have served Brigitte Bardot and Laurence Olivier, but it's the number of Greeks who come here that testifies to Psarra's appeal. Oil-oregano octopus and marinated *gavros* (a small fish) are good appetizers. Simple, tasty entrées include rooster in wine, *arnaki pilino* (lamb baked in clay pots), and pork chops with ouzo. Can't make up your mind? Try the *ouzokatastasi* ("ouzo situation"), a plate of tidbits to nibble while you decide. ⊠*Erechtheos 16, at Erotokritou, Plaka* ☎*210/321–8733* ▤*AE, MC, V.*

$-$$ ✕**O Platanos.**
Fodor'sChoice Set on a picturesque corner, this is one of the oldest tav-
★ ernas in Plaka, and it's a welcome sight compared with the many over-priced tourist traps in the area. A district landmark—it is set midway between the Tower of the Winds and the Museum of Greek Popular Musical Instruments—it warms the eye with its pink-hue house, nicely color-coordinated with the bougainvillea-covered courtyard. Although the rooms here are cozily adorned with old paintings and photos, most of the crowd opts to relax under the courtyard's plane trees (which give the place its name). Platanos is packed with locals, who flock here because the food is good Greek home cooking and the waiters fast and polite. Don't miss the oven-baked potatoes, roasted lamb, fresh green beans in savory olive oil, and the exceptionally cheap but delicious barrel retsina. ⊠*Diogenous 4, Plaka* ☎*210/322–0666* ▤*No credit cards* ⊗*Closed Sun.*

$-$$ ✕**Taverna Xynos.** Stepping into the courtyard of this Plaka taverna is like entering a time warp back to Athens in the 1950s. In summer, tables move outside and a guitar duo drops by, playing ballads of yesteryear. Loyal customers say little has changed since then—although diners' demands have, making the setup seem somewhat dated. Start with the classic stuffed-grape-leaf appetizer, and then move on to the taverna's strong suit—dishes such as lamb *yiouvetsi* (baked in ceramic dishes with tomato sauce and barley-shape pasta), livers with sweet-

Continued on page 126

EAT LIKE A GREEK

Hailed for its healthfulness, heartiness, and eclectic spicing, Greek cuisine remains one of the country's greatest gifts to visitors. From gyros to galaktoboureko, moussaka to myzthira, and soutzoukakia to snails, food in Greece is rich, exotic, and revelatory.

To really enjoy communal meals of fresh fish, mama's casseroles, flavorful salads, house wine, and great conversation, keep two ground rules in mind.

ORDER LIKE A NATIVE

Go for "*tis oras*" (grilled fish and meat) or "*piato tis imeras*" (or "plate of the day," often stews, casseroles, and pastas). Remember that fish is always expensive but avoid frozen selections and go for the freshest variety by asking the waitstaff what the day's catch is (you can often inspect it in the kitchen). Note that waiters in Greece tend to be impatient—so don't waffle while you're ordering.

DINE LIKE A FAMILY

Greeks share big plates of food, often piling bites of *mezedes*, salads, and main dishes on small dishes. It's okay to stick your fork into communal platters but not in each other's personal dishes (unless you're family or dear friends).

GRECIAN BOUNTY

Greece is a country of serious eaters, which is why there are so many different kinds of eateries. Here is a list of types to seek out.

Estiatorio: You'll often find fine tablecloths, carefully placed silverware, candles, and multipage menus at an *estiatorio*, or restaurant; menus range from traditional to nouvelle.

Oinomageirio: Now enjoying a retro resurgence, these simple eateries were often packed with blue-collar workers filling up on casseroles and listening to *rembetika*, Greece's version of the blues.

Taverna: This is vintage Greece—family-style eateries noted for great spreads of grilled meat "tis oras" (of the hour), thick-cut fried potatoes, dips, salads, and wine—all shared around a big table and with a soundtrack of *bouzouki* music.

Psarotaverna: Every bit like a regular taverna, except the star of the menu is fresh fish. Remember that fish usually comes whole; if you want it filleted, ask "*Mporo na exo fileto?*" Typical fish varieties include *barbounia* (red mullet), *perka* (perch), *sardella* (sardine), *bakaliaros* (cod), *lavraki* (sea bass), and *tsipoura* (sea bream).

Mezedopoleia: In this Greek version of tapas bars, you can graze on a limited menu of dips, salads, and hot and cold mezedes. Wildly popular with the pre-nightclub crowd.

Ouzeri and Rakadiko: *Ouzo* and the Cretan firewater *raki* (also known as *tsikoudia*) are the main attractions here, but there's always a generous plate of hot or cold mezedes to go with the spirits. A mix of old-timers and young scenesters make for great people-watching.

Kafeneio (café): Coffee rules here—but the food menu is usually limited to sandwiches, crepes, *tiropites* (cheese pies), and *spanakopites* (spinach pies).

Zacharoplasteio (patisserie): Most dessert shops are "to go," but some old-style spots have a small klatch of tables to enjoy coffee and that fresh slice of *galaktoboureko* (custard in phyllo dough).

TAKING IT TO THE STREETS

Greeks are increasingly eating on the go, since they're working longer (right through the afternoon siesta that used to be a mainstay). Fortunately, eateries have adapted to this lifestyle change. *Psitopoleia* (grill shops) have the most popular takeaway food: the wrapped-in-pita *souvlaki* (pork, lamb, or chicken chunks), *gyros* (slow-roasted slabs of pork and lamb, or chicken), or *kebabs* (spiced, grilled ground meat). Tzatziki, onions, tomatoes, and fried potatoes are also tucked into the pita. Toasted sandwiches and tasty hot dogs are other yumptious options.

THE GREEK TABLE

Mezedes ΜεΖέδες **(appetizers):** Eaten either as a first course or as full meals, they can be hot (pickled octopus, chickpea fritters, dolmades, fried squid) or cold (dips like *tzatziki; taramosalata,* puree of salted mullet roe or the spicy whipped feta called *htipiti*). Start with two or three, then keep ordering to your heart's content.

Tzatziki (cucumber in yogurt)

Salata Σαλάτα **(salad):** No one skips salads here since the vegetables burst with flavor, texture, and aroma. The most popular is the *horiatiki,* or what the rest of the world calls a "Greek salad"—this country-style salad has tomato, onion, cucumber, feta, and Kalamata olives. Other popular combos include *maroulosalata* (lettuce tossed with fresh dill and fennel) and the Cretan *dakos* (bread rusks topped with minced tomato, feta, and onion).

Horiatiki (Greek salad)

Kyrios Piato Κύριο Πιάτο **(main course):** Main dishes were once served family-style, like mezedes, but the plates are now offered as single servings at many restaurants. Some places serve the dishes as they are ready while more Westernized eateries bring all the plates out together. Order all your food at the same time, but be sure to tell the waiter if you want your main dishes to come after the salads and mezedes. Most grilled meat dishes come with a side of thick-cut fried potatoes, while seafood and casseroles such as *moussaka* are served alone. *Horta,* or boiled greens, drenched in lemon, are the ideal side for grilled or fried fish.

Sardines with rice, potatoes, and salad

Epidorpio Επιδόρπιο **(dessert):** Most restaurants give diners who have finished their meals a free plate of fresh seasonal fruit or some homemade *halva* (a cinnamony semolina pudding-cake with raisins).

Krassi Κρασί **(wine):** Greeks almost always have wine with a meal, usually sharing a carafe or two of *hima* (barrel or house wine) with friends. Bitter resinated wine, or *retsina,* has become less common in restaurants. Instead, the choice is often a dry Greek white wine that goes well with seafood or poultry.

Moussaka

Psomi Ψωμί **(bread):** Bread, often pita-fashion, comes with a meal and usually costs 1 to 2 euros—a *kouver* (cover) charge—regardless of whether you eat it.

Nero Νερό **(water):** If you ask for water, waitstaff will usually bring you a big bottle of it—and charge you, of course. If you simply want tap water (free and safe to drink) ask for a *kanata*—or a pitcher.

Galaktoboureko (custard filled phyllo pastry)

LIKE MAMA USED TO MAKE

Nearly all Greek restaurants have the same homey dishes that have graced family dinner tables here for years. However, some are hardly ever ordered by locals, who prefer to eat them at home—most Greeks avoid moussaka and pastitsio unless they're made fresh that day. So if you order the following foods at restaurants, make sure to ask if they're fresh ("*tis imeras*").

■ Dolmades—grape leaves stuffed with rice and herbs

■ Kotopoulo lemonato—whole chicken roasted with thickly sliced potatoes, lemon, and oregano

■ Moussaka—a casserole of eggplant and spiced beef topped with béchamel

■ Pastitsio—tube-shaped pasta baked with spiced beef, béchamel, and cheese

Best bet: Grape leaves

■ Psari plaki—whole fish baked with tomato, onions, garlic and olive oil

■ Soupa avgolemono—an egg-lemon soup with a chicken stock base

COFFEE CULTURE

Greeks go out for coffee not because of caffeine addiction but because they like to spend at least two hours mulling the world with their friends. *Kafeneia*, or old-style coffeehouses, are usually full of courtly old men playing backgammon and sipping a tiny but strong cup of *elliniko* (Greek coffee). Modern cafés (*kafeterias*) are more chic, packed with frappé-loving office workers, freddo-swilling college students, and arty hipsters nursing espressos. Order your coffee *sketos* (without sugar), *metrios* (medium sweet), or *glykos* (sweet).

Frappé—a frothy blend of instant coffee (always Nescafe), cold water, sugar, and evaporated milk.

Elliniko—the strong traditional coffee made from Brazilian beans ground into a fine powder.

Freddo—an iced cappuccino or espresso.

Nes—instant coffee, often served with froth.

Frappé

breads in vinegar and oregano, and piquant *soutzoukakia,* meatballs fried, then simmered in a cinnamon-laced tomato sauce. The entrance is down the walkway next to Glikis Kafenion. ⊠ *Aggelou Geronda 4, Plaka* ☏ *210/322–1065* ⊟ *No credit cards* ⊘ *Closed weekends and July. No lunch.*

¢–$ ✕ **Sholarhio.** A favorite with university students, artists, and grizzled workers, this open-hearted tavern offers a tasty daily platter of all the best in home-cooked Greek cuisine. Waiters bring a giant tray of the day's offerings, which include such favorites as taramosalata, tzatziki, cuttlefish stewed with onions, *lahanodolmades* (cabbage rolls), eggplant dip, fried calamari, and *bekri mezedes* (wine-marinated pork cutlets). You can also order a wide range of seafood, pasta, and meat dishes from the menu. Order a carafe of wine and enjoy the feast on the bloom-filled deck. All in all, a great option for lunch or dinner after a day of sightseeing. ⊠ *Tripodon 14, Plaka* ☏ *210/322–0666* ⊕ *www. sholarhio.gr* ⊟ *No credit cards.*

MONASTIRAKI & THISSION ΜΟΝΑΣΤΗΡΑΚΙ & ΘΗΣΕΙΟ

Northwest of Plaka, Monastiraki and Thission retain the gritty charm of an Anatolian bazaar and magnetize the city's hardcore café and bar crowd.

$$$$ ✕ **Pil Poul et Jerome Serres.** A century ago, customers arrived on foot
Fodor'sChoice or in horse-drawn carriages for fittings at this elegant Jazz Age hab-
★ erdasher, but today they drive up in SUVs to sample lobster with passion fruit or pan-roasted rooster breast with shallot confit. The prices definitely make this restaurant—which chef Jerome Serres has made one of the best in the city—one for special occasions, but just stepping onto its marble terrace makes it one: the view of the Parthenon is so spectacular you may not fully savor your grouper with lemongrass and winter truffles. White linens and candlelight enhance the romantic aura of this beautifully restored neoclassic building at the edge of the Apostolou Pavlou promenade. If you're just interested in soaking up the atmosphere, stake a spot in the lively ground-floor cocktail lounge. ⊠ *Apostolou Pavlou 51 and Poulopoulou, Thission* ☏ *210/342–3665* ⊟ *AE, MC, V* ⊘ *Closed Mon.*

$$$–$$$$ ✕ **Kuzina.** Sleek, dazzlingly decorated, and moodily lighted, this bistro
Fodor'sChoice attracts many style-conscious Athenians but Kuzina isn't just a pretty
★ face. The food—especially the inventive seafood and pasta dishes—is among the best in Athens, especially on touristy Adrianou. Happily, the decor is almost as delicious as the Sikomaida fig tart marinated in anise seed and ouzo. Past an outdoor table setting, the main room soars skyward, glittering with birdcage chandeliers and factory ducts, with a vast lemon-yellow bar set below a spotlighted wall lined with hundreds of wine bottles. The menu showcases newfangled Greek as well as old faves; best bets include the grilled and cured octopus with fennel shavings, the soffritto of salted cod, and the beef tenderloin with black truffles. Whether you sit outside on the street, in the spectacular main dining room, or opt for a table on the roof (offering a fantastic view of the Acropolis), finish your meal off with a stroll to the small but

impressive art gallery, Porta, on the second floor. Kuzina's Web site is a winner, too—take a look. ⊠*Adrianou 9, Thission* ☎*210/324–0133* ⊕*www.kuzina.gr* ⊟*AE, MC, V.*

$$–$$$ ✕**Filistron.** In warm weather it's worth stopping by this place just to have a drink and enjoy the delightful, painterly scene from the roof garden—a sweeping view of the Acropolis and Mt. Lycabettus. In cooler weather, take a seat in the sunny, cheerful dining room off a pedestrian walkway. The long list of mezedes has classics and more unusual dishes: codfish croquettes with herb and garlic sauce; pork with mushrooms in wine sauce; grilled potatoes with smoked cheese and scallions; and an array of regional cheeses, washed down with a flowery white *hima* (barrel wine). The service is top-notch. ⊠*Apostolou Pavlou 23, Thission* ☎*210/346–7554 or 210/342–2897* ⊟*MC, V* ⊙*Closed 1 wk in Aug. No lunch.*

¢–$ ✕**Bairaktaris.** Run by the same family for more than a century, this is one of the best places to eat in Monastiraki Square. After admiring the painted wine barrels and black and white stills of Greek film stars, go to the window case to view the day's *magirefta* (stove-top cooked dish, usually made earlier)—maybe beef *kokkinisto* (stew with red sauce) and *soutzoukakia* (oblong meatballs simmered in tomato sauce) spiked with cloves. Or sit down and order the gyro platter. Appetizers include small cheese pies with sesame seeds, tender mountain greens, and fried zucchini with tzatziki garlic dip. ⊠*Monastiraki Sq. 2, Monastiraki* ☎*210/321–3036* ⊟*AE, MC, V.*

¢–$ ✕**Steki tou Ilias.** Athenians who love fresh-grilled lamb chops and thick-cut fried potatoes that could have come from *yiayia's* (grandma's) very kitchen flock to this taverna along a quiet pedestrianized street in Thission. It's a place to relax with friends: split a giant plate of *paidakia* (lamb chops), fries, creamy tzatziki, and fava bean spread. ⊠*Thessalonikis 7, Thission* ☎*210/342–2407* ⊟*No credit cards.*

CENTRAL ATHENS, PSIRRI & OMONIA SQUARE
ΑΘΗΝΑ (ΚΕΝΤΡΟ), ΨΥΡΡΗ & ΠΛΑΤΕΙΑ ΟΜΟΝΟΙΑΣ

Located north of Monastiraki, Omonia, the city's main square, is busy by day and seedy by night, but it bursts with cultural diversity and the kaleidoscopic Central Market. The former warehouse district of Psirri, which is between Omonia and Monastiraki, is party central for Athens.

$$$$ ✕**Hytra.** Don't let the understated bistro ambience fool you: this is one of the city's most fashionable eateries. Applying his French training to his Cretan background, chef Yiannis Baxevanis has created an imaginative menu that has caught the attention of the international press. If you find it hard to choose, sample the range of his culinary combinations—fish soup garnished with sea urchin, the classic lamb in egg-lemon sauce—with a tasting menu of 15 dishes. The wine list features an intriguing selection of vintages to accompany your meal, or you can stick with chilled raki, the traditional tipple of Crete. ⊠*Navarhou Apostoli 7, Psirri* ☎*210/331–6767* ⊛*Reservations essential* ⊟*AE, DC, V* ⊙*Closed Sun. and June–Sept.*

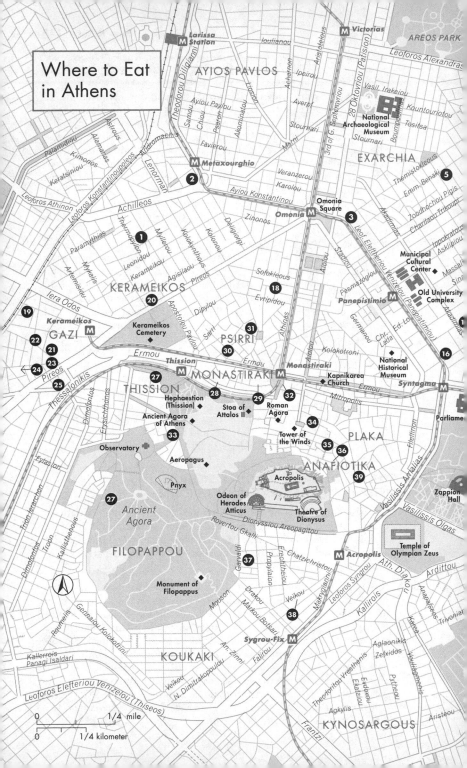

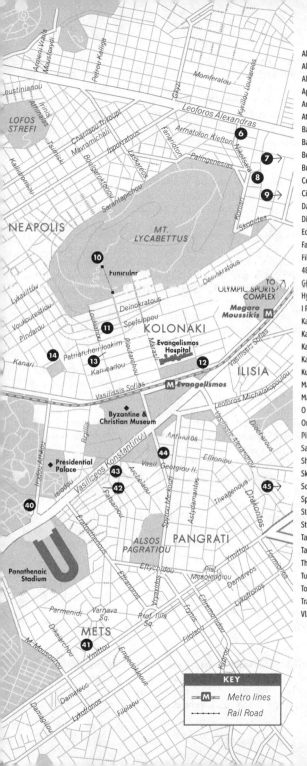

$$$–$$$$ ✕**Archaion Gefseis.** The epicurean owners of "Ancient Flavors" combed through texts and archaeological records in an effort to re-create foods eaten in antiquity—not to mention how they were eaten, with spoon and knife only. Dishes like pancetta seasoned with thyme and squid cooked in its ink prove, if anything, the continuity between ancient and modern Greek cuisine. There's an undeniable kitsch factor in the setting: in a torch-lighted garden, waiters in flowing chitons serve diners reclining on couches. ⊠ *Kodratou 22, Karaiskaki Sq., Metaxourgeio* ☎ *210/523–9661* ◭ *Reservations essential* ▭ *AE, MC, V* ☾ *Closed Sun.*

$$$–$$$$
Fodor'sChoice
★   ✕**To Varoulko.** Not one to rest on his Michelin star, acclaimed chef Lefteris Lazarou is constantly trying to outdo himself, with magnificent results. Rather than use the menu, give him an idea of what you like and let him create your dish from what he found that day at the market. Among his most fabulous compilations are octopus simmered in sweet red *mavrodafni* wine and served with mousse made from a sourdough pasta called *trahana,* crayfish dolmas wrapped in sorrel leaves, and red snapper with black truffle and eggplant mousse. Some dishes fuse traditional peasant fare like the Cretan *gamopilafo* ("wedding rice" flavored with boiled goat) with unusual flavors like bitter chocolate. The multilevel premises stand next to the Eridanus Hotel; in summer, dinner is served on a rooftop terrace with a wonderful Acropolis view. ⊠ *Pireos 80, Gazi* ☎ *210/522–8400* ◭ *Reservations essential* ▭ *AE, DC, V* ☾ *Closed Sun. No lunch.*

$$–$$$ ✕**To Zeidoron.** This usually crowded Psirri hangout has decent mezedes, but the real draw is its strategic location. Metal tables line the main pedestrian walkway, great for watching all the world go by and for enjoying the sight of the neighborhood's illuminated churches and alleys. Small dishes include hot feta sprinkled with red pepper, grilled green peppers stuffed with cheese, eggplant baked with tomato and pearl onions, shrimp with ouzo, and an impressive array of dips and spreads. The wines are overpriced; opt for ouzo instead. ⊠ *Taki 10, at Ayion Anargiron, Psirri* ☎ *210/321–5368* ▭ *No credit cards* ☾ *Closed Aug.*

$–$$ ✕**Abyssinia Cafe.** Facing hoary Abyssinia Square, where scores of merchants sell wares such as antique furniture and gleaming bouzoukis, this timeworn but exceptional eatery is popular with locals who want home-cooked traditional food and endless servings of the excellent barrel wine. Try the mussels and rice pilaf, the wine-marinated octopus with pasta, or any of the dips, including the spicy feta-and-garlic spread. Keep this is mind for a great place to relax after a day of shopping at the flea market. Although usually only open 10:30 AM to 2 PM for lunch, it is sometimes open for dinner but call ahead to be sure. ⊠ *Plateia Abyssinias, Psirri* ☎ *210/321–7047* ▭ *V* ▭ *No credit cards.*

$–$$
★   ✕**Athinaikon.** Choose among classic specialties at this mezedopoleio: grilled octopus, shrimp croquettes, broad beans simmered in thick tomato sauce, and *ameletita* (sautéed lamb testicles). All goes well with the light barrel red. The decor is no-nonsense ouzeri, with marble tables, dark wood, and framed memorabilia. It's a favorite of

attorneys and local office workers. ⊠*Themistokleous 2, Omonia Sq.* ☎*210/383–8485* ▭*No credit cards* ⊘*Closed Sun. and Aug.*

$–$$ ✗**Maritsa's.** Brokers from the Athens Stock Exchange just a couple of doors down the street have made this mezedopoleio their lunchtime haunt. Choose from classic taverna dishes—pickled octopus, grilled sardines, or deep-fried zucchini—and see if you can catch some insider gossip on the day's trading. ⊠*Sofokleous 17–19, Omonia Sq.* ☎*210/325–1421* ▭*MC, V.*

¢–$ ✗**Diporto.** Through the years, everyone in Omonia has come here for lunch—butchers from the Central Market, suit-clad brokers from the nearby stock exchange, artists, migrants, and even bejeweled ladies who lunch; they're often sitting at the same tables when it gets crowded. Owner-chef Barba Mitsos keeps everyone happy with his handful of simple, delicious, and dirt-cheap dishes. There's always an exceptional *horiatiki* (Greek salad), sometimes studded with fiery-hot green pepperoncini; other favorites are his buttery *gigantes* (large, buttery white beans cooked in tomato sauce), *vrasto* (boiled goat, pork, or beef with vegetables), warming chickpea soup, and fried finger-size fish. Wine is drawn directly from the barrels lining the walls. ⊠*Theatrou and Sofokleous, Central Market* ☎*No phone* ▭*No credit cards* ⊘*No dinner.*

SYNTAGMA SQUARE & KOLONAKI
ΠΛΑΤΕΙΑ ΣΥΝΤΑΓΜΑΤΟΣ & ΚΟΛΩΝΑΚΙ

Located east of Plaka, Kolonaki is an old-money neighborhood that's a haunt for politicians, expats, and high-maintenance ladies who lunch (and shop). Syntagma, a pretty central square between Parliament and Ermou Street, is also popular with tourists.

$$$$ ✗**Cibus.** The lush Zappion Gardens have always been a tranquil green
★ oasis for stressed-out Athenians, who head here to gaze at the distant views of the Parthenon and Temple of Olympian Zeus, or catch an open-air cinema showing, or chill out at the landmark café. Now, the café is gone and a chic new restaurant is luring both fashionables and families. The food has an Italian touch, thanks to chef Mauro Peressini, and it's expensive but fantastic (reservations are essential for dinner). Try the ravioli with red radicchio and almonds, with a fondue of Montasio cheese and truffles, or one of several outstanding risotto dishes, including one with crayfish and tomatoes. After dinner, have a drink and listen to the latest grooves with the beautiful people at the neighboring Lallabai club. ⊠*Zappion Gardens, National Garden* ☎*210/336–9364* ▭*AE, DC, MC, V.*

$$$–$$$$ ✗**Cellier Le Bistrot.** On the same spot occupied by Apotsos, an ouzeri
★ that was a fixture on the Athenian social scene for decades, Cellier Le Bistrot has introduced an upmarket eatery fashioned around wine. The bistro has one of the largest selections of by-the-glass wines in the city, which you can sample with a light dish from the ever-changing menu: maybe fresh pasta, salad, or seafood. The decor is both timeless and contemporary, with leather banquettes and mahogany surfaces. The service is as impeccable as the wine list, which is culled from the

finest vintages from nearby Cellier, one of the city's top wineshops. ⊠*Panepistimiou 10, in the arcade, Syntagma Sq.* ☎*210/363–8525* ⊟*AE, MC, V.*

$$$–$$$$ ✕**Orizontes.** Have a seat on the terrace atop Mt. Lycabettus: the Acropolis glitters below, and, beyond, Athens unfolds like a map out to the Saronic Gulf. It's tough to compete with such a view and, at times, the food and the service (or both) fail to match it. But best bets include the black sea bream with silver beet, mussels, grated tomato, and sea-urchin roe, or the beef paillard with yogurt risotto and glazed tomato. No road goes this high: the restaurant is reached by cable car. ⊠*Mt. Lycabettus, Kolonaki* ☎*210/721–0701 or 210/722–7065* ⚐*Reservations essential* ⊟*AE, DC, MC, V.*

$$ ✕**Kafenio.** A Kolonaki institution, this ouzeri reminiscent of a French bistro is slightly fancier than the normal mezedopoleio, with cloth napkins, candles on the tables, a handsome dark-wood interior, and society matrons taking a break from retail therapy. The enormous menu offers many unusual creations. For the freshest dishes, ask the waiter for the day's specials, which include traditional fare such as *kolokithokeftedes* (fried zucchini balls), marinated octopus, and pork cooked in wine, as well as more-modern twists such as a mixed greens salad with pomegranates. ⊠*Loukianou 26, Kolonaki* ☎*210/722–9056* ⊟*No credit cards* ☉*Closed Sun. and 3 wks in Aug.*

$–$$ ✕**Dakos.** This sleek new restaurant—named after a scrumptious Cretan salad made of bread rusks, shaved tomato, onions, feta, and olive oil—offers a broad menu of delicacies from Greece's largest island. Some of the best dishes include *hortopitakia* (pies made of wild greens), grilled meats (with excellent sausage), *sfakianopita* (a flat pita stuffed with a ricotta-like cheese and drizzled with honey), and, of course, the *dakos* salad. Wash it all down with a shot of raki, the extremely potent spirit made from grape must. The service is excellent, the waiters informed and very polite, and the decor minimalist and relaxing. ⊠*Tsakalof 6, Kolonaki* ☎*210/360–4020* ⊟*No credit cards.*

$–$$ ✕**Sophia's Cafe Valaoritou.** This chic-yet-homey bistro opened recently next to its more-famous sister, the Valaoritou Brasserie, where chef Lefteris Lazarou wins Michelin stars and creates works of art like his cuttlefish risotto with caramelized garlic. Here, the salads are generous and delicious, especially those with the bistro's well-spiced grilled chicken, and there are also a range of pasta dishes and traditional Greek fare like lemon-oregano chicken, lamb, and seafood. But save room for the fabulous desserts, especially the lemon pie and the amazing galaktoboureko made with Camembert cheese instead of the traditional custard. ⊠*Valaoritou 15, Kolonaki* ☎*210/364–1530* ⊟*MC, V.*

$–$$ ✕**Taverna Filipou.** This unassuming taverna is hardly the sort of place you'd expect to find in chic Kolonaki, yet its devotees include cabinet ministers, diplomats, actresses, and film directors. The appeal is simple, well-prepared Greek classics, mostly *ladera* (vegetable or meat casseroles cooked in an olive-oil–and–tomato sauce), roast chicken, or fish baked in the oven with tomatoes, onions, and parsley. Everything's home-cooked, so the menu adapts to what's available fresh at the open-air produce market. In summer and on balmy spring or autumn evenings, choose a table on the pavement; in winter, seating is in a cozy dining room a few steps below street level. ⊠ *Xenokratous 19, Kolonaki* ☎ *210/721–6390* ⊟ *No credit cards* ⊘ *Closed Sat. and mid-Aug.*

PANGRATI & KAISARIANI ΠΑΓΚΡΑΤΙ & ΚΑΙΣΑΡΙΑΝΗ

Urbane without being snobby or expensive, Pangrati and Kaisariani are havens for academics, artists, and expats who bask in the homey warmth of these neighborhoods.

$$$$
Fodor's Choice
★
✕ **Spondi.** One of Athens's most intensely designed temples to great food, Spondi is a feast for both the eyes and the taste buds. One salon shimmers with arty Swarovski chandeliers, walls of hot pink and cool aubergine, and chic black leather couches; for less glamour opt for the white-linen vaulted room, a beige-on-beige sanctorum; or, in summer, chill in the vast, bougainvillea-draped courtyard. No matter where you sit, however, you'll be able to savor the transcendentally delicious creations of Arnaud Bignon and consultant chef Eric Frechon (of Paris's Hotel Bristol fame). Highlights of their French-inspired Mediterranean menu (which change every summer and winter) include eggplant with tuna, fillet of sea bass in vanilla sauce, black ravioli with honeyed leeks and shrimp, and a feta-and-coriander-flavor ice cream. You may wish to opt for a taxi ride out to Pangrati—but isn't one of the best meals in all of Greece worth it? ⊠ *Pirronos 5, Varnava Sq., Pangrati* ☎ *210/752–0658* 🖷 *210/756–4021* ⊕ *www.spondi.gr* 🖑 *Reservations essential* ⊟ *AE, DC, MC, V* ⊘ *No lunch.*

$$–$$$
✕ **Trata O Stelios.** The owner works directly with fishermen, guaranteeing that the freshest catch comes to the table. Just point to your preference and it will soon arrive in the way Greeks insist upon: grilled with exactitude, coated in the thinnest layer of olive oil to seal in juices, and accompanied by lots of lemon. Even those who scrunch up their nose at fish soup will be converted by this version of the dense yet delicate *kakavia*. Stelios is also one of the few remaining places you can get real homemade taramosalata. Avoid the place during Sunday lunch; it's packed with Athenian families. ⊠ *Anagenniseos Sq. 7–9, off Ethnikis Antistaseos, Kaisariani* ☎ *210/729–1533* ⊟ *No credit cards* ⊘ *Closed 10 days at Orthodox Easter.*

$–$$
✕ **Aphrodite.** This mezedopoleio's menu changes more often than the faces of its regulars, a mix of locals, politicians, and intellectuals who have elevated this cozy neighborhood square into a city insider's alternative to Kolonaki. Sip the complimentary raki and crunch on bread sticks dipped in olive paste while deciding whether to order the day's special or a round of mezedes: roasted red peppers stuffed with goat cheese, bite-size fried pies with a filling of wild greens, whole grilled squid, marinated anchovies, and a range of salads in season. In warm weather tables go out on the *platia* (square); in winter, seating is in a split-level dining room with a casual island ambience. ⊠ *Ptolemeon and Amynta 6, Proskopon Sq., Pangrati* ☎ *210/724–8822* ⊟ *MC, V.*

$–$$
✕ **Fatsio.** Don't be fooled by the Italian name: the food at this old-fashioned restaurant is all home-style Greek. Walk past the kitchen and point at what you want before taking a seat. Favorites include a "souffle"

CLOSE UP

Greek Fast Food

Souvlaki is the original Greek fast food: spit-roasted or grilled meat, tomatoes, onions, and garlicky *tzatziki* wrapped in a pita to go. Greeks on the go have always eaten street food such as the endless variations of cheese pie, *koulouri* (sesame-covered bread rings), roasted chestnuts or ears of corn, and palm-size paper bags of nuts. But modern lifestyles and the arrival of foreign pizza and burger chains have cultivated a taste for fast food—and spawned several local brands definitely worth checking out. **Goody's** serves burgers and spaghetti as well as some salads and sandwiches. Items like baguettes with grilled vegetables or seafood salads are seasonal additions to the menu. At **I Pitta tou Pappou** you can sam-ple several takes on souvlaki: grilled chicken breast or pork-and-lamb patties, each served with a special sauce. **Everest** is tops when it comes to *tost*—oval-shape sandwich buns with any combination of fillings, from omelets and smoked turkey breast to fries, roasted red peppers, and various spreads. It also sells sweet and savory pies, ice cream, and desserts. Its main rival is **Grigoris**, a chain of sandwich and pie shops that also runs the City Espresso Bars. If you want to sit down while you eat your fast food, look for a **Flocafe Espresso Bar**. Along with espresso, frappé, *filtro* (drip), and cappuccino, they also serve a selection of pastries and sandwiches, including brioche with mozzarella and pesto.

that is actually a variation on baked macaroni-and-cheese, with pieces of ham and slices of beef and a topping of eggplant and tomato sauce. Quick service and good value for the money is the reason for Fatsio's enduring popularity among both elder Kolonaki residents and office workers seeking an alternative to fast food. ✉*Effroniou 5–7, off Rizari, Pangrati* ☎210/721–7421 ▭*No credit cards* ✆*Closed 1 wk mid-Aug. No dinner.*

$-$$

★ ✕**Karavitis.** The winter dining room is insulated with huge wine casks; in summer there is garden seating in a courtyard across the street (get there early so you don't end up at the noisy sidewalk tables). The classic Greek cuisine is well prepared, including pungent tzatziki, *bekri mezedes* (lamb chunks in zesty red sauce), lamb ribs (when in season), *stamnaki* (beef baked in a clay pot), and melt-in-the-mouth meatballs. This neighborhood favorite is near the Panathenaic Stadium. ✉*Arktinou 35, at Pausaniou, Pangrati* ☎210/721–5155 ▭*No credit cards* ✆*Closed 1 wk mid-Aug. No lunch.*

GAZI, KERAMEIKOS, & ROUF ΓΚΑΖΙ, ΚΕΡΑΜΕΙΚΟΣ, & ΡΟΥΦ

West of Psirri, the greater Gazi district has turned into the city's hottest art, culture, and nightlife zone. The new Kerameikos metro station has also made it ultra-convenient.

$$$–$$$$ ✕**Thalatta.** Walking into this charming renovated house off the factory-lined streets of Gazi feels like stumbling upon a wonderful secret. Owner Yiannis Safos, an islander from Ikaria, has transformed the space into a fresh, modern dining room with a colorful tile-paved

courtyard. He fills the menu with fish pulled daily from the Aegean; ask about the selection, from sea urchins to clams. Perhaps try grilled octopus with pureed pumpkin and sun-dried tomatoes, monkfish carpaccio with wild fennel, or salmon with champagne sauce. Finish with homemade lemon sorbet—bits of zest are left in for added bite. ⊠ *Vitonos 5, Gazi* ☎*210/346–4204* ⚲ *Reservations essential* ▤*MC, V* ⊘ *Closed Sun. No lunch.*

\$\$–\$\$\$ ✕ **Aleria.** Athenian trend-watchers are so enthusiastic about the gritty-cool neighborhood of Metaxourgeio that they say it will soon be like Paris's boho-chic Marais district. Restaurants like Aleria, a gem of neoclassic design and inventive Mediterranean fusion cuisine, are one reason the area's star is rising. Try the canelloni stuffed with shrimp, mussels and carrots in a mango and pineapple sauce, or the pork fillets in ouzo sauce. ⊠ *Meg. Alexandrou 57, Metaxourgeio* ☎*210/522–2633* ⚲ *Reservations essential* ▤*AE, MC, V* ⊘ *Closed Sun. No lunch.*

\$\$–\$\$\$ ✕ **The Butcher Shop.** A carnivore's paradise, this sleek and simple tavern does its meats superbly. Try the steaks, sausages, and the juicy, gigantic hamburgers. Don't miss the crispy home fries and specialty cheeses from around Greece. For sides, go for a plate of fresh, vinegary beets or the seasonal salads. The menu also offers a selection of cheeses from around Greece as well as an eclectic selection of local wines. ⊠ *Persefonis 19, Gazi* ☎*210/341–3440* ▤ *No credit cards.*

\$\$ ✕ **Mamacas.** This restaurant started the wave of "modern tavernas," which offer new takes on traditional Greek food amid the chicness of minimalist decor. Mamacas, which means "the mommies" in Greek, was also the first restaurant to spark the rebirth of Gazi, the once-forlorn neighborhood around what was once a gas foundry. Since it opened in 1998, Mamacas has consistently offered fresh, delicious home cooking such as pork with prunes, tomatoes, and peppers stuffed with rice and raisins, and, when they make it, arguably the best walnut cake in town. After hours, the restaurant turns into a bar and draws a flashy crowd of miniskirted young women and open-shirted men who strike poses as if the whole world is looking. Now that the new Kerameikos metro station has opened, it's easier than ever to go to the restaurant that helped turn Gazi into the hottest spot in Athens. ⊠ *Persefonis 41, Gazi* ☎*210/346–4984* ▤ *MC, V* ⊘ *Closed Mon.*

\$\$ ✕ **Sardelles.** If you love seafood and don't want to pay a fortune for it, don't miss this wonderful and beautifully designed eatery next to Mamacas. The simple lines of Greek island decor are evident in wooden *kafeneion* (coffeehouse) tables and 1950s-style metal-frame garden chairs picked up at auctions and painted dazzling white. Try the cod cutlets, the grilled fish drizzled with mastic-flavored sauce, and the house specialty, the sardines ("sardelles") in rock salt. Also recommended are any of the house salads, especially the mixed greens with goat cheese and pomegranate seeds. Top it off with a shot of *mastiha*, or mastic-flavor liqueur, and a slice of lemon or chocolate tart. ⊠ *Persefonis 15, Gazi* ☎*210/347–8050* ▤ *No credit cards.*

\$–\$\$ ✕ **Kanella.** Housed in a sleek, airy building with modern and traditional touches, this lively restaurant is infused with Gazi's energy. The superb home cooking includes the braised beef in tomato sauce with spaghetti, the simmered pork with mushrooms and mashed potatoes, the Kefalonia-style rooster in red sauce, and an excellent salad with boiled zucchini, sliced avocado, and grated Graviera cheese. Wine comes in beautifully designed glass carafes. Warning: when the place gets busy, it gets almost psychedelically loud. ⊠ *Konstantinoupoleos 70 and Evmolpidon, Gazi* ☎ *210/347–6320* ▭ *No credit cards.*

$–$$ ✕ **Skoufia.** This pretty, high-quality restaurant has some of the best food in town—and at reasonable prices. Menus are the royal-blue lined notebooks used by Greek schoolchildren; the proprietors have handwritten the Cretan-inspired offerings on the pages. Enjoy Skoufia's signature roasted lamb, which is so tender it just falls off the bone, on one of the tables outside. Other excellent choices include braised beef with eggplant puree, wild-greens pie, and syrupy *ravani* cake with mastic-flavor *kaimaki* ice cream. ⊠ *Vasileiou Megalou 50, Rouf* ☎ *210/341–2252* ▭ *No credit cards.*

ATHENS NORTH & EAST ΑΘΗΝΑ, ΒΟΡΕΙΑ & ΑΝΑΤΟΛΙΚΗ

$$$$ ✕ **Balthazar.** With its airy neoclassic courtyard—paved with original painted tiles, canopied by huge date palms, and illuminated by colored lanterns—Balthazar truly feels like an oasis in the middle of Athens. The crowd is hip, moneyed, and beautiful, so you might wish to come for dinner, then stay to mingle as the DJ picks up the beat. Talented young chef Yiorgos Tsiktsiras keeps the quality and flavor high on the up-to-the-minute menu, with prices to match. Try any of the creative salads, the East-meets-West fish dishes, and the homemade desserts, especially the grape sorbet. ⊠ *Tsoha 27, at Soutsou, Ambelokipi* ☎ *210/644–1215* ⋀ *Reservations essential* ▭ *AE, MC, V* ☺ *Closed Sun. No lunch.*

$$$$ ✕ **48.** One of the best and most atmospheric restaurants in Athens, 48
Fodor's Choice   takes the best of traditional Greek fare and transforms it into food so
★   experiential that you will remember it forever. Inspired by the setting—this cavernous space was previously an art gallery—French-trained chef Christophoros Peskiaschas created a menu with definite visual appeal. Rather than fusing Greek recipes with nouvelle ingredients, he has re-created old favorites but given them a twist. Try the sea bass with marinated cucumber and fish roe sauce, the raw and marinated fresh fish platter, or the lamb simmered with artichokes. The desserts are almost orgasmic, especially anything made with chocolate. ⊠ *Armatolon and Klefton 48, between Leoforos Alexandras and Mt. Lycabettus, Ambelokipi* ☎ *210/641–1082* ⋀ *Reservations essential* ▭ *AE, DC, V* ☺ *Closed Sun.*

$$$–$$$$ ✕ **Boschetto.** The thick greenery of a small urban park, the pampering
★   of an expert maître d', and the flavors of Italian nouvelle cuisine make you forget you're in the center of Athens. The specialty here is fresh pasta, such as the excellent papardelle with rooster ragout and Marsala sauce. Also on the menu is scorpion fish with lobster sauce, as well as more typical (but just as outstanding) fare such as the rack of lamb with polenta and smoked scamorza cheese, and the risotto with lime, mushrooms, and Dry Martini. The desserts, especially the tiramisu and pan-

acotta, are also dreamy, and they go down well with a cup of espresso, the best in Athens. ⊠ *Evangelismos Park, near the Hilton, Ilisia, 10676* ☎ *210/721–0893 or 210/722–7324* ⚐ *Reservations essential* ☐ *AE, V* ⊙ *Closed Sun. and 2 wks in Aug. No lunch Oct.–Aug.*

$$$ ✕**Giantes.** The menu here definitely has a modern streak, but meals are served in a lovely flower-filled courtyard. The taverna is co-owned by one of Greece's foremost organic farmers, so almost everything is fresh and delicious, though a little pricier than the norm. The Byzantine pork and chicken with honey, raisins, and coriander are perennial favorites. ⊠ *Valtetsiou 44, Exarchia* ☎ *210/330–1369* ☐ *AE, DC, MC, V* ⊙ *Closed Mon. and 1st 2 wks in Aug.*

$–$$ ✕**Vlassis.** Relying on traditional recipes from Thrace, Roumeli, Thessaly, and the islands, cooks whip up what may be the best Greek home-style cooking in Athens. There's no menu: pick from the tray of 20 or so small dishes brought to your table. They're all good, but best bets include *tirokafteri* (a peppery cheese dip), lahanodolmades (cabbage rolls), *pastitsio* (meat pie with macaroni and béchamel sauce), *katsiki ladorigani* (goat with oil and oregano), and the octopus stifado, which is tender and sweet with lots of onions. For dessert, order the halvah or a huge slice of galaktoboureko (custard in phyllo). ⊠ *Paster 8, Mavili Sq.* ☎ *210/646–3060* ⚐ *Reservations essential* ☐ *No credit cards* ⊙ *Closed Aug.–mid-Sept. No dinner Sun.*

Fodor's Choice ★

$$ ✕**Alexandria.** Egyptian spice infuses Greek cuisine with an exotic, eclectic, and dynamic menu at this superb restaurant. The choices include simple but stunning fare such as a tomato salad with thick yogurt and caramelized onions as well as a tender lamb cooked with dried plums and apricots. If you're an adventurous foodie, don't miss Alexandria's signature dish: tender, wine-simmered baby octopus on a creamy bed of fava. The wine list is extensive and well priced, and the service is outstanding. The relaxing, clean-white interior design recalls the cosmopolitan flair of the Egyptian Greeks. ⊠ *Metsovou 13 and Rethymnou, behind Park Hotel, near Archaeological Museum, Exarchia* ☎ *210/821–0004* ☐ *No credit cards* ⊙ *Closed Sun. No lunch.*

Fodor's Choice ★

$–$$ ✕**Kainari.** Handwoven throws and an odd collection of photographs and mementos adorn the walls of this cozy neighborhood taverna, where you'll rub elbows—literally—with businessmen, doctors, students, and other regulars. But what it lacks in space, it makes up for with an extensive menu combining daily specials (ask the fishmonger sipping ouzo at the next table) and favorites, like spicy grilled pancetta, twisted pites, and hand-cut fries cooked in olive oil. ⊠ *Xiromerou 20, behind Archaeological Museum, Erithros Stavros, Ambelokipi* ☎ *210/698–3011* ☐ *No credit cards* ⊙ *Closed Sun. and Aug.*

WHERE TO STAY

As a result of the 2004 Olympics, Athens's hotels have risen both in quality and number of rooms. Nearly every hotel in town underwent a renovation before the games, with luxury hotels paying serious attention to style and design and many adding spas, pools, and gyms. Concept hotels like the Semiramis in Kifissia and Periscope in Kolonaki have not escaped the notice of the international media. Athens's budget hotels—once little better than dorms—now often have air-conditioning and television, along with prettier public spaces. Perhaps best of all is the increase in the number of good-quality, middle-rank family hotels, of which there was long a shortage.

The most convenient hotels for tourists are in the city center. Some of the older hotels in Plaka and near Omonia Square are comfortable and clean, their charm inherent in their age. But along with charm may come leaking plumbing, sagging mattresses, and other lapses in the details—take a good look at the room before you register. The thick stone walls of neoclassic buildings keep them cool in summer, but few of the budget hotels have central heating, and it can be devilishly cold in winter. A buffet breakfast is often served for a few euros extra: cold cuts and cheese, even poached eggs and other meat, but nothing cooked to order.

PRICES

Along with higher quality have come higher hotel prices: room rates in Athens are not much less than in many European cities. Still, there are bargains to be had. Paradoxically, you may get up to a 20% discount if you book the hotel through a local travel agent; it's also a good idea to bargain in person at smaller hotels, especially off-season. When negotiating a rate, bear in mind that the longer the stay, the lower the nightly rate, so it may be less expensive to spend six consecutive nights in Athens rather than staying for two or three nights at either end of your trip through Greece.

WHAT IT COSTS IN EUROS					
	¢	$	$$	$$$	$$$$
FOR 2 PEOPLE	under €80	€80–€150	€150–€200	€200–€250	over €250

Hotel prices are for a standard double room in high season, including taxes. Hotels operate on the European Plan (EP, with no meal provided) unless we note that they use the Continental Plan (CP, with Continental breakfast) or Breakfast Plan (BP, with a full breakfast). Hotel rooms have air-conditioning, room phones, and TVs unless otherwise noted.

ACROPOLIS & SOUTH ΑΚΡΟΠΟΛΗ & ΠΡΟΣ ΤΑ ΝΟΤΙΑ

Under Athens's iconic landmark, newly chic neighborhoods such as Koukaki and Philopappou offer both historic vibes and hipsterious ambience.

$$$$ ⚐ **Ledra Marriott.** The Ledra's main calling cards are its high-performance staff and its style. Guest rooms are gorgeously modern-chic, furnished in warm reds and oranges with feather duvets, with overstuffed armchairs, marble bathrooms, and vast closet space. The fourth-floor executive lodgings are even more spacious and include a private check-in and lounge. The lobby piano bar sits below a spectacular 1,000-crystal chandelier; Kona Kai, the Polynesian restaurant, is excellent; and the Zephyros Café has a bountiful Sunday brunch. While you

can enjoy a gorgeous Acropolis view from the rooftop pool, you'll note you are some distance from the city center. ⊠*Syngrou 115, Neos Kosmos, 11745* ☎*210/930–0000* 🖷*210/935–8603* ⊕*www.marriott. com* ⊷*259 rooms, 11 suites* ♿*In-room: safe, Ethernet. In-hotel: 3 restaurants, bars, pool* ▤*AE, DC, MC, V.*

$$$–$$$$ 🖼**Herodion Hotel.** A good compromise between the area's budget venues and deluxe digs, this hospitable hotel is down the street from the Odeon of Herodes Atticus, where Hellenic Festival performances are held, and a few minutes from the Acropolis. Service is friendlier and more efficient here than at most other Plaka neighborhood hotels, while the marble in the renovated lobby lends a touch of grandeur. Guest rooms are done in light-wood furnishings and muted olive-color walls. The complimentary buffet breakfast is served in a peaceful, tree-shaded atrium; on the roof, there is a terrace with deck chairs and a Parthenon panorama. Take full advantage of the hotel's location and ask for a room with an Acropolis view. ⊠*Rovertou Galli 4, Acropolis, 11742* ☎*210/923 6832 through 210/923–6836* 🖷*210/923–5851* ⊕*www.herodion.gr* ⊷*86 rooms, 4 suites* ♿*In-room: refrigerator. In-hotel: restaurant, bar* ▭*DC, MC, V* ❐❶*BP.*

$$–$$$ 🖼**Philippos Hotel.** Just around the corner from its sister hotel, the Herodion, the Philippos shares its good qualities: a quiet location convenient to the Acropolis and friendly, efficient service. Modular dark-veneer beds (in smallish rooms) are offset by pale green carpets and draperies. You can sip a coffee in the light-filled atrium with comfortable couches and patio tables. Prices are kept down by details like the complimentary Continental (rather than full) breakfast, but the overall experience is just as positive. ⊠*Mitseon 3, Makriyianni, 11742* ☎*210/922–3611* 🖷*210/922–3615* ⊕*www.philipposhotel.gr* ⊷*46 rooms, 2 suites* ♿*In-room: refrigerator. In-hotel: public Internet* ▤*MC, V* ❶*CP.*

$–$$ 🖼**Acropolis Select.** For only €10 more than many basic budget options,
Fodor'sChoice you get to stay in a slick-looking hotel with a lobby full of Philippe
★ Starck–like furniture. Bright, comfortable guest rooms have cheery yellow bedspreads with an abstract red poppy design. Similar in color choice, the dramatic restaurant has daffodil-color walls and contemporary, scroll-back chairs in tomato red. About a dozen rooms look toward the Acropolis: ask for Rooms 401–405 for the best views. There are only 10 no-smoking rooms in the hotel, all on the fifth floor. The residential neighborhood of Koukaki, south of Filopappou Hill, is a 10-minute walk from the Acropolis. ⊠*Falirou 37–39, Koukaki, 11742* ☎*210/921–1610* 🖷*210/921–1610* ⊕*www.acropoliselect.gr* ⊷*72 rooms* ♿*In-room: refrigerator. In-hotel: restaurant, bar* ▤*AE, DC, MC, V.*

$–$$ 🖼**Art Gallery Pension.** A handsome house on a residential street, this pension is comfortably old-fashioned, with family paintings on the muted white walls, comfortable beds, hardwood floors, and ceiling fans. Many guest rooms have balconies with views of Filopappou or the Acropolis. A congenial crowd of visiting students and single travelers fills the place. In winter, lower rates are available to long-term guests, some of whom stay on for a few months. Rates with and without breakfast are available. Though the residential neighborhood, a

10-minute walk south of the Acropolis, lacks the charm of Plaka, it has many fewer tourists and the metro offers easy access to many of the city's sights. ⊠*Erechthiou 5, Koukaki, 11742* ☎*210/923–8376 or 210/923–1933* 🖷*210/923–3025* ✐*ecotec@otenet.gr* ⇨*21 rooms, 2 suites* ♿*In-room: dial-up. In-hotel: bar* ⊟*No credit cards.*

¢ 🖭**Marble House.** This popular pension has a steady clientele—even in winter, when it has low monthly and weekly rates. Guest rooms are clean and quiet, with ceiling fans and rustic wooden furniture. Rooms with air-conditioning and private bath cost a few euros extra. The international staff is always willing to help out and the courtyard is a lovely place to relax. It is a little off the tourist circuit, but it's still possible to walk to most ancient sights (it's about 20 minutes from the Acropolis). It's also close to the metro and the Zinni stop on Trolley 1, 5, or 9 from Syntagma. ⊠*Andreou Zinni 35, Koukaki, 11741* ☎*210/923–4058 or 210/922–6461* ⊕*www.marblehouse.gr* ⇨*16 rooms, 11 with bath* ♿*In-room: no a/c (some), no phone, kitchen (some), refrigerator, no TV* ⊟*No credit cards.*

PLAKA ΠΛΑΚΑ

Northeast of the Acropolis, Plaka and Anafiotika are Athens's old-world villages, replete with winding alleys and a bevy of cafés and shops.

$$$–$$$$ 🖭**Electra Palace.** If you want simple elegance, excellent service, and a ★ great location in Plaka, this is the hotel for you. Located on an attractive street close to area museums, its guest rooms are comfortable and beautifully decorated, with ample storage space. Rooms from the fifth floor up have a view of the Acropolis–which you can also enjoy from the rooftop garden bar. Before setting out in the morning, fill up with one of the city's best buffet breakfasts—sausage, pancakes, and home fries. In the evening, relax in a steam bath in the hotel spa. ⊠*Nikodimou 18–20, Plaka, 10557* ☎*210/337–0000* 🖷*210/324–1875* ⊕*www.electrahotels.gr* ⇨*131 rooms, 19 suites* ♿*In-room: refrigerator, Wi-Fi. In-hotel: restaurant, pool* ⊟*AE, DC, MC, V* ⦿*BP.*

$$–$$$ 🖭**Plaka Hotel.** Tastefully decorated, with deep-blue velvet curtains that **Fodor's**Choice match the upholstery on the wood-arm easy chairs, the guest rooms in ★ this charming hotel are a comfortable place to rest while in the heart of old Athens. This hotel, part of the family-owned chain that includes the hotels Hermes and Achilleas, flourishes in its location; some rooms have views of the Acropolis, which you can also enjoy from the roof garden. The staff is helpful, the rooms small but well kept, and breakfast is served in a glassed-in, taverna-style space overlooking the shopping thoroughfare of Ermou, Syntagma, and the Monastiraki metro. ⊠*Kapnikareas 7, Plaka, 10556* ☎*210/322–2706 or 210/322–2707* 🖷*210/322–2412* ⊕*www.plakahotel.gr* ⇨*67 rooms* ♿*In-room: refrigerator* ⊟*AE, DC, MC, V* ⦿*BP.*

$$ 🖭**Hermes Hotel.** Athens's small, modestly priced establishments have generally relied on little more than convenient central locations to draw visitors. Not so at the Hermes: sunny yellow guest rooms with wardrobes and tufted comforters feel warm and welcoming. Breakfast is served in the cheerful dining room, and you can enjoy a sunset cocktail

at the cozy roof-garden bar before setting off to sample the city's night-life. CHAT tours has an office in the lobby and can help you arrange day trips. Pros: Great staff, happy decor, central location. Con: Small rooms. ⊠*Apollonos 19, Plaka, 10557* ☎*210/323–5514* 🖷*210/323–2073* ⊕*www.hermeshotel.gr* 🗢*45 rooms* ⚴*In-room: no TV (some)* 🗏*AE, MC, V* †◎|*BP.*

$–$$ 🏨**Adrian.** This comfortable pension offers friendly service and an excellent location in the heart of Plaka. Incurable romantics should ask for one of just three rooms looking toward the Acropolis; if you like being in the thick of things, enjoy the Acropolis view from the shaded roof garden and ask instead for one of the rooms with the spacious balconies overlooking the café-lined square. Some room rates include breakfast. ⊠*Adrianou 74, Plaka, 10556* ☎*210/325–0454* 🖷*210/325–0461* ⊕*www.douros-hotels.com* 🗢*22 rooms* ⚴*In-room: refrigerator. In-hotel: bar, public Internet* 🗏*MC, V.*

¢–$ 🏨**Student and Travellers' Inn.** Not only is it cheap, this place is in the
★ pricey Plaka! Wood floors, regular spruce-ups, and large windows make this spotless hostel cheerful and homey. The renovated house on an attractive and bustling street in Plaka has private rooms and shared dorm bedrooms. You pay extra for a private bathroom, but all rooms have a sink and mirror. There are also public computers with Internet access, and a small garden café. One caveat: the owners forbid food, drinks, or visitors in the rooms. The inn does not accept credit cards for payment, but a credit card number is required to make a reservation. ⊠*Kidathineon 16, Plaka, 10658* ☎*210/324–4808* 🖷*210/321–0065* ⊕*www.studenttravellersinn.com* 🗢*35 rooms, 14 with bath* ⚴*In-room: no a/c, no phone, no TV. In-hotel: public Internet* 🗏*No credit cards.*

MONASTIRAKI, PSIRRI & THISSION
ΜΟΝΑΣΤΗΡΑΚΙ, ΨΥΡΡΗ & ΘΗΣΕΙΟ

Northwest of Plaka, Monastiraki and Thission conjure up the gritty charm of an Anatolian bazaar and yet attract the city cognoscenti to hardcore cafés and bars.

$$$–$$$$ 🏨**Ochre & Brown.** A beautiful boutique hotel with a soothing, sleek
Fodor'sChoice design and an outstanding restaurant-bar, Ochre & Brown opened its
★ doors in early 2006 and has quickly become one of the most talked-about new hotels in town. The guest rooms—from relaxing suites to a dazzling penthouse (with its own terrace)—are all little havens of urban cool; think flat-screen TVs, personal stereo/DVD systems, Pascal Morabito bath products, high-drama color schemes, black minimalistic headboards, and soft white Egyptian cotton sheets. The service is wonderful—you get champagne and fresh fruit when you arrive—and the staff keeps you up to date with all the latest happenings in the area, which are quite a few, since Psirri's legendary nightlife and flea market are right outside your door. ⊠*Leokoriou 7, Psirri, 10554* ☎*210/331–2950* 🖷*210/331–2942* ⊕*www.ochreandbrown.com* 🗢*9 rooms, 2 suites* ⚴*In-room: refrigerator. In-hotel: restaurant, bar* 🗏*AE, MC, V* †◎|*BP.*

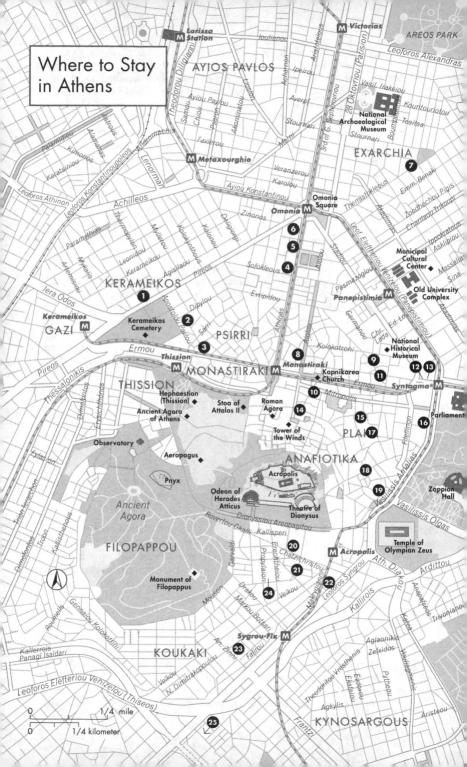

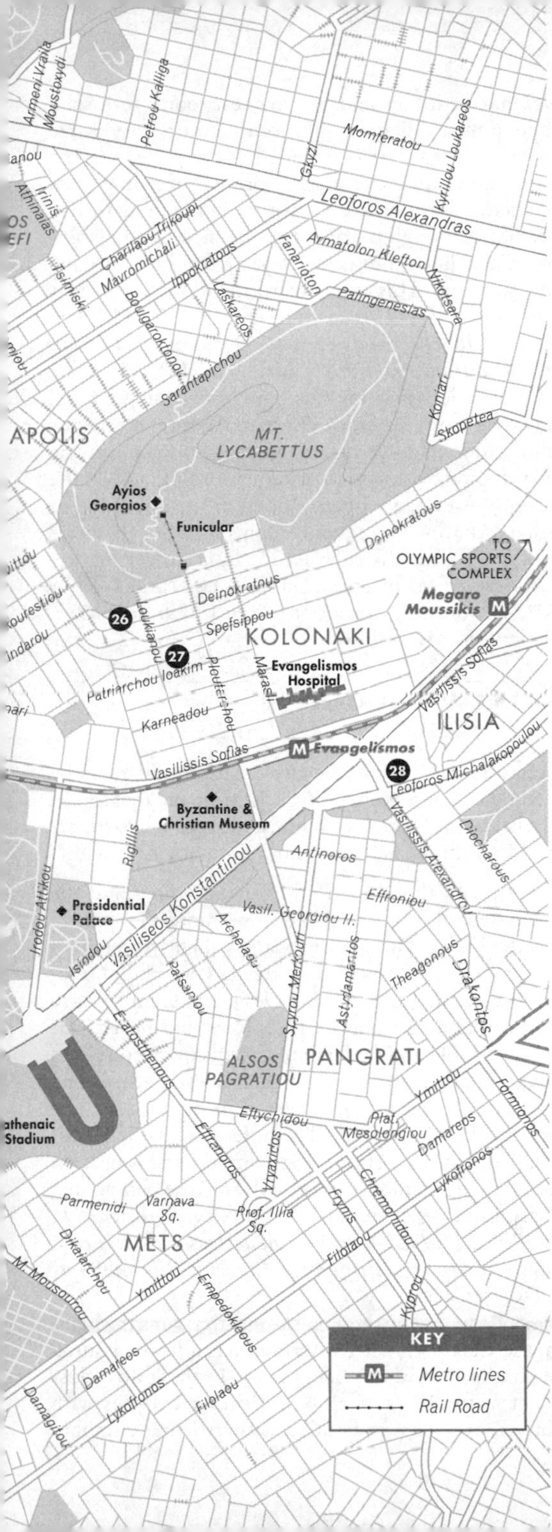

3

APOLIS

MT. LYCABETTUS

Ayios Georgios

Funicular

KOLONAKI

Megaro Moussikis Ⓜ

TO OLYMPIC SPORTS COMPLEX

Evangelismos Hospital

ILISIA

Ⓜ Evaagelismos

Byzantine & Christian Museum

Presidential Palace

PANGRATI

ALSOS PAGRATIOU

athenaic Stadium

METS

KEY

Ⓜ —— *Metro lines*

········ *Rail Road*

$–$$ ⚏**Jason Inn.** The cool marble lobby leads up to guest rooms furnished in warm peaches and pinks. All have mini-refrigerators, good-size closets, and safes. A buffet breakfast is included in the price, and the rooftop garden restaurant has an intriguing panorama spreading from the Acropolis to the ancient Kerameikos Cemetery to the modern-day warehouse district of Gazi. Though it's on a run-down, seemingly out-of-the-way little corner, the Jason Inn is steps away from the buzzing nightlife districts of Psirri and Thission, not to mention the ancient Agora. ✉*Ayion Assomaton 12, Thission, 10553* ☎*210/325–1106* ⊞*210/324–3132* ⊕*www.douros-hotels.com* ➾*57 rooms* ⚭*In-room: refrigerator. In-hotel: restaurant, bar* ⊟*AE, MC, V* ⍥*BP.*

⚏**Hotel Tempi.** It's all about location for this bare-bones budget hotel just a short, pleasant stroll from Plaka, the Roman Agora, and Psirri's nightlife. Guest room windows have double-glazing to keep out the noise—an especially welcome feature on weekday mornings, when the shops on pedestrians-only Aiolou are open. Rooms at the lower end of the rate scale have shared baths, and several rooms have lovely views to the church of Ayia Irini, which is surrounded by a flower market most mornings. ✉*Aiolou 29, Monastiraki, 10558* ☎*210/321–3175* ⊞*210/325–4179* ➾*24 rooms, 12 with bath* ⚭*In-room: no phone, kitchen. In-hotel: bar* ⊟*AE, MC, V.*

CENTRAL ATHENS, GAZI & OMONIA SQUARE
ΑΘΗΝΑ (ΚΕΝΤΡΟ) & ΠΛΑΤΕΙΑ ΟΜΟΝΟΙΑΣ

Located north of Monastiraki, Omonia, the city's main square roars by day and is seedy by night, but offers multi-culti excitement and that foodie fave, the Central Market. The former warehouse district of Psirri, set between Omonia and Monastiraki, is party central for many Athenians.

$$$–$$$$ ⚏**Baby Grand.** Fun yet posh, this dream pad for the young and the
Fodor'sChoice young-at-heart is a crazy/cool boutique hotel—just note the vintage
★ convertible parked in the lobby. Though its locale is slightly sketchy if you're not fond of inner-city grit, it is also strategic: City Hall, Omonia, and the Central Market are all close by. Designers seem to have gone a bit overboard with neon art and graffiti pieces, but never fear: guest rooms can be comfortable and understated, with curvaceous lines and art deco modeling. Another array of rooms, however, are among the most dazzling in Europe, with walls covered in psychedelic-like clouds in one or pop art olives in another. The hotel's fantastic restaurant, Meat Me, specializing in juicy steaks and hamburgers, is near an upmarket bar for the champagne and Moët crowd. For true pampering, head to the on-site Carita spa. ✉*Athinas 65 & Lykourgou, Kotzia Sq., 10551* ☎*210/325–0900* ⊞*210/325–0900* ⊕*www.classicalhotels.com* ➾*65 rooms, 11 suites* ⚭*In-room: refrigerator, Ethernet. In-hotel: restaurant, spa* ⊟*AE, DC, MC, V.*

$$$ ⚏**Classical Athens Acropol.** Owned by the same family that runs the high-class Grecotel chain, the Classical Athens Acropol has a fresh, assured aesthetic that's style-conscious without being fussy. In the lobby, clusters of cylindrical light fixtures cast a glow on leather couches with beaded fuchsia cushions, and glass pots filled with growing bamboo.

Spacious, quiet rooms are done in olive and cream, with pale patterned coffee tables, art deco–esque armchairs, and other retro details. ⊠*Pireos 1, Omonia Sq., 10552* ☎*210/528–2100* 🖷*210/523–1361* ⊕*www.grecotel.gr* ➾*164 rooms, 3 suites* ⌂*In-room: refrigerator, Ethernet. In-hotel: restaurant* ⊟*AE, DC, MC, V.*

$$$
Fodor's Choice
★

Eridanus. Dazzling modern art, a sparkling staircase, luscious beds, top-line bath products—this lovely hotel on the edge of the rising-star neighborhood of Gazi has it all. The building has a neoclassic vibe but the interiors are cool/hot 21st century, thanks to a dramatic, white minimalistic lobby, bedrooms that are designed for the *Wallpaper* crowd, and some high-style marble bathrooms. There are also some stunning antique touches, such as carved wood armoires and a bar lined with vintage Grecian rugs. You can see the Acropolis from seven of the rooms, especially from the gorgeous rooftop suite. The in-house restaurant, Parea, is a great place for meat-lovers (note: the city's best seafood is right next door at the Michelin-starred To Varoulko). Eridanus's staff is professional and well informed and can fill you in on all the hippest happenings in Gazi, a transitioning neighborhood that looks a bit pockmarked in places. ⊠*Pireos 78, Kerameikos, 10435* ☎*210/520–5360* 🖷*210/520–0550* ⊕*www.eridanus.gr* ➾*27 rooms, 3 suites* ⌂*In-room: refrigerator. In-hotel: restaurant* ⊟*AE, DC, MC, V.*

$–$$

Fresh Hotel. Reveling in minimalist glam, this attractive boutique hotel has relaxing and expertly decorated rooms, a plugged-in staff, and a fabulous in-house bar-bistro that features wonderful nouvelle (some might say experimental) Greek cuisine. The nabe is slightly dodgy at night and unattractive by day—the Athens Central Market and Omonia Square are nearby—but this Athenian madness is forgotten quickly as you soak in the hotel's ninth-floor swimming pool or the in-house sauna and steam rooms. ⊠*Sofokleous 26, near Kotzia Sq., 10552* ☎*210/524–8511* 🖷*210/524–8517* ⊕*www.freshhotel.gr* ➾*133 rooms* ⌂*In-room: refrigerator. In-hotel: restaurant, pool, gym, public Wi-Fi* ⊟*AE, DC, MC, V.*

SYNTAGMA SQUARE & KOLONAKI
ΠΛΑΤΕΙΑ ΣΥΝΤΑΓΜΑΤΟΣ & ΚΟΛΩΝΑΚΙ

Located east of Plaka, Kolonaki is a posherie favored by politicians, expats, and the ladies who lunch. Syntagma, on the other hand, is a pretty central square, near Parliament, that is a fave with tourists.

$$$$

Amalia Hotel. Depending on your needs, the Amalia's best and worst feature is its location: right on one of Athens's biggest, busiest streets, directly across from Parliament. The minute you step outside, you're swept up in the noise and chaos of central Athens—fortunately, double-glazed windows and a view to the pretty National Garden keep things peaceful inside. The newly remodeled rooms are fresh and inviting, and the hotel is close to transport: the airport shuttle is next door, the metro and tram just a few steps away. ⊠*Amalias 10, Syntagma Sq., 10557* ☎*210/323–7301* 🖷*210/607–2135* ⊕*www.amalia.gr* ➾*98 rooms, 1 suite* ⌂*In-room: refrigerator, Internet. In-hotel: restaurant, bar, public Wi-Fi* ⊟*AE, DC, MC, V.*

$$$$ ⊡**Grande Bretagne.** Rest on custom-made silk ottomans in the lobby;
Fodor'sChoice drink tea from gold-leafed porcelain in the atrium; call your personal
★ butler 24 hours a day from your room—the landmark Grande Bretagne,
built in 1842, remains the most exclusive hotel in Athens. The guest list
includes more than a century's worth of royals, rock stars, and heads
of state. An all-out-luxury renovation, completed in 2003, recaptured
the original grandeur, restoring 19th-century oil paintings, antiques,
and hand-carved details as they were a century earlier. There's also a
lovely spa where you can pamper yourself with indulgences such as
ouzo-oil massages. ⊠*Vasileos Georgiou A' 1, Syntagma Sq., 10564*
☎*210/333–0000, 210/331–5555 through 210/331–5559 reservations*
🖨*210/322–8034, 210/333–0910 reservations* ⊕*www.grandebretagne.
gr* ⤶*290 rooms, 37 suites* ₺*In-room: refrigerator, Ethernet. In-hotel:
3 restaurants, bars, pools, gym, spa* ⊟*AE, DC, MC, V.*

$$$$ ⊡**King George II Palace.** A spacious lobby done in marble, mahogany,
★ velvet, leather, and gold trim lures you into a world where antique
crystal lamps and frosted glass shower stalls with mother-of-pearl tiles
raise standards of luxury to dizzying heights. Each room is individually
furnished with one-of-a-kind handcrafted furniture, antique desks, and
raw silk upholstery. Heavy brocade curtains are no more than a decorative flourish: the rooms are soundproofed and their lighting calibrated
to the natural light. At the Tudor Hall restaurant, savor Mediterranean
delicacies and a view of the city skyline stretching from the Panathenaic
Stadium to the Parthenon. ⊠*Vasileos Georgiou A' 2, Syntagma Sq.,
10564* ☎*210/322–2210* 🖨*210/325–0564* ⊕*www.grecotel.gr* ⤶*77
rooms, 25 suites* ₺*In-room: refrigerator, Ethernet. In-hotel: restaurant, bars, spa* ⊟*AE, DC, MC, V.*

$$$–$$$$ ⊡**St. George Lycabettus.** This small, luxurious hotel on the wooded
Fodor'sChoice slopes of Mt. Lycabettus, in upscale Kolonaki, is steps from Athens's
★ museum row and designer shops. Meticulously decorated, most rooms
have splendid views (although some have blah ones). Each floor has its
own theme, and rooms are designed accordingly, with looks ranging
from jewel-tone art nouveau to sleek black-and-white minimalism to
soothing neutrals with bamboo. The rooftop pool bar and Le Grand
Balcon restaurant have an unbeatable panoramic view. Downstairs the
postmodern 1970s-style lounge, Frame, is one of the hottest night-
spots in town and also serves a decadent weekend brunch. ⊠*Kleom-
enous 2, Kolonaki, 10675* ☎*210/729–0711 through 210/729–0719*
🖨*210/729–0439 or 210/724–7610* ⊕*www.sglycabettus.gr* ⤶*162
rooms, 5 suites* ₺*In-room: dial-up. In-hotel: 2 restaurants, bar, pool,
gym, some pets allowed* ⊟*AE, DC, MC, V.*

$$$ ⊡**Athens Cypria Hotel.** This modest, friendly oasis in the city center is a
good bet for families. It has reasonable prices (considering the location
off Syntagma Square) and discounts for children up to 12 years old.
Cribs are provided free of charge. There are also several connecting
family rooms. Modern, clean, simple blue-and-white rooms overlook a
quiet street, but if you'd like a view ask for one of the three rooms looking toward the Acropolis. Breakfast is an American-style buffet (with
eggs, not just cold meats). Broadband is being added to some rooms
at press time. ⊠*Diomias 5, Syntagma Sq., 10563* ☎*210/323–8034*

🖨210/324–8792 ✒diomeia@hol.gr 🛏71 rooms ⚘In-room: refrigerator, dial-up (some). In-hotel: bar ▤AE, MC, V ⑩BP.

$$–$$$ ⊡**Periscope.** Like Ochre & Brown, this sleek concept hotel combines minimalist urban-chic design, amenity-filled rooms, and exceptional service for a truly relaxing experience. Business travelers and urbane globe-trotters love the efficient staff, spotless rooms, and the old-money neighborhood of Kolonaki. Guest rooms are a bit small with disappointing views but no one will complain about the flat-screen TVs. Many of the city's best restaurants and cafés are here, and it's only a short walk to the metro. ⊠*Haritos 22, Kolonaki, 10675* 🖨*210/729–7200* ⊕*www.periscope.gr* 🛏*17 rooms, 4 junior suites* ⚘*In-room: refrigerator. In-hotel: bar, public Internet* ▤*AE, DC, MC, V.*

$$ ⊡**Hotel Achilleas.** Like its sisters, the Hermes and Plaka hotels, the Achilleas combines interesting design with the friendly, personal service that comes from being family-run—and a price at the lower end of its category. Black and white diamond tiles alternate down the center of the long, sleek lobby lined by opposing black and white armchairs. The spicy mustard-color guest-room walls contrast nicely with dusky blue bedding and leopard-print curtains. The buffet breakfast is served in a stylish interior courtyard. ⊠*Lekka 21, Syntagma Sq., 10562* 🖨*210/322–5826* 🖨*210/322–2412* ⊕*www.achilleashotel.gr* 🛏*50 rooms* ⚘*In-room: refrigerator, dial-up* ▤*AE, DC, MC, V* ⑩BP.

¢–$ ⊡**Hotel Dioskouros.** The real draws of Dioskouros over similarly cheap, downtown spots are its amicable staff, central but quiet location at Plaka's edge, and its shaded garden, where you can relax with a beer at the end of the day. It's a students' and independent travelers' favorite. Many of the basic rooms have space for the two twin beds and not much more. ⊠*Pittakou 6, Syntagma Sq., 10558* 🖨*210/324–8165* 🖨*210/321–9991* ⊕*www.consolas.gr* 🛏*18 rooms without bath* ⚘*In-room: no TV, no room phones* ▤*AE, DC, MC, V* ⑩CP.

ATHENS NORTH & EAST ΑΘΗΝΑ, ΒΟΡΕΙΑ & ΑΝΑΤΟΛΙΚΗ

$$$$ ⊡**Athens Hilton.** The Hilton reflects the trend sweeping through most of Athens's high-end properties, whose recent revamps have left them with modern, clean-lined, and minimal design. The once-traditional lobby is now a vast expanse of white marble punctuated by sleek, mod benches. Guest rooms are fitted out in light wood, brushed metal, etched glass, and crisp white duvets. Facilities are business-oriented, with a stylish executive check-in lounge and huge conference rooms. Along with a spa, the hotel has the biggest hotel pool in Athens. It also boasts a branch of Estatorio Milos, Manhattan's luxe Greek restaurant. ⊠*Vasilissis Sofias 46, Ilisia, 11528* 🖨*210/728–1000, 210/728–1100 reservations* ⊕*www.athens.hilton.com* 🛏*498 rooms, 19 suites* ⚘*In-room: refrigerator, Ethernet. In-hotel: 4 restaurants, bars, pool, gym* ▤*AE, DC, MC, V.*

¢ ⊡**Exarcheion.** Smack in the center of a lively bohemian bar and café district, this hotel has been a fixture on the international backpacking circuit for years. Guest rooms are plain and slightly worn, but the fact that the National Archaeological Museum is just around the corner makes this a good value. ⊠*Themistokleous 55, Exarchia, 10683* ☎*210/380–256* 🖷*210/380–3296* 🕾*49 rooms* ♿*In-room: refrigerator* ▭*MC, V.*

NIGHTLIFE & THE ARTS

From ancient Greek tragedies in quarried amphitheaters to the chicest disco clubs, Athens rocks at night. Several of the former industrial districts are enjoying a renaissance, and large spaces have filled up with galleries, restaurants, and theaters—providing one-stop shopping for an evening's entertainment. The Greek weekly *Athinorama* covers current performances, gallery openings, and films, as do the English-language newspapers *Athens News*, published Friday, and *Kathimerini*, inserted in the *International Herald Tribune*, available Monday through Saturday. The monthly English-language magazine *Insider* has features and listings on entertainment in Athens, with a focus on the arts. *Odyssey*, a glossy bimonthly magazine, also publishes an annual summer guide in late June, sold at newsstands around Athens with the season's top performances and exhibitions.

NIGHTLIFE

Athens's heady nightlife starts late. Most bars and clubs don't get hopping until midnight and they stay open at the very least until 3 AM. Drinks are rather steep (about €6–€10), but generous. Often there is a cover charge on weekends at the most popular clubs, which also have bouncers. In summer many major downtown bars and clubs close their in-town location and move to the seaside. Ask your hotel for recommendations and summer closings. For a uniquely Greek evening, visit a club featuring rembetika music, a type of blues, or the popular *bouzoukia* (clubs with live bouzouki, a stringed instrument, music). Few clubs take credit cards for drinks.

BARS

★ **Balthazar.** Athenians of all ages come to escape the summer heat at this bar-restaurant in a neoclassic house with a lush garden courtyard and subdued music. ⊠*Tsoha 27, Ambelokipi* ☎*210/644–1215 or 210/645–2278.*

Baraonda. Beautiful people, breakneck music, and a VIP vibe have made this club a perennial favorite. The food here is also top-line and there's a beautiful garden when you need a breather. ⊠*Tsoha 43, Ambelokipi* ☎*210/644–4308.*

Mad. Dance in manic fun to '80s pop and all eras of rock at this fun and popular club in the hot Gazi district. ⊠*Persefonis 53, Gazi* ☎*210/346–2007.*

Memphis. Gregarious is the word for this Athens classic. The music is predominantly 1980s, with some Gothic theme nights and occasional live bands. ⊠*Ventiri 5, behind Hilton, Ilisia* ☎*210/722–4104.*

Fodor's Choice **Parko.** With low-key music and a romantic setting, Parko is a summer
★ favorite. ⊠*Eleftherias Park, Ilisia* ☎*210/722–3784.*

Sodade. This gay-friendly bar-club-lounge attracts a standing-room-only crowd every weekend. The draw is the great music, the joyous vibe, and the very fact that it's in Gazi, the hottest place in central Athens. ✉*Triptolemou 10, Gazi* ☎*210/346–8657.*

Soul Garden. Popular Soul Garden is unquestionably hip but also friendly. Relax with a cocktail and snacks in the plant-filled, lantern-lighted courtyard; after 1 AM the dance floor inside picks up pace. ✉*Evripidou 65, Psirri* ☎*210/331–0907.*

Stavlos. All ages feel comfortable at the bar in what used to be the Royal Stables. Sit in the courtyard or in the brick-wall restaurant for a snack like Cretan *kalitsounia* (similar to a calzone), or dance in the long bar. Stavlos often hosts art exhibits, film screenings, miniconcerts, and other happenings, as the Greeks call them, throughout the week. ✉*Iraklidon 10, Thission* ☎*210/345–2502 or 210/346–7206.*

BOUZOUKIA

Many tourists think Greek social life centers on large clubs where live bouzouki music plays while patrons smash up the plates. Plate-smashing is now prohibited, but plates of flowers are sold for scattering over the performer or your companions when they take to the dance floor. Upscale bouzouki clubs line the lower end of Syngrou and stretch out to the south coast, where top entertainers command top prices. Be aware that bouzouki food is overpriced and often second-rate. There is a per-person minimum (€30) or a prix-fixe menu; a bottle of whiskey costs around €200. For those who choose to stand at the bar, a drink runs about €15 to €20 at a good bouzouki place.

Fever. One of Athens's most popular bouzouki clubs showcases the most popular singers of the day, including the ageless Anna Vissi, Greece's own answer to Madonna. It's open Wednesday through Sunday. ✉*Syngrou 259, Neos Kosmos* ☎*210/942–7580 through 210/942–7583.*

Rex. Over-the-top is the way to describe a performance at Rex—it's a laser-light show, multi–costume-change extravaganza, with head-lining pop and bouzouki stars. ✉*Panepistimiou 48, Central Athens* ☎*210/381–4591.*

CLUBS

Nightclubs in Greece migrate with the seasons. From October through May, they're in vast, throbbing venues in central Athens and the northern suburbs; from June through September, many relocate to luxurious digs on the south coast. The same spaces are used from year to year, but owners and names tend to bounce around. Before heading out, check local listings or talk to your concierge. Most clubs charge a cover at the door and employ bouncers, aptly called "face-control" by Greeks because they tend to let only the "lookers" in. One way to avoid both of these, since partying doesn't get going until after 1 AM, is to make an earlier dinner reservation at one of the many clubs that have restaurants as well.

Akrotiri Lounge. Luxurious Akrotiri has as much of a reputation for chef Christophe Clessienne's excellent food—think foie-gras bonbons with sautéed pears and spices—as it does for its runway-beautiful clientele, sea views, and a poolside dance floor. ⊠ *Vasileos Georgiou 11, Agios Kosmas, Kalamaki* ☎ *210/985–9147* ⊕ *www.akrotirilounge.gr.*

Bios Basement. All the coolest artists, grunge-rockers, revolutionaries, and experimental philosophers hang out in the cavernous basement of this Bauhaus building in the Kerameikos neighborhood, part of

> **LEAVE THE DRIVING TO THEM**
>
> In summer, the best way to get to Athens's seaside nightclubs is by taxi—driving on the coastal road can be a nightmare. Just tell the taxi the name of the club; drivers quickly learn the location of the major spots once they open each year.

the greater Gazi district. Expect to hear the best electronica music in town. ⊠ *Piraios 84, Gazi.*

★ **Bo.** A seaside club that actually has a permanent address, Bo is in a huge old beachfront mansion. The beautiful tile floors haven't lost their luster after years of serving as a platform for gyrating club kids. The place is also open during the day for drinks and coffee, served on the terrace. ⊕ *8 km (5 mi) south of Athens,* ⊠ *Konstantinou Karamanli 14, Voula* ☎ *210/895–9645.*

Central-Island. From September to May, Athens's hippest people make an appearance at this designer-styled club to groove to ambient music, nibble on sushi, and languidly sip fancy cocktails. From May to September, Central is closed in town; it reopens on the coast as Island, in an atmospheric space in the sunny suburb of Varkiza. ⊠ *Kolonak Sq. 14, Kolonaki* ☎ *210/724–5938* ⊕ *www.island-central.gr Island* ⊠ *On Km 27 of Athens-Sounio Ave., Varkiza* ☎ *210/892–5000.*

Venti. This successful Psirri club is now open in summer, one of the few in the city center to do so. Its open-air style comes complete with a canopy of olive and palm trees while the crowd dances to a furious beat of Greek pop music. ⊠ *Lepeniotou 20, Psirri* ☎ *210/325–4504.*

JAZZ & BLUES CLUBS

The jazz scene has built up momentum, and there are several venues from which to choose. Tickets to shows can be purchased at the clubs or major record stores.

Half Note Jazz Club. The original and best venue in town is the place for serious jazz sophisticates. It's a good idea to reserve a table ahead of time, especially for one near the stage; latecomers can always stand at the bar in back. ⊠ *Trivonianou 17, Pangrati* ☎ *210/921–3310 or 210/923–2460.*

House of Art. This laid-back venue hosts small, mostly blues, groups. ⊠ *Santouri 4, at Sarri, Psirri* ☎ *210/321–7678.*

Parafono. Leave the big names at other clubs and tap into the homegrown jazz circuit here instead. ⊠ *Asklipiou 130A, Exarchia* ☎ *210/644–6512* ⊕ *www.parafono.gr.*

REMBETIKA

The Greek equivalent of the urban blues, rembetika is rooted in the traditions of Asia Minor and was brought to Greece by refugees from Smyrna in the 1920s. It filtered up from the lowest economic levels to become one of the most enduring genres of Greek popular music, still enthralling clubgoers today. At these thriving clubs, you can catch a glimpse of Greek social life and even join the dances (but remember, it's considered extremely rude to interrupt a solo dance). The two most common dances are the *zeimbekikos,* in which the man improvises in circular movements that become ever more complicated, and the belly-dance-like *tsifteteli.* Most of the clubs are closed in summer; call in advance. Drink prices range from €5 to €8, a bottle of whiskey from €50 to €70, but the food is often expensive and unexceptional; it's wisest to order a fruit platter or a bottle of wine.

Anifori. This friendly, popular club plays both rembetika and *dimotika* (Greek folk music). It's open Friday through Sunday nights. ✉ *Vasileos Georgiou A' 47, Pasalimani, Piraeus* ☎ *210/411–5819*

Boemissia. Usually crowded and pleasantly raucous, Boemissia attracts many young people, who quickly start gyrating in various forms of the tsifteteli. Doors are shut Monday. ✉ *Solomou 19, Exarchia* ☎ *210/384–3836 or 210/330–0865.*

Mnisikleous. The authentic music of gravel-voiced Bobbis Tsertos, a popular *rembetis* (rembetika singer), draws audience participation Thursday through Sunday. ✉ *Mnisikleous 22, at Lyceiou, Plaka* ☎ *210/322–5558 or 210/322–5337.*

★ **Stoa ton Athanaton.** "Arcade of the Immortals" has been around since 1930, housed in a converted warehouse in the meat-market area. Not much has changed since then. The music is enhanced by an infectious, devil-may-care mood and the enthusiastic participation of the audience, especially during the best-of-rembetika afternoons (3:30–7:30). The small dance floor is always jammed. Food here is delicious and reasonably priced, but liquor is expensive. Make reservations for evening performances, when the orchestra is led by old-time rembetis greats. The club is closed Sunday. ✉ *Sofokleous 19, Central Market* ☎ *210/321–4362 or 210/321–0342.*

Taximi. At one time or other, most of Greece's greatest rembetika musicians have played at this old-time bar; many of their black-and-white pictures are on the smoke-stained walls. ✉ *Isavron 29, at Harilaou Trikoupi, Exarchia* ☎ *210/363–9919.*

TAVERNAS WITH MUSIC

Klimataria. At this century-old taverna, a guitarist (as well as an accordion player in winter) plays sing-along favorites much appreciated by the largely Greek audience. The price of this slice of old-style Greek entertainment is surprisingly reasonable. ✉ *Klepsidras 5, Plaka* ☎ *210/324–1809 or 210/321–1215.*

Stamatopoulou Palia Plakiotiki Taverna. Enjoy good food and an acoustic band with three guitars and bouzouki playing old Athenian songs in an 1822 house. In summer the show moves to the garden. Greeks will often get up and dance, beckoning you to join them, so don't be shy. ⊠*Lysiou 26, Plaka* ☎*210/322–8722 or 210/321–8549.*

THE ARTS

Athens's energetic year-round performing arts scene kicks into a higher gear from June through September, when numerous stunning outdoor theaters host everything from classical Greek drama (in both Greek and English), opera, symphony, and ballet, to rock, pop, and hip-hop concerts. In general, dress for summer performances is fairly casual, though the city's glitterati get decked out for events such as a world premiere opera at the Odeon of Herodes Atticus. From October through May, when the arts move indoors, the Megaron Mousikis/Athens Concert Hall is the biggest venue. Athenians consider the Megaron a place to see and be seen, and dress up accordingly. Performances at outdoor summer venues, stadiums, and the Megaron tend to be priced between €20 to €120 for tickets, depending on the location of seats and popularity of performers.

CONCERTS, DANCE & OPERA

Dora Stratou Troupe. The country's leading folk dance company performs Greek folk dances from all regions, as well as from Cyprus, in eye-catching authentic costumes. The programs change every two weeks. Performances are held Tuesday through Sunday from the end of May through September at 9:30 PM and Sunday at 8:15 PM at the Dora Stratou Theater. Tickets cost €13 and can be purchased at the box office before the show. ⊠*Arakinthou and Voutie, Filopappou* ☎*210/921–4650 theater, 210/324–4395 troupe's office* 🖨*210/324–6921* ⊕*www.grdance.org.*

Megaron Mousikis/Athens Concert Hall. World-class Greek and international artists take the stage at the Megaron Mousikis to perform in concerts and opera from September through June. Information and tickets are available weekdays 10–6 and Saturday 10–4. Prices range from €18 to €90; there's a substantial discount for students and those 8 to 18 years old. Tickets go on sale a few weeks in advance, and many events sell out within hours. On the first day of sales, tickets can be purchased by cash or credit card only in person at the Athens Concert Hall. From the second day on, remaining tickets may be purchased by phone, in person from the downtown box office (weekdays 10–4), and online. ⊠*Vasilissis Sofias and Kokkali, Ilisia* ☎*210/728–2333* 🖨*210/728–2300* ⊕*www.megaron.gr Downtown box office* ⊠*Omirou 8, Central Athens* ☎*No phone.*

Philippos Nakas Conservatory. Inexpensive classical music concerts are held November through May at the conservatory. Tickets cost about €11. ⊠*Ippokratous 41, Central Athens* ☎*210/363–4000* 🖨*210/360–2827.*

FESTIVALS

★ **Hellenic Festival.** The city's primary artistic event, the Hellenic Festival (formerly known as the Athens Festival), runs from June through September at the Odeon of Herodes Atticus. The festival has showcased performers such as Norah Jones, Dame Kiri Te Kanawa, Luciano Pavarotti, and Diana Ross; such dance troupes as the Royal London Ballet, the Joaquin Cortes Ballet, and Maurice Béjart; symphony orchestras; and local groups performing ancient Greek drama. Usually a major world premiere is staged during the festival. The Odeon theater makes a delightful backdrop, with the floodlighted Acropolis looming behind the audience and the Roman arches behind the performers. The upper-level seats have no cushions, so bring something to sit on, and wear low shoes, since the marble steps are steep. For viewing most performances the Gamma zone is the best seat choice. Tickets go on sale two weeks before performances but sell out quickly for popular shows; they are available from the festival box office. Prices range from €16 to as high as €120 for the big names; student and youth discounts are available. *Odeon of Herodes Atticus* ⊠*Dionyssiou Areopagitou, Acropolis* ☏*210/323–2771, 210/323–5582 box office* ⊕*www.greekfestival.gr Festival box office* ⊠*Panepistimiou 39, Syntagma Sq.* ☏*210/322–1459.*

> ## MOONLIGHT SERENADES
>
> Every year, on the night of the full moon in August (believed to be the brightest and most beautiful moon of the year), Athens holds an August Moon Festival. The Acropolis, Roman Agora, Odeon of Herodes Atticus, and sometimes other sites are open to the public for free, and performances of opera, Greek dance, and classical music take place amid the ancient columns by moonlight. If you're in Athens in August, this is a must-do. The main venue is the Odeon of Herodes Atticus, at Dionyssiou Areopagitou, phone: 210/323–2771, 210/323–5582 box office.

Lycabettus Theater. A few Elliniko Festival events are held at the Lycabettus Theater, set on a pinnacle of Mt. Lycabettus. The specialty here is popular concerts; past performers have included B. B. King, Bob Dylan, Massive Attack, and Paco de Lucia. Since buses travel only as far as the bottom of the hill, and taxi drivers often won't drive to the top, buy a one-way ticket on the funicular and walk about 10 minutes to the theater. ⊠*At top of Mt. Lycabettus, Kolonaki* ☏*210/322–1459, 210/727–2233, 210/722–7209 theater box office.*

Vyronas Festival. Performances by well-known Greek musician Dimitris Mitropanos, international acts such as the Beijing Opera, and ancient Greek theater classics are staged in an old quarry, now the Theatro Vrahon. Shows begin around 9:30 PM. Buy tickets (€10–€15) at the theater before the show, or at any of the chain of Metropolis music stores. ⊠*Tatoulon, where Trolley 11 ends, Vyrona* ☏*210/765–5748 or 210/765–3775.*

FILM

Films are shown in original-language versions with Greek subtitles (except for major animated films), a definite boon for foreigners. Downtown theaters have the most advanced technology and most comfortable seats. Tickets run about €7. Check the *Athens News* or *Kathimerini* in the *International Herald Tribune* for programs, schedules, and addresses and phone numbers of theaters, including outdoor theaters. The Hellenic-American Union (www.hau.gr) and the British Council (www.britishcouncil.gr) screen films for free (screenings are usually published in local English-language media).

Unless theaters have air-conditioning, they close from June through September, making way for *therina* (open-air theaters), an enchanting, uniquely Greek entertainment that offers instant escapism under a starry sky. A feature of postwar Mediterranean countries that has survived only in Greece, open-air cinemas saw their popularity decline after the arrival of television. There's been a resurgence in their appeal, and about 75 now operate in the greater Athens area.

Attikon Cinemax Class. With its old-fashioned red-velvet and gold-trim embellishments, huge crystal chandelier, wide screen, enormous seats, and central location, this is the best theater in all of Athens. It screens world premieres and classic rereleases. ⊠*Stadiou 19, Syntagma Sq.* ☎*210/322–8821.*

Cine Paris. Kitschy posters of old Greek movies are for sale in the lobby of this rooftop garden theater. It's close to many hotels, on Plaka's main walkway, but the place uses regular stereo instead of Dolby Digital sound. ⊠*Kidathineon 22, Plaka* ☎*210/322–2071 or 210/324–8057.*

Elly. Frequent Elly for independent and art films that don't make it to Greece's more-mainstream cinemas. ⊠*Akadimias 64, Syntagma Sq.* ☎*210/363–2789.*

Thission. Films at this open-air theater compete with a view of the Acropolis. It's on the Unification of Archaeological Sites walkway. ⊠*Apostolou Pavlou 7, Thission* ☎*210/342–0864 or 210/347–0980.*

SHOPPING

For serious retail therapy, most natives head to the shopping streets that branch off central Syntagma and Kolonaki squares. Syntagma is the starting point for popular Ermou, a pedestrian zone where large, international brands like Esprit and Marks & Spencer's have edged out small, independent retailers. You'll find local shops on streets parallel and perpendicular to Ermou: Mitropoleos, Voulis, Nikis, Perikleous, and Praxitelous among them. Poke around here for real bargains, like strings of freshwater pearls, loose semiprecious stones, or made-to-fit hats. Much ritzier is the Kolonaki quarter, with boutiques and designer shops on fashionable streets like Anagnostopoulou, Tsakalof, Skoufa, Solonos, and Kanari. Voukourestiou, the link between Kolonaki and Syntagma, is where you'll find Louis Vuitton, Ralph Lauren, and similar brands. In Monastiraki, coppersmiths have their shops on Ifestou. You can pick up copper wine jugs, candlesticks, cookware, and more for next to nothing. The flea market centered on Pandrossou and Ifestou operates on Sunday mornings and has practically everything, from secondhand guitars to Russian vodka. No matter how low the price, always bargain.

ANTIQUES & ICONS

Antiques are in vogue now, so the prices of these items have soared. Shops on Pandrossou sell small antiques and icons, but keep in mind that many of these are fakes. You must have government permission to export genuine objects from the ancient Greek, Roman, or Byzantine periods.

Alekos Kostas. This *palaiopolio* (junk dealer) is especially popular among collectors of old radio sets and vintage toys, and carries wonderfully quirky items such as mechanized piggy banks. ⊠*Abyssinia Sq. 3, Monastiraki* ☎*210/321–1580.*

Kiritisis. Old coins, from Greece and around the world, are for sale at Kiritisis, along with stamps and medals. ⊠*Areos 1, at Pandrossou, Monastiraki* ☎*210/324–0544.*

Martinos. Serious antiques collectors should head here to look for items such as exquisite dowry chests, old swords, and Venetian glass. ⊠*Pandrossou 5, Monastiraki* ☎*210/321–3110* ⊠*Pindarou 24, Kolonaki* ☎*210/360–9449.*

Nasiotis. With a little perseverance, you can make some interesting finds in this huge basement stacked with books, engravings, old magazines, and first editions. ⊠*Ifestou 24, Monastiraki* ☎*210/321–2369.*

Pylarinos. Stamp and coin collectors love this packed shop, which also has a good selection of 19th-century engravings. ⊠*Panepistimiou 18, Syntagma Sq.* ☎*210/363–0688.*

CLOTHING

Greece is known for its well-made shoes (most shops are clustered around the Ermou pedestrian zone and in Kolonaki), its furs (Mitropoleos near Syntagma), and its durable leather items (Pandrossou in Monastiraki). In Plaka shops you can find fishermen's caps—always a good present—and the natural wool undershirts and hand-knit sweaters worn by fishermen; across the United States these have surfaced at triple the Athens price.

★ **Afternoon.** Prices are lower than what you'll find abroad at this shop with an excellent collection of fashions by Greece's best new designers, including Sophia Kokosalaki, whose work has often graced the pages of *Vogue*. Look for labels from up-and-comers like Deux Hommes, Vasso Consola, and Pavlos Kyriakides. ⊠*Deinokratous 1, Kolonaki* ☎*210/722–5380.*

Kaplan Furs. Despite animal rights campaigns, Mitropoleos is lined with fur shops. Kaplan has everything from pieced-together stoles to full-length minks, often from the northern city of Kastoria. ⊠*Mitropoleos 22–24, Syntagma Sq.* ☎*210/322–2226.*

Me Me Me. Whether you're shopping around for a new cocktail dress or for funky accessories, this is the place to head for trendsetting creations by emerging Greek designers. ⊠*Haritos 19, Kolonaki* ☎*210/722–4890.*

Occhi. Art and the latest clothes and accessories by young Greek designers are displayed side-by-side in this gallery-style shop. ⊠*Sarri 35, Psirri* ☎*210/321–3298.*

Stavros Melissinos. A legendary poet and gentle soul, as well as shoe-maker, Stavros outfits many tourists with his handmade sandals. The Beatles once visited his shop. ⊠*Ayias Theklas 2, Monastiraki* ☎*210/321–9247.*

GIFTS

Athens has great gifts, particularly handmade crafts. Better tourist shops sell copies of traditional Greek jewelry, silver filigree, Skyrian pottery, onyx ashtrays and dishes, woven bags, attractive rugs (including *flokati*, or shaggy goat-wool rugs), and little blue-and-white pendants designed as amulets to ward off the *mati* (evil eye).

Baba. Greeks can spend hours heatedly playing *tavli* (backgammon). To take home a game set of your own, look closely for this hole-in-the-wall, no-name shop, which sells boards and pieces in all sizes and designs. ⊠*Ifestou 30, Monastiraki* ☎*210/321–9994.*

Bead Shop. From pinhead-size "evil eyes" to 2-inch-diameter wood beads, you'll find a dizzying selection of beads to string your own *komboloi* (worry beads) or bracelet. ⊠*Pal. Venizelou 6, Mitropolis* ☎*210/322–1004.*

Fodor'sChoice **Benaki Museum Gift Shop.** The museum shop has excellent copies of
★ Greek icons, jewelry, and folk art—at fair prices. ⊠*Koumbari 1, at Vasilissis Sofias, Kolonaki* ☎*210/362–7367.*

Diplous Pelekys. Wool totes, pillow covers with hand-embroidered folk motifs, and, of course, pins featuring the Cretan double-headed ax (*diplous pelekys*) make excellent, and affordable, gifts. ⊠*Voulis 7 and Kolokotroni 3, Syntagma Sq.* ☎*210/322–3783.*

Fresh Line. Among the solid shampoo cakes, body oils, and face packs are a tremendous number of Greek-made soaps that are sliced from big blocks or wheels as though they were cheese; you pay by weight. The strawberries-and-cream soap, Rea, contains real berries; the Orpheus and Eurydice soap for sensitive skin is made with vanilla, milk, and rice, just like Greek *rizogalo* (rice pudding). ⊠*Skoufa 10, Kolonaki* ☎*210/364–4015.*

Goutis. One of the more-interesting stores on Pandrossou, Goutis has an eclectic jumble of jewelry, costumes, embroidery, and old, handcrafted silver objects. ⊠*Dimokritou 40, Kolonaki* ☎*210/361–3557.*

Ilias Kokkonis. This century-old store stocks any flag you've always wanted, large or small, from most any country. ⊠*Stoa Arsakeiou 8, enter from Panepistimiou or Stadiou, Omonia Sq.* ☎*210/322–1189 or 210/322–6355.*

Korres. Natural beauty products blended in traditional recipes using Greek herbs and flowers have graced the bathroom shelves of celebrities like Nicole Kidman. In Athens they are available at most pharmacies for regular-folk prices. For the largest selection of basil-lemon shower gel, coriander body lotion, olive-stone face scrub, and wild-rose eye cream, go to the original Korres pharmacy behind the Panathenaic Stadium. ⊠*Eratosthenous and Ivikou, Pangrati* ☎*210/722–2744.*

Mastiha Shop. Medical research lauding the healing properties of gum mastic, a resin from trees only found in an area of Chios, has spawned a range of products, from chewing gum and cookies to cosmetics.

✉ *Panepistimiou 6, Syntagma Sq.*
☎ *210/363–2750.*

Riza. You can pick up wonderful lace, often handmade, in romantic designs at Riza. The shop also carries fabric at fair prices, and decorative items such as handblown glass bowls and brass candlesticks. ✉ *Voukourestiou 35, at Skoufa, Kolonaki* ☎ *210/361–1157.*

The Shop. A plain or brightly colored olive-oil pourer, traditional *kafeneion* (coffeehouse) trays, and *fanaria* (birdcagelike contraptions in which to store fresh food) are just some of the items available here that embody Greek village life. Some of the aluminum pieces are handmade. ✉ *Lysikratous 3, Plaka* ☎ *210/323–0350.*

Tanagrea. Hand-painted ceramic pomegranates, a symbol of fertility and good fortune, are one of the most popular items in one of the city's oldest gift shops. ✉ *Voulis 26 and Mitropoleos 15, Syntagma Sq.* ☎ *210/322–3366.*

Thiamis. Iconographer Aristides Makos creates beautiful hand-painted, gold-leaf icons on wood and stone. He also paints patron saints to order. ✉ *Apollonos 12, Plaka* ☎ *210/331–0337.*

HANDICRAFTS

Amorgos. Wood furniture, hand-carved and hand-painted by the shop's owners, has motifs from regional Greek designs. Needlework, hanging ceiling lamps, shadow puppets, and other decorative accessories are also for sale. ✉ *Kodrou 3, Plaka* ☎ *210/324–3836.*

★ **Center of Hellenic Tradition.** The Center is an outlet for quality handicrafts—ceramics, weavings, sheep bells, and old paintings. Take a break from shopping in the center's Oraia Ellada café, in clear view of the Parthenon. ✉ *Mitropoleos 59 and Pandrossou 36, Monastiraki* ☎ *210/321–3023, 210/321–3842 café.*

Lykeio Ellinidon. Resident weavers seated at two looms copy folk motifs from the costumes in the upstairs museum run by the Greek Women's Lyceum. This cozy shop stocks a range of handicrafts, starting at €5, and you can even custom-order a woven tapestry or bedcover. ✉ *Dimokritou 7a, basement, Kolonaki* ☎ *210/361–1607.*

Oikotechnia. Craftspeople throughout Greece provide folk crafts for sale here by the National Welfare Organization: stunning handwoven carpets, flat-weave kilims, and tapestries from original designs. Hand-embroidered tablecloths and wall decorations make handsome presents; flokati rugs are also for sale. ✉ *Filellinon 14, Syntagma Sq.* ☎ *210/325–0240.*

ARE YOU GIFTED?

An inexpensive but unusual gift is a string of *komboloi* (worry beads) in plastic, wood, or stone. You can pick them up very cheaply in Monastiraki or look in antiques shops for more expensive versions, with amber, silver, or black onyx beads. Reasonably priced natural sponges from Kalymnos also make good presents. Look for those that are unbleached, since the lighter ones tend to fall apart quickly. They're usually sold in front of the National Bank on Syntagma and in Plaka souvenir shops. The price is set by the government, so don't bother to bargain.

JEWELRY

Prices are much lower for gold and silver in Greece than in many Western countries, and the jewelry is of high quality. Many shops in Plaka carry original pieces available at a good price if you bargain hard enough (a prerequisite). For those with more-expensive tastes, the Voukourestiou pedestrian mall off Syntagma Square has a number of the city's leading jewelry shops.

Byzantino. Great values in gold, including certified copies of ancient Greek pieces and many original works designed in the on-site workshop, can be purchased here. ⊠*Adrianou 120, Plaka* ☎*210/324–6605.*

Elena Votsi. Elena Votsi designed jewelry for Gucci before opening her own boutique, where she sells exquisite creations in coral, amethyst, aquamarine, and turquoise. ⊠*Xanthou 7, Kolonaki* ☎*210/360–0936.*

Fanourakis. Original gold masterpieces can be had at these shops, where Athenian artists use gold almost like a fabric—creasing, scoring, and fluting it. ⊠*Patriarchou Ioakeim 23, Kolonaki* ☎*210/721–1762* ⊠*Evangelistrias 2, Mitropolis* ☎*210/324–6642* ⊠*Panagitsas 6, Kifissia* ☎*210/623–2334.*

Goulandris Cycladic Museum. Exceptional modern versions of ancient jewelry designs are available here. ⊠*Neofitou Douka 4, Kolonaki* ☎*210/724–9706.*

Lalaounis. A world-famous Greek jeweler experiments with his designs, taking ideas from nature, biology, and ancient Greek pieces—the last are sometimes so close to the original that they're mistaken for museum artifacts. ⊠*Panepistimiou 6, Syntagma Sq.* ☎*210/361–1371* ⊠*Athens Tower, Sinopis 2, Ambelokipi* ☎*210/770–0000.*

Pentheroudakis. Browse among the classic designs; there are even less-expensive trinkets, like silver worry beads that can be personalized with cubed letters in Greek or Latin and with the stone of your choice. ⊠*Voukourestiou 19, Kolonaki* ☎*210/361–3187.*

★ **Sagianos.** For five generations, the Sagianos family's creations have adorned the fingers, necks, and ears of well-to-do Athenian matrons. The tradition continues, but with more-modern, one-of-a-kind pieces inspired by ordinary objects like bar codes and buttons. ⊠*Makriyianni 3, Makriyianni* ☎*210/362–5822.*

Xanthopoulos. Shop for traditional gold, silver, and jewels at this store. ⊠*Voukourestiou 4, Kolonaki* ☎*210/322–6856.*

Zolotas. This jeweler, Lalaounis's main competitor, is noted for its superb museum copies. ⊠*Pandrossou 8, Plaka* ☎*210/323–2413* ⊠*Stadiou 9, Syntagma Sq.* ☎*210/322–1212.*

MUSIC

Metropolis. Take your pick of a huge selection of all-Greek music, from rembetika to the latest Greek club hits, all by Greek artists. ⊠*Panepistimiou 54, Omonia Sq.* ☎*210/380–8549.*

ATHENS ESSENTIALS

TRANSPORTATION

Many major sights, as well as hotels, cafés, and restaurants, are within a fairly small central area of Athens. It's easy to walk everywhere, though sidewalks are sometimes obstructed by parked cars. Most far-flung sights, such as beaches, are reachable by metro, bus, and tram. Check the Organization for Urban Public Transportation (OASA) Web site (⇨ *By Bus & Tram Within Athens*) for English-language information on how to use public transport to get to sights around the city. OASA also answers questions about routes (usually only in Greek). The office, open weekdays 7:30–3, distributes maps of bus routes with street names in Greek; these are also distributed at the white ticket kiosks at many bus terminals.

The price of public transportation has risen steeply, but it is still less than that in other western European capitals. Riding during rush hours is definitely not recommended. Upon boarding, validate your ticket in the orange canceling machines at the front and back of buses and trolleys and in metro stations. Keep your tickets until you reach your destination, as inspectors occasionally pop up to check that they have been canceled and validated. They are strict about fining offenders, including tourists. You can buy a day pass covering the metro, buses, trolleys, and trams for €3, a weekly pass for €10, or, at the beginning of each month, a monthly pass for €38.

BY AIR

The opening of Athens's sleek Eleftherios Venizelos International Airport has made air travel around the country much more pleasant and efficient. Greece is so small that few in-country flights take more than an hour or cost more than €200 round-trip. Aegean Airlines and Olympic Airways have regular flights between Athens, Thessaloniki, and most major cities and islands in Greece. *For further information, see Air Travel in the Essentials chapter.*

AIRPORTS & *For information about Eleftherios Venizelos International Airport near*
TRANSFERS *Athens, see Airports in the Essentials chapter.* The best way to get to the airport from downtown Athens is by metro or light-rail. Single tickets cost €6 and include transfers (within 90 minutes of the ticket's initial validation; don't forget to validate the ticket again) to bus, trolley, or tram. Combined tickets for two (€10) and three (€15) passengers are also available; if you're making a stopover in Athens, opt for a round-trip ticket (€10), valid for trips to and from the airport made during a single 48-hour period.

In Athens three reliable express buses connect the airport with the metro (Ethniki Amyna station), Syntagma Square, and Piraeus. These buses are air-conditioned and have space for luggage. Express buses leave the arrivals level of the airport every 10 minutes and operate 24 hours a day. Bus E95 will take you to Syntagma Square (Amalias avenue); E94 goes to the bus terminus at the Ethniki Amyna metro stop (Line 3), which will get you into Syntagma within 10 minutes. Bus E96 takes the Vari–Koropi road inland and links with the coastal road, passing through Voula, Glyfada, and Alimo; it then goes on to Piraeus (opposite Karaiskaki Square).

The Attiki Odos and the expansion of the city's network of bus lanes has made travel times more predictable, and on a good day the E94 can get you to Ethniki Amyna in 40 minutes. Tickets to and from the airport cost €2.90 and are valid on all forms of transportation in Athens for 24 hours from the time of validation. Purchase tickets from the airport terminal, kiosks, metro stations, or even on the express buses. The Greek National Tourism Organization (GNTO, or EOT in Greece) dispenses schedules. You can also obtain brochures at the airport with bus schedules and routes.

Taxis *(⇨ Taxis)* are readily available at the arrivals level of the Athens airport; it costs an average of €22 to get into downtown Athens (including tolls). Limousine Service and Royal Prestige Limousine Service provide service to and from Athens; an evening surcharge of up to 50% often applies, and you should call in advance. Prices start at €80 for one-way transfer from the airport to a central hotel.

Limousines **Limousine Service** (☎ *210/970–6416* ⊕ *www.limousine-service.gr*). **Royal Prestige Limousine Service** (☎ *210/988–3221* ☷☷ *210/983–0378*).

BY BOAT & FERRY

Boat travel in Greece is common and relatively inexpensive. Every weekend thousands of Athenians set off on one- and two-hour trips to islands like Aegina, Hydra, and Andros, while in summer ferries are weighed down with merrymakers on their way to Mykonos, Rhodes, and Santorini. Cruise ships, ferries, and hydrofoils from the Aegean and most other Greek islands dock and depart every day from Athens's main port, Piraeus, 10 km (6 mi) southwest of Athens. Ships for the Ionian islands sail from ports nearer to them, such as Patras and Igoumenitsa. Connections from Piraeus to the main island groups are good, connections from main islands to smaller ones within a group less so, and services between islands of different groups or areas—such as Rhodes and Crete—are less frequent.

Travel agents *(⇨ Travel Agents)* and ship offices in Athens and Piraeus have details. Boat schedules are published in *Kathimerini,* inserted in the *International Herald Tribune;* EOT *(⇨ Visitor Information)* distributes boat schedules updated every Wednesday. You can also call a daily Greek recording (listed below) for ferry departure times. Timetables change according to seasonal demand, and boats may be delayed by weather conditions, so your plans should be flexible. Buy your tickets two or three days in advance, especially if you are traveling in summer or taking a car. Reserve your return journey or continuation soon after you arrive. *For further information, see Boat & Ferry Travel in the Essentials chapter.*

To get to and from Piraeus harbor, you can take the green line metro (Line 1) from central Athens directly to the station at the main port.

The trip takes 25–30 minutes. A taxi takes longer because of traffic and costs around €12–€15.

Athens's other main port is Rafina, which serves some of the closer Cyclades and Evia. KTEL buses run every 30 minutes between the port and the Mavromateon terminal in central Athens, from about 5:30 AM until 9:30 PM, and cost €2 *(⇨ By Bus & Tram Within Athens)*. At Rafina, the buses leave from an area slightly uphill from the port. The trip takes about one hour.

Contacts Ferry departures (☎ *1440*). **Piraeus** (✉ *Port Authority, Akti Miaouli, Piraeus* ☎ *210/451–1311 through 210/451–1317*). **Rafina** (☎ *22940/22300*).

BY BUS TO & FROM ATHENS

Travel around Greece by bus is inexpensive, usually comfortable, and relatively fast. The journey from Athens to Thessaloniki takes roughly the same time as the regular train, though the InterCity Express train covers the distance 1¼ hours faster. To reach the Peloponnese, buses are speedier than trains. Information and timetables are available at tourist information offices. Make reservations at least one day before your planned trip, earlier for holiday weekends.

Terminal A is the arrival and departure point for bus lines that serve parts of northern Greece, including Thessaloniki, and the Peloponnese destinations of Epidauros, Mycenae, Nafplion, Olympia, and Corinth. Each destination has its own phone number; EOT offices distribute a list. Terminal B serves Evia, most of Thrace, and central Greece, including Delphi. EOT provides a phone list *(⇨ Visitor Information)*. Tickets for these buses are sold only at this terminal, so you should call to book seats well in advance in high season or holidays.

To get to the city center from Terminal A, take Bus 051 to Omonia Square; from Terminal B, take Bus 024 downtown. To get to the stations, catch Bus 051 at Zinonos and Menandrou off Omonia Square (for Terminal A) and Bus 024 on Amalias in front of the National Garden (for Terminal B). International buses drop their passengers off on the street, usually in the Omonia or Syntagma Square areas or at Stathmos Peloponnisou (train station).

Information Terminal A (✉ *Kifissou 100* ☎ *210/512–4910 or 210/512–4911*). **Terminal B** (✉ *Liossion 260* ☎ *210/831–7096 for Delphi, 210/831–7173 for Livadia [Ossios Loukas via Distomo], 210/831–1431 for Trikala [Meteora]*).

BY BUS & TRAM WITHIN ATHENS

See the Athens Planner at front of this chapter.

BY CAR

Greece's main highways to the north and the south link up in Athens; both are called Ethnikis Odos (National Road). Take the Attiki Odos, a beltway around Athens that also accesses Eleftherios Venizelos International Airport, to speed your travel time entering and exiting the city.

At the city limits, signs in English clearly mark the way to both Syntagma Square and Omonia Square in the city center. Leaving Athens, routes to the highways and Attiki Odos are well marked; signs usually name Lamia for points north, and Corinth or Patras for points southwest. From Athens to Thessaloniki, the distance is 515 km (319 mi); to Kalamata, 257 km (159 mi); to Corinth, 84 km (52 mi); to Lamia, 214 km (133 mi); to Patras, 218 km (135 mi); to Igoumenitsa, 472 km (293 mi).

CAR RENTAL   If you are coming to Athens from abroad, especially the United States or Canada, and are planning to rent a car from a major international chain, it's almost always cheaper to book from your home country. Agencies are grouped around Syngrou and Syntagma Square in central Athens, and at the arrivals area of the airport. *For further information, see Car Rental in the Essentials chapter.*

DRIVING IN   Driving in Athens is not recommended unless you have nerves of steel;
ATHENS   it can be unpleasant and even unsafe. It's fairly easy to get around the city with a combination of public transportation and taxis; save car rentals for excursions out of town. Red traffic lights are frequently ignored, and motorists often pass other vehicles while driving on hills and while rounding corners. Driving is on the right, and although the vehicle on the right has the right-of-way, don't expect this or any other driving rule to be obeyed. The speed limit is 50 kph (31 mph) in town. Traffic tends toward gridlock or heart-stopping speeding; parking in most parts of the city could qualify as an Olympic sport. Seat belts are compulsory, as are helmets for motorcyclists, though many natives ignore the laws. In downtown Athens do not drive in the bus lanes marked by a yellow divider; if caught, you may be fined.

Downtown parking spaces are hard to find, and the few downtown garages—including ones in vacant lots—are both expensive and perpetually full. You're better off leaving your car in the hotel garage and walking or taking a cab. Gas pumps and service stations are everywhere, and lead-free gas is widely available. Be aware that all-night stations are few and far between.

EMERGENCIES   *For information about the Automobile Touring Club of Greece (ELPA), see Car Travel in the Essentials chapter.*

BY METRO
See the Athens Planner at the front of this chapter.

BY TAXI
Most drivers in Athens speak basic English. Although you can find an empty taxi on the street, it's often faster to call out your destination to one carrying passengers; if the taxi is going in that direction, the driver will pick you up. Likewise, don't be alarmed if your driver picks up other passengers (although he should ask your permission first, and he will never pick up another fare if you are a woman traveling alone at night). Each passenger pays full fare for the distance he or she has traveled.

Taxi rates are still affordable compared to fares in other European capitals. Most taxi drivers are honest and hardworking, but a few con artists infiltrate the ranks at the airports and near popular restaurants and clubs frequented by foreigners. Get an idea from your hotel how much the fare should be, and if there's trouble, ask to go to a police station (most disagreements don't ever get this far, however). Make sure the driver turns on the meter and that the rate listed in the lower corner is 1, the normal rate before midnight; after midnight, the rate listed is 2.

Taxi drivers know the major central hotels, but if your hotel is less well known, show the driver the address written in Greek and make note of the phone number and, if possible, a nearby landmark. If all else fails, the driver can call the hotel from his mobile phone or a kiosk. Athens has thousands of short side streets, and few taxi drivers have maps, although newer taxis have GPS installed. Neither tipping nor bargaining is generally practiced; if your driver has gone out of the way for you, a small gratuity (10% or less) is appreciated.

FARES The meter starts at €1, and even if you join other passengers, you must add this amount to your final charge. The minimum fare is €2.65. The basic charge is €0.26 per kilometer (½ mi); this increases to €0.50 between midnight and 5 AM or if you go outside city limits. There are surcharges for holidays (€0.50), trips to and from the airport (€2), and rides to (but not from) the port, train stations, and bus terminals (€0.70). There is also a €0.29 charge for each suitcase over 10 kilograms (22 pounds), but drivers expect €0.29 for each bag they place in the trunk anyway. Waiting time is €7.10 per hour. Radio taxis charge an additional €3 to €5 for the pickup. Athina 1, Ermis, Hellas, and Parthenon are reliable radio taxi services.

Taxi Companies Athina 1 (☎ *210/921–7942*). **Ermis** (☎ *210/411–5200*). **Hellas** (☎ *210/645–7000 or 210/801–4000*). **Parthenon** (☎ *210/532–3300*).

BY TRAIN

The *proastiakos* ("suburban"), a light rail network offering travelers a direct link from Athens airport to Corinth for €8, is introducing Athenians to the concept of commuting. The trains now serve the city's northern and eastern suburbs as well as western Attica. The Athens-to-Corinth fare is €6; lower fares apply for points in between. Upgrades are also being made to the segments linking Athens with Halkidha and Thebes. If you plan on taking the train while in Athens, call the Greek Railway Organization (OSE) to find out which station your train leaves from, and how to get there. At this writing, Stathmos Peloponnisou, where the trains from the Peloponnese arrive, has been temporarily closed and operations transferred to the Ayii Anaryiri station. Trains from the north and international trains arrive at, and depart from, Stathmos Larissis, which is connected to the metro. If you want to buy tickets ahead of time, it's easier to visit a downtown railway office. *For further information, see Train Travel in the Essentials chapter.*

Information Greek Railway Organization (OSE) (☎ *210/529–7777*) ⊕ *www.ose. gr*. **OSE buses** (☎ *210/513–5768 or 210/513–5769*). **Proastiakos** (☎ *210/529– 7777* ⊕ *www.proastiakos.gr*). **Railway Offices** (✉ *Karolou 1, Omonia Sq.* ☎ *210/529–7006 or 210/529–7007* ✉ *Sina 6, Kolonaki* ☎ *210/529–8910* ✉ *Filellinon 17, Syntagma Sq.* ☎ *210/323–6747*). **Stathmos Larissis** (☎ *210/529–8837*). **Stathmos Peloponnisou** (☎ *210/529–8735*).

CONTACTS & RESOURCES

EMERGENCIES

You can call an ambulance in the event of an emergency, but taxis are often faster. For car accidents, call the city police.

Contacts Ambulance (☎ 166). **City Police** (☎ 100). **Coast Guard** (☎ 108). **Fire** (☎ 199). **Tourist Police** (✉ Dimitrakopoulou 77, Koukaki ☎ 171).

DOCTORS & DENTISTS Most hotels will call a doctor or dentist for you; you can also contact your embassy for referrals to either. For a doctor on call 2 PM–7 AM on Sunday and holidays, dial 105 (in Greek).

HOSPITALS Dial 106 (in Greek), check the *Athens News* or the English-language *Kathimerini,* inserted in the *International Herald Tribune,* or ask your hotel to check the Greek papers to find out which emergency hospitals are open; not all hospitals are open nightly. Hygeia Hospital is considered one of the best in Greece, as is its sister maternity hospital, Mitera; both have some English-speaking staff. Children go to Aglaia Kyriakou Hospital or Ayia Sofia Hospital. Note that children's hospitals answer the phone with "Pedon" and not the specific name of the institution.

Contacts Aglaia Kyriakou Hospital (✉ Levadias 3 and Thivon, Goudi ☎ 210/777-5611 through 210/777-5619). **Asklepion Hospital** (✉ Vasileos Pavlou 1, Voula ☎ 210/895-8301 through 210/895-8306). **Ayia Sofia Hospital** (✉ Mikras Asias and Thivon, Goudi ☎ 210/777-1811 through 210/777-1816). **Hygeia Hospital** (✉ Erythrou Stavrou 4, at Kifissias, Maroussi ☎ 210/686-7000 ⊕ www.hygeia. gr). **KAT Hospital** (✉ Nikis 2, Syntagma Sq. ☎ 210/801-4411, 166 for accidents). **Mitera** (✉ Erythrou Stavrou 6, at Kifissias, Maroussi ☎ 210/686-9000). **Ygeia** (✉ Erythrou Stavrou 4, at Kifissias, Maroussi ☎ 210/682-7940 through 210/682-7949).

Contacts Late-night pharmacy hotline (in Greek) (☎ 107). **Thomas** (✉ Papadiamantopoulou 6, near Hilton and Holiday Inn, Ilisia ☎ 210/721-6101).

ENGLISH-LANGUAGE MEDIA

English-language books, newspapers, and magazines are readily available in central Athens; international bookstores and kiosks in Kolonaki and Syntagma stock everything from the *Wall Street Journal* to *Wallpaper.* Local English-language publications include the weekly *Athens News,* which offers a mix of politics, features, travel, and style articles written by both Greek and international journalists; the English-language translation of the respected Greek broadsheet *Kathimerini,* sold as an insert with the *International Herald Tribune; Odyssey* magazine, a glossy bimonthly on politics, sports, travel, and events in Greece and among Greeks abroad; and *Insider,* a monthly magazine on lifestyle and entertainment in Athens, with a focus on shopping, art exhibits, restaurants, and nightlife.

MARRIED, WITH CHILDREN

The concept of babysitting agencies hasn't really taken hold in Athens, in part because Greeks are used to taking their children almost everywhere, including restaurants and late-night cafés and cinemas. High-end hotel chains can arrange for staff to babysit children in your hotel for between €10 and €15 per hour.

3

INTERNET CAFÉS

Though Greeks use the Internet far less than their European Union counterparts, there are still plenty of places to check your e-mails in Athens. Many hotels offer Internet access, but it's usually expensive. If your laptop has a wireless adapter, you can use the Athens Wireless Metropolitan Network for free. A good stop for free Web surfing is the quiet café on the top floor of the Eleftheroudakis bookstore on Panepistimiou Street. If you don't have a laptop, go to the following cafés. Expect to pay between one and two euros an hour.

Internet & Mail Information Arcade (⊠ *Stadiou 5Center* ☎ *210/321–0701*). **Bits & Bytes Net** (⊠ *Akadimias 78Center* ☎ *210/330–6590*). **Quick Net Café** (⊠ *Gladstonos 4Omonia* ☎ *210/380–3771*).

MAIL & SHIPPING

There are post offices all over Athens; ask your hotel how to get to the closest one. The city's two central post offices are in Syntagma Square and off Omonia Square; both are infamous for long lines and slow service. Avoid all post offices during the first week of the month, when Greeks line up to pay their utility bills. Post offices are open weekdays 8–2; some also open Saturday morning. If you want to mail a letter, you can do it from the yellow mailboxes outside post offices; there are separate boxes for international and domestic mail.

Post Offices Omonia Square (⊠ *Tritis Septemvriou 28, Omonia Sq.* ☎ *210/522–4949* ◷ *Weekdays 7:30 AM–8 PM*). **Syntagma Square** (⊠ *Corner of Mitropoleos and Filellinon, Suite 134, Syntagma Sq.* ☎ *210/323–7573* ◷ *Weekdays 7:30 AM–8 PM, Sat. 7:30–2, Sun. 9–1:30*).

SIGHTSEEING TOURS

BUS TOURS For Athens guided bus tours, see the Athens Planner at the front of this chapter.

EXCURSION TOURS Most agencies *(⇨ Travel Agents)* offer excursions at about the same prices, but CHAT is reputed to have the best service and guides. Common excursion tours include a half-day trip to the Temple of Poseidon at Sounion (€29); a half-day tour to the Isthmus and ancient Corinth (€48); a full-day tour to Delphi (€76, €66 without lunch); a two-day trip to Delphi (€116 including half-board—meaning breakfast and dinner—in first-class hotels); a three-day tour taking in Delphi and the monasteries of Meteora with half-board in first-class hotels (€273); a one-day tour to Nafplion, Mycenae, and Epidauros (€76, €66 without lunch); a two-day tour to Mycenae, Nafplion, and Epidauros (€116 including half-board in first-class hotels); a four-day tour covering Nafplion, Mycenae, Epidauros, Olympia, and Delphi (€378 with half-board in first-class hotels); and a five-day "classical" tour covering all major sights in the Peloponnese, as well as Delphi and Meteora (€492 with half-board in first-class hotels). Most tours run two to three times a week, with reduced service in winter. It's best to reserve a few days in advance.

PERSONAL GUIDES Major travel agencies *(⇨ Travel Agents)* can provide English-speaking guides to take you around Athens's major sights. The Union of Official

Guides provides licensed guides for individual or group tours, starting at about €120, including taxes, for a four-hour tour of the Acropolis and its museum. Hire only guides licensed by the EOT—they have successfully completed a two-year state program.

Contact Union of Official Guides (✉ *Apollonos 9A, Plaka* ☎ *210/322-9705 or 210/322-0090* 🖷 *210/923-6884*).

TRAVEL AGENTS

Several travel agents and tour services in Athens are listed below. Closer to Omonia, try Condor Travel, CHAT tours, or Pharos Travel and Tourism.

Contacts American Express (✉ *Ermou 2, Syntagma Sq.* ☎ *210/324-4975* 🖷 *210/322-7893*). **Amphitrion Travel LTD** (✉ *Syngrou 7, Central Athens* ☎ *210/924-9701* 🖷 *210/924-9671* ✉ *Deuteras Merachias 3, Pasalimani, Piraeus* ☎ *210/411-2045 through 210/411-2049* 🖷 *210/417-0742* ⊕ *www.amphitrion. gr*). **CHAT** (✉ *Stadiou 4, Syntagma Sq.* ☎ *210/322-2886* 🖷 *210/323-5270*). **Condor Travel** (✉ *Stadiou 43, Central Athens* ☎ *210/321-2453 or 210/321-6986* 🖷 *210/321-4296*). **Dolphin Hellas** (✉ *Syngrou 16, Makriyianni* ☎ *210/922-7772* 🖷 *210/923-2101* ⊕ *www.dolphin-hellas.gr*). **Key Tours** (✉ *Kallirois 4, Central Athens* ☎ *210/923-3166* 🖷 *210/923-2008* ⊕ *www.keytours.gr*). **Magic Travel Service (Magic Bus)** (✉ *Filellinon 20, Syntagma Sq.* ☎ *210/323-7471* 🖷 *210/322-0219* ⊕ *www.magic.gr*). **Pharos Travel and Tourism** (✉ *Triti Septemvriou 18, Patissia* ☎ *210/523-3403 or 210/523-6142* 🖷 *210/523-3726*). **Travel Plan** (✉ *Christou Lada 9, Syntagma Sq.* ☎ *210/323-8801 through 210/323-8804* 🖷 *210/322-2152* ⊕ *www.travelplan.gr*).

VISITOR INFORMATION

Greek National Tourism Organization (GNTO; EOT in Greece) offices generally close around 2 PM. The English-speaking tourist police can answer questions about transportation, steer you to an open pharmacy or doctor, and locate phone numbers of hotels and restaurants. The Web site of the city of Athens has a small but growing section in English.

Contacts City of Athens Web site (⊕ *www.cityofathens.gr*). **Greek National Tourism Organization (EOT)** (✉ *Tsochas 7, Ambelokipi, near National Garden and Syntagma Square* ☎ *210/870-7000* ✉ *Eleftherios Venizelos International Airport, arrivals area* ☎ *210/354-5101* ✉ *EOT Bldg., 1st fl., Zea Marina, Pasalimani, Piraeus* ☎ *210/452-2591 or 210/452-2586* ⊕ *www.gnto.gr*). **Tourist Police** (✉ *Veikou 43, 4th fl., Koukaki* ☎ *171*).

The Saronic Gulf Islands

AEGINA, HYDRA & SPETSES

Hydra Island

WORD OF MOUTH

"You will not find many 'sights' on Hydra. But you will find beautiful whitewashed homes and shops. Lots of winding, narrow, cobbled streets [and a] great little harbor with small fishing boats and cafés. . . . You can do some swimming off the island—but it is not a traditional beach, just a rocky cove."

—tastravel

WELCOME TO THE SARONIC GULF ISLANDS

TOP REASONS TO GO

★ **Handsome Hydra:** The place for the jet-setter who appreciates walking more than showing off new wheels, Hydra offers both tranquility or sociability—a bustling main town and abundant walking trails.

★ **Ship-shape Spetses:** A fine jumping-off point for the Peloponnesian shore, Spetses is famed for its Spetsiot seafaring tradition—not surprisingly, the old-town harbor is picture-perfect.

★ **Ancient Aegina:** Not far from this vast island's medieval Palaiachora—with nearly 20 churches—is the Temple of Aphaia, one of Greece's best preserved Archaic sites. Aegina's isle is the closest Saronic island to Athens' port of Piraeus.

★ **Pistachio Perfection:** You can already taste them—salty, sweet, mellow, and the best pistachio nuts anywhere may come from Aegina.

The beautiful harbor of Hydra

1 Aegina. The largest of Saronic islands, Aegina is a land of contrasts—from its crowded beach towns to its isolated, rugged mountain peaks, scattered ruins, and forgotten monasteries. Take in the main town's famous fish market, visit the pre-Hellenic Temple of Aphaia, then explore the ghost town of Palaiachora, still spirit-warm thanks to its 20 chapels.

2 Hydra. Noted for its 19th-century *archontika* (mansions), its crescent-shaped waterfront, and fashionable boutiques, Hydra has been catnip for decades for writers and artists—visit the isle's galleries or bring along your easel and let your own creative juices flow. For Hydriot splendor in excelsis, visit the 1780 Lazaros Koundouriotis Mansion or buy a glittering jewel or two at Elena Votsi's harbor-front jewelry shop.

Thisvi

Gulf of Corinth

Perakhora

Korinthos

Sofikon

Nafplion

Portochelion

Kosta

Spetses **3**

SPETSES

SPETSOPOULA

Aegina's popular Marina Beach

4

GETTING ORIENTED

Only have a few days in Greece but need to taste island life? One of the Saronic isles offers the perfect solution. Called the "offshore islands" by day tripping Athenians, they are treasured for their proximity to the burly city. Aegina is the closest—just south of Piraeus, it still feels like another world. Heading southward you'll find Hydra, a fitting stage for one of Sophia Loren's first forays into Hollywood and, finally, Spetses, anchored off mainland Kosta.

The Doric-style Temple of Aphaia on Aegina

3 Spetses. The island, with regular boat service to pine-lined beaches, is perfect for beach-hopping. It's also top contender for the most dining and nightlife offerings of the Saronic isles. As for sights, Bouboulina's House in the main town offers fascinating details about the island's storied history.

SARONIC GULF ISLANDS PLANNER

How's the Weather?

The weather on the islands tends to be the same as in Athens, though the heat can feel more intense on the arid peaks of Aegina and Hydra.

The island breeze—felt on all the Saronic isles, particularly later in the day—makes these vacation destinations more refreshing than the mainland on summer evenings (and in the winter, more bitter, due to the colder humidity).

Due to the risk of summer fires, do not wander into forested areas in the hot-weather months.

And check the forecast before heading to Aegina, Hydra, or Spetses at any time of year—bad weather in the off-season or strong August winds (meltemia) may strand you on the island you only intended to visit briefly.

How's the Water?

Ask at small hotels if solar water heaters are used in summer; if so, find out when it's best to bathe—otherwise you may be forced to choose between taking a freezing cold shower or not bathing at all.

Finding a Place to Stay

Accommodations on the Saronic Gulf islands range from elegant 19th-century mansions—usually labeled as "traditional settlements"—and boutique-style hotels to spare rental rooms overlooking a noisy waterfront. Rented rooms can be less expensive than hotels, and an easy option for fly-by-the-seaters: just follow signs, or solicitors who show up when boats come in. (And note that it's OK to check out the room before committing.) From June to September, book far in advance. Off-season (October–April), you'll have fewer hotels to choose from, as many close during the colder months. Souvala and Agia Marina are suitable lodging alternatives to Aegina's main town, but on the other islands, if you'd like choices when it comes to eating and nightlife, make sure to stay in the main ports. If you want to plan a great off-season trip with minimum hassle, putting your itinerary in the hands of a professional is your best bet. On Aegina we recommend Karagiannis Klimi Travel (*Kanari 2, Aegina town 22970/25664 ⊕ www.aegina-travel.com*). Also note that during certain times of the year (most notably summer) you may get better deals on weekdays than on Athenian-heavy weekends.

Dining & Lodging Prices in Euros

	¢	$	$$	$$$	$$$$
Restaurants	Under €8	€8–€15	€15–€20	€20–€25	Over €25
Hotels	Under €80	€80–€120	€120–€160	€160–€200	Over €200

Restaurant prices are for one main course at dinner, or for two mezedes (small dishes). Hotel prices are for a standard double room in high season, including taxes. Hotels operate on the European Plan (EP, with no meal provided) unless we note that they use the Continental Plan (CP, with Continental breakfast); Breakfast Plan (BP, with a full breakfast); Modified American Plan (MAP, with breakfast and dinner); or the Full American Plan (FAP, with all meals). Inquire when booking if these meal plans (which can entail higher rates) are mandatory. Guest rooms have air-conditioning, room phones, and TVs unless otherwise noted.

Festivals of Fire and Water

Think February's Greek Karnavali (Carnival) is the hottest festival in the country? Consider nautical Hydra and Spetses, which both light up—in flame!—with festivals to commemorate the Greek War of Independence. On Hydra, the Miaoulia is held over a three-day span in mid- to late June, building up to a reenactment of Admiral Miaoulis's torching of an enemy ship. And if that's not enough sizzle for you, there are celebratory fireworks and dancing as well. On Spetses for a couple of days in early to mid-September, there's more ship-torching—with another naval battle and locals in period costume. For more info about these events, contact the municipalities of Hydra (22980/52210 or www.hydra.gr) or Spetses (22980/72225)

Making the Most of Your Time

The Saronic isles make fabulous day trips, though an overnight stay—or hop to a second isle—is recommended. To ease into the pace of island life probably requires at least two days per island. However, it's doable to visit all the islands within a week, or even four days. A day trip is best spent at any of the island's main-port towns (Aegina—the closest to Piraeus, with the most regular traffic to and fro—is a good choice if your time is very limited). All of the Saronic islands have bathing places close to the main ports, so you can squeeze a dip in, too, though it's doing Spetses's greatest beaches an injustice if you rush your swimming there. In three days you can explore most of Hydra or Spetses, or really get to know Aegina. However, if you wish to visit more than one island, you can start with a day or two on the beaches of Spetses before setting sail for another destination. Keep in mind that if it's natural variety you're after, each of the islands have their very distinctive terrain. Island-hopping on your agenda? First, check your budget: a three-island trek will hit your wallet harder than choosing two islands and exploring them in depth. If funds aren't an issue, try starting in Spetses and working your way north to Aegina. (Note that from Oct.–Apr., there are fewer daily boats and hydrofoils between the islands, so check the whole route in advance with a travel agent or boat company.) Our recommended itinerary: Devote the first two days to Spetses's small main town and beautiful beaches. In the next two, wander Hydra's port town, and if you're ambitious (and in shape), hike to a monastery. Then give Aegina its day's due.

Getting Around

A car is only truly useful on Aegina, and cars are prohibited on the islands of Hydra and (except by special permit) Spetses. Renting scooters, mopeds, and bicycles is popular with tourists on Aegina and Spetses, but extreme caution is advised: the equipment may not be in good condition, roads can be narrow and treacherous, and many drivers scorn your safety. Wear a helmet. If braving the road isn't part of your plan, never fear: on Aegina, there is regular bus service between towns and beaches. On Hydra, you can travel by mule or donkey and on Spetses by buggy and boat—but, as with any personal transportation in Greece, it's best to confirm prices first, so you don't get taken for a different kind of ride.

Ahoy, Mateys!

If you're traveling in a group, consider pushing off in your own vessel to see these isles by water. Six people can rent a sailboat, complete with skipper, from Vernicos Yachts (210/989-6000, www.vernicos.com). At about 100 euros a head per night (excluding fuel) for a week, it's less expensive than staying in some hotels, and you won't have to contend with the oft-postponed ferries. Sailors at various Saronic ports offer to ferry folks to isolated beaches—just remember to arrange for your return so you're not stranded!

4

Updated
by Angelike
Contis and
Natasha
Giannousi

BOUNDED ON THREE SIDES BY SEA, Atikí (Attica) has an indented, sun-gilt coastline fringed with innumerable sandy beaches and rocky inlets. Just to the south of Athens, straddling the gulf between its bustling port of Piraeus and the Peloponnese are the Saronic Gulf islands, the aristocracy of the Greek isles. Set with coves and natural harbors ideal for seafaring, they're enveloped in a patrician aura that is the combined result of history and their more-recent cachet as the playgrounds of wealthy Athenians. Owing to their proximity and beauty, the main islands of Aegina, Hydra, and Spetses (along with lesser-visited Poros) can get swamped with vacationers during the summer months yet they retain their distinct cultural traditions, perhaps best appreciated out of season.

Aegina's pretty country villas have drawn shipping executives, who commute from the island to their offices in Piraeus. Here pine forests mix with groves of pistachio trees, a product for which Aegina is justly famous. Water taxis buzz to Poros, more like an islet, from the Peloponnese, carrying weary locals eager to relax on its beaches and linger in the island cafés. The island's rustic clay-tile roofs have a cinematic beauty that has inspired poets, writers, and musicians who have lived here. Hydra and Spetses are farther south and both ban automobiles. Hydra's stately mansions, restaurants, and boutiques cater to the sophisticated traveler. Spetses has both broad forests and regal, neoclassic buildings. Rather than being spoiled by tourism, all four islands have managed to preserve their laid-back attitude, well suited to the hedonistic lifestyle of weekend pleasure-seekers arriving by yacht and hydrofoil.

EXPLORING THE SARONIC GULF ISLANDS

The Saronic Gulf islands, whose ancient city-states rivaled Athens, are now virtually a part of the capital. Aegina, one of the most-visited islands in Greece because of its proximity to the capital city, is just 30 minutes from Piraeus by hydrofoil, while Spetses, the most "remote" and the greenest of the Saronic islands, is 90 minutes away. South of the Argolid, the peninsula that divides the Saronic Gulf from the Gulf of Argolis, rests Hydra, poor in beaches but rich in charm.

AEGINA ΑΙΓΙΝΑ

30 km (19 mi) south to Aegina town from Athens's port of Piraeus.

Although it may seem hard to imagine, by the Archaic period (7th to 6th century BC), Aegina was a mighty maritime power. It introduced the first silver coinage (marked with a tortoise) and established colonies in the Mediterranean. By the 6th century BC, Aegina had become a major art center, known in particular for its bronze foundries—worked by such sculptors as Kallon, Onatas, and Anaxagoras—and its ceramics, which were exported throughout the Mediterranean. This powerful island, lying so close off the coast of Attica, could not fail to come into conflict with Athens. As Athens's imperial ambitions grew,

Saronic Gulf Islands

Salamina

Aegina

Souvala
Vaia
Vathy
Messagros
Livádi
Aegina town
Temple of Aphaia
Fáros
Omorfi Ekklisiá
Palaiachora
Marathonas
Portes
Sfikári
Perdika

Korfos

Kounoupitsa

Epidaurus

Gulf of Epidauros

Ligourio
Epidauros
Fanari
Trahia
Kaloni
Methana
Poros
Troezen
Galatas
Leukaiti
Poros town
Didima
Metochi
Piepi
Kranidi
Ermioni
Dokos
Hydra town
Hydra
Ydra
Kamini
Mandraki
Vlichos
Molos
Profitis Elias
Moni
Ayios Nikolas Monastery
Episkopi
Petassi
Bilsi
Porto Heli
Kosta
Zogeria
Agia Paraskevi
Vrellas
Agii Anargyri
Spetses town
Spetses
Spetsopoula

Saronic Gulf

Piraeus
TO ATHENS

TO ALL AEGEAN ISLANDS

TO CRETE

0 — 50 miles
0 — 75 km

KEY
Ferry lines

Aegina became a thorn in its side. In 458 BC Athens laid siege to the city, eventually conquering the island. In 455 BC the islanders were forced to migrate from the island, and Aegina never again regained its former power.

From the 13th to the 19th century, Aegina ping-ponged between nations. A personal fiefdom of Venice and Spain after 1204, it was fully claimed by Venice in 1451. Less than a century later, in 1537, it was devastated and captured by the pirate Barbarossa and repopulated with Albanians. Morosini recaptured Aegina for Venice in 1654, but Italian dominance was short-lived: the island was ceded to Turkey in 1718. Its Greek roots were brushed off in the early 19th century, when it experienced a rebirth as an important base in the 1821 War of Independence, briefly holding the fledgling Greek nation's government (1826–28). The first modern Greek coins were minted here. At this time many people from the Peloponnese, plus refugees from Chios and Psara, emigrated to Aegina, and many of the present-day inhabitants are descended from them.

AEGINA TOWN ΑΙΓΙΝΑ (ΠΟΛΗ)

84 km (52 mi) southwest of Piraeus.

The eastern side of Aegina is rugged and sparsely inhabited today, except for Ayia Marina, a former fishing hamlet now studded with hotels. The western side of the island, where Aegina town lies, is more fertile and less mountainous than the east; fields are blessed with grapes, olives, figs, almonds, and, above all, the treasured pistachio trees. Idyllic seascapes, and a number of beautiful courtyard gardens, make Aegina town attractive. A large population of fishermen adds character to the many waterfront café-taverna hybrids serving ouzo and beer with pieces of grilled octopus, home-cured olives, and other *mezedes* (appetizers). Much of the ancient city lies under the modern. Although some unattractive contemporary buildings mar the harborscape, a number of well-preserved neoclassic buildings and village houses are found on the backstreets. It takes between 60 and 90 minutes for ferries from Piraeus to dock at Souvala, a sleepy fishing village on the island's northern coast, or at the main port in Aegina town. Hydrofoils reach Aegina town in 35 minutes.

As you approach from the sea, your first view of Aegina town takes in the sweep of the harbor, punctuated by the tiny white chapel of **Ayios Nikolaos.** ⊠*Harbor front, Aegina town.*

During the negotiations for Greece during the War of Independence, Ioannis Kapodistrias, the first president of the country, conducted meetings in the medieval **Markelon Tower.** Today the tower houses the town's cultural center and the Spyros Alexiou Center for Social Issues. ⊠*Town center, Aegina town.*

The **Archaeological Museum** is small, but it was the first to be established in Greece (1829). Finds from the Temple of Aphaia and excavations throughout the island, including early– and middle–Bronze Age pottery, are on display. Among the Archaic and classical pottery is the distinctive Ram Jug, depicting Odysseus and his crew fleeing the Cyclops, and a 5th-century BC sphinx. Also notable is a Hercules sculpture from the Temple of Apollo. Just above the Archaeological Museum is the ancient site of the acropolis of Aegina, the island's religious and political center. The settlement was first established in the Copper Age, and was renamed **Kolona**, or "column," in modern times, after the only remaining pillar of the Temple of Apollo that once stood there. You can examine ruins and walls dating back to 1300–1600 BC, as well as Byzantine-era buildings. ⊠*Harbor front, 350 ft from ferry dock, Aegina town* ☎22970/22248 ☜€3 ☉*Tues.–Sun. 8:30–3:30.*

NEED A BREAK?

Having a bite to eat at the *psaragora* (fish market) is a must in Aegina town. A small dish of grilled octopus at the World War II–era taverna Agora (*market* ⊠ *Within market on Panayi Irioti, Aegina town* ☎22970/27308) is perfect with an ouzo—if you aren't averse to the smell of raw fish wafting over. Inside, fishermen gather mid-afternoon and early evening, worrying their beads while seated beside glistening octopus hung up to dry—as close to a scene from the film *Zorba the Greek* as you are likely to see in modern Greece.

The haunting remains of the medieval **Palaiachora** *(Old Town)*, built in the 9th century by islanders whose seaside town was the constant prey of pirates, are set on the rocky, barren hill above the monastery. Capital of the island until 1826, Palaiachora has the romantic aura of a mysterious ghost town, a miniature Mistras that still has more than 20 churches. They are mostly from the 13th century, and a number of them have been restored and are still in use. They sit amid the ruins of the community's houses abandoned by the inhabitants in the early 19th century. Pick up a booklet from the Aegina Tourist Police that provides a history of the settlement and directs you to several of the most interesting churches. Episkopi (often closed), Ayios Giorgios, and Metamorphosi have lovely but faded (by dampness) frescoes. The frescoes of the church of Ayioi Anargyroi are especially fascinating because they are of pagan subjects, such as the mother goddess Gaia on horseback and Alexander the Great. The massive Ayios Nektarios Monastery, 1 km (½ mi) west of Palaiachora, is one of the largest in the Balkans. ⊠*7 km (4½ mi) south of Aegina town center.*

The small, somewhat-overrun port of **Ayia Marina** has many hotels, cafés, restaurants, and a family-friendly beach. ⊠*13 km (8 mi) east of Aegina town, via small paved road below Temple of Aphaia.*

From the **Temple of Aphaia,** perched on a promontory, you have superb views of Athens and Piraeus across the water—with binoculars you can see both the Parthenon and the Temple of Poseidon at Sounion. This site has been occupied by many sanctuaries to Aphaia; the ruins visible today are those of the temple built in the early 5th century BC. Aphaia was apparently a pre-Hellenic deity, whose worship eventually converged with that of Athena. The temple, one of the finest extant examples of Archaic architecture, was adorned with an exquisite group of pedimental sculptures that are now in the Munich Glyptothek. Twenty-five of the original 32 Doric columns were either left standing or have been reconstructed. You can visit the museum for no extra fee. The exhibit has many fragments from the once brilliantly colored temple interior and inscriptions of an older temple from the 6th and 5th centuries BC, as well as drawings that show a reconstruction of the original building. From Aegina

NO-SWEAT TIP

In July and August visit archaeological sites like the Temple of Aphaia as early in the day as possible. There is little shade at such sites, and the midday heat can be withering. Plus, an early start may help you avoid crowds.

town, catch the bus for Ayia Marina on Ethniyersias Square, the main Aegina town bus station; ask the driver to let you off at the temple. A gift and snack bar is a comfortable place to have a drink and wait for the return bus to Aegina town or for the bus bound for Ayia Marina. ⊠*15 km (9 mi) east of Aegina town, Ayia Marina* ☎*22970/32398* ⊕*www.culture.gr* ⊠*€4* ⊙*Temple Apr.–Nov., daily 8–7:15; Dec.–Mar., daily 8:15–5; museum Tues.–Sun. 8–2:15.*

Follow the lead of the locals and visiting Athenians, and for an excursion, take a bus (a 20-minute ride from Ethniyersias Square) to the pretty village of **Perdika** to unwind and eat lunch at a seaside taverna. Places to eat in Perdika have multiplied over the years but are still low-key and have a strong island flavor, transporting you light-years away from the bustle of much of modern Greece. Try O Nontas, the first fish taverna after the bus station, for a meal on the canopied terrace overlooking the little bay and the islet of Moni. Antonis, the famous fish tavern, draws big-name Athenians year-round. Other interesting year-round cafés include the inviting Liotrivi, with its corner view on the port, beachside tables, and the antique olive press it's named after on display inside; the Kioski, in a little stone building; and mainstream bar Cafe Aigokeros. There's also a small sand cove with shallow water safe for young children to swim in. ⊠*9 km (5½ mi) south of Aegina town.*

BEACHES

There are no broad coasts, and most beaches on Aegina are slivers of sand edging the coastal roads. Aegina town's beaches, and notably the pine-surrounded **Kolona** beach (⊠*Near Kolona monument*), are pleasant enough, though crowded. There's a good swimming spot at the sandy **Marathonas** beach (⊠*6 km [4 mi] south of Aegina town*). After Marathonas, **Aiginitissa** (⊠*7 km [4½ mi] south of Aegina town*) is a small, sandy bay that has its own café-restaurant and is lined with umbrellas and lounge chairs. **Klima** (⊠*10 km [6 mi] south of Aegina town*), a semi-secluded sandy beach, has a finely pebbled bay of crystal-clear waters. To reach it, turn left at the intersection before entering Perdika. **Ayia Marina's beach** (⊠*15 km [9 mi] east of Aegina town*) is popular with the parenting set, as the shallow water is ideal for playing children.

WHERE TO STAY & EAT

$$$-$$$$ ✗**Antonis.** Seafood is the word at this famed taverna run by Antonis and his sons. The octopus grilled in front of the establishment lures bathers and other visitors who tuck into options ranging from teeny fried smelt to enormous lobsters. People-watching is as much of a draw as the food, since the tables afford a view of all the comings and goings of the harbor's small boats as well as some sleek yachts. Bouillabaisse is a good starter. ⊠ *Waterfront, Perdika* ☎ *22970/61443* ▤ *MC, V.*

$$-$$$ ✗**Taverna O Kostas.** Hollowed-out wine barrels used for displaying wines and serving food are more kitsch than antique, but they match the lightheartedness of this country tavern. Cooks showily prepare saganaki (fried kasseri cheese) over live flames by the table as waiters pull wine from the barrels lining the walls. The menu is solid Greek fare, slightly tweaked for non-Greek palates in search of a "genuine" taverna experience. Yes, it's touristy, but it's also fun. ⊠ *Aegina–Alones road, Ayia Marina* ☎ *22970/32424* ▤ *No credit cards.*

$$-$$$ ✗**Vatsoulia.** Ask a local to name the best restaurant in Aegina, and the response is invariably Vatsoulia. In summer the garden is a pleasant oasis, scented with jasmine and honeysuckle; in winter, nestle inside the cozy dining room. Eggplant in garlic sauce and zucchini croquettes are can't-go-wrong starters. Continue with taverna classics such as veal in red sauce; thick, juicy grilled pork chops; or moussaka enlivened with cinnamon and a wonderfully fluffy béchamel. In winter try the hare stew. A 10-minute walk from Aegina town center gets you to this rustic taverna. ⊠ *Aphaias 75, Aegina town* ☎ *22970/22711* ⌲ *Reservations essential* ▤ *AE, MC, V* ☺ *Closed Mon., Tues., Thurs., and Fri.*

$-$$ ✗**Ela Mesa.** It may have relocated to the elegant hotel of the same name, but Ela Mesa hasn't changed its inventive approach to food. Crisp, deep-fried zucchini puffs give va-va-voom to the typically sliced and fried squash starter. And entrées like golden shrimp *bourekia* (wrapped in phyllo, deep-fried, and served in a cream base) and *midopilafo* (mussel risotto) will sate your inner foodie while sparing your wallet. ⊠ *Souvala* ☎ *22970/53158* ⊕ *www.elamesa.gr* ▤ *AE, MC, V.*

¢-$ ✗**Tsias.** For a light bite, try this harborside ouzeri-meze restaurant that's a hangout for locals as well as tourists passing through. Except for the 30 varieties of ouzo, everything is homemade in this small establishment whose warm yellow walls are decorated with stencils. Vouta Vouta *(Dip Dip)*, a shrimp-and-pink-spicy-sauce concoction is a palate pleaser, but the real don't-miss dishes are baked apple in cognac and the custom omelets for breakfast. Reservations recommended at night. ⊠ *Harbor road (Dimokratias), Aegina town* ☎ *22970/23529* ▤ *MC, V.*

BEACH BUMMED?

If Aegina's beaches don't wow you, climb aboard one of the many daily boats from Aegina's harbor to the smaller, nearby isle of **Angistri**. Without cars, but with food, drink, and small coves to swim in, Angistri has a relaxed, out-of-the-way feel, and more than its share of lovely beaches, which range from sandy stretches to pine-surrounded pebble beaches, all lapped by crystal waters.

4

$ 🏨 **Hotel Apollo.** Take advantage of the beachside location by relaxing on the restaurant terrace or renting a boat to water-ski. Steps lead down from the sundeck to the sand. Spartan guest rooms at this white, block-shape hotel all have balconies and sea views. The town center of overdeveloped Ayia Marina is a 10-minute walk from the hotel; a bus stop is 750 feet from the hotel. ✉ *Ayia Marina beach, 18010 Ayia Marina* ☎ *22970/32271 through 22970/32274, 210/323-4292 winter in Athens* ⊕ *www.apollohotel.gr* ➲ *107 rooms* ♨ *In-room: refrigerator. In-hotel: restaurant, pool* ☰ *AE, DC, MC, V* ⊘ *Closed Nov.–Mar.* ⦿ *BP.*

$ 🏨 **Pension Rena.** Come home to the handmade lace curtains and the
★ wood and marble furnishings lovingly tended by friendly proprietor Rena Kappou. The breakfast of homemade cakes, jams, and fresh juice is served family-style in the dining room or courtyard. With an advance request, Rena will cook dinner for you. Her specialties: *yiouvetsaki* (meat baked in ceramic dishes with tomato sauce and barley-shape pasta) and *kasseropita* (a pie made from kasseri cheese). Bonus: all rooms have a balcony. Pension Rena is a 10-minute walk from the town harbor. ✉ *Parodos Ayias Irinis, Faros, 18010 Aegina town* ☎ *22970/24760 or 22970/22086* ⊟ *22970/24244* ➲ *8 rooms* ♨ *In-room: refrigerator* ☰ *AE, MC, V* ⦿ *BP.*

$ 🏨 **Rastoni.** Quiet and secluded, this hotel's peaceful quality is height-
Fodor'sChoice ened by the landscaped Mediterranean garden, which has pistachio
★ trees, wood pergolas and benches, and rattan armchairs where you can curl up with a book or just spend the day staring out at sea. A sense of space and reliance on Asian wood trims and furniture adds to the Zen appeal. Rooms have a sleek, minimalist feel, in addition to private verandas with panoramic views. Rastoni overlooks the beach and the Kolona promontory, a short walk (about 900 feet) north of the town center. ✉ *Dimitriou Petriti 31, 18010 Aegina town* ☎ *22970/27039* ⊕ *www.rastoni.gr* ➲ *11 studios* ♨ *In-room: refrigerator. In hotel: no elevator* ☰ *AE, MC, V* ⦿ *BP.*

FESTIVALS

Two of the most important festivals held at **Ayios Nektarios Monastery** (✉ *7 km [4½ mi] southeast of Aegina town* ☎ *22970/53806*) are Whitmonday, or the day after Pentecost (the seventh Sunday after Easter), and the November 9 saint's day, when the remains of Ayios Nektarios are brought down from the monastery and carried in a procession through the streets of town, which are covered in carpets and strewn with flowers. On the Assumption of the Virgin Mary, August 15—the biggest holiday of summer—a celebration is held at **Panayia Chrysoleontissa** (✉ *6 km [4 mi] east of Aegina town*), a mountain monastery. On September 6 and 7, the feast of the martyr Sozon is observed with a two-day *paniyiri* (saint's day festival), celebrated at **Ayios Sostis** (✉ *9 km [5½ mi] south of Aegina town, Perdika*).

NIGHTLIFE

Greek bars and clubs frequently change names, so it's sometimes hard to keep up with the trends. The ever-popular **Avli** (✉ *Panayi Irioti 17, Aegina town* ☎ *22970/26438*) serves delicious appetizers in a small courtyard that goes from café-bistro by day to bar (playing Latin rhythms) by night. On the outskirts of Aegina town, multilayered **Inn on the Beach** (⊠*1 km [½ mi] north of center, Aegina town* ☎*22970/25116*) draws an early crowd with its sunset cocktails and chill-out music, before notching up the music to a beach-party tempo. An Aegina mainstay since 1996, beach bar **Aqua Loca** (⊠*1½ km [1 mi] north of Aegina town, on road toward Perdika, Agios Vasilios* ☎*69426/96709*) promises great cocktails (ask for the house special) with some of the best sunsets of your life. Consider nibbling on a *poikilia mezedon* (an hors d'oeuvre assortment) or the shrimp and sea urchin salad.

THE OUTDOORS

Aegina is one of the best islands for hiking, since the interior is gently undulating, older dirt trails are often still marked by white paint markings, and the terrain has many landscapes. Those who are ambitious might want to hike from Aegina town to the Temple of Aphaia or on the unspoiled eastern coast from Perdika to Ayia Marina, two routes described in detail in Gerald Thompson's *A Walking Guide to Aegina*, available at local gift and bookshops.

SHOPPING

Aegina's famous pistachios, much coveted by Greeks, can be bought from stands along the town harbor. They make welcome snacks and gifts. A treat found at some of the Aegean town bakeries behind the harbor is *amigdalota*, rich almond cookies sprinkled with orange flower water and powdered sugar. If you want to have a picnic lunch on the island or on the ferryboat while en route to another Saronic island, check out the luscious fruit displayed on several boats in the center of the harbor.

Cheap secondhand items from lamps to undergarments can be found at the **Animal Respect** (⊠*Panayi Irioti 73, behind town hall, Aegina harbor* ☎*22970/27049*) charity shop. Run by the nonprofit organization that cares for stray animals on the island, the shop also sells fashionable pet accessories.

Flip-flops, shoes, and bikinis; jewelry; papier-mâché figures; dangling Turkish charms; and kitchenware form a rainbow of items available at **Fistiki** (⊠*Panayi Irioti 15, Aegina town* ☎*22970/28327*). The shop's small entrance opens into a maze of boxy rooms filled with everything you could ever need to stay stylish on your trip.

HYDRA Ύδρα

139 km (86 mi) south of Aegina town port.

As the full length of Hydra stretches before you when you round the easternmost finger of the northern Peloponnese, your first reaction might not, in fact, be a joyful one. Gray, mountainous, and barren, the island has the gaunt look of a saintly figure in a Byzantine icon. But as the island's curved harbor—one of the most picturesque in all of

Greece—comes into view, delight will no doubt take over. Because of the nearly round harbor, the town is only visible from a perpendicular angle, a quirk in the island's geography that often saved the island from attack, since passing ships completely missed the port.

In the middle of the 20th century the island became a haven for artists and writers like Canadian singer-songwriter Leonard Cohen and the Norwegian novelist Axel Jensen. In the early 1960s, an Italian starlet named Sophia Loren emerged from Hydra's harbor waters in the Hollywood flick *A Boy and a Dolphin*. The site of an annex of Athens's Fine Arts School, today Hydra remains a favorite haunt of new and established artists. In summer there are continual small art exhibits.

HYDRA TOWN ΎΔΡΑ (ΠΟΛΗ)

146 km (91 mi) south of Aegina.

Even though the harbor is flush with bars and boutiques, Hydra town seems as fresh and innocent as when it was "discovered." The two- and three-story gray and white houses with red tile roofs, many built from 1770 to 1821, climb the steep slopes around Hydra town harbor. The noble port and houses have been rescued and placed on the Council of Europe's list of protected monuments, with strict ordinances regulating construction and renovation.

Although Hydra has a landmass twice the size of Spetses, only a fraction is habitable, and after a day or so on the island, faces begin to look familiar. All motor traffic is banned from the island (except for several rather noisy garbage trucks). When you arrive by boat, mule tenders in the port will rent you one of their fleet to carry your baggage—or better yet, you—to your hotel, for around €10. ■**TIP→ Make sure to agree on a price before you leave**. Mule transport is the time-honored and most practical mode of transport up to the crest; you may see mules patiently hauling anything from armchairs and building materials to cases of beer.

Impressed by the architecture they saw abroad, shipowners incorporated many of the foreign influences into their *archontika,* old, gray-stone mansions facing the harbor. The forbidding, fortresslike exteriors are deliberately austere, the combined result of the steeply angled terrain and the need for buildings to blend into the gray landscape. One of the finest examples of this Hydriot architecture is the **Lazaros Koundouriotis Mansion,** built in 1780 and beautifully restored in the 1990s as a museum. The interior is lavish, with hand-painted ceiling borders, gilt moldings, marquetry, and floors of black-and-white marble tiles. Some rooms have pieces that belonged to the Koundouriotis family, who played an important role in the War of Independence; other rooms have exhibits of costumes, jewelry, wood carvings, and pottery from the National Museum of Folk History. The basement level has three rooms full of paintings by Periklis Vyzantinos and his son. ✉*On a graded slope over port, on west headland, Hydra town* ☎*22980/52421* 💶*€3* ⏱*Mar.–Oct., Tues.–Sun. 10–4:30.*

Hydra Historical Archives and Museum has a collection of historical arti-facts and paintings dating back to the 18th century. A small first-floor room contains figureheads from ships that fought in the 1821 War of Independence. There are old pistols and navigation aids, as well as portraits of the island's heroes and a section devoted to local costume, including the dark *karamani,* pantaloons worn by Hydriot men. There are also temporary Greek-art exhibits. ⊠ *On east end of harbor, Hydra town* ☎ *22980/52355* ⊠ *€4* ⊗ *Daily 9–4:30 and 7–9.*

Founded in 1643 as a monastery, the **Church of the Dormition** has since been dissolved and the monks' cells are now used to house municipal offices and a small **ecclesiastical museum.** The church's most notice-able feature is an ornate, triple-tier bell tower made of Tinos marble, likely carved in the early 19th century by traveling artisans. There's also an exquisite marble iconostasis. ⊠ *Along central section of har-bor front, Hydra town* ☎ *22980/54071 museum* ⊠ *Church: dona-tions accepted; museum: €2* ⊗ *Church daily 10–3 and 6–8; museum Mar. Nov, daily 10–3*

Kamini, a small fishing hamlet built around a shallow inlet, has much of Hydra town's charm but none of its bustle—except on Orthodox Good Friday, when the entire island gathers here to follow the funerary procession of Christ. On a clear day, the Peloponnese coast is plainly visible across the water, and spectacular at sunset. Take the 15-minute stroll from Hydra town west; a paved coastal track gives way to a staggered, white path lined with fish tavernas. ⊠ *1 km (½ mi) west of Hydra town.*

From Kamini, the coastal track continues to **Vlichos,** another pretty vil-lage with tavernas, a historic bridge, and a rocky beach on a bay. It's a 5-minute water-taxi ride from the Hydra town port or a 40-minute walk (25 minutes past Kamini). ⊠ *6 km (4 mi) west of Hydra town.*

OFF THE BEATEN PATH

Hydra's monasteries. If you're staying for more than a day, you have time to explore Hydra's monasteries. Hire a mule (■ TIP→ **again, check prices first, as they can soar to more than €70**) for the ascent up Mt. Klimaki, where you can visit the **Profitis Ilias Monastery** (about two hours on foot from Hydra town) and view the embroidery work of an inhabitant of the nearby nunnery of **Ayia Efpraxia.** Experienced hikers might be tempted to set off for the **Zourvas Monastery** at Hydra's tip. It's a long and difficult hike, but compensation comes in the form of spectacular views and a secluded cove for a refreshing dip. An alterna-tive: hire a water taxi to Zourvas.

The convent of **Ayios Nikolaos Monastery** is to the southeast of Hydra town, after you pass between the monasteries of Agios Triadas and Agias Matronis (the latter can be visited). Stop here for a drink and a sweet (a donation is appropriate), and to see the beautiful 16th-century icons and frescoes in the sanctuary. When hiking wear sturdy walking shoes, and in summer start out early in the morning—even when travel-ing by mule—to minimized exposure to the midday sun. Your reward: stunning vistas over the island (resplendent with wildflowers and herbs in spring), the western and eastern coasts, and nearby islets on the way to area monasteries.

BEACHES

Beaches are not the island's main attraction; the only sandy stretch is an activity-centered beach by the Mira Mare hotel (☎22980/52300), near Mandraki. There are small, shallow coves at Kaminia and Vlichos, west of the harbor. At **Hydronetta** (✉ *Western edge of harbor, Hydra town*) the gray crags have been blasted and laid with cement to form sundecks. Sunbathing and socializing at the beach bars take priority over swimming, but diving off the rocks into the deep water is exhilarating. Boats ferry bathers from Hydra town harbor near the Mitropolis church to pebble beaches on the island's **southern coast**, including **Bisti** and **Ayios Nikolaos**, where there are sun beds and umbrellas. Large boats have set fees posted for particular beaches; water taxis, whose rates you should negotiate in advance, start at €10.

WHERE TO STAY & EAT

$$$$ ✕ **Enalion.** A charming young trio of owners—Fanis, Kostas, and Alexandros—imbues the place with energy and attentive service. Their light, imaginative approach to Mediterranean cuisine includes dishes like *skordopitakia* (garlic bread with tomato and shrimp) and mussels flavored with saffron, as well as a good selection of vegetarian options, including spinach and broccoli tarts. All go perfectly with a glass of house wine and the accompanying Mediterranean tunes. ✉*2½ km (1½ mi) west of Hydra town, 100 ft from beach, Vlichos* ☎*22980/29680* ▤*AE, MC, V* ☉*Closed Dec.–Mar.*

$$$–$$$$ ✕ **Kondylenia's.** In a whitewashed fisherman's cottage on a promontory
★   overlooking the little harbor of Kaminia, the restaurant is irresistibly charming (if a little pricey). Peek into the kitchen below the terrace to see what's cooking: a whole fish may be char-grilling. When available, order *kritamos* (rock samphire), vegetation which grows on the island's rocky coast, or share an order of fresh-caught grilled squid. ✉*1 km (½ mi) west of Hydra town, on headland above harbor, Kaminia* ☎*22980/53520* ▤*No credit cards* ☉*Closed Nov.–Mar.*

$$$–$$$$ ✕**Omilos.** The spot where Aristotle Onassis and Maria Callas once danced is now a vision in white, reopened in 2007 by one of Enalion's owners. Tables nestle in the small, high-ceiling Hydra Nautical Club and wind around the deck outside, which affords an exquisite sea view. An extensive salad menu joins tempting starters such as Greek caviar with fava bean mash and caramelized onions. Try the risotto entrée with sea urchins or select from six different sauces for grilled meats. By day bathers sip coffee on the deck; by night the feel is more formal, before all reserve melts away in the wee hours of summer mornings, when the restaurant turns club. ✉*Hydra port, on the way to Hydronetta* ☎*22980/53800* ▰*Reservations essential* ▤*MC, V* ☉*Closed Mon.–Thurs. Oct.–Apr.*

$$ ✕ **To Geitoniko.** Christina and her husband, Manolis, cook home-style
★   Greek dishes in a cozy old Hydriot house with stone floors and wooden ceilings. Try the octopus *stifado* (stew) with pearl onions, beef with quince, or eggplant stuffed with ground meat. Grilled meats and fresh

fish, including the island's own calamari, are also available. Scrumptious desserts include baklava, and two types of halvah. It's a good idea to arrive before 9 PM for dinner; there are only 20 tables under the open-air vine-covered pergola upstairs, and they fill up. ✉ *Spiliou Harami, opposite Pension Antonis, Hydra town* ☎ 22980/53615 ☰ *No credit cards* ☉ *Closed Dec.–Feb.*

$-$$ ✗ **Kyria Sofia.** This home-based eatery is so popular you have to call to make an appointment. The oldest restaurant in Hydra, it sports bright green, original woodwork inside and, outside, a terrace with half a dozen tables that are quickly

WORD OF MOUTH

"I stayed at Angelica hotel . . . and loved it. Very clean, comfortable, and reasonably priced. The hotel itself also looked very nice. It's in a great location—close enough to the main drag to be convenient, but far enough up the hill to give you a glimpse of island life. It's around the corner from two grocery stores and the pharmacy (which is also the Internet café), so that was very convenient."

—DenverDice

snapped up by those in the know. Owner Leonidas lived in New York for many years, and he's more than happy to share his culinary stories as he serves your meal. For tasty appetizers try the small cheese pies with cinnamon, and fresh salads. ✉ *Miaouli 60, past Miranda hotel, Hydra town* ☎ 22980/53097 ⚲ *Reservations essential* ☰ *No credit cards* ☉ *Closed mid-Jan.–mid-Mar. No lunch (except big parties).*

$$$$ ▦ **Angelica Hotel** It's composed of two island villas with Hydra stone, garden areas, and red barrel-tile roofs. The 13-room main villa is currently undergoing extensive reconstruction to bring it up to the high standards of its fully renovated sister, now called the V.I.P. There, streamlined wood furniture and soft neutral colors predominate in eight spacious rooms with names like Sappho and Amazon, each with unique decor. Perks include hot tubs, plasma TVs, and Korres beauty products. It's a three-minute walk from the port. ✉ *Miaouli 42, 18040 Hydra town* ☎ 22980/53202 or 22980/53264 ⊕ *www.angelica. gr* ☞ *21 rooms* ⚷ *In-room: refrigerator. In hotel: no elevator* ☰ *AE, DC, MC, V* ⦿|*BP.*

$$$$ ▦ **Orloff.** Commissioned in 1796 by Catherine the Great for her lover Count Orloff, who came to Greece with a Russian fleet to try to dislodge the Turks, this *archontiko* (old mansion) retains its splendor. The thick white walls and white linens are offset by cornflower blue on the deep window wells and matching blue guest-room carpets. Antiques in the public (and some private) rooms have been carefully chosen—curvaceous walnut sofas, chairs, dining sets, and highboys; old paintings and lithographs; and gilt mirrors. Superior rooms are suites with a couch; all rooms have views of the town or the courtyard shaded by a mulberry tree. ✉ *Rafalia 9, 350 ft from port, 18040 Hydra town* ☎ 22980/52564, 22980/52495, 210/522–6152 winter in Athens ⊕ *www.orloff.gr* ☞ *5 rooms, 4 suites* ⚷ *In room: refrigerator. In-hotel: no elevator* ☰ *AE, MC, V* ☉ *Closed Nov.–late Mar.* ⦿|*BP.*

$$$–$$$$ ▦ **Bratsera.** An 1860 sponge factory was transformed into this posh hotel,
   ★   with doors made out of old packing crates still bearing the "Piraeus"

stamp. Hints of the building's rustic past are visible in the Hydriot gray stonework, exposed-timber ceilings, and wide-plank floors. Some guest rooms have four-poster ironwork beds, others have cozy lofts, and all are decorated with portraits and engravings. The restaurant operates in the oleander- and bougainvillea-graced courtyard, and its kitchen, which specializes in European cuisine, is considered one of the island's best. Bar-restaurant tables spill out poolside, and quiet Greek music plays on weekends. ⊠ *On left leaving port, near Hydra Tours office, 18040Hydra town* ☎ *22980/53971 through 22980/53975, 22980/52794 restaurant, 210/721–8102 winter in Athens* ⊕ *www.bratserahotel.com* ⌁ *25 rooms, 3 suites* ♿ *In-room: refrigerator. In-hotel: restaurant, bar, pool, no elevator, public Wi-Fi* ▤ *AE, DC, MC, V* ⊗ *Closed Nov.–Mar.* †⊙| *BP.*

> ### WORD OF MOUTH
>
> "It is not necessary to take a donkey ride to get to your hotel if you are staying at the Bratsera. We are still laughing about being taken by that tourist trap. However, our friends love the pictures and the story." —AKNIC

$$–$$$ ⚏ **Miranda.** Art collectors might feel right at home among the interest-
★ ing 18th- and 19th-century furniture and art (Oriental rugs, wooden chests, nautical engravings) at the sparkling clean Miranda. This traditional Hydriot home was built in 1821 by a Captain Danavasis and is now classified by the Ministry of Culture as a national monument. The two suites on the top floor have huge balconies, sea views, and graceful ceiling frescoes done by Venetian painters. There are also paintings by esteemed Greek painters Panagiotis Tetsis and Christos Karras. The large breakfast is served in the interior courtyard, full of fragrant lemon blossoms, jasmine, and bougainvillea. ⊠ *Miaouli, 2 blocks inland from port center, 18040Hydra town* ☎ *22980/52230, 22980/53953, 210/804–3689 winter in Athens* ⊕ *www.mirandahotel. gr* ⌁ *12 rooms, 2 suites* ♿ *In-room: refrigerator. In hotel: no elevator* ▤ *MC, V* ⊗ *Closed Nov.–Feb.* †⊙| *BP.*

FESTIVALS

Status as a weekend destination has made Hydra a popular venue for all sorts of events, from international puppet festivals to open-air performances by British theater troupes. Exhibits, concerts, and performances are usually held June–August; details are available from the **municipality** (⊠ *Main street, Hydra town* ☎ *22980/52210*).

The island celebrates its crucial role in the War of Independence with the **Miaoulia,** which takes place the third week of June. Festivities include dancing, and culminate in a reenactment of the night Admiral Miaoulis loaded a vessel with explosives and sent it upwind to the Turkish fleet. Naturally, the model enemy's ship goes down in flames.

NIGHTLIFE

Bars often change names, ownership, and music—if not location—so check with your hotel for what's in vogue. On the ground floor of an early-19th-century mansion, **Amalour** (⊠ *Tombazi, behind port, Hydra town* ☎ *22980/53125*) attracts a thirtysomething crowd who sip expertly made cocktails and listen to ethnic, jazz, soul, and funk music. The trendy **Nautilus Bar** (⊠ *West of the harbor, Hydra town* ☎22980/52687) hosts Greek music jam sessions.

Café-bar **Pirate** (⊠*South end of harbor, Hydra town* ☎22980/52711) has been a fixture of the island's nightlife since the late 1970s. It got a face-lift, added some mainstream dance hits to its rock music–only play-list, and remains popular and raucous. Drinks include the fruity Tropical Sin. The **Saronicos** (⊠*Harbor front, Hydra town* ☎22980/52589), which plays primarily Greek music, goes wild after midnight and is ideal for die-hard partygoers. The club's easy to spot: there's a fishing boat "sofa" out front.

The minuscule **Hydronetta** (⊠ *West of Hydra town, on the way to Kamini, past Kanoni* ☎22980/54160) has an enchanting view from its perch above the harbor. It's jammed during the day and it is *the* place to enjoy an ouzo or fruity long drink at sunset. **Spilia** (☎22980/54166), tucked into the seaside rocks just below the Hydronetta bar, provides a nice escape from the midday sun and is a popular nocturnal haunt, too. It offers both coffee and drinks.

SHOPPING

A number of elegant shops (some of them offshoots of Athens stores) sell fashionable and amusing clothing and jewelry, though you won't save much by shopping here. Worth a visit is the stylish store of local jewelry designer **Elena Votsi** (⊠*Ikonomou 3, Hydra town* ☎22980/52637). Exquisite handmade pieces are more work of art than accessory. Her designs sell well in Europe and New York.

SPETSES ΣΠΕΤΣΕΣ

24 km (15 mi) southwest of Hydra town port.

In the years leading up to the revolution, Hydra's great rival and ally was the island of Spetses. Lying at the entrance to the Argolic Gulf, off the mainland, Spetses was known even in antiquity for its hospitable soil and verdant pine-tree-covered slopes. The pines on the island today, however, were planted by a Spetsiot philanthropist dedicated to restoring the beauty stripped by the shipbuilding industry in the 18th and 19th centuries. There are far fewer trees than there were in antiquity, but the island is still well watered, and the many prosperous Athenians who have made Spetses their second home compete to have the prettiest gardens and terraces. The island shows evidence of continuous habitation through all of antiquity. From the 16th century, settlers came over from the mainland and, as on Hydra, they soon began to look to the sea, building their own boats. They became master sailors, successful merchants, and, later, in the Napoleonic Wars, skilled blockade runners, earning fortunes that they poured into building larger boats and grander houses. With the outbreak of the War of Independence in 1821, the Spetsiots dedicated their best ships and brave men (and women) to the cause.

SPETSES TOWN ΣΠΕΤΣΕΣ (ΠΟΛΗ)

91 km (56 mi) southwest of Hydra.

By most visitors' standards, Spetses town is small—no larger than most city neighborhoods—yet it's divided into districts. Kastelli, the oldest quarter, extends toward Profitis Ilias and is marked by the 18th-century Ayia Triada church, the town's highest point. The area along the coast to the north is known as Kounoupitsa, a residential district of pretty cottages and gardens with pebble mosaics in mostly nautical motifs. A water-taxi ride here from Kosta, across the channel on the mainland, takes about 15 minutes.

THE AUTO "BAN" EXPLAINED

Unlike on Hydra, cars are not banned outright on Spetses; residents are permitted to ferry their autos to the island. In some rare cases, for medical or professional reasons, it's possible for nonresidents to get a car permit from the port authority (☎ 22980/72245), but it must be obtained at least two days prior to arrival.

Ships dock at the modern harbor, **Dapia**, in Spetses town. This is where the island's seafaring chieftains met in the 1820s to plot their revolt against the Ottoman Turks. A protective jetty is still fortified with cannons dating from the War of Independence. Today, the town's waterfront strip is packed with cafés; and the navy-blue-and-white color scheme adopted by Dapia's merchants hints of former maritime glory. The harbormaster's offices, to the right as you face the sea, occupy a building designed in the simple two-story, center-hall architecture typical of the period and this place.

The waterfront's 1914 **Hotel Poseidonion** was the scene of glamorous Athenian society parties and balls in the era between the two world wars, and was once the largest resort in the Balkans and southeastern Europe. It is currently closed for renovation. ⊠ *West side of Dapia, Spetses town.*

In front of a small park is **Bouboulina's House,** where you can take a 45-minute guided tour (available in English) and learn about this interesting heroine's life. Laskarina Bouboulina was the bravest of all Spetsiot revolutionaries, the daughter of a Hydriot sea captain, and the wife—then widow—of two more sea captains. Left with a considerable inheritance and nine children, she dedicated herself to increasing her already substantial fleet and fortune. On her flagship, the *Agamemnon,* the largest in the Greek fleet, she sailed into war against the Ottomans at the head of the Spetsiot ships. Her fiery temper led to her death in a family feud many years later. It's worth visiting the mansion just for the architectural details, like the carved-wood Florentine ceiling in the main salon. Hours are unpredictable but are posted along with tour times on the door. ⊠ *Behind Dapia, Spetses town* ☎22980/72416 ⚐€5 ☉ *Late Mar.–Oct., daily 9:45–2:30 and 3:45–9* ⊕*www.bouboulinamuseum-spetses.gr.*

A fine late-18th-century archontiko, built in a style that might be termed Turko-Venetian, contains Spetses's **museum.** It holds articles from the period of Spetses's greatness during the War of Independence, including Bouboulina's bones and a revolutionary flag. A small collection of ancient artifacts is mostly ceramics and coins. As this book went to press, the museum was closing indefinitely for renovation work. ✉ *Archontiko Hatziyianni-Mexi, 600 ft south of harbor, Spetses town* ☎ *22980/72994.*

Spetses actually has two harbors; the **Paleo Limani** *(Old Harbor),* also known as Baltiza, slumbers in obscurity. As you stroll the waterfront, you might imagine it as it was in its 18th- and 19th-century heyday: the walls of the mansions resounding with the noise of shipbuilding and the streets humming with discreet whisperings of revolution and piracy. Today, the wood keels in the few remaining boatyards are the backdrop for trendy bars, cafés, and restaurants. ✉ *Waterfront, 1½ km (1 mi) southeast of Dapia, Spetses town.*

The promontory is the site of the little 19th-century church, **Ayios Mamas.** ✉ *Above harbor, Spetses town.*

On the headland sits **Ayios Nikolaos,** the current cathedral of Spetses, and a former abbey. Its lacy white-marble bell tower recalls that of Hydra's port monastery. It was here that the islanders first raised their flag of independence. ✉ *On road southeast of waterfront, Spetses town.*

Anargyios and Korgialenios School is known as the inspiration for the school in John Fowles's *The Magus.* It was established in 1927 as an English-style boarding school for the children of Greece's Anglophilic upper class. Today tourism management students study amid the elegant amphitheaters, black-and-white-tile floors, and huge windows. Visitors can take a peek (free) inside the school throughout the year. ✉ *½ km (¼ mi) west of Dapia, Spetses town* ☎ *22980/74306.*

Walk along the coast to **Analipsi,** the old fisherman's village. At Easter, instead of setting off fireworks at midnight to celebrate the resurrection, local tradition dictates that a boat is set afire and put out to sea. Excavations here unearthed pottery shards and coins from the 7th century. ✉ *1 km (½ mi) south of Spetses town.*

BEACHES

Water taxis at Dapia make scheduled runs to the most-popular outlying beaches but can also be hired for trips to more-remote coves. **Scholes Kaiki** (✉ *1 km [½ mi] southeast of Spetses town center, in front of Anargyios and Korgialenios School*) is a triangular patch of sand beach that draws a young crowd with its beach volleyball courts, water sports, and bars. The beach at **Ayia Marina** (✉ *2 km [1 mi] southeast of Spetses town*) is the home of the elegant Paradise Bar. You can hire a horse-drawn buggy from town to arrive in style.

Spetses's best beaches are on the west side of the island, and most easily reached by water taxi or the daily boats from Spetses town. **Ayioi Anargyroi** (✉ *6 km [4 mi] west of Spetses town*) is clean and cosmopolitan, with umbrellas and lounge chairs. The gently sloped seabed has deep waters suitable for snorkeling, waterskiing, and other water sports (rentals available). **Zogeria** (⊠7½ *km [4¾ mi] west of Spetses town*), a pine-edged cove with deep sapphire waters, has a gorgeous natural setting that more than makes up for the lack of amenities—there's just a tiny church and a modest taverna. On a clear day you can see all the way to Nafplion. Pine trees, tavernas, and umbrellas line **Ayia Paraskevi** (⊠8 *km [5 mi] west of Spetses town*), a sheltered beach with a mostly sandy shore.

WHERE TO STAY & EAT

$$$ ✕ **Patralis.** Sit on a seaside veranda and savor seafood mezedes and fresh
★   fish—fried, grilled, or baked. The house specialties are the fish soup, *astakomakaronada* (lobster with spaghetti), and a kind of paella with mussels, shrimp, and crayfish. *Magirefta* (oven-baked dishes) include stuffed peppers and tomatoes; oven-baked lamb; and *papoutsakia* (literally, "little shoes"), sliced eggplant with minced meat or with tomatoes and onion. The chef makes a mean baked apple for dessert, and the service is especially friendly. ⊠*Kounoupitsa, near Spetses Hotel, Spetses town* ☎22980/72134 ▭AE, MC, V ⊗*Closed Nov. and Dec.*

$$ ✕ **Exedra.** Called Sioras or Giorgos by locals (all three names are on the sign), this waterside taverna lets you ogle mooring yachts while digging into a well-prepared, and thoroughly Greek meal. Mussels saganaki and a dish called Argo, shrimp and lobster baked with feta, are among the specialties, and if you've been stalking the elusive *gouronopoulo kokkinisto* (suckling pig slow-cooked in tomato sauce), your hunt can end here. Fresh fish is always available, and you can also order meats such as souvlaki and even schnitzel. ⊠*At edge of Old Harbor, Spetses town* ☎22980/73497 ▭MC, V ⊗*Closed Nov.–Feb.*

$–$$ ✕ **Lazaros.** A boisterous local crowd fills the small tables—which spill onto the street in summer—and old family photos and barrels of retsina line the walls. A small selection of well-prepared dishes includes some daily specials, such as goat in lemon sauce, chicken kokkinisto, grilled meats, and, occasionally, fresh fish at good prices. Tasty appetizers include homemade *tzatziki* (cucumber-yogurt dip), *taramosalata* (fish roe dip), *mavromatika* (black-eyed pea salad), and tender beets with *skordalia* (potato dip). Order the barrel retsina, priced by the kilo. ⊠*Kastelli, 900 ft up hill from harbor, Spetses town* ☎22980/72600 ▭*No credit cards* ⊗*Closed mid-Nov.–mid-Mar. No lunch.*

$$$$ ▦ **Archondiko Economou.** Captain Mihail Economou's heirs have converted his 1851 stone mansion into a beautiful seaside spot. The main building's airy rooms feature iron beds and a sprinkling of antiques: the old ship safe, for instance, houses board games. The pebbled gardens contain a small, pretty swimming pool and a handful of live tortoises. The building's additions are less glamorous but feature pluses—in one case, a generous balcony with a cannon facing the sea. Note: no children under 16 are permitted. ⊠*Harbor road, near town hall, 18050 Spetses town* ☎22980/73400 ⊕*www.spetsestravel.gr* ⤴*2 suites, 2 studios, 4 apartments* ⚷*In-room: kitchen (some), refrigerator. In-hotel: no elevator, public Wi-Fi* ▭*AE, MC, V* ⊗*BP.*

$$$ ▦ **Spetses Hotel.** Enjoy both privacy—surrounded by greenery, beach, and water—and a short walk's distance to town. Here waiters bring

drinks to your lounge chair in the sand, and breakfast can be taken in bed, on your balcony, or in the terrace restaurant. Blue-carpeted rooms have wood-veneer beds covered in plaid spreads, and balconies with either a sea or a town view. The staff can help you arrange excursions to mainland sights. ⊠*Beachfront, 1 km (½ mi) west of Dapia, 18050 Spetses town* ☎*22980/72602 through 22980/72604, 210/821–3126 winter in Athens* ⊕*www.spetses-hotel.gr* ⇆*77 rooms* ♦*In-room: refrigerator, dial-up. In-hotel: restaurant, bar, public Wi-Fi* ⊟*MC, V* ⊗*Closed Nov.–Mar.* ⊺⊙*BP.*

$ ★ ⊞**Niriides Apartments.** With cheerful exteriors surrounded by myriad flowers, these four-bed apartments a short walk from the main harbor are a good value, especially in the off-season. Old-fashion wood shutters and beds with wrought-iron frames are just the right accents to set off the cool white, minimalist interiors. ⊠*Near square with clock tower, Dapia, 18050 Spetses town* ☎*22980/73392, 210/984–1851 winter in Athens* ⊕*www.niriides-spetses.gr* ⇆*7 apartments* ♦*In-room: kitchen, Wi-Fi. In hotel: no elevator* ⊟*MC, V* ⊺⊙*CP.*

FESTIVAL

Spetses puts on an enormous harbor-front reenactment of a **War of Independence naval battle** for one week in early September, complete with costumed fighters and burning ships. Book your hotel well in advance if you wish to see this popular event. There are also concerts and exhibitions the week leading up to it.

NIGHTLIFE

For the newest "in" bars, ask your hotel or just stroll down to the Old Harbor, which has the highest concentration of clubs.

Surviving many years and with ever bigger dimensions, including a seaside patio, is **Baltiza** (⊠*Old Harbor, Spetses town* ☎No phone). International rhythms play earlier in the evening; late at night, it's packed with writhing bodies, and when the music switches to Greek at midnight, as the Greeks say, *ginete hamos*—chaos reigns. **Bratsera** (⊠*Waterfront, Spetses town* ☎No phone) is a popular mainstream bar in the middle of Dapia.

SPORTS

The lack of cars and the predominantly level roads make Spetses ideal for bicycling. One good trip is along the coastal road that circles the island, going from the main town to Ayia Paraskevi beach.

Ilias Rent-A-Bike (⊠*Ayia Marina road, by Analipsis Sq., Spetses town* ☎69738/86407) rents well-maintained bikes, motorbikes, and equipment.

SARONIC GULF ISLANDS ESSENTIALS

TRANSPORTATION

BY BOAT & FERRY

The islands of Poros and Spetses are so close to the Peloponnese mainland that you can drive there, park, and ferry across the channel in any of a number of caïques (price negotiable) at the ports, but to get to them from Athens or to visit the other Saronic Gulf islands, you must take to the sea in a ferry.

Saronikos Ferries carries you and your car from the main port in Piraeus (Gate E8, which is about 400 m (1,312 ft) from the train station, beyond Karaiskaki Square, to Aegina (1 hour) or you alone—no cars allowed—to Hydra (3 hours, 15 minutes) and Spetses (4 hours, 25 minutes). You can get a weekly boat schedule from the Greek National Tourism Organization (GNTO or EOT). There are approximately a half dozen departures per day, and fares range from about €5 per person for Aegina to about €11 for Spetses. Car rates are usually three to four times the passenger rate. Hydra and Spetses are also serviced by Euroseas' catamarans. Ferries are the leisurely and least-expensive way to travel; however, most people prefer the speedier Hellenic Seaways hydrofoils (faster than the catamarans; no cars allowed) that also depart from Piraeus, at Gate E8 or E9. You can get to Aegina in 40 minutes (€12), to Hydra in 90 minutes (€21.50), and to Spetses (€29.50) in just under two hours. There are about a half dozen departures daily to each island, but make reservations ahead of time—boats fill quickly. You can also reserve through a travel agent.

BETWEEN THE ISLANDS

Hellenic Seaways' Flying Dolphins travel regularly, year-round, from Piraeus to Hydra and Spetses (and back again). There are about five such daily rounds from October to April, more the rest of the year. In the summer, Saronikos Ferries has a daily boat between all four islands. But plan your Argo-Saronic island-hopping carefully in the off-season, as boats between the islands are much less frequent, and you may have to do a ferry-and–Flying Dolphin or catamaran combination.

Contacts **Blue Star Ferries** (☎ 210/891-9800 ⊕ www.bluestarferries.com). **Euroseas** (☎ 210/413-2188 ⊕ www.euroseas.com). **Hellenic Seaways** (☎ 210/419-9000 for flying dolphin tickets, 210/411-7341 for ferry tickets ⊕ www. hellenicseaways.gr). **Saronikos Ferries** (☎ 210/417-1190 or 210/411-7341).

BY BUS

Buses in Aegina leave from the main port for spots around the island, including Ayia Marina and Perdika. There are no public buses on Hydra or Spetses. Bus service on the islands becomes more infrequent, and the last bus tends to run earlier, from late October to early May.

Information **Aegina bus station** (⊠ Harbor road, across from ferries, Aegina town, Aegina ☎ 22970/22787).

BY CAR

On Aegina, there is a good network of mostly narrow rural roads (two lanes at best). Drivers should be prepared for occasional abrupt turns; major towns and sites are well marked. Karagiannis Klimis Travel, on Aegina, rents both cars and motorcyles. Cars are not allowed on Hydra and Spetses.

Agencies Karagiannis Klimis Travel (⊠ *Kanari 2, Aegina town* ☎ *22970/25664* 🖷 *22970/28779*).

CONTACTS & RESOURCES

EMERGENCIES

Keep in mind that hailing a cab may be faster than calling and waiting for an ambulance. The Automobile Touring Club of Greece (ELPA) assists tourists with breakdowns free of charge if they belong to AAA or to ELPA; otherwise, there is a charge. Patients are admitted to regional hospitals according to a rotating system; call the duty hospital number, or in an emergency, an ambulance.

Information Ambulance (☎ *166*). **Duty Hospitals and Clinics** (☎ *1434*). **ELPA** (☎ *104 emergency, 210/606–8800* ⊕ *www.elpa.gr*). **Fire** (☎ *199*). **Forest Fires** (☎ *191*). **Police** (☎ *100*). **Tourist Police** (☎ *22970/27777 on Aegina, 22980/52205 on Hydra, 22980/73100 on Spetses*).

INTERNET, MAIL & SHIPPING

Internet cafés are scattered throughout the main port towns; they range in services offered. In Hydra town, Rafaleas pharmacy, a fascinating mix of old and new, has speedy Internet connection in an 1890 landmark building—worth skipping the coffee for. Post offices are open weekdays from 7:30 AM–2 PM. You can arrange with the Athens branches of other couriers for special deliveries to and from the islands.

Information Aegina Post Office (⊠ *Ethnegersias Sq., Aegina town* ☎ *22970/22398*). **DHL** (☎ *210/989–0000 in Athens* ⊕ *www.dhl.gr*). **E-global Internet café** (⊠ *Phaneromenis 7, across municipal stadium, Aegina town* ☎ *22970/ 27819*). **1800 Bar & Internet Café** (⊠ *Harbor road, Kounoupitsa, Spetses town* ☎ *22980/29497*). **Federal Express** (☎ *210/662–0222 in Athens* ⊕ *www.fedex. com*). **Hellenic Post** (⊕ *www.elta.gr*). **Hydra Post Office** (⊠ *Off main port, Hydra town* ☎ *22980/52262*). **Rafaleas Pharmacy** (⊠ *Harbor, behind clock tower, near Angelica Hotel, Hydra town*). **Spetses Post Office** (⊠ *On side street off Dapia harbor road, Dapia, Spetses town* ☎ *22980/72228*).

TOUR OPTIONS

Most agencies run tour excursions at about the same prices, but CHAT and Key Tours have the best service and guides. A full-day cruise from Piraeus, with either CHAT or Key Tours, visits Aegina, Poros, and Hydra, and costs around €93 (including buffet lunch on the ship).

Contacts CHAT (⊠ *Xenofontos 9, Syntagma, Athens* ☎ *210/322–2886 or 210/323 0827* ⊕ *www.chatours.gr*). **Key Tours** (⊠ *Kallirois 4, Syntagma, Athens* ☎ *210/923–3166 or 210/923–3266* ⊕ *www.keytours.gr*).

VISITOR INFORMATION

Contacts Aegina Municipality (⊠ *Town hall, Aegina* ☎ *22970/22220 or 22970/22391*). **Aegina Tourist Police** (⊠ *Leonardou Lada 11, Aegina town* ☎ *22970/27777*). **Greek National Tourism Organization** (⊕ *www.gnto.gr*). **Hydra Tourist Police** (⊠ *Port, Hydra town* ☎ *22980/52205*). **Poros Police** (⊠ *Dimosthenous, off Iroon Sq., Poros town* ☎ *22980/22462*). **Spetses Police** (⊠ *Hatziyianni-Mexi, near museum, Spetses town* ☎ *22980/73744 or 22980/73100*).

The Sporades

SKIATHOS, SKOPELOS & SKYROS

Skyros

WORD OF MOUTH

"Skiathos—out of season—is still the quaint, lovely, quiet, and very green island people have fond memories of. The town is still cobbled and whitewashed, old caïques line the harbor quay, fishermen still mend their nets in the mornings and head out to sea to ply their trade. In summer, the nightlife grinds on through the night, and it's a very European, younger crowd, though nothing like Ios or Mykonos. And never are there crowds like there are on Santorini."   —djuna

WELCOME TO THE SPORADES

The hub of Skopelos island is Skopelos t

TOP REASONS TO GO

★ **Sun-and-fun Skiathos:** Thousands of international sunseekers head here to enjoy famous beaches and then work on their neon tans in the buzzing nightclubs.

★ **Skyros's Style:** Set against a dramatic rock, the main town of Skyros is a showstopper of Cycladic houses colorfully set with folk wood carvings and embroideries.

★ **Sylvan Skopelos:** Not far from the verdant forests lie 40 picturesque monasteries and Skopelos town, looking like a Sporades Positano.

★ **Beachy Keen:** The beaches are best on Skiathos, the star location being Koukounaries, whose golden sands are famous throughout Greece.

★ **"Forever England":** The grave of Edwardian poet Rupert Brooke draws pilgrims to Vouno on Skyros.

1 Skiathos. The 3,900 residents are eclipsed by the 50,000 visitors who come here each year for clear blue waters and scores of beaches, including the world-famous Koukounaries. Close to the mainland, this island has some of the aura of the Pelion peninsula, with red-roof villages and picturesque hills. Beauty spots include the monastery of Evangelistria and Lalaria beach. Skiathos draws a lot of artists for its scenic villages and spiritual energy.

2 Skopelos. Second largest of the Sporades, this island is lushly forested and more prized by ecologists than funseekers. The steep streets of Skopelos town needs mountain-goat negotiating skills, but the charming alleys are irresistible, as are the island's monasteries, the famous cheese pies, and the traditional *kalivia* farmhouses around Panormos bay.

Celebrants of Clean Monday, Skyros

GETTING ORIENTED

This small cluster of islands off the coast of central Greece is just a short hop from the mainland and, consequently, often overrun in high season. Obviously, the Cyclades aren't the only Greek islands that serve up a cup of culture and a gallon of hedonism to travelers looking for that perfect tan. Each of the Sporades is very individual in character. Due east of tourism-oriented Skiathos are eco-blessed Skopelos and folk-craft-famous Skyros.

5

PSATHOURA

GIOURA

PIPERI

PELAGOS

Aegean Sea

SKANTZOURA

SPORADES

Atsitsa   SKYROS

3

Skyros Town

SKYROPOULA   Linaria
      ERINIA   Vouno
   VALAXA

SARAKINA

3 Skyros. Located at the virtual center of the Aegean sea, this Sporades Shangri-la is the southernmost of the island group. The top half is covered with pine forests and is home to Skyros town, a Cycladic cubic masterpiece, which climbs a spectacular rock peak and is a tangle of lanes, whitewashed houses, and Byzantine churches. The arid southern half has the site of the grave of the noted Edwardian poet Rupert Brooke at Vouno.

A view of spectacular Skyros town

SPORADES PLANNER

How to Choose?

If you're the can't-sit-still type and think crowds add to the fun, Skiathos is your island. By day you can take in the beautiful, thronged beaches and Evangelistria Monastery or the fortress-turned-cultural-center, and at night stroll the port to find the most hopping nightclub. Day people with a historical bent should explore Skopelos's many monasteries and churches and its 19th-century Folk Art Museum. Skyros should be at the top of your list if you're a handicraft collector, as the island's furniture and pottery is known throughout the country.

Festival Fun

The Carnival (Feb.) traditions of Skopelos, although not as exotic as those of Skyros, parody the expulsion of the once-terrifying Barbary pirates. August 15 is the Panayia (Festival of the Virgin), celebrated on Skyros at Magazia beach and on Skopelos in Skopelos town; its cultural events continue to late August. Skiathos hosts cultural events in summer, including a dance festival in July. Feast days? Skiathos: July 26, for St. Paraskevi; Skopelos: February 25, for St. Reginos.

Finding a Place to Stay

Accommodations reflect the pace of tourism on each particular island: Skopelos has a fair number of hotels, Skiathos a huge number, but there are far fewer on Skyros. Most hotels close from October or November to April or May. Reservations are a good idea, though you may learn about rooms in pensions and private homes when you arrive at the airport or ferry landing. The best bet, especially for those on a budget, is to rent a converted room in a private house—look for the Greek National Tourism Organization (EOT or GNTO) license displayed in windows. Owners meet incoming ferries to tout their location, offer rooms, and negotiate the price.

In Skyros most people take lodgings in town or along the beach at Magazia and Molos: you must choose between being near the sea or the town's bars and eateries. Accommodations are basic, and not generally equipped with television sets. In Skiathos tourists are increasingly renting private apartments, villas, and minivillas through local island travel agents. Rates fluctuate from season to season; the August high-season prices may drop by more than half between October and May. Always negotiate off-season.

Dining & Lodging Prices in Euros

	¢	$	$$	$$$	$$$$
Restaurants	under €8	€8– €11	€11– €15	€15– €20	over €20
Hotels	under €60	€60– €90	€90– €120	€120– €160	over €160

Restaurant prices are for one main course at dinner, or for two mezedes (small dishes). Hotel prices are for a standard double room in high season, including taxes. Hotels operate on the European Plan (EP, with no meal provided) unless we note that they use the Continental Plan (CP, with Continental breakfast); Breakfast Plan (BP, with a full breakfast); Modified American Plan (MAP, with breakfast and dinner); or the Full American Plan (FAP, with all meals). Inquire when booking if these meal plans (which can entail higher rates) are mandatory. Guest rooms have air-conditioning, room phones, and TVs unless otherwise noted.

Getting Around

The road networks on Skiathos, Skopelos, and Skyros are so rudimentary that cars are not really needed.

Still, it's not a bad idea to rent one for a day to get a feel for the island, then use public transport or a scooter thereafter. Car rentals cost €28–€33 per day, while scooters cost about €15–€20 (with full insurance).

If you rent a scooter, however, be extra cautious: many of those for hire are in poor condition. The locals are not used to the heavy summer traffic on their narrow roads, and accidents provide the island clinics with 80% of their summer business.

Bus service is available throughout the Sporades, although some islands' buses run more frequently than others.

Caïques leave from the main ports for the most popular beaches, and interisland excursions are made between Skiathos and Skopelos. You can also hire a caïque (haggle over the price) to tour around the islands; they are generally the preferred way to get around by day.

For popular routes, captains have signs posted showing their destinations and departure times. On Skyros, check with Skyros Travel (See ⇨ Tour Options in Essentials) for caïque tours.

Making the Most of Your Time

Inveterate island-hoppers might spend one night on each island, although your trip might be more comfortable if you plant yourself on one. There are regular cruises that travel around the Sporades in three to four days, but as each of the four islands are so very varied, it's worth spending at least two days on each. That noted, you can get around Skiathos and Skopelos in a total of two days, since there are daily ferry connections between them and they are relatively near each other. Traveling between these islands and Skyros, however, requires advance planning, since ferries and flights to Skyros are much less frequent. Also, make sure that you are arriving and leaving from the correct harbor; some islands, such as Skopelos, have more than one from which to depart. Five days can be just enough for touching each island in summer; off-season you need more days to accommodate the ferry schedule.

When to Go

Winter is least desirable, as the weather turns cold and rainy; most hotels, rooms, and restaurants are closed, and ferry service is minimal. If you do go from November through April, book in advance and leave nothing to chance. The same advice applies to July and August peak season, when everything is open but overcrowded, except on Skyros. The meltemi, the brisk northerly summer wind of the Aegean, keeps things cooler than on the mainland even on the hottest days. Late spring and early summer are ideal, as most hotels are open, crowds have not arrived, the air is warm, and the roadsides and fields of flowers are incredible; September is also mild.

Eating Well

Eating and drinking out in the Sporades is as much about savoring the ambiance as consuming the fresh island food; if in doubt, eat where the locals do; few hangouts geared specifically to tourists are as good. Ask your waiter for suggestions about local specialties—you won't go wrong with the catch of the day. Octopus and juicy prawns, grilled with oil and lemon or baked with cheese and fresh tomatoes, are traditional dishes. Skyros is especially noted for spiny lobster, which is almost as sweet as the North Atlantic variety.

Updated by
Adrian Vrettos
and Alexia
Amvrazi

LIKE EMERALD BEADS SCATTERED ON SAPPHIRE SATIN, the verdant Sporades islands of Skiathos and Skopelos, and a nearby host of tiny, uninhabited islets are resplendent with pines, fruit trees, and olive trees. The lush countryside, marked with sloping slate roofs and wooden balconies, strongly resembles that of the neighboring Pelion peninsula, to which the islands were once attached. Only on Skyros, farther out in the Aegean, will you see a windswept, treeless landscape, or the cubist architecture of the Cyclades. Sitting by itself east of Evia, Skyros is neither geographically nor historically related to the other Sporades.

The Sporades have changed hands constantly throughout history, and wars, plunder, and earthquakes have eliminated all but the strongest ancient walls. A few castles and monasteries remain, but these islands are now geared more for having fun than for sightseeing. Skiathos is the most touristy, to the point of overkill, while less-developed Skopelos has fewer beaches and much less nightlife, but has a main town that is said to be the most beautiful in the Sporades. Late to attract tourists, Skyros is the least traveled of the Sporades. It's also the most remote and quirky, with well-preserved traditions.

The Sporades are (with the exception of Skyros) quite easily reached from the mainland; even so, many parts remain idyllic. They may be close to each other, yet they remain different in character, representing a spectrum of Greek culture, from towns with screaming nightlife to hillsides where the tinkle of goat bells may be the only sound for miles. Quintessential Greek-island delights beckon: sun, sand, and surf, along with starlit dinners. Almost all restaurants have outside seating, often under leafy trees, where you can watch the passing Greek dramas of daily life: lovers arm-in-arm, stealing a kiss; animated conversations between restaurateur and patron that may last for the entire meal; fishermen cleaning their bright yellow nets and debating and laughing as they work. Relax and immerse yourself in the blue-and-green watercolor of it all.

EXPLORING THE SPORADES

Little mentioned in mythology or history, the Sporades confidently rely on their great natural beauty to attract visitors. Some locals poetically claim them to be the handful of colored pebbles the gods were left with after creating the world, and as an afterthought, they flung them over the northwestern Aegean. Bustling with tourists, Skiathos sits closest to the mainland; it has a pretty harbor area and the liveliest nightlife, international restaurants and pubs, and resort hotels. Due east is Skopelos, covered with dense, fragrant pines, where you can visit scenic villages, hundreds of churches, and lovely beaches. The least progressive of the islands, it is the most naturally beautiful and has a fascinating old hill town.

Some visitors return year after year to mythical Skyros, southeast of the other islands, for its quiet fishing villages, expansive beaches, and stunning cubist rabbit warren of a town that seems to spill down a

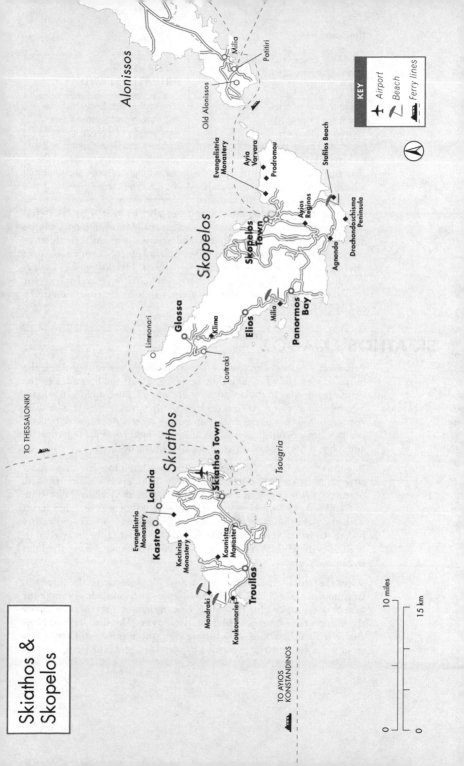

Skiathos & Skopelos

Skiathos

Lalaria

Evangelistria Monastery

Kastro

Kechrias Monastery

Kounistra Monastery

Mandraki

Koukounaries

Troullos

Skiathos Town

Tsougria

TO THESSALONIKI

Skopelos

Limonari

Loutraki

Glossa

Klima

Elios

Milia

Panormos Bay

Skopelos Town

Ayios Reginos

Agnonda

Drachondoschisma Peninsula

Stafilos Beach

Evangelistria Monastery

Ayia Varvara

Prodromou

Alonissos

Milia

Palitiri

Old Alonissos

TO AYIOS KONSTANDINOS

KEY
✈ Airport
⚓ Beach
⎯ Ferry lines

0   10 miles

0   15 km

hill. As a current citadel of Greek defense Skyros also has the bonus of an airport.

Regular air shuttles and boat service have brought the aptly named Sporades ("scattered ones") closer together. The islands are connected by ferry and sometimes hydrofoil, although some are infrequently scheduled, especially November to April. A number of uninhabited islands in the Sporades archipelago can also be visited by chartered boat. If you are taking it easy, you can generally just jump on a caïque and island-hop. If time is limited and you want to do something in particular, it's best to plan your schedule in advance. Olympic Airways offers a weekly flight to Skyros from Athens. Flying Dolphin hydrofoils and Olympic flight timetables are available from travel agents; for regular ferries, consult the Greek National Tourism Organization (EOT or GNTO), in Athens.

> ## YOUR OWN PRIVATE ISLAND
>
> Nine idyllic islets lush with pines and olive groves surround Skiathos, and two lie across the main harbor, with safe anchorage and a small marina. You can sail over, or hire a caïque, to swim and sun on the isolated beaches.

SKIATHOS ΣΚΙΑΘΟΣ

Part sacred (scores of churches), part profane (active nightlife), the hilly, wooded island of Skiathos is the closest of the Sporades to the Pelion peninsula. It covers an area of only 42 square km (16 square mi), but it has some 70 beaches and sandy coves. A jet-set island 25 years ago, today it teems with European—mostly British—tourists on package deals promising sun, sea, and late-night revelry. Higher prices and a bit of Mykonos's attitude are part of the deal, too.

In winter most of the island's 5,000 or so inhabitants live in its main city, Skiathos town, built after the War of Independence on the site of the colony founded in the 8th century BC by the Euboean city-state of Chalkis. Like Skopelos and Alonissos, Skiathos was on good terms with the Athenians, prized by the Macedonians, and treated gently by the Romans. Saracen and Slav raids left it virtually deserted during the early Middle Ages, but it started to prosper during the later Byzantine years.

When the Crusaders deposed their fellow Christians from the throne of Constantinople in 1204, Skiathos and the other Sporades became the fief of the Ghisi, knights of Venice. One of their first acts was to fortify the hills on the islet separating the two bays of Skiathos harbor. Now connected to the shore, this former islet, the Bourtzi, still has a few stout walls and buttresses shaded by some graceful pine trees.

SKIATHOS TOWN ΣΚΙΑΘΟΣ (ΠΟΛΗ)

2½ hrs from Agios Konstantinos.

Though the harbor is picturesque from a distance—especially from a ferry docking at sunset, when a purple light casts a soft glow and the lights on the hills behind the quay start twinkling like faint stars—Skiathos town close-up has few buildings of any distinction. Many traditional houses were burned by the Germans in 1944, and postwar development has pushed up cement apartments between the pleasant, squat, red-roof older houses. Magenta bougainvillea, sweet jasmine, and the casual charm of brightly painted balconies and shutters camouflage most of the eyesores as you wander through the narrow lanes and climb up the steep steps that serve as streets. Activity centers on the waterfront or on Papadiamantis, the main drag, with banks, travel agents, telephones, post offices, police and tourist police stations, plus myriad cafés, fast-food joints, postcard stands, tacky souvenir shops, tasteful jewelry stores, and car- and bike-rental establishments. Shops, bars, and restaurants line the cobbled side streets, where you can also spot the occasional modest hotel and rooms-to-rent signs. The east side of the port (more commonly known as the new port), where the larger boats and Flying Dolphin hydrofoils dock, is not as interesting. The little church and clock tower of Ayios Nikolaos watch over it from a hill reached by steps so steep they're almost perpendicular to the earth.

Papadiamantis Museum is devoted to one of Greece's finest writers, Alexandros Papadiamantis (1851–1911), who wrote passionately about traditional island life and the hardships of his day. Skiathos plays a part in his short stories; his most famous novel, *The Murderess,* has been translated to English. Three humble rooms with his bed, the low and narrow divan where he died, some photos, and a few personal belongings are all that is exhibited. ⊠ *Right of Papadiamantis at fork* ☎ *24270/23843* ⬛ *24270/23841* ⬛ *€1* ☙ *July and Aug., daily 9:30–1:30 and 5–8:30; Sept.–June, Tues.–Sun. 9:30–1:30 and 5–8:30.*

The **Bourtzi** (⊠ *End of causeway extending from port*) is a piney islet that was once a fortress. It divides the harbor and now is a cultural center with periodic events and activities. In July and August, art and antiquities exhibitions and open-air performances are held here. West of the waterfront is the fishing port and the dock where caïques depart for round-the-island trips and the beaches. The sidewalk is filled with cafés and *ouzeri* (casual bars) catering more to people-watchers than to serious culinary aficionados. At the far end of the port, beginning at the square around the 1846 church of Trion Hierarchon, fancier restaurants spread out under awnings, overlooking the sea. A few good restaurants and bars are hidden on backstreets in this neighborhood, many of them serving foreign foods.

BEACHES

Skiathos is known for its beaches, but as has happened so many times before, popularity has a way of spoiling special places. Since the arrival of English expatriates in the early 1960s, the beautiful, piney 14-km (9-mi) stretch of coast running south of town to famed, gold-sand Koukounaries has become one almost continuous ribbon of villas, hotels, and tavernas. One beach succeeds another, and in summer the asphalted coast road carries a constant stream of cars, buses, motorbikes, and pedestrians buzzing beach to beach, like frenzied bees sampling pollen-laden flowers. To access most beaches, you must take little, usually unpaved, lanes down to the sea. Along this coast, the beaches, **Megali Ammos, Vassilias, Achladia, Tzaneria, Vromolimnos,** and **Platania,** all offer water sports, umbrellas, lounge chairs, and plenty of company.

WHERE TO STAY & EAT

$$–$$$ ✕**The Windmill.** Sit outdoors at this well-preserved 1880 mill–turned–
★ unpretentiously elegant restaurant and a nighttime trek to the hill above Ayios Nikolaos is rewarded with spectacular views of the dimly lighted harbor. White terraces have dark, rough-hewn wood rails, and small balconies poke out from the mill building. The Windmill's friendly and clued-in staff, under the direction of Scottish co-owners Pamela Dance and Karen McCann, serves creative dinners like Thai fish cakes with sweet chili sauce and duck with a honey-and-orange sauce, along with exotic cocktails and a variety of fine Greek and foreign wines. Follow signs to the top of the short but steep staircase. ⊠*Above clock tower* ☎24270/24550 ⌖*Reservations essential* ▤*MC, V* ⊙*Closed mid-Oct.–mid-May. No lunch.*

$–$$ ✕**Amphiliki.** Sprawled on a balcony overlooking Siferi bay, this restaurant, open for three meals a day, pairs an inviting breeze with one of the best views in town. The menu's pairings are less reliable: a Mediterranean-fusion approach works for some dishes, like mouthwatering prawns and mushrooms dressed in a zingy lemon sauce. But for others (like mussels drowned in cheese) it detracts from the purity of the fresh ingredients. Service is attentive and the white house wine crisp and cool. Leave space for the feather-light *ekmek* (custard cake) with mastic ice cream if you arrive for lunch or dinner. ⊠*Opposite health center* ☎24270/22839 ▤*MC, V* ⊙*Oct.–May.*

$–$$ ✕**Don Quijote Tapas Bar Restaurant.** Mediterranean ingredients inspire at one of the few tapas bars in Greece. Its impressive selection of hot and cold tapas include baked feta in foil, spicy prawns, paella, *jamon* (Spanish crude ham), and tortillas. Between nibbles, sip a traditional Spanish wine, or a refreshing margarita, mojito, or caipirinha. Catalan cream (the Spanish version of crème brûlée) and chocolate soufflé make for a sweet end. Have a question about a dish? The cheerful, friendly waitstaff is happy to answer. Sitting on the cozy, vibrantly colored rooftop terrace allows you to view the harbor's bustle with the sound turned down. ⊠*East harbor* ☎24270/21600 ▤*MC, V* ⊙*Closed Nov.–Apr.*

$–$$ ✕**Ta Psarädika.** You can't get any closer to the fish market than this
★ old port taverna, and the fresh seafood dishes (served grilled or fried) prove it. Fish is caught daily by local fishermen expressly for the restaurant, which is family-owned and run. Sit at an outside table facing the sea and sip an icy ouzo while sampling the *mezedes* (appetizers) and finny creatures. ⊠*Far end of old port* ☎24270/23412 ▤*AE, MC, V* ⊙*Closed Dec. and Jan.*

$–$$ ✗▣**Fresh.** The warm, inviting owners, Astergios and Spyros, can be counted on to entertain while imparting their in-depth knowledge of Skiathos. Many of the simple studios with modern furnishings have great views of the harbor. For Greek food—*pastitsio* (pasta with aromatic meat sauce and béchamel), moussaka—reasonable prices, and great service, don't pass up the casual boardwalk café (¢), also fun for people-watching. ⊠*Portside, 37002* ☎*24270/21998* ☞*10 studios* ☖*In-room: kitchen. In-hotel: restaurant, no elevator* ▭*AE, DC, MC, V* ☾*Closed Nov.–Apr.* ⏴❘*CP.*

¢ ✗▣**Mouria Hotel and Taverna.** A wonderful choice for budget travelers,
★ Mouria first opened in 1830 as a market and taverna and is today an inn and restaurant run by the great-grandchildren of the original owners. Guest rooms, some of which can accommodate up to six people, have air-conditioning as well as access to kitchen and laundry facilities. Ask for a room with a balcony overlooking the courtyard, where Papadiamantis once came to write stories. The reasonably priced taverna ($–$$) serves traditional Greek food and fish brought in from the hotel's own boat. ⊠*Areti Ioannou, behind National Bank, 37002* ☎*24270/23069* ☒*24270/23859* ☞*12 rooms* ☖*In-room: no phone. In-hotel: restaurant, laundry facilities* ▭*MC, V.*

$$ ▣**Alkyon.** Don't be disappointed by the boxy exterior and the lack of architectural embellishments—this is a discreet, light-filled hotel with many rooms offering lovely views of the new harbor. It's just enough away from the motion and commotion of Skiathos's main artery to provide some tranquillity, but it's also within easy walking distance of terrific nightlife. The rooms are comfortable and sunny (all come with private balconies), and the lounge areas are spacious and inviting. ⊠*New port, 37002* ☎*24270/22981 through 24270/22985* ☒*24270/21643* ☞*89 rooms* ☖*In-room: kitchen, no TV. In-hotel: bar, pool* ▭*AE, MC, V* ☾*Closed Nov.–Mar.* ⏴❘*CP.*

NIGHTLIFE

Skiathos is filled with night owls, and for good reason. Bars for all tastes line main and side streets, from pubs run by Brits to quintessential Greek bouzouki joints in beach tavernas. Most of the nightlife in Skiathos town is centered along the waterfront and on Papadiamantis, Politechniou, and Evangelistrias streets. The most active season, as you might expect, is June through August, when nightclubs catering to all tastes open along the new port.

MUSIC & NIGHTCLUBS For late-night action along a row of hopping clubs, head to **Kahlua** (⊠*Tasos Antonaros [new port]* ☎*24270/23205* ☾*Closed Oct.–Apr.*), which has indoor and outdoor dancing and is open in summer until at least 3 AM. The popular **Kentavros Bar** (⊠*Papadiamantis Sq.* ☎*24270/22980* ☾*Closed Oct.–Apr.*) entertains a young professional crowd with rhythm and blues, funk, soul, and rock starting at 9:30 PM.

Rock 'n' Roll (⊠*Old port* ☎*24270/22944* ☾*Closed Oct.–Apr.*) is a trendy bar that serves more than 100 cocktails and has a DJ after 9:30 PM. At the funky, white-hot **Slip Inn** (⊠*Old port* ☎*24270/21006*) you can indulge in an amazing fresh passion-fruit margarita as you lounge, Dionysian style on multicolor floor cushions.

SPORTS & THE OUTDOORS

SAILING For multiday charters with or without crew, contact *Active Yachts* (⊠ *Portside* ☎ *69722/45391* ✐ *activeyachts@ath.forthnet.gr* ☾ *Closed Oct.–Apr.*), which also rents out motorboats by the day.

SCUBA DIVING Popular beaches often have diving-equipment rental and instructors on hand. Skiathos is the only Sporades island with scuba-diving schools. The first in operation, **Dolphin Diving Center** (⊠ *Porto Nostos beach [off bus stop 12]* ☎ *24270/21599* 🖷 *24270/22525* ⊕ *www.ddiving. gr* ☾ *Closed Nov.–Apr.*) offers single or multiple dives, as well as full-certification programs.

SHOPPING

ANTIQUES & The **Archipelago** (⊠ *Near Papadiamantis Museum* ☎ *24270/22163*) CRAFTS is the most impressive shop on the island. Browse here among the antiques, pottery, jewelry made from fossils, and embroideries. **Galerie Varsakis** (⊠ *Trion Hierarchon* ☎ *24270/22255*) has kilims, embroideries, jewelry, icons, and hundreds of antiques, set off by the proprietor's surrealistic paintings. **Loupos and His Dolphins** (⊠ *Papadiamantis Sq.* ☎ *24270/23777*) is two adjacent shops that sell museum copies of Byzantine jewelry, ceramics made in Volos, furniture, and antiques. **Skia** (⊠ *Off Papadiamantis, behind National Bank* ☎ *24270/21728*) sells original paintings, sculptures, and ceramics handcrafted by the owners, Milena and Vladislav.

JEWELRY **Odysseus Jewelry** (⊠ *Papadiamantis* ☎ *24270/24218*) sells gold and silver pieces. **Seraïna** (⊠ *Near Papadiamantis Museum* ☎ *24270/22039*) sells jewelry, ceramic plates, and lamp shades. **Simos** (⊠ *Papadiamantis* ☎ *24270/22916*) has unique silver and gold designs.

KALAMAKI PENINSULA ΚΑΛΑΜΑΚΙ (ΧΕΡΣΟΝΗΣΟΣ)

6 km (4 mi) south of Skiathos town.

The less-developed area on the south coast of Skiathos is the Kalamaki peninsula, where the British built their first villas. Some are available for rent in summer, many above tiny, unfrequented coves. Access here is by boat only, so you can usually find your own private beach to get away from the crowds. Motor launches run at regular intervals to the most popular beaches from Skiathos town, and you can always hire a boat for a private journey.

WHERE TO STAY

$$$$ 🖽 **Skiathos Princess.** Flanking virtually the whole of Platania bay below Ayia Paraskevi, Skiathos Princess has all the expected amenities of a luxury resort and friendly, professional service to match. The lobby is minimal, airy, and polished. Rooms that look lifted from a magazine have tile floors, elegant marble bathrooms, and patios or balconies—most with garden views, some facing the sea. A poolside bar serves light snacks. Open only for lunch, the property's chic seaside taverna is worth a visit; the unimaginative buffet dinner at the main restaurant is less enticing. ⊠ *8 km (5 mi) from Skiathos town, 37002 Ayia Paraskevi* ☎ *24270/49731* 🖷 *24270/49740* ⊕ *www.skiathosprincess.com*

131 rooms, 25 suites, 2 apartments ⚘*In-room: safe, refrigerator. In-hotel: 2 restaurants, bars, pool, spa, no elevator, parking (no fee)* ▭*AE, MC, V* ⊘*Closed Nov.–Apr.* ❍❘*BP.*

TROULLOS ΤΡΟΥΛΛΟΣ

4 km (2½ mi) west of Kalamaki peninsula, 8 km (5 mi) west of Skiathos town.

On the coast road west of Kalamaki peninsula lies Troullos bay, a resort area. Continue west and you come to Koukounaries beach—famous, beautiful, and overcrowded.

The dirt road north of Troullos leads to beaches and to the small, and now deserted, **Kounistra Monastery** (✉*4 km [2½ mi] north of Troullos*). It was built in the late 17th century on the spot where an icon of the Virgin miraculously appeared, swinging from a pine tree. The icon spends most of the year in the church of Trion Hierarchon, in town, but on November 20 the townspeople parade it to its former home for the celebration of the Presentation of the Virgin the following day. You can enter the deserted monastery church any time, though its interior has been blackened by fire and its 18th-century frescoes are hard to see.

BEACHES

Though **Koukounaries** (✉*4 km [2½ mi] northwest of Troullos, 12 km [8 mi] west of Skiathos town*) has been much touted as Greece's best beach, photos displaying it must either have been taken a long time ago or on a brilliant, deserted winter's day. All summer it is so packed with umbrellas, beach chairs, and blistering tourists that you can hardly see the sand. The multitudes can be part of the fun, however: think of this as an international Greek island beach party. Water activities abound, with waterskiing, sailing (laser boats), paddleboats, and banana-boat rides all available. The beach can only be reached from its ends, as a lagoon separates it from the hinterland.

Around the island's western tip are **Ayia Eleni** and **Krasa** (✉*1 km [½ mi] west of Koukounaries beach, 13 km [8 mi] west of Skiathos town*), facing the Pelion peninsula, which looms close by. These beaches are also known as Big and Little Banana, perhaps because sun worshippers—mainly gay men on Little Banana—often peel their clothes off. Rocky coves provide some privacy.

Mandraki (✉*5 km [3 mi] northwest of Troullos bay, 12 km [7½ mi] west of Skiathos town*) has privacy because the beach is a 25-minute walk from the road. Sometimes called Xerxes's harbor, this is where the Persian king stopped on his way to ultimate defeat at the battles of Artemisium and Salamis. The reefs opposite are the site of a monument Xerxes supposedly erected as a warning to ships, the first such marker known in history.

Megalos Aselinos and Mikros Aselinos (✉*7 km [4½ mi] north of Troullos, 8 km [5 mi] west of Skiathos town*), north of Mandraki beach, can be reached by car or bike.

WHERE TO STAY

$$$$ ☷**Aegean Suites.** In a league of its own on Skiathos, this luxurious
★ boutique hotel pampers eclectic and demanding guests ages 18 and up
in what resembles a Mediterranean grand villa. Suites are separated by
stairs weaving through a lush garden, and each accommodation has
a separate living room and bedroom and its own audacious, original
Greek artwork. Balconies peer over the Aegean Sea near Troullos. The
beach lies close by, and the outdoor candlelit restaurant, Pelagos, shares
the rooms' blue-green sea views. Expect outstanding service and such
perks as a champagne bar, Jacuzzi dinners, yacht cruises, helicopter
transfers, and occasional wine tastings or barbecue nights. ⊠*Megali
Ammos beach* ⬭ *Winter address: Santikmos Hotels & Resorts, 40
Ag. Konstantinou, Aethrio Centre, Office A40, 15124 Maroussi, Athens* ☏*24270/24069* 🖷*24270/24070* ⊕*www.aegeansuites.com* ⬱*20
suites* ⅃*In-room: safe, refrigerator, Wi-Fi. In-hotel: 3 restaurants, bar,
pool, no elevator, parking (no fee)* ⊟*AE, D, MC, V* ☉*Closed Nov.–
Apr.* ꙮ*BP.*

$ ☷**Troullos Bay.** Quiet and peaceful, this homey beachfront hotel invites
reading, chatting, and relaxing in bamboo chairs around the lobby's
fireplace. Bedrooms have wood furniture, striped duvets, tile floors,
and colorful prints. Most rooms have balconies and views of the pretty
beach. The restaurant, decorated with bamboo and chintz, serves a combination of good Greek and international food and opens onto the lawn
near the sand's edge. ⊠*Troullos, 37002Troullos Bay* ☏*24270/49390
or 24270/49391* 🖷*24270/49218* ⬱*43 rooms* ⅃*In-room: refrigerator. In-hotel: restaurant, bar* ⊟*MC, V* ☉*Closed Nov.–Apr.*

KASTRO ΚΑΣΤΡΟ

*13 km (8 mi) northeast of Troullos, 9 km (5½ mi) northeast of Skia-
thos town.*

Also known as the old town, Kastro perches on a forbidding promontory high above the water, accessible only by steps. Skiathians founded
this former capital in the 16th century when they fled from the pirates
and the turmoil on the coast to the security of this remote cliff—staying
until 1829. Its landward side was additionally protected by a moat and
drawbridge, and inside the stout walls they erected 300 houses and 22
churches, of which only 2 remain. The little Church of the Nativity has
some icons and must have heard many prayers for deliverance from the
sieges that left the Skiathians close to starvation.

You can drive or take a taxi or bus to within 325 feet of the old town,
or wear comfortable shoes for a walk that's mostly uphill. Better, take
the downhill walk back to Skiathos town; the trek takes about three
hours and goes through orchards, fields, and forests on the well-marked
paths of the interior.

Four kilometers (2½ mi) southwest of Kastro is the deserted **Kechrias
monastery,** an 18th-century church covered in frescoes and surrounded
by olive and pine trees. Be warned: the road to Kechrias from Skiathos

town and to the beach below is tough going; stick to a four-wheel-drive vehicle.

LALARIA ΛΑΛΑΡΙΑ

Fodor's Choice *2 km (1 mi) east of Kastro, 7 km (4½ mi) north of Skiathos town.*
★

The much-photographed, lovely Lalaria beach, on the north coast, is flanked by a majestic, arched limestone promontory. The polished limestone and marble add extra sparkle to the already shimmering Aegean. There's no lodging here, and you can only reach Lalaria by taking a boat from the old port in Skiathos town, where taxi and tourist boats are readily available. In the same area lie **Skoteini (Dark) cave, Galazia (Azure) cave,** and **Halkini (Copper) cave.** If taking a tour boat, you can stop for an hour or two here to swim and frolic. Bring along a flashlight to turn the water inside these grottoes an incandescent blue.

★ The island's best-known and most beautiful monastery, **Evangelistria,** sits on Skiathos's highest point and was dedicated in the late 18th century to the Annunciation of the Virgin by monks from Mt. Athos. It encouraged education and gave a base to revolutionaries, who pledged an oath to freedom and first hoisted the blue-and-white flag of Greece here in 1807. Looming above a gorge, and surrounded by pines and cypresses, the monastery has a high wall that once kept pirates out; today it encloses a ruined refectory kitchen, the cells, a small museum library, and a magnificent church with three domes. A gift shop sells the monastery's own Alypiakos wine, olive oil, preserves, and icons. It's close to Lalaria, and about a 10-minute drive, or an hour's walk, from Skiathos town. ⊠*2 km (1 mi) south of Lalaria, 5 km (3 mi) north of Skiathos town* ☎No phone ✉Donations accepted ☉Daily 9–7.

■ **NEED A**
BREAK?

A couple of miles south of Evangelistria Monastery, the dirt road veers off toward the north and northwest of the island. Follow this track for a quick repast; about 2 km (1 mi) on, an enterprising soul has set up a café and snack bar, Platanos (⊠*Off main road south of Evangelistria Monastery* ☎No phone ☉Closed Oct.–Apr.), where you can stare at the astounding view of the harbor for as long as you like.

SKOPELOS ΣΚΟΠΕΛΟΣ

This triangular island's name means "a sharp rock" or "a reef"—a fitting description for the terrain on its northern shore. It's an hour away from Skiathos by hydrofoil and is the second largest of the Sporades. Most of its 122 square km (47 square mi), up to its highest peak on Mt. Delphi, are covered with dense pine forests, olive groves, and orchards. On the south coast, villages overlook the shores, and pines line the pebbly beaches, casting jade shadows on turquoise water. Although this is the most populated island of the Sporades, with two major towns, Skopelos remains peaceful and absorbs tourists into its life rather than

5

giving itself up to their sun-and-fun desires. It's not surprising that ecologists claim it's the greenest island in the region.

Legend has it that Skopelos was settled by Peparethos and Staphylos, colonists from Minoan Crete, said to be the sons of Dionysus and Ariadne, King Minos's daughter. They brought with them the lore of the grape and the olive. The island was called Peparethos until Hellenistic times, and its most popular beach still bears the name Stafilos. In the 1930s a tomb believed to be Staphylos's was unearthed, filled with weapons and golden treasures (now in the Volos museum on the Pelion peninsula).

The Byzantines were exiled here, and the Venetians ruled for 300 years, until 1204. In times past, Skopelos was known for its wine, but today its plums and almonds are eaten rather than drunk, and incorporated into the simple cuisine. Many artists and photographers have settled on the island and throughout summer are part of an extensive cultural program. Little by little, Skopelos is cementing an image as a green and artsy island, still unspoiled by success.

SKOPELOS TOWN ΣΚΟΠΕΛΟΣ (ΠΟΛΗ)

3 hrs from Agios Konstantinos, ½ hr from Skiathos town.

Pretty Skopelos town, the administrative center of the Sporades, overlooks a bay on the north coast. On a steep hill below, scant vestiges of the ancient acropolis and medieval castle remain. The town works hard to stay charming—building permits are difficult to obtain, signs must be in native style, pebbles are embedded into the walkways. Three- and four-story houses rise virtually straight up the hillside, reached by flagstone steps, where women sit chatting and knitting by their doorways. The whitewashed houses look prosperous and cared for, their facades enlivened by brightly painted or brown timber balconies, doors, and shutters. Flamboyant vines and potted plants complete the picture. Interspersed among the red-tile roofs are several with traditional gray fish-scale slate—too heavy and expensive to be used much nowadays.

Off the waterfront, prepare for a breath-snatching climb up the almost perpendicular steps in Skopelos town, starting at the seawall. You will encounter many churches as you go—the island has over 300. The uppermost, located near the castle and said to be situated on the ruins of the ancient temple of Minerva, is the 11th-century Ayios Athanasios with a typically whitewashed exterior and an interior that includes 17th-century Byzantine murals. At the stairs' summit you're standing within the walls of the 13th-century castle erected by the Venetian Ghisi lords who held all the Sporades as their fief. It in turn rests upon polygonal masonry of the 5th century BC, as this was the site of one of the island's three ancient acropoli. Once you've admired the view and the stamina of the old women negotiating the steps like mountain goats, wind your way back down the seawall steps by any route you choose. Wherever you turn, you may spy a church; Skopelos claims some 360, of which 123 are in the town proper. Curiously, most of them seem to be locked, but the exteriors are striking—some incorporating ancient artifacts, Byzantine plates or early Christian elements, and slate-capped domes.

★ For a glimpse of the interior of a Skopelan house, visit the **Folk Art Museum,** a 19th-century mansion with period furniture and traditional tools. Check out the example of an elaborate women's festive costume: a silk shirt embroidered with tiny flowers, a velvet coat with wide embroidered sleeves, and a silk head scarf. Even today, women in the villages dress this way for special occasions. ✉ *Hatzistamatis* ☎ *24240/23494* 💶 *€3* ⊙ *May–Sept., daily 10–10.*

> ## PILGRIMAGE WITH A VIEW
>
> A few of Skopelos's 40 monasteries—dazzling white and topped with terra-cotta roofs—are perched on the nearby mountainside, circling in tiers to the shore. Most offer spectacular views of the town; some are deserted, but others are in operation and welcome you to visit (dress appropriately: no bare legs or arms, and women must wear skirts). You can drive or go by bike, but even by foot, with a good walking guide, you can visit them all in a few hours.

Evangelistria Monastery was founded in 1676 and completely rebuilt in 1712. It contains no frescoes but has an intricately carved iconostasis and an 11th-century icon of the Virgin with Child, said to be miraculous. ✉ *On mountainside opposite Skopelos town, 1½ km (1 mi) to the northeast* ☎ *24240/23230* 💶 *Free* ⊙ *Daily 9–1 and 3–5.*

★ The **Prodromou** *(Forerunner)*, dedicated to St. John the Baptist, now operates as a convent. Besides being of an unusual design, its church contains some outstanding 14th-century triptychs, an enamel tile floor, and an iconostasis spanning four centuries (half carved in the 14th century, half in the 18th century). The nuns sell elaborate woven and embroidered handiwork. Opening days and hours vary. ✉ *2½ km (1½ mi) east of Skopelos town.*

The tiny port of **Agnonda** has many tavernas along its pebbled beach. It is named after a local boy, Agnonas, who returned here from Olympia in 546 BC wearing the victor's wreath. ✉ *5 km (3 mi) south of Skopelos town.*

The road from the beach at Stafilos runs southwest through the rounded **Drachondoschisma peninsula,** where, legend has it, St. Reginos dispatched a dragon that was picking off the islanders. ✉ *5 km (3 mi) south of Skopelos town.*

BEACHES

Most beaches lie on the sheltered coast, south and west of the main town, and are reached from the road by footpath. The water in this area is calm, and pines grow down to the waterfront. Scattered farms and tavernas, houses with rooms for rent, and one or two pleasant hotels line the road to the beach at **Stafilos** (✉ *8 km (5 mi) southeast of Skopelos town)*, the closest to town and the most crowded. Prehistoric walls, a watchtower, and an unplundered grave suggest that this was the site of an important prehistoric settlement. **Velania** (✉*1 km [½ mi] east of Stafilos*), reachable by footpath, takes its name from the *valanium* (Roman bath) that once stood here, which has since disintegrated under the waves. It's a nude beach today.

WHERE TO STAY & EAT

$-$$ ✕**Alexander Garden Restaurant.** If you've had enough of the waterfront, follow the signs up to this little garden restaurant in the hills for a made-to-order meal. Especially recommended are *orektika* (appetizers) such as fried eggplant or zucchini, served with *tzatziki* (garlic and yogurt dip) or *tirosalata* (cheese dip). A 200-year-old well in the center of the elegant, leafy terrace produces its own natural spring water, which you can enjoy while dining here. ✉*Odhos Manolaki; turn inland after corner shop Armoloi* ☎*24240/22324* ▭*MC, V* ⊙*No lunch.*

$-$$ ✕**Perivoli.** An elegant, imaginative meal awaits at this local favorite with a candlelit garden. The varied menu is chock-full of delicious options; standouts include rolled pork with mushrooms in wine sauce, seafood risotto, and any of the beef fillets. Make sure to leave room for dessert, as the *amigdalopita* (almond cake with chocolate and fresh cream) is a winner. The secret is out, though—this place is usually crowded. Follow the signs up from Platanos Square (aka Souvlaki Square). ✉*Off Platanos Sq.* ☎*24240/23758* ▭*MC, V* ⊙*Closed Oct.–May. No lunch.*

$ ✕**Molos.** The best of the cluster of tavernas near the ferry dock, Molos serves excellent grilled meat, stuffed grape leaves, meatballs, and *magirefta* (dishes cooked ahead in the oven, and often served at room temperature). It's one of the few places in town open for lunch, especially delightful at an outdoor table. ✉*Waterfront* ☎*24240/22551* ▭*No credit cards* ⊙*Closed Nov.–Mar.*

¢-$ ✕**Mihalis.** Come here for the delicious *Skopelitiki tiropita* (Skopelos cheese pie), or splurge on *rizogalo* (rice pudding). Bougainvillea lines the walls of the courtyard, where you hear the warble of canaries. Opposite stands a barbershop that embodies the charm of another era. ✉*East side of port, 3 blocks inland from bank* ☎*24240/22014* ▭*No credit cards.*

$$$-$$$$ ▦**Skopelos Village.** If sprawling is your style, try one of these spacious
ↄ bungalows. Each sleeps from two to six people and has a balcony or
★ patio, kitchen, large bedroom(s), and living room. The design is traditional northern Greece, with white stucco exterior and interior walls, orange barrel-tile roofs, and rustic pine beds. A sparkling pool is the focus of the central courtyard, and lounge chairs sit poolside. The hotel is steps away from the beach and about a 15-minute walk from the town center. ✉*1 km (½ mi) west of center, 37003* ☎*24240/23011 or 24240/22517* ☎*24240/22958* ⊕*www.skopelosvillage.gr* ⇄*36 suites* ⚅*In-room: safe, kitchen. In-hotel: restaurant, bar, pool, no elevator* ▭*MC, V* ⊙*Closed Nov.–Apr.*

$$ ▦**Alkistis.** Geared toward families or couples with cars, this complex of
ↄ four buildings amid a grove of olive trees makes an agreeable alternative to a beach or town hotel. The cheerful apartments' exteriors are pastel-contemporary; lounges and dining terraces are more traditional,

though airy and bright. Housekeeping is included, and the large pool has a swim-up bar. Room TVs are provided upon request. ⊠ *2 km (1 mi) southeast of town on road to Stafilos, 37003* ☎24240/23006 *through 24240/22517* 🖨24240/22116 ⚓*25 apartments* ⚑*In-room: kitchen. In-hotel: restaurant, bar, pool, no elevator* ▤*No credit cards* ⊘*Closed Oct.–May.*

¢ 🏨**Pension Sotos.** This cozy, restored old Skopelete house on the water-front is inexpensive and extremely casual. Tiny rooms look onto one of the hotel's two courtyard terraces. Breakfast is not offered, although you are welcome to bring your own food and use the communal kitchen. ⊠ *Waterfront, 37003* ☎24240/22549 🖨24240/23668 ⚓*12 rooms* ⚑*In-room: no a/c (some), no phone, refrigerator (some), no TV (some). In hotel: no elevator* ▤*No credit cards.*

THE OUTDOORS

A big caïque captained by a knowledgeable local guide makes day cruises from Skopelos to Alonissos and the National Marine Park. The tour includes a visit to Patitiri, the port of Alonissos, and to the island of Kyra Panayia, where you can walk, swim, snorkel, and visit a post-Byzantine monastery. You can make reservations at Madro Travel (⇨ *Tour Options in Sporades Essentials*).

NIGHTLIFE

Nightlife on Skopelos is more sedate than it is on Skiathos. There's a smattering of cozy bars playing music of all kinds, and each summer at least one nightclub operates (look for advertisements). The *kefi* (good mood) is to be found at the western end of the waterfront, where a string of bar-nightclubs come to life after midnight. Take an evening *volta* (stroll); most bars have tables outside, so you really can't miss them.

At **Anatoli** (⊠ *Old kastro* ☎2 12 10/22051), tap into a truly Greek vein with proprietor Giorgo Xithari, who strums up a storm on his bou-zouki and sings *rembetika*, traditional Greek acoustic blues (without the benefit of a microphone). Sometimes other musicians join in, some-times his sons, and with enough ouzo, you might, too.

Venture into the back alleys and have a drink at **Ionos Blue Bar** (⊠ *Skopelos town* ☎24240/23731), which offers cool jazz and blues. **Mercurius** (⊠ *Skopelos town* ☎24240/24593), along the waterfront, is an artsy jazz bar with a candlelit terrace and unbeatable sea view. **Platanos Jazz Club** (⊠ *Next to ferry dock, Skopelos town* ☎24240/23661), on the eastern part of the harbor, is atmospheric and quietly popular.

SHOPPING

The town's tiny shops are tucked into a few streets behind the central part of the waterfront. Handicrafts include loom-woven textiles made by nuns.

CLOTHING **Mythos** (⊠ *Behind port, next to post office* ☎24240/23943) sells fash-ionable Greek and international styles for women. Try **Pragmata** (⊠ *Be-hind port, above Verdo Bldg.* ☎24240/22866) for clothes, shoes, and other accessories.

LOCAL CRAFTS   **Archipelago** (✉ *Waterfront* ☎24240/23127), the sister shop of Archipelago on Skiathos, has modern ceramics and crafts, great jewelry, handbags, and a wonderful selection of pricey antiques. **Armoloi** (✉ *Waterfront* ☎24240/22707), one of the neatest shops, displays ceramics made by local potters, tapestries, embroideries, and bags crafted from fragments of old Asian rugs and kilims. Kilims, bags, hand-painted T-shirts, and jewelry are among the wares at **Ploumisti** (✉ *Waterfront* ☎24240/22059). **Yiousouri** (✉ *Waterfront* ☎24240/23983) sells decorative ceramics.

PANORMOS BAY ΌΡΜΟΣ ΠΑΝΟΡΜΟΥ

6 km (4 mi) west of Skopelos town, 4 km (2½ mi) northwest of Agnonda.

Due northwest of Agnonda is Panormos bay, the smallest of the ancient towns of Peparethos, founded in the 8th century BC by colonists from Chalkis. A few well-concealed walls are visible among the pine woods on the acropolis above the bay. With its long beach and its sheltered inner cove ideal for yachts, this is fast becoming a holiday village, although so far it retains its quiet charm. Inland, the interior of Skopelos is green and lush, and not far from Panormos bay traditional farmhouses called *kalivia* stand in plum orchards. Some are occupied; others have been turned into overnight stops or are used only for feast-day celebrations. Look for the outdoor ovens, which baked the fresh plums when Skopelos was turning out prunes galore. This rural area is charming, but the lack of signposts makes it easy to get lost, so pay attention.

BEACHES

Pebbly **Milia** (✉ *2 km [1 mi] north of Panormos bay*) Skopelos's longest beach, is considered by many to be its best. Though still secluded, Milia bay is up and coming—parasols and recliners are lined across the beach ready and waiting for the summer crowd. There's an enormous taverna, thankfully ensconced by pine trees; the food is only decent, but cold drinks and ice cream are a luxury in the noonday sun. No matter what, Milia is breathtaking, and if you want to minimize the distance between you and the deep blue sea, locate the owner of one of the villas for rent right on the beach. They're well tended and a few short strides from the water's edge. Next to Milia, accessible through the Adrina Beach hotel, **Adrina beach** has gorgeous turquoise water and a feeling of seclusion. Dassia, the verdant islet across the bay, was named after a pirate who drowned there—a woman.

WHERE TO STAY

$$$$ 🏨 **Adrina Beach.** Atop a picture-book cove, this terraced hotel has unin-
★   terrupted views of Panormos bay from every level. Outside there is multihued bougainvillea; indoors, the blue-and-white scheme is carried throughout, complemented by terra-cotta floors. Plates adorn the walls, amphorae (large clay vessels that usually held wine) the corners. The only fly on the baklava might be the many stairs between the private beach, pool, restaurant (which serves scrumptious home-style

food made from local products), and your room, and the steep walk back from the little town. ⊠*1 km (½ mi) northwest of Panormos bay, 37003Adrina* ☎*24240/23371 or 24240/23373* 🖷*24240/23372* ⊕*www.adrina.gr* ⤙*42 rooms, 10 suites* ⚲*In-room: refrigerator. In-hotel: restaurant, bar, pool, spa, no elevator, parking (no fee)* ☰*AE, DC, MC, V* ☺*Closed Nov.–Apr.* 🍽️*BP.*

$ ⛁ **Panormos Beach.** The owner's attention to detail shows in the beautifully tended flower garden, the immaculate rooms with pine furniture and handwoven linens, the country dining room, and the entrance case displaying his grandmother's elaborate costume. The lobby even looks like a little museum decorated with antiques and traditional clothes. This exceptionally peaceful hotel is a five-minute walk from the beach. ⊠*Beachfront, 37003* ☎*24240/22711* 🖷*24240/23366* ⤙*34 rooms* ⚲*In-room: refrigerator. In-hotel: no elevator* ☰*No credit cards* ☺*Closed Nov.–Apr.*

ELIOS ΈΛΙΟΣ

10 km (6 mi) north of Panormos bay, 25 km (16 mi) west of Skopelos town.

Residents of Klima who were dislodged in 1965 by the same earthquake that devastated Alonissos now live here. The origin of its name is more intriguing than the village: legend has it that when St. Reginos arrived in the 4th century to save the island from a dragon that fed on humans, he demanded, "Well, where in *elios* (God's mercy) is the beast?"

Klima (⊠*3 km [2 mi] north of Elios*) means "ladder," and in this village Kato (Lower) Klima leads to Ano (Upper) Klima, clinging to the mountainside. Some houses destroyed in the 1965 earthquake have not been restored and are still for sale. If you crave an island retreat, this could be your chance.

WHERE TO STAY

$ ⛁ **Zanétta.** These simple, peaceful apartments are surrounded by pine trees and are close to the sea. Two-bedroom apartments host four people and the three-bedrooms can accommodate six. The white hotel with yellow trim and red barrel-tile roof is about a five-minute walk from the water. ⊠*Hovolo beach, 37005* ☎*24240/33140* 🖷*24240/33717* ⤙*16 apartments* ⚲*In-room: no a/c (some), kitchen. In-hotel: tennis court, pool, no elevator* ☰*MC, V* ☺*Closed Nov.–Apr.*

EN ROUTE

Loutraki is the tiny port village where the ferries and hydrofoils stop to and from Skiathos, and it is not very charming.

Three hundred yards from the port are the remains of the acropolis of Selinous, the island's third ancient city. Unfortunately, everything lies buried except the walls.

GLOSSA ΓΛΩΣΣΑ

38 km (23 mi) northwest of Skopelos town, 14 km (8 mi) northwest of Elios, 3 km (1½ mi) northwest of Klima.

Delightful Glossa is the island's second-largest settlement, where white-washed, red-roof houses are clustered on the steep hillside above the harbor of Loutraki. Venetian towers and traces of Turkish influence remain; the center is closed to traffic. This is a place to relax, dine, and enjoy the quieter beaches. Just to the east, have a look at Ayios Ioannis monastery, dramatically perched above a pretty beach. There's no need to tackle the series of extremely steep steps to the monastery, as it is not open to visitors.

WHERE TO EAT

$ ✕**Restaurant Agnanti.** With breathtaking views of the sea below, cre-
★ ative dishes, and reasonable prices, this restaurant, opened in a restored home in 1953, has stayed true to the spirit that gave it its renown. Fresh produce and local wines underscore the high quality. Begin with a sun-dried tomato and smoked cheese salad, and move on to the lemon chicken, pork with plums, or goat in a tomato sauce. ✉*Above bus stop, on left side of Agiou Riginou* ☎*24240/33076* ▤*MC, V* ☉*Closed Nov.–Apr.*

SKYROS ΣΚΥΡΟΣ

Even among these unique isles, Skyros stands out. Its rugged terrain looks like a Dodecanese island, and its main town, occupied on and off for the last 3,300 years and filled with mythical ghosts, looks Cycladic. It has military bases, and an airport with periodic connections to Athens, yet it remains the most difficult ferry connection in the Sporades. With nothing between it and Lesbos, off the coast of Turkey, its nearest neighbor is the town of Kimi, on the east coast of Evia.

Surprisingly beguiling, this southernmost of the Sporades is the largest (209 square km [81 square mi]). A narrow, flat isthmus connects Skyros's two almost-equal parts, whose names reflect their characters—*Meri* or *Imero* ("tame") for the north, and *Vouno* (literally, "mountain," meaning tough or stony) for the south. The heavily populated north is virtually all farmland and forests. The southern half of the island is forbidding, barren, and mountainous, with Mt. Kochilas its highest peak (2,598 feet). Its western coast is outlined with coves and deep bays dotted with a series of islets.

Until Greece won independence in 1831, the population of Skyros squeezed sardine-fashion into the area under the castle on the inland face of the rock. Not a single house was visible from the sea. Though the islanders could survey any movement in the Aegean for miles, they kept a low profile, living in dread of the pirates based at Treis Boukes bay on Vouno.

Strangely enough, although the island is adrift in the Aegean, the Skyrians have not had a seafaring tradition, and they have looked to the

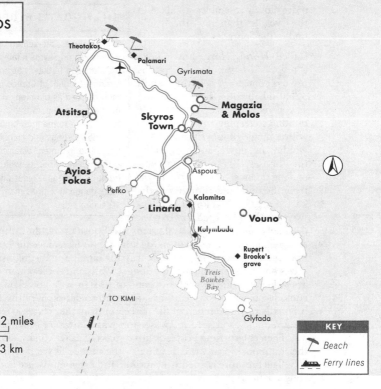

Skyros

Theotokos
Palamari
Gyrismata
Atsitsa
**Skyros
Town**
**Magazia
& Molos**
**Ayios
Fokas**
Aspous
Pefko
Linaria
Kalamitsa
Kolymbada
Vouno
**Rupert
Brooke's
grave**
*Treis
Boukes
Bay*
TO KIMI
Glyfada

0   2 miles
0   3 km

KEY
Beach
Ferry lines

land for their living. Their isolation has brought about notable cultural differences from the other Greek islands, such as pre-Christian Carnival rituals. Today there are more than 300 churches on the island, many of them private and owned by local families. An almost-extinct breed of pony resides on Skyros, and exceptional crafts—carpentry, pottery, embroidery—are practiced by dedicated artisans whose creations include unique furniture and decorative linens. There are no luxury accommodations or swank restaurants: this idiosyncratic island makes no provisions for mass tourism, but if you've a taste for the offbeat, you may feel right at home.

SKYROS TOWN ΣΚΥΡΟΣ (ΧΩΡΙΟ)

Fodor's Choice ★ *1 hr 40 mins from Kimi to Linaria by boat, 30 mins from Linaria by car*

As you drive south from the airport, past brown, desolate outcroppings with only an occasional goat as a sign of life, Skyros town suddenly looms around a bend. It resembles a breathtaking imaginary painting by Monet, Cézanne, or El Greco: blazing white, cubist, dense, and otherworldly, clinging, precipitously it seems, to the precipitous rock beneath it and topped gloriously by a fortress-monastery. This town more closely resembles a village in the Cyclades than any other you'll find in the Sporades.

Called *Horio, Hora,* and *Chora* ("town") by the locals, Skyros town is home to 90% of the island's 3,000 inhabitants. The impression as you get closer is of stark, simple buildings creeping up the hillside, with a tangle of labyrinthine lanes winding up, down, and around the tiny houses, Byzantine churches, and big squares. As you stroll down from the ruins and churches of the kastro area, or explore the alleyways off the main drag, try to peek

> **BILLY GOAT'S BLUFF**
>
> The **Apokries**, pre-Lenten Carnival revelry, on Skyros relates to pre-Christian fertility rites and is famous throughout Greece. Young men dressed as old men, maidens, or "Europeans" roam the streets teasing and tormenting onlookers with ribald songs and clanging bells. The "old men" wear elaborate shepherd's outfits, with masks made of baby-goat hides and belts dangling with as many as 40 sheep bells.

discreetly into the houses. Skyrians are house-proud and often leave their windows and doors open to show off. In fact, since the houses all have the same exteriors, the only way for families to distinguish themselves has been through interior design. Walls and conical mantelpieces are richly decorated with European- and Asian-style porcelain, copper cooking utensils, wood carvings, and embroideries. Wealthy families originally obtained much of the porcelain from the pirates in exchange for grain and food, and its possession was a measure of social standing. Then enterprising potters started making exact copies, along with the traditional local ware, leading to the unique Skyrian style of pottery. The furniture is equally beautiful, and often miniature in order to conserve interior space.

Farther up the hill, the summit is crowned with three tiny cubelike churches with blue and pink interiors, and the ruined Venetian cistern, once used as a dungeon. From there you have a spectacular view of the town and surrounding hills. The roofs are flat, the older ones covered with a dark gray shale that has splendid insulating properties. The house walls and roofs are interconnected, forming a pattern that from above looks like a magnified form of cuneiform writing. Here and there the shieldlike roof of a church stands out from the cubist composition of white houses that fills the hillside—with not an inch to spare.

Most commercial activity takes place in or near the agora (the market street), familiarly known as Sisifos, as in the myth, because of its frustrating steepness. Found here are the town's pharmacies, travel agencies, shops with wonderful Skyrian pottery, and an extraordinary number of tiny bars and tavernas but few boutiques and even less kitsch. In the summer heat, all shops and restaurants close from 2 PM to 6 PM, but the town comes alive at night.

★ The best way to get an idea of the town and its history is to follow the sinuous cobbled lanes past the mansions of the old town to the *kastro*, the highest point, and the 10th-century fortified **Monastery of St. George,** which stands on the site of the ancient acropolis and Bronze Age settlement. Little remains of the legendary fortress of King Lykomedes, portrayed in Skyros's two most colorful myths, though lower down on the north and southwest face of the rock are the so-called Pelagian bastions of immense rectangular fitted blocks, dated to the classical period or later.

A white marble lion, which may be left over from the Venetian occupation, is in the wall above the entrance to the monastery. This classical symbol is a reminder of when Skyros was under Athenian dominion and heavily populated with Athenian settlers to keep it that way. This part of the castle was built on ancient foundations (look right) during the early Byzantine era and reinforced in the 14th century by the Venetians. The monastery itself was founded in 962 and radically rebuilt in 1600. Today it is inhabited by a sole monk.

> ## MYTHIC SKYROS
>
> In the legends of The *Iliad*, before the Trojan War, Theseus, the deposed hero-king of Athens, sought refuge in his ancestral estate on Skyros. King Lykomedes, afraid of the power and prestige of Theseus, took him up to the acropolis one evening, pretending to show him the island, and pushed him over the cliff—an ignominious end. In ancient times, Timon of Athens unearthed what he said were Theseus's bones and sword, and placed them in the Theseion—more commonly called the Temple of Hephaistion—in Athens, in what must be one of the earliest recorded archaeological investigations.

Unfortunately, the once splendid frescoes of the Monastery of St. George are now mostly covered by layers of whitewash, but look for the charming St. George and startled dragon outside to the left of the church door. Within, the ornate iconostasis is considered a masterpiece. The icon of St. George on the right is said to have been brought by settlers from Constantinople, who came in waves during the iconoclast controversy of the 9th century. The icon has a black face and is familiarly known as Ayios Georgis o Arapis ("the Negro"); the Skyrians view him as the patron saint not only of their island but of lovers as well. ✉ *1 km (½ mi) above waterfront.*

Take the vaulted passageway from St. George's Monastery courtyard to the ruined church of **Episkopi,** the former seat of the bishop of Skyros, built in 895 on the ruins of a temple of Athena. This was the center of Skyros's religious life from 1453 to 1837. You can continue up to the summit from here. ✉ *Above St. George's Monastery.*

The tiny **archaeological museum** (on the way to Magazia beach as you begin to descend from the town) contains finds, mostly from graves dating from Neolithic to Roman times. Weapons, pottery, and jewelry are represented. ✉ *Rupert Brooke Sq. (at far end of Sisifos)* ☎22220/91327 ✆€2 ⏲ *Tues.–Sun. 8:30–3.*

★ The **Faltaits Historical and Folklore Museum** has an outstanding collection of Skyrian decorative arts. Built after independence by a wealthy family who still owns it, the house is far larger than the usual Skyros dwelling, and it's almost overflowing with rare books, costumes, photographs, paintings, ceramics, local embroideries, Greek statues, and other heir-looms. The embroideries are noted for their flamboyant colors and vivacious renderings of mermaids, hoopoes (the Skyrians' favorite bird), and human figures whose clothes and limbs sprout flowers. A handwritten copy of the Proclamation of the Greek Revolution against the Ottoman Empire is among the museum's historical documents. The informative guided tour is well worth the extra euros. ⊠ *Rupert Brooke Sq.* ☎ *22220* ✉ *€2; tour €5* ⊙ *Daily 10–2 and 6–9.*

It'd be hard to miss the classical bronze statue, *To Brooke,* dedicated to the English poet Rupert Brooke. Every street seems to lead either to it or to the kastro, and the statue stands alone with a 180-degree view of the sea behind it. In 1915, Brooke was 28, on his way to the Dardanelles to fight in World War I when he died of septicemia on a French hospital ship off Skyros. Brooke was a socialist, but he became something of a paragon for war leaders such as Churchill. ⊠ *Rupert Brooke Sq.*

BEACH

Around the northern end of the island is a dirt road to **Theotokos** (⊠ *15 km [9 mi] northwest of Skyros town*). The large Greek air base near the northern tip of the beach is off-limits.

WHERE TO STAY & EAT

$–$$ ✕ **Margetis Taverna.** A vest-pocket taverna wedged in among shops on the main drag, Margetis is known locally as the best place for fish on the island. It's popular, so get here early (8–8:30). Though fish and lobster are always pricey, they are worth it here, as is the roast pork loin, lamb, or goat chops. Try the flavorful barrel wine, sit outside under the big tree, and watch the folks walk by. ⊠ *Agora* ☎ *22220/91311* ▭ *No credit cards* ⊙ *No lunch.*

¢–$ ✕ **Papous Ki'Ego.** "My Grandfather and I," as the name translates in
★ English, serves terrific Greek cuisine in an eclectic dining room decorated with hanging spoons, bottles of wine and ouzo, and whole heads of garlic. The proud grandson suggests that diners order a selection of mezedes and share with others at the table. The best include fried pumpkins with yogurt, tzatziki, zucchini croquettes, and meatballs doused with ouzo and served flambé. If you want a single dish, the baby goat served as a casserole tastes delicious. ⊠ *Agora* ☎ *22220/93200* ▭ *MC, V* ⊙ *Closed Nov. and Dec. No lunch.*

$$–$$$ ✕▦ **Nefeli.** This superb little hotel is decorated in Cycladic white and
Fodor$Choice soft green trim, with a dazzling pool and elegant bar terrace. The three
★ buildings reflect unique styles, including modern, traditional, and antique, and the guest rooms have handsome furniture and sophisticated amenities. The suites come with hydro-massage baths. Nefeli's restaurant ($–$$) serves organic food from its own local farm, with outstanding service; breakfast is served à la carte. The hotel is about a five-minute walk from the town center and the beach. ⊠ *Plageiá, 34007* ☎ *22220/91964, 22220/92060, or 22220/91481* 🖷 *22220/92061* ⊕ *www.skyros-nefeli.gr* ➫ *4 apartments, 7 studios, 8 rooms, 2 suites* ⊸ *In-room: kitchen (some), refrigerator. In-hotel: restaurant, bar, pool, no elevator* ▭ *AE, DC, MC, V.*

NIGHTLIFE

Skyros town's bars are seasonal affairs, offering loud music in summer. **Apokalypsis** (⊠*Next to post office*) plays hits from the '60s and '70s. Jazz and blues are the standards at **Calypso** (⊠*Agora*), the oldest bar-club.

At **Rodon** (⊠*Agora*), the owner, Takis, is also the DJ spinning the best tunes in town. **Stone** (⊠*South of Skyros town*) is popular with the disco crowd.

SHOPPING

Want to buy something really unusual for a shoe lover? Check out the multi-thong *trohadia,* worn with pantaloons by Skyrian men as part of their traditional costume. Just as unique, Skyrian pottery and Skyrian furniture are famous around the country. The pottery is both utilitarian and decorative, and the distinctive wooden furniture is easily recognizable by its traditional carved style. Although you will see it all over town, the best places to shop are all on the agora. Skyrian furniture can be shipped anywhere. Don't try to shop between 2 and 6 PM, as all stores close for siesta.

CLOTHING You can find the conversation-stopping trohadia at the **Argo Shop** (⊠*Off Rupert Brooke Sq.* ☎*No phone*).

FURNITURE The workshop of **Lefteris Avgoklouris** (⊠*About 100 yds from Rupert Brooke Sq. on right side of road heading down hill* ☎*22220/91106*), a carpenter with flair, is open to visitors. Ask around to find other master carpenters and craftspersons who make original furniture and other artistic handicrafts.

POTTERY The best store selling Skyrian handmade ceramics and imports is **Ergastiri** (⊠*Agora* ☎*22220/91559*).

MAGAZIA & MOLOS ΜΑΓΑΖΙΑ & ΜΩΛΟΣ

1 km (½ mi) northeast of Skyros town.

Coastal expansions of the main town, these two resort areas are the places to stay if you love to swim. Magazia, where the residents of Horio used to have their storehouses and wine presses, and Molos, a bit farther north, where the small fishing fleet anchors, are both growing fast. You can sunbathe, explore the isolated coastline, and stop at sea caves for a swim. Nearby are rooms to rent and tavernas serving the day's catch and local wine. From here, Skyros town is only 15 minutes away, along the steps that lead past the archaeological museum to Rupert Brooke Square.

At the August 15 **Panagia** *(Festival of the Virgin)* on the beach at Magazia, children race on the island's domesticated small ponies, similar to Shetland ponies.

BEACHES

From **Molos** to **Magazia** is a long, sandy beach. A short walk south of Magazia, **Pourias** offers good snorkeling, and nearby on the cape is a small treasure: a sea cave turned into a chapel. North of Molos, past low hills, fertile fields, and the odd farmhouse, a dirt road leads to the beach at **Palamari.**

WHERE TO STAY

$–$$ ⚏ **Perigiali.** Unlike other options in this area, Perigiali has many of the comforts of home and a few that home may be lacking—like private terraces and a pretty, verdant garden with plenty of shade, where you can relax over breakfast or drinks in summer. Located near Magazia beach, the accommodations are simple, and simply decorated with traditional touches. Breakfast isn't included, but fridges and cookers in rooms mean you can prep your own with a trip to the nearby minimarket. ⊠ *On the beachfront at the foot of Skyros town 34007Magazia* ☎*22220/91889 or 22220/92075* 🖷*22220/92770* ⊕*www.perigiali. com* 🛏*12 rooms* △*In-room: refrigerator. In-hotel: restaurant, pool, no elevator* ▭*AE, MC, V.*

$–$$ ⚏ **Skiros Palace.** With a big freshwater pool and a gorgeous, isolated beach, this is a water lover's dream. Separate white, low-rise cubist buildings have arched windows and flat roofs. Rooms decorated with traditional Aegean furnishings offer simple wood beds, chairs, desks, and verandas; upstairs rooms also have air-conditioning. ⊠*North of Molos, 34007Girismata, Kambos* ☎*22220/91994 or 22220/92212* 🖷*22220/92070* ⊕*www.skiros-palace.gr* 🛏*80 rooms* △*In-room: no a/c (some), refrigerator, no TV. In-hotel: restaurant, pool, no elevator* ▭*AE, MC, V* ☉*Closed Oct.–June* ⦿*CP.*

NIGHTLIFE

For late-night dancing, the best club is **Skiropoulo** (⊠*On beach before Magazia* ☎*No phone* ☉*Closed Oct.–Apr.*). Music is Western at first and later on, Greek. A laser lighting system illuminates the rocks of the acropolis after the sun has gone down. The club can be reached from Rupert Brooke Square by descending the steps past the archaeological museum.

ATSITSA ΑΤΣΙΤΣΑ

14 km (9 mi) west of Molos.

On the northwest coast, pine forests grow down the rocky shore at Atsitsa. The beaches north of town—Kalogriá and Kyra Panagia—are sheltered from the strong northern winds called the *meltemi.*

The road south from Atsitsa deteriorates into a rutted track, nerve-wracking even for experienced motorbike riders. If you're feeling fit and the weather's good, however, consider the challenging 6-km (4-mi) trek around the headland to **Ayios Fokas** (⊠*5 km [3 mi] south of Atsitsa*). There are three lovely white-pebbled beaches and a small taverna where Kyria Kali serves her husband's just-caught fish with her own vegetables, homemade cheese, and bread. She also rents out a couple of very basic rooms without electricity or plumbing.

On July 27, the chapel of **Ayios Panteleimon** (✉ *On dirt road south of Atsitsa*) holds a festival in honor of its patron saint.

Skyros Centre, founded in 1978, was the first and remains the foremost center in Europe for holistic vacations. Participants come for a two-week session, staying in straw huts or in the main building, all surrounded by pines and facing the sea, and can take part in activities as diverse as windsurfing, creative writing with well-known authors, art, tai chi, yoga, massage, dance, drama, and psychotherapy. Courses also take place in Skyros town, where participants live in villagers' traditional houses. Skyros Centre's courses are highly reputed. Contact the London office well in advance of leaving for Greece. ✉ *Atsitsa coast* ✆ *Prince of Wales road 92, LondonNW5 3NE, U.K.* ☎ *207/267–4424 or 207/284–3065* 🖷 *207/284–3063* ⊕ *www.skyros.co.uk.*

> ### THE WAY THE WIND BLOWS
>
> As of this writing, government and conservationists are locked in battle over putting a 100-turbine wind farm in the island's barren southeast. While the government sees it as a means to increase the country's sustainable energy sources, conservationists say it could be the death knell for the rare Skyrian horses and bird species that live there.

EN ROUTE All boats and hydrofoils to Skyros dock at the tiny port of **Linaria** (✉ *18 km [11 mi] southeast of Atsitsa, 10 km [6 mi] south of Skyros town*) because the northeast coast is either straight, sandy beach, or steep cliffs. A bus to Skyros town meets arrivals. To get to the otherwise inaccessible sea caves of Pentekáli and Diaryptí, you can take a caïque from here. This dusty area offers scenes of fishermen tending their bright-yellow nets and not much more.

VOUNO ΒΟΥΝΟ

Via Loutro, 5 km (3 mi) northwest of Linaria; access to southern territory starts at Ahilli, 4 km (2½ mi) south of Skyros town and 25 km (15 ½ mi) from Atsitsa.

In the mountainous southern half of Skyros, a passable dirt road heads south at the eastern end of the isthmus, from Aspous to Ahilli. The little bay of Ahilli (from where legendary Achilles set sail with Odysseus) is a yacht marina. Some beautiful, practically untouched beaches and sea caves are well worth the trip for hard-core explorers.

Thorny bushes warped into weird shapes, oleander, and rivulets running between sharp rocks make up the landscape; only goats and Skyrian ponies can survive this desolate environment. Many scholars consider the beautifully proportioned, diminutive horses to be the same breed as the horses sculpted on the Parthenon frieze. They are, alas, an endangered species, and only about 100 survive.

Pilgrims to **Rupert Brooke's grave** should follow the wide dirt road through the Vouno wilderness down toward the shore. As you reach the valley, you can catch sight of the grave in an olive grove on your left. He was buried the same night he died on Skyros, and his marble grave was immortalized with his prescient words, "If I should die think only this of me:/ That there's some corner of a foreign field/ That is forever England." Restored by the British Royal Navy in 1961, the grave site is surrounded by a stout wrought-iron and cement railing. You also can arrange for a visit by taxi or caïque in Skyros town.

BEACHES
The beach of **Kalamitsa** is 4 km (2½ mi) along the road south from Ahilli. Three tavernas are at this old harbor. The inviting, deserted **Kolymbada** beach is 5 km (3 mi) south of Kalamitsa.

SPORADES ESSENTIALS

TRANSPORTATION

BY AIR
CARRIERS Olympic Airways flies daily in summer to Skiathos from Athens International Airport. The trip takes 50 minutes; the fare is €65 one way. In summer there are also weekly Olympic Airways flights from Athens to Skyros Airport. The flight takes 35 minutes; the fare is €40 one way. Skopelos has no air service.

Contact Olympic Airways (☎ *80111/44444 within Greece, 210/966–6666 in Athens* ⊕ *www.olympicairlines.gr*).

AIRPORTS Skiathos Airport handles direct charter flights from many European cities.

Contacts Athens International Airport (✉ *Spata* ☎ *210/353–0000*). **Skiathos Airport** (✉ *1 km [½ mi] northeast of Skiathos town* ☎ *24270/22049 or 24270/23300*). **Skyros Airport** (✉ *11 km [7 mi] northwest of Skyros town* ☎ *22220/91600*).

BY BOAT & FERRY
Ferry travel to Skiathos and Skopelos requires that you drive or take a bus to Agios Konstantinos, located a couple of hours north of Athens, near Volos. Altogether, there are at least two or three ferries per day (regular, or the fast Flying Dolphin hydrofoils) in summer from Agios Konstantinos to Skiathos and Skopelos; fewer in winter. There are also some ferries from Volos and Thessaloniki. For all ferries, it's best to call a travel agency (Alonissos Travel for Thessaloniki and Agios Konstantinos, Vlaikos Travel for Volos and Agios Konstantinos) ahead of time to check schedules and prices, which change seasonally. Tickets are available from several travel agents on the dock. The fast ferry from Agios Konstantinos costs €23 to Skiathos and takes one hour; the fare is higher to continue on to Skopelos (€27). The regular ferry takes twice as long and costs half as much.

Getting to Skyros is equally tricky. You must drive or take a bus to Kimi—on the large Sporades island of Evia—and then catch one of the two daily ferries, or the weekly hydrofoil, to Skyros. You can buy ferry tickets at the Kimi dock when you get off the bus; the trip to Skyros takes two hours and costs €8.30. Should you choose to book your return when you get to Skyros, note that Skyros Travel (⇨ *Tour Options*) has a virtual monopoly on hydrofoil tickets.

BETWEEN THE ISLANDS
Regular ferries connect Skiathos and Skopelos; between Skyros and the other Sporades there is no regular boat service. The once-per-week Flying Dolphin hydrofoil that travels from Kimi, on the large nearby island of Evia, to all the Sporades is by far the quicker, more reliable way to travel between the islands. Because schedules change frequently, check the times listed outside travel agencies in each of the port towns; the agents sell tickets. Connecting through Kimi is the easiest way to get between Skyros and the other islands (the alternative is to fly through Athens).

ON THE ISLANDS
On all islands, caïques leave from the main port for the most popular beaches, and interisland excursions are made between Skiathos and Skopelos. You can also hire a caïque (haggle over the price) to tour around the islands; they are generally the preferred way to get around by day. For popular routes, captains have signs posted showing their destinations and departure times. On Skyros, check with Skyros Travel for caïque tours.

Contacts Flying Dolphin (☎ *21041/99000* ⊕ *www.hellenicseaways.gr*). **Port Authority** (☎ *22350/31759 in Agios Konstantinos, 22220/22606 in Kimi, 24270/22017 in Skiathos town, 24240/22180 in Skopelos town, 22220/91475 in Skyros town*).

Vlaikos Travel (☎ *24240/65220*).

BY BUS
From central Athens, buses to Agios Konstantinos, the main port for the Sporades (except Skyros), cost €11.50 and take about 2½ hours. Buses from Athens to Kimi, on Evia island (the only port where boats depart for Skyros), cost €11 and take 2½ hours. For those connecting to Agios Konstantinos from Halkidha, on Evia island, the bus costs €8 and takes 1½ hours. Check the **KTEL** (⊕ *www.ktel.org*) site for schedules.

Buses on Skiathos leave Skiathos town to make the beach run as far as Koukounaries every 30 minutes from early morning until 11:30 PM. Buses on Skopelos run six times a day from Skopelos town to Glossa and Loutraki, stopping at the beaches. Skyros buses carry ferry passengers between Linaria and Horio, stopping in Molos in summer.

Information Athens to Agios Konstantinos (☎ *210/831–7147 in Athens*). **Athens to Skyros** (☎ *210/831–7163 in Athens*). **Ceres Lines bus** (☎ *210/428–0001 in Piraeus*). **KTEL bus station** (☎ *22210/22026 in Halkidha*).

CLOSE UP

Paradise Found: The Pelion Peninsula

An incredibly charming landscape of stone churches, elegant houses adorned with rose arbors, and storybook town squares lies across the water from Skiathos on the mainland, about 320 km (200 mi) northeast of Athens.

The Pelion peninsula—three hours by ferry or 1½ hrs by hydrofoil traveling east of Skiathos town—looms large in myth and legend. Jason and the Argonauts are said to have embarked from the port of ancient Iolkos, once set opposite modern Volos, on the northwestern tip of the peninsula, to make good a vague claim to the Golden Fleece.

Mt. Pelion, still thickly wooded with pine, cypress, and fruit trees, was the home of the legendary Centaurs, those half-man–half-horse beings notorious for lasciviousness and drunkenness. Here, too, on a cypress-clad hill overlooking Volos, was the site of the wedding banquet of the nymph Peleus and the mortal Thetis. Uninvited, the goddess of discord, Eris, flung a golden apple between Athena and Aphrodite, asking Prince Paris of Troy to decide who was the fairest (and thereby giving Homer one heck of a plot).

Today the peninsula is much more peaceful, dotted with no fewer than 24 lovely villages. As you leave Volos (having explored its waterfront esplanade and splendid archaeological museum), you ascend along serpentine roads into the cooler mountains, enjoying great views over Volos Bay.

Some roads wind down to beautiful white-sand or round-stone beaches, such as Horefto and Milopotamos. Nestled among the forests are villages such as Tsangarades, Milies (with the

beautifully frescoed Ag Taxiarchis church), and Vyzitsa, while high above Volos is exquisite Portaria, whose kokkineli (fresh red wine) has to be consumed on the spot, as it does not stand up well to transport.

Neither visitors nor locals complain of this. Separated from Portaria by a deep ravine is Makrynitsa, incredibly rich in local color. The village square is straight out of fairyland: the large, paved terrace overhangs the town and gulf below, yet feels intimate thanks to a backdrop of huge plane trees that shade a small Byzantine church and a lulling fountain.

Most of the Pelion villages have archetypal Greek houses—replete with bay windows, stained glass, and ornamentation—whose elegance cannot be bettered.

To get to Pelion from Skiathos by car, take the three-hour ferry down to Volos; you can also board the hydrofoil and rent a car in Pelion. There is daily train service to Volos from Athens's Stathmos Larissa station (this ride takes six hours).

For information on the Pelion peninsula and accommodations in the lovely government-renovated village inns, contact the **EOT** (⊠ *Riga Fereous, Volos* ☎ *24210/23500* ☾*open weekdays 7–2:30).*

Embarking on a latter-day *Odyssey*: Yalos harbor, Symi, the Dodecanese.

The glory that was Athens can be found at the Parthenon (top); Greek soul—icons for sale in Athens's Plaka district (bottom).

Set on Corfu, Pontikonisi is some enchanted islet (top); Hydra is a car-less universe (bottom).

A dip into the turquoise waters of Lalaria Beach, Skiathos (top); a bar on the beach in Kastro, Skiathos, the Sporades (bottom).

Fish tales are often told at Molyvos on Lesbos (top); Viewing Crete's pretty coastline is a shore thing (bottom).

A volcanic survivor, Santorini has come back from the brink (top); Ia, one of the island's main towns, is a symphony in blue and white (bottom).

Many villages of the Dodecanese are at "see" level (top); Mykonos street view; Avenue of the Lions on Delos (bottom).

Have your camera ready: the church of Agios Spiridon, in the old quarter of Corfu town.

BY CAR

To get to Skiathos and Skopelos by car you must drive to the port of Agios Konstantinos (Agios) and from there take the ferry. The drive to Agios from Athens takes about two hours. For high-season travel you might have to reserve a place on the car ferry a day ahead.

For Skyros you must leave from the port of Kimi on the big Sporades island of Evia. From Athens, take the Athens–Lamia National Road to Skala Oropou and make the 30-minute ferry crossing to Eretria on Evia (every half hour in the daytime). No reservations are needed. Because it is so close to the mainland, you can skip the ferry system and drive directly to Evia over a short land bridge connecting Agios Minas on the mainland with Halkidha. From Athens, about 80 km (50 mi) away, take the National Road 1 to the Schimatari exit, and then follow the signs to Halkidha. Beware that weekend crowds can slow traffic across the bridge.

ROAD CONDITIONS The road networks on all three islands are so rudimentary that cars are not really needed, but it's not a bad idea to rent one for a day to get a feel for the island, then use the bus or a scooter thereafter. Car rentals usually cost €30–€50 per day, while scooters cost about €15–€25. Four-wheel drives, cars, scooters, and motorbikes can be rented everywhere. If you rent a scooter, however, be extra cautious: many of those for hire are in poor condition. The locals are not used to the heavy summer traffic on their narrow roads, and accidents provide the island clinics with 80% of their summer business. Check with the travel agencies for rental information.

BY TAXI

Taxis wait at the ferry landings on all the islands. They are unmetered, so negotiate your fare in advance.

CONTACTS & RESOURCES

EMERGENCIES

The most efficient way to get to a medical center is to ask a taxi driver to take you to the nearest facility. Emergency services are listed by island.

Skiathos Tourist Police (☎ *24270/23172 in Skiathos town*). **Medical Center** (☎ *24270/22040 in Skiathos town*).

Skopelos Police (☎ *24240/33333 in Glossa, 24240/22235 in Skopelos town*). **Medical Center** (☎ *24240/22222 in Skopelos town*).

Skyros Police (☎ *22220/91274 in Skyros town*). **Medical Center** (☎ *22220/92222 in Skyros town*).

INTERNET, MAIL & SHIPPING

Contacts Skiathos Sixth Element Internet Café (✉ *15 G. Panora St., across from National Bank of Greece, Skiathos town* ☎ *24270/29040* ⊙ *9 AM–2 AM*). **Skopelos Net Café** (✉ *In town, Skopelos town* ☎ *24240/23093*). **Internet Café** (✉ *In Patitiri on road going up from port toward Milia and Old Town, Alonissos town*). **Hellenic Postal Services** (✉ *3 Papadiamadi St., Skiathos town* ☎ *24270/22011*). **Hellenic**

Postal Services (✉ *Skopelos Town Center, Skopelos town* ☎ *24240/22203*). **Hellenic Postal Services** (✉ *Skyros highstreet, Skyros town* ☎ *22240/91208*). **DHL Services** (☎ *210/9890-000 in Athens, 24270/29058 in Skiathos, 22210/20004 in Evia Prefecture [Chalkida]*).

BOATING   On Skiathos, small motorboats can be rented at the Marine Center. Boats can also be rented at the Marine Center in Alonissos.

Contacts Marine Center–Skiathos (✉ *Near airport runway* ☎ *24270/22888* 🖷 *24270/23262*).

TOUR OPTIONS

Thalpos Holidays has a number of boat excursions that start from the island of Skopelos.

Contacts Creator Tours (✉ *New port, Skiathos* ☎ *24270/22385 or 24270/21384* 🖷 *24270/21136*). **Madro Travel** (✉ *Waterfront, Skopelos town* ☎ *24240/22145* ⊕ *www.madrotravel.com*). **Skyros Travel** (✉ *Agora, Skyros town* ☎ *22220/91123 or 22220/91600* 🖷 *22220/92123* ⊕ *www.skyrostravel.com*). **Thalpos Holidays** (✉ *Paralia Skopelou, Skopelos town* ☎ *24240/22947* 🖷 *24240/23057* ⊕ *www. holidayislands.com*).

VISITOR INFORMATION

The Greek National Tourism Organization is the authority on the Sporades. Contact the tourist police in Skiathos town for information on the island. In Skopelos, try the Skopelos Municipality.

Contacts Greek National Tourism Organization (GNTO or EOT) (✉ *Tsoha 7, Athens* ☎ *210/870–7000* ⊕ *www.gnto.gr*). **Skiathos Municipality** (✉ *Odos Papadiamndiou, Skiathos town* ☎ *24270/22200* ⊕ *www.n-skiathos.gr*). **Skopelos Municipality** (✉ *Waterfront, Skopelos town* ☎ *24240/22205* ⊕ *www.skopelosweb. gr*). **Skyros official Web site** (⊕ *www.skyros.gr*).

Corfu

Spianada Promenade, The Liston, Corfu Town

WORD OF MOUTH

"I loved Corfu . . . it's quite different from the dry islands with the white houses that you see in photos. It is lush with greenery and olive trees, for one thing, and also it has such a varied history (various empires owned it at one time or another) that you can go into Corfu town, sit under a Venetian-style arcade, eat Greek food, and hear a discussion about a game of cricket."

—elaine

WELCOME TO CORFU

TOP REASONS TO GO

★ **Corfu Town:** No matter how clogged the streets or how sophisticated the resorts, this little beauty of a city glows with a profusion of picturesque remnants of its Venetian, French, and British colonies.

★ **Some Enchanted Islet:** Hero of a 1,001 travel posters, Pontikonisi is crowned by a white-washed chapel—could tiny "Mouse Island" really be Odysseus's ship turned to stone by Poseidon?

★ **The Achilleion:** A neo-classic white elephant, this Corfu villa built for Empress Elizabeth of Austria is more than redeemed by its enchanting seaside gardens.

★ **Homer's City of the Phaeacians:** Once hallowed by Odysseus, Paleokastritsa is still a spectacle of grottoes, cliffs, and turquoise waters.

★ **Hiking Heaven:** The fully marked Corfu Trail runs 220 km (137 mi) from Lake Korisia to Mt. Pantokrator.

Enchanting Corfu town

1 Corfu Town. Along the east coast mid-island, Corfu town occupies the central prong of a three-pronged peninsula; on the southern prong is Paleopolis (Old Town) and on the northern is the Old Fortress. Between the two is the gorgeous and elegant Esplanade, from which extend stage-set streets lined with Venetian and English Georgian houses and Corfiot cafés.

2 South Corfu. Just south of Corfu town is a region that crowned heads—and heads that were once crowned—once made their own. Mon Repos was the summer residence of the British lord high commissioners (and birthplace of Queen Elizabeth II's husband). Another 16 km (10 mi) south is Gastouri, site of the Achilleion, a 19th-century extravaganza studded with a bewildering number of neoclassic statues. To remind yourself you're really in Greece, take in the famed vista of the chapel-covered Mouse Island.

3 West-Central & North Corfu. Corfu town is great for a day or three of sightseeing but you really need to head into the island interiors to find your personal niche. Many head to Paleokastritsa, where you'll discover one of Greece's best beaches; rent a boat to visit the nearby caves. Head inland to Ano Korakiana—"Little Venice"—before chilling out at the picturesque harbor town of Agni.

Hellenic temple on Corfu island

GETTING ORIENTED

Scattered along the western coast of Greece the Ionian islands derive their name from the Ionian Greeks, their first colonizers. The proximity of these isles to Italy and their sheltered position on the East–West trade routes tempted many an occupier to the main island jewel, Corfu. Never subjected to Turkish rule, the Corfiots were greatly influenced by the graciousness of Venetian settlers as well as the civilized formality of its 19th-century British Protectorate. With its fairy-tale setting, Corfu (Kerkyra in Greek) is connected by numerous ferries with Italy's Brindisi and is the gateway to Greece for many European travelers.

6

West-Central Corfu is famous for its beaches

0   15 mi
0   15 km

CORFU PLANNER

Where to Start?

Whether arriving by ferry from the mainland or another island or directly by plane, the best place to start your exploration of the island is Corfu town.

Catch your breath by first relaxing in the shaded Liston arcade over coffee and a Ionian spoon sweet—the island's specialty is kumquat—then stroll the narrow lanes of the pedestrians-only medieval quarter.

For an overview of the immediate area, and a quick tour of the Mon Repos palace, hop on the little tourist train.

Corfu town has a different feel at night, so book a table at one of its famed tavernas near the Town Hall to savor Corfu's unique cuisine.

Getting Around

You need a car to get to some of Corfu's loveliest and most inaccessible places, and the island's gentle climate and rolling hills make Corfu ideal motorbike country.

Your can rent cars and motorbikes in Corfu town. If you only plan to visit a few of the major sights and towns, the inexpensive local bus system will do.

Taxis can be hired for day trips from Corfu town.

Making the Most of Your Time

Corfu is often explored in a day—most people pass through quickly as part of a cruise of the Greek islands. Two days allows enough time to visit Corfu town and its nearby and most famous sites. With four days you can spend time exploring the island's other historic sites and natural attractions along both coasts. Six days allows you time to get a closer look at the museums, churches, and forts and perhaps even take a day trip to Albania. Because Corfu is small, you could make day trips to outlying villages and return to accommodations in Corfu town if you wish. Alternatively, you could spend a night at the hilltop Pelekas or farther north at the seaside Paleokastritsa. Don't forget to see the ruins of Angelokastro in the mountains at Lakones. Take the coast road northeast around the bay to the most mountainous part of the island and historic Kassiopi. Spend the night there so you can explore the northern beaches of Roda and Sidari, or head into the mountains to stay near Ano Korakiana.

Dining & Lodging Prices in Euros

	¢	$	$$	$$$	$$$$
Restaurants	under €8	€8– €15	€15– €20	€20– €25	over €25
Hotels	under €80	€80– €120	€120– €160	€160– €200	over €200

Restaurant prices are for one main course at dinner, or for two mezedes (small dishes). Hotel prices are for a standard double room in high season, including taxes. Hotels operate on the European Plan (EP, with no meal provided) unless we note that they use the Continental Plan (CP, with Continental breakfast); Breakfast Plan (BP, with a full breakfast); Modified American Plan (MAP, with breakfast and dinner); or the Full American Plan (FAP, with all meals). Inquire when booking if these meal plans (which can entail higher rates) are mandatory. Guest rooms have air-conditioning, room phones, and TVs unless otherwise noted.

Finding a Place to Stay

Corfu has both bed-and-breakfasts in renovated Venetian town houses and sleek resorts with children's camps and spas.

The explosion of tourism in recent years has led to prepaid, low-price package tours, and the largest hotels often cater to groups.

These masses can get rowdy and overwhelm otherwise pleasant surroundings, mainly in towns along the southeast coast.

Budget accommodation is scarce, though it can be found with effort; the Greek National Tourism Organization (GNTO or EOT) can often help.

Corfu is popular year-round so reservations are strongly recommended, especially as many hotels are closed from the end of October through March.

At Easter, the island is crammed with Greek tourists, and the availability of charter flights directly from the United Kingdom and other European cities means there's a steady flow of tourists from early spring through fall.

How's the Weather?

Corfu enjoys a temperate climate, with a relatively long rainy season that lasts from late fall through early spring.

Winter showers bring spring flowers, and the countryside is positively abloom starting in April, when the air is perfumed with the fragrances of orange blossoms, jasmine, and wildflowers.

The weather begins warming in May, although nights can be cool—be sure to pack a thick sweater—but even this early in the season the sun can be quite warm, especially when trekking through sights during the day.

By late May swimming is possible, and by June the waters have warmed considerably. July and August are the hottest months and can also be a little humid.

September is gloriously warm and dry, with warm evenings and the occasional cool breeze.

Swimming is often possible through mid-October, although after that the water can be quite cool. Late September through late October are good for hiking and exploring the countryside.

Great Flavors

Corfiot food specialties, which tend to reflect the island's Venetian heritage, are served at most restaurants and tavernas.

Those worth a try are *soffritto* (veal cooked in a sauce of vinegar, parsley, and plenty of garlic) served with rice or potatoes; *pastitsada* (a derivation of the Italian dish *spezzatino*—layers of beef and pasta, called *macaronia* in Greek, cooked in a rich and spicy tomato sauce and topped off with béchamel sauce).

Other tantalizing treats include *bourdetto* (firm-flesh fish stewed in tomato sauce with lots of hot red pepper) and *bianco* (whole fish stewed with potatoes, herbs, black pepper, and lemon juice).

Corfu doesn't have many vineyards, but if you find a restaurant that has its own barrel wine, try it—you'll rarely be disappointed.

Two drinks that are legacies of the British are *tsitsibira* (ginger-beer), often drunk while watching cricket, and the bright-orange liqueur made from kumquats, which the colonists first planted on the island.

Note: locals say the liqueur, available at any tourist shop, is an aphrodisiac.

Bottled water can and should be bought everywhere—Corfu's tap water is *not* one of its pleasures.

6

Updated by
Diane Shugart

THE IONIAN ISLANDS ARE ALL LUSH AND LOVELY, but Kerkyra (Corfu) is the greenest and, quite possibly, the prettiest of all Greek islands—emerald mountains, ocher and pink buildings, shimmering silver olive leaves. The turquoise waters lap rocky, pine-rimmed coves, and plants like bougainvillea, scarlet roses, and wisteria spread over cottages. Homer's "well-watered gardens" and "beautiful and rich land" were Odysseus's last stop on his journey home. Corfu is also said to be the inspiration for Prospero's island in Shakespeare's *The Tempest*. This northernmost of the major Ionian islands has, through the centuries, inspired other artists, as well as conquerors, royalty, and, of course, tourists.

Today more than a million—mainly British—tourists visit every year, and in summer crowd the evocative capital city of Corfu town (population 100,000). As a result, the town has a number of stylish restaurants and hotels, and coastal areas are crammed with package-tour resorts, which blight areas of its beauty. Still, the interior remains largely unspoiled, and the entire island has gracefully absorbed its many layers of history, creating an alluring mix of neoclassic villas and extensive resorts, horse-drawn carriages and Mercedes, simplicity and sophistication.

Corfu's proximity to Europe, 72 km (45 mi) from Italy and 2 km (1 mi) or so from Albania, and its position on an ancient trade route, assured a lively history of conquest and counter-conquest. In classical times, Corinth colonized the northern Ionian islands, but Corfu, growing powerful, revolted and allied itself with Athens, a fateful move that triggered the Peloponnesian War. Subjection followed: to the tyrants of Syracuse, the kings of Epirus and of Macedonia, in the 2nd century BC to Rome, and from the 11th to the 14th century to Norman and Angevin kings. Then came the Venetians, who protected Corfu from Turkish occupation and provided a 411-year period of development. Napoléon Bonaparte took the islands after the fall of Venice. "The greatest misfortune which could befall me is the loss of Corfu," he wrote to Talleyrand, his foreign minister. Within two years he'd lost it to a Russo-Turkish fleet.

For a short time the French regained and fortified Corfu from the Russians, and their occupation influenced the island's educational system, architecture, and cuisine. Theirs was a Greek-run republic—the first for modern Greece—which whetted local appetites for the independence that arrived later in the 19th century. In 1814 the islands came under British protection; roads, schools, and hospitals were constructed, and commercialism developed. Corfu was ruled by a series of eccentric lord high commissioners. Nationalism finally prevailed, and the islands were ceded to Greece in 1864.

Indeed, when you look at Corfu in total, it's hard to believe an island of its size could generate such a large history. The classical remains have suffered from the island's tempestuous history and also from earthquakes; architecture from the centuries of Venetian, French, and British rule is most evident, leaving Corfu with a pleasant combination of contrasting design elements. And although it was bombed during the Italian and Nazi occupation in World War II, the town of Corfu remains one of the loveliest in all of Greece: every nook and cranny tells a story, every street meanders to a myth. The island's northeast section has become geared to tourism, but there are inland farming villages that seem undisturbed by the civilizations that have come and gone. Corfu today is a vivid tapestry of cultures—a sophisticated weave, where charm, history, and natural beauty blend.

CORFU TOWN ΠΟΛΗ ΤΗΣ ΚΕΡΚΥΡΑΣ

34 km (21 mi) west of Igoumenitsa, 41 km (26 mi) north of Lefkimmi.

This lovely capital and cultural, historical, and recreational center is off the middle of the island's east coast. All ships and planes lead to Corfu town, on a narrow strip of land hugged by the Ionian Sea. Though beguilingly Greek, much of Corfu's old town displays the architectural styles of many of its conquerors—molto of Italy's Venice, a soupçon of France, and more than a tad of England. A multi-sight ticket (€8), available at any of the sights, includes admission to the Archaeological Museum, the Museum of Asiatic Art, the Byzantine Museum, and the Old Fortress.

6

WHAT TO SEE

🔞 **Archaeological Museum.** Examine finds from ongoing island excavations; most come from Kanoni, the site of Corfu's ancient capital. The star attraction is a giant relief of snake-coiffed Medusa, depicted as her head was cut off by the hero Perseus—at which moment her two sons, Pegasus and Chrysaor, emerged from her body. The 56-foot-long sculpture once adorned the pediment of the 6th-century BC Temple of Artemis at Kanoni and is one of the largest and best-preserved pieces of Archaic sculpture in Greece. ⊠ *Vraila 1, off Leoforos Dimokratias, past Corfu Palace hotel* ☎26610/30680 ⊠€3 ⊙ *Tues.–Sun. 8:30–3.*

British Cemetery. Flowers—rare orchids and lilies, cultivated cyclamens, snowdrops, tulips, and hundreds of wildflowers—bloom in this over-grown cemetery established in 1814, as do fascinating stories told by the stone angels, Celtic crosses, and quirky inscriptions atop the nearly 600 memorials. Along the cypress-lined paths (Greeks believe the pointed trees help guide souls to heaven) are tombs of the British colonizers, soldiers who died during the Crimean and two world wars, and more recently, Brits who so fell so in love with Corfu that they were buried here years after they'd returned home. ⊠ *Kolokotroni 22* ⊠*Free* ⊙ *Daily 9–dusk.*

🔟 **Byzantine Museum.** Panagia Antivouniotissa, an ornate church dating from the late 15th century, houses an outstanding collection of Byzantine religious art. More than 85 icons from the 13th to the 17th century hang on the walls as the ethereal sounds of Byzantine chants are piped in overhead. Look for works by the celebrated icon painters Tzanes and Damaskinos; they are perhaps the best-known artists of the Cretan style of icon painting, with unusually muscular, active (and sometimes

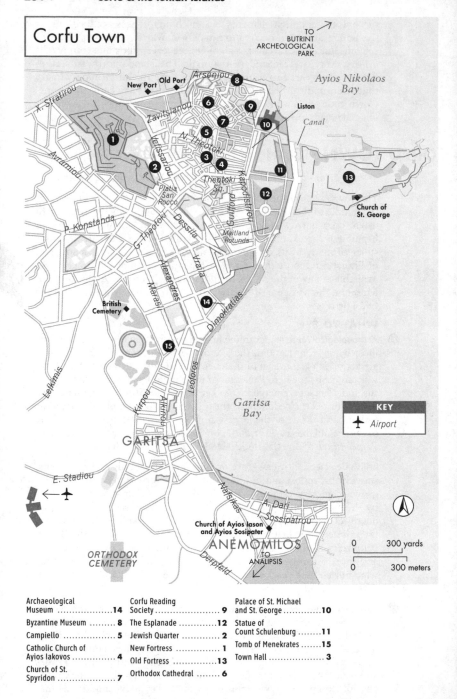

Corfu Town

TO
BUTRINT
ARCHEOLOGICAL
PARK

*Ayios Nikolaos
Bay*

New Port Old Port
Arseniou
X. Stratirou
Zavitsianou
Avramiou
Velissariou
N. Theotoki
Liston
Canal
Theotoki
Sq.
*Platia
San
Rocco*
P. Konstanda
G. Theotoki
Dessila
Vraila
*Maitland
Rotunda*
Church of
St. George
Kapodistriou
Platia
Alexandras
Marasi
British
Cemetery
Dimokratias
Lefkimis
Kirrou
Aikinou
Leoforos
*Garitsa
Bay*

KEY

✈ *Airport*

E. Stadiou
GARITSA

Narfkas
A. Dari
Sossipatrou
Church of Ayios Iason
and Ayios Sosipater
ANEMOMILOS
TO
ANALIPSIS

*ORTHODOX
CEMETERY*

Derpfeld

0 ————— 300 yards
0 ————— 300 meters

CORFU TOWN: STEP-BY-STEP

Arriving from mainland Greece by ferry, you dock at the new port, adjacent to the new port, adjacent to the **New Fortress**, with its British citadel. East of the fortress is the area of Velissariou, one of Corfu town's main streets, and the western edge of the historical center. Here is the former **Jewish Quarter**, with its old synagogue. From Velissariou, go southeast toward Voulgareos, turn left on G. Theotoki, and follow the street for about 10 minutes until you reach Theotoki Square. Ahead is the ornate, marble, 17th-century **Town Hall**. Note the elaborate Venetian design, popular throughout the town. Adjacent is the neoclassic **Catholic Church of Ayios Iakovos**, more commonly known as the Cathedral of San Giacomo. Go north on Theotoki to Filarmonikis, four blocks through the medieval area of **Campiello**—narrow winding streets filled with artisans' shops and restaurants—to the **Orthodox Cathedral**. From the cathedral, look up to see the nearby red bell tower of the **Church of St. Spyridon**, dedicated to the island's patron saint. Head north to the waterfront to explore the fascinating **Byzantine Museum**; then backtrack to the cathedral area.

Southeast from the museum, in Kapodistriou, is the historic **Corfu Reading Society**, with its grand outside staircase. From here go south two blocks to Ayios Ekaterinis. East are the colonnade of the **Palace of St. Michael and St. George** and the arcades of the Liston area. Along the central path is the **Statue of Count Schulenburg**, hero of the siege of 1716. The southern half of the **Esplanade** has a Victorian bandstand, Ionic rotunda, and a statue of Ioannis Kapodistrias, a Corfu resident and the first president of modern Greece. Relax a while, and then cross over the bridge to the **Old Fortress** on the northeastern tip of Corfu town. In the southern section of the fort is the Church of St. George, with views of Albania.

6

visserally gruesome) depictions of saints. Their paintings more closely resemble Renaissance art—another Venetian legacy—than traditional, flat orthodox icons. ⊠ *Arseniou Mourayio* ☎26610/38313 ⊡€2 ♥*Tues.–Sun. 8:30–3.*

❺ **Campiello.** Narrow, winding streets and steep stairways make up the Campiello, the large, traffic-free medieval area of the town. Laundry lines connect balconied Venetian buildings bearing marble porticoes engraved with the original occupant's coat of arms to multistory, neoclassic 19th-century ones built by the British. Small cobbled squares anchored by central wells and surrounded by high-belfry churches and alleyways that lead nowhere and back add to the utterly lovely urban space. ⊠ *West of the Esplanade, northeast of New Fortress.*

❹ **Catholic Church of Ayios Iakovos.** Built in 1588 and consecrated 50 years later, this elegant cathedral was erected to provide a grand place of worship for Corfu town's Catholic occupiers. If you use the Italian name, San Giacomo, locals will know it. When it was bombed by the Nazis in 1943, the cathedral's original neoclassic facade of pediments, friezes, and columns was practically destroyed; only the bell tower remained intact. ⊠ *Dimarcheiou Sq. next to Town Hall* ☎*No phone.*

Church of Ayios Iason and Ayios Sosipater. The suburb of Anemomilos is crowned by the ruins of the Paleopolis church and by the 11th-century Church of Ayios Iason and Ayios Sosipater. It was named after two of St. Paul's disciples, St. Jason and St. Sosipater, who brought Christianity to the island in the 1st century. The frescoes are faded, but the icons are beautiful, and the exterior is dramatic among the unspoiled greenery. This is one of only two Byzantine churches on the island; the other is in the northern coastal village of Ayios Markos. ⊠ *Anemomilos at south end of Garitsa Bay* ☎ *No phone.*

❼ Church of St. Spyridon. Built in 1596, this church is the tallest on the island, thanks to its distinctive red-domed bell tower, and is filled with

Fodor's Choice   silver treasures. The patron saint's internal remains—smuggled here

★   after the fall of Constantinople—are contained in a silver reliquary and carried in procession four times a year, along with his mummified body, which can be seen through a glass panel. His slippered feet are actually exposed during the procession so that the faithful can venerate them. The saint was not a Corfiot but a shepherd from Cyprus, who became a bishop before his death in AD 350. His miracles are said to have saved the island four times: once from famine, twice from the plague, and once from the hated Turks. During World War II, a bomb fell on this holiest place on the island but didn't explode. Maybe these events explain why it seems every other man on Corfu is named Spiros. If you keep the tower in sight you can wander as you wish without getting lost around this fascinating section of town. ⊠ *Agiou Spyridon* ☎ *No phone.*

❾ Corfu Reading Society. The oldest cultural institution in modern Greece, the Corfu Reading Society was founded in 1836. The building, filled with the archives of the Ionian islands, stands opposite the High Commissioner's Palace and has an impressive exterior staircase leading up to a loggia. ⊠ *Kapodistriou* ☎ *26610/39528* 🎟 *Free* ☉ *Weekdays 9:15–1:45 and 5:30–8, Sat. 9:15–1:45.*

⓬ The Esplanade. Central to the life of the town, this huge, open parade ground on the land side of the canal is, many say, the most beautiful *spianada* (esplanade) in Greece. It is bordered on the west by a street lined with seven- and eight-story Venetian and English Georgian houses, and arcades, called the **Liston.** The name refers to a list that the Venetians kept of lucky upper-class townspeople who were allowed to walk and linger here. Today, happily, its beauty can be enjoyed by all. Cafés spill out onto the passing scene, and Corfiot celebrations, games, and trysts occur in the sun and shadows. Sunday cricket matches, a holdover from British rule, are sometimes played on the northern half of the Esplanade, which was once a Venetian firing range. On the southern half is an ornate **Victorian bandstand** and a **statue of Ioannis Kapodistrias,** a Corfu resident and the first president of modern Greece. He was also, unfortunately, the first Greek president to be assassinated, in 1831. The restored **Ionic rotunda** was built in honor of Sir Thomas Maitland, the not-much-loved first British lord high commissioner who was appointed in 1814 when the island became a protectorate of Britain. ⊠ *Between Old Fortress and old town.*

② **Jewish Quarter.** This twist of streets was home to the area's Jewish population from the 1600s until 1940, when the community was decimated, most sent to Auschwitz by the occupying Nazis. Fewer than 100 of 5,000 Jews survived. At the southern edge of the ghetto, a 300-year-old synagogue with an interior in Sephardic style still proudly stands. ⊠ *Parados 4, off Velissariou, 2 blocks from New Fortress.*

① **New Fortress.** Built in 1577–78 by the Venetians, the New Fortress was constructed to strengthen town defenses—only three decades after the construction of the "old" fortress. The French and the British subsequently expanded the complex to protect Corfu town from a possible Turkish invasion. You can wander through the maze of tunnels, moats, and fortifications, and the moat (dry now) is the site of the town's marketplace. A classic British citadel stands at its heart. At the top, there is an exhibition center as well as the trendy Morrison Café, which has stunning views by day and international DJs spinning cool, ambient tunes at night. The best time to tour is early morning or late afternoon. ⊠ *Solomou on promontory northwest of Old Fortress* ☎ 26610/27370 ☎ €2 ⊙ *June–Oct., daily 9* AM–9:30 PM.

⑬ **Old Fortress.** Corfu's entire population once lived within the walls of the
★ Old Fortress, or Citadel, built by the Venetians in 1546 on the site of a Byzantine castle. Separated from the rest of the town by a moat, the fort is on a promontory mentioned by Thucydides. Its two heights, or *korypha* ("bosom"), gave the island its Western name. Standing on the peaks, you have a gorgeous view west over the town and east to the mountainous coast of Albania. Inside the fortress, many Venetian fortifications were destroyed by the British, who replaced them with their own structures. The most notable of these is the quirky **Church of St. George,** built like an ancient Doric temple on the outside and set up like a Greek Orthodox church on the inside. In summer there are folk-dancing performances in the fortress, and in August sound-and-light shows tell the fortress's history. ⊠ *On northeastern point of Corfu town peninsula* ☎ 26610/48310 ☎ €4 ⊙ *Weekdays 8–7, weekends 8:30–3.*

⑥ **Orthodox Cathedral.** This small, icon-rich cathedral was built in 1577. It is dedicated to St. Theodora, the island's second saint. Her headless body lies in a silver coffin by the altar; it was brought to Corfu at the same time as St. Spyridon's remains. Steps lead down to the harbor from here. ⊠ *Southwest corner of Campiello, east of St. Spyridon* ☎ 26610/39409.

⑩ **Palace of St. Michael and St. George.** Admire Ming pottery in an ornate
Fodor'sChoice colonial palace as Homer's Ionian Sea shimmers outside the windows.
★ This elegant, colonnaded, 19th-century Regency structure houses the **Museum of Asiatic Art,** a notable collection of Asian porcelains and Sino-Japanese art, as well as the **Municipal Art Gallery,** which displays work by Corfiot artists and depictions of the island's history and famous figures. The building was constructed as a residence for the lord high commissioner and headquarters for the order of St. Michael and St. George; it was abandoned after the British left in 1864 and precisely renovated about a hundred years later by the British ambassador

6

to Greece. Before entering the galleries, stop at the Art Café in the shady courtyard, where you may have trouble tearing yourself away from the fairy-tale view of the lush islet of Vido and the mountainous coast of Albania. ⊠*North end of the Esplanade* ☎*26610/30443 Museum of Asiatic Art, 26610/48690 Municipal Art Gallery* ☜*€3* ⊙*Tues.–Sun. 8:30–3.*

⓫ **Statue of Count Schulenburg.** The hero of the siege of 1716, an Austrian mercenary, is immortalized in this statue. The siege was the Turks' last (and failed) attempt to conquer Corfu. ⊠*Along central path of Esplanade.*

⓯ **Tomb of Menekrates.** Part of an ancient necropolis, this site held funerary items that are now exhibited in the Archaeological Museum. ⊠*South around Garitsa Bay, to right of obelisk dedicated to Sir Howard Douglas.*

❸ **Town Hall.** The rich marble, 17th-century Town Hall was built as a Venetian loggia and converted in 1720 into Greece's first modern theater—a far cry from the classic amphitheater pioneered in Epidaurus. A second story was added by the British before it became a grand town hall early in the 20th century. Note the sculpted portraits of Venetian dignitaries over the entrance—one is actually a lion, the symbol of Venice. ⊠*Theotoki Sq.* ☎*26610/40401* ☜*Free* ⊙*Weekdays 9–1.*

WHERE TO EAT

$$$–$$$$ ✕**To Dimarcheio.** Menu items like marinated salmon with fennel and
★ veal carpaccio reflect the chef's classic French training. But ask the waiter what else is in the kitchen, and he may reel off a list of hearty village favorites that includes a rich *soffritto* (veal cooked in a sauce of vinegar, parsley, and plenty of garlic), *pastitsada* (a derivation of the Italian dish *spezzatino*—layers of beef and pasta, called *macaronia* in Greek, cooked in a rich and spicy tomato sauce and topped off with béchamel sauce), and pork stewed with celery, leeks, and wine. You won't go wrong choosing from among them. In June you can sit beneath a jacaranda tree's electric-blue flowers; year-round the outdoor tables of the Town Hall restaurant overlook the comings and goings at that elegant building. Reservations are recommended on weekends. ⊠*Dimarcheiou Sq.* ☎*26610/39031* ☐*AE, DC, MC, V.*

$$$–$$$$ ✕**Venetian Well.** Tables organized around a 17th-century well, a staff that tiptoes past lingering lovers—the scene is as delicious as the food. In a Venetian building, on the most charming little square in the old town, operatic and traditional music accompanies the Greek and international specialties. Creative entrées include crepes with spinach and green-tea sauce, and wild boar. ⊠*Kremasti Sq. across from Church of the Panagia* ☎*26610/44761* ☜*Reservations essential* ☐*MC, V* ⊙*No lunch Sun.*

$$–$$$$ ✕**Bellisimio.** Contrary to its Italian-sounding name, this is a traditional, family-run Greek taverna where owner Stavros invites you into the kitchen to look at the available food. Here you can relax, away from the bustling crowds, on a quiet square and eat traditional favorites such as *briam* (a mixture of eggplant, zucchini, and potatoes in olive oil and

tomato sauce). Only Corfiot wine is sold, in order to keep prices afford-able. ⊠*Lemonia Sq. off N. Theotoki* ☎*26610/41112* ⊟*No credit cards* ⊘*Closed Nov.–Apr. No lunch Sun.*

$$–$$$ ✗**Aegli.** More than 100 different dishes, both local and international, are on the menu. Start with a plate of baked artichokes, then move on to perfectly executed Corfiot classics such as spicy swordfish *bourdetto* (firm-flesh fish stewed in tomato sauce with lots of hot red pepper), or the more-unusual *arnaki kleftiko* (lamb cooked as the *kleftes,* War of Independence fighters, liked it), with onions, olives, mustard, and feta cheese. Tables in front, with comfortable armchairs and spotless tablecloths, overlook the nonstop parade on the Esplanade at Liston. Aegli keeps late hours, serving drinks and sweets midnight until 2 AM. ⊠*Kapodistriou 23, Liston* ☎*26610/31949* ⊟*AE, MC, V.*

$$–$$$ ✗**Gerekos.** One of the island's most famous seafood tavernas, Gerekos's raw materials are supplied daily by the family's own fishing boats. The menu varies according to the catch and the season, but the friendly staff will guide your choice. For a light *meze,* opt for a table on the terrace and try the whitefish *me ladi* (cooked in olive oil, garlic, and pepper) with a salad and some crisp white wine while deciding. ⊠*Kondokali Bay, 6 km (4 mi) north of Corfu town* ☎*26610/91281* ⚓*Reservations essential* ⊟*AE, V.*

$$–$$$ ✗**Rex.** A friendly Corfiot restaurant in a 19th-century town house, Rex
★ has been a favorite for nearly 100 years, and with good reason. Classic local specialties such as a hearty and meaty pastitsada, *stifado* (meat stewed with sweet onions, white wine, garlic, cinnamon, and spices), and *stamna* (lamb baked with potatoes, rice, beans, and cheese) are reliably delicious. Dishes such as rabbit stewed with fresh figs and chicken with kumquats are successful twists on the regional fare. Outside tables are perfect for people-watching on the Liston. ⊠*Kapodistriou 66, west of Liston* ☎*26610/39649* ⊟*AE, V.*

WHERE TO STAY

$$$$ ▥**Corfu Palace.** Get away from the town center, and gaze out over
★ the bay from spacious rooms decorated with Louis XIV–style furni-ture. Every room has a sea-view balcony and a huge marble bathroom. The two restaurants both have seating in the lush gardens adjacent to the sprawling pool, and once a week there's a barbecue. You can book a tennis court at the nearby Corfu Tennis Club and hire facili-ties at the Corfu Yacht Club. Three days a week a shuttle runs to the beach at Glyfada on the west coast. ⊠*Leoforos Dimokratias 2, 49100* ☎*26610/39485* ╠*26610/31749* ⊕*www.corfupalace.com* ↩*101 rooms, 11 suites* ⚘*In-room: refrigerator. In-hotel: 2 restaurants, bars, pool, spa* ⊟*AE, DC, MC, V.*

$$$–$$$$ ▥**Corfu Imperial.** A deluxe resort complex—run by top Greek chain Gre-cotel—juts into Komeno Bay atop a 14-acre peninsula. Luxury rooms, bungalows, and villas (several with private pools), provide comfortable elegance—and balconies with sea views. The eight suites, all different, have large living rooms and bathrooms with whirlpool tubs, and the Presidential Suite also has a dining room and a dramatic view across the Ionian Sea to the shores of Albania. Though extensive, the prop-

6

erty blends harmoniously with the lush landscape of olive, palm, and cypress trees and colorful gardens. ⊠*Komeno Bay, 10 km (6 mi) north of Corfu town, 49100* ☎*26610/88400* ☎☎*26610/91481* ⊕*www.grecotel.gr* ⌨*184 rooms, 119 bungalows, 8 suites, 21 villas* ♿*In-hotel: 2 restaurants, bars, pool* ☰*AE, DC, MC, V* ☉*Closed Nov.–Apr.*

$$$–$$$$ **Daphnila Bay.** Yet another dazzling member of the Grecotel chain, the Daphnila Bay has as its star attraction the impressive Elixir Thalasso Spa, which specializes in thalassotherapy and aromatherapy. Family-oriented guest rooms are large and brightly decorated with spacious balconies; the public lounges are an elegant mix of sophisticated, high-tech design with traditional folk elements. The property is in an olive grove and surrounded by verdant pines, which sweep down to the edge of a beach. The hotel operates on an all-inclusive-rate basis only. ⊠*11 km (7 mi) north of Corfu town, 49100Dassia* ☎*26610/91520* ☎*26610/91026* ⊕*www.grecotel.gr* ⌨*126 rooms, 134 bungalows, 2 suites* ♿*In-room: refrigerator. In-hotel: 3 restaurants, bar, pools, spa* ☰*AE, D, MC, V* ☉*Closed Nov.–Mar.*

$$–$$$ **Kontokali Bay.**When you tire of exploring the streets and museums in town, this hotel is a fine place to relax away from it all. The pastel guest rooms, with modern wood appointments, are cheerful and sunlit, with balconies facing the sea, the mountains, or the lake. Umbrellas and chaise lounges wait for you on the two beaches. A buffet and a grill restaurant serve Greek and Italian cuisine, or you can order a snack from the beach bar. ⊠ *Kondokali Bay, 6 km (4 mi) north of Corfu town, 49100* ☎*26610/90500 through 26610/90509, 26610/99000 through 26610/99002* ☎*26610/91901* ⊕*www.kontokalibay.com* ⌨*158 rooms, 83 bungalows* ♿*In-room: safe. In-hotel: 3 restaurants, bars, pool, public Internet* ☰*AE, DC, MC, V* ☉*Closed Nov.–Mar.*

$–$$ **Cavalieri Hotel.** Ask for a room on the fourth or fifth floor, with a number ending in 2, 3, or 4, for a breathtaking view of the Old Fortress near the Liston. The building is swank yet graceful and chock-full of history—it was built in the 18th century and is a landmark of old Corfu. Rooms have polished wood furniture and old brass fixtures, though the bathrooms are a little cramped. The highlight is the roof garden, where, over a drink at sunset, you have the most glorious view in town. Be warned though, the service is not always top-notch. ⊠*Kapodistriou 4, 49100* ☎*26610/39041* ☎*26610/39283* ⊕*www.cavalieri-hotel.com* ⌨*50 rooms* ♿*In-hotel: restaurant, bar* ☰*AE, DC, MC, V.*

$–$$ **Hotel Bella Venezia.** This colorful two-story Venetian town house in the center of town was operated as a hotel as early as the 1800s. The large lobby has a marble floor; a rich, polished wood ceiling; and chandeliers. The high-ceiling rooms are small but have elegant furniture, and some have canopy beds. Enjoy the buffet breakfast in the huge garden. There are no views, but that's what keeps it affordable. ⊠*Zambelli 4, behind Cavalieri Hotel, 49100* ☎*26610/20707 or 26610/44290* ☎*26610/20708* ⌨*30 rooms, 1 suite* ♿*In-room: refrigerator. In-hotel: bar* ☰*AE, DC, MC, V* ⦿*BP.*

¢   **Hotel Hermes.** The bare-bones Hermes is popular with backpackers because it has clean rooms, comfortable beds (a double, two twins, or a single), and cheap rates (as little as €28 for a double). It's not bad for a short stay, but not the best choice for a summer holiday if you value creature comforts, views, and being near the beach (the hotel is in town). The nearby daily produce market is convenient for stocking up for picnics, but it makes the hotel a bit noisy in the morning. ⊠*G. Markora 14, 49100* ☎*26610/39268* ⌂*25 rooms* ⌂*In-room: no a/c, no TV* ⊟*MC, V* ⫼*BP.*

NIGHTLIFE & THE ARTS

Past the commercial center, 3 km (2 mi) west of town is a string of discos that really don't start swinging

> ## A MUSICAL TRADITION
>
> Corfu has a rich musical tradition, partly the result of the Italian, French, and British influences evident throughout the island. The town's numerous marching bands take part in all official ceremonies, even religious observances. Throughout the summer on Sunday you can catch the local philharmonic in concert on the Esplanade in Corfu town.

until after midnight. They have names like Privelege, Hippodrome, and Apocalypsis, and they throb with the latest Euro-pop and dance hits. Incredibly loud sound systems and futuristic designs are just what the young, flesh-baring crowd wants for dancing into the wee hours. Most of the clubs have a cover charge, which includes the first drink. Greek clubs come and go by the minute, so be sure to ask the concierge and locals for the current hot spots.

BARS & CLUBS For sunsets with your ouzo and *mezedes* (appetizers), try the **Aktaion Bar** (⊠*South of Old Fortress* ☎*No phone*) on the water. The rooftop bar at the **Cavalieri Hotel** (⊠*Kapodistriou 4* ☎*26610/39041*) is hard to beat for views. Hotel guests happily mingle with locals as the scene slowly enlivens from a mellow, early-evening cocktail crowd to a more energetic partylike atmosphere.

Hip but relaxed **Cofineta** (⊠*Liston, north end* ☎*26610/25642*) has cane chairs out on the cobblestones and a good view not of nature, but of decked-out promenade strollers. At **Ekati** (⊠*Alykes Potamou* ☎*No phone*) crowds are sophisticated and older, but the volume of the live music is nevertheless high at this chichi club, where excessive baubles and Paris designer labels are in evidence. Ekati is at the end of the disco strip west of the commercial center.

Have a drink from the bar at **Internet Cafe Netoikos** (⊠*Kalokeretou 12–14* ☎*26610/47479*) while you do business online from 10 AM to midnight every day except Sunday, when the place opens at 6 PM. At the top of the New Fortress, **Morrison Café** (⊠*Solomou, on northwest town promontory* ☎*No phone*) overlooks the water and has Corfu's best DJs, who favor cool acid jazz. It stays open long after the rest of the fortress is closed to the public.

FILM Corfu town's **Foinikas** (⊠*Akadimias* ☎*No phone*) is said to be the oldest outdoor cinema in Greece. It shows undubbed international movies in a pretty courtyard from June to September. In summer, shows generally start at 9 PM and 11 PM; selections change every two to three weeks.

SHOPPING

Corfu town has myriad tiny shops. Increasingly, designer boutiques, shoe shops, and accessory stores are opening up in every nook and cranny of the town. For traditional goods, head for the narrow streets of the Campiello, where olive wood, lace, jewelry, and wineshops abound. For perishable products such as liqueurs and candies, you may do better checking out the supermarkets than buying in the old town. Most of the shops listed below are in the Campiello and are open May to October, from 8 AM until late (whenever the last tourist leaves); they're generally closed September to April. Stores in outlying shopping areas tend to close Monday, Wednesday, and Saturday afternoons at 2:30 PM, and all day Sunday.

Alexis Traditional Products. For locally made wines and spirits, including kumquat liqueur and marmalade, go to Alexis Traditional Products. Traditional sweets, local olive oil, olives, and olive oil soap—as well as honey, herbs, and spices—are also sold. ⊠*Solomou 10–12, Spilia* ☎*26610/21831.*

Katafigio. You can take a replica of your favorite museum artifact home with you from this shop. There's also a display of chess sets, some of which have pieces depicting ancient Greek heroes. ⊠*N. Theotoki 113* ☎*26610/43137.*

Mironis Olive Wood. Bowls, sculptures, wooden jewelry, and much more are crammed into two tiny family-run shops. Smaller items are made as you watch. ⊠*Filarmonikis 27* ☎*26610/40621* ⊠*Agiou Spyridon 65* ☎*26610/40364.*

Nikos Sculpture and Jewellery. Nikos makes original gold and silver jewelry designs, and sculptures in cast bronze; they're expensive, but worth it. ⊠*Paleologou 50* ☎*26610/31107* ⊠*N. Theotoki 54* ☎*26610/32009* ⊕*www.nikosjewellery.gr.*

Rolandos. Visit the talented artist Rolando and watch him at work on his paintings and handmade pottery. ⊠*N. Theotoki 99* ☎*26610/45004.*

SOUTH CORFU ΝΟΤΙΑ ΚΕΡΚΥΡΑ

Outside Corfu town, near the suburb of Kanoni, are several of Corfu's most unforgettable sights, including the lovely view of the island of Pontikonisi. The nearby palace and grounds of Mon Repos were once owned by Greece's royal family and are open to the public as a museum. A few villages south of Benitses, and some on the island's southern tip, are usually overrun with raucous package-tour groups. If you seek a hard-drinking, late-night crowd, and beaches chockablock with activities and tanning bodies, head there. If you're looking for more-solitary nature in the south, take a trip to Korisia.

KANONI KANONI

5 km (3 mi) south of Corfu town.

At Kanoni, the site of the ancient capital, you may behold Corfu's most famous view, which looks out over two beautiful islets. Keep in mind that though the view *of* the islets has sold a thousand postcards, the view *from* the islets is that of a hilly landscape built up with resort hotels and summer homes and of the adjacent airport, where planes take off directly over the churches.

The suburb of Kanoni was once one of the world's great beauty spots, made deservedly famous by countless pictures. The name derives from a French cannon that once stood here, no doubt utterly incongruous in this once sublimely peaceful landscape. The open sea is separated by a long, narrow causeway from the lagoon of Halikiopoulou, with the intensely green slopes of Mount Agia Deka as a backdrop. A shorter breakwater leads to the white convent of Moni Vlahernes on a tiny islet. Beyond, tall cypresses guard **Pontikonisi**, or Mouse Island, a rock rising dramatically from the clear water and topped by a 13th-century chapel—one of the most picturesque setpieces in all Greece. Legend has it that the island is really Odysseus's ship, which an enraged Poseidon turned to stone: the reason why Homer's much-traveled hero was shipwrecked on Phaeacia (Corfu) in The *Odyssey*. June to August a little motorboat runs out to Pontikonisi every 20 minutes.

FodorsChoice
★

The island's only casino is in the sleek and curving hotel, **Corfu Holiday Palace.** The nearly 5,500 square feet of gaming space is open daily noon–3 AM. ⊠ *Kanoni* ☎*26610/46941.*

★ The royal palace of **Mon Repos** is surrounded by gardens and ancient ruins. It was built in 1831 by Sir Frederic Adam for his wife, and it was later the summer residence of the British lord high commissioners. Prince Philip, the duke of Edinburgh, was born here. After Greece won independence, it was used as a summer palace for the royal family of Greece, but it was closed when the former king Constantine fled the country in 1967, after which the Greek government expropriated it. Throughout the '90s, the estate was tangled in an international legal battle after Constantine petitioned to have the property returned; the Greek government finally paid him a settlement and opened the fully restored palace as a museum on the island's rich history. After touring the palace, wander around the extensive grounds, which include ruins of temples from the 7th and 6th centuries BC as well as the small but lovely beach that was once used exclusively by the Greek royal family and is now open to the public. Ask museum officials for maps and information; the pamphlets are free and useful but aren't handed out unless requested. Opposite Mon Repos are ruins of Ayia Kerkyra, the 5th-century church of the Old City. ⊹*1 km (½ mi) north of Kanoni, near Mon Repos beach* ☎*26610/41369* ☎*€3* ☉*Tues.–Sun. 8:30–7.*

6

GASTOURI ΓΑΣΤΟΥΡΙ

19 km (12 mi) southwest of Corfu town.

The village of Gastouri, still lovely despite the summer onrush of day-★ trippers, is the site of the **Achilleion.** Although in remarkably bad taste (Lawrence Durrell called it "a monstrous building"), the palace is redeemed by lovely gardens stretching to the sea. Built in the late 19th century by the Italian architect Rafael Carita for Empress Elizabeth of Austria, this was a retreat for her to nurse her health and her heartbreak over husband Franz Josef's numerous affairs. Elizabeth named the palace after her favorite hero, Achilles, whom she identified with her son. After she was assassinated, Kaiser Wilhelm II bought it and lived here until the outbreak of World War I, during which he still used it as a summer residence. After the armistice, the Greek government received it as a spoil of war.

The interior contains a pseudo-Byzantine chapel, a pseudo-Pompeian room, and a pseudo-Renaissance dining hall, culminating in a vulgar fresco called *Achilles in His Chariot.* One of the more-interesting furnishings is Kaiser Wilhelm II's saddle seat, used at his desk. On the terrace, which commands a superb view over Kanoni and the town, is an Ionic peristyle with a number of statues in various degrees of undress. The best is *The Dying Achilles.* In 1962 the palace was restored, leased as a gambling casino, and later was the set for the casino scene in the James Bond film *For Your Eyes Only.* The casino has since moved to the Corfu Holiday Palace. The exhibits on the ground floor contain mementos and portraits. ✉ *Main street* ☎ *26610/56210* €6 ⏲ *June–Aug., daily 8–7; Sept.–May, daily 9–4.*

WHERE TO STAY & EAT

$$$$ ✕ **Taverna Tripas.** Taken in the right spirit, this most famous (and most touristed) of Corfu's tavernas can be fun. The festivity kicks in when the live music and local dancers fill the courtyard (patrons join in, too), and it's not uncommon to see Greek politicians and their retinues dining here. The fixed menu has a choice of tasty *mezedakia* (small appetizers); the pastitsada and beef *kokkinisto* (roasted in a clay pot with garlic and tomatoes) are especially good. ✉ *2 km (1 mi) northwest of Gastouri, Kinopiastes* ☎ *26610/56333* 🌐 *www.tripas.gr* ✍ *Reservations essential* 💳 *No credit cards* ⏲ *No lunch.*

$$$–$$$$ **Marbella Hotel.** In an olive grove near the emerald waters of Agios Ioannis south lies the deluxe Marbella Hotel complex and bungalows. The spacious, sophisticated Mediterranean-style accommodation has amazing views of the sea or the garden from balconies that adjoin the rooms. Single rooms are available, and prices drop almost by half off-season. The Marbella is on the coast road between Benitses and Moraitika. ✉ *10 km (6 mi) south of Gastouri, 49084Agios Ioannis Peristeron* ☎ *26610/71183* 📠 *26610/71189* 🌐 *www.marbella.gr* *375 rooms, 21 suites* *In-room: refrigerator. In-hotel: 5 restaurants, pool, public Internet, parking (no fee)* 💳 *AE, D, MC, V* ⏲ *Closed Nov.–Apr.* 🍽 *MAP.*

$$ ⊞**San Stefano.** Close to Achilleion palace and 900 feet from the beach, this modern hotel commands a hill overlooking the water in 35 acres of garden. Rooms have standard hotel furniture and are rather uninspiring, but most have balconies from which to savor the coastline vistas. Bungalows have kitchenettes with refrigerators. It's hard to get bored here: there are many activities and water sports available through the hotel, and the beach lies just below. ⊠*1 km (½ mi) south of Gastouri, 49084Benitses* ☎*26610/71123* 🖷*26610/71124 or 26610/72272* ⊕*www.ellada.net/sanstef* 🖃*216 rooms, 4 suites, 39 bungalows* ⚴*In-hotel: 2 restaurants, bars, pool, some pets allowed* ▭*AE, DC, MC, V* ⊘*Closed Nov.–Mar.*

WEST-CENTRAL CORFU
ΔΥΤΙΚΗ-ΚΕΝΤΡΙΚΗ ΚΕΡΚΥΡΑ

The agricultural Ropa Valley divides the sandy beaches and freshwater lagoon of the lower west coast past Ermones from the dramatic mountains of the northwest. Hairpin bends take you through orange and olive groves, over the mountainous spine of the island to the rugged bays and promontories of the coast. The road descends to the sea, where two headlands near Paleokastritsa, 130 feet high and covered with trees and boulders, form a pair of natural harbors.

6

PELEKAS ΠΕΛΕΚΑΣ

11 km (7 mi) northwest of Gastouri, 13 km (8 mi) west of Corfu town.

Inland from the coast at Glyfada is Pelekas, a hilltop village that overflows with tourists because of its much-touted lookout point, called **Kaiser's Throne.** German kaiser Wilhelm II enjoyed the sunset here when not relaxing at Achilleion Palace. The rocky hilltop does deliver spectacular views of almost the entire island and sea beyond.

North across the fertile Ropa Valley is the resort town of **Ermones** (⊠*8 km [5 mi] north of Pelekas*), with pebbly sand beaches, heavily wooded cliffs, water with plentiful fish, large hotels, and a backdrop of green mountains. The Ropa River flows into the Ionian Sea here.

BEACHES

The beach at **Pelekas** has soft, golden sand and clear water but is developed and tends to be crowded. There's a huge resort hotel next to it. Free minibuses regularly transport people to the beach from the village, which is a long and steep walk otherwise. The large, golden beaches at **Glyfada** (⊠*2 km [1 mi] south of Pelekas*) are the most famous on the island. Though the sands are inevitably packed with sunbathers—some hotels in Corfu town run daily beach shuttles to Glyfada—many still come. Sun beds, umbrellas, and water-sports equipment is available for rent and there are several tourist resorts.

The isolated **Myrtiotissa** (⊠*3 km [2 mi] north of Pelekas*) beach, between sheer cliffs, is known for its good snorkeling—and its nude sunbathing. Backed by olive and cypress trees, this sandy stretch was called by Lawrence Durrell in *Prospero's Cell* (with debatable overenthusiasm) "perhaps the loveliest beach in the world." Alas, summer crowds are the norm.

WHERE TO STAY & EAT

$$$$ ✕**Spiros and Vassilis.** Escape the in-town tourist hordes and venture to a timeless restaurant on farmland belonging to the Polimeri family. Steak is a big winner on the classic French menu, as are frogs' legs and escargots. An extensive wine list and truly efficient, discreet service add to the pleasure. ⊠*9 km (6 mi) west of Corfu town on road to Pelekas, Agios Ioannis* ☏*26610/52552 or 26610/52438* ▤*AE, D, MC, V* ⊘*No lunch.*

$$–$$$$ ✕**Jimmy's.** Only fresh ingredients and pure local olive oil are used at this family-run restaurant serving traditional Greek food. Try *tsigareli*, a combination of green vegetables and spices, or some of Jimmy's own Corfiot meat dishes. There's a nice choice of vegetarian dishes and of sweets. The place opens early in the morning for breakfast and stays open all day. ⊠*Pelekas* ☏*26610/94284* ▤*MC, V* ⊘*Closed Nov.–Apr.*

$$$ 🏨**Pelekas Country Club.** The old family mansion of Nikos Velianitis, ★ amid 200 acres of olive and cypress trees, forms the core of this idyllic retreat. Seven impeccably furnished bungalows and four suites are decorated with antiques and family heirlooms from England and Russia; all have large verandas overlooking the gardens. Olive Press House and the François Mitterrand Suite are recommended. Breakfast treats include fresh-squeezed fruit juices and homemade jams served in the mansion dining room. ⊠*Kerkyra–Pelekas road, 49100* ☏*26610/52239 or 26610/52917* 📠*26610/52919* ⊕*www.countryclub.gr* ⏎*7 studios, 4 suites* ⑂*In-room: no a/c (some), kitchen (some). In-hotel: bar, pool* ▤*No credit cards* ⑩*BP.*

$ 🏨**Levant Hotel.** Guest rooms have small balconies to enjoy the breathtaking views (and sunsets) over the Adriatic Sea and across silver-green olive groves. The neoclassic Levant retains a touch of romance in the traditional Corfiot style: canopies hang over the beds in comfortable rooms. Start off your day with a soul-warming breakfast served on the main terrace. This hotel is under Kaiser Wilhelm II's favorite lookout point. ⊠*Near Kaiser's Throne, 49100* ☏*26610/94230 or 26610/94335* 📠*26610/94115* ⊕*www.levanthotel.com* ⏎*24 rooms, 1 suite* ⑂*In-hotel: restaurant, bar, pool* ▤*MC, V* ⑩*BP.*

PALEOKASTRITSA ΠΑΛΑΙΟΚΑΣΤΡΙΤΣΑ

21 km (13 mi) north of Pelekas, 25 km (16 mi) northwest of Corfu town.

Identified by archaeologists as the site of Homer's city of the Phaeacians, this spectacular territory of grottoes, cliffs, and turquoise waters has a big rock named Kolovri, which resembles the mythological ship that brought Ulysses home. The natural beauty and water sports of Paleo, as Corfiots call it, have brought hotels, tavernas, bars, and shops to the hillsides above the bays, and the beaches swarm with hordes of people on day trips from Corfu town. You can explore the quiet coves in peace with a pedal boat or small motorboat rented at the crowded main beach. There are also boat operators that go around to the prettiest surrounding beaches; ask the skipper to let you off at a beach that appeals to you and to pick you up on a subsequent trip.

Paleokastritsa Monastery, a 17th-century structure, is built on the site of an earlier monastery, among terraced gardens overlooking the Adriatic Sea. Its treasure is a 12th-century icon of the Virgin Mary, and there's a small museum with some other early icons. Note the Tree of Life motif on the ceiling. Be sure to visit the inner courtyard (go through the church), built on the edge of the cliff, dappled white, green, and black by the sunlight on the stonework, vine leaves, and habits of the hospitable monks. Under a roof of shading vines you look precipitously down to the placid green cove and the torn coastline stretching south. ⊠ *On northern headland* ☎ *No phone* ✉ *Donations accepted* ⊘ *Daily 7–1 and 3–8.*

The village of **Lakones** is on the steep mountain behind the Paleokastritsa Monastery. Most of the current town was constructed in modern times, but the ruins of the 13th-century **Angelokastro** also loom over the landscape. The fortress was built on an inaccessible pinnacle by a despot of Epirus during his brief rule over Corfu. The village sheltered Corfiots in 1571 from attack by Turkish wannabe conquerors. Look for the chapel and caves, which served as sanctuaries for hermits. The road to this spot was reputedly built by British troops in part to reach Lady Adam's favorite picnic place, the Bella Vista terrace (there's a café here now). Kaiser Wilhelm also came here to enjoy the magnificent view of Paleokastritsa's coves. ⊠ *5 km (3 mi) northeast of Paleokastritsa.*

WHERE TO STAY & EAT

$$$–$$$$ ✕ **Vrahos** *(The Rock).* Overlooking the rock of the bay in Paleokastritsa, where Homer's wine-dark sea touches forest-green mountains, the view here is one of those Greek keys that explain all. As for the food, the lobster and spaghetti is delicious, and the house salad is a tasty mix of rocket lettuce, spinach, and cabbage with mushrooms and croutons. The prices are reasonable considering the fantastic views. ⊠ *North end of beach* ☎ *26630/41233* ▤ *AE, MC, V* ⊘ *Closed Nov.–May.*

¢ ▦ **Casa Lucia.** The stone buildings of an olive press have been converted into individually decorated guest cottages, each overlooking a tranquil garden filled with hibiscus, olive trees, and bougainvillea. Cottages have two to five beds with colorful striped linens and a few antiques, and most have their own small kitchens and courtyard. Tai chi and yoga sessions are held out in the garden by the pool. ⊠ *Corfu–Paleokastritsa road, 13 km (8 mi) northwest of Corfu town, 49083 Sgombou* ☎ *26610/91419* ⊕ *www.casa-lucia-corfu.com* ▭ *9 cottages* ⟡ *Inroom: no a/c, no phone, no TV. In-hotel: pool* ▤ *AE, D, MC, V.*

6

NORTH CORFU
BOPEIA KEPKYPA

The main roads along the northeast coast above Corfu town are crowded with hotels, gas stations, touristy cafés, and shops. But head inland a bit and there are more-peaceful settings—dusty villages where olives, herbs, and home-brewed wine are the main products, and where goats roam the squares and chickens peck at the roadsides. Steep Mt. Pantokrator ("ruler of all")—at 2,970 feet the highest peak on Corfu—forms the northeast lobe of the island. The northern coastal area is replete with pretty coves, and it has the longest sand beach in Corfu, curving around Roda to Archaravi.

> ### HIKING CORFU
>
> Corfu's verdant, varied interior is excellent hiking terrain. There are trails to the summit of Mt. Pantokrator from the villages of Strinylas, Spartylas, and Old Perithia. The fully marked Corfu Trail runs 220 km (137 mi), winding through Corfu's most beautiful scenery, from the lake at Korisia to Mt. Pantokrator. It takes about 10 days to hike the entire trail (there are hotels and tavernas along the way), but it's possible to explore small chunks of it in a day or two. For info, read *The Companion Guide to the Corfu Trail* and *The Second Book of Corfu Walks* written by Hilary Whitton Paipeti.

ANO KORAKIANA ΆΝΩ ΚΟΡΑΚΙΑΝΑ

★ *6 km (4 mi) northeast of Paleokastritsa, 19 km (12 mi) north of Corfu town.*

Corfiots call this beautiful village Little Venice, for its narrow lanes winding through old Venetian houses painted in fading peach and ocher. Instead of watery canals, they're set against the silvery-green olive-tree-covered slopes of Mt. Pantokrator, and filled with gardens of pomegranate and lemon trees and brilliantly colored flowers. Life is quiet but happy here: old men bring their chairs out to the square, where they can drink coffee and gossip while looking out to the sea; heavenly aromas drift out from the bakeries, said to make the island's best bread; and some afternoons the town marching band strikes up a tune in the square.

WHERE TO EAT

$$$ ✕**Etrusco.** Hidden in the old mansion of a tree-filled village is one of the
Fodor'sChoice best restaurants in Greece; it's mentioned regularly on the prestigious
★ Golden Chef's Cap Awards list. Etrusco is run by the Italian-Corfiot Botrini family, whose passion for both cuisines, combined with flawless technique and creativity, results in truly memorable dinners. Chef Ettore Botrini delights with dishes like homemade *pappardelle* (flat pasta with rippled edges) with duck and truffles, and medallions of fish cooked in Triple Sec and sesame seeds. For starters try the extraordinary home-cured meats and marinated fish—particularly delicious is the salmon in aromatic oil and poppy seeds. Ettore's wife, Monica, prepares the desserts; her terrine of peaches and white chocolate is sublime. ⊠ *1 km (½ mi) east of Ano Korakiana, Kato Korakiana* ☎ *26610/93342* ⚏ *Reservations essential* ☰ *MC, V* ☻ *No lunch.*

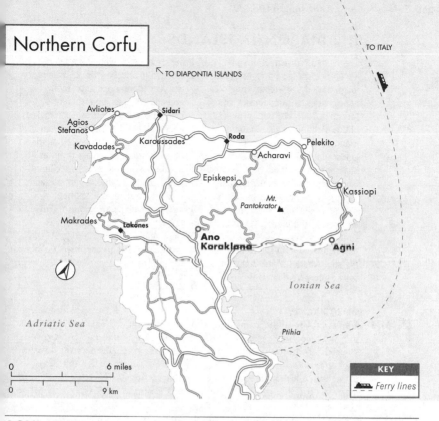

Northern Corfu

TO ITALY

↖ TO DIAPONTIA ISLANDS

Avliotes
Agios Stefanos
Kavadades
Karoussades
Sidari
Roda
Acharavi
Pelekito
Episkepsi
Kassiopi
Mt. Pantokrator
Makrades
Lakones
Ano Korakiana
Agni
Ionian Sea
Adriatic Sea
Ptihia

0   6 miles
0   9 km

KEY
Ferry lines

AGNI ΑΓΝΗ

7 km (4½ mi) north of Ano Korakiana, 28 km (17 mi) north of Corfu town.

Tiny, clear-water Agni is little more than a scenic fishing cove. Like the rest of Corfu's coast, it has good swimming, and you can rent small boats to go exploring on your own. What makes it a don't-miss destination is its three outstanding restaurants, all lining the pretty harbor. If you're doing a drive around Corfu's north coast, try to stop at Agni for lunch or dinner—or both.

The harbor town at **Kouloura**, 3 km (2 mi) south of Agni, is on a U-shape bay enclosed by cypress, eucalyptus, and palm trees and has a small shingle beach with close views of the Albanian coastline. This coastline is part of the Corfu immortalized by the Durrell brothers—much of Lawrence Durrell's writing of *Prospero's Cell* was done in what is now a taverna called the White House, south in Kalami. Donkeys still plod the roads, cafés serve local wine, and life here on the lower slopes of Mt. Pantokrator holds its sweet charm, even when besieged by tourists in July and August.

THE DIAPONTIA ISLANDS

Even with a four-wheel drive and a map of dirt roads, it can still be tough to find a stretch of truly pristine coast on cosmopolitan Corfu. Less than 7 km (4.5 mi) northwest of Corfu, the three tiny Diapontia islands look more like the untouched landscape evoked by Homer and Shakespeare. All three have beaches where you won't see anything at all beyond water, white sand, and hilltops where wild herbs and flowers wave in the breeze. The island of Othonoi also has a few ruined Venetian castles, and a cave said to be the spot where Calypso held Odysseus captive. Verdant Erikoussa has excellent fishing and a thickly wooded inland. Mathraki, where the year-round population rarely exceeds 100, has long, solitary, stunningly beautiful beaches. Each makes a memorable day trip. If you want to stay longer, each also has a handful of small hotels; there are tavernas at the harbors where boats dock from Corfu. Boats for the Diapontia islands leave three times a week from Agios Stefanos. San Stefano Travel (18 km [11 mi] northwest of Kassiopi, Agios Stefanos, 26630/51910, steftrav@otenet.gr) can help arrange trips to the islands.

WHERE TO EAT

$$$-$$$$ ✕ **Taverna Agni.** The quintessential island taverna, Taverna Agni sits on a white-pebble beach near shallow turquoise waters, with cypress-covered mountains as backdrop. The food—stuffed zucchini flowers, chicken cooked in champagne, grilled fish caught earlier that day—is just as much a reason to stop here as the setting. ⊠*North end of Agni beach* ☎*26630/91142* ⚄*Reservations essential* ⊟*MC, V* ☉*Closed Nov.–Apr.*

$$$-$$$$ ✕ **Toula's.** Of the Agni restaurants, Toula's gets the most creative with the abundant fresh seafood and seasonal produce. Many declare the fragrant shrimp pilaf to be the best they've ever tasted—cooked with lots of garlic, parsley, and chili, and a secret spice Toula's refuses to reveal. The pasta with lobster or prawns is also excellent, as are simpler dishes, like fresh grilled bream and mussels cooked in broth. ⊠*Waterfront* ☎*26630/91350* ⊟*MC, V* ☉*Closed Nov.–Apr.*

$$-$$$ ✕ **Taverna Nicholas.** Which Corfiot village dishes are available at Taverna Nicholas depends on what produce has been brought down from the mountains, and what fish out of the sea, that day. Likely as not, there will be an exemplary soffritto, cod with garlic sauce, and chicken in white wine with freshly picked herbs. The simple, whitewashed beachfront terrace restaurant has been serving food for several generations. ⊠*South end of Agni cove* ☎*26630/91243* ⊟*AE, MC, V* ☉*Closed Nov.–mid-Apr.*

CORFU ESSENTIALS

TRANSPORTATION

BY AIR

Olympic Airlines and Aegean Airlines both have two or three flights a day from Athens to Corfu town. Fares change, but the hour-long flight starts at about €180 round-trip. AirSea Lines has connections to the islands of Paxos, Ithaki, and Lefkas, and to Ioannina and Patras on the mainland; it also connects the region with the Italian port of Brindisi. Between April and October many charter flights arrive in Corfu directly from the United Kingdom and northern Europe.

Carriers Aegean Airlines (☎ *210/998–8350, 210/998–8300 in Athens* ⊕ *www. aegeanairlines.gr*). **AirSea Lines** (☎ *26610/99316* ⊕ *www.airsealines.com*). **Olympic Airlines** (☎ *26610/38694, 26610/38695, 26610/49484, or 26610/49485* ⊕ *www.olympicairlines.com*).

AIRPORTS Corfu Airport is northwest of Kanoni, 3 km (2 mi) south of Corfu town. A taxi from the airport to the town center costs around €8; there is no airport bus. Taxi rates are on display in the arrivals hall.

Information Corfu Airport (☎ *26610/89600*).

BY BOAT & FERRY

There are no ferries from Piraeus to Corfu town; you need to drive to Patras or to the northwestern city of Igoumenitsa, to catch one of the daily ferries for Corfu. You can buy tickets at the ports, or book in advance through the ferry lines or travel agents. For the most up-to-date information on boat schedules, call the port authority in the city of departure or check the Greek ferry information Web site.

Ferries from Patras to Corfu town (six to seven hours) generally leave around 11 PM or midnight. The ferries are run by Minoan, ANEK, and Blue Star lines and tickets cost about €25 per person, €70 per car, and €40 per person for a cabin. Kerkyra Lines and Cruises runs ferries between Igoumenitsa and Corfu town (two hours); tickets are €8 per person and €32 per car. Petrakis Lines and Cruises hydrofoils go from Igoumenitsa to Corfu town (45 minutes) on Sunday and Corfu town to Igoumenitsa on Tuesday (€12). International ferries between Greece and Italy stop in Corfu town at least several times a week; check with Minoan Lines.

Boat & Ferry Lines ANEK Lines (✉ *Akti Kondili 22, Piraeus* ☎ *210/419–7438* ⊕ *www.anek.gr*). **Argostoli Port Authority** (☎ *26710/22224*). **Blue Star Ferries** (✉ *Amalias 30, Athens* ☎ *210/891–9800* ⊕ *www.bluestarferries.com*). **Corfu Port Authority** (☎ *26610/32655*). **Greek ferry info** (⊕ *www.greekferries.gr*). **Igoumenitsa Port Authority** (☎ *26650/22235*). **Kerkyra Lines and Cruises** (✉ *Eleftheriou Venizelou 32, Corfu town* ☎ *26610/23874*). **Minoan Lines** (✉ *25th August 17, Iraklio* ☎ *2810/399800* ⊕ *www.minoan.gr*). **Patras Port Authority** (☎ *2610/341002*). **Petrakis Lines and Cruises** (✉ *Venizelou 9, new port, Corfu town* ☎ *26610/31649*).

6

BY BUS

KTEL buses leave Athens Terminal A for Corfu town (10 hours, €35 one way), via Patras and the ferry, three or four times a day. The inexpensive local bus network covers Corfu island, with reduced service Sunday, holidays, and off-season. Green KTEL buses leave for long-distance destinations from the Corfu town terminal near the new port. Blue local buses (with destinations including Kanoni and Gastouri) leave from San Rocco Square. You can get timetables and information at both bus depots and in the English-language news magazine *The Corfiot*.

Contacts Corfu local buses (⊠ *San Rocco Sq., Corfu town* ☎ *26610/31595*). **KTEL Corfu buses** (⊠ *Avramiou, Corfu town* ☎ *26610/39862 or 26610/30627* ⊠ *Terminal A, Kifissou 100, Athens* ☎ *210/512–4190 or 210/512–9443*).

BY CAR & MOTORBIKE

The best route from Athens is the National Road via Corinth to Igoumenitsa (472 km [274 mi]), where you take the ferry to Corfu. In winter, during severe weather conditions, the ferries from Igoumenitsa may stop running.

There is little or no system to Greek driving, and "Depend on the other guy's brakes" best expounds the basic philosophy of many drivers. The road surfaces deteriorate as the tourist season progresses, and potholes abound.

As on all Greek islands, exercise caution with regard to steep, winding roads, and fellow drivers equally unfamiliar with the terrain.

RENTALS Corfu town has several car-rental agencies, most clustered around the ports. There's a gamut of options, ranging from international chains offering luxury four-wheel drives to local agencies offering cheap deals on basic wheels. Prices can range from €35 a day for a Fiat 127 (100 km [62 mi] minimum) to €120 a day for a four-wheel-drive jeep with extras. Expect additional charges of around €20 for insurance, delivery, and so forth. It's definitely worth it to shop around: chains have a bigger selection, but the locals will usually give a cheaper price. Don't be afraid to bargain, especially if you want to rent a car for several days. In Corfu town, Ocean Car Hire has good bargains, and Reliable Rent-a-Car has dozens of options. Other agencies include Top Cars and Olympus Rent-a-Car.

A 50cc motorbike can be rented for about €25 a day and €110 a week, or a 125cc motorbike for about €30 a day and €160 a week, but you can bargain, especially if you want it for longer. Helmets are rarely provided, and then only on request. Check the lights, brakes, and other mechanics before you accept a machine. In Corfu town, try Easy Rider; rentals are available in even the most-remote villages.

Contacts Budget Zakynthos (☎ *26950/51337*). **Easy Rider** (⊠ *Eleftheriou Venizelou 50, Corfu town* ☎ *26610/43026*). **Kefalonia Rent-A-Car** (☎ *26710/27313*). **Ocean Car Hire** (⊠ *New port, Corfu town* ☎ *26610/44017* ⊕ *www.oceancar.gr*). **Olympus Rent-a-Car** (⊠ *National Stadium 29, Corfu town* ☎ *26610/36147*). **Reliable Rent-a-Car** (⊠ *Donzelot 5, Corfu town* ☎ *26610/35740*). **Top Cars** (⊠ *Donzelot, Corfu town* ☎ *26610/35237* ⊕ *www.topcars.gr*).

BY TAXI

Taxis are available 24 hours a day, and rates, which are set by the government, are reasonable—when adhered to. Many drivers speak English and know the island well. If you want to hire a cab and driver on an hourly or daily basis, negotiate the price before you travel. In Corfu town, taxis wait at Sarokou Square, Theotoki Square, the Esplanade, and the ports.

Contact Corfu Taxis (☎ *26610/33811, 26610/30383, or 26610/39911*).

CONTACTS & RESOURCES

EMERGENCIES

In Corfu town there's always one pharmacy open 24 hours; call the 24-hour information line to find out which one.

Information Corfu Tourist Police (✉ *Kapodistriou 1, Corfu town* ☎ *26610/30265*). **Hospital** (✉ *Andreadi, Corfu town* ☎ *26610/45811*). **Police** (✉ *Alexandras 19, Corfu town* ☎ *100*). **24-Hour Pharmacy Information** (☎ *107*).

MEDIA

The monthly English news magazine *The Corfiot*, written mostly by and for ex-pats, has information on events; restaurant reviews; and bus, boat, and plane schedules. It's available at newsstands and at English-language bookshops, the largest of which is Lykoudis, which also has memoirs and novels related to the island. Lykoudis also runs a kiosk that sells English-language periodicals, from *Financial Times* to *Seventeen*.

English-Language Bookstores Lykoudis (✉ *Polimnias Skaramgka Sq., Corfu town* ☎ *26610/39845* Kiosk ✉ *Kapodistriou 11, Corfu town* ☎ *No phone*).

TOUR OPTIONS

Many travel agencies run half-day tours of Corfu's old town, and tour buses go daily to all the sights on the island; All-Ways Travel is reliable. Charitos Travel has more than 50 tours of the island and can create custom tours for groups of five or more. International Tours arranges hiking, mountain biking, horseback riding, jeep trips, and other such excursions around the island. Cosmic Travel has east-coast boat trips as well as sunset and moonlight cruises from Kassiopi.

Contacts All-Ways Travel (✉ *G. Theotoki 34, Corfu town* ☎ *26610/33955* ⊕ *www.allwaystravel.com*). **Charitos Travel** (✉ *Arseniou 35, Corfu town* ☎ *26610/44611* ⊕ *www.charitostravel.gr*). **Cosmic Travel** (✉ *Kassiopi* ☎ *26630/81624* ⊕ *www.cosmic-kassiopi.com*). **International Tours** (✉ *Eleftheriou Venizelou 32, Corfu town* ☎ *26610/39007 or 26610/38107*). **Petrakis Lines and Cruises** (✉ *Ethnikis Antisaseos 4, Corfu town* ☎ *26610/31649*).

VISITOR INFORMATION

Information Greek National Tourism Organization (GNTO or EOT) (✉ *San Rocco Sq., Corfu town* ☎ *26610/20733* ⊕ *www.gnto.com*).

6

The Cyclades

TINOS, MYKONOS, DELOS, NAXOS, PAROS,
SANTORINI, FOLEGANDROS, SIFNOS & SYROS

Ia, Santorini

WORD OF MOUTH

"I'd always heard that Naxos has the best beaches in the Cyclades
and our visit there last year confirmed it."

—repete

"Yes, I would bring the ring to Santorini . . . suggest a romantic
restaurant with a sunset view of the caldera. Catch her at that
moment! If she loves you and has a pulse she can't say no."

—worldinabag

WELCOME TO THE CYCLADES

Fishing harbors dot the coast of Sifnos

TOP REASONS TO GO

★ **Atlantis Found?:** Volcanic, spectacular Santorini is possibly the last remnant of the "lost continent"—the living here is as high as the towns' cliff-top perches.

★ **Ariadne's Island:** Mythic haunt of the ancient Minoan princess, Naxos is the largest of the Cyclades and is noted for its 16th-century Venetian homes.

★ **Lively, Liberated Mykonos:** The rich arrive by yacht, the middle class by plane, the backpackers by boat—but everyone is out to enjoy the golden sands and Dionysian nightlife.

★ **Cubism, Cycladic Style:** The smiling island of Sifnos is studded with mirage-like, white clusters of houses that tumble down hillsides like so many cubist sculptures.

★ **Tantalizing Antiparos:** Hiding within the shadow of its mother island of Paros, this long-forgotten jewel has been discovered by Hollywood high-rollers like Tom Hanks and Brad Pitt.

1 Tinos. Among the most beautiful of the Cyclades, Tinos's charms remains largely unheralded but include the "Greek Lourdes"—the Panayia Evangelistria church—1,000 traditional stone dovecotes, and idyllic villages like Pirgos.

2 Mykonos. Party Central because of its nonstop nightlife, the chief village of Mykonos, called Mykonos town, is the Cyclades's best preserved—a maze of flatstone streets lined with white houses and flower-filled balconies. A short boat ride away is hallowed Delos, sacred to Apollo.

3 Naxos. Presided over by the historic port of Naxos town, largely the creation of the Venetian dukes of the archipelago, Naxos has a landscape graced with time-stained villages like Sangri, Chalki, and Apeiranthos, many with Venetian-era towers.

4 Paros. West of Naxos and known for its fine beaches and fishing villages, as well as the pretty town of Naousa, Paros often takes the summer overflow crowd from Mykonos. Today, crowds head here for Paros town and its Hundred Doors Church and great ferry harbor.

5 Santorini. Once the vast crater of a volcano, Santorini's spectacular bay is ringed by black-and-red cliffs that rise up a thousand feet over the sea. The main towns of Fira and Ia cling inside the rim in dazzling white contrast to the somber cliffs. South lies the "Greek Pompeii" that is ancient Akrotiri.

6 Folegandros. Tides of travelers have yet to discover this stark island, which makes it all the more alluring to Cyclades lovers, particularly those who prize its stunning cliff scenery.

7 Sifnos. In ancient days famed for its silver mines, Sifnos is now noted for its Siphnian cooking, its traditional pottery, and perfect Cycladic houses. The capital of Apollonia extends over three hills, offering jaw-dropping vistas.

Korissia
Kea
KEA

Merihas
KYTHNOS

Livad
SERIFOS

Adamas
MILOS

GETTING ORIENTED

Set in the heart of the Grecian Mediterranean, these nearly 2,000 islands and islets are scattered like a ring (Cyclades is the Greek word for "circling ones") around the sacred isle of Delos, birthplace of the god Apollo. All the top spots—Santorini, Naxos, Paros, Mykonos, Tinos, Sifnos, and Folegandros—are beloved for their postcard-perfect olive groves, stark white-washed cubist houses, and bays of lapis lazuli. Gateways to this Aegean archipelago include the airports on Mykonos and Santorini and the harbors of Paros and Syros.

8 Syros. The commercial hub of the Cyclades, the impressive port city of Ermoupoli is a 19th-century neoclassic spectacular, replete with opera house and town hall palace climbing up two mountain peaks.

Man climbing stairs on his donkey, Santorini

7

THE CYCLADES PLANNER

Water, Water, Everywhere

When it comes to the Cyclades, anyone who invests in a mask, snorkel, and flippers has entry to intense, serene beauty.

But even without this underwater gear, this archipelago is a swimmer's paradise.

Most of the Cycladic islands gleam with beaches, from long blond stretches of sand to tiny pebbly coves.

The best beaches are probably those on the southwest coast of Naxos, though the ones on Mykonos are trendier.

Beaches on Tinos tend to be less crowded than those on other islands in the Cyclades.

The strands on Santorini, though strewn with plenty of bathers, are volcanic; you can bask on sands that are strikingly red and black.

As for water sports, there are many options that entice many sunseekers.

Waterskiing, parasailing, scuba diving, and especially windsurfing have become ever more popular.

Note that many water sports venues change from season to season.

When to Go

The experience of the Cyclades is radically different summer and winter. In summer all services are operating on overload, the beaches are crowded, the clubs noisy, the restaurants packed, and the scene swinging. Walkers, nature lovers, and devotees of classical and Byzantine Greece would do better to come in spring and fall, ideally in late April–June or September–October, when temperatures are lower and tourists are fewer. But off-season travel means less-frequent boat service; in fact, there is sometimes no service at all between November and mid-March, when stormy weather can make the seas too rough for sailing. In winter, many shops, hotels, and restaurants are closed, and the open cafés are full of locals recuperating from summer's intensities. The villages can feel shuttered and the nightlife zilch. Cultural organizations, film clubs, concerts of island music, and religious festivals become more important. The temperature will often seem colder than the thermometer indicates: if it is in the low fifties, cloudy, drizzling, and windy, you will feel chilled and want to stay indoors, and Greece is at her best outdoors.

Making the Most of Your Time

The Cyclades are more for lazing around than for booknosed tourism. Start with the livelier islands (Mykonos, Santorini), add one or two of the larger islands (Naxos, Paros), and finish up with an untouristy one (Sifnos, Folegandros). While it is true that feverish partying can overwhelm the young in summer, in other seasons the temptations are fewer, gentler, and more profound. If you move fast, you will see little, and the beauty is in the general impression of sea, sky, mountain, and village, and in the details that catch your eye: an ancient column used as a building block, an octopus hung to dry in the sun, a wedding or baptism in a small church you are stopping into (welcome, stranger), a shepherd's mountain hut with a flagstone roof—they are endless. There are important sites such as Delos's ruins but just enjoying the island rhythms often proves as soul-satisfying.

Dining à la Cyclades

Dishes in the Cyclades are often wonderfully redolent of garlic and olive oil. Many of the islands are still more geared to agriculture than to tourism, so you can expect the freshest vegetables. Grilled seafood is a favorite, and you should try grilled octopus with ouzo at least once. Lamb is a staple in the Cyclades and a simply grilled lamb chop can be a memorable meal; lamb on a skewer and keftedes (spicy meatballs) are on many menus. Likewise, a light meal of fresh fried calamari with a salad garnished with locally made feta cheese is the Cyclades equivalent of fast food but is invariably excellent.

Finding a Place to Stay

Overall, the quality of accommodations in the Cyclades is high, whether they be tiny pensions, private houses, or luxury hotels. The best rooms and service (and noticeably higher prices) are on Mykonos and Santorini, where luxury resort hotels are mushrooming. Wherever you stay in the Cyclades, make a room with a view, and a balcony, a priority. Unless you're traveling at the very height of the season (July 15–August 30), you're unlikely to need advance reservations; often the easiest way to find something is to head for a tourist office and describe your needs and price range. Remember few hotels have elevators, and even Santorini's best often have breathlessly picturesque cliffside staircases and no porters.

Dining & Lodging Prices in Euros

	¢	$	$$	$$$	$$$$
Restaurants	Under €8	€8–€11	€11–€15	€15–€20	Over €20
Hotels	Under €60	€60–€90	€90–€120	€120–€160	Over €160

Note that luxury hotel and restaurant prices in Santorini and Mykonos are more comparable to the Athens price chart. Restaurant prices are for one main course at dinner, or for two mezedes (small dishes). Hotel prices are for a standard double room in high season, including taxes. Hotels operate on the European Plan (EP, with no meal provided) unless we note that they use the Continental Plan (CP, with Continental breakfast); Breakfast Plan (BP, with a full breakfast); Modified American Plan (MAP, with breakfast and dinner); or the Full American Plan (FAP, with all meals). Inquire when booking if meal plans (which can entail higher rates) are mandatory. Guest rooms have air-conditioning, room phones, and TVs unless otherwise noted.

Getting There and Around

Transportation to the islands is constantly improving. Five of the Cyclades have airports, and the flight is short. But if you want to understand where you are, you really should travel by boat—after all, these are islands in the fabled Aegean, inhabited even before the days of Homer. But remember that boat schedules depend on Poseidon's weather-whims, and also on the tippling gods of holidays, when they adjust. If you come for Easter, better buy tickets to and from in advance. For details on getting to the Cyclades from mainland Greece and on using island buses, see the Essentials section at the end of this chapter.

Hiking Heaven

The Cyclades are justly famous for their hiking. Ancient goat and donkey trails go everywhere—through fields, over mountains, along untrodden coasts. Since tourists crowd beaches, clubs, and ancient sites, walking is uncrowded even in July and August. Prime walking months, though, are April and May, when temperatures are reasonable, wildflowers seem to cover every surface, and birds migrate. October is also excellent for hiking—plus, olive groves provide their own sort of spectacle when dozens of "gatherers" descend upon them with nets.

7

Updated by
Jeffrey and
Elizabeth
Carson

THE MAGICAL WORDS "GREEK ISLANDS" conjure up beguiling images. If for you they suggest blazing sun and sea, bare rock and mountains, olive trees and vineyards, white rustic architecture and ancient ruins, fresh fish and fruity oils, the Cyclades are isles of quint-essential plenty, the ultimate Mediterranean archipelago. "The islands with their drinkable blue volcanoes," wrote Odysseus Elytis, winner of the Nobel Prize for poetry, musing on Santorini. That Homer—who loved these islands—is buried here is unverifiable but spiritually true.

The major stars in this constellation of islands in the central Aegean Sea—Tinos, Mykonos, Naxos, Paros, Sifnos, and Santorini—are the archetypes of the islands of Greece. Swinging Mykonos and spectacular Santorini remain the most popular of the islands, with relaxing Paros and fertile Naxos right behind them. Delicate Sifnos, the potter's island, is getting more crowded all the time, and for good reason. Tinos is espe-cially beloved by Greeks, while Syros has the Cyclades's only real city, with many notable buildings. Little Folegandros—the smallest of our islands—is for purists. No matter which of these islands you head for it always seems—at least in summer—that Zeus's sky is faultlessly azure, Poseidon's sea warm, and Dionysus's nightlife swinging (especially in Mykonos's clubs). The prevailing wind is the northern *vorias*; called *meltemi* in summer, it cools the always-sunny weather. In a magnificent fusion of sunlight, stone, and sparkling aqua sea, the Cyclades offer both culture and hedonism: ancient sites, Byzantine castles and muse-ums, lively nightlife, shopping, dining, and beaches plain and fancy.

These arid, mountainous islands are the peaks of a deep, submerged plateau; their composition is rocky, with few trees. They are volcanic in origin, and Santorini (also known as Thira), southernmost of the group, actually sits on the rim of an ancient drowned volcano that exploded about 1600 BC. The dead texture of its rock is a great contrast to the living, warm limestone of most Greek islands. Santorini's basic geological colors—black, pink, brown, white, pale green—are not in themselves beautiful; as you arrive by boat, little shows above the cliff tops but a string of white villages—like teeth on the vast lower jaw of some giant monster. Still, the island was called Kállisti, "Loveliest," when it was first settled, and today, appreciative visitors find its mix-ture of vaulted cliff-side architecture, European elegance, and stunning sunsets all but irresistible.

A more-idyllic rhythm of life can still be found on many of the other Cyclades (and, of course, off-season in Santorini). Tinos has stayed authentically Greek, since its heavy tourism is largely owing to its mira-cle-working icon, not to its beautiful villages. In the town of Mykonos, the whitewashed houses huddle together against the meltemi winds, and backpackers rub elbows with millionaires in the mazelike white-marble streets. The island's sophistication level is high, the beaches fine, and the shopping varied and upscale. It's also the jumping-off place for a mandatory visit to tiny, deserted Delos. That windswept islet, birth-place of Apollo, still watched over by a row of marble lions, was once the religious and commercial center of the eastern Mediterranean.

Naxos, greenest of the Cyclades, makes cheese and wine, raises livestock, and produces potatoes, olives, and fruit. For centuries a Venetian stronghold, it has a shrinking aristocratic Roman Catholic population, Venetian houses and fortifications, and Cycladic and Mycenaean sites. Paros, a hub of the ferry system, has reasonable prices and is a good base for trips to other islands. It's also good for lazing on long, white-sand beaches and for visiting fishing villages. Of course, throughout the Cyclades, there are countless classical sites, monasteries, churches, and villages to be explored. The best reason to visit them may be the beauty of the walk, the impressiveness of the location, and the hospitality you will likely find off the beaten track.

Despite its depredations, the presence of automobiles has brought life back to Cycladic villages. Many shuttered houses are being authentically restored, and much traditional architecture can still be found in Ia on Santorini, Kardiani on Tinos, and Apeiranthos on Naxos—villages that are part of any deep experience of the islands. In the countryside, many of the sites and buildings are often or permanently closed, though the fencing around sites may have fallen, and monks and nuns may let you in if you are polite and decently dressed—the gods may still be out there.

EXPLORING THE CYCLADES

Each island in the Cyclades differs significantly from its neighbors, so how you approach your exploration of the islands will depend on what sort of experience you are seeking. The busiest and most-popular islands are Santorini, with its fantastic volcanic scenery and dramatic cliff-side towns of Fira and Ia, and Mykonos, a barren island that insinuates a sexy jet-set lifestyle, flaunts some of Greece's most famous beaches, and has a perfectly preserved main town.

> **BEEP BEEP**
>
> When your feet prove less than bionic, it may be time to rent wheels. Many people opt for scooters, but be careful—island hospitals are frequently filled with people with serious-looking injuries from scooter travels. ATV's are the safest bets, while many places now rent Smart Cars for about 25 to 40 euros a day: these two-seaters are way-cool for getting around.

7

These two islands have the fanciest accommodations. Naxos has the best mountain scenery and the longest, least-developed beaches, and Andros, too, is rugged and mountainous, covered with forests and laced with waterfalls. Tinos, the least visited and most scenic of the Cyclades, is the place to explore mountain villages, hundreds of churches, and fancifully decorated dovecotes (*peristeriónes*). Sifnos has more than 360 churches, all of which celebrate their name day, and is the most scrupulously whitewashed.

All these islands are well connected by ferries and faster boats, with the most frequent service being scheduled in summer. Schedules change frequently, and it can be difficult to plan island-hopping excursions in advance. So be flexible and the islands are yours.

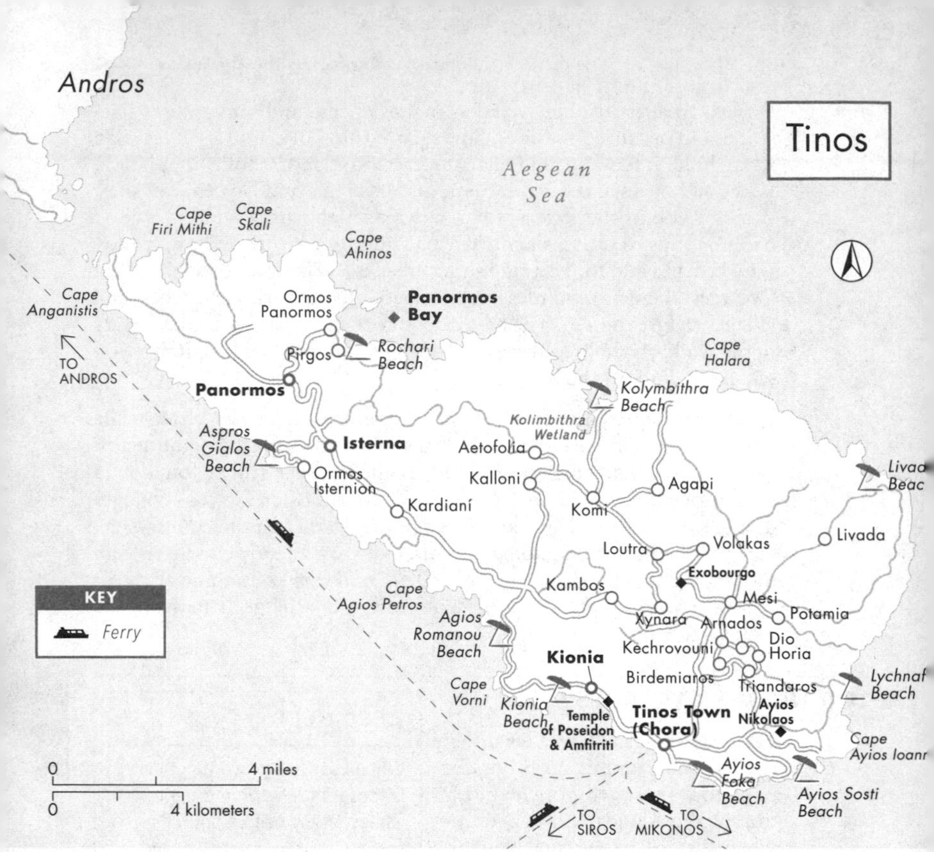

Andros

Tinos

Aegean Sea

Cape Firi Mithi
Cape Skali
Cape Ahinos
Cape Anganistis
TO ANDROS
Ormos Panormos
Panormos Bay
Pirgos
Rochari Beach
Panormos
Aspros Gialos Beach
Isterna
Ormos Isternion
Kardianí
Aetofolia
Kolimbithra Wetland
Kalloni
Komi
Kolymbithra Beach
Cape Halara
Agapi
Livada Beac
Livada
Loutra
Volakas
Exobourgo
Kambos
Cape Agios Petros
Mesi
Potamia
Xynara
Arnados
Dio Horia
Agios Romanou Beach
Kechrovouni
KEY
Ferry
Cape Vorni
Kionia
Kionia Beach
Birdemiaros
Triandaros
Lychnaf Beach
Temple of Poseidon & Amfitriti
Tinos Town (Chora)
Ayios Nikolaos
Cape Ayios Ioanr
0   4 miles
0   4 kilometers
Ayios Faka Beach
Ayios Sosti Beach
TO SIROS
TO MIKONOS

TINOS ΤΗΝΟΣ

Tinos (or, as archaeologists spell it, Tenos) is among the most beautiful and most fascinating of the major Cyclades. The third largest of the island group after Naxos and Andros, with an area of 195 square km (121 square mi), it is inhabited by nearly 10,000 people, many of whom still live the traditional life of farmers or craftsmen. Its long, mountainous spine, rearing amid Andros, Mykonos, and Syros, makes it seem forbidding, and in a way it is. It is not popular among tourists for several reasons: the main village, Tinos town (Chora), lacks charm; the beaches are undeveloped; there is no airport; and the prevailing north winds are the Aegean's fiercest (passing mariners used to sacrifice a calf to Poseidon—ancient Tinos's chief deity—in hopes of avoiding shipwreck). But for Greeks, a visit to Tinos is essential: its great Church of the Evangelistria is the Greek Lourdes, a holy place of pilgrimage and miraculous cures; 799 other churches adorn the countryside. Encroaching development here is to accommodate those in search of their religious elixir and not, as on the other islands, the beach-and-bar crowd.

Tinos is dotted with possibly the loveliest villages in the Cyclades, which, for some welcome reason, are not being abandoned. The dark arcades of Arnados, the vine-shaded sea views of Isternia and Kardiani, the Venetian architecture of Loutra, the gleaming marble squares of Pirgos: these, finally, are what make Tinos unique. A map, available at kiosks or rental agencies, will make touring these villages by car or bike somewhat less confusing, as there are nearly 50 of them. Note that of all the major islands, Tinos is the least developed for sports—the strong winds discourage water sports, and sports outfitters come and go.

> ### LOVEY-DOVEY MCMANSIONS
>
> Tinos is also renowned for its 1,300 dovecotes (*peristeriónes*), which, unlike those on Mykonos or Andros, are mostly well maintained; in fact, new ones are being built. Two stories high, with intricate stonework, carved-dove finials, and thin schist slabs arranged in intricate patterns resembling traditional stitchery, the dovecotes have been much written about—and are much visited by doves.

TINOS TOWN ΤΗΝΟΣ (ΧΩΡΑ)

55 km (34 mi) southeast of Andros's port.

Civilization on Tinos is a millennium older than Tinos town, or Chora, founded in the 5th century BC. On weekends and during festivals, Chora is thronged with Greeks attending church, and restaurants and hotels cater to them. As the well-known story goes, in 1822, a year after the War of Independence began (Tinos was the first of the islands to join in), the Virgin sent the nun Pelagia a dream about a buried icon of the Annunciation. On January 30, 1823, such an icon was unearthed amid the foundations of a Byzantine church, and it started to heal people immediately.

Fodor's Choice
★ The Tiniots, hardly unaware of the icon's potential, immediately built the splendid **Panayia Evangelistria,** or Church of the Annunciate Virgin, on the site, in 1823. Imposing and beautiful, framed in gleaming yellow and white, it stands atop the town's main hill (*chora*), which is linked to the harbor via Megalochais, a steeply inclined avenue lined with votive shops. Half Venetian, half Cypriot in style, the façade (illuminated at night) has a distinctive two-story arcade and bookend staircases. Lined with the most costly stones from Tinos, Paros, and Delos, the church's **marble courtyards** (note the green-vein Tiniot stone) are paved with pebble mosaics and surrounded by offices, chapels, a health station, and **seven museums.** Inside the **upper three-aisle church** dozens of beeswax candles and precious tin and silver-work votives—don't miss the golden orange tree near the door donated by a blind man who was granted sight—dazzle the eye. You must often wait in line to see the little icon, encrusted with jewels, which was donated as thanks for cures. To beseech the icon's aid, a sick person sends a young female relative or a mother brings her sick infant. As the pilgrim descends from

Traditional Festivals

All over Greece, villages, towns, and cities have traditional celebrations that vary from joyous to deeply serious, and the Cyclades are no exception. In Tinos town on Tinos, the healing icon from Panayia Evangelistria church is paraded with much pomp on Annunciation Day, March 25, and especially Dormition Day, August 15. As it is carried on poles over the heads of the faithful, cures are effected, and religious emotion runs high. On July 23, in honor of St. Pelagia, the icon is paraded from Kechrovouni Nunnery, and afterward the festivities continue long into the night, with music and fireworks.

If you're on Santorini on July 20, you can partake in the celebration of St. Elias's name day, when a traditional pea-and-onion soup is served, followed by walnut and honey desserts and folk dancing.

Naxos has its share of festivals to discover and enjoy. Naxos town celebrates the Dionysia festival during the first week of August, with concerts, costumed folk dancers, and free food and wine in the square. During Carnival, preceding Lent, "bell wearers" take to the streets in Apeiranthos and Filoti, running from house to house making as much noise as possible with strings of bells tied around their waists. They're a disconcerting sight in their hooded cloaks, as they escort a man dressed as a woman

from house to house to collect eggs. In Apeiranthos, villagers square off in rhyming-verse contests: on the last Sunday of Lent, the *paliomaskari*, their faces blackened, challenge each other in improvising *kotsakia* (satirical couplets). On July 14, Ayios Nikodemos Day is celebrated in Chora with a procession of the patron saint's icon through town, but the Dormition of the Virgin on August 15 is, after Easter and Christmas, the festival most widely celebrated, especially in Sangri, Filoti (where festivities take place on August 4), and Apeiranthos.

On Paros each year on August 23, eight days after the huge festival in Parikia at the Church of a Hundred Doors, Naoussa celebrates the heroic naval battle against the Turks, with children dressed in native costume, great feasts, and traditional dancing. The day ends with 100 boats illuminated by torches converging on the harbor. On June 2 there is much feasting in Lefkes for the Holy Trinity.

On Sifnos, which has more than 360 churches, the Ascension (a movable feast in May or June) is celebrated especially fervently at Chrysopigi Monastery. Many people also make the trek on June 26 to Ayios Panteleimon in Cheronisos.

On Syros, you can attend Easter services (except when they coincide) in both the Catholic and Orthodox cathedrals: how different they are!

the boat, she falls to her knees, with traffic indifferently whizzing about her, and crawls painfully up the faded red padded lane on the main street—1 km (½ mi)—to the church. In the church's courtyards, she and her family camp for several days, praying to the magical icon for a cure, which sometimes comes. This procedure is very similar to the ancient one observed in Tinos's temple of Poseidon. The **lower church,** called the Evresis, celebrates the finding of the icon; in one room a baptismal font is filled with silver and gold votives. The chapel to the left commemorates the torpedoing by the Italians, on Dormition Day, 1940, of the Greek ship *Helle*; in the early stages of the war, the roused Greeks amazingly overpowered the Italians. ⊠ *At end of Megalohari* ☎ *22830/22256* 🎫 *Free* ⊙ *Daily 8:30–3.*

On the main street, near the church, is the small **Archaeological Museum**; its collection includes a sundial by Andronicus of Cyrrhus, who in the 1st century BC also designed Athens's Tower of the Winds. Here, too, are Tinos's famous huge, red storage vases, from the 8th century BC. ⊠ *Megalohari* ☎ *22830/22670* 🎫 *€4* ⊙ *Tues.–Fri. 8–2.*

Just 1½ km (¾ mi) from Chora you'll see a copse of pines shading a small parking lot, from which a path leads down to Stavros (Holy Cross) chapel; right on the water is the unmarked **Markos Velalopoulos's Ouzeri** (⊠ *Under church* ☎ *22830/23276*), which serves *strophia* (raki), ouzo, and traditional snacks such as fried cheese or figs with sesame. This is Tinos's most romantic spot to watch the sunset. It is also good for swimming. Note that the sunken breakwater along the coastal road in front of the *ouzeri* (casual bar) is ancient.

The **Cultural Center,** in the large and splendid neoclassic building at the south end of the quay, finally opened in 2007 and has a full schedule of traveling exhibitions and a permanent exhibition of the sculptures of Iannoulis Chalepas (➪ *Pirgos, below*). ☎ *22830/22742* 🎫 *€3* ⊙ *Wed.– Mon. 10–2 and 7–9.*

OFF THE BEATEN PATH

Mountain Villages Above Chora. At night the lights of the hill villages surrounding Tinos's highest mountain, Mt. Tsiknias—2,200 feet high and the ancient home of Boreas (the wind god)—glitter over Chora like fireworks. By day they are worth visiting. Take the good road that runs through Dio Horia and Monastiri, which ascends and twists around switchbacks while passing fertile fields and a few of Tinos's most fanciful old dovecotes. After 9 km (5½ mi) you reach **Kechrovouni,** or Monastiri, which is a veritable city of nuns, founded in the 10th century. One cell contains the head of St. Pelagia in a wooden chest; another is a small icon museum. Though a nunnery, Kechrovouni is a lively place, since many of the church's pilgrims come here by bus. Out front, a nun sells huge garlic heads and braids to be used as charms against misfortune; the Greeks call these "California garlic." One kilometer (½ mi) farther on, Tinos's telecommunications towers spike the sky, marking the entrance to **Arnados,** a strange village 1,600 feet up, overlooking Chora. Most of the streets here are vaulted, and thus cool and shady, if a bit claustrophobic; no medieval pirate ever penetrated this warren. In one alley is the **Ecclesiastical Museum,** which displays icons from local churches. Another 1½ km (¾ mi) farther on are the **Dio Horia** (Two Villages), with a marble fountain house, unusual in Tinos. The spreading plane tree in front of it, according to the marble plaque, was planted in 1885. Now the road starts winding down again, to reach **Triandaros,** which has a good restaurant. Many of the pretty houses in this misty place are owned by Germans. Yannis Kyparinis, who made the three-story bell tower in Dio Horia, has his workshop and showroom here.

BEACHES

There is a series of beaches between Chora and Kionia (and beyond, for walkers). **Stavros** is the most romantic of the area beaches. **Ayios Yannis** (⊠*Near Porto*) is long, sandy, and peaceful. **Pachia Ammos** (⊠*Past Porto, reached by a dirt road*) is undeveloped and sparkling.

WHERE TO STAY & EAT

$$$ ✕**Metaxi Mas.** On a trellised lane by the harbor, Euripides Tatsionas's restaurant, the best in Tinos, turns out to be no more expensive than a taverna. The name means "between us," and a friendly air prevails. The decor is traditional—pale yellow walls, wooden furniture, high stone arches—and the staff is welcoming. From starters to desserts, the food is homemade, but with an haute-Athenian flair. For a starter, try deep-fried sun-dried tomatoes or hot eggplant slices wrapped around cheese, mint, and green pepper. Among the main dishes, the spicy lamb cooked in paper is especially succulent; the beef fillet with peppers is also exceptional. With a fireplace in winter and an air conditioner for summer, this place stays open year-round. ⊠*Kontogiorgi alley* ☎22830/25945 ▤*AE, MC, V.*

$$ ✕**Symposion.** Yorgos Visdalis's café and restaurant occupies the prettiest and best-kept neoclassic building on Evangelistria street, which is closed to traffic. Its second- and third-floor terraces overlook the Turkish fountain and the passing scene, Tinos's liveliest during shop hours. Marble stairs lead to rooms with elegant furnishings in pastel colors. The second-floor café, open all day, serves snacks and drinks. The third floor is an excellent restaurant. You might start with the ambrosia salad and follow it with burger á la crème (with mushrooms and basmati rice). His mixed plates, combining local meats and vegetables, are perfect to accompany an ouzo on the terrace. The wine list is big and Greek. ⊠*Evangelistrias 13* ☎22830/24368 ▤*AE, MC, V* ☾*Closed Nov.–Mar.*

$ ✕**Zefki.** It may say Zeyki on the sign out front but no matter the spelling, locals—who always know where to find the freshest food—love this place. Andreas Levantis has converted this old wineshop into an attractive room. The local wines and the raki are carefully chosen. He is a specialist with omelets (local eggs, of course). His main dishes include roasted local goat. The desserts are homemade and change with the season. To find Zefki, walk up Evangelistria street and take your second right. Open all year. ⊠*Alex. Lagourou 6* ☎22930/22231 ▤*AE, MC, V* ☾*Closed Nov.–Mar.*

$$$ ▥**Porto Tango.** This ambitiously up-to-date resort-hotel strives for the best in decor and service. Greece's late prime minister, Andreas Papandreou, stayed here during his last visit to Tinos. Modular Cycladic architecture lends privacy; the lobby, where an art exhibition is usually on display, has a wooden ceiling, marble floors, and Tiniot furnishings,

both modern and antique. Rooms are simple, white, and private, with basic wood furniture. There are extensive spa facilities, for ultimate relaxation. The price includes transfers. This is an out-of-town resort; you need transportation to go anywhere. ✉ *Follow signed road up hill, 84200Porto (Agios Ioannis)* ☎ *22830/24411 through 22830/24415* 📠 *22830/24416* 🌐 *www.tinosportotangohotel.com* 🛏 *55 rooms, 7 suites* ♖ *In-room: refrigerator. In-hotel: restaurant, bar, pool, gym, spa* 💳 *AE, D, MC, V* ⏲ *Closed Nov.–Mar.* 🍴 *BP.*

$$–$$$ 🏨 **Favie Suzanne Hotel.** Sleek, posh, and convenient, too: if you are willing to give up a sea view, this is the best place to stay in Tinos town. Set right in the heart of the busy town, it has two wings, with the fancier new section added in 2007. From fanlights to dovecotes, the decoration incorporates many Tiniot details. Guest rooms have massage showers and big plasma TVs. The pool, the first in town, is adjacent to a spa area. Breakfast and transfer are included in the main room rate. ✉ *Antoniou Sochou 22, 84200* ☎ *22830/22693* 📠 *22830/25993* 🌐 *www.faviesuzanne.gr* 🛏 *32 rooms, 2 suites* ♖ *In-room: Ethernet (some). In-hotel: public Internet* 💳 *AE, MC, V* ⏲ *Closed Nov.–Feb.* 🍴 *BP.*

$$ ★ 🏨 **Alonia Hotel.** Ordinary looking from the road, this is Tinos's most pleasant hotel. Comfortable, family-run, and quietly efficient, it is for you if you dislike snazzy resorts and want to be out of (but still convenient to) hectic Chora. The fairly large rooms all have dazzling views (those overlooking the pool are best) over palms and olive trees to the sea; the bathrooms have bathtubs, a rarity in island hotels. Tinos's largest freshwater pool is surrounded by lawns, trees, and gardens—not baking cement. The price includes transfers. The restaurant (¢) serves home-style meals prepared by the owners, especially son Vangelis. To start, try pita stuffed with meat or vegetables. Entrées include chicken breasts stuffed with bacon, cheese, and herbs, or beef stew with wine and onions—the menu changes, so ask what's available that day. The barrel wine is excellent. Vangelis also has inexpensive (€50) rooms in town by the church. ✉ *2 km (1 mi) from Chora toward Porto (Agios Ioannis), 84200* ☎ *22830/23541 through 22830/23543* 📠 *22830/23544* 🌐 *www.aloniahotel.gr* 🛏 *34 rooms, 4 suites* ♖ *In-hotel: restaurant, bar, pool, no elevator* 💳 *AE, MC, V* 🍴 *BP.*

$ 🏨 **Akti Aegeou.** The family that runs this little resort is lucky to own such a valuable piece of property. Akti Aegeou, or "Aegean Coast," is right on the uncrowded beach at Porto—a very pretty location (too bad there are so many modern villas being built here). All the airy rooms come with sea-view balconies, marble floors, and traditional rag rugs. The good restaurant specializes in fresh fish. A fishing caïque is set up next to the saltwater pool, which looks out to Delos. ✉ *Beach of Ayios Ioannis, 84200 Porto (Agios Ioannis)* ☎ *22830/24248* 📠 *22830/23523* 🌐 *www.aktiaegeou.gr* 🛏 *5 rooms, 6 apartments* ♖ *In-room: kitchen. In-hotel: restaurant, bar, pool, no elevator* 💳 *AE, MC, V* ⏲ *Closed Nov.–Mar.* 🍴 *BP.*

$ 🏨 **Anna's Rooms.** The best bet on Tinos for those on a budget, this is a healthful 10-minute walk from town and 5 minutes from Stavros beach. Families like this small pension since each apartment has a full kitchen. The apartments, arranged around a green courtyard, all have balconies with sea views. Except for fresh bread, there is no breakfast. The price includes transfers. ⊠ *Kiona road, about ½ km (¼ mi) outside town, 84200* ☎ *22830/22877* ⊕ *www.tinos.nl* 🖙 *10 rooms* ⟡ *In-room: kitchen. In-hotel: no elevator, public Internet* ⊟ *No credit cards.*

NIGHTLIFE

Tinos has fewer bars and discos than the other big islands, but there is plenty of late-night bar action behind the waterfront between the two boat docks. People go back and forth among the popular clubs **Syvilla, Volto,** and **Metropolis,** on the street behind the fish market next to the Archeio Bar.

SHOPPING

FARMERS' & FLEA MARKETS
Tinos is a rich farming island, and every day but Sunday, farmers from all the far-flung villages fill the **square** (⊠ *Between 2 docks*) with vegetables, herbs, and *kritamos* (pickled sea-plant leaves). In a square near town, the local pelican (a rival to Mykonos's Petros) can often be found cadging snacks from the **fish market.**

Tinos produces a lot of milk. A short way up from the harbor, on the right, is the little store of the **Enosis** (*Farmers' Cooperative* ⊠ *Megalohari, up from harbor* ☎ *22830/23289*), which sells milk, butter, and cheeses, including sharp kopanistí, perfect with ouzo; local jams and honeys are for sale, too.

JEWELRY
At **Artemis d and b** (⊠ *Evangelistria 18* ☎ *22830/24312*), owned by the Artemis brothers, Christos paints the seascapes; Dimitris, a retired captain, makes ship models; and the classic jewelry is all by Teniots. The selection at **Ostria** (⊠ *Evangelistria 20* ☎ *222830/23893* 🖷 *22830/24568*) is especially good; in addition to delicate silver jewelry, it sells silver icon covers, silver plate, and 22-karat gold.

WEAVINGS
The 100-year-old weaving school, or **Biotechniki Scholi** (⊠ *Evangelistria, three-quarters of the way up from sea* ☎ *22830/22894*), sells traditional weavings—aprons, towels, spreads—made by its students, local girls. The largest of its three high-ceiling, wooden-floor rooms is filled with looms and spindles.

KIONIA KIONIA

2½ km (1¼ mi) northwest of Tinos town.

The reason to come to this small community outside Tinos town is to visit the large, untended **Sanctuary of Poseidon** (⊠ *Northwest of Tinos town*), also dedicated to the bearded sea god's sea-nymph consort, Amphitrite. The present remains are from the 4th century BC and later, though the sanctuary itself is much older. The sanctuary was a kind of hospital, where the ailing came to camp and solicit the god's help. The marble dolphins in the museum were discovered here. According to the Roman historian Pliny, Tinos was once infested with serpents (goddess symbols) and named Serpenttown (Ophiousa), until supermasculine Poseidon sent storks to clean them out. The sanctuary functioned well into Roman times.

BEACH

The Kiona road ends at a long, sheltered beach, which is unfortunately being worn away by cars heading for the two pretty coves beyond, including the Gastrion cave, whose entrance bears Byzantine inscriptions.

WHERE TO EAT

$ ✗ **Tsambia.** Abutting the Sanctuary of Poseidon and facing the sea, this multilevel taverna home makes traditional fare. For starters try the indigenous specialties: *louza* (smoked pork), local Tiniot cheeses rarely sold in stores (especially fried local goat cheese), and homegrown vegetables. Fresh fish is available, depending on the weather. Tried-and-true are pork in red wine with lemon, or goat casserole with oregano. To get here, follow signs for TRADITIONAL TAVERNA before the Sanctuary of Poseidon. ✉ *Cement road* ☏ *22830/23142* ▭ *No credit cards.*

ISTERNIA ΙΣΤΕΡΝΙΑ

24 km (15 mi) northwest of Tinos town.

The village of Isternia (Cisterns) is verdant with lush gardens. Many of the marble plaques hung here over doorways—a specialty of Tinos—indicate the owner's profession, for example, a sailing ship for a fisherman or sea captain. A long, paved road winds down to a little port, **Ayios Nikitas,** with a beach and two **fish tavernas**; a small boat ferries people to Chora in good weather.

PIRGOS ΠΥΡΓΟΣ

★ *32 km (20 mi) northwest of Tinos town, 8 km (5 mi) north of Isternia.*

The village of Pirgos, second in importance to Chora, is inland and up from the little harbor of Panormos. Tinos is famous for its marble carving, and Pirgos, a prosperous town, is noted for its sculpture school (the town's highest building) and marble workshops, where craftsmen make fanlights, fountains, tomb monuments, and small objects for tourists; they also take orders. The village's main square is aptly crafted of all marble; the five cafés, noted for *galaktoboureko* (custard pastry), and one taverna are all shaded by an ancient plane tree. The quarries for the green-vein marble are north of here, reachable by car. The cemetery here is, appropriately, a showplace of marble sculpture.

The marble-working tradition of Tinos survives here from the 19th century and is going strong, as seen in the two adjacent museums **Museum Iannoulis Chalepas** and **Museum of Tenos Artists,** which house the work of Pirgos's renowned sculptor, and other works. ✉ *1 block from bus stop* ☏ *22830/31262* 🎟 *€5* ⊙ *Daily 10–2 and 6–8.*

BEACHES

The **beaches next to Panormos** are popular in summer.

7

SHOPPING

A number of marble carvers are, appropriately, found in Pirgos. You may visit the shop of probably the best master carver, **Lambros Diamantopoulos** (✉*Near main square* ☎*22830/31365*), who accepts commissions for work to be done throughout Greece. He makes and sells traditional designs to other carvers, who may bring a portable slab home to copy, and to visitors.

PANORMOS BAY ΌΡΜΟΣ ΠΑΝΟΡΜΟΥ

35 km (22 mi) northwest of Tinos town, 3 km (2 mi) north of Pirgos.

Panormos bay, an unpretentious port once used for marble export, has ducks and geese, a row of seafood restaurants, and a good beach with a collapsed sea cave. More coves with secluded swimming are beyond, as is the islet of Panormos. There are many rooms to rent.

WHERE TO EAT

$$ ✗**The Fishbone.** When any Tinos restaurant features fish from Panormos bay, they tell you; happily, the Fishbone always does (that is, when weather permits). This small taverna, decorated with lots of blue and two Tiniot fanlights, is on the quay; boats right out front bring in fresh fish, which owners Belasarius Lais and Nikos Menardos, brothers-in-law, serve with flare. Among the appetizers are small fish pies and mussels in mustard sauce. Fresh fish wrapped in paper to preserve succulence is a specialty; sole with mushrooms is also a top choice. ✉*Panormos* ☎*22830/31362* ▭*V* ☺*Closed Nov.–Apr.*

MYKONOS & DELOS ΜΥΚΟΝΟΣ & ΔΗΛΟΣ

From backpackers to the superrich, from day-trippers to yachties, from gays to celebrities (who head here by helicopter), Mykonos has become one of the most popular of the Aegean islands. Today's scene is a weird but attractive cocktail of tradition, beauty, and glitz, but travelers from all over the world have always been drawn to this dry, rugged island—at 16 km (10 mi) by 11 km (7 mi), one of the smallest of the Cyclades—thanks to its many stretches of sandy beach, its thatched windmills, and its picturesque port town. One thing is certain: Mykonos knows how to maintain its attractiveness, how to develop it, and how to sell it. Complain as you will that it is touristy, noisy, and overdeveloped, you'll be back.

Happily, the islanders seem to have been able to fit cosmopolitan New Yorkers, Londoners, and Athenians gracefully into their way of life. You may see, for example, an old island woman leading a donkey laden with vegetables through the town's narrow streets, greeting the suntanned vacationers walking by. The truth is, Mykonians regard a good tourist season the way a fisherman inspects a calm morning's catch; for many, the money earned in July and August will support them for the rest of the year. Not long ago Mykonians had to rely on what they could scratch out of the island's arid land for sustenance, and some remember suffering from starvation under Axis occupation during World War II. In the 1950s a few tourists began trickling into Mykonos on their way to see the ancient marvels on the nearby islet of Delos, the sacred isle.

For almost 1,000 years Delos was the religious and political center of the Aegean and host every four years to the Delian games, the region's greatest festival. The population of Delos actually reached 20,000 at the peak of its commercial period, and throughout antiquity Mykonos, eclipsed by its holy neighbor, depended on this proximity for income (it has been memorably described as Delos's "bordello"), as it partly does today. Anyone interested in antiquity should plan to spend at least one morning on Delos, which has some of the most striking sights preserved from antiquity, including the beautiful Avenue of the Lions or the eye-knocking sight of the enormous stone phalli at the entrance to the Sanctuary of Dionysus.

MYKONOS TOWN ΜΥΚΟΝΟΣ (ΧΩΡΑ)

16 km (10 mi) southeast of Tinos town.

Put firmly on the map by Jackie O. in the 1960s, Mykonos town—called Hora by the locals—remains the Saint-Tropez of the Greek islands. The scenery is memorable, with its whitewashed streets, Little Venice, the Kato Myli ridge of windmills, and Kastro, the town's medieval quarter. Its cubical two- or three-story houses and churches, with their red or blue doors and domes and wooden balconies, have been long celebrated as some of the best examples of classic Cycladic architecture. Luckily, the Greek Archaeological Service decided to preserve the town, even when the Mykonians would have preferred to rebuild, and so the authentic old town has been impressively preserved. Pink oleander, scarlet hibiscus, and trailing green pepper trees form a contrast amid the dazzling whiteness, whose frequent renewal with whitewash is required by law. Any visitor who has the pleasure of getting lost in its narrow streets (made all the narrower by the many outdoor stone staircases, which maximize housing space in the crowded village) will appreciate how its confusing layout was designed to foil pirates—if it was designed at all. After Mykonos fell under Turkish rule in 1537, the Ottomans allowed the islanders to arm their vessels against pirates, which had a contradictory effect: many of them found that raiding other islands was more profitable than tilling arid land. At the height of Aegean piracy, Mykonos was the principal headquarters of the corsair fleets—the place where pirates met their fellows, found willing women, and filled out their crews. Eventually the illicit activity evolved into a legitimate and thriving trade network.

Today, Mykonos makes its living from tourism, though the fishing boats still go out in good weather. The summer crowds have turned one of the poorest islands in Greece into one of the richest. Old Mykonians complain that their young, who have inherited stores where their grandfathers once sold eggs or wine, get so much rent that they have lost ambition, and in summer sit around pool bars at night with their

7

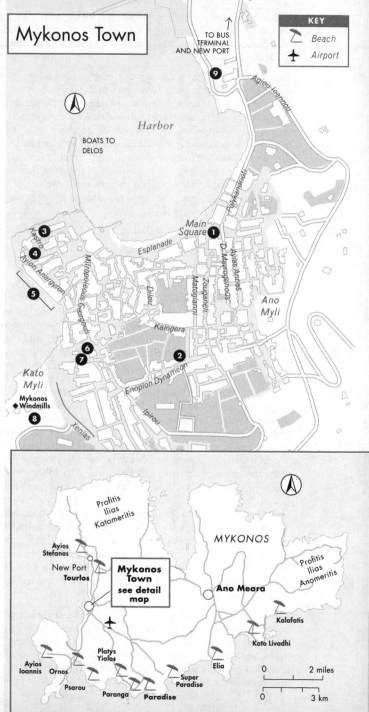

Mykonos Town

KEY

Beach

Airport

TO BUS
TERMINAL
AND NEW PORT

Harbor

BOATS TO
DELOS

9

Agiou Ioannou

3
4

Kastro

Ayion Anargyron

5

Mitropoleos Georgouli

Main
Square **1**

Esplanade

Diliou

Kalogera

Zouganeli
Matogianni

D. Mavrogenous

Ayias Annas

Ioannou Voinovits

*Ano
Myli*

6
7

*Kato
Myli*

◆ Mykonos
Windmills

8

Enoplon Dynameon

2

Ipirou

Xenias

*Profitis
Ilias
Katomeritis*

MYKONOS

Ayios
Stefanos

New Port
Tourlos

**Mykonos
Town**
see detail
map

Ano Meara

*Profitis
Ilias
Anomeritis*

Kalafatis

Kato Livadhi

Elia

**Platys
Yialos**

Ayios
Ioannis   Ornos

Psarou

Paranga   **Paradise**

**Super
Paradise**

| 0 | | 2 miles |

| 0 | | 3 km |

friends, and hang out in Athens in winter when island life is less scintillating, rather than on Paros, Naxos, Andros, or Tinos.

Morning on the main town quay is busy with deliveries, visitors for the Delos boats, lazy breakfasters, and street cleaners dealing with the previous night's mess. In late morning the cruise-boat people arrive, and the shops are all open. In early afternoon, shaded outdoor tavernas are full of diners eating salads (Mykonos's produce is mostly imported); music is absent or kept low. In mid- and late afternoon, the town feels sleepy, since so many

THE PRANCE OF THE PELICAN

By the time morning's open-air fish market picks up steam in Mykonos town, Petros the Pelican—the town mascot—preens and cadges eats. In the 1950s a group of migrating pelicans passed over Mykonos, leaving behind a single exhausted bird; Vassilis the fisherman nursed it back to health, and locals say that the pelican in the harbor is the original Petros (though there are several).

people are at the beach, on excursions, or sleeping in their air-conditioned rooms; even some tourist shops close for siesta. At sunset, people have come back from the beach, having taken their showers and rested. At night, the atmosphere in Mykonos ramps up. The cruise-boat people are mostly gone, coughing three-wheelers make no deliveries in the narrow streets, and everyone is dressed sexy for summer and starting to shimmy with the scene. Many shops stay open past midnight, the restaurants fill up, and the bars and discos make ice cubes as fast as they can.

❶ Start a tour of Mykonos town (Hora) on the main square, **Mando Mavrogenous Square** (sometimes called Taxi Square). Pride of place goes to a bust of Mando Mavrogenous, the island heroine, standing on a pedestal. In the 1821 War of Independence the Mykonians, known for their seafaring skills, volunteered an armada of 24 ships, and in 1822, when the Ottomans landed a force on the island, Mando and her soldiers forced them back to their ships. After independence, a scandalous love affair caused the heroine's exile to Paros, where she died. An aristocratic beauty who becomes a great revolutionary war leader and then dies for love may seem unbelievably Hollywoodish, but it is true.

The main shopping street, **Metoyanni** (✉ *Perpendicular to harbor*), is lined with jewelry stores, clothing boutiques, chic cafés, and candy shops. Owing to the many cruise ships that disgorge thousands of shoppers daily in season, the rents here rival Fifth Avenue's, and the more-interesting shops have skedaddled to less-prominent side streets.

The **Public Art Gallery** (✉ *Metoyanni* ☎22890/27190) is also here, with exhibitions changing often.

❷ The charming **Aegean Maritime Museum** contains a collection of model ships, navigational instruments, old maps, prints, coins, and nautical memorabilia. The backyard garden displays some old anchors and ship wheels and a reconstructed 1890 lighthouse, once lighted by oil. ✉ *Enoplon Dynameon* ☎22890/22700 ✉€3 ☉ *Daily 10:30–1 and 6:30–9.*

Take a peek into **Lena's House,** an accurate restoration of a middle-class Mykonos house from the 19th century. ⊠*Enoplon Dynameon* ☎*22890/22591* ⊴*Free* ⊙*Apr.–Oct., daily 7 PM–9 PM.*

The **Mykonos Agricultural Museum** displays a 16th-century windmill, traditional outdoor oven, waterwheel, dovecote, and more. ⊠*Petassos, at top of Mykonos town* ☎*22890/22591* ⊴*Free* ⊙*June–Sept., daily 4–6 PM.*

❸ The **Folk Museum,** housed in an 18th-century house, exhibits a bedroom furnished and decorated in the fashion of that period. On display are looms and lace-making devices, Cycladic costumes, old photographs, and Mykoniot musical instruments that are still played at festivals. ⊠*South of boat dock* ☎*22890/22591 or 22890/22748* ⊴*Free* ⊙*Mon.–Sat. 4–8, Sun. 5:30–8.*

Mykonians claim that exactly 365 churches and chapels dot their land-scape, one for each day of the year. The most famous of these is the **❹ ★ Church of Paraportiani** (*Our Lady of the Postern Gate* ⊠*Ayion Anargyron, near folk museum*). The sloping, whitewashed conglomeration of four chapels, mixing Byzantine and vernacular idioms, looks fantastic, it is solid and ultimately sober, and its position on a promontory facing the sea sets off the unique architecture.

Many of the early ship's captains built distinguished houses directly on the sea here, with wooden balconies overlooking the water. Today **❺ ★** this neighborhood, at the southwest end of the port, is called **Little Venice** (⊠*Mitropoleos Georgouli*). This area, architecturally unique and one of the most attractive in all the islands, is so called because its handsome houses, which once belonged to shipowners and aristocrats, rise from the edge of the sea, and their elaborate buttressed wooden balconies hang over the water—there are no Venetian marble palazzi reflected in still canals. Many of these fine old houses are now elegant bars specializing in sunset drinks, or cabarets, or shops, and crowds head to the cafés and clubs, many found a block inland from Little Venice. These are usually soundproofed (Mykonians are still sad that a rent fight closed Pierro's, the Mediterranean's most famous gay bar, though maybe residents who lived nearby aren't).

❻ The **Greek Orthodox Cathedral of Mykonos** (⊠*On square that meets both Ayion Anargyron and Odos Mitropolis*) has a number of old icons of the post-Byzantine period.

❼ Next to the Greek Orthodox Cathedral is the **Roman Catholic Cathedral** (⊠*On square that meets both Ayion Anargyron and Odos Mitropolis*) from the Venetian period. The name and coat of arms of the Ghisi family, which took over Mykonos in 1207, are inscribed in the entrance hall.

Across the water from Little Venice, set on a high hill, are the famous **❽ Mykonos windmills,** echoes of a time when wind power was used to grind the island's grain. The area from Little Venice to the windmills is called **Alefkandra,** which means "whitening": women once hung their laundry here. A little farther toward the windmills the bars chockablock on shoreside decks are barely above sea level, and when the north wind is up (often) surf splashes the tables. Further on, the shore spreads into an unprepossessing beach, and tables are placed on sand or pebbles. After dinner (there are plenty of little tavernas here), the bars turn up their music, and knowing the beat thumps into the night, older tourists seek solace elsewhere.

Before setting out on the mandatory boat excursion to the isle of

> **A SEASIDE MILKY WAY**
>
> The best time to visit Mykonos's central harbor is in the cool of the evening, when the islanders promenade along the esplanade to meet friends and visit the numerous cafés. Mykonians, when they see the array of harbor lights from offshore, call it the String of Pearls, though more and more lights are fuzzing the dazzle.

9 Delos, check out the **Archaeological Museum,** set at the northern edge of town. It affords insight into the intriguing history of its ancient shrines. The museum houses Delian funerary sculptures, many with scenes of mourning; most were moved to Rhenea when the Athenians cleansed Delos in the 6th century, during the sixth year of the Peloponnesian war, and, under instruction from the Delphic Oracle, the entire island was purged of all dead bodies. The most significant work from Mykonos is a 7th-century BC *pithos* (storage jar), showing the Greeks in the Trojan horse and the sack of the city. ✉*Ayios Stefanos, between boat dock and town* ☎*22890/22325* ✆*€3* ☉*Wed.–Mon. 8:30–2:30.*

BEACHES

There is a beach for every taste in Mykonos. Beaches near Mykonos town, within walking distance, are **Tourlos** and **Ayios Ioannis. Ayios Stefanos,** about a 45-minute walk from Mykonos town, has a mini-golf course, water sports, restaurants, and umbrellas and lounge chairs for rent. The south coast's **Psarou,** protected from wind by hills and surrounded by restaurants, offers a wide selection of water sports and is often called the finest beach. Nearby **Platys Yialos,** popular with families, is also lined with restaurants and dotted with umbrellas for rent. **Ornos** is also perfect for families; boats leave from here for more-distant beaches, and there is lively nightlife patronized by locals as well as visitors. **Paranga, Paradise, Super Paradise,** and **Elia** are all on the southern coast of the island, and are famously nude, though getting less so; one corner of Elia is gay. **Super Paradise** is half gay, half straight, and swings at night. The scene at Paradise's bars throbs till dawn. All have tavernas on the beach. At the easternmost end of the south shores is **Kalafatis,** known for package tours, and between Elia and Kalafatis there's a remote beach at **Kato Livadhi,** which can be reached by road.

WHERE TO STAY & EAT

$$$$ ✕**La Maison de Catherine.** This hidden restaurant's Greek and French
FodorsChoice   cuisine and hospitality—Katerina is still in charge—are worth the
★   search through the Dilou quarter of Mykonos. The splendid air-conditioned interior mixes Cycladic arches and whitewash with a French feeling and a faded 16th-century tapestry from Constantinople. Candles and classical music set the tone for baby squid stuffed with rice and

Greek mountain spices, or soufflé, puffed to perfection and loaded with cheese, mussels, and prawns. For entrées, try leg of lamb with mint sauce or pasta with lobster. The apple tart is divine. ⊠ *Ayios Gerasimos, Dilou, 84600* ☎ *22890/22169* 🖷 *22890/26946* ⚖ *Reservations essential* ▤ *AE, DC, MC, V.*

$$$-$$$$ ✕ **Tagoo.** High Mykonian style can be yours at the eatery of this noted hotel. Haute cuisine is served up in either an all-white room or at outdoor tables, with Mykonos bay on one side and an infinity pool on the other. Start with local louza (smoked pork) with grilled tomatoes and bean mash, seasoned with thyme and marjoram, or with bass carpaccio marinated in olive oil, lemon, and fennel. Other home runs include the sea bream fillet with spinach, rice, and yogurt, or the baby beef fillet with vin santo and coriander. Fish is always fresh and delicately prepared. To top things off, opt for the warm chocolate fondant with ice cream and vanilla sauce. The sommelier helps with the large selection of wines. The restaurant is open April through October. ⊠ *Hotel Cavo Tagoo, 84600 (15 mins by foot north of Mykonos town on sea road)* ☎ *22890/23692 through 22890/23694* ⚖ *Reservations essential* ▤ *AE, DC, MC, V.*

$$$ ✕ **Chez Maria's.** Dine at this 30-year-old garden restaurant for lively atmosphere—sometimes with live music and dancing—for the zest of Greek living in a lovely candlelit garden. Octopus in wine, great cheese pies, and the fillet of beef with cheese and fresh vegetables will keep you in the mood. So will the apple tart with ice cream and walnuts. ⊠ *Kalogera 30, 84600* ☎ *22890/27565* ▤ *AE, MC, V.*

$$$ ✕ **Sea Satin Market–Caprice.** If the wind is up, the waves sing at this
★ magical spot, set on a far tip of land below the famous windmills of Mykonos. The preferred place for Greek shipowners, Sea Satin Market sprawls out onto a seaside terrace and even onto the sand of the beach bordering Little Venice. When it comes to fish, prices vary according to weight. Shellfish is a specialty, and everything is beautifully presented. In summer, live music and dancing add to the liveliness. ⊠ *On seaside under windmills* ☎ *22890/24676* ▤ *AE, MC, V.*

$$ ✕ **El Greco.** A fixture for 30 years in Mykonos town's Three Wells district, El Greco has now moved to Tourlos, near the new harbor. Its quiet terrace overlooks the bay (and sunset), although you can go formal in the indoor dark-wood dining room, which has a wine cellar to explore. While wife Barbara provides gracious service, owner Giorgos Rizopoulos cooks "Greek with imagination" and he has a remarkable culinary sensitivity for fresh herbs, which come from the adjacent garden. You might start with *soupies politikes* (cuttlefish, Constantinople style), cooked in their ink and moschato wine; the plate of Mykonos specialties, such as cheeses and cured meats, is the best in town. For a main dish, try rabbit in wine, parsley, and vinegar; or monkfish fricassee (with lettuce and dill). For a fine finale, Giorgos turns his orchard's lemons into an aromatic mousse. Set in the Tourlos suburb, El Greco is located right on the main harbor, about a 20 minute walk from the center of Mykonos town. ⊠ *Tourlos* ☎ *22890/22074* ▤ *No credit cards.*

$–$$ ✕ **Kounelas.** This long-established fresh-fish taverna is where many fishermen themselves eat, for solid, no-frills food. The menu depends on the weather—low winds means lots of fish. Note: even in simple places such as Kounelas, fresh fish can be expensive. ⊠*Off port near Delos boats* ☎*22890/28220* ☰*No credit cards.*

$-$$ ✕**Lotus.** For more than 30 years, Giorgos and Elsa Cambanis have lovingly run this tiny restaurant. Elsa is the cook, so compliment her on the fine starter, the mushroom "Lotos" with cream and cheese. The roast leg of lamb with oregano, lemon, and wine is succulent, and the moussaka is almost too good to be traditional. For dessert, have *pralina*, which resembles tiramisu. It's open year-round for dinner only: the porch is covered with bougainvillea in summer, and there's a fireplace in winter. ⊠*Metoyanni 47, 84600* ☎*22890/22881* ☰*No credit cards* ⊘*No lunch.*

¢–$ ✕**Angolo Bar.** Run by Italians, this place has been serving Mykonos's best espresso for years. In the evening, they also prepare light Italian meals (their full-fledged restaurant is directly across the street). During the day the music is less loud. Set in Mykonos town's busy Lakka area, Angolo can be found 50 yards from the bus stop. ⊠*Lakka, 84600* ☎*22890/24207* ☰*No credit cards.*

$$$$ 🏨**Belvedere.** You may not have to go to Greece once you view the
Fodor's Choice "movie" presentation on this hotel's Web site—it is almost as relaxing,
★ blue-and-white, and high style as this hotel (but not quite). Favored by the hip, replete with Matsuhisa Mykonos—an outpost of famed sushi chef Nobu—and designed in the best dreamy manner, the Belevedere has a clublike atmosphere, convenient location, and view over Mykonos town and harbor that ensures this hotel's popularity. In the restaurants and bars, you can cut the "cool" attitude with a knife—but when you want to slip off your Tods, repair to the dramatically decorated guest rooms, white-on-white sanctums with sailcloth drapes, rope accents, and a beautifully laid-back touch. Some have magical views, a trade-off for the small dimensions of some of the rooms. For stylishness and class, it's hard to top this one. ⊠*School of Fine Arts district, 84600* ☎*22890/25122* 🖶*22890/25126* ⊕*www.belvederehotel.com* ⇄*42 rooms, 6 suites* ⚴*In-room: refrigerator. In-hotel: restaurant, bar, pool, spa, public Internet* ☰*AE, MC, V* ⊘*Closed Nov.–Mar.* ⁍❙*BP.*

$$$$ 🏨**Cavo Tagoo.** Completely redesigned in 2007 in a "barefoot chic"
★ esthetic by the architect-owner, the Cavo Tagoo climbs the hill over the bay in sensuous white curves, with natural projecting rock on the winding path to the guest rooms. The two public pools (one a 38-foot-long eternity) and many private pools make it feel island-aqueous. Drama is on tap in the pool bar where a 43-foot-long aquarium comes stocked with sharks (PETA-lovers, beware). The medley of white cubical suites are furnished in high-drama minimalism, with a

stark white palette enlivened by hot red or cool blue; palm-leaf futons, plasma TVs, and luxurious bathrooms add luxe. Longtime manager Tasos Didimiotis keeps it all gracious. It's a 15-minute walk to town. ⊠*Follow coast road, north of port, 84600* ☏*22890/23692 through 22890/23695* 🖷*22890/24923* ⊕*www.cavotagoo.gr* ⌨*68 rooms, 5 suites* ⚿*In-room: Ethernet, Wi-Fi. In-hotel: restaurant, bar, pool, no elevator* ⊟*AE, MC, V* ⊗*Closed Nov.–Mar.* ⊺⊙*BP.*

$$$$ ⊞**Deliades.** Away from the fray, the Deliades (which translates as
★   "Delian nymphs") is a welcome escape from Mykonos's heat. But these cool Cycladic white cubes offer a lovely retreat made all the more appealing because manager Steve Argiriadis had a hand in their design. The capacious, airy guest rooms (many with beautiful wood beams and 19th-century-style lanterns) all have sea views and terraces, the marble carvings were made especially for this hotel, and the stark white of the architecture is softened with accents in muted sand and sea shades. Eating dinner at the quiet poolside café-restaurant, overlooking the bay, is especially pleasant and it is only a short walk to Ornos beach. The price includes transfers. ⊠*Far end of Ornos beach, follow road up 30 yards, 84600 Ornos* ☏*22890/79430 or 22890/79470* 🖷*22890/26996* ⊕*www.hoteldeliadesmykonos.com* ⌨*30 rooms* ⚿*In-room: refrigerator, dial-up. In-hotel: restaurant, bar, pool, no elevator* ⊟*AE, MC, V* ⊗*Closed Nov.–Mar.* ⊺⊙*BP.*

$$$$ ⊞**Hotel Mykonos Adonis.** Set on the edge of town (behind the bus stop) overlooking the sea, this recently renovated option is both convenient and out of the fray. Completely eschewing Mykonos glitz, this place is thoughtfully planned to produce a homelike atmosphere. Result? The clientele, many of them artists and writers, return year after year to let owners Michalis and Roz Apostolou (he's Mykonian, she's American) take care of them. The guest rooms all have balconies, many with views of the sea and the hotel gardens—some of the staffers are passionate gardeners. Breakfast and transfers included. ⊠*Chora, 84600* ☏*22890/23433* 🖷*22890/23449* ⊕*www.mykonosadonis.gr* ⌨*12 rooms, 12 suites* ⚿*In-room: refrigerator. In-hotel: no elevator* ⊟*AE, D, MC, V* ⊗*Closed Nov.–Mar.* ⊺⊙*BP.*

$$$$ ⊞**Kivotos Clubhotel.** Beautifully designed with a vast stonework facade,
★   topped with its usual Cycladic whitewashed house, Spyros Michopoulos's deluxe hotel is architecturally ambitious and designed around an impressive pool. The main floor is all done in a richly decorative island style, with statues in niches and mosaic work, and unexpected little courtyards with bright flowers. The guest rooms, all individually decorated, display local crafts and dazzling objects—ship steering wheels, Fortunyesque pleated fabrics, fine antiques, and sea views all catch the eye. A hotel minibus runs into town, and to the airport. ✛*2 km (1 mi) from Mykonos town* ⊠*Ornos bay, 84600* ☏*22890/25795 or 22890/25796* 🖷*22890/22844* ⊕*www.kivotosclubhotel.gr* ⌨*35 rooms, 5 suites* ⚿*In-room: refrigerator, Ethernet, dial-up. In-hotel: 2 restaurants, bars, pools, no elevator* ⊟*AE, D, MC, V* ⊗*Closed Nov.–Mar.* ⊺⊙*BP.*

$$$$ ⊞**Royal Myconian.** You may never leave this light-filled, luxurious hotel, a 20-minute drive from Mykonos town, set high on the bare mountain overlooking quiet Elia beach. A vast fantasia of stone terraces, bou-

gainvillea, Cycladic whitewash, green shutters, spa pools, and sea-view dining, this place may be large enough to boast a vast business convention center but it is also designed with excellent taste. Guest rooms have light teak-wood trim, sheer beige curtains, and Cycladic accents. Their terraces overlook the sea, and suites have private Jacuzzis. The restaurant is elegant inside and out. The price includes transfers. ✉*Elia beach, 84600* ☎*22890/72000* 🖶*22890/72027* ⊕*www. royal-myconian.gr* ⇱*129 rooms, 20 suites* ♿*In-room: refrigerator. In-hotel: 2 restaurants, pool, spa, public Internet* ▤*AE, D, MC, V* ⊘*Closed Nov.–Mar.* ⦿⦿*BP.*

$$$$ 🖼**Semeli.** A carved-marble entrance doorway leads to an old stately
★ home that has been expanded into an elegant hotel in the high Mykoniot style. Named after a Greek nymph, the hotel is now a rambling complex, threaded by stone paths running through sweet gardens. A welcoming lobby allures with coved archways and pretty island handcrafts. Each of the large guest rooms, some with sea views, is differently and traditionally furnished. Though convenient to the town, the pool area, with its terraces and garden view, will tempt you to linger. But the rooms could be larger. ✉*On ring road, 84600* ☎*22890/27466 or 22890/27471* 🖶*22890/27467* ⊕*www.semelihotel.gr* ⇱*42 rooms, 3 suites* ♿*In-room: refrigerator. In-hotel: restaurant, bar, pool, no elevator, public Internet* ▤*AE, MC, V* ⦿⦿*BP.*

$$$ 🖼**Omiros.** Looking for an inexpensive, attractive, convenient, slightly out-of-town accommodation on a hill overlooking the bay? Try this spot, set in the Tagoo area, a 10-minute walk from town (but longer to the center, and the walk back is uphill), on the upper road. The guest rooms are fairly small and simply furnished, some with balconies, and the public terraces lend a convivial atmosphere. Owner Yannis Koukas is efficient, dynamic, and friendly, and a useful expert on Mykonos's less-expensive restaurants; he also edits the local newspaper. Breakfast and transfers are included. ✉*Chora, 84600* ☎*22890/23328* 🖶*22890/24369* ⊕*www.hotelomiros.gr* ⇱*10 rooms* ♿*In-hotel: no elevator, public Internet.* ▤*AE, D, MC, V* ⊘ ⦿⦿*BP.*

$$$ 🖼**Villa Konstantin.** This complex of small apartments, studios, and rooms, located on the ring road, is a 765-yard downhill walk to the town—a theoretically walkable distance, but really not. The owners themselves live here all year, and go to lengths to make it attractive and friendly, as their many returning customers attest. The decor is traditional Mykoniot with built-in furniture, and all rooms have terraces or balconies with sea views. The lovely pool was added in 2006. ✉*Box 1030, 84600* ☎*22890/26204* 🖶*22890/26205* ⊕*www.villakonstan-tin-mykonos.gr* ⇱*19 units* ♿*In-room: kitchen, dial-up. In-hotel: no elevator* ▤*MC, V* ⊘*Closed Nov.–Mar.*

$ 🖼**Philippi.** Of the inexpensive hotels scattered throughout town, this is the most attractive. The rooms have balconies that overlook the garden—owner Christos Kontizas is a passionate gardener. You can't get there by vehicle, but once there you are in the center of things. If you want to get away from it all, go elsewhere. ✉*Kalogera 25, 84600* ☎*22890/22294* 🖶*22890/24680* ✐*chriko@otenet.gr* ⇱*13 rooms* ♿*In-room: refrigerator. In hotel: no elevator* ▤*AE, MC, V* ⊘*Closed Nov.–Mar.*

7

NIGHTLIFE & THE ARTS

Whether it's bouzouki music, break beat, or techno, Mykonos's night-life beats to an obsessive rhythm until undetermined hours—little wonder Europe's gilded youth comes here *just* to enjoy the night scene. After midnight, they often head to the techno bars along the Paradise and Super Paradise beaches. Some of Little Venice's nightclubs become gay in more than one sense of the word, while in the Kastro, convivial bars welcome all for tequila-*sambukas* at sunset. What is "the" place of the moment? The scene is ever-changing—so you'll need to track the buzz once you arrive.

BARS &
DISCOS

Little Venice is a good place to begin an evening, and Damianos Gripar-is's **Galleraki** (⊠ *Little Venice* ☎22890/27118) is one of the best cocktail bars in town; it's so close to the water you may get wet when a boat passes. Upstairs in the old mansion (Delos's first archaeologists lived here), you'll find an art gallery—a handy sanctum for drinks on windy nights. Kostas Karatzas's long-standing **Kastro Bar** (⊠ *Behind Paraportiani* ☎22890/23072 ⊕ *www.kastrobar.com*), with heavy beamed ceilings and island furnishings, creates an intimate environment for enjoying the evening sunset over the bay; classical music sets the tone. **Montparnasse** (⊠ *Agion Anargyron 24, Little Venice* ☎22890/23719 ⊕ *www.thepianobar.com*) hangs paintings by local artists; its superb sunset view precedes nights of live cabaret and musicals.

El Pecado–Remezzo (⊠ *North of waterfront*) is a high-tech, wild dance club.

SPORTS & THE OUTDOORS

DIVING

Mykonos Diving Center (⊠ *Psarou* ☎22890/24808 ⊕ *www.dive.gr*) has a variety of scuba courses and excursions at 30 locations.

WATER
SPORTS

The windy northern beaches on Ornos bay are best for water sports; you can rent surfboards and take lessons. There's windsurfing and waterskiing at Ayios Stefanos, Platys Yialos, and Ornos. **Aphrodite Beach Hotel** (⊠ *Kalafati beach* ☎28890/71367 🖷22890/71525) has water sports. The program at **Surfing Club Anna** (⊠ *Agia Anna* ☎22890/71205) is well organized.

SHOPPING

FASHION

Yiannis **Galatis** (⊠ *Mando Mavrogenous Square, opposite Lalaounis* ☎22890/22255) has outfitted such famous women as Elizabeth Taylor, Ingrid Bergman, and Jackie Onassis. Yiannis will probably greet you personally and show you some of his coats and costumes, hostess gowns, and long dresses. He also has men's clothes. His memoirs capture the old days on Mykonos, when Jackie O. was a customer. **Jella's** (⊠ *Nikiou 5* ☎22890/24153 ⊕ *www.mykonos-web.com*), a tiny boutique filled with custom-made silk knits that drape with special elegance, and silk slippers from Turkistan, is next to La Maison de Catherine restaurant; the nearby area is rife with shops. **Loco** (⊠ *Kalogera 29 N* ☎22890/23682) sells cotton and linen summer wear in lovely colors. The Marla knits are from the family factory in Athens. **Parthenis** (⊠ *Alefkandra Square* ☎22890/23080 ⊕ *www.orsalia-parthenis. gr*) was opened by Dimitris Parthenis in 1978 but now features designs by his daughter Orsalia, all showcased in a large Mykonian-style building on the up side of Alefkandra Square in Little Venice. The collection of cotton and silk garments in white and soft neutral colors are very popular for their soft draping and clinging wrap effect.

FINE &
DECORATIVE
ART

Soula Papadakou's **Venetia** (✉ *Ayion Anargyron 16, Little Venice* ☎ 22890/24464) carries authentic copies of traditional handmade embroideries in clothing, tablecloths, curtains, and such, all in white; the women who work for her come from all over Greece, including a nunnery in Ioannina. Mykonos used to be a weaver's island, where 500 looms clacked away. Two shops remain. In **Nikoletta** (✉ *Little Venice*), Nikoletta Xidakis sells her skirts, shawls, and bedspreads made of local wool. **Ioanna Zouganelli** (☎ 22890/22309), whose father used to sell the family's weavings from a trunk on his Delos excursion boat, makes mohair shawls and traditional Mykonian weavings in her tiny shop on the square in front of Paraportiani.

JEWELRY

Ilias Lalaounis (✉ *Polykandrioti 14, near taxis* ☎ 22890/22444 🖷 22890/24409 ⊕ *www.lalaounismykonos.com*) is known internationally for jewelry based on classic ancient Greek designs, reinterpreted for the modern woman. There are always new variations; the shop is as elegant as a museum. **Precious Tree** (✉ *Dilou 2* 🖷 2289024685) is a tiny shop aglitter in gems elegantly set here and in its workshop in Athens; in its creativity, it hardly resembles Mykonos's mainline shops.

ANO MERA ΆΝΩ ΜΕΡΑ

8 km (5 mi) east of Mykonos town.

Monastery buffs should head to Ano Mera, a village in the central part of the island, where the **Monastery of the Panayia Tourliani**, founded in 1580 and dedicated to the protectress of Mykonos, stands in the central square. Its massive baroque iconostasis (altar screen), made in 1775 by Florentine artists, has small icons carefully placed amid the wooden structure's painted green, red, and gold-leaf flowers. At the top are carved figures of the apostles and large icons depicting New Testament scenes. The hanging incense holders with silver molded dragons holding red eggs in their mouths show an Eastern influence. In the hall of the monastery, an interesting **museum** displays embroideries, liturgical vestments, and wood carvings. A good taverna is across the street. The monastery's big festival—hundreds attend—is on August 15. ✉ *On central square* ☎ 0289/71249 ☉ *By appointment only; call in advance.*

DELOS ΔΗΛΟΣ

Fodor'sChoice ★

25-min caïque ride southwest from Mykonos.

Arrive at the mythical, magical, and magnificent site of Delos and you might wonder how this barren islet, which had virtually no natural resources, became the religious and political center of the Aegean. One answer is that Delos provided the safest anchorage for vessels sailing between the mainland and the shores of Asia; another answer is that it had no other utilization. A third is provided if you climb Mt. Kynthos to see that the isle is shielded on three sides by other islands. Indeed, this is how the Cyclades—the word means "circling ones"—got their name: they circle around the sacred island. Delos's amazing saga begins back in the times of myth:

Zeus fell in love with gentle Leto, the Titaness, who became pregnant. When Hera discovered this infidelity, she forbade Mother Earth to give Leto refuge and ordered the Python to pursue her. Finally Poseidon, taking pity on her, anchored the poor floating island of Delos with four diamond columns to give her a place to rest. Leto gave birth first to the virgin huntress Artemis on Rhenea and then, clasping a sacred palm on a slope of Delos's Mt. Kynthos, to Apollo, god of music and light.

By 1000 BC the Ionians, who inhabited the Cyclades, had made Delos their religious capital. Homeric Hymn 3 tells of the cult of Apollo in the 7th century BC. One can imagine the elegant Ionians, whose central festival was here, enjoying the choruses of temple girls—"Delian korai, who serve the Far-Shooter"—singing and dancing their hymn and displaying their graceful tunics and jewelry. But a difficult period began for the Delians when Athens rose to power and assumed Ionian leadership. In 543 BC an oracle at Delphi conveniently decreed that the Athenians purify the island by removing all the graves to Rhenea, a dictate designed to alienate the Delians from their past.

After the defeat of the Persians in 478 BC, the Athenians organized the Delian League, with its treasury and headquarters at Delos (in 454 BC the funds were transferred to the Acropolis in Athens). Delos had its most prosperous period in late Hellenistic and Roman times, when it was declared a free port and quickly became the financial center of the Mediterranean, the focal point of trade, where 10,000 slaves were sold daily. Foreigners from as far as Rome, Syria, and Egypt lived in this cosmopolitan port, in complete tolerance of one another's religious beliefs, and each group built its various shrines. But in 88 BC Mithridates, the king of Pontus, in a revolt against Roman rule, ordered an attack on the unfortified island. The entire population of 20,000 was killed or sold into slavery. Delos never fully recovered, and later Roman attempts to revive the island failed because of pirate raids. After a second attack in 69 BC, Delos was gradually abandoned.

In 1872, the French School of Archaeology began excavating on Delos—a massive project, considering that much of the island's 4 square km (1½ square mi) is covered in ruins. The work continues today. Delos remains dry and shadeless; off-season, the snack bar is often closed; most guards leave on the last boat to Mykonos in the early afternoon. But if on the way to Mykonos you see dolphins leaping (it often happens), you'll know Apollo is about and approves.

❶ On the left from the harbor is the **Agora of the Competialists** (circa 150 BC), members of Roman guilds, mostly freedmen and slaves from Sicily who worked for Italian traders. They worshipped the *Lares Competales,* the Roman "crossroads" gods; in Greek they were known as Hermaistai, after the god Hermes, protector of merchants and the

Delos

Harbor

0 — 100 yards

0 — 100 meters

2 crossroads. The **Sacred Way,** east of the agora, was the route, during the holy Delian festival, of the procession to the Sanctuary of **3** Apollo. The **Propylaea,** at the end of the Sacred Way, were once a monumental white marble gateway with three portals framed by four Doric columns. Beyond the Propylaea is **4** the **Sanctuary of Apollo;** though little remains today, when the Propylaea were built in the mid-2nd century BC, the sanctuary was crowded with altars, statues, and temples—three of them to Apollo. Inside the sanc- **5** tuary and to the right is the **House of**

A SITE TO SEE BY SEA

Most travel offices in Mykonos town run guided tours to the ancient isle of Delos that cost about €35, including boat transportation and entry fee. Alternatively, take one of the small passenger boats that visit Delos daily from the port: the round-trip costs about €12, and entry to the site (with no guide) is €6. They leave between 8:30 AM and 1 PM and return noon to 2 PM.

the Naxians, a 7th- to 6th-century BC structure with a central colonnade. Dedications to Apollo were stored in this shrine. Outside the north wall a massive rectangular **pedestal** once supported a colossal statue of Apollo (one of the hands is in Delos's Archaeological Museum, and a piece of a foot is in the British Museum). Near the pedestal a bronze palm tree was erected in 417 BC by the Athenians to commemorate the palm tree under which Leto gave birth. According to Plutarch, the palm tree toppled in a storm and brought the statue of Apollo down with it. Odysseus in The Odyssey compares the Phaeacian princess Nausicaa to the palm he saw on Delos, when the island was wetter.

6 Southeast of the Sanctuary of Apollo are the ruins of the **Sanctuary of the Bulls,** an extremely long and narrow structure built, it is thought, to display a trireme, an ancient boat with three banks of oars, dedicated to Apollo by a Hellenistic leader thankful for a naval victory. Maritime symbols were found in the decorative relief of the main halls, and the head and shoulders of a pair of bulls were part of the design of an interior entrance. A short distance north of the Sanctuary of the Bulls **7** is an oval indentation in the earth where the **Sacred Lake** once sparkled. It is surrounded by a stone wall that reveals the original periphery. According to islanders, the lake was fed by the River Inopos from its source high on Mt. Kynthos until 1925, when the water stopped flow- **8** ing and the lake dried up. Along the shores are two ancient **palaestras,** buildings for physical exercise and debate. One of the most evocative **9** sights of Delos is the 164-foot-long **Avenue of the Lions.** These are replicas; the originals are in the museum. The five Naxian marble beasts crouch on their haunches, their forelegs stiffly upright, vigilant guardians of the Sacred Lake. They are the survivors of a line of at least nine lions, erected in the second half of the 7th century BC by the Naxians. One, removed in the 17th century, now guards the Arsenal of Venice **10** (though with a later head). Northeast of the palaestras is the **gymnasium,** a square courtyard nearly 131 feet long on each side. "Gym" means naked in Greek, and here men and boys stayed in shape (and, in those heavily Platonic days, eyed each other). The long, narrow **11** structure farther northeast is the **stadium,** the site of the athletic events

of the Delian Games. East of the stadium site, by the seashore, are the
⑫ remains of a **synagogue built by Phoenician Jews** in the 2nd century BC.
⑬ A road south from the gymnasium leads to the **tourist pavilion,** which
⑭ has a meager restaurant and bar. The **Archaeological Museum** is also on
the road south of the gymnasium; it contains most of the antiquities
found in excavations on the island: monumental statues of young men
and women, stelae, reliefs, masks, and ancient jewelry. Immediately to
⑮ the right of the museum is a small **Sanctuary of Dionysus,** erected about
300 BC; outside it is one of the more-boggling sights of ancient Greece:
several monuments dedicated to Apollo by the winners of the choral
competitions of the Delian festivals, each decorated with a huge phallus, emblematic of the orgiastic rites that took place during the Dionysian festivals. Around the base of one of them is carved a lighthearted
representation of a bride being carried to her new husband's home. A
marble phallic bird, symbol of the body's immortality, also adorns this
corner of the sanctuary. Beyond the path that leads to the southern part
⑯ of the island is the **ancient theater,** built in the early 3rd century BC in the
elegant residential quarter inhabited by Roman bankers and Egyptian
and Phoenician merchants. Their one- and two-story **houses** were typically built around a central courtyard, sometimes with columns on all
sides. Floor mosaics of snakes, panthers, birds, dolphins, and Dionysus
channeled rainwater into cisterns below; the best-preserved can be seen
⑰⑱⑲ in the **House of the Dolphins,** the **House of the Masks,** and the **House of the
Trident.** A dirt path leads east to the base of Mt. Kynthos, where there
⑳ are remains from many **Middle Eastern shrines,** including the **Sanctuary of the Syrian Gods,** built in 100 BC. A flight of steps goes up 368 feet
㉑ to the summit of **Mt. Kynthos** (after which all Cynthias are named), on
whose slope Apollo was born. ✉ *Delos island and historic site, take
a small passenger boat from Mykonos town* ☎22890/22259 ⊕*www.
culture.gr* 🎫*€5* ⊙*Apr.–Oct., Tues.–Sun. 8:30–3.*

NAXOS ΝΑΞΟΣ

"Great sweetness and tranquillity" is how Nikos Kazantzakis, premier
novelist of Greece, described Naxos, and indeed a tour of the island
leaves you with an impression of abundance, prosperity, and serenity.
The greenest, largest, and most fertile of the Cyclades, Naxos, with its
many potato fields, its livestock and its thriving cheese industry, and its
fruit and olive groves framed by the pyramid of Mt. Zas (3,295 feet,
the Cyclades's highest), is practically self-sufficient. Inhabited for 6,000
years, the island has memorable landscapes—abrupt ravines, hidden
valleys, long and sandy beaches—and towns that vary from a Cretan mountain stronghold to the seaside capital that strongly evokes its
Venetian past. It is full of history and monuments—classical temples,
medieval monasteries, Byzantine churches, Venetian towers—and its
huge interior offers endless magnificent hikes, not much pursued by
summer tourists, who cling to the lively capital and the developed western beaches, the best in the Cyclades.

Continued on page 292

MYTH,
BEHAVIN'

GREECE'S GODS AND HEROES

Superheroes, sex, adventure: it's no wonder Greek myths have reverberated throughout Western civilization. Today, as you wander ancient Greece's most sacred sites—such as Delos, island birthplace of the sun god Apollo—these ageless tales will come alive to thrill and perhaps haunt you.

Whether you are looking at 5th century BC pedimental sculptures in Olympia or ancient Red-Figure vase paintings in Athens, whether you are reading the epics of Homer or the tragedies of Euripides, you are in the presence of the Greek mythopoetic mind. Peopled with emblems of hope, fear, yearning, and personifications of melting beauty or of petrifying ugliness, these ancient myths helped early Greeks make sense of a chaotic, primitive universe that yielded no secrets.

Frightened by the murder and mayhem that surrounded them, the Greeks set up gods in whom power, wisdom, and eternal youth could not perish. These gods lived, under the rule of Zeus, on Mount Olympus. Their rivalries and intrigues were a primeval, superhuman version of *Dynasty* and *Dallas*. These astounding collections of stories not only pervaded all ancient Greek society but have influenced the course of Western civilization: How could we imagine our culture—from Homer's *Iliad* to Joyce's *Ulysses*—without them?

IN GODS WE TRUST

To the ancient Greeks, mythology was more than a matter of literature, art, philosophy, and ethics. For them, the whole countryside teemed with spirits and powers. Besides the loftier Olympian gods there were spirits of mountain, sea, trees, and stream—oreads, nereids, dryads, and naiads. The ancients preferred to personify natural phenomena than to depict them realistically.

Nymphs, for example, were primarily personifications of nature—oak trees, pools, sea waves, caves, peaks, isles. Monsters did the same; Scylla, who ate six of Odysseus' men, was the symbolic personification of a shipwrecking cliff in the Straits of Messina. In the darkness of the night (or of the mind), the ancients' ancestral fears and perverse desires became embodied in a world of brutal minotaurs, evil chimeras, mischievous sphinxes, terrifying centaurs, and ferocious Furies. To combat them, people looked to the gods, promoters of peace and justice at home, success in trade and war, and fertility.

YE GODS!

WHO'S WHO IN GREEK MYTHOLOGY

ZEUS
Latin Name: Jupiter
God of: Sky, Supreme God
Attribute: Scepter, Thunder
Roving Eye: Zeus was the ruler of Mount Olympus but often went AWOL pursuing love affairs down on earth with nymphs and beautiful ladies; his children were legion, including Hercules.

DEMETER
Latin Name: Ceres
Goddess of: Earth, Fecundity
Attribute: Sheaf, Sickle
Most Dramatic Moment: After her daughter Persephone was kidnapped by Zeus, Demeter decided to make all plants of the earth wither and die.

ATHENA
Latin Name: Minerva
Goddess of: Wisdom
Attribute: Owl, Olive
Top Billing: The goddess of reason, she gave the olive tree to the Greeks; her uncle was Poseidon, and the Parthenon in Athens was built in her honor.

ARTEMIS
Latin Name: Diana
Goddess of: Chastity, Moon
Attribute: Stag
Early Feminist: Sister of Apollo, she enjoyed living in the forest with her court, frowned on marriage, and, most notoriously, had men torn apart by her hounds if they peeked at her bathing.

HEPHAESTOS
Latin Name: Vulcan
God of: Fire, Industry
Attribute: Hammer, Anvil
Pumping Iron: The best-preserved Doric style temple in Athens, the Hephaestaion, was erected to this god in the ancient Agora marketplace; today, ironmongers still have shops in the district there.

APOLLO
Latin Name: Phoebus
God of: Sun, Music, and Poetry
Attribute: Bow, Lyre
Confirmed Bachelor: Born at Delos, his main temple was at Delphi; his love affairs included Cassandra, to whom he gave the gift of prophecy; Calliope, with whom he had Orpheus; and Daphne, who, fleeing from his embrace, changed into a tree.

The twelve chief gods formed the elite of Olympus. Each represented one of the forces of nature and also a human characteristic. They also had attributes by which they can often be identified. The Romans, influenced by the arts and letters of Greece, largely identified their own gods with those of Greece, with the result that Greek gods have Latin names as well. Here are the divine I.D.s of the Olympians.

HERA

Latin Name: Juno

Goddess of: Sky, Marriage

Attribute: Peacock

His Cheating Heart: Hera married her brother Zeus, wound up having a 300-year honeymoon with him on Samos, and was repaid for her fidelity to marriage by the many love affairs of her hubby.

HESTIA

Latin Name: Vesta

Goddess of: Hearth, Domestic Values

Attribute: Eternal Fire

Hausfrau: A famous virgin, she was charged with maintaining the eternal flame atop Olympus; the Vestal Virgins of ancient Romans followed in her footsteps.

POSEIDON

Latin Name: Neptune

God of: Sea, Earthquakes

Attribute: Trident

Water Boy: To win the affection of Athenians, Poseidon and Athena were both charged with giving them the most useful gift, with his invention of the bubbling spring losing out to Athena's creation of the olive.

APHRODITE

Latin Name: Venus

Goddess of: Love, Beauty

Attribute: Dove

And the Winner Is: Born out of the foam rising off of Cyprus, she was given the Golden Apple by Paris in the famous beauty contest between her, Athena, and Hera, and bestowed the love of Helen on him as thanks.

HERMES

Latin Name: Mercury

God of: Trade, Eloquence

Attribute: Wings

Messenger Service: Father of Pan, Hermes was known as a luck-bringer, harbinger of dreams, and the messenger of Olympus; he was also worshipped as the god of commerce and music.

ARES

Latin Name: Mars

God of: Tumult, War

Attribute: Spear, Helmet

Antisocial: The most famous male progeny of Zeus and Hera, he was an irritable man; considering his violent temper, few temples were erected in his honor in Greece.

7

MYTH BEHAVIN'

TOGA PARTY

Was all human life doomed to disaster and woe? Zeus, many believed, had two jars—one of good fortune and one of ill—which he dipped into when making his decisions. To most people he distributed portions fairly equally—but Zeus himself often fell prey to pride and envy, and the latter often got this chronic double-dater into trouble. No matter that he had seven wives: He was a very "Your honey or your wife" philanderer and his endless seductions provided innumerable scandals.

One notable case was Leda, queen to King Tyndareus of Sparta. Zeus saw her shapely naked limbs, seduced her by assuming the form of a swan, and she then gave birth to two eggs, one of which hatched with the Dioscuri, Castor and Pollux, the other with Clytemnestra and Helen of Troy, women of serious trouble. Clytemnestra married Agamemnon, king of Mycenae, and Helen married Menelaos, king of Sparta. The Trojan War followed and the rest is history (or something like history). The whole story, embracing fantasy, politics, and cult has been retold endlessly in poems from Homer to Yeats and images from Leonardo to Gustave Moreau's surrealist paintings. The ancient myths turn out to be as modern as today.

GREEK LIGHTNING

Today, historians point to tribal origin-heroes and local cult figures of the ancient Near East as influencing the earliest Greek myths, first professed in the preliterate second millennium BC. Capturing primeval energies from the past that are still in us, these stories provide the back story to great sites like Delos, the legendary birthplace of the god Apollo. The ancients believed that the sun crossed the sky in Apollo's chariot. Other gods were considered the cause of many phenomena. What caused earthquakes? Poseidon with his trident. Who used lighting bolts as weapons? Zeus. Who invented fire? Prometheus brought it down from Olympus. How did pain and sickness come into the world? Through the curiosity of Pandora (that other Eve). Before long, in the non-factual, gravity-free world of the ancient Greek imagination, the deeds of the gods became moralistic parables about man. Is gold the best thing of all? Consider Midas. Would it be a good thing to fly? Icarus did not find it so. Would you like to be married to Helen of Troy, or to Jason, the winner of the Golden Fleece? Consult Menelaus and Medea. How wonderful to be the supremely powerful and popular ruler of a fabulously great city! Not for Oedipus. Without some understanding of the ancient myths, half the meaning of Greece will elude you.

HERCULES THE FIRST ACTION HERO

Greece's most popular mythological personage was probably Heracles, a hero who became a god, and had to work hard to do it. This paragon of masculinity was so admired by the Romans that they vulgarized him as Hercules, and modern entrepreneurs have capitalized on his popularity in silly sandal epics and sillier Saturday morning cartoons. His name means "glory of Hera," though the goddess hated him because he was the son of Zeus and the Theban princess Alcmene. The Incredible Bulk proved his strength and courage while still in the cradle, and his sexual prowess when he impregnated King Thespius' fifty daughters in as many nights. But the twelve labors are his most famous achievement. To expiate the mad murder of his wife and his three children, he was ordered to:

1. Slay the Nemean Lion
2. Kill the Lernaean Hydra
3. Capture the Cerynean Hind
4. Trap the Erymanthian Boar
5. Flush the Augean stables of manure
6. Kill the obnoxious Stymphalian Birds
7. Capture the Cretan Bull, a Minoan story
8. Steal the man-eating Mares of Diomedes
9. Abscond with the Amazon Hippolyta's girdle
10. Obtain six-armed Geryon's Cattle
11. Fetch the Golden Apples of the Hesperides, which bestowed immortality
12. Capture three-headed Cerberus, watchdog of Hades.

In other words, he had to rid the world of primitive terrors and primeval horrors. Today, some revisionist Hellenistic historians considered him to be a historical king of Argos or Tiryns and his main stomping ground was the Argolid, basically the northern and southern Peloponnese. Travelers can today still trace his journeys through the region, including Lerna (near the modern village of Myli), not far from Nafplion, where the big guy battled the Hydra, now seen by some historians as a symbol for the malarial mosquitoes that once ravaged the area. Herc pops up in the myths of many other heroes, including Jason, who stole the Golden Fleece; Perseus, who killed Medusa; and Theseus, who established Athens' dominance. And his constellation is part of the regularly whirling Zodiac that is the mythological dome over all our actions and today's astrology.

Facing page: left, Disney's *Hercules* (2000); middle, *Apollo*, Olympia Museum; right, Antigone leads Oedipus out of Thebes. Left: *Hercules Farnese*. National Archaeological Museum, Naples

7

MYTH BEHAVIN'

NAXOS TOWN ΝΑΞΟΣ (ΧΩΡΑ)

7 hrs by ferry from Piraeus; 35 km (22 mi) east of Paros town.

As your ferry chugs into the harbor, you see before you the white houses of Naxos town (Chora) on a hill crowned by the one remaining tower of the Venetian castle, a reminder that Naxos was once the proud capital of the Venetian semi-independent Duchy of the Archipelago.

> **LOOK, DON'T TOUCH**
>
> If you put on a mask and flippers for a swim in Delos's pellucid water, remember that the site guards will check you, as the offshore waters here are gleaming with shards of Delos past.

The tiny church of **Our Lady of Myrtle** (⊠*Perched on sea rock off waterfront*) watches over the local sailors, who built it for divine protection.

★ While the capital town is primarily beloved for its Venetian elegance and picturesque blind alleys, Naxos's most famous landmark is ancient: the **Portara** (⊠*At harbor's far edge*), a massive doorway that leads to nowhere. The Portara stands on the islet of **Palatia,** which was once a hill (since antiquity the Mediterranean has risen quite a bit) and in the 3rd millennium BC was the acropolis for a nearby Cycladic settlement. The Portara, an entrance to an unfinished Temple of Apollo that faces exactly toward Delos, Apollo's birthplace, was begun about 530 BC by the tyrant Lygdamis, who said he would make Naxos's buildings the highest and most glorious in Greece. He was overthrown in 506 BC, and the temple was never completed; by the 5th and 6th centuries AD it had been converted into a church; and under Venetian and Turkish rule it was slowly dismembered, so the marble could be used to build the castle. The gate, built with four blocks of marble, each 16 feet long and weighing 20 tons, was so large it couldn't be demolished, so it remains today, along with the temple floor. Palatia itself has come to be associated with the tragic myth of Ariadne, princess of Crete.

Ariadne, daughter of Crete's King Minos, helped Theseus thread the labyrinth of Knossos and slay the monstrous Minotaur. In exchange, he promised to marry her. Sailing for Athens, the couple stopped in Naxos, where Theseus abandoned her. Jilted Ariadne's curse made Theseus forget to change the ship's sails from black to white, and so his grieving father Aegeus, believing his son dead, plunged into the Aegean. Seeing Ariadne's tears, smitten Dionysus descended in a leopard-drawn chariot to marry her, and set her bridal wreath, the Corona Borealis, in the sky, an eternal token of his love.

The myth inspired one of Titian's best-known paintings, as well as Strauss's opera *Ariadne auf Naxos*.

North of Palatia, **underwater remains of Cycladic buildings** are strewn along an area called **Grotta**. Here are a series of large worked stones, the remains of the waterfront quayside mole, and a few steps that locals say go to a tunnel leading to the islet of Palatia; these remains are Cycladic (before 2000 BC).

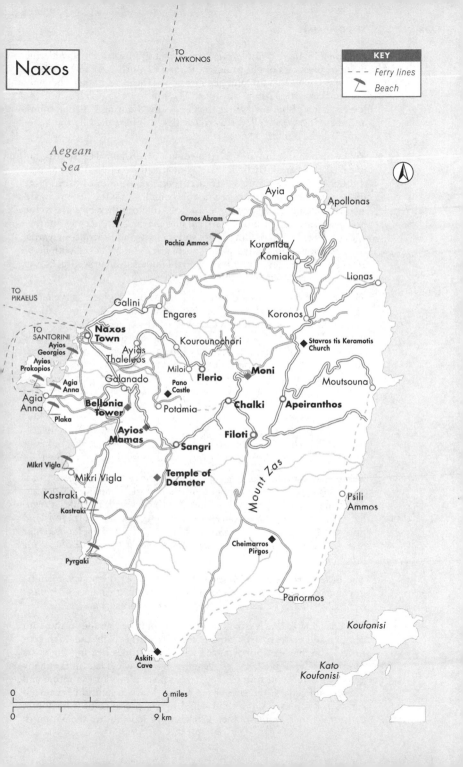

Naxos

KEY

- - - Ferry lines

Beach

TO
MYKONOS

*Aegean
Sea*

TO
PIRAEUS

Ayia

Apollonas

Ormos Abram

Pachia Ammos

Koronida/
Komiaki

Lionas

Galini

Engares

Koronos

TO SANTORINI

Ayios
Georgios

Ayios
Prokopios

**Naxos
Town**

Ayias
Thaleleos

Kourounochori

Stavros tis Keramotis
Church

Agia
Anna

Galanado

Miloi

Flerio

Moni

Moutsouna

Agia
Anna

Plaka

**Bellonia
tower**

Pano
Castle

Chalki

Apeiranthos

**Ayios
Mamas**

Potamia

Mikri Vigla

Sangri

Filoti

Kastraki

Mikri Vigla

**Temple of
Demeter**

Mount Zas

Psili
Ammos

Kastraki

Pyrgaki

Cheimarros
Pirgos

Panormos

Koufonisi

*Kato
Koufonisi*

**Askiti
Cave**

0   6 miles

0   9 km

Old town (⊠ *Along quay, left at 1st big square*) possesses a bewildering maze of twisting cobblestone streets, arched porticoes, and towering doorways, where you're plunged into cool darkness and then suddenly into pockets of dazzling sunshine. The old town is divided into the lower section, **Bourgos,** where the Greeks lived during Venetian times, and the upper part, called **Kastro** (castle), still inhabited by the Venetian Catholic nobility.

★ You won't miss the gates of the **castle** (⊠ *Kastro*). The south gate is called the **Paraporti** (side gate), but it's more interesting to enter through the northern gate, or **Trani** (strong), via Apollonos street. Note the vertical incision in the gate's marble column—it is the Venetian yard against which drapers measured the bolts of cloth they brought to the noblewomen. Step through the Trani into the citadel and enter another age, where sedate Venetian houses still stand around silent courtyards, their exteriors emblazoned with coats of arms and bedecked with flowers. Half are still owned by the original families; romantic Greeks and foreigners have bought up the rest.

The entire citadel was built in 1207 by Marco Sanudo, a Venetian who, three years after the fall of Constantinople, landed on Naxos as part of the Fourth Crusade. When in 1210 Venice refused to grant him independent status, Sanudo switched allegiance to the Latin emperor in Constantinople, becoming duke of the archipelago. Under the Byzantines, "archipelago" had meant "chief sea," but after Sanudo and his successors, it came to mean "group of islands," i.e., the Cyclades. For three centuries Naxos was held by Venetian families, who resisted pirate attacks, introduced Roman Catholicism, and later rebuilt the castle in its present form. In 1564 Naxos came under Turkish rule but, even then, the Venetians still ran the island, while the Turks only collected taxes. The rust-color Glezos tower was home to the last dukes; it displays the coat of arms: a pen and sword crossed under a crown.

The **Domus Venetian Museum,** in the 800-year-old Dellarocca-Barozzi house, lets you, at last, into one of the historic Venetian residences. The house's idyllic garden, built into the Kastro wall, provides a regular venue in season for a concert series, from classical to jazz to island music. ⊠ *At Kastro north gate* ☎ *22850/22387* ✐ *venetian@acn.gr* ⛆ *€4, tour €6* ⊘ *June–Aug., daily 10–3 and 7–10; check ahead for other times.*

The little **Naxos Folklore Museum** shows costumes, ceramics, farming implements, and other items from Naxos's far-flung villages. ⊠ *Roubel Sq.* ☎ *22850/25531* ⛆ *€3* ⊘ *Hours not set at press time.*

The **Cathedral** (⊠ *At Kastro's center*) was built by Sanudo in the 13th century and restored by Catholic families in the 16th and 17th centuries. The marble floor is paved with tombstones bearing the coats of arms of the noble families. Venetian wealth is evident in the many gold and silver icon frames. The icons reflect a mix of Byzantine and Western influences: the one of the Virgin Mary is unusual because it shows a Byzantine Virgin and Child in the presence of a bishop, a cathedral benefactor. Another 17th-century icon shows the Virgin of the Rosary surrounded by members of the Sommaripa family, whose house is nearby.

Today the historic convent and school of the Ursulines houses the **Naxos Archaeological Museum,** best known for its Cycladic and Mycenaean finds. During the early Cycladic period (3200 BC–2000 BC) there were settlements along Naxos's east coast and outside Naxos town at Grotta. The finds are from these settlements and graveyards scattered around the island. Many of the vessels exhibited are from the early Cycladic I period, hand-built of coarse-grain clay, sometimes decorated with a herringbone pattern. Though the museum has too many items in its glass cases to be appreciated in a short visit, you should try not to miss the white marble Cycladic statuettes, which range from the early "violin" shapes to the more-detailed female forms with their tilted flat heads, folded arms, and legs slightly bent at the knees. The male forms are simpler and often appear to be seated. The most common theory is that the female statuettes were both fertility and grave goddesses, and the males servant figures. ⊠ *Kastro* ☎ *22850/22725* ⊕ *www.culture. gr* ⊡ *€3* ⊙ *Tues.–Sun. 8:30–3.*

The **Greek Orthodox cathedral** (⊠ *Bourgos*) was built in 1789 on the site of a church called Zoodochos Pigis (Life-giving Source). The cathedral was built from the materials of ancient temples: the solid granite pillars are said to be from the ruins of Delos. Amid the gold and the carved wood, there is a vividly colored iconostasis painted by a well-known iconographer of the Cretan school, Dimitrios Valvis, and the Gospel Book is believed to be a gift from Catherine the Great of Russia.

The **Ancient Town of Naxos** was directly on the square in front of the Greek Orthodox cathedral. You'll note that several of the churches set on this square, like the cathedral itself, hint at Naxos's venerable history as they are made of ancient materials. In fact, this square was, in succession, the seat of a flourishing Mycenaean town (1300–1050 BC), a classical agora (when it was a 167-foot by 156-foot square closed on three sides by Doric stoas, so that it looked like the letter "G"; a shorter fourth stoa bordered the east side, leaving room at each end for an entrance), a Roman town, and early Christian church complex. Although much of the site has been refilled, under the square a **museum** (⊡ *Free* ⊙ *Tues.–Sun. 8–2:30*) gives you a well-marked sampling of the foundations. City, cemetery, tumulus, hero shrine: no wonder the early Christians built here. For more of ancient Naxos, explore the nearby precinct of Grotta.

BEACHES

The southwest coast of Naxos, facing Paros and the sunset, offers the Cyclades's longest stretches of beaches. All these have tavernas and rooms. They are listed, in order, heading south. **Ayios Georgios** is now part of town and very developed. **Ayios Prokopios** has a small leeward harbor and lagoons with waterfowl. **Ayia Anna,** very crowded, has a small harbor with connections to Paros. **Plaka,** ringed by sand dunes and bamboo groves, is about 8 km (5 mi) south of town. **Mikri Vigla** is sandy and edged by cedar trees. Seminude **Kastraki** has white marble sand. **Pyrgaki** is the least-developed beach, with idyllic crystalline water.

WHERE TO STAY & EAT

$$
✗**Old Inn.** Berlin-trained chef Dieter von Ranizewski serves German food informed by Naxos. In a courtyard under a chinaberry tree, with rough whitewashed walls and ancient marbles, two of the old church's interior sides open into the wine cellar and gallery; on the fourth side, with beams and wood paneling, is a fireplace. The menu is extensive. For starters you might try sausages with beer sauce, smoked ham, or liver pâté—all homemade. For entrées, have the

signature steak with tomatoes, olives, Roquefort, and bacon-flecked roast potatoes. Barbecue spareribs are also especially good. For dessert the mousse beckons voluptuously. There is a children's menu and small playground. ✉*Naxos town; take car road off waterfront, turn right into 2nd alley* ☎22850/26093 ▭*No credit cards.*

$ ✗**Apolafsis.** Rightly named "Enjoyment," Lefteris Keramideas's second-floor restaurant offers a balcony with a great view of the harbor and sunset. You'll enjoy live music (always in summer; often in winter), as well as a large assortment of appetizers (try spinach or zucchini tart), local barrel wine, and fresh fish. The sliced pork in wine sauce is good, too. ✉*Naxos town waterfront* ☎22850/22178 ▭*AE, MC, V.*

$ ✗**Gorgona.** Bearded Dimitris and Koula Kapris's beachfront taverna is popular both with sun worshippers on Ayia Anna beach and locals from Chora, who come here winter and summer to get away and sometimes to dance until the late hours, often to live music. The menu is extensive and fresh daily—the fresh fish comes from the caïques that pull up at the dock right in front every morning. Two good appetizers are *kakavia* (fish stew) and shrimp *saganaki* (with cooked cheese), while spaghetti with crab is a fine entrée. The barrel wine is their own (they also bottle it). The small hotel next door is also theirs. ✉*Ayia Anna near dock* ☎22850/41007 ▭*No credit cards.*

$ ✗**Labyrinth.** Opened in 2006 in the middle of the old town, Labyrinth was an immediate success with locals. Its more-than-simple food, its cozy flagstone garden, and its good service are all praiseworthy. Good appetizers include a tomato and feta quiche, and crepe rolls with smoked salmon and avocado. Among main dishes are chicken fillet with shrimp, potatoes, and herbs; and roast lamb with tomatoes and mint. And don't miss out on the light and summery lemon mousse. ☎22850/22253 ▭*No credit cards* ☉*Closed Oct.–Apr. No lunch.*

$$$ ▣**Galaxy.** All whitewash and marble, this hotel is perfect if you want to be on the beach (and don't mind the crowds at the seaside in summer). Its three buildings have wide stone arches and wooden doors in

shades of green and blue, and balconies with grillwork depicting swans. Archways also span the large rooms, which have beamed ceilings and orange accessories, plus plants, kitchenettes, and dining areas. Most rooms have ocean views (the beach is a minute away). The carefully tended grounds glow with yellow roses and a fountain. Too bad this hotel isn't more convenient to town. ⊠*Ayios Georgios beach, 84300* ☎*22850/22422 or 22850/22423* ☎*22850/22889* ⊕*www.hotel-galaxy.com* ⇨*43 studios, 11 rooms* ⚘*In-room: kitchen, Ethernet. In-hotel: pool, no elevator* ⊟*AE, MC, V* ⊗*Closed Nov.–Mar.* ⬤❘*BP.*

$ 🏨**Abram Village.** If you love island nature and dislike crowds, this is your place. Set on Naxos's northern coast (the developers only moved in a few years ago when the road was finally paved), Panyiotis Albertis's rooms and villas recline in a green garden on beautiful Abram beach. The scenery is extraordinary and there are many coves with beaches. Most of the accommodations here are rooms, with no TV, air-conditioners (it's cool), or telephones; in addition, there are two villas (which have all these amenities and sleep up to eight; they run about €160), both rooms and villas have balconies with sea views. The inexpensive restaurant, where Panyiotis's mother and wife cook, features traditional food from local products. *Tiliktera* (meatballs with eggplants and spicy sauce) is especially good—and the rosé wine and raki are Panyiotis's own. ⊹*20 km (33 mi) from Chora* ⊠*Abram 84300* ☎*22850/63244* ☎*22850/63223* ⊕*www.abram.gr* ⇨*20 rooms, 2 villas* ⚘*In-hotel: no elevator, public Internet* ⊟*MC, V* ⊗*Closed Oct.–Apr.*

$ 🏨**Apollon.** In addition to being comfortable, attractive, and quiet (it's
★ a converted marble workshop), this hotel, set in the Fontana quarter, is convenient to everything in town. Even better, it offers parking facilities, a rarity in town. The lobby blends wood, warm marble, deep greens, and many plants. The rooms are simple and have balconies; bathrooms are small. The outside, of ocher plaster and stone, is adorned with a feast of marble decoration. ⊠*Behind Orthodox cathedral, car entrance on road out of town, 84300Fontana, Chora* ☎*22850/22468* ☎*22850/25200* ⊕*www.apollonhotel-naxos.gr* ⇨*12 rooms, 1 suite* ⚘*In-hotel: no elevator, parking* ⊟*AE, MC, V.*

$ 🏨**Chateau Zevgoli.** If you stay in Chora, try to settle in here. Each room in Despina Kitini's fairy-tale pension, in a comfortable Venetian house, is distinct. The living room is filled with dark antique furniture, gilded mirrors, old family photographs, and locally woven curtains and tablecloths. One of the nicest bedrooms has a private bougainvillea-covered courtyard and pillows handmade by Despina's great-grandmother; the honeymoon suite has a canopy bed, a spacious balcony, and a view of the Portara. Despina also has roomy studios, in Chora's old town, including several on the kastro—stay a day and you'll stay a month. The only downside: The hotel is uphill and you must walk. ⊠*Chora old town (follow signs stenciled on walls), 84300* ☎*22850/22993 or 22850/26143* ☎*22850/25200* ⊕*www.apollonhotel-naxos.gr* ⇨*8 rooms, 1 suite* ⚘*In-room: refrigerator. In-hotel: no elevator, public Internet* ⊟*AE, MC, V.*

NIGHTLIFE & THE ARTS

BARS   Nightlife in Naxos is quieter than it is on Santorini or Mykonos, but there are several popular bars at the south end of Chora. Popularity changes fast, so keep your ears open for the latest places. **Ocean Dance** (⊠*Chora* ☎*22850/26766*) opens at 11:30 PM, all year round. Head for **Abyss** (⊠*Grotta road, Chora*) for a large, soundproof space with a Portara view; it's active till dawn.

> ### A TOP TIME-OUT
>
> Naxos Café (22850/26343) is one of a number of cafés in Naxos's old town trying for charm and authenticity, and succeeding. It stays open late and there is usually live jazz on Wednesday nights.

ARTS EVENTS   The 17th-century **Bazeos tower** (⌖*12 km [18 mi] from Chora toward Chalki,* ☎*22850/31402* ⊕*www.bazeostower.gr*) is one of the island's most beautiful 17th-century Venetian-era monuments and is worth a visit in itself (during high season it is open daily 10–5) but also offers a calendar of exhibitions, concerts, and seminars every summer. The **Catholic Cultural Center** (⊠*Kastro, near church* ☎*22850/24729*), among other things, runs art exhibitions; watch for posters. The **Domus Venetian Museum** (⊠*At Kastro north gate, Chora* ☎*22850/22387*), in the 800-year-old Dellarocca-Barozzi house, offers a summer concert series in its lovely garden. The **Town Hall Exhibition Space** (⊠*Chora's south end* ☎*22850/37100*) offers an ambitious program of art exhibitions, concerts, and other events.

SPORTS & THE OUTDOORS

SAILING & WATER SPORTS   For windsurfing rental and lessons near Chora, contact **Naxos-Surf Club** (⊠*Ayios Yorgios beach* ☎*22850/29170*). For windsurfing on distant, paradisiacal Plaka beach, contact **Plaka Watersports** (⊠*Plaka beach* ☎*22850/41264*).

SHOPPING

ANTIQUES   Eleni Dellarocca's shop, **Antico Veneziano** (⊠*In Kastro, down from museum* ☎*22850/26206 or 22850/22702*), is in the basement of her Venetian house, built 800 years ago. The columns inside come from Naxos's ancient acropolis. In addition to antiques, she has handmade embroideries, porcelain and glass, mirrors, old chandeliers, and vintage photographs of Naxos. One room is an art gallery.

BOOKS   At Eleftherios Primikirios's bookstore **Zoom** (⊠*Chora waterfront* ☎*22850/23675 or 22850/23676* ✉*prizoom@otenet.gr*), there's an excellent selection of English-language books about Naxos and much else. No other island bookstore is this well stocked.

CLOTHING   Vassilis and Kathy Koutelieris's **Loom** (⊠*Dimitriou Kokkou 8, in old market, off main square, 3rd street on right* ☎☎*22850/25531* ✉*loom.naxos@gmail.com*) sells casual clothes made from organically grown Greek cotton (including the Earth Collection in muted natural colors).

JEWELRY   At **Midas** (⊠*Old town, up main street behind Promponas on Chora waterfront* ☎*22850/24852*), owner Fotis Margaritis creates talismans in different settings. All include a "Naxos eye," which is the operculum, or door, of a seashell with a spiral design that fishermen bring him. The workshop of **Nassos Papakonstantinou** (⊠ *Ayiou Nikodemou street, on old town's main square* ☎☎*22850/22607*) sells one-of-a-kind pieces both sculptural and delicate. His father was a woodcarver; Nassos has inherited his talent. The shop has no sign—that is Nassos's style.

> ### DAYS FOR WINE & THYME
>
> A large selection of the famous *kitro* (citron liqueur) and preserves, as well as Naxos wines and thyme honey, packed in attractive gift baskets, can be found at Promponas Wines and Liquors, located on the Chora waterfront (22850/22258). It has been around since 1915 and free glasses of kitro are offered.

TRADITIONAL CRAFTS, CARPETS & JEWELS The embroidery and knitted items made by women in the mountain villages are known throughout Greece. They can be bought at **Techni** (⊠ *Persefonis street, old town* ☎*22850/24767* ⊕*www.techni.gr*). Techni's two shops, almost facing each other, also sell carpets, jewelry in old designs, linens, and more.

BELLONIA TOWER ΠΥΡΓΟΣ ΜΠΕΛΟΝΙΑ

5 km (3 mi) south of Naxos town.

The graceful Bellonia tower (Pirgos Bellonia) belonged to the area's ruling Venetian family, and like other fortified houses, it was built as a refuge from pirates and as part of the island's alarm system. The towers were located strategically throughout the island; if there was an attack, a large fire would be lighted on the nearest tower's roof, setting off a chain reaction from tower to tower and alerting the islanders. Bellonia's thick stone walls, its Lion of St. Mark emblem, and flat roofs with zigzag chimneys are typical of these pirgi. The unusual 13th-century **"double church"** of **St. John** (⊠ *In front of Bellonia tower*) exemplifies Venetian tolerance. On the left side is the Catholic chapel, on the right the Orthodox church, separated only by a double arch. A family lives in the tower, and the church is often open. From here, take a moment to gaze across the peaceful fields to Chora and imagine what the islanders must have felt when they saw pirate ships on the horizon.

AYIOS MAMAS ΆΓΙΟΣ ΜΑΜΑΣ

3 km (2 mi) south of Bellonia tower, 8 km (5 mi) south of Naxos town.

A kilometer (½ mi) past a valley with unsurpassed views is one of the island's oldest churches (9th century), Ayios Mamas. St. Mamas is the protector of shepherds and is regarded as a patron saint in Naxos, Cyprus, and Asia Minor. Built in the 8th century, the stone church was the island's cathedral under the Byzantines. Though it was converted into a Catholic church in 1207, it was neglected under the Venetians and is now falling apart. You can also get to it from the Potamia villages.

SANGRI ΣΑΓΚΡΙ

3 km (2 mi) south of Ayios Mamas, 11 km (7 mi) south of Naxos town.

Sangri is the center of an area with so many monuments and ruins spanning the Archaic to the Venetian periods it is sometimes called little Mystras, a reference to the famous abandoned Byzantine city in the Peloponnese.

The name Sangri is a corruption of Sainte Croix, which is what the French called the town's 16th-century monastery of **Timios Stavros** *(Holy Cross)*. The town is actually three small villages spread across a plateau. During the Turkish occupation, the monastery served as an illegal school, where children met secretly to learn the Greek language and culture.

Above the town, you can make out the **ruins of Kastro Apilarou** (⊠ *On Mt. Profitis Ilias*), the castle Sanudo first attacked. It's a hard climb up.

TEMPLE OF DEMETER ΝΑΟΣ ΤΗΣ ΔΗΜΗΤΡΑΣ

★ *5 km (3 mi) south of Sangri.*

Take the asphalt road right before the entrance to Sangri to reach the Temple of Demeter, a marble Archaic temple, circa 530 BC, lovingly restored by German archaeologists during the 1990s. Demeter was a grain goddess, and it's not hard to see what she is doing in this beautiful spot. There is also a small museum here (admission is free).

CHALKI ΧΑΛΚΙ

6 km (4 mi) northeast of Sangri, 17 km (10½ mi) southeast of Naxos town.

You are now entering the heart of the lush Tragaia valley, where in spring the air is heavily scented with honeysuckle, roses, and lemon blossoms and many tiny Byzantine churches hide in the dense olive groves. In Chalki is one of the most important of these Byzantine churches: the white, red-roofed **Panagia Protothrone** *(First Enthroned Virgin Church)*. Restoration work has uncovered frescoes from the 6th through the 13th century, and the church has remained alive and functioning for 14 centuries. The oldest layers, in the apse, depict the Apostles. ⊠ *On main road* ☉ *Mornings.*

Chalki itself is a pretty town, known for its neoclassic houses in shades of pink, yellow, and gray, which are oddly juxtaposed with the plain but stately 17th-century Venetian **Frangopoulos tower.** ⊠ *Main road, next to Panagia Protothrone* 💰*Free* ☉ *Sometimes open in morning.*

MONI ΜΟΝΗ

6 km (4 mi) north of Chalki, 23 km (14¼ mi) east of Naxos town.

Owing to a good asphalt road, Moni ("monastery"), high in the mountains overlooking Naxos's greenest valley, has become a popular place for a meal or coffee on a hot afternoon. Local women make embroideries for Chora's shops. Just below Moni is one of the Balkans's most important churches, **Panayia Drosiani** (☎*22850/31003*), which has faint, rare Byzantine frescoes from the 7th and 8th centuries. Its name means Our Lady of Refreshment, because once during a severe drought, when all the churches took their icons down to the sea to pray for rain, only the icon of this church got results. The fading frescoes are visible in layers: to the right when you enter are the oldest—one shows St. George the Dragon Slayer astride his horse, along with a small boy, an image one usually sees only in Cyprus and Crete. According to legend, the saint saved the child, who had fallen into a well, and there met and slew the giant dragon that had terrorized the town. Opposite him is St. Dimitrios, shown killing barbarians. The church is made up of three chapels—the middle one has a space for the faithful to worship at the altar rather than in the nave, as became common in later centuries. Next to that is a very small opening that housed a secret school during the revolution. It is open mornings and again after siesta; in deserted winter, ring the bell if it is not open.

7

FILOTI ΦΙΛΟΤΙ

6½ km (4 mi) south of Moni, 20 km (12½ mi) southeast of Naxos town.

Filoti, a peaceful village on the lower slopes of Mt. Zas, is the interior's largest. A three-day festival celebrating the Dormition starts on August 14. In the center of town are another Venetian tower that belonged to the Barozzi and the Church of Filotissa (Filoti's Virgin Mary) with its marble iconostasis and carved bell tower. There are places to eat and rooms to rent.

SPORTS & THE OUTDOORS

Filoti is the starting place for several walks in the countryside, including the climb up to **Zas cave** (✉*Southeast of town on small dirt track*), where obsidian tools and pottery fragments have been found; lots of bats live inside. Mt. Zas, or Zeus, is one of the god's birthplaces; on the path to the summit lies a block of unworked marble that reads *Oros Dios Milosiou*, or "Boundary of the Temple of Zeus Melosios." (Melosios, it is thought, is a word that has to do with sheep.) The islanders say that under the Turks the cave was used as a chapel, and two stalagmites are called the Priest and the Priest's Wife, who are said to have been petrified by God to save them from arrest.

APEIRANTHOS ΑΠΕΙΡΑΝΘΟΣ

★ *12 km (7½ mi) northeast of Filoti, 32 km (20 mi) southeast of Naxos town.*

Apeiranthos is very picturesque, with views and marble-paved streets running between the Venetian Bardani and Zevgoli towers. As you walk through the arcades and alleys, notice the unusual chimneys—no two are alike. The elders sit in their doorsteps chatting, while packs of children shout "Hello, hello" at any passerby who looks foreign.

A very small **Archaeological Museum,** established by a local mathematician, Michael Bardanis, displays Cycladic finds from the east coast. The most important of the artifacts are unique gray marble plaques from the 3rd millennium BC with roughly hammered scenes of daily life: hunters and farmers and sailors going about their business. If it's closed, ask in the square for the guard. ⊠ *Off main square* 🎫 *Free* ⊙ *Daily 8:30–3.*

TOWERING VIEWS

The Cheimarros Pirgos (Tower of the Torrent), a cylindrical Hellenistic tower, can be reached from Filoti by a road that begins from the main road to Apeiranthos, outside town, or by a level, 3½-hour hike with excellent views. The walls, as tall as 45 feet, are intact, with marble blocks perfectly aligned. The tower, which also served as a lookout post for pirates, is often celebrated in the island's poetry: "O, my heart is like a bower/And Cheimarros's lofty tower!"

PAROS & ANTIPAROS ΠΑΡΟΣ & ΑΝΤΙΠΑΡΟΣ

In the classical age, the great sculptor Praxiteles prized the incomparably snowy marble that came from the quarries at Paros; his chief rival was the Parian Scopas. Between them they developed the first true female nude and gentle voluptuousness seems a good description of this historic island. Today, Paros is favored by people for its cafés by the sea, golden sandy beaches, and charming fishing villages. It may lack the chic of Mykonos and have fewer top-class hotels, but at the height of the season it often gets Mykonos's overflow. The island is large enough to accommodate the traveler in search of peace and quiet, yet the lovely port towns of Paroikía, the capital, and Naousa also have an active nightlife (overactive in August). Paros is a focal point of the Cyclades ferry network, and many people stay here for a night or two while waiting for a connection. Paros town has a good share of bars and discos, though Naousa has a more-chic island atmosphere. And none of the islands has a richer cultural life, with concerts, exhibitions, and readings, than does Paros. For this, check the English monthly, *Paros Life,* available everywhere (⊕*www.paroslife.gr*, and also ⊕*www.parosweb.com*).

Like all the bigger islands, Paros is developing too fast. In the last 15 years 2,000 new homes have been built on the island, which has a population of 14,000. Another thousand are underway—and this equals the total number of homes ever built here. You'll understand why: you're likely to want to build a little house here yourself. The

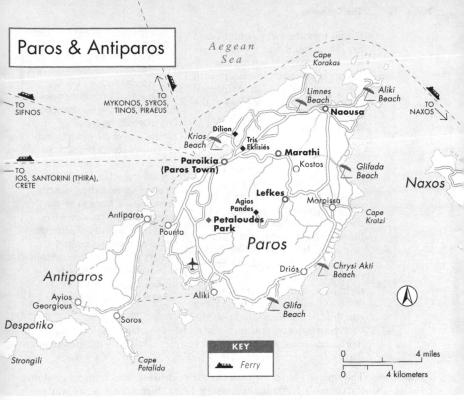

Paros & Antiparos

Aegean
Sea

TO SIFNOS

TO MYKONOS, SYROS, TINOS, PIRAEUS

TO IOS, SANTORINI (THIRA), CRETE

Cape Korakas

Limnes Beach

Aliki Beach

Naousa

TO NAXOS

Krios Beach

Dilion

Tris Eklisiés

Paroikía (Paros Town)

Marathi

Kostos

Glifada Beach

Naxos

Lefkes

Agios Pandes

Marpissa

Antiparos

Cape Kratzi

◆ **Petaloudes Park**

Pounta

Paros

Antiparos

Driós

Chrysi Akti Beach

Ayios Georgious

Aliki

Glifa Beach

Despotiko

Soros

Strongili

Cape Petalida

KEY
🛳 Ferry

0   4 miles

0   4 kilometers

overflow of visitors is such that it has now washed up on Paros's sister, Antiparos: this island forgetaway still has an off-the-beaten-track vibe, even though the rich and famous—Dolly Goulandris, Brad Pitt, and Tom Hanks, to name three—have discovered it.

PAROIKIA ΠΑΡΟΙΚΙΑ (ΠΑΡΟΣ)

35 km (22 mi) west of Naxos town, 10 km (6 mi) southwest of Naousa.

First impressions of Paroikía (Paros town), pretty as it is, will not necessarily be positive. The port is clogged with too many boats and the traffic problem, now that Athenian families bring two cars and local families own two cars, is insoluble; the new parking area on landfill is one of the Cyclades's disasters. The waterfront is lined with travel agencies, a multitude of car and motorbike rental agencies, and *"fast-food-adika"*—the Greek word means just what you think it does. Then, if you head east on the harbor road, you'll see a lineup of bars, tourist shops, and coffee shops—many, as elsewhere on the more-prosperous islands, rented by Athenians who come to Paros to capitalize on the huge summer influx. Past them are the fishing-boat dock, a partially excavated ancient graveyard, and the post office; then start the beaches (shaded and over-popular), with their hotels and tavernas.

But go the other way straight into town and you'll find it easy to get lost in the maze of narrow, stone-paved lanes that intersect with the streets of the quiet residential areas. The new marble plaza at the town's entrance, finished in 2007, is full of strollers and playing children in the evening (during the day, you can fry eggs on this shadeless space). As you check your laptop (Paroikía is Wi-Fi) along the market street chockablock with tourist shops, you'll begin to traverse the centuries: ahead of you looms the seaside Kastro, the ancient acropolis. In 1207 the Venetians conquered Paros, which joined the Duchy of Naxos, and built their huge marble castle wall out of blocks and columns from three temples. At the crest, next to the church of Saints Constantine and Helen (built in 1689), are the visible foundations of a late-Archaic temple to Athena—the area remains Paros's favorite sunset spot.

> ## PRIDE GOETH BEFORE A FALL
>
> At one point, Justinian the Great (who ruled the Byzantine Empire in 527-65) had the Hundred Doors Church rebuilt. He appointed Isidorus, one of the two architects of Constantinople's famed Hagia Sophia, to design it, but Isidorus sent his apprentice, Ignatius, in his place. On inspection, Isidorus discovered the dome to be so magnificent that, consumed by jealousy, he pushed the apprentice off the roof. Ignatius grasped his master's foot and the two tumbled to their death together. Look for the folk sculpture at the sanctuary's left portal of the two men.

Fodor'sChoice
★ The square above the port, to the northwest, was built to celebrate the church's 1,700th anniversary. From there note a white wall with two belfries, the front of the former monastic quarters that surround the magnificent **Panayia Ekatontapyliani** *(Hundred Doors Church)*, the earliest remaining proto-Byzantine church in Greece and one of the oldest unaltered churches in the world. As such, it is of inestimable value to architecture buffs (such as Prince Charles, who has been spotted here).

The story began in 326, when St. Helen—the mother of Emperor Constantine the Great—set out on a ship for the Holy Land to find the True Cross. Stopping on Paros, she had a vision of success and vowed to build a church there. Though she died before it was built, her son built the church in 328 as a wooden-roof basilica. Two centuries later, Justinian the Great (who ruled the Byzantine Empire in 527–65) comissioned the splendid dome.

According to legend, 99 doors have been found in the church and the 100th will be discovered only after Constantinople is Greek again—but the name is actually older than the legend. Inside, the subdued light mixes with the dun, reddish, and green tufa (porous volcanic rock). The columns are classical and their capitals Byzantine. At the corners of the dome are two fading Byzantine frescoes depicting six-winged seraphim. The 4th-century iconostasis (with ornate later additions) is divided into five frames by marble columns. One panel contains the 14th-century icon of the Virgin, with a silver covering from 1777.

The Virgin is carried in procession on the church's crowded feast day, August 15, the Dormition. The adjacent **Baptistery,** nearly unique in Greece, also built from the 4th to the 6th century, has a marble font and bits of mosaic floor. During Easter services, thousands of rose petals are dropped from the dome on the singing celebrants. The church **museum,** at right, contains post-Byzantine icons. ✉ *750 ft east of dock* ☎ *22840/21243* 🖃 *€2* ⊙ *Daily 8* AM–*10* PM.

The **Archaeological Museum** contains a large chunk of the famed Parian chronicle, which recorded cultural events in Greece from about 1500 BC until 260 BC (another chunk is in Oxford's Ashmolean Museum). It interests scholars that the historian inscribed detailed information about artists, poets, and playwrights, completely ignoring wars and shifts in government. Some primitive pieces from the Aegean's oldest settlement, Saliagos (an islet between Paros and Antiparos), are exhibited in the same room, on the left. A small room contains Archaic finds from the ongoing excavation at Despotiko—and they are finding a lot. In the large room to the right rests a marble slab depicting the poet Archilochus in a banquet scene, lying on a couch, his weapons nearby. The ancients ranked Archilochus, who invented iambic meter and wrote the first signed love lyric, second only to Homer. When he died in battle against the Naxians, his conqueror was cursed by the oracle of Apollo for putting to rest one of the faithful servants of the muse. Also there are a monumental Nike and three superb pieces found in the last decade: a waist-down kouros, a gorgon with intact wings, and a dancing-girl relief. ✉ *Behind Hundred Doors Church* ☎ *22840/21231* 🖃 *€3* ⊙ *Tues.–Sun. 8:30–2:30.*

At the **Anthemion Museum,** the Kontogiorgos family has lovingly gathered a large, valuable collection of books, manuscripts, prints, coins, jewels, embroideries, weapons, ceramics, and much more, mostly pertaining to Paros, and lovingly displays it in this house-turned-museum. ✉ *Airport road, before Punta split* ☎ *22840/91010* 🖃 *€5* ⊙ *Tues.– Sun. 8:30–2:30.*

The **Scropios Museum** is set next to a garden full of large models of traditional Parian windmills, dovecotes, churches, and other such things, making for an utterly charming setting. It showcases the creations of fisherman Benetos Skiadas, who loves to make detailed models of ships, including his own, and his scrupulous craftsmanship is on view here; you can also order a model of your own design. ✉ *On road to Aliki, just past airport* ☎ *22840/91129* 🖃 *€2* ⊙ *May–Sept., changeable hrs.*

BEACHES

From Paros town, boats leave throughout the day for beaches across the bay: to sandy **Krios** and the quieter **Kaminia. Livadia,** a five-minute walk, is very developed but has shade. In the other direction, Delfini has a club with live music, and Parasporos has two music bars.

WHERE TO STAY & EAT

$$ ✕**Levantis.** Owner George Mavridis does his own cooking—always a
★ good sign. Though this spot looks like a garden taverna and, amazingly,
is priced like one, the food is sophisticated and eclectic, as George often
returns from winter travels with exotic new recipes. Two intriguing
starters are roasted eggplant tart with salsa verde, and Greek mussels
with a spicy ouzo sauce. Top entrées include handmade ravioli stuffed
with gingered beets, goat cheese, and pesto or the caramelized calves'
liver with roasted grapes. Then choose, if you can, between banana
toffee and cream pie or lemon sorbet with roasted figs and sweet wine.
Unusual in Greece, Levantis has a nonsmoking section. ⊠ *Central mar-
ket street* ☎ *22840/23613* ⊟ *AE, MC, V* ⊘ *Closed Nov.–Apr.*

$–$$ ✕**Porphyra.** Yannis Gouroyannis knows everything about fish; he fishes,
★ dives, prepares, and greets you with a plate of marinated fish, and his
oysters, clams, and urchins couldn't be fresher. The mussels are always
superb, and the kakavia (fish soup with a whole fish in each plate) and
fresh fish (it changes) in an aromatic white sauce remind you that Paros
is seagirt. The interior is simple and authentic, while the outdoor tables
border a romantic ancient ruin. All ingredients are local and of the
highest quality in Paros's best seafood restaurant. ⊠ *Along waterfront
toward post office* ☎ *22840/23410* ⊟ *AE, MC, V.*

¢ ✕**Gelato Sulla Luna.** Many of the evening strollers on the waterfront
of Paroikía cannot pass this authentic gelateria; their willpower melts
faster than the gelato. Denise Marinucci's father made ice cream in
New Jersey, and Denise continues the tradition, but her recipes come
from Venice. She makes everything on the premises. Have another.
⊠ *Waterfront* ☎ *22840/22868* ⊕ *www.parosweb.com/sullaluna* ⊟ *No
credit cards* ⊘ *Closed Dec.–Mar.*

$$$$ ▦**Bicycle House.** The name comes from the bicycle (of the noted late
★ dancer Vasilis Iakoumis) mounted to the front of this house, which
contains three lovely units. The complex overlooks the sea and sunset,
is surrounded by greenery, and is scrupulously designed in island style
with the addition of modern comforts. Owners Len and Marilyn Rooks
are warm and helpful and visitors tend to return, if only to hear more
about Len's own cycling exploits (guests are often regaled with these
stories at his garden barbecues). You should have your own transportation, though there is a bus. Unusually for a place at this price range, no
credit cards are taken. It's open all year. ✛ *8 km (12 mi) from Paroikía
on airport road* ⊠ *84400* ☎ *22840/92203* ⊕ *www.paroshome.com/
roshome.com* ⇖ *3 apartments* ⚹ *In-room: kitchen, Ethernet. In-hotel:
no elevator* ⊟ *No credit cards.*

$$$ ▦**Pandrossos Hotel.** If you want a good night's sleep away from the
pulse of Paros town but you don't want to give up shopping, nightlife,
restaurants, and cafés, the Pandrossos—built on a hill with a splendid
view overlooking Paros bay—is the best choice. The lobby, restaurant,
and terrace form one great expanse of marble, perfect for sunset watch-
ing—unless you're watching it from your room's sea-view balcony. Note
that some of the rooms are on the small side. To get to this hotel's hill
location, take the seaside road from Paros town. ⊠ *On hill at south-
west edge of Paros town, 84400* ☎ *22840/22903* ⊟ *22840/22904*

⊕*www.pandrossoshotel.gr* ⌖*41 rooms, 5 suites* ♿*In-room: Ethernet. In-hotel: restaurant, bar, pool, no elevator* ▤*AE, MC, V* ⊗*Closed Nov.–Mar.* ❍❙*BP.*

$ ⊡**Parian Village.** This shady, quiet hotel at the far edge of Livadia beach has small rooms, all with balconies or terraces, most with spectacular views over Paroikía bay. The pool is pretty, but the sea is close. Breakfast is included. ⊠*25-min sea walk from center of Paros town, 84400* ☎*22840/23187* 🖷*22840/23880* ⊕*www.paros-accommodations.gr/ parianvillage* ⌖*28 rooms* ♿*In-room: refrigerator. In-hotel: pool, no elevator* ▤*MC, V* ⊗*Closed Nov.–Apr.* ❍❙*BP.*

$ ⊡**Pension Evangelistria.** Voula Maounis's rooms, all with balconies,
★ are usually full of returnees—archaeologists, painters, and the like—who enjoy its central location near the Hundred Doors Church, olive trees, and gracious welcome. The house is built over a Roman-period ruin; the hotel is open all year. ⊠*Near dock, 84400* ☎*22840/21481* 🖷*22840/22464* ✐*parosrealmarket@otenet.gr* ⌖*9 rooms* ♿*In-room: kitchen. In-hotel: no elevator* ▤*No credit cards.*

NIGHTLIFE & THE ARTS

MUSIC & BARS Turn right along the waterfront from the port in Paros town to find the town's famous bars; then follow your ears. At the far end of the Paralia is the laser-light-and-disco section of town, which you may want to avoid. In the younger bars, cheap alcohol, as everywhere in tourist Greece, is often added to the more-colorful drinks. For a classier alternative to noisy bars, head for **Pebbles** (⊠*On Kastro hill* ☎*22840/22283*), which often has live jazz (Greece's best jazz guitarist, Vasilis Rakopoulos, who summers on Paros, likes to drop by with local bassist Petros Varthakouris) and overlooks the sunset.

THE ARTS The **Aegean Center for the Fine Arts** (⊠*Main cross street to market street* ☎*22840/23287* ⊕*www.aegeancenter.org*), a small American arts college, hosts readings, concerts, lectures, and exhibitions in its splendidly restored neoclassic mansion. Director John Pack, an American photographer, lives on the island with his family. Since 1966 the center has offered courses (two three-month semesters) in writing, painting, photography, and classical voice training.

The **Archilochos Cultural Society** (⊠*Near bus stop* ☎*22840/23595* ⊕*www.archilochos.gr*) runs a film club in winter and offers concerts, exhibitions, and lectures throughout the year.

The **Paros Summer Musical Festival** brings musicians from around the world to perform at the Archilochos Hall. Watch for posters for upcoming events.

Of all the islands Paros has the liveliest art scene (check *Paros Life* for openings and events), with dozens of galleries and public spaces presenting exhibitions. Many artists, Greek and foreign, live on the island or visit regularly—painters Jane Pack and Neva Bergmann, sculptor Britt Spillers, photographers Stavros Niflis and Elizabeth Carson, mosaicist Angelika Vaxevanidou, and ceramist Stelios Ghikas are just a few—and the Aegean Center has proved a strong stimulant. Set on an enchanting alley in the historic Kastro area of Paroikía is the former wine storage space now known as the **Apothiki** (⊠*Near bus stop* ☎*22840/28226* ⊕*www.apothiki.com*); artists include sculptor Richard King and painter Ellen Shire, and it's worth a visit just for the beauty of its space.

The **Orange Door Gallery** (⊠*Market street* ☎*22840/21590* ⊕*www. orangedoorgallery.com*) is set in a whitewashed town house and has a fine stable of artists, including some great photographers.

SPORTS & THE OUTDOORS

WATER SPORTS Many beaches offer water sports, especially windsurfing. **Aegean Diving College** (⊠*Golden beach* ☎☎*22840/43347*) offers scuba lessons and takes you to reefs, shipwrecks, and caves. Director Peter Nikolaides, who discovered the oldest shipwreck known, is a marine biologist involved in many of Greece's ecological projects. Every summer the **F2 Windsurfing Center** (⊠*New Golden beach, at Philoxenia Hotel, near Marpissa* ☎*22840/41878*) hosts the International Windsurfing World Cup.

SHOPPING

CERAMICS On Market street, look for the house with the beautifully carved Parian marble facade to find Paros's most elegantly designed shop, **Yria Interiors** (⊠*Start of Market street* ☎*22840/24359* ⊕*www.yriaparos.com*). Here Stelios and Monique Ghikas display their pottery from Studio Yria, as well as a carefully chosen range of stylish household items mostly from France.

JEWELRY Vangelis Skaramagas and Yannis Xenos have been making their own delicate, precious jewelry at **Jewelry Workshop** (⊠*End of market street* ☎*22840/21008*) for more than 20 years. Local Phaidra Apostolopoulou, who studied jewelry in Athens, now has a tiny shop, **Phaidra** (⊠*Near Zoodochos Pyghi church* ☎*22840/23626*), where she shows her silver pieces, many lighthearted for summer.

LOCAL FOODS **Enosis** (*Agricultural Cooperative's shop* ⊠*Mando Mavrogenous Sq. at front of Paros town under police station* ☎*22820/22181*) sells homemade pasta, honey, cheeses, and especially Paros's renowned wines. The varietal wine Monemvasia (officially rated "Appellation of High Quality Origin Paros") is made from white monemvasia grapes, indigenous to Paros. You can visit the winery for an evocative slide show, a photography exhibition of Paros's agricultural traditions, and a wine tasting. For an appointment call Alexis Gokas at 22840/22235.

EN ROUTE Halfway from Paros town to Naousa, on the right, the 17th-century **Monastery of Longovarda** (☎*22840/21202*) shines on its mountainside. The monastic community farms the local land and makes honey, wine, and olive oil. Only men, dressed in conservative clothing, are allowed inside, where there are post-Byzantine icons, 17th-century frescoes depicting the Twelve Feasts in the Life of Christ, and a library of rare books; it is usually open mornings.

NAOUSA ΝΑΟΥΣΑ

★ *10 km (6 mi) northeast of Paroikía.*

Naousa, impossibly pretty, long ago discovered the benefits of tourism. Its outskirts are mushrooming with villas and hotels that exploit it further. Along the harbor—which thankfully maintains its beauty and function as a fishing port—red and navy-blue boats knock gently against one another as men repair their nets and foreigners relax in the ouzeri—Barbarossa being the traditional favorite—by the water's edge. From here the pirate Hugue Crevelliers operated in the 1570s, and Byron turned him into the Corsair. Navies of the ancient Persians, flotillas from medieval Venice, and the imperial Russian fleet have anchored in this harbor. The half-submerged ruins of the Venetian fortifications still remain; they are a pretty sight when lighted up at night. Compared to Paroikía, the scene in Naousa is somewhat more chic, with a more-intimate array of shops, bars, and restaurants, but in winter the town shuts down. Unobtrusive Paros's gay scene is here, if it is anywhere.

BEACHES

A boat goes regularly to **Lageri** (⊠*North of Naousa*), a long, sandy beach with dunes. The boat that goes to Lageri also travels to **Santa Maria** (⊠*Northeastern shore of Paros*), the windsurfers' beach. A boat crosses the bay to **Kolimbithres** (⊠*Directly across bay from Naousa*), noted for its anfractuous rock formations, water sports, a choice of tavernas, and two luxury hotels. **Ayios Ioannis** (⊠*Across from Naousa*), served by the boat that goes to Kolimbithres, is a quiet locale, offering a pretty 15-minute walk along a path to a lighthouse.

WHERE TO STAY & EAT

$$$$ ✕**Poseidon.** Eat here for elegant dining away from the fray, on a spacious terrace with two pools, dozens of palm trees, and the bay of Naousa in front of you. The vegetables are from their own garden, the fish is fresh, and the food has a French accent. To start, try beef (fresh from France) carpaccio in a crush of herbs and spices with arugula and Parmesan, or scallops St-Jacques with parsley butter. Two excellent main courses would be French beef fillet with pepper sauce, sautéed oyster mushrooms, and broccoli; or Dover sole fillet with Mozambique prawns, leeks, and sautéed spinach, and wild rice with a bouillabaisse sauce. If you can still manage dessert (you will want to sit here a long time), try the chocolate pyramid with passion-fruit cream. ⊠*Astir Hotel, Kolimbithres* ☎*22840/51976* ⊕*www.astirofparos.gr* ▤*AE, MC, V* ⊗*Closed Nov.–Apr.*

$$$$ ✕**Taverna Christos.** For more than 25 years Christos has been Naousa's
Fodor'sChoice best restaurant; it still is. Its cool, white, spacious garden—the walls
★ are an art gallery—has an easy elegance; the service is both efficient and gracious. Excellent first courses include fresh sardines rolled in vine leaves with yogurt and saffron, and risotto with fresh cuttlefish in its ink. Among entrées, try the fine veal fillet with fresh tomatoes and basil, and roast lamb with lentils and caramelized onions. Fresh strawberry mousse on chocolate slabs is sinful, to say nothing of the chocolate "Trilogy," with Madagascar vanilla ice cream and caramel sauce. Chris-

tos always has local specialties, so ask. ✉ *Up hill from central square, 84401* ☎ *22840/51442* ⊕ *www. christos-restaurant.gr* ⊟ *AE, MC, V* ⊙ *Closed Oct.–May.*

$$$ ✗ **Mario.** Good food is enhanced
★ here by the pretty location, a few feet from the fishing boats on Naousa's harbor. The taverna specializes in fresh fish and also such dishes as eggplant confit, or pastry rolls stuffed with shrimp and soft cheese. For a main dish, have fresh fish wrapped in bacon, or a fillet

of beef on potato puree in wine sauce. The fresh strawberry liquor will keep you sitting longer. ✉ *On fishing-boat harbor* ☎ *22840/51047* ✉ *tsachoo@hotmail.com* ⚐ *Reservations essential* ⊟ *AE, MC, V.*

$$$$ 🏨 **Astir of Paros.** Across the bay from Naousa twinkle the lights of this deluxe resort hotel, a graceful and expensive retreat (expensive for Paros, not for Mykonos), with green lawns, tall palm trees, extensive lush gardens, and an art gallery. Guest rooms are elegant and spacious, a vibrant mix of antiques and boldly colored modern paintings, which lose a little compared to the window views of sparkling Naousa bay. The hotel's bars (one set by the sea) are popular and its two restaurants are ambitious. As you stroll through the vast gardens—note the historic Chapel of St. Nicholas (and its Byzantine-era murals) church carefully rebuilt on 12th-century foundations—the bustle of Paros is very far away indeed. ✉ *Take Kolimbithres road from Naousa, 84401* ☎ *22840/51976 or 22840/51984* ☎ *22840/51985* ⊕ *www.astirofparos.gr* ➷ *11 rooms, 46 suites* ⚒ *In-room: refrigerator, Ethernet. In-hotel: 2 restaurants, bars, tennis court, pool, gym, no elevator* ⊟ *AE, DC, MC, V* ⊙ *Closed Nov.–Mar.* ⊤⊙*BP.*

$ 🏨 **Svoronos Bungalows.** These bungalow apartments always seem to be fully occupied. The friendly Sovronos family tends the lush garden, and the comfortable apartments and Cycladic whitewashed courtyards are decorated with antiques and objects from the family's extensive travels. Though quiet, the hotel is within easy reach of Naousa's lively shopping and nightlife. There is no air-conditioning, but it is cool. ✉ *Behind big church, 1 block in from Santa Maria road, 84401* ☎ *22849/51211 or 22840/51409* ☎ *22840/52281* ⊕ *www.parosweb.gr/svoronos* ➷ *19 apartments* ⚒ *In-room: no a/c, kitchen, no TV. In-hotel: bar, no elevator* ⊟ *MC, V* ⊙ *Closed Nov.–Apr.*

NIGHTLIFE & THE ARTS

BARS **Linardo's** (✉ *At fishing harbor*) is lively and is open into the wee hours. **Agosta** (✉ *At fishing harbor*) is a pretty spot.

DANCE The group **Music–Dance "Naousa Paros"** (☎ *22840/52284* ⊕ *www.users. otenet.gr/~parofolk/index_en.html*), formed in 1988 to preserve the traditional dances and music of Paros, performs all summer long in Naousa in the costumes of the 16th century and has participated in dance competitions and festivals throughout Europe. Keep an eye out for posters.

SPORTS & THE OUTDOORS

If you're traveling with children, **Aqua Paros Waterpark** (⊠ *Kolimbithres, next to Porto Paros Hotel* ☎ 22840/53271), with its 13 waterslides big and small, will cool a hot afternoon. Admission is €12. **Santa Maria Surf Club** (⊠ *Santa Maria beach, about 4 km [2½ mi] north of Naousa*) is popular, with windsurfing, jet-skiing, waterskiing, and diving.

SHOPPING

ART & JEWELRY Paros is an art colony and exhibits are everywhere in summer. Petros Metaxas's **Metaxas Gallery** (⊠ *On 2nd street from harbor toward main church* ☎ 22840/52667) is especially devoted to the jewelry of Aristotelis and Lilly Bessis, who run it, too. There are also exhibits by local artists, and a selection of antiques from Albania.

FASHION Kostas Mouzedakis's **Tango** (⊠ *On 2nd street from harbor toward main church* ☎ 22840/51014) has been selling classic sportswear for two decades; its most popular line is its own Tangowear.

MARATHI ΜΑΡΑΘΙ

10 km (6 mi) east of Paros town.

During the classical period the island of Paros had an estimated 150,000 residents, many of them slaves who worked the ancient marble quarries in Marathi. The island grew rich from the export of this white, granular marble known among ancient architects and sculptors for its ability to absorb light. They called it *lychnites* ("won by lamplight").

Marked by a sign, **three caverns** (⊠ *Short walk from main road*) are bored into the hillside, the largest of them 300 feet deep. The most recent quarrying done in these mines was in 1844, when a French company cut marble here for Napoléon's tomb.

SHOPPING

At **Studio Yria** (✛ *1½ km [¾ mi] east of Marathi, above road to Kostos village* ☎ 22840/29007 ⊕ *www.yriaparos.com*) master potters Stelios and Monique Ghikas and other craftspeople can be seen at work. Marble carvers, metalsmiths, painters, and more all make for a true Renaissance workshop. Both the ceramic tableware and the works of art make use of Byzantine and Cycladic motifs in their designs; they have even made ceramic designs for the prince of Wales. Easily accessible by bus, taxi, and rental car, the studio is usually open daily 8–8; call ahead in the off-season.

LEFKES ΛΕΥΚΕΣ

6 km (4 mi) south of Marathi, 10 km (6 mi) southeast of Paros town.

Rampant piracy in the 17th century forced thousands of people to move inland from the coastal regions; thus for many years the scenic village of Lefkes, built on a hillside in the protective mountains, was the island's capital. It remains the largest village in the interior and has maintained a peaceful, island feeling, with narrow streets fragrant of jasmine and honeysuckle. These days, the old houses are being restored, and in summer the town is full of people. Farming is the major source of income, as you can tell from the well-kept stone walls and olive groves. For one of the best walks on Paros, take the ancient Byzantine road from the main lower square to the lower villages.

Two **17th-century churches** of interest are **Ayia Varvara** (St. Barbara) and Ayios Sotiris (Holy Savior).

The big 1830 neo-Renaissance **Ayia Triada** *(Holy Trinity)* is the pride of the village.

BEACHES
Piso Livadi (⊠ *On road past Lefkes*) was the ancient port for the marble quarries and today is a small resort town convenient to many beaches; the harbor, where boats leave for Naxos and Delos, is being expanded.

WHERE TO STAY & EAT
$ ✕ **Taverna Klarinos.** You go to Nikos and Anna Ragousis's place for the real thing. Nikos grows the vegetables, raises the meat, makes the cheese (even the feta) from his own goats, and makes the wine from his own vineyards; Anna cooks. Traditional dishes such as fried zucchini or beets with garlic sauce are the best you'll taste, and the grilled meats make the gods envious. ⊠ *Main entrance street, opposite square, on 2nd fl.* ☎ *22840/41608* ▤ *No credit cards* ☾ *Closed Oct.–May.*

$$$ ⊞ **Lefkes Village.** All the rooms in this elegant hotel are white, and the
★   wooden furniture and fabrics are reproductions of traditional styles; all have balconies with magnificent views down the olive-tree valley and over the sea to Naxos. The restaurant is noted for its traditional Greek food; the folk museum here is chockablock with interesting objects. ⊠ *East of Lefkes on main road, 84400* ☎ *22840/41827* 昌 *22840/42398* ⊕ *www.lefkesvillage.gr* ⤶ *20 rooms* ⟁ *In-room: refrigerator. In-hotel: restaurant, bar, pool, no elevator, public Internet* ▤ *AE, DC, MC, V* ☾ *Closed Nov.–Mar.* ℠ *BP.*

SHOPPING
WEAVINGS   On the main street above the lower café square, Nikoletta Haniotis's shop, **Anemi** (☎ *22840/41182*), sells handwoven weavings colored with natural dyes and local designs. Also for sale are iron pieces made by her father, Lefkes's blacksmith.

PETALOUDES PARK ΠΕΤΑΛΟΥΔΕΣ

4 km (2½ mi) south of Paros town.

A species of moth returns year after year to mate in Petaloudes (the Valley of the Butterflies), a lush oasis of greenery in the middle of this dry island. In May, June, and perhaps July, you can watch them as they lie dormant during the day, their chocolate-brown wings with yellow stripes still against the ivy leaves. In the evening they flutter upward to the cooler air, flashing the coral-red undersides of their wings as they rise. A notice at the entrance asks visitors not to disturb them by taking photographs or shaking the leaves. ⊠*Petaloudes* 🖼€3 ☉*Mid-May–mid-Sept., daily 9–8.*

NEED A BREAK?

Even when the butterflies are not there, it is pleasant to have coffee in the small *kafeneio* (*coffeehouse* ⊠ *Inside entrance to park*) and enjoy the shade of the cypress, olive, chestnut, mulberry, and lemon trees.

On the summit of a hill beyond the garden reigns a lopped **Venetian tower.** Its founder's name, Iakovos Alisafis, and the date, 1626, are inscribed on it.

WHERE TO EAT

$$$ ★ ✕**Thea.** From the terrace of this fine restaurant you can enjoy the view over the Antiparos strait and the little ferries that ply it. The interior is all of wood and hundreds of bottles of wine shelved from floor to high ceiling. Owner Nikos Kouroumlis is, in fact, a wine fanatic, and Thea has one of the most varied wine lists in all of Greece; his own wine is excellent. In winter, a good bottle of the grape and a warm fire keep Thea popular. Nikos and family hail from northern Greece and Constantinople and so does their food: Caesaria pie, hot and spicy with cheeses, salted meat, and tomatoes; Cappodocian lamb, cooked with dried apricots; Constantinopolitan chicken, with plums, raisins, and rice; or one of their famous T-bone steaks. Save room for one of the traditional Greek sweets, especially the *ekmek* served up with mastic ice cream. Reservations are recommended in summer. ⊠ 🕿*22840/91220* 🖃*MC, V.*

EN ROUTE

A 15-minute walk or 2-minute drive back toward Paros town from the Valley of the Butterflies leads to the convent known as **Christos sto Dasos** (*Christ in the Wood*), from where there's a marvelous view of the Aegean. The convent contains the tomb of St. Arsenios (1800–77), who was a schoolteacher, an abbot, and a prophet. He was also a rainmaker whose prayers were believed to have ended a long drought, saving Paros from starvation. The nuns are a bit leery of tourists. If you want to go in, be sure to wear long pants or skirt and a shirt that covers your shoulders, or the sisters will turn you away.

ANTIPAROS ΑΝΤΙΠΑΡΟΣ

Fodor's Choice ★

5 km (2 mi) southwest of Paroikía.

The smaller, sister isle of Paros, Antiparos is developing all too rapidly, though recent visitors, such as Tom Hanks and Brad Pitt, want to keep this place a secret. Twenty-five years ago you went to the Paros hamlet of Pounta, went to the church, opened its door (as a signal), and waited for a fishing caïque to chug over. Now, 30 car ferries ply the channel all day and a lovely seven-minute ride wafts you from Paros (from Pounta; the ride from Paroikía takes about 20 minutes) to Antiparos. The green, inhabited islet on the way belongs to Dolly Goulandris, benefactress of the Goulandris Cycladic Museum in Ath-

7

ens (and much else). A causeway once crossed the Antiparos strait, which would be swimmable but for the current, and on one of its still emergent islets, Saliagos, habitations and objects have been found dating back almost to 5,000 BC.

Antiparos's one town, also called Antiparos, has a main street and two centers of activity: the quay area and the main square, a block or two in. At both are restaurants and cafés. To the right of the square are houses and the kastro's 15th-century wall. At the other end of the quay from the ferry dock a road goes to an idyllic sandy beach (it is 10 minutes by foot); you can wade across to the islet opposite, Fira, where sheep and goats graze.

BEACHCOMBERS' PARADISE

Pounta is not even a village, just a few houses, three restaurants (one fine one), and a tiny harbor, whence the ferries leave for Antiparos. The road that turns left just before you get there continues on to many beaches. And beyond—it is a beautiful drive—are the peaceful harbor towns of Aliki and Dryos, both with fine beaches and restaurants, especially Faragas. Beyond Dryos toward Naousa are the windsurfers' long beaches, Golden beach and New Golden beach.

In the 19th century the most famous sight in the Aegean was the **Antiparos cave** (9 km [5½ mi] from town), and it still deservedly attracts hundreds of visitors a year. Four hundred steps descend into huge chambers, pass beneath enormous pipe-organ stalactites, and skirt immense stalagmites. In 1673 the French ambassador famously celebrated Christmas Mass here with 500 guests, who feasted for three days. Look for Lord Byron's autograph. Outside is the church of Agios Ioánnis Spiliótis, built in 1774.

It is pleasant to go around to the other side of Antiparos on the good road to Ayios Georgios, where there are three excellent taverns, perfect after a swim. On request a boat will take you to the nearby islet of **Despotikon,** uninhabited except for seasonal archaeologists excavating a late-Archaic marble temple complex to Apollo. In autumn the hills are fragrant with purple flowering heather. A great source of information about Antiparos, with a complete listing of hotels can be found at www.antiparos-isl.gr.

WHERE TO EAT

$$　✕**Akrogiali.** Far from the madding crowd, you sit and look across the strait to the sacred isle of Despotikon, and, after a swim, eat the fish from right here. The bells you hear belong to the goats of the Pipinos family (yes, they occasionally end up on the table here). Vegetables come from the garden. This is one of three good restaurants by the little dock. ⊘ *Closed Oct.–Apr.* ▭ *No credit cards.*

SANTORINI (THERA) ΣΑΝΤΟΡΙΝΗ (ΘΗΡΑ)

Undoubtedly the most extraordinary island in the Aegean, crescent-shape Santorini remains a mandatory stop on the Cycladic tourist route—even if it's necessary to enjoy the sensational sunsets from Ia, the fascinating excavations, and the dazzling white towns with a million other travelers. Called Kállisti (the "Loveliest") when first settled, the island has now reverted to its subsequent name of Thera, after the 9th-century BC Dorian colonizer Thiras. The place is better known, however, these days—outside Greece, that is—as Santorini, a name derived from its patroness, St. Irene of Thessaloniki, the Byzantine empress who restored icons to Orthodoxy and died in 802.

You can fly conveniently to Santorini, but don't: the boat trip here provides a spectacular, almost mandatory introduction, a literal rite of passage. After the boat sails between Sikinos and Ios, your deck-side perch approaches two close islands with a passage between them. The bigger one on the left is Santorini, and the smaller on the right is Thirassia. Passing between them, you see the village of Ia adorning Santorini's northernmost cliff like a white geometric beehive. You are in the caldera (volcanic crater), one of the world's truly breathtaking sights: a demilune of cliffs rising 1,100 feet, with the white clusters of the towns of Fira and Ia perched along the top. The bay, once the high center of the island, is 1,300 feet in some places, so deep that when boats dock in Santorini's shabby little port of Athinios, they do not drop anchor. The encircling cliffs are the ancient rim of a still-active volcano, and you are sailing east across its flooded caldera. On your right are the Burnt Isles, the White Isle, and other volcanic remnants, all lined up as if some outsize display in a geology museum. Hephaestus's subterranean fires smolder still—the volcano erupted in 198 BC, about 735, and in 1956.

Indeed, Santorini and its four neighboring islets are the fragmentary remains of a larger landmass that exploded about 1600 BC: the volcano's core blew sky high, and the sea rushed into the abyss to create the great bay, which measures 10 km by 7 km (6 mi by 4½ mi) and is 1,292 feet deep. The other pieces of the rim, which broke off in later eruptions, are Thirassia, where a few hundred people live, and deserted little Aspronissi ("White Isle"). In the center of the bay, black and uninhabited, two cones, the Burnt Isles of Palea Kameni and Nea Kameni, appeared between 1573 and 1925.

There has been too much speculation about the identification of Santorini with the mythical Atlantis, mentioned in Egyptian papyri and by Plato (who says it's in the Atlantic), but myths are hard to pin down. (For the full scoop, *see* our special photo feature, "Santorini: The Lost Atlantis?" in this chapter). This is not true of old arguments about whether or not tidal waves from Santorini's cataclysmic explosion destroyed Minoan civilization on Crete, 113 km (70 mi) away. The latest carbon-dating evidence, which points to a few years before 1600 BC for the eruption, clearly indicates that the Minoans outlasted the eruption by a couple of hundred years, but most probably in a

Continued on page 320

SANTORINI:
THE LOST ATLANTIS?

View of Santorini's
waters caldera from
the town of Ia

Did Atlantis, "the island at the center of the earth," ever really exist? And if it did, where? Big-budget Hollywood films have placed it in the middle of the Atlantic Ocean. Several historians think it was located in the Bay of Naples; others that it was a Sumerian island in the Persian gulf, or a sunken island in the Straits of Gibraltar. Nowadays, more and more experts are making a case for the island of Santorini—and therein lies a tale.

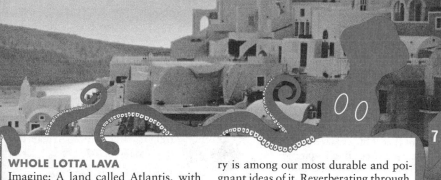

WHOLE LOTTA LAVA

Imagine: A land called Atlantis, with a vast, spectacular city adorned with hanging gardens, gigantic palaces, and marble colossi of Poseidon, ancient god of the sea. One fateful day, more than 3,500 years ago, an enormous earthquake triggers a cataclysmic volcano that destroys the capital. In the space of a few hours, a towering tidal wave washes all traces of this civilization into a fiery cauldron. All, that is, except for a rocky fragment framing a watery caldera. Historical detectives, archaeologists, and volcanologists have long wondered if Greece's fabled isle of Santorini could be that last remnant of Atlantis. But is this theory more fable than fact?

For those who consider Atlantis merely a symbol or metaphor, the question is not important. Surfacing like a rising island in a deep bay, the notion of a Golden Age is ever-present in the human imagination, and the Atlantis story is among our most durable and poignant ideas of it. Reverberating through Western culture and dazzling the mind, the name "Atlantis" glitters with glamour; it titles hotels, Web sites, towns, submarines, book and film companies, even a pop song by Donovan. But historians today remain divided on whether Atlantis was a funtastic shooting-star of history or just a legend with a moral lesson.

PLATO VERSUS THE VOLCANO

Plato (427–347 BC), the most fearless, and the most substantive writer, of all the ancient Greek philosophers, would have supported the latter option. He liked to end his famous Dialogues with a myth, and Atlantis shows up in both his "Timaeus" and his "Critias," as a parable (and history?) of good and bad government. Plato says that the great 6th-century lawgiver-poet of Athens, Solon (630–560 BC), went to Egypt, and there heard

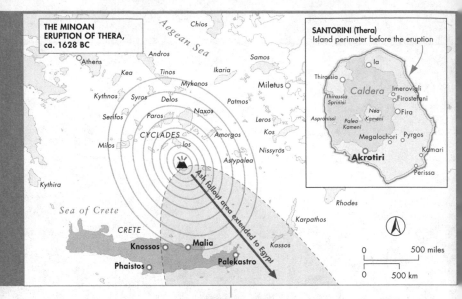

THE MINOAN
ERUPTION OF THERA,
ca. 1628 BC

Aegean Sea

Chios

Athens
Andros
Samos
Kea
Tinos
Ikaria
Mykonos
Miletus
Kythnos
Syros
Delos
Patmos
Serifos
Paros
Naxos
Leros
Kos
Milos
CYCLADES
Ios
Amorgos
Nissyros
Astypalea
Kythira

Sea of Crete

CRETE
Knossos
Malia
Phaistos
Palekastro
Kassos
Karpathos
Rhodes

Ash fallout area extended to Egypt

0   500 miles
0   500 km

SANTORINI (Thera)
Island perimeter before the eruption

Thirassia
Ia
Thirassia
Sprinisi
Caldera
Imerovigli
Firostefani
Aspronissi
Nea
Kameni
Fira
Palea
Kameni
Megalochori
Pyrgos
Kamari
Akrotiri
Perissa

stories of Atlantis. They told him that 9,000 years ago Athens defeated the empire of Atlantis, a huge island in the Atlantic Ocean, in battle.

Then a natural cataclysm destroyed the island in one day, "and Atlantis disappeared in the sea depths." Atlantis was created by and belonged to Poseidon, god of the sea and of earthquakes, and he made it a paradise ruled by his son, King Atlas, with the guidance by wise counselors. When later generations on the island abandoned his prudent ways, catastrophe struck: you mustn't love Power more than you love the Gods. The Bible had Sodom and Gomorrah; Plato had Atlantis.

Some authors claim the story of Atlantis is history, not fantasy. They believe that Solon misread 9,000 years as 900. If so, Atlantis would have flourished at the same time as Santorini, which, as we know and the classical Greeks suspected, was destroyed by earthquakes followed by a cataclysmic volcanic

eruption, probably just before 1600 BC—some historians point to the date of 1628 BC.

THE MINOAN CONNECTION

In the late 1960s, when archaeologist Spyridon Marinatos's excavations of Santorini's caldera revealed the ruin of Akrotiri, preserved under 25 feet of volcanic ash, the island's claim to be Atlantis began to outweigh all others. The buried town had been large, comfortable, and attractive, the art beautiful and gentle, and its high Bronze Age civilization resembled Minoan Crete's, 47 miles south. Since a tsunami from the volcano must have devastated the larger island, it is not surprising that Crete, whose dimensions chime better with Plato's, is also called Atlantis.

Crete and its satellite, Santorini (don't call it this to a Santorini scholar, but it's true) were "feminine" civilizations. They worshipped the goddess of fertility; disliked depictions of war and

Imaginary view of Santorini's submerged volcano in eruption in 1866, (below) Akrotiri frescoes.

weapons; kept their towns unwalled; loved magnificent jewelry; and their art eschews the monumental for spontaneous natural forms, such as swallows, octopi, dolphins, and palm trees. They liked pretty people. The women's elaborate costumes exposed their breasts, and the men, nearly naked, wore gold jewelry and fancy hairstyles. They worshipped not in temples, but in caves, springs, and mountaintops. From our sparse evidence, it seems it was indeed a golden age, when "the earth bore freely all the aromatic substances it bears today, roots, herbs, bushes and gums exuded by flowers or fruit." Perfume was as popular here as in Egypt. A mural preserved in Athens from Akrotiri shows blue monkeys opening doors à la Wizard of Oz. Plato, the stern taskmaster, would probably have disapproved.

... ET TU, SANTORINI?

Today, archaeological excavation continues at Akrotiri, situated high— 1,300 feet—over the whitecaps of the Aegean Sea. What was Santorini like when the great bay was terra firma, lush with olive trees and abundant harvests? Santorini's own Prehistoric Museum is studying the possibilities, as the writings of historians, poets, and philosophers provide food for thought. The fact remains that the evidence is not all in: there is a possibility that Santorini could, in fact, reawaken from its long slumber and once again erupt, and then subside again. The key to Atlantis's existence may lie in the once and future fury of this fascinating island.

very weakened state. In fact, the island still endures hardships: since antiquity, Santorini has depended on rain collected in cisterns for drinking and irrigating—the well water is often brackish—and the serious shortage is alleviated by the importation of water. However, the volcanic soil also yields riches: small, intense tomatoes with tough skins used for tomato paste (good restaurants here serve them); the famous Santorini fava beans, which have a light, fresh taste; barley; wheat; and white-skin eggplants.

Sadly, unrestrained tourism has taken a heavy toll on Santorini. Fira, and now Ia, could almost be described as "a street with 40 jewelry shops"; many of the natives are completely burned out by the end of the peak season (the best times to come here are shoulder periods); and, increasingly, business and the loud ringing of cash registers have disrupted the normal flow of Greek life here. For example, if a cruise ship comes in during afternoon siesta, all shops immediately open. And you will have a pushy time walking down Fira's main street in August, so crowded is it. Still and all, if you look beneath the layers of gimcrack tourism, you'll find Greek splendor. No wonder Greece's two Nobel poets, Giorgios Seferis and Odysseus Elytis, wrote poems about it. For you, too, will be "watching the rising islands / watching the red islands sink" (Seferis) and consider, "With fire with lava with smoke / You found the great lines of your destiny" (Elytis).

FIRA ΦΗΡΑ

10 km (6 mi) west of the airport, 14 km (8½ mi) southeast of Ia.

Tourism, the island's major industry, adds more than 1 million visitors per year to a population of 7,000. As a result, Fira, the capital, midway along the west coast of the east rim, is no longer only a picturesque village but a major tourist center, overflowing with discos, shops, and restaurants. Many of its employees, East Europeans or young travelers extending their summer vacations, hardly speak Greek. But it soon becomes clear what brings the tourists here: with its white, cubical houses clinging to the cliff hundreds of feet above the caldera, Fira is a beautiful place.

To experience life here as it was until only a couple of decades ago, walk down the much-photographed, winding **staircase** that descends from town to the water's edge—walk or take the cable car back up, avoiding the drivers who will try to plant you on the sagging back of one of their bedraggled-looking donkeys.

The modern Greek Orthodox cathedral of **Panayia Ypapantis** (⊠ *Southern part of town*) is a major landmark; the local priests, with somber faces, long beards, and black robes, look strangely out of place in summertime Fira.

Along **Eikostis Pemptis Martiou** (*25th of March street* ⊠ *East of Panayia Ypapantis*), you'll find inexpensive restaurants and accommodations.

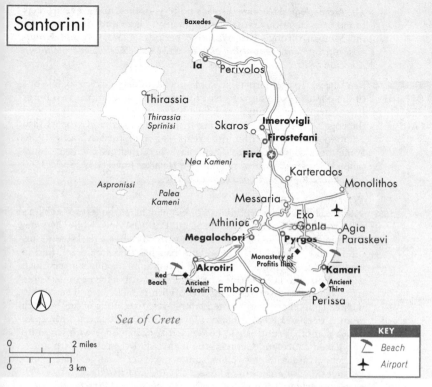

Santorini

Baxedes

Ia Perivolos

Thirassia

Thirassia
Sprinisi

Skaros **Imerovigli**
Firostefani

Fira

Nea Kameni

Karterados

Aspronissi Monolithos

Palea
Kameni

Messaria

Athinios Exo
Gonia Agia
Paraskevi

Megalochori **Pyrgos**

Monastery of
Profitis Ilias

Red
Beach **Akrotiri** **Kamari**

Ancient
Akrotiri Emborio Ancient
Thira

Perissa

Sea of Crete

0   2 miles

0   3 km

KEY	
🏖	Beach
✈	Airport

The blocked-off Ypapantis street (west of Panayia Ypapantis) leads to **Kato Fira** *(Lower Fira)*, built into the cliff side overlooking the caldera, where prices are higher and the vista wonderful. For centuries the people of the island have been digging themselves rooms-with-a-view right in the cliff face—many bars and hotel rooms now occupy the caves.

★ The **Museum of Prehistoric Thera** displays pots and frescoes from the famed excavations at Akrotiri. Note the fresco fragments with the painted swallows (who flocked here because they loved the cliffs) and the women in Minoan dresses. The swallows, which still come in spring, remain the island's favorite design motif. The fossilized olive leaves from 60,000 BC prove the olive to be indigenous. ✉ *Mitropoleos, behind big church* ☎22860/23217 ⊕*www.culture.gr* ✉*€5 including Archaeological Museum; €8 including Archeological Museum and Akrotiri* ♡*Tues.–Sun. 8:30–3.*

WALK ON BY

Tourist touts still like to promote mules as a mode of transport to take you up the zigzag cliff path to the island capital of Fira. But animal rights groups would prefer you didn't. And you should be aware of another reason: the mules on Santorini are piously believed to contain souls of the dead, who are thus doing their purgatory. It is an arduous ascent.

The **Archaeological Museum** displays pottery, statues, and grave artifacts found at excavations mostly from ancient Thera and Akrotiri, from the Minoan through the Byzantine periods. ⊠*Stavrou and Nomikos, Mitropoleos, behind big church* ☏*22860/22217* ☑*€5 including Museum of Prehistoric Thera* ☉*Tues.–Sun. 8:30–3.*

OFF THE BEATEN PATH

Nea Kameni. To peer into a live, sometimes smoldering volcano, join one of the popular excursions to Nea Kameni, the larger of the two Burnt Isles. After disembarking, you hike 430 feet to the top and walk around the edge of the crater, wondering if the volcano is ready for its fifth eruption during the last hundred years—after all, the last was in 1956. Some tours continue on to Therassia, where there is a village. Tours (about €15) are scheduled regularly by **Nomikos Travel** (☏*22860/23660* ☏*22860/23666* ⊕*www.nomikosvillas.gr*).

WHERE TO STAY & EAT

$$$$ ✕**Selene.** No wonder weddings are popular here: the terrace at Fira's most romantic restaurant has a splendid caldera view, while the time-burnished cliff house is a beaut, with vaulted ceilings, dark-wood furniture, and "Thera-style" banquette benches (the sort you'll find in traditional island homes). The menu is full of interesting starters, such as zucchini with langoustine salad and slices of botargo (roe of tuna), or mixed seafood wrapped in phyllo with fennel sauce. The entrées include lamb chops and roasted lamb—yes, two kinds of lamb—with yogurt, rice, and local tomatoes layered in a mold; beef with green olives is another subtle dish. For dessert try zabaglione with vin santo and flaked chocolate. Georgia, the maître d', oversees all with grace, efficiency, and knowledge. In summer, owner George Hatziyianakis gives daylong cooking classes. ⊠*Cliff-side walkway, 310 ft left of Hotel Atlantis* ☏*22860/22249* ⊕*www.selene.gr* ⌲*Reservations essential* ☰*AE, DC, MC, V* ☉*Closed Nov.–Mar.*

$$$$ ✕**Sphinx.** When Fira locals want more than a taverna, they come to this pretty vaulted room, which glows with spotlighted Cycladic sculptures and blush-pink walls. As lush as this is, however, few can resist an outdoor terrace table, thanks to the striking caldera views in one direction and a vista of the giant cathedral in the other. Owner George Psichas is his own chef, and every dish is evidence of his loving care—even the bread and pasta are homemade. Starters include smoked salmon with fresh asparagus and brik caviar with hollandaise sauce, or artichokes with lemon and feta. Fresh fish is usually available—try the fresh grouper steak with grape and grappa sauce. Other high-style delights include the scallops and shrimps with pink peppercorn sauce and the steak fillet with mushrooms, truffle oil, arugula, and Parmesan flakes. Desserts change day by day, but rich chocolate soufflé is always available. The wine list is long and Greek (and the "cave" is very much worth a look). ⊠*Cliff-side walkway in front of Panayia Ypapantis* ☏*22860/23823* ⊕*www.sphinx-santorini.com* ⌲*Reservations essential in summer* ☰*AE, MC, V.*

$$ ✕**Naoussa.** This family taverna, owned by Kyriakos and Stelios Selios, is easily Fira's most popular among the locals. The food is freshly prepared daily (most tavernas cook in advance, then freeze and

microwave), and so here is the right place to get moussaka, stuffed vegetables, and other Greek specialties; there is always a daily specialty. Winning best bets include the small spinach pies with egg, feta, and spring onions and the walnut-studded eggplant salad. Naoussa can be found on the second-floor terrace on the main shopping street near the Archaeological Museum. ⊠ *LaGoudera Shopping Center (near cable car)* ☎ *22860/22869* ⊕ *www.naoussa-restaurant.gr* 🖃 ⊘ *Closed Dec.–mid-Mar.*

$ ✕ **Nicholas.** This is Santorini's oldest taverna, where you'll find the natives camped out in winter. Island dishes are prepared well and served in a simple, attractive room. Try the local yellow lentils and the lamb fricassee with an egg-lemon sauce. ⊠ *2 streets in from cliff side on Erythrou Stavrou* ☎ *No phone* 🖃 *No credit cards.*

$$$$ 🏨 **Aigialos.** For a taste of old aristocratic Santorini, venture to Aigialos

Fodor'sChoice ("seashore"), a cluster of buildings from the 18th and 19th centuries.

★ The most comfortable and discreetly luxurious—as well as the most poetic and serenely quiet—place to stay in Fira, it comprises an array of one- and two-bedroom villas. Outside, various abodes are built in traditional volcanic stone, lime-washed in heavenly pastels. Inside, you'll find marble floors, magnificently beautiful antique furniture, and walls festooned with 19th-century engravings. Nearly all guest rooms have sublime terraces or balconies overlooking the caldera—no need to venture out at sunset. There's maid service twice daily, impeccable 24-hour service, and fresh flowers. The restaurant serves its Mediterranean cuisine only to residents, and you can eat on your private terrace. Breakfast, included, is served in a deep cave, on the pool terrace, or on your balcony. Note that this complex does have a lot of steps, even for Santorini. ⊠ *South end of cliff-side walkway, 84700* ☎ *22860/25191 through 22860/25195* 🖶 *22860/22856* ⊕ *www.aigialos.gr* 🛏 *17 villas* △ *In-room: refrigerator. In-hotel: bar, pool, spa, no elevator, public Internet* 🖃 *AE, DC, MC, V* ⊘ *Closed Nov.–Mar.* ⦿| *BP.*

$$$$ 🏨 **Hotel Aressana.** Though the Aressana lacks a view of the caldera, its own slant of sea view is effulgent (and helps make you forget the Las Vegas–like hotel sign). The large freshwater pool, spacious lobby with traditional furnishings and wood-panel bar, excellent service, famous breakfast, and location in central Fira make this a popular option. The Aressana specializes in traditional wedding receptions and provides charming bridal suites—so don't be surprised by how many Americans honeymoon here. Renovated in 2007, this is a large full-service hotel, with no steps and an elevator. ⊠ *South end of cliff-side walkway, 84700* ☎ *22860/23900 or 22860/23901* 🖶 *22860/23902* ⊕ *www. aressana.gr* 🛏 *42 rooms, 8 suites* △ *In-room: dial-up. In-hotel: bar, pool, no elevator, public Internet, parking* 🖃 *AE, DC, MC, V* ⊘ *Closed Nov.–Mar.* ⦿| *BP.*

$$$ 🏨 **Aroma Suites.** For a caldera view, this new (2006) accommodation is an exceptional value. The small white cave-rooms with vaulted ceilings are decorated with warm touches of color and sleek marble fixtures. The common terrace overlooks the caldera, and you will want to sit here mornings and evenings. Transfers and breakfast are extra, and there are stairs, but it is very attractive, small, and friendly. Pool privileges can be

had at the nearby Loizos Apartments. To get to Aroma Suites, head to the southern end of Fira's caldera walkway, then follow the signs down. ⊠ *Caldera walkway, 84700* 🕾 *22860/24112* 🖷 *22860/24116* ⊕ *www. aromasuites.gr* 🔊 *4 rooms, 4 suites* ⌂ *In-room: refrigerator. In-hotel: no elevator, public Wi-Fi* ⊟ *AE, MC, V.*

$$$ 🔂 **Dream Island Hotel.** Opened in 2006, well appointed, and family run, this complex of 15 rooms looks like a complete Cycladic village, presiding over a vast (somewhat forlorn) pool terrace and an almost cinematic vista over ancient Thera. Sorry, the view doesn't include the watery caldera (guest rooms take in the view over the sea, in the opposite direction) but that fact helps make this place less expensive than it looks. The rooms (all with plasma satellite TV) and cavernous spacious lobby are decorated in light beige tones with strong color accents. Outside, the pool's terrace is paved with volcanic rock. Breakfast is extra; transfers are included. Owners Roussetos and Georgia Karamelogos are very accommodating. Some other pluses: there are no steps and off-season prices are very low. To get to the hotel, walk north (toward Ia) five minutes from the main (Theotokopoulou) square and turn right at the sign. ⊠ *Off Martiou St., 84700* 🕾 *22860/24122* 🖷 *22860/23922* ⊕ *www.dreamislandhotel.gr* 🔊 *15 rooms* ⌂ *In-hotel: no elevator, public Internet, parking* ⊟ *MC, V*

$$ 🔂 **Costa Marina Villas.** Set in a tranquil neighborhood, surrounded by
★   a garden, and vaulted and shimmering-white in archetypal Cycladic fashion, this is a nifty option (built in 2002). Although just a block or so from the main square, the immediate precinct is a quiet, domestic neighborhood. Most guest rooms have a tiny balcony overlooking the garden or with an eastern sea view; "family" rooms (which anyone can book) are most spacious, thanks to their impressive double-height loft ceilings. A bit of luxury: some rooms have a Jacuzzi. Great value for the money, Costa Marina may be a hike from the caldera, but it is romantic all the same. ⊠ *Along road leading to camping grounds, 84700* 🕾 *22860/28923* 🖷 *22860/28926* ⊕ *www.santorini.org/hotels/cost-amarina-hotel* 🔊 *21 rooms* ⌂ *In-room: refrigerator, kitchen (some). In-hotel: no elevator* ⊟ *MC, V* 🍴 *BP.*

$$ 🔂 **Pelican Hotel.** Just down from the busy main (Theotokopoulou) square on Danezi street, this small hotel is in the center of the commercial part of town. Although not in a picturesque neighborhood, few can complain about the convenient location. Happily, most rooms are sound-insulated, making for an oasis of quiet. The vaulted lobby and white guest rooms are furnished with dark traditional wooden furniture. Some rooms have balconies over a lovely garden. Breakfast is included, but not transfers. There is a self-service laundry room. ⊠ *On cobbled road up from main traffic street, near town hall, 84700* 🕾 *22860/23133* 🖷 *22860/23514* ⊕ *www.pelican.gr* 🔊 *18 rooms* ⌂ *In-room: Wi-Fi. In-hotel: pool, no elevator, public Internet* ⊟ *AE, D, MC, V.*

$ 🔂 **Loizos Apartments.** Lefteris Anapliotis's pension, located in a quiet and convenient section of Fira, is the perfect budget choice. The rooms, some with sea views, are spacious and the garden is pretty. The price includes transfers. The excellent breakfast costs €5. Lefteris also runs the even cheaper Loizos Hotel, 3 km (2 mi) outside town. Lefteris makes this place special—he's got lots of handy tips to spread around (just ask him about Santorini wine). ⊠ *On cobbled road up from main traffic street, near town hall, 84700* ☎ *22860/24046* 🖷 *22860/25118* ⊕ *www.loizos.gr* ⮐ *23 rooms* ♿ *In-room: refrigerator. In-hotel: pool, no elevator, public Internet, public Wi-Fi* ▭ *AE, MC, V.*

> ## A "PRIVATE" BALCONY?
>
> Remember that many of Santorini's hotel cliffside balconies elbow each other out of the way for the best view and, with footpaths often running above and aside them, privacy is often hard to come by.

$ 🖭 **Pension Delphini I.** Vassilis Rousseas's pension, on the busy main traffic street, is well run, inexpensive, friendly, and open all year. His mother tends the lovely little garden. Although an excellent budget choice, the front rooms are on the noisy car road and a few rooms lack air conditioning. ⊠ *Main traffic street, opposite Piraeus Bank, 84700* ☎ *22860/22780* 🖷 *22860/22371* ⊕ *www.delfini-santorini.gr* ⮐ *10 rooms* ♿ *In-room: refrigerator, dial-up. In-hotel: no elevator* ▭ *No credit cards.*

NIGHTLIFE & THE ARTS

DANCING The **Koo Club** (⊠ *North end of cliff-side walkway* ☎ *22860/22025*) is Fira's most popular outdoor disco by far. **Santorinia** (⊠ *Next to Nomikos Conference Center* ☎ *22860/23777*) is the place for live Greek music and dancing. Nothing happens before midnight. **Casablanca Soul** (⊠ *Fira* ☎ *22860/24008*) is in the maze to the north; there is often live music.

FESTIVALS The **Bellonia Cultural Center**, on the main car crossroads, contains a small auditorium, the latest audiovisual equipment, and a large library. In summer, it presents concerts, readings, and theater festivals; in winter, it becomes an educational center. Thank pianist Athena Capodistria for September's **Santorini Music Festival** (⊠ *Nomikos Conference Center* ☎ *22860/22220*), which always includes internationally known musicians. In 2007 the **Santorini Jazz Festival** (⊠ *Open-air Cinema Kamari* ⊕ *www.jazzserver.nl/festivals/?letter=s*) celebrated its 10th anniversary.

MUSIC The popular **Franco's Bar** (⊠ *Below cliff-side walkway* ☎ *22860/24428* ⊕ *www.francos.gr*) plays classical music and serves champagne cocktails. It has a caldera view.

SHOPPING

EMBROIDERY **Costas Dimitrokalis** and Matthew Dimitrokalis sell locally made embroideries of Greek linen and Egyptian cotton, rugs, pillowcases in hand-crocheted wool with local designs, and more. Purchases can be mailed anywhere. ⊠ *1 block from cable car* ☎ *22860/22957* ▭ *AE, D, MC, V.*

GALLERIES **Art and Glass Gallery.** Aris Carreris's gallery represents seven Greek artists whose crafts range from icons on wood to glass in both sleek modern and traditional designs. He ships everywhere. ⊠ *On block that runs*

down from Archaeological Museum to main car street ☎*22860/25977.*
Phenomenon. Christoforos Asimis studied painting at Athens University,
and has had many exhibitions there and abroad. The nearby cathedral's
murals are his. His paintings specialize in the light and landscape of
his home island. His wife, Eleni, who also studied in Athens, shows
sculptures, ceramics, and jewelry; her jewelry, in elegant designs both
classic and modern, is executed with the highest craftsmanship. Few
of Fira's proliferating jewelry shops have work to compare with this.
✉*Ypapantis walkway, Palia Fabrika* ☎*22860/23041* ⊕*www.san-
torini.info/paliafabrika/index.html.*

JEWELRY **Bead Shop.** Marina Tsiagkouri's shop has expanded, but beads are
still the main reason to go. Who can resist her unique beads made
from Santorini's volcanic rock? ✉*Opposite entrance to Museum of
Prehistoric Thera* ☎*22860/25176.* **Kostas Antoniou Jewelry.** Many of
Kostas's original pieces were inspired by ancient Thera; some solid
gold necklaces are magnificent enough to earn their own names, such
as Earth's Engravings, Ritual, and Motionless Yielding. The work is
both classic and creative. ✉*In Spiliotica shopping area, near Archaeological Museum* ☎☎*22860/22633* ⊕*www.antoniou-santorini.com*
▭*AE, MC, V.*

SPORTS & THE OUTDOORS
SAILING The **Santorini Sailing Center** (✉*Merovigli* ☎*22860/23058 or
22860/23059*), near Fira, arranges charters and runs weekly two- to
three-day sailing trips around the Cyclades for groups of up to 10.

FIROSTEFANI ΦΗΡΟΣΤΕΦΑΝΙ

Firostefani used to be a separate village, but now it is an elegant suburb
north of Fira. The 10-minute walk between them, along the caldera, is
one of Santorini's highlights. From Firostefani's single white cliff-side
street, walkways descend to traditional vaulted cave houses, which are
fast becoming pensions. Though close to the action, Firostefani feels
calm and quiet.

WHERE TO STAY & EAT
$$$ ✕**Vanilia.** Set in a windmill—built in 1872 and preserved by the gov-
★ ernment after the 1956 earthquake—Vanilia also encompasses pretty
terraces, on which to enjoy the good food. You might start with San-
torini fava served with onions, cherry tomatoes, and capers. Home-
made pasta, such as ravioli stuffed with Cretan graviera cheese and
served with yogurt, is a specialty. An intriguing entrée is grilled pork
fillet in thyme-honey sauce. Kazas-tipi (cream custard on cinnamon
sugar) will make you want to linger at this friendly place. ✉*Main
square* ☎*22860/25631* ▭*AE, D, MC, V* ⊗*Closed Nov.–Apr.*

$$ ✕**Aktaion.** In his tiny taverna, Vangelis Roussos uses mostly his grand-
★ father's recipes. The paintings on the walls are Vangelis's own. Salad
Santorini, his mother's recipe, has raw cod flakes, caper leaves, and seasonal ingredients. The moussaka, made with white eggplant, is incomparable. ✉*Main square* ☎*22860/22336* ▭*MC, V.*

$$$$
Fodor'sChoice
★ **Tsitouras Hotel.** Architectural Digest–worthy decor and earthy Cycladic charm collide here at this complex of six apartments, and the result is true Santorinian splendor. Little wonder these apartments have been homes-away-from-homes for the likes of Gianni Versace, Joan Kennedy, Harvey Keitel, Nana Mouskouri, and Jean-Paul Gaultier. There's no sign; guests are met (at the airport or harbor) and brought to these sparkling white cubes with volcanic stone trimmings built around an 18th-century mansion. Inside, the decor is a fantasia of Chippendale armchairs, ancient amphorae, Byzantine icons, Corfiot mariner's chests, Picasso ceramics, and gilt-framed engravings; the glowing color schemes were cooked up by legendary British designer David Hicks. Salons are picturesquely dotted with domes, skylights, and interior windows—the showpiece is the "House of the Winds," where the Oscar winner is the grand, double-height, cathedral-roofed living room ashimmer with elegant antiques and robin's-egg-blue walls. The elegant terrace overlooks the caldera, but many choose to enjoy dinner on their own terrace. All this luxe comes at a stiff price, but no doubt many will think their pennies—rates run from €470 to €790—well spent. ⊠ *Firostefani cliff face, next to St. Mark's, 84700* ☎ *22860/23747* 🖷 *22860/23918* ⊕ *www.tsitouras.gr* 📞 *6 apartments* ⟁ *In-room: refrigerator. In-hotel: restaurant, no elevator, public Internet* ⊟ *AE, D, MC, V* ⦿ *BP.*

> **WORD OF MOUTH**
>
> "Just next to Fira on Santorini is Firostefani, sometimes not designated as a separate village. This is a much shorter walk from Fira than Imerovigli, so if you can get a hotel there you will have the quiet and caldera view without the crowds."
>
> —brotherleelove2004

$$–$$$$
★ **Reverie Traditional Apartments.** Georgios Fytros has converted his family home into an inexpensive and attractive hotel, all cream color with marble insets. Each of the large rooms, white with dark-toned wood furniture, has a winding staircase to a balcony with a metal frame bed. The roof garden has a caldera view. ⊠ *Between Firostefani walkway and main traffic road, 84700* ☎ *22860/23322* 🖷 *22860/23044* ⊕ *www.reverie.gr* 📞 *13 rooms, 2 suites* ⟁ *In-room: refrigerator. In-hotel: pool, no elevator, public Internet* ⊟ *D, MC, V*

IMEROVIGLI ΗΜΕΡΟΒΙΓΛΙ

Set on the highest point of the caldera's rim, Imerovigli (the name means Watchtower), is what Firostefani was like a decade and a half ago. It is now being developed, and for good reasons: it is quiet, traditional, and less expensive. The 25-minute walk from Fira, with incredible views, should be on everyone's itinerary. The lodgments, some of them traditional cave houses, are mostly down stairways from the cliffside walkway. The big rock backing the village was once crowned by Skaros Castle, whence Venetian overlords reigned after 1207. It collapsed in an earthquake, leaving only the rock. A trail descending from the church of Ayios Georgios crosses the isthmus and encircles Skaros;

7

it's only 10 minutes to the castle top. After 1 km (½ mi) it reaches the small chapel of Theoskepasti with a memorable caldera view.

WHERE TO STAY & EAT

$$$ ✗**Blue Note.** You can't go wrong with the location: a deck extended over the cliff, a panoramic caldera view, and a sunset as dessert. For a starter try Gruyère flambé. For a main dish, lamb *klephtiko* (stewed in wine and herbs in a ceramic dish) is a good choice, as is shrimp Blue Note (a secret recipe). Blue Note is open for lunch and dinner. ⊠*On main walkway near Maltesa.* ☎*22860/23771* ▤*MC, V.*

$$ ✗**Skaros Fish Taverna.** This rustic open-air taverna, one of three restaurants in Imerovigli, has spectacular caldera views. It serves fresh fish and Santorini specialties, such as octopus in onion sauce, and mussels with rice and raisins. ⊠*On cliff-side walkway* ☎*22860/23616* ▤*AE, MC, V* ☉*Closed Nov.–Mar.*

$$$ ▥**Spiliotica Apartments and Suites.** With his lively vibe, Tony Spiliotis (a Greek-American) has created an attractive hideaway that attracts everyone from families to celebrities. Cascading steeply down the cliff side, these cave rooms are individually theme-decorated, with baths built into the deep rock recesses. All rooms have caldera views and little terraces where you can watch the sunset. Breakfast is included; transfers are extra. Beware: there are a lot of steep steps. ⊠*On cliff-side walkway, behind church of Panaghia Maltesa, near parking and bus stop, 84700* ☎*22860/22637* ▤*22860/23590* ⊕*www.spiliotica. com* ⬏*4 houses* ⬥*In-hotel: pool, no elevator, public Internet* ▤*MC, V* ☉*Closed Nov.–Mar.* ⎮⎮*BP.*

$$ ▥**Annio.** The rooms in this cliff-side lodgment are attractive and simple, with local furnishings both new and old. All have terraces and caldera views, making this a good deal (if you don't care about a pool). Christos Nomikos built it himself on his family property, and his daughter Katerina runs it. They don't provide transfers, but rather lots of beauty, peace, comfort, and quiet. Breakfast costs extra. ⊠*Imerovigli, 84700* ☎*22860/24714* ▤*22860/23550* ⊕*www.annioflats.gr* ⬏*11 rooms* ⬥*In-room: refrigerator, Ethernet. In-hotel: no elevator* ▤*MC, V* ☉*Closed Nov.–Apr.*

$$ ▥**Heliades Apartments.** Owner Olympia Sarri knows she has something special. Her father mostly built the apartments, consisting of four cave houses, white with blue-green accents, with verandas and caldera views. The couches and loft beds are traditional, and the arches are outlined in Santorini tufa; the living room areas are especially spacious. Unbelievably, there are just a few steps. Breakfast is extra. ⊠*On cliff-side walkway, behind church of Panaghia Maltesa, near parking and bus stop, 84700* ☎*22860/24102* ▤*22860/25587* ⊕*www.heliades-apts. gr* ⬏*4 houses* ⬥*In-room: kitchen. In-hotel: no elevator.* ▤*No credit cards* ☉*Closed Nov.–Mar.*

IA OIA

Fodor's Choice
★

14 km (8½ mi) northwest of Fira.

At the tip of the northern horn of the island sits Ia (or Oia), Santorini's second-largest town and the Aegean's most photographed village. Ia is more tasteful than Fira (for one thing, no establishment here is allowed to play music that can be heard on the street), and the town's cubical white houses (some vaulted against earthquakes) stand out against the green-, brown-, and rust-color layers of rock, earth, and solid volcanic ash that rise from the sea. Every summer evening, travelers from all over the world congregate at the caldera's rim—sitting on white-washed fences, staircases, beneath the town's windmill, on the old **kastro**—each looking out to sea in anticipation of the performance: the Ia sunset. The three-hour rim-edge walk from Ia to Fira at this hour is unforgettable.

In the middle of the quiet caldera, the volcano smolders away eerily, adding an air of suspense to an already awe-inspiring scene. The 1956 eruption caused tremendous earthquakes (7.8 on the Richter scale) that left 48 people dead (thankfully, most residents were working outdoors at the time), hundreds injured, and 2,000 houses toppled. The island's west side—especially Ia, until then the largest town—was hard hit, and many residents decided to emigrate to Athens, Australia, and America. And although Fira, also damaged, rebuilt rapidly, Ia proceeded slowly, sticking to the traditional architectural style. The perfect example of that style is the restaurant 1800, a renovated ship-captain's villa. In 1900, Ia had nearly 9,000 inhabitants, mostly mariners who owned 164 seafaring vessels and seven shipyards. Now there are about 500 permanent residents, and more than 100 boats. Many of these mariners use the endless flight of stairs from the kastro to descend down to the water and the small port of **Ammoudi,** where the pebble beach is home to some of the island's nicest fish tavernas. Head east to find the fishing port of **Armeni,** home to all those excursion boats that tour the caldera.

Ia is set up like the other three towns—Fira, Firostefani, and Imerovigli—that adorn the caldera's sinuous rim. There is a car road, which is new, and a cliff-side walkway (Nikolaos Nomikou), which is old. Shops and restaurants are all on the walkway, and hotel entrances mostly descend from it—something to check carefully if you cannot negotiate stairs easily. In Ia there is a lower cliff-side walkway writhing with stone steps, and a long stairway to the tiny blue bay with its dock below. Short streets leading from the car road to the walkway have cheaper eateries and shops. There is a parking lot at either end, and the northern one marks the end of the road and the rim. Nothing is very far from anything else.

The main walkway of Ia can be thought of as a straight river, with a delta at the northern end, where the better shops and restaurants are. The most-luxurious cave-house hotels are at the southern end, and a stroll by them is part of the extended evening promenade. Although it is not as crowded as Fira, where the tour boats deposit their thousands of hasty shoppers, relentless publicity about Ia's beauty and tastefulness, accurate enough, are making it impassable in August. The sunset in Ia may not really be much more spectacular than in Fira, and certainly not better than in higher Imerovigli, but there is something tribally satisfying at the sight of so many people gathering in one spot to celebrate pure beauty. Happily, the night scene isn't as frantic as Fira's—most shop owners are content to sit out front and don't cotton to the few revelers' bars in operation. In winter, Ia feels pretty uninhabited.

The **Naval Museum of Thera** is in an old neoclassic mansion, once destroyed in the big earthquake, now risen like a phoenix from the ashes. The collection displays ships' figureheads, seamen's chests, maritime equipment, and models—all revealing the extensive nautical history of the island, Santorini's main trade until tourism took over. ⊠ *Near telephone office* ☎ *22860/71156* ⊠€*4* ☉ *Tues.–Sun. 8:30–3.*

BEACH

There are no beautiful beaches close to Ia, but you can hike down Ia's cliff side or catch a bus to the small sand beach of **Baxedes** (⊠ *Port of Armoudhi*).

WHERE TO STAY & EAT

$$$$ ✕ **1800.** Clearly, some of Santorini's old sea captains lived graciously, as
Fodor's Choice   you'll note when dining at one of Santorini's most famous restaurants,
★   1800 (the name refers to the date when the house was built). Owner, architect, and restaurateur John Zagelidis has lovingly restored this magnificent old captain's house with original colors (white, olive green, and gray) and furnishings, including antique sofas, wooden travel chests, and a hand-painted Venetian bed. To top it all off, a superlative roof terrace was constructed, with a vista framed by Ia's most-spectacular church cupolas—a perfect perch on hot nights for taking in the famous Ia sunset. Maître d' Eleni Economou is efficient, knowledgeable, and charming, while the chef, Thanasis Sfougkaris—winner of Greece's prestigious Golden Toque award in 2004—does full honor to the beautiful surroundings. For starters try red mullet baked in vine leaves with tapenade sauce, spring onion coulis, and capers with their leaves; or tomato and mozzarella tart with basil and bell pepper dressing. Entrées include fillet of white grouper with celery mousse, artichokes, capers, and botargo sauce; and baked lamb cutlets with fennel, young peas, and porcini sauce. ⊠ *Main street, 84702* ☎ *22860/71485* 🖷 *22860/72317* ⊕ *www.oia-1800.com* ⊟ *AE, DC, MC, V.*

$$–$$$ ✕ **Red Bicycle.** Once featured on Giada De Laurentis's Food Network show, this sophisticated café, wine bar, and art gallery is located at the north end of Ia's main walkway, just down the steps; its big terrace with sail-like white awnings overlooks the bay. Owner Chara Kourti loves "Chara's Pie" (ground beef, carrots, pistachios, pine nuts baked in phyllo with tahini sauce), and no one will complain about the delicious quiches or large wine list. Desserts are a specialty; try *galaktoboureko* (warm custard pie with dates, raisins, and rosewater syrup). ⊠ *Ia* ☎ *22860/71918* ⊟ *No credit cards.*

$–$$ ✕**Kastro.** Spyros Dimitroulis's restaurant is primarily patronized for its
★ view of the famous Ia sunset, and at the magical hour it is always filled.
Happily, the food makes a fitting accompaniment. A good starter is
olives stuffed with cream cheese dipped in beer dough and fried, served
on arugula with a balsamic sauce. For a main dish try lamb scallops in
wine and rosemary sauce, or pappardelle with asparagus and a sauce
of dried tomato and garlic. Lunch is popular. ⊠*Near Venetian castle*
☎*22860/71045* ⊟*AE, MC, V.*

$$$$ 🏨**Katikies.** Sumptuously appointed, this immaculate white cliff-side
complex layered on terraces has sleek modern design, including Andy
Warhol wall prints, stunning fabrics, and handsome furniture. Chic as
the surroundings are, the barrel-vaulted ceilings and other architectural
details lend a traditional air to the place. Suites and villas are small and
private; all have private terraces that overlook the caldera and are luxu-
riously appointed. The restaurant terrace sports a great caldera view,
strikingly framed by sleek white columns and chairs slip-covered in the
whitest linen. Note: there are a lot of stairs for the weary. ⊠*Ia cliff face,
edge of main town, 84702* ☎*22860/71401* 🖷*22860/71129* ⊕*www.
kutikies.com* ⟲*7 rooms, 33 suites, 7 villas* &*In-room: kitchen. In-
hotel: 3 restaurants, bars, pools, no elevator, public Internet* ⊟*AE,
MC, V* ⊘*Closed Nov.–Mar.* ⊺◎⊺*BP.*

$$$$ 🏨**Lampetia Villas.** This EOT Traditional Settlement, 800 feet up the cliff
from the sea, offers charm, comfort, and friendliness. The owner, Tom
Alafragis, has a charm all his own. Each of the accommodations—all
have private balconies with a view—is different in size and furnishings.
⊠*Nomikou, Ia cliff face, down from main street* ☎🖷*22860/71237*
⊕*www.lampetia.gr* ⟲*8 houses* &*In-room: kitchen. In-hotel: pool, no
elevator* ⊟*AE, MC, V* ⊘*Closed Nov.–Mar.* ⊺◎⊺*BP.*

$$$$ 🏨**Perivolas.** Immortalized as one of the most famous infinity pools
★ on earth (thanks to nearly a dozen magazine covers), the cliff-hanger
here seems to make you feel you could easily swim off the edge into
the caldera's blue bay 1,000 feet below. The pool is the jewel in the
crown of these 17 houses (all connected by flights of stairs), one of
the first hotel complexes built after the big 1956 earthquake. Inside,
guest rooms have been converted from old wineries and renovated in
archetypal *skafta* (vaulted cave) fashion, with clever nooks for beds,
sculpted walls, and full kitchens; all are simply but stunningly furnished with handmade wooden pieces and weavings. Each house has
its own terrace. ⊠*Nomikou, Ia cliff face, 15 mins by foot from cliff-
side street, 84702* ☎*22860/71308* 🖷*22860/71309* ⊕*www.perivolas.
gr* ⟲*17 houses* &*In-room: kitchen. In-hotel: restaurant, bar, pool, no
elevator* ⊟*AE, MC, V* ⊘*Closed Nov.–Mar.* ⊺◎⊺*BP.*

$ 🏨**Delfini Villas.** If you think a comfortable, convenient room in Ia with
a caldera view and terrace has to be expensive, think again: Rena
Halari's place is affordable and warmly charming. This is a great buy,
so don't expect a lot of service. ⊠*Lower main traffic street, opposite
Piraeus Bank, 84702* ☎*22860/71600* 🖷*22860/71601* ⊕*www.delfini-
villas.com* ⟲*6 rooms, 4 apartments* &*In-room: kitchen, refrigerator.
In hotel: no elevator* ⊟*AE, MC, V* ⊘*Closed Nov.–Mar.*

7

NIGHTLIFE

There are the usual cafés, bars, and pastry shops along the main street but a peaceful note is struck by the fact that establishments are forbidden to play loud music. The bar at Santorini's most sophisticated restaurant, **1800** (⊠ *Main street* ☎ *22860/71485*), gets lively late, when diners leave. With a balcony overlooking the caldera, **Skiza** (☎ *22860/71569*) is well known for the excellence of its pastries. Those in search of a happy-hour beer go to **Zorba's** (⊠ *On cliff side*).

> **THE REAL DEAL**
>
> Ia mostly abjures the jewelry madness of Fira, and instead offers a variety of handcrafted items. Since the shops are not so dependent on cruise ships, a certain sophistication reigns in the quiet streets. Art galleries, "objets" shops, crafts shops, and icon stores set the tone. More open every year.

SHOPPING

ACCESSORIES You'll know the **Silk Shop** (⊠ *Main shopping street* ☎ *22860/71923*), a tiny outlet near the Red Bicycle restaurant, from the spectacular array of brilliant rainbow colors. Judy Neaves and Theodore Xenos sell woven silk scarves, shawls, and small handmade purses.

ANTIQUES & Manolis and Chara Kourtis's **Loulaki** (⊠ *Main shopping street*
COLLECTIBLES ☎ *22860/71856*) sells antiques, odd pieces, jewelry, and art; exploring the shop is a pleasure. Alexandra Solomos's painted plates are a favorite.

ART **Art Gallery** (⊠ *Main shopping street* ☎☎ *22860/71448*) sells large, three-dimensional representations of Santorini architecture by Bella Kokeenatou and Stavros Galanopoulos. Their lifelike depth invites the viewer to walk through a door or up a flight of stairs.

BOOKS **Atlantis Books** (⊠ *North end of main shopping street* ☎ *22869/72346* ⊕ *www.atlantisbooks.org*) is a tiny English bookshop that would be at home in New York's Greenwich Village or London's Bloomsbury; its presence here is a miracle. Only good literature makes it onto the shelves. Writers stop by to chat and give readings.

PYRGOS ΠΥΡΓΟΣ

5½ km (3½ mi) south of Fira.

Though today Pyrgos has only 500 inhabitants, until the early 1800s it was the capital of the island. Stop here to see its medieval houses, stacked on top of one another and back to back for protection against pirates. The beautiful neoclassic building on the way up is a luxury hotel. The view from the ruined Venetian castle is panoramic. And reward yourself for the climb up the picturesque streets, which follow the shape of the hill, with a stop at the panoramic terrace of the Café Kastelli, for Greek coffee and homemade sweets. In Pyrgos you are really in old Santorini—hardly anything has changed.

The **Monastery of Profitis Ilias** is at the highest point on Santorini, which spans to 1,856 feet at the summit. From here you can see the surrounding islands and, on a clear day, the mountains of Crete, more than 100 km (66 mi) away. You may also be able to spot ancient Thera on the peak below Profitis Ilias. Unfortunately, radio towers and a NATO radar installation provide an ugly backdrop for the monastery's wonderful bell tower.

Founded in 1711 by two monks from Pyrgos, Profitis Ilias is cherished by islanders because here, in a secret school, the Greek language and culture were taught during the dark centuries of the Turkish occupation. A **museum** in the monastery contains a model of the secret school in a monk's cell, another model of a traditional carpentry and blacksmith shop, and a display of ecclesiastical items. The monastery's future is in doubt because there are so few monks left. ⊠ *At highest point on Santorini* 🚏*Free* 🕐 *No visiting hrs; caretaker is sometimes around.*

> **VIN BEATS EAU**
>
> The locals say that in Santorini there is more wine than water, and it may be true; Santorini produces more wine than any two other Cyclades islands (Paros is second). The volcanic soil, high daytime temperatures, and humidity at night produce 36 varieties of grape, and these unique growing conditions are ideal for the production of distinctive white wine now gaining international recognition. Farmers twist the vines into a basketlike shape, in which the grapes grow, protected from the wind. A highlight of any Santorini trip is a visit to one of its many wineries—log on to www.santorini.org/wineries/ for a helpful intro.

MEGALOCHORI ΜΕΓΑΛΟΧΩΡΙ

4 km (2½ mi) east of Pyrgos, 9 km (5½ mi) southwest of Fira.

Megalochori is a picturesque, half-abandoned town set. Many of the village's buildings were actually *canavas,* wine-making facilities. The tiny main square is still lively in the evening.

On your way south from Megalochori to Akrotiri, stop at **Antoniou Winery** (⊠ *Megalochori* ☎ *22860/23557* ⊕ *www.antoniou-santorini.com*) and take a tour of the multilevel old facility. It's so beautiful, local couples get married here. An enologist leads a wine tasting with snacks, and a slide show describes local wine production; it costs €5. Many think Antoniou's white wines are Santorini's best—and that's saying a lot.

WHERE TO STAY

$$$$ ★ 🏨 **Vedema.** Angelina Jolie, Oliver Stone, Susan Sarandon, Danny DeVito … and now you? Those A-Listers head here because the black-lava environs keep crowds and paparazzi at bay—but you, too, may enjoy the peace of this distant and deluxe outpost. A world unto itself, it was built up around a beautiful 15th-century winery. Trouble is, it kept expanding and expanding, and now tops out at 42 villas, almost like a "planned" gated community in Florida. Inside, the leitmotif is minimalism-meets-Mediterranean: SoHo stone tables below vintage

island-style mirrors, with some guest rooms done in such shocking blues and pinks you may soon be reaching for your Visine. Still, the old vaulted dining room is one of the prettiest on Santorini; the wine cellar, with its many valuable wines, is worth exploration (there are wine tastings nightly). The spacious suites all have marble bathrooms and terraces. Vedema is not cheap, but you'll get what you're paying for, in spades—everyone raves about the food and service. Although the location is relatively isolated, a handy shuttle service ferries you to other parts of the island. ⊠84700Megalochori ☎22860/81796 or 22860/81797 🖷22860/81798 ⊕www.vedema.gr ⤳35 rooms, 7 suites ⚏In-room: kitchen (some). In-hotel: 2 restaurants, pool, no elevator ⊟AE, D, MC, V ⊙Closed Nov.–Mar. ⧄BP.

AKROTIRI ΑΚΡΩΤΗΡΙ

7 km (4½ mi) west of Pyrgos, 13 km (8 mi) south of Fira.

★ If Santorini is known as the "Greek Pompeii" and is claimant to the title of the lost Atlantis, it is because of the archaeological site of **ancient Akrotiri,** near the tip of the southern horn of the island. At this writing (winter 2007), the site was closed temporarily for structural repairs, so check ahead before you plan your visit.

In the 1860s, in the course of quarrying volcanic ash for use in the Suez Canal, workmen discovered the remains of an ancient town. The town was frozen in time by ash from an eruption 3,600 years ago, long before Pompeii's disaster. In 1967 Spyridon Marinatos of the University of Athens began excavations, which occasionally continue. It is thought that the 40 buildings that have been uncovered are only one-thirtieth of the huge site and that excavating the rest will probably take a century.

Marinatos's team discovered great numbers of extremely well-preserved frescoes depicting many aspects of Akrotiri life, most now displayed in the National Archaeological Museum in Athens; Santorini wants them back. Meanwhile, postcard-size pictures of them are posted outside the houses where they were found. The antelopes, monkeys, and wildcats they portray suggest trade with Egypt.

Culturally an outpost of Minoan Crete, Akrotiri was settled as early as 3000 BC and reached its peak after 2000 BC, when it developed trade and agriculture and settled the present town. The inhabitants cultivated olive trees and grain, and their advanced architecture—three-story frescoed houses faced with masonry (some with balconies) and public buildings of sophisticated construction—is evidence of an elaborate lifestyle. ⊠South of modern Akrotiri, near tip of southern horn ☎22860/81366 ⊕www.culture.gr ⊡€5 ⊙Tues.–Sun. 8:30–3.

BEACH

Red beach (⊠On southwest shore below Akrotiri) is quiet and has a taverna.

KAMARI ΚΑΜΑΡΙ

6½ km (4¼ mi) east of Akrotiri, 6 km (4 mi) south of Fira.

★ Archaeology buffs will want to visit the site of **ancient Thera.** There are relics of a Dorian city, with 9th-century BC tombs, an engraved phallus, Hellenistic houses, and traces of Byzantine fortifications and churches. At the sanctuary of Apollo, graffiti dating to the 8th century BC record the names of some of the boys who danced naked at the god's festival (Satie's famed musical compositions, *Gymnopedies,* reimagine these). To get here, hike up from Perissa or Kamari or take a taxi up **Mesa Vouna.** On the summit are the scattered ruins, excavated by a German archaeology school around the turn of the 20th century; there's a fine view. ☒*On a switchback up mountain right before Kamari, 2,110 ft high* ☎*22860/31366* ⊕*www.culture.gr* ☒*€5* ⊗*Tues.–Sun. 8:30–3.*

BEACH

The black-sand beach of **Kamari** is a natural treasure of Santorini and crowds head here to rent deck chairs and umbrellas. They also flock to Kamari because tavernas and refreshment stands abound—despite an attractive wooden walkway and lively nightlife, Kamari is the epitome of overdevelopment.

FOLEGANDROS ΦΟΛΕΓΑΝΔΡΟΣ

7

If Santorini didn't exist, little, bare Folegandros (⊕*www.folegandros. gr*) would be world famous. Its gorgeous Cycladic main town of Chora, built between the walls of a Venetian fort, sits on the edge of a beetling precipice: this hilltop setting represents, with the exception of Santorini, the finest cliff scenery in the Cyclades. Beyond this, the island does not seem to have much to offer on paper—but in person it certainly does. Beautiful and authentic, it has become the secret island of Cyclades lovers, who want a pure dose of the magic essence of the Aegean every year or so. Only 31 square km (12 square mi) in area and 64 km (40 mi) in circumference, it lacks ruins, villages, green valleys, trees, country houses, and graceful cafés at the edge of the sea. But what it does have—one of the most stunning Chora towns; deliberately downplayed touristic development; several good beaches; quiet evenings; traditional local food; and respectful visitors—make it addictive. There are no discos, no bank, but the sea is shining and, in spring, much of the island is redolent of thyme and oregano.

Visitors to Folegandros—historians are divided on whether the name immortalizes the Cretan explorer Pholegandrus or comes from the Phoenician term for "rock-strewn"—all stay in the main town, and hang around the town's three squares. A walk, a swim at the beach, a visit to the little Folklore Museum at Ano Meria, meeting other people who love the essence of the Greek islands: these require few arrangements. Unless you want to stop on the side of the road to look at views (the island does offer an array of interesting hiking trails), the bus is adequate. There are a number of beaches—Angali and Ayios Nikolaos are especially good. Because Folegandros is so small, it fills up fast in

August, and despite the absence of raucous nightlife, it somewhat loses its special flavor. For travel services and booking boat trips, check out Tours in the Essentials section at the end of this chapter.

A TASTE OF ITALY

The island's Italian vibe lingers at Flavio Facciolo's Café dei Viaggiatori. Found on the first bus square, Flavio and his wife offer a selection of good Italian wines, serve light Venetian-flavored snacks, and serve the best espresso on the isle.

CHORA ΧΩΡΑ

42 km (27 mi) northwest of Santorini, 164 km (102 mi) southeast of Athens.

As the boat approaches the little port of Karavostasi, bare, sun-scoured cliffs—with a hint of relieving green in wet winter but only gray glare in summer—let you know where you are. Leaving the port immediately, since there is hardly anything here, visitors climb the road 3 km (2 mi) to Chora on buses (which meet all ferries). On the rugged way up, you'll see the spectacular, whitewashed **church of Koímisis tis Theotókou** (or Dormition of the Mother of God) dominating the town on the high cliff where the ancient settlement first stood. On Easter Sunday the chief icon is carried through the town.

After a steep ride, cliff-top Chora comes into view. Its sky-kissing perch is well out of sight of the port, an important consideration in the centuries when the seas here were plagued by marauding pirate raiders. Today, Chora—small, white, old, and preserved lovingly by the islanders—is less hidden and is known as the main reason to visit the island. Its main street, starting at the bus stop (past which most streets are pedestrianized) meanders through five little squares—the middle three are the main ones—each with a few restaurants and cafés shaded by bougainvillea and hibiscus. Some of the buildings, including a hotel and café, are set into the walls of the Venetian fort, or kastro, built by the Venetian duke of Naxos in the 13th century. The second street circles the kastro and the precipice on which the town stands and is strikingly lined with two-story cube houses that form a wall atop the towering cliff. The glory days of Venice came to an end in 1715, when the ruling Turks sacked Folegandros and sold the captives as slaves. The old families go back to 1780, when the island was repopulated. As for dining and lodging, the new fancier places at the edge of town miss the meaning of the island. Opt, instead, for the simple tavernas in Chora, all family run. Next to one another and competitive, they are all good.

ANO MERIA ΆΝΩ ΜΕΡΙΑ

The paved road connects the port, the capital, and, after 5 km (3 mi), Ano Meria. On the way there, you can see terraces where barley was coaxed seemingly from stone, though they are hardly farmed now. The tiny town is a smaller version of Chora, and the cafés are perfect places for a drink. Exhibits in the little **Folklore Museum** (*Free* *July–mid-*

Sept., daily 10–6,) reconstruct traditional farming life. The church of Agios Panteleimon celebrates on July 27, and almost everyone goes.

WHERE TO STAY & EAT

¢ ✕ **I Piazze.** A middle-square eatery, this popular option has tables set out under trees. Specialties include kalasouna cheese pies and home-made noodles (called *matsata*) with pork or lamb. They also sell their own aromatic thyme honey. ⊠*Middle square* ☎*No phone* ⊟*No credit cards.*

¢ ✕ **O Kritikos.** Set under a tree and abutting a Byzantine church, Kritikos serves exclusively local meats and vegetables. Souroto, a local cheese, makes a fitting appetizer. Kontosouli is usually pork on the spit; here it is a mixture of lamb and pork, and delicious. ⊠*Middle square* ☎*22860/41219* ⊟*No credit cards.*

$$$ ▦ **Anemomilos Apartments.** Much the best place to stay in Folegandros (it is up to the right as you enter the main town), Anemomilos is the friendly domain of Dimitris and Cornelia Patelis. Perched on the cliff overlooking the sea and set amid a series of small garden terraces (perfect for breakfast and drinks), the complex is faced with attractive island-style stonework. The apartments beckon in traditional blue and white; all have terraces, half with sea view. Breakfasts and transfers are extra. ⊠*Chora, 84011* ☎*22860/41309* ⎙*22860/41407* ⊕*www.anemomilosapartments.com* ⟿*23 rooms* ⌂*In-room: refrigerator, Wi-Fi. In-hotel: pool, no elevator* ⊟*MC, V* ⊙*Closed mid-Oct.–Easter.*

$ ▦ **Meltemi.** If you want a simple, inexpensive, family place to stay, Meltemi does the job. Clean, white, simple, convenient, with good-size rooms, it is open March through October. ⊠*Chora, 84011* ☎*22860/41425* ⊕*www.greekhotel.com/cyclades/folegand/chora/meltemi* ⟿*11 rooms* ⌂*In-hotel: no elevator, public Wi-Fi* ⊟*No credit cards* ⊙*Closed Nov.–Feb.*

SHOPPING

JEWELRY Open April through September, **Jewelry Creations** (⊠*Middle square* ☎*22860/41524*) features the jewelry of Apostolos and Eleni, who have been creating their striking jewels, often with Greek stones, for 20 years.

SIFNOS ΣΙΦΝΟΣ

Sifnos is a *kore*—one of those elegantly draped young female figures that the Archaic islanders liked to carve out of the finest marble. Her beauty is graceful and modest. Unlike her parched neighbor Seriphos, just 19 km (12 mi) northwest, Sifnos is well watered and fertile, a garden island. But to passing boats she appears formidable, for her sweetness is guarded by steep cliffs, broken suddenly by only a few deep-cut bays with safe anchorage. The main towns of the island, Apollonia and Artemonas, are found along the central ridge, while the popular beaches are in the south; the north, where the ancient silver mines were, is sparsely inhabited. Because Sifnos is small (2,000 people) and relatively undeveloped (though ministers, ambassadors, and artists

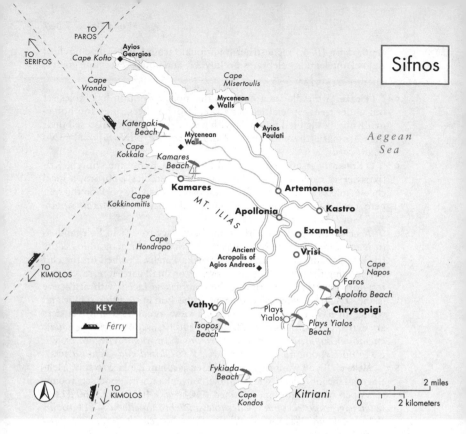

Sifnos

TO PAROS
TO SERIFOS
Cape Kofto
Ayios Georgios
Cape Vronda
Cape Misertoulis
Mycenean Walls
Katergaki Beach
Mycenean Walls
Ayios Poulati
Cape Kokkala
Kamares Beach
Aegean Sea
Kamares
Artemonas
Cape Kokkinomitis
MT. ILIAS
Apollonia
Kastro
Exambela
Cape Hondropo
Vrisi
Ancient Acropolis of Agios Andreas
Cape Napos
Faros
Apolofto Beach
TO KIMOLOS
Vathy
Plays Yialos
Chrysopigi
Plays Yialos Beach

KEY
Ferry

TO KIMOLOS
Tsopos Beach
Fykiada Beach
Cape Kondos
Kitriani

0   2 miles
0   2 kilometers

have houses here), her 35,000 tourists yearly overwhelm resources in August, when the beaches are clogged and the buses packed.

The history of the island is fabled. Ancient Sifnos enjoyed a brief period of great prosperity when gold was found here; the remains of the Siphnian treasury which was erected at Delphi are impressive. The Siphnians were supposed to give Apollo at Delphi a golden egg annually: once they tried to fob him off with a gilded stone, and in anger, he sent tidal waves to swamp their mines (a drier account simply has them running dry). The island's name, not insignificantly, means "empty."

Buses run regularly all day from Apollonia's clogged central square to the outlying villages and some of the beaches, and this is probably the best way to get around Sifnos. Taxis (22840/33300) start here, too; bikes, quads, and cars are available, but useful only for unusual locations, and if you're heading to some of the beaches, you'll want to access them via small boats from Kamares. Aegean Thesaurus Travel and Tourism (*see* Tours in this chapter's Essentials section) is on the main square; they handle accommodations, tickets, rentals, and are especially good on hiking trips, a chief reason to visit Sifnos. The sights of Sifnos (⊕*www.sifnos.gr*) can easily be seen in three days; to be seen well, they require years.

KAMARES ΚΑΜΑΡΕΣ

50 km (31 mi) northwest of Fole-gandros, 105 km (65 mi) northwest of Santorini.

The most protected of Sifnos's anchorages is the port of Kamares, a small white town on a bay on the west coast with high cliffs on either side, a good beach with tamarisk trees, and a narrow green valley whose road takes you to the interior. You'll find some handy travel agencies and rental-car offices here (as well as in the island's main towns). A couple of potters' studios still function, and there is a mining establishment at the north end, in one of whose shafts relics of ancient temples were found. Indeed, the old fishermen who still reside here whisper about Nereids—and they don't mean the scantily clad tourists who lunch at the beachside fish tavernas. Today, however, Kamares is a hectic tourist port, with new Athenian villas, and you'll want to move on quickly to the island interior.

The bus ride from Kamares southeast up to Apollonia (5 km [3 mi]) provides a sweet initiation into Sifnos's enchanting landscape. You will see two-story dovecotes, delicate chapels hugging the hillside, ruined windmills, and very narrow terraces with golden wheat, glinting olive trees, or low grape vines buttressed by elegant stone walls that prevent them from washing into the ravines below during winter storms. In spring the hillsides are so yellow with Spanish broom they are hard to look at in bright sunlight. The most notable and numerous accents dotting the landscape are the Hellenistic watchtowers—the *pirgis*. Sifnos has remains of more than 40, testament to the ferocity of Venetian, Maltese, and Turkish pirate raids of centuries gone by.

APOLLONIA ΑΠΟΛΛΩΝΙΑ

1 km (2 ½ mi) southeast of Kamares.

Apollonia, capital of Sifnos since 1836, seems at first glance a gentle, disheveled sprawl on the high undulation of the island's saddle. Once you reach the central crossroads, and take in a jaw-dropping vista of the surrounding countryside, you'll find it is actually a whitewashed constellation of six villages and blue-dome churches. The bus stops at the lively main square, the busy central crossroads for all Sifnos (gridlocked in August). The big building in the central Iroon Square (Heroes' Square) houses the **Folklore Museum,** full of traditional weavings, embroideries, and vestments, a Sifnos specialty. Also on view are examples of ancient Siphnian pottery, which was made at several places on the island, always by the sea, so that it could be shipped with ease. ⊠ *Iroon Sq.* ☎ *22840/33730* 🖼 *€2* ◷ *July–mid-Sept., Mon.–Sat., 10–1 and 6–9.*

With their mazelike streets closed to vehicles, the best and only way to explore these villages is on foot. From the main square a main street locals call the Steno winds upward to traverse the prettiest sections of the old town. On the right (east) side of the street, through an archway, gleams the **Panayia Ouranophora,** called the Church of the Heaven-Bearing Virgin. The marble carvings around the door give the date 1767, but the church itself is older; the relief overhead depicts St. George and the Dragon. The marble column by the courtyard well is from the 7th-century BC temple to Apollo, Apollonia's namesake. To fast-forward several millennia: most of Sifnos's nightlife is on the Steno—just follow your aching ears. The street, more officially called Stilianou Proukou, is lined with cafés and shops but debouches, in timeless Greek fashion, at a mammoth cathedral, the Agios Spirídonos (restored 1901) .

Then the road crosses into **Ano Petali,** quiet and pristine, tucked between its larger neighbors, and presided over by the Italianate-style Agios Ioánnis church (not far away is the Panayia Ta Gournía, which has impressive murals and icons). The islanders' scrupulous dedication to whitewash makes the villages of Sifnos seem daintier than those of the other Cyclades. The flagstones here are carefully delineated with very thin white lines reapplied weekly (much more time consuming than the thicker lines preferred elsewhere). It is on Sifnos that the Cycladic cubic type of architecture, seen with small variations in so many islands, is found in its greatest perfection. Here a projecting ledge, over every door or window, adds to the interest of the exteriors (a feature also to be seen on Folegandros, where the houses are also very beautiful).

NEED A BREAK? At the lower end of the Steno, between it and the car road, is the Gerontopoulos Sweetshop and Café (☎ *22840/32220*); its *bourekia,* a kind of sweetmeats, are to die for.

WHERE TO STAY & EAT

$$ ✕**Odos Oneiron.** "Dream Street" is one of Sifnos's few restaurants that depart from local cuisine. A good starter is tomato croquettes with grilled haloumi cheese and arugula oil. For a main dish, try stuffed pork fillet with Cyprian white cheese, olive paste, tomato sauce, and mint. The special of the day is always top-notch, as is the dessert of yogurt pie. ⊠*On square behind Taxiarch church on Steno* ☎*22840/23002* ⊟ *No credit cards.*

$$$$
Fodor's Choice
★
🏨 **Petali Hotel.** On a hilltop offering spectacular views over several villages, the sea, and Antiparos clear in the distance, the open-all-year Petali is a mini-Cycladic village. Although built recently, it blends in beautifully with its ageless surrounds. Inside, the decor is picture-perfect, with wood-beam ceilings, four-posters, tablecloth drapes, antiques, and a very cozy sense of style; many of the room balconies are exquisitely embowered in ivy. The restaurant is serious, there's a vast and relaxing terrace around a pool, and the amenities are worth the price. Transfers are extra. The Petali is not far from the bustling center of Apollonia, but it's far enough for true peace and quiet: it's located on the pedestrian street leading to Artemonas—there is a sign to it

on the car road, halfway up. ✉*Ano Petali, 84003* ☎*22840/33024* 🖷*22840/33391* ⊕*www.hotelpetali.gr* ⮧*23 rooms* ⚫*In-room: refrigerator, Ethernet. In-hotel: restaurant, pool, no elevator, public Internet* ☰*MC, V* ❢❶*BP.*

ARTEMONAS ΑΡΤΕΜΩΝΑΣ

3 km (1 mi) northeast of Apollonia.

The flagstone street from Apollonia's Ano Petali district descends slightly to cross a stone bridge over the seasonal Marinou River. Artemonas, named after Apollo's virginal sister, Artemis, is the most beautiful village on Sifnos. The walls of the **church of the Virgin of the Troughs**, on the rock outcropping to the left, were frescoed in the primitive style by a monk 150 years ago. Inside, note the marble tombstones set into the floor.

Beyond lies the small square built to honor Nicholas Chrysogelos, a local teacher who led a contingent in the 1821 revolution who later became Greece's first minister of education. His marble bust reigns over the tiny town hall and impressive town houses. Soon the same street reaches Artemonas's capacious main square, where the bus turns to go back down to Apollonia. The 18th-century church here, with its ghostly white stairway, is dedicated, like the square, to Saints Constantine and Helen. Right next to the church is an excellent taverna, the Manganas, and the comfortable Hotel Artemon, with a garden restaurant. The main stone-paved street of the town is lined with large neoclassic houses, with gardens in front of them, built by wealthy shipowner families of the late 19th century. The quiet coexistence of elegant edifices and small houses, many with the characteristic Siphnian chimney caps of multi-spouted inverted pots, all united by fresh whitewash, gives Artemonas its graceful appearance. Strolling by the mansions, you'll notice on the main street Katerina Theodorou's Sweet Shop, where she makes her traditional almond sweets and nougat by hand; the shop is in a preserved sitting room of old Sifnos, full of curios.

The main street leads to Artemonas's multi-domed chief church, the **Kochi**. In its courtyard, where Artemis's temple once stood, the Siphnian Cultural Society presents readings and concerts in summer. Just past Kochi, turning left down a narrow lane, you reach, on the right after about 30 yards, a little two-story house marked by a plaque as the place where poet John Gryparis (1871–1942), indifferent to the world's praise (but not, gossip the Siphnians, to his bossy wife's), wrote mournful sonnets. In May, perfumed Easter lilies bloom on every porch in this district—lined with traditional houses and elegant neoclassic mansions—and as you stand here it is easy to see where Gryparis got his inspiration.

WHERE TO STAY & EAT

$ ✕**Lenbessis.** Artemonas's best, Lenbessis is part of chef Stamatis Len-
★ bessis's family hotel (happily, it is open all year). In this quiet garden restaurant, the meat, vegetables, and wine come from Dad's organic

farm. Quiche with sun-dried tomatoes starts things off properly, rabbit stew with onions and lamb wrapped in phyllo with cheese and herbs make a hearty main course, and where else can you find crème caramel made from cream fresh from the cow? ⊠*Near end of Artemonas's car road* ☎*22830/13103* ▭*No credit cards.*

$ ✕**Liotrivi.** For 50 years, the famed, beloved outpost of Liotrivi has
★ excelled in traditional Siphnian fare. Caper salad and chickpea cro-
quettes are found everywhere on Sifnos; eat them here. Zucchini stuffed with meat and grilled seafood are specialties. It's open year-round. ⊠*In carless entrance square to Artemonas* ☎*22840/31246* ▭*No credit cards.*

$$ ▦**Hotel Artemon.** A true home-away-from-home, this is entirely a family outfit (just note all the memorabilia in the lobby), and many visitors—artists, writers, and hikers among them—come back yearly. Inside the modern, motel-like structure, guest rooms are comfortable and quiet; all come with balconies, with the views particularly nice on the second floor. Be sure to compliment owner-manager Voula Lem-bessis on her lovely flowering plants. ⊠*Near end of car road, 84003* ☎*22840/31303* 🖷*22840/32385* ⊕*www.hotel-artemon.com* ⇦*26 rooms* ⚐*In-room: Wi-Fi (some). In-hotel: public Internet* ▭*MC, V.*

SHOPPING

POTTERY With a grand hilltop vista at its feet, **Kalogirou** (⊠*On car road to Ayia Anna, follow sign from Artemonas* ☎*22840/33090* ⊕*www. theworkshops.gr*), also called the Workshops, mostly showcases ceram-ics made by fifth-generation potter Andonis (whose life has included a 30-year stay in New Jersey, where his creations won prizes in art exhibitions); now returned to his home island, he works with his son, while mother and daughter make traditional weavings and patchwork. **Lembesis** (⊠*Between Apollonia and Artemonas, closer to Artemonas* ☎*22840/23010*) shows work made in the family's pottery located on the nearby hill of Ayia Anna, which you can also visit. The designs and glazes are in the old Siphnian tradition. If you want to find the most traditional of Sifnos's potteries, head to the beach of Cheronisos at the northern end of the island; the clay is dug up right there.

KASTRO ΚΑΣΤΡΟ

★ *4 km (2 mi) east of Apollonia.*

An acropolis overlooking a little bay, the hilltop, whitewashed Kastro (Castle) was already a thousand years old when Herodotus knew it. The site of ancient Sifnos, it was wrested by the Da Corogna family from Naxos's control in 1307 and it did not fall to the Turks until 1617. Before 1833 it was the island's capital city, with a population of 2,000. All this history has left much of interest behind, most notably some of the Cyclades's most idiosyncratic architecture; you'll find that one street can pass over the roof of one-story buildings below, then join up by bridges to the upper stories of the opposite houses. Many houses bear Venetian coat of arms and have Italian-style balconies. Today, only 30 families remain all year, but cafés and a restaurant now welcome the many visitors who pass through the five town gates, superb remnants of the former Venetian fortified town. The classical sarcophagi in the main street were brought up from the riverbed below, where they had been used to water cows. Kastro's main **church of the Virgin of Mercy** was last restored in 1635, the date on the marble lintel. The **church of the Dormition of the Virgin,** 1593, is elaborately inlaid in Siphnian style—note the marble holy table, a classical altar adorned with Dionysian bulls' heads and swags. Elsewhere, notably on the promontories near the outskirts of town, are some hyper-picturesque churches with great sea views (and sunrises)—the most famous is the **Eftamartyres** (Seven Martyrs). In the middle of the town, in a Venetian-era building, the **Archaeological Museum** displays locally found objects from pre-Christian times. ☎22840/31022 🖼Free ⊙Tues.–Sat. 9–2, Sun. 10–2.

Sifnos has some of the Cyclades's most stunningly beautiful monasteries, including Chrysopigi (⇨below). A healthy hike from Kastro lies
Fodor'sChoice magical **Panagia Pouláti,** a whitewashed sculpture, whose blue dome
★ and soaring bell tower are dazzlingly set off by the dramatic cliffs and rocky bay that surround it—have your Nikon handy. The most famous monastery is the **Profitis Ilias,** an abandoned Byzantine extravaganza that sits atop the island's highest mountain, which you can see after a two-hour hike up from the village of Katavati, just south of Apollonia (a monk can tour you around). Needless to say, the panoramic sea view here stops all conversation. The main feast day honoring the Prophet Elijah falls on either July 19, 20, or 21, and is celebrated with a torch-lighted procession.

EXAMBELA AND VRISI ΕΞΑΜΠΕΛΑ & ΒΡΥΣΗΣ

From Apollonia three paved roads lead to three coastal villages. The road south to Platys Yialos passes through the villages of Katavati and Exambela. Exambela is especially pretty and white, with flowers by every stoop. In Turkish times (from 1617 to 1830) Exambela was considered a hot night spot, renowned for its songs. The ruined neoclassic buildings were schools, and at the edge of the village are the ruins of a Hellenistic watchtower. On the Hill of St. Andrew to the southwest lies an ancient acropolis, but not much is left. Objects from 3,000 to 400 BC keep turning up, but little of Sifnos's ancient splendor has survived to the present day. A bit farther along, whitewash steps climb to the **Vrisi (Fountain) Monastery,** cared for by the Lambrinos family: a deep vaulted gateway opens into the courtyard and church, whose arcaded porch employs classical Doric columns from an earlier temple. Inside is a small museum devoted to religious arts. Vrisi's flowing water is considered the best on Sifnos.

CHRYSOPIGI ΧΡΥΣΟΠΗΓΗ

8 km (5 mi) southeast of Apollonia.

Fodor'sChoice Between the famed beach of Platys Yialos and the harbor of Faros
★ lies Chrysopigi, the spectacular site of the **Golden Wellspring Monastery**

(1650), winner of Sifnos's "Most Picturesque" award. Its dramatic Cape Petálos perch—a rocky peninsula with seagirt views—overlooks the long, sandy beach of Apokofto (home to an excellent taverna). The Siphnians think of the monastery, built in 1650, as paradise, and the simple rooms it rents are booked way in advance. The chief icon here, which fishermen discovered gleaming in the waves, saved Sifnos in 1675 from plague and in 1928 from locusts. The gape in the entranceway, through which the sea whistles and hisses, was cut by another miracle. One dawn some local maidens who came to tend the church found seven pirates asleep. When the brigands awakened and pursued them with impure intentions, the maidens prayed to the Virgin. Aristomenes Provelengios, who often wrote in a cell here, described what took place: "Suddenly a great quake shook the cape and cut it from the shore … the women fell to their knees and glorified the Virgin for her grace."

WHERE TO EAT

$ ✗ **Chrisopigi.** This taverna, owned by George Lembesis, features top Siphnian specialties, such as caper salad and chickpea croquettes, all freshly made, as well as cooked and grilled dishes. ⊠*Apokofto beach* ☎*22840/71295* ⊟*No credit cards.*

BEACHES

This region of the island is home to its most beautiful beaches, including **Platys Yialos** (Broad beach), the most developed and popular stretch of sand hereabouts, thanks to its hotels and cafés. Once a potters' beach, it still has potteries, where you can buy what you see being made. The most notable is the shop of the brothers **Apotolides** (☎*22840/71358*), which offers ceramics based on traditional but modernized designs.

VATHY ΒΑΘΥ

★ *8 km (5 mi) southeast of Apollonia.*

Formerly one of the more-isolated and unblemished districts of Sifnos, Vathy is a green isolated valley leading to a beautiful, crescent-shape bay with a beach looking toward Kimolos. Here, the whitewashed **Taxiarhis Monastery** (16th century) looms into view on its stone mole perch over the water, offering a lovely vision of white domes and cubic blocks. The valley road was laid only in 1997; before that, the village here was accessible only by caïque or donkey, and frequented by potters who worked on the beach (a few remain). Inevitably undergoing development—now including the island's fanciest hotel—it remains one of Sifnos's prettiest and quietest spots to swim, or to lunch on the beach at one of the several tavernas.

WHERE TO STAY

$$$$
FodorsChoice
★

⛉ **Elies Resort.** Since 2003, little ole Sifnos boasts one of the fanciest hotels in the western Cyclades, a retreat now favored by some big-time Athenian politicians and celebs. Elies (it means "olive trees") climbs a terraced hill with the usual Cycladic village sprawl of white-on-white villas around a pool. In this case, sleekness has nearly steamrolled traditional Siphnian style, so get ready to vibe with white-on-gray color schemes, spare and elegant furniture, and glittering, cubistic bathrooms. The pool, superfluous so near the sea, is large; the restaurant is Iranian-caviar ambitious; the bar is stocked with Cuban cigars; and all guest rooms have terraces and balconies (and suites have private pools). Although a bit isolated from the island center, the hotel does reach out, offering guests speedboat tours, pottery-making lessons, and photo safaris—bravo! After the time-stained, millennia-old charm of Sifnos, the suave luxury of Elies may be exactly what the doctor ordered. Price includes transfer. ⊠ *Vathy bay, 84003* ☎ *22840/34000* 🖶 *22840/34070* ⊕ *www.eliesresorts.com* ↪ *20 rooms, 12 suites* ♿ *In-room: refrigerator, Ethernet. In-hotel: gym, spa, no elevator, public Internet* ☰ *AE, MC, V* ☽ *Closed Nov.–Mar.* ⦿| *BP.*

SHOPPING

POTTERY **Andonis and Yannis Atsonios** (☎ *22840/71194*) have a shop right by the main bus stop filled with traditional wares (their work atelier is nearby). The island's **Potter's Union** (15 potteries) has an annual exhibit of local wares, July 15 to August 30, at the Monastery of Phyrogia in Vathy. Foreign painters, photographers, jewelers, and ceramists also participate by invitation.

SYROS ΣΥΡΟΣ

The mercantile bustle of modern Ermoupoli—Syros's port, capital, and the archipelago's business hub since the 18th century—often makes people do a double take. Seen from a far distance out at sea, the city looks like a Cycladic village—one, however, raised to the nth dimension, with thousands of houses climbing their way up twin conical hills. The closer you get, the more impressive things get. As you pull up to the harbor, lined with big mansions and towering churches, you see that Hermesopolis—the city was originally named after Hermes, the god of trade—is a 19th-century neoclassic jewel. A palatial marble town hall, a grand city square that looks airlifted from Paris, an opera house modeled after La Scala; and a British-run gambling casino: these are just a few of the flourishes that announce Ermoupoli as the centuries-old administrative hub of the Cyclades. Partly colonized by one of Greece's largest Catholic populations, Syros is home to more than half the residents of the island chain.

Though it seems arid, Homer praised the island in Book XV of The *Odyssey,* and Markos Vamvakaris, the great Syrian rebetis (performer of rembetika music), wrote a song celebrating the beauty of its women of Venetian and Frankish descent, the "Frankosyriani," perhaps the most popular of all *bouzouki* songs. Herman Melville, writing in 1856–57, gave the men equal time: "Lithe fellows tall with gold-shot eyes, Sunning themselves as leopards may."

Near the center of the Cyclades, due east of Kythnos and west of Mykonos, rocky Syros covers an area of 135 square km (52 square mi). Some might say that Ermoupoli is the only real reason for a stopover on Syros—but it is so architecturally rich that it should not be missed. Also, the island's untouristy urbanity and long, exciting history, much of it visible, make it worthwhile.

ERMOUPOLI ΕΡΜΟΥΠΟΛΗ

35 km (21 mi) west of Mykonos, 135 km (83 mi) northwest of Santorini, 154 km (95 mi) southeast of Athens.

Ermoupoli spills like multicolor lava from the twin colonial hills of Ano Syros and Vrodado, topped respectively by churches Roman Catholic (St. George, on the left-hand peak when viewed from the harbor) and Greek Orthodox (Resurrection, on the right). Capital not only of the island but of the entire Cycladic island group, Ermoupoli was the main port of Greece for half a century after its conception in 1822, during the War of Independence. During the struggle refugees fleeing from the Turkish massacres chose the site of the ancient "town of Hermes," god of travelers and merchants, on which to raise their new city, and crowned it with Vrodado's blue-dome Resurrection church. Following the war, Syros became so important it was seriously considered as a site for the fledgling nation's first capital. Starting at that time, waves of rich immigrants from Smyrna, Chios, Hydra, Psara, and Crete made the island into a cultural and commercial center.

The full splendor of Syros's heyday is on view on Miaoúli Square, located two blocks up Venizelou street from the quay. The square's showpiece is the frescoed Municipal Palace, which today houses the capital's administrative offices and courts. Designed by the noted beaux arts European architect Ernst Ziller in 1876, it also houses two museums, one devoted to historic fire engines, the other Syros's noted **Archaeological Museum.** Located on the left side of the town hall, this contains artifacts from the island's rich ancient history. The collection stretches back to the Neolithic era, with important finds taken from the prehistoric acropolis at Kastri to the north. Particularly illustrious are the Early Cycladic objects from Chalandriani (just south of Kastri), which indicate an advanced culture in the 3rd millennium BC. The museum, while not extensive, is one of the oldest in Greece. ⊠ *Plateia Miaouli* ☎ *22860/86900* ✆ *€3* ⊙ *Tues.–Sun. 8:30–2.*

Like the Municipal Palace, the palm-ringed **Miaoúli Square,** or Plateia Miaouli, was the creation of Ernst Ziller (who also is credited with Athens's famous Grande Bretagne hotel). Here a band shell with nine sculpted Muses, and a statue of revolutionary war hero Admiral Andreas Miaoulis, ornament a vast expanse of marble pavement. Families patrician and not still stroll back and forth on their evening *voltes* (strolls), displaying their marriageable members, while skateboarding children skid around them.

Across from the Municipal Palace on Miaoúli Square is another testament to Syros's wealth: the **Apollon Theater** (⊕ *www.festivaloftheaegean.com*), 1861, a small-scale version of Milan's La Scala. It is, after decades of restoration, again offering operas and other cultural events in July and August; its third floor displays a collection of cultural memorabilia. Although money poured into Syros since the days of Italian rule after 1207, the high-rollers and opera divas really began to arrive in the 19th century, after the Turkish period, when Ermoupoli became the main port between Europe, the Black Sea, and the Levant. When commerce boomed, Greece's first high school (Eleftherios Venizelos, Greece's greatest modern politician, attended) and first shipyard were established on Syros. Around Miaoúli Square are streets lined with two- and three-story mansions with graceful wrought-iron fanlights washed in pastels; here, too, in the streets to the right of Miaoúli Square (facing the palace), you can find a high-quality concentration of Syros's tavernas.

One of the two towering peaks that rise over town, **Ano Syros** was greatly expanded by Venetians in the 13th century, who erected a walled town over the ancient acropolis, immuring themselves against pirates. From the Roman Catholic bishopric of the church of St. George crowning the hill on down, this lofty retreat maintains its 13th-century integrity. Take a taxi up and walk down, with Ómiros street a handy thoroughfare through this picturesque quarter, dotted with castle walls and stone alleyways. High atop the hill is the looming Capuchin Monastery (1633), where visitors on official religious business may enjoy a sojourn in the jasmine-scented garden overlooking all Ermoupoli. Not far away is a belvedere—the town's high point—where a bronze bust of Pherekides commemorates that imaginative 6th-century BC Syrian philosopher, Pythagoras's teacher, who reputedly invented the sundial and was the first to write Greek prose. The bishopric, where bishops have presided since the time of Irenaios (AD 343, is downhill from the monastery. Farther down is the Jesuit Monastery, founded in 1747, and the adjacent church of the Virgin of Carmel. As you can see, the hill of Ano Syros remains mostly Catholic, but just across the townscape is the hill of Vrodado, which reminds us that Syros is now two-thirds Greek Orthodox (happily, relations remain cordial). The Catholic-flavored Venetian influence has given the island's culture and architecture a distinctive flavor: having welcomed so many religious refugees to its shores, Syros came under the protection of Louis XIII in 1640, which accounts for the French-flavored influence.

WHERE TO STAY & EAT

$$$ ✗**Lilis Taverna.** On a clear day you can flee forever to this spot high
★ above the city on the peak of Ano Syros. You can also see forever—or at least to the shores of Mykonos—if you grab a front-row table on the stone terrace. One of Ermoupoli's top food-with-a-view options, these vistas are yours if you climb the big flight of steps past the Hotel Omiros (or opt for a cab). Grilled meats and fish are the house specialties, but the chef knows his stuff and you can't go wrong no matter what you order. Sometimes *rembetika* musicians play late. ✉ *Ano Syros* ☎*22810/88087* ▭*No credit cards* ☼*No lunch.*

$$ ✗**Thalami.** Although this spot, ensconced in a neoclassic mansion, is a top choice for fresh seafood, it is the view that makes Thalami special. Perched on a sea cliff, its two terraces offer vistas as delicious as the

fresher-than-fresh shellfish. Opt for the squid stuffed with feta and green pepper or, if you have a chubby wallet, splurge on the fresh fish of the day. Open March to October; in summer, it's best to make dinner reservations. ⊠ *Kalemenopoulo 1 (next to neoclassic Nomarch bldg.)* ☎22810/85331 ⊟*AE, MC, V* ⊘ *Closed Nov.–Feb.*

$ ✕**Kouzina.** Set in a wood-trim
★ taverna setting, with a vast courtyard semi-embowered in pink bougainvillea, Kouzina is a showcase for top Cyprus cuisine, thanks to chef-owner Pavlos Grivas. He pays homage to his homeland with stylish twists, including a wicked beef carpaccio marinated in black truffle oil and lemon garnished with arugula and Parmesan. Top main dishes include the *afelia,* dried pork cooked slowly in red wine and coriander, served with bulgur and minted yogurt. For a different change of pace (and another €10) Pavlos will cook you fresh Argentine beefsteaks. Don't miss out on his exceptional homemade bitter-chocolate ice cream with Talisker whiskey, cardamom, and chili. The wine list is international; ask Pavlos's wife Andrea for some recommendations (although the house wine is excellent). Kouzina is located at the far end of restaurant-lined Stephanou street; walk up Venizelou toward Miaoúli Square and take the third left. ⊠*Androu 5* ☎*22840/34000* ⊕*www.kouzinasyros.gr* ⊟*AE, MC, V.*

¢ ✕**To Kastri.** Located in the central market, To Kastri is run by the Women's Union of Syros. A group comprising 28 women, they cook 10 dishes a day—home cooking so good that local housewives secretly buy food for their midday meals here. Open 9–5 (all year), this cafeteria often sells out by early afternoon. Beef stew, stuffed zucchini, stuffed cuttlefish, and beef in lemon sauce are what you would expect—but better. ⊠*Parou 13 (a small side street off Chiou)* ☎*22810/83140* ⊟*No credit cards.*

$$ ▦**Nisaki.** Convenient and comfortable, this modern three-story building is set amid neoclassic ones and is nestled next to a little park overlooking the sea. The lobby is comfy-traditional, with modular white furniture and green plants galore. Accessed by elevator, guest rooms all have balconies, half of which have town vistas and half unencumbered and exhilarating sea views. Most customers are Greek, which makes it lively (but they smoke). Breakfast is included. ⊠*E. Padadam 1, 84100* ☎*22810/88200* ⊟*22810/82000* ⊕*www.hotelnisaki.gr* ⇔*14 rooms* ⌂*In-room: no TV, refrigerator. In-hotel: restaurant, public Internet* ⊟*AE, MC, V* ⍣❙*BP.*

> ## I LOVE THE NIGHTLIFE
>
> Siros is known for its *rembetika* music—the noted songster Markos Vamvakaris was a native. The best places to hear traditional songs are the cafés way up on the Ano Syros hill (reservations needed) but you'll also find fine cafés down by the harbor, including To Rebetadio, a noted restaurant on Eptanisou street (one block up from the waterfront), where, late at night, the music begins to wail. Other nighttime options: the open-air Pallas Cinema (east of Miaoúli Square), concerts at Apollon Theater, or the elegant British-run casino on the quay.

$ ★ ☰Hotel Omiros. Perched on a steep hill just above Miaoúli Square and alluringly set in a yellow-stucco neoclassic mansion, Omiros is a friendly place to experience both comfort and old Syros. The lobby's two handsome sitting rooms are much used; the one used in winter looks like a whitewashed farmhouse living room, complete with sculpted Cycladic fireplace and rough stonework walls. Take the spiral staircase up to the guest rooms, many adorned with furniture and marble decorations from the 19th century (some have balconies). Omiros, or Homer, is up the street from the Metamorphosis church. A bar and cafeteria are adjacent; breakfast is extra. ✉43 Omirou Metamorfosi, 84100 ☎22810/84910 🖶22810/89266 ⊕www.greekhotel.com/cyclades/syros ⇦11 rooms, 2 suites ⚹In-hotel: no elevator, parking ☰AE, MC, V.

MACHO GREEK FLAVORING

When Athenians want *real* Greek food, they often head to Siros, which has long been known for its culinary brio. Not only was Greece's first cookbook published here in 1828, famed foodie Elizabeth David earned her toques in Mediterranean cooking here. Flavors are strong and accented with cheese, tomato, and fennel. Check out the lemon-and-anise-flavored *loukanika* sausages, the cured-pork louza tenderloin soaked in wine and cloves, the *marathopita*, lemon-herb and fennel bread, and the *kopanisti*, the island's tangy cheese.

BEACHES

Athough its beaches don't equal those of Andros, Mykonos, Paros, and Naxos, Syros has plenty of pleasant stretches of sand. Almost all of these are being developed, and villas, some truly hideous, are going up by the dozen. **Megas Yialos, Poseidon** (or **Dellagrazia**), **Finikas,** and **Galisas** all offer beachfront accommodations and tavernas. No one can deny that eating some fresh squid at a seaside taverna, watching the ducks bob, and having a swim are a pleasant respite from the big-city excitement of Ermoupoli.

7

CYCLADES ESSENTIALS

TRANSPORTATION

BY AIR

Schedules change seasonally and are often revised; reservations are always a good idea. There are no airports on Tinos, Sifnos, or Folegandros.

CARRIERS   Olympic Airways has six flights daily to Mykonos (10 daily during peak tourist season). There are also summer flights between Mykonos and Heraklion (on Crete), and between Mykonos and Rhodes. The Olympic Airways offices in Mykonos are at the port and at the airport. Olympic Airways has two flights daily between Athens and Naxos airport. Olympic also offers five daily flights to the Paros Airport from Athens (up to seven a day in high season) and six daily flights to Santorini Airport from Athens in peak season. Syros has two flights daily. In summer there are flights to Mykonos and Salonica about three times per week.

Aegean Airlines has five daily flights to Mykonos and four to Santorini in summer, but their schedules are often subject to change. Some European countries now have charter flights to Mykonos.

Contacts Aegean Airlines (☎ 210/626–1000 ⊕ www.aegeanair.com). **Olympic Airways** (✉ Port, Mykonos town ☎ 22890/22490 or 22890/22495 ⊕ www.olympic-air.com ✉ Ayia Athanassiou, Santorini, Fira ☎ 22860/22493 or 22860/22793).

AIRPORTS   **Information Mykonos Airport** (✉ 4 km [2½ mi] southeast of Mykonos town ☎ 22890/22327). **Naxos Airport** (✉ 1 km [½ mi] south of Naxos town ☎ 22850/23969). **Paros Airport** (✉ Near Alyki village, 9 km [5½ mi] south of Paros town ☎ 22840/91257). **Santorini Airport** (✉ On east coast, 8 km [5 mi] from Fira, Monolithos ☎ 22860/31525). **Syros Airport** (✉ 5 km [3 mi] south of Ermoupoli ☎ 22810/82634).

BY BIKE & QUADS

All the major islands have car- and bike-rental agencies at the ports and in the business districts. Motorbikes and scooters start at about €10 a day, including third-party liability coverage. Don't wear shorts or sandals, insist on the helmet (which the law requires), and get a phone number, in case of breakdown. Quads feel safer, but overturn easily.

BY BOAT & FERRY

Most visitors use the island's extensive ferry network, which is constantly being upgraded. Ferries sail from Piraeus (Port Authority) and from Rafina, 35 km (22 mi) northeast of Athens (Port Authority). Leaving from Rafina cuts traveling time by an hour; buses leave for the one-hour trip from Rafina to Athens every 20 minutes 6 AM–10 PM. Traveling time from Piraeus varies with the speed (and price) of the boat.

Economy-class boat tickets cost roughly one-third the airfare, and passengers are restricted to seats in the deck areas and often-crowded indoor seating areas. High-speed boats are more expensive (and there are no scenic outdoor decks). A first-class ticket, which sometimes buys a private cabin and better lounge, costs about half an airplane ticket. For information on interisland connections, contact local travel agents. High season is June through September; boats are less frequent in the off-season. All schedules must be checked soon before departure, as they change with the season, for major holidays, for weather, and for reasons not ascertainable. Many Web sites give official long-range schedules: ⊕ *holidaytravel.forth-crs.gr/english/npgres.exe?PM=BO* and ⊕ *www.openseas.gr/OPENSEAS/index_en.vm* are two good examples, as they try to update every five days. Port authorities, who have expertise, generally send you to a travel agent as the best bet for booking the right kind of boat and ticket for you.

On all islands, caïques leave from the main port for popular beaches and interisland trips. For popular routes, captains have posted signs showing their destinations and departure times.

Contacts Piraeus Port Authority (☎ *210/451–1311 or 210/415–1321*). **Rafina Port Authority** (☎ *22940/22300*).

Contact Andros Port Authority (☎ *22820/22250*).

FOLEGANDROS Two boats a day (not all ferries, as some might be catamarans or steamers) leave from Piraeus. Boats from here also call at Santorini, Paros, Naxos, Ios, and Syros.

Contact Folegandros Port Authority (☎ *22860/41530*).

MYKONOS In summer, there are two to three ferries daily to Mykonos from Piraeus and Rafina. There are daily departures to Paros, Syros, Tinos, Naxos, Santorini, and Andros. Destinations are widening monthly. Check which dock they leave from, as there are both new and old docks. For complete information, you must check here with several agencies.

Contact Mykonos Port Authority (✉ *Harbor, above National Bank* ☎ *22940/22218*).

NAXOS In summer, ferries leave Piraeus for Naxos at least three times a day. (The trip takes about four to seven hours.) Boats go daily from Naxos to Mykonos, Ios, Paros, Syros, Tinos, and Santorini; check for other places served.

Contact Naxos Port Authority (☎ *22850/22300*).

PAROS About three ferries leave Piraeus for Paros every day in summer. Paros has daily ferry service to Santorini, Mykonos, Tinos, Andros, Syros, and Naxos; there are also weekly boats to Ikaria, Samos, Folegandros, and other islands. Antiparos excursion boats leave from Parikia, car ferries leave from Pounta. Cruise boats leave daily from Paros town and Naousa for excursions to Delos and Mykonos.

Contact Paros Port Authority (☎ *22840/21240*).

SANTORINI Santorini is served at least thrice daily from Piraeus; from Santorini, ferries make frequent connections to the other islands—daily to Paros, Naxos, Ios, Anaphi, and Crete. All ferries dock at Athinios port, where taxis and buses meet the boats. Travelers bound for Ia and other towns change at Fira. The port below Fira is used only by cruise ships and small craft. Passengers disembarking here face a half-hour hike, or they can take the cable car (just use the traditional transport donkeys for photo ops).

Contact **Santorini Port Authority** (☎ *22860/22239*).

SIFNOS   There are four to five boats daily from Piraeus, mostly ferries and the occasional steamer or catamaran. Sifnos has daily connections with Seriphos and Mylos. There are also boats to Syros and Paros.

Contact **Sifnos Port Authority** (☎ *22840/33617*).

SYROS   There are four or five boats, most of them ferries, daily from Piraeus. There are daily connections with Andros, Tinos, and Mykonos, and regular connections with Paros, Naxos, Sifnos, Santorini, and other islands.

Contact **Syros Port Authority** (☎ *22810/82690*).

TINOS   Tinos is served in summer by four boats a day from Rafina and Piraeus. There are daily connections with Andros, Syros, Paros, Naxos, and Mykonos and regular boats to Santorini, and sometimes other islands. An excursion boat goes daily to nearby Delos, returning in the afternoon. Only Sea Jets and excursion boats stop at the old dock. For information, you must check with several agencies.

Contact **Tinos Port Authority** (☎ *22830/22348*).

BY BUS

FOLEGANDROS   Buses go from the little port to Chora every hour or so throughout the day; buses meet the boats. Buses go almost as often to the southern beaches and to Ano Meria.

MYKONOS   In Mykonos town the Ayios Loukas station in the Fabrica quarter at the south end of town has buses to Ornos, Ayios Ioánnis, Platys Yialos, Psarou, Paradise beach, the airport, and Kalamopodi. Another station near the Archaeological Museum is for Ayios Stefanos, Tourlos, Ano Mera, Elia, Kalafatis, and Kalo Livadi. Schedules are posted.

NAXOS   On Naxos, the bus system is reliable and fairly extensive. Daily buses go from Chora (near the boat dock) to Engares, Melanes, Sangri, Filoti, Apeiranthos, Koronida, and Apollonas. In summer there is added daily service to the beaches, including Ayia Anna, Pyrgaki, Ayiassos, Pachy Ammos, and Abram. All the many villages have bus service. Schedules are posted.

PAROS   From the Paros town bus station, just west of the dock, there is service every hour to Naousa and less-frequent service to Alyki, Pounta, and the beaches at Piso Livadi, Chrysi Akti, and Drios. Schedules are posted.

SANTORINI   On Santorini buses leave from the main station in central Fira (Deorgala) for Perissa and Kamari beaches, Ia, Pyrgos, and other villages. Schedules are posted.

SIFNOS   Buses meet the boats in Kamares and go to Apollonia, the capital. From Apollonia there are hourly connections to Artemonas, Kastro, and Platys Yialos, and less frequently to Vathy. Schedules are posted.

SYROS   From the seaside station between the boat dock and the main street, buses run at least every hour from Ermoupoli to all the other villages. Schedules are posted.

TINOS   On Tinos, buses run several times daily from the quay of Chora to nearly all the many villages in Tinos, and in summer buses are added for beaches.

Information Bus Information (☎ *22820/22316 in Andros, 22860/41425 in Folegandros, 22890/23360 in Mykonos, 22850/22440 in Naxos, 22840/21133 in Paros, 22890/25404 in Santorini, 22840/31210 in Sifnos, 22810/82575 in Syros, 22830/22440 in Tinos).*

BY CAR

To take cars on ferries you must make reservations. Though there is bus service on the large and mountainous islands of Andros and Naxos, it is much more convenient to travel by car.

Although islanders tend to acknowledge rules, many roads on the islands are poorly maintained, and tourists sometimes lapse into vacation inattentiveness. Drive with caution, especially at night, when you may well be sharing the roads with motorists returning from an evening of drinking.

All the major islands have car- and bike-rental agencies at the ports and in the business districts. Car rentals cost about €45 per day, with unlimited mileage and third-party liability insurance. Full insurance costs about €6 a day more. Four-wheeled semi-bikes (quads), that look—but are not—safer than bikes, are also available everywhere. Choose a dealer that offers 24-hour service and a change of vehicle in case of a breakdown. Most will take you from and to your plane or boat. Beware: all too many travelers end up in Athenian hospitals owing to poor roads, slipshod maintenance, careless drivers, and excessive partying.

FOLEGANDROS   There is not much reason to rent a vehicle in tiny Folegandros; buses will do. The few agencies have offices in the port and in the capital of Apollonia.

Local Agency Diaplous Travel (✉ ☎ *22860/41158* 📠 *22860/41159* ⊕ *www. diaploustravel.gr).*

MYKONOS   No cars are permitted in town. Many car rentals line the street above the bus terminal, and in the Maouna area near the windmills. Beware of sharp dealing. For friendly, trustworthy service go to Apollon Rent a Car, run by the Andronikos family. They'll meet you at the boat with a car, or bring one to your hotel; they also have offices at Mykonos Airport and at Ornos. Their in-town parking is a boon.

Local Agency Apollon Rent a Car (✉ *Maouna, Mykonos* ☎ *22890/24136* 🖶 *22890/23447* ⊕ *www.apolloncars.com*).

NAXOS   Car-rental outfits are concentrated in the Chora new town: try Naxos Vision. Or let Despina Kitini, of the Tourist Information Centre (⇨ *Tour Options*), make arrangements for you.

Local Agency Naxos Vision (✉ *Chora, near post office* ☎ *22850/26200* 🖶 *22850/26201* ⊕ *www.naxosvision.com*).

PAROS   It is a good idea to rent a vehicle here, because the island is large; there are many beaches to choose from, and taxis are in demand. There are many reputable agencies near the port. Nick Boyatzis's Acropolis is reliable and friendly, and will meet boats and planes.

Major Agency Sixt (✉ *Car-rental desk in Polos Travel, by OTE office, Paros town* ☎ *22840/21309* ⊕ *www.polostours.gr/english/rentacar* ✉ *Naousa* ☎ *22840/51544*).

Local Agency Acropolis Rent a Car (✉ *On waterfront, 2 blocks east of the port, Parikia* ☎ *22840/21830* 🖶 *22840/24344*).

SANTORINI   Europcar has offices in Fira and at Santorini Airport. Ia's Drossos delivers anywhere.

Major Agency Europcar (☎ *22860/24610 in Fira, 22860/33290 airport* ⊕ *www.europcar.com.gr*).

Local Agency Drossos (☎ *22860/71492, 22860/71668 at port* ⊕ *www.drossos.gr*).

SIFNOS   Buses go everywhere, but cars will definitely come in handy if you want to stop at the many little roadside chapels.

Local Agency Aegean Thesaurus Travel and Tourism (✉ *Apollonia* ☎ *22840/33151* 🖶 *22840/32190* ⊕ *www.thesaurus.gr*); there is also a branch office in Kamares port ☎ *22840/33527*.

SYROS   The main sights in Syros are in Ermoupoli, and buses go frequently everywhere else; a car is probably superfluous.

Local Agency Gaviotis Travel (✉ *Main quay, Ermoupoli* ☎ *22810/86644* 🖶 *22810/88755* ⊕ *www.syros.com.gr/companies/rentacar/gaviotis/gaviotis_en.htm*).

TINOS   Vidalis Rent-a-Car and Dimitris Rental, almost next door to each other, are reliable.

Local Agencies Dimitris Rental (✉ *Alavanou, Tinos town* ☎ *22830/23585* 🖶 *22830/22744* ⊕ *www.tinosrentacar.com/index.html*). **Vidalis Rent-a-Car** (✉ *Alavanou 16, Tinos town* ☎ *22830/24300* 🖶 *22830/25995* ⊕ *www.vidalisrentacar.gr*).

BY TAXI

Taxis are privately owned. Taxis on Folegandros meet boats and a stand is at the town entrance. Meters are not used on Mykonos; instead, standard fares for each destination are posted on a notice bulletin board. There is a taxi stand on Naxos near the harbor, and in Paros, there is one across from the windmill on the harbor. Note that in high season taxis are often busy. The main taxi station on Santorini is near Fira's central square (25th of March street). Taxis on Sifnos meet boats, and there is a stand in the main square of Apollonia. On Syros they wait on the quay and on Miaoúli Square. In Tinos, taxis wait near the central boat dock, on the quay.

Contacts Taxis (☎ *22820/22171 in Andros, 22890/22400 or 22860/41048 in Fole-gandros, 22810/31272 in Kythnos, 22890/23700 in Mykonos, 22850/22444 in Naxos, 22840/21500 in Paros, 22860/22555 in Santorini, 22840/31656 or 22840/33570 for 2 of Sifnos's 10 taxis, 22810/86222 in Syros, 22830/22470 in Tinos*).

EMERGENCIES

FOLEGANDROS **Contacts Health Center** (☎ *22860/41222*). **Police** (☎ *22860/41249*).

MYKONOS The hospital in Mykonos has 24-hour emergency service with patholo-gists, surgeons, pediatricians, dentists, and X-ray technicians.

Contacts First Aid (✉ *Ano Mera* ☎ *22890/71395*). **Hospital** (✉ *Mykonos town* ☎ *22890/23998 or 22890/23994*). **Police** (☎ *2289/22235*).

NAXOS The Health Center outside Chora is open 24 hours a day.

Contacts Health Center (☎ *22850/23333 or 2285/23676*). **Medical Center of Naxos** (✉ *Quay, Chora* ☎ *22850/23234* 📠 *22850/23576*). **Police** (☎ *22850/22100 in Chora, 22850/31244 in Filoti*).

PAROS **Contacts Medical Center** (☎ *22840/22500 in Paros town, 22840/51216 in Naousa, 22840/61219 in Antiparos*). **Police** (☎ *22840/23333 in Paros town, 22840/51202 in Naousa*).

SANTORINI **Contacts Medical assistance** (☎ *22860/22237 in Fira, 22860/71227 in Ia*). **Police** (☎ *22860/22649 in Fira*).

SIFNOS **Contacts Medical assistance** (☎ *22840/31315 in Apollonia*). **Police** (☎ *22840/31210 in Fira*).

SYROS Syros has the islands' most fully equipped hospital.

Contacts Hospital (✉ *Near Iroon Sq., Ermoupoli* ☎ *22810/86666*). **Police** (☎ *22810/82610 on Miaoúli Sq.*).

TINOS **Contacts Medical assistance** (✉ *East end of town, Chora* ☎ *22830/22210* ✉ *Isternia* ☎ *22830/31206*). **Police** (☎ *22830/22255 in Chora, 22830/31371 in Pirgos*).

TOUR OPTIONS

Contact Colours Travel (✉ *Main square, Batsi* ☎ *22820/41252* 📠 *22820/41608* ⊕ *www.bookandros.com*).

FOLEGANDROS Flavio Facciolo's Sottovento arranges boat trips and general informa-tion graciously.

Contact Maraki Travel and Tours (✉ *Chora* ☎ *22860/41273* ✍ *maraki@syr. forth.gr.*). **Sottovento** (✉ *Main square, Chora* ☎ *22860/41444* 📠 *22820/41608* ⊕ *www.sottovento.eu*).

MYKONOS   Windmills Travel takes a group every morning for a day tour of Delos
(€35). The company also has half-day guided tours of the Mykonos
beach towns, with a stop in Ano Mera for the Panayia Tourliani Monastery (€20). Windmills also provides excursions to nearby Tinos (€40–
€50); arranges private tours of Delos and Mykonos and off-road jeep
trips (€50); charters yachts; and, in fact, handles all tourist services.
John van Lerberghe's office, the Mykonos Accommodations Center, is
small, but he can tailor your trip from soup to nuts.

Contacts The Mykonos Accommodation Center (✉ *In picturesque old building, up steep staircase Enoplon Dynameon 10, Mykonos town* ☎ *22890/23160*
🖷 *22890/24137* ⊕ *mykonos-accommodation.com*). **Windmills Travel** (✉ *Fabrica*
☎ *22890/26555 or 22890/23877* 🖷 *22890/22066* ⊕ *www.windmillstravel.com*).

NAXOS   The Tourist Information Centre, run by Despina Kitini of the Chateau
Zevgoli, offers round-the-island tours (€20). Despina can usually tell
exactly what you want after a short discussion and then swiftly arrange
it. Zas Travel runs two good one-day tours of the island sights with
different itineraries, each costing about €20, and one-day trips to Delos
(about €40) and Mykonos (about €35).

Contacts Tourist Information Centre (✉ *Waterfront, Chora* ☎ *22850/22993*
🖷 *22850/25200* ✐ *info@naxostownhotels.com*). **Zas Travel** (✉ *Chora*
☎ *22850/23330 or 22850/23331* 🖷 *22850/23419* ✉ *Ayios Prokopios*
☎ *22850/24780* ✐ *zas-travel@nax.forthnet.gr*).

PAROS   Trips by land and sea, such as a tour around Antiparos, are arranged
by Kostas Akalestos's Paroikia Tours. Erkyna Travel runs many excursions by boat, bus, and foot. For yacht and other VIP services, check
out Nikos Santorineos's office.

Contacts Erkyna Travel (✉ *On main square, Naousa* ☎ *22840/22654,
22840/22655, or 22840/53180* ⊕ *www.erkynatravel.com/islands/paros.htm*).
Paroikia Tours (✉ *Market street, Paros town* ☎ *22840/22470 or 22840/22471*
🖷 *22840/22450* ✐ *parikiatours@parosweb.com*). **Santorineos Travel Services** (✉ *Quay, Paros town* ☎ *22840/24245* 🖷 *22840/23922* ✐ *nikos@par.
forthnet.gr*).

SANTORINI   Pelican Travel runs coach tours, wine tastings, and visits to Ia; it also
has daily boat trips to the volcano and Thirassia (half day €12, full day
€25) and arranges private tours. Nomikos Travel has tours to the same
sights and to the island's wineries and the Monastery of Profitis Ilias.
This is the place to sign up for a caldera submarine trip (€60).

Contacts Nomikos Travel (✉ *Fira* ☎ *22860/23660* 🖷 *22860/23666* ⊕ *www.
nomikosvillas.gr*). **Pelican Travel** (✉ *Fira* ☎ *22860/22220* 🖷 *22860/22570*
✐ *info@pelican.gr* ⊕ *www.pelican.gr*).

SIFNOS   Aegean Thesaurus Travel handles private tours, walking tours (€15),
cooking classes (€32), and much more.

Contact Aegean Thesaurus Travel (✉ *Apollonia* ☎ *22840/33151* 🖷 *22840/32190*
✐ *aegean@thesaurus.gr* ⊕ *www.thesaurus.gr*).

SYROS   Konstantinos Gaviotis has a number of tours and excursions.

Contact **Gaviotis Travel** (✉ *Apollonia* ☏ *22810/86644* 📠 *22810-88755* ✎ *gaviotistravel@syr.forthnet.gr* ⊕ *www.syros.com.gr/companies/rentacar/gaviotis/gaviotis_en.htm*).

TINOS Sharon Turner at Windmills Travel runs daily guided bus tours of the island for €15, specialty tours by jeep, and unguided Delos–Mykonos trips (€25).

Contact **Windmills Travel** (✉ *Above outer dock, behind playground, Chora* 📠📠 *22830/23398* ✎ *sharon@otenet.gr* ⊕ *www.windmillstravel.com*).

VISITOR INFORMATION

Contacts Colours Travel (✉ *Batsi main square* ☏ *22820/41252* 📠 *22820/41608* ⊕ *www.bookandros.com*). **Police Station** (✉ *Across from ferry dock, Gavrio* ☏ *22820/71220*).

FOLEGANDROS Flavio Facciolo's Sottovento handles tickets and all other arrangements.

Contact **Sottovento** (✉ *Main square, Chora* ☏ *22860/41444* 📠 *22820/41608* ⊕ *www.sottovento.eu*).

MYKONOS Very personal service can be found at John van Lerberghe's Mykonos Accommodations Center, and all services at Windmills Travel.

Contacts Mykonos Accommodation Center (✉ *In picturesque old building, up steep staircase Enoplon Dynameon 10, Mykonos town* ☏ *22890/23160* 📠 *22890/24137* ⊕ *mykonos-accommodation.com*). **Tourist police** (✉ *Mykonos town harbor, near departure point for Delos* ☏ *22890/22716*). **Windmills Travel** (✉ *Fabrica* ☏ *22890/26555 or 22890/23877* 📠 *22890/22066* ⊕ *www.windmills travel.com*).

NAXOS Despina Kitini's Tourist Information Centre has free booking service, bus and ferry schedules, international dialing, luggage storage, laundry service, and foreign exchange at bank rates. You can also book airline tickets and rent Kastro houses.

Contact **Tourist Information Centre** (✉ *Waterfront, Chora* ☏ *22850/24525, 22285/24358, or 22850/22993* 📠 *222850/25200* ✎ *info@naxostownhotels.com*).

PAROS For efficient and friendly service—tickets, villa rentals for families, apartments, and quality hotel reservations—try Kostas Akalestos's Paroikia Tours. Kostas, efficient and full of the Greek spirit, has many repeat customers. Polos Tours is big, inclusive, and efficient and will deliver tickets to your Athens hotel. Nikos and Clara Santorineos are very helpful.

Contacts Paroikia Tours (✉ *Market street, Paros town* ☏ *22840/22470 or 22840/22471* 📠 *22840/22450*). **Polos Tours** (✉ *Next to dockside OTE office, Paros town* ☏ *22840/22333* 📠 *222840/21983*). **Santorineos Travel Services** (✉ *Quay, Paros town* ☏ *22840/24245* 📠 *22840/23922* ✎ *nikos@par.forthnet.gr*).

SANTORINI Nomikos Travel, which has offices in Fira and Perissa, can handle most needs.

Contact **Nomikos Travel** (☏ *22860/23660* 📠 *22860/23666* ⊕ *www.nomikos villas.gr*).

SIFNOS   Aegean Thesaurus Travel is much the best travel office in Sifnos.

Contact Aegean Thesaurus Travel (✉ *Apollonia* ☎ *22840/33151* 🖷 *22840/32190* ✐ *aegean@thesaurus.gr* ⊕ *www.thesaurus.gr*).

SYROS   Konstantinos Gaviotis gives good service for most travel needs.

Contact Gaviotis Travel (✉ *Apollonia* ☎ *22810/86644* 🖷 *22810/88755* ✐ *gaviotistravel@syr.forthnet.gr* ⊕ *www.syros.com.gr/companies/rentacar/gaviotis/gaviotis_en.htm*).

TINOS   For all tourist services (schedules, room bookings, tours, happenings), see friendly Sharon Turner, manager of Windmills Travel; she's a gold mine of information—there's nothing she doesn't know about her adopted island.

Contact Windmills Travel (✉ *Above outer dock, behind playground, Chora* 🖷☎ *22830/23398* ✐ *sharon@otenet.gr* ⊕ *www.windmillstravel.com*).

Crete

Matala

WORD OF MOUTH

"Under most circumstances, I would consider it a no-brainer to stay in Hania rather than Heraklion. But if all you want to do is visit the [Archaeological] Museum and [the Palace of] Knossos, you should definitely stay in Heraklion . . . you will want to allow yourself a few hours at the museum in Heraklion. It contains all the best artifacts, wall frescoes, etc. that were removed from Knossos for better preservation and safety, including quite a few pieces of world renown."

—Marilyn

WELCOME TO CRETE

The fabled ruins of the Palace of Knoss

TOP REASONS TO GO

★ **Minoan Magnificence:** At the Palace of Knossos, get up-close to the mysteries—and the throne room's dazzling murals—of the 3,500-year-old civilization of the Minoans.

★ **Getting Your Sea Major:** From palm-backed Vai to remote Elafonisi, some of the finest beaches in Greece are lapped by Crete's turquoise waters.

★ **Crete's Venice:** Although it has its bright city lights, Rethymnon is most noted for its time-burnished Venetian quarter, threaded with narrow lanes leading to palazzos, fountains, and shady squares.

★ **Walk on the Wild Side:** With its snowcapped peaks and deep gorges, craggy Crete offers lots of escapes for those who want to get away from it all.

★ **Suite Temptation:** New palatial resorts let you live like royalty in a Venetian palace or—at the Elounda Mare—sun-worship the day away in your own private pool.

1 Eastern Crete. Knossos, the most spectacular of the Minoan palaces and Crete's most popular attraction, is here in the east. Just as this sprawling complex was the hub of island civilization 3,500 years ago, nearby Heraklion is Crete's bustling modern capital. Farther east along the coast is the Elounda peninsula, the island's epicenter of luxury, where some of the world's most-sumptuous resort getaways are tucked along a stunning shoreline. The east isn't all hustle, bustle, and glitz, though—the beach at Vai is just one example of the natural beauty that abounds here in the east, and in mountain villages like Kritsa, old traditions continue to thrive.

Traditional red-roofed Cretan church

Life's a beach on Crete

GETTING ORIENTED

Crete is long and slender, approximately 257 km (159 mi) long and only 60 km (37 mi) at its widest. The most development is present on the north shore; for the most part, the southern coast remains blessedly unspoiled. The island's three major cities, Heraklion, Rethymnon, and Hania, are in the north, and are connected by the island's major highway, an east–west route that traverses most of the north coast. All three cities are served by ferry from Piraeus, and Heraklion and Hania have international airports. By car or bus, it's easy to reach other parts of the island from these gateways.

8

2 Western Crete. The scenery gets more rugged as you head west, where the White mountains pierce the blue sky with snowcapped peaks then plunge into the Libyan Sea along dramatic, rocky shorelines. Mountain scenery and remote seacoast villages—some, like Loutro, accessible only on foot or by boat—attract many visitors to the west. Others come to enjoy the urban pleasures of Rethymnon and Hania, gracious cities that owe their harbors, architectural jewels, and exotic charms to Venetian and Turkish occupiers.

Tread carefully through the Samaria Gorge

CRETE PLANNER

The Serendipitous Shopper

You still occasionally come across the heavy scarlet-embroidered blankets and bedspreads that formed the basis of a traditional dowry chest.

All the villages on the Lasithi plateau have shops selling embroidered linens, made in front of the stove during the cold months.

All over the island, local craftspeople produce attractive copies of Minoan jewelry in gold and silver, as well as some with original modern designs.

A Cretan knife, whether plain steel or with a decorated blade and handle, makes a handy kitchen or camping implement (remember to pack it in your checked luggage when you fly home).

Boot makers in Heraklion and Hania can make you a pair of heavy Cretan leather knee boots to order.

In the village of Thrapsano, potters make terra-cotta vases, candlesticks, and other objects, including pithoi, tall earthenware jars used by the Minoans for storing wine and oil that are popular as flowerpots.

Making the Most of Your Time

Enticing as Crete's beaches are, there is much more to the island than sand and surf. Archaeological sites in Crete open at 8 or 8:30 in summer, so get an early start to wander through the ruins before the sun is blazing. You'll also want to visit some of the folklife museums that pay homage to the island's traditional past. One of the finest collections is in Vori, southwest of Heraklion; there are also excellent folk collections at the Historical and Folk Art Museum in Rethymnon and the Historical Museum of Crete in Heraklion. An evening should begin with a stroll around the shady squares that grace every Cretan town and village, or along a waterfront promenade—those in Hania, Ayios Nikolaos, and Siteia are especially picturesque and jammed with locals. Most evenings are spent over a long meal, almost always eaten outdoors in the warm weather. For entertainment, seek out a *kentron* (a taverna that hosts traditional Cretan music and dancing). The star performer is the *lyra* player, who can extract a surprisingly subtle sound from the small pear-shape instrument, held upright on the thigh and played with a bow. Ask at your hotel where lyra players are performing.

Dining & Lodging Prices in Euros

	¢	$	$$	$$$	$$$$
Restaurants	under €8	€8–€11	€11–€15	€15–€20	over €20
Hotels	under €60	€60–€90	€90–€120	€120–€160	over €160

Note that luxury resort prices on Crete are more comparable to the Athens price chart. Restaurant prices are for one main course at dinner, or for two mezedes (small dishes). Hotel prices are for a standard double room in high season, including taxes. Hotels operate on the European Plan (EP, with no meal provided) unless we note that they use the Continental Plan (CP, with Continental breakfast); Breakfast Plan (BP, with a full breakfast); Modified American Plan (MAP, with breakfast and dinner); or the Full American Plan (FAP, with all meals). Inquire when booking if meal plans (which can entail higher rates) are mandatory. Guest rooms have air-conditioning, room phones, and TVs unless otherwise noted.

Dining à la Crete

Cretans tend to take their meals seriously, and like to sit down in a taverna to a full meal. Family-run tavernas take pride in serving Cretan cooking, and a number of the better restaurants in cities now also stress Cretan produce (the fruit is famous) and traditional dishes. One way to dine casually is to sample the mezedes (small plates) served at some bars and tavernas. These often include such Cretan specialties as tyropita (cheese-filled pastry), and a selection of cheeses: Cretan graviera, a hard, smooth cheese, is a blend of pasteurized sheep's and goat's milk that resembles Emmentaler in flavor and texture—not too sharp, but with a strong, distinctive flavor—and Mizythra (a creamy white cheese).

As main courses, Cretans enjoy grilled meat, generally lamb and pork, but there is also plenty of fresh fish. Cretan olive oil is famous throughout Greece; it's heavier and richer than other varieties. The island's wines are special: look for Boutari Kritikos, a crisp white; and Minos Palace, a smooth red. Make sure you try the tsikouthia (also known as raki), the Cretan firewater made from fermented grape skins, which is drunk at any hour, often accompanied by a dish of raisins or walnuts drenched in honey. Many restaurants offer raki free of charge at the end of a meal. Lunch is generally served from 1 to 3 or so. Dinner is an event here, as it is elsewhere in Greece, and is usually served late; in fact, when non-Greeks are finishing up around 10:30 or so, locals usually begin arriving.

Where to Stay

Some of Greece's finest resorts line the shores of Elounda peninsula, offering sumptuous surroundings and exquisite service. Although the atmosphere at these resorts is more international than Greek, you'll find authentic surroundings in the Venetian palaces and old mansions that are being sensitively restored as small hotels, especially in Hania and Rethymnon. For the most authentic experience on Crete, opt for simple, whitewashed, tile-floor rooms with rustic pine furniture in the ubiquitous "room to rent" establishments in mountain and seaside villages. Another common term is "studio," which implies the presence of a kitchen or basic cooking facilities. Standards of cleanliness are high in Crete, and service is almost always friendly.

When to Go

The best times for visiting Crete are April and May, when every outcrop of rock is ablaze with brilliant wildflowers, or September and October, when the sea is still warm and the light golden but piercingly clear.

A spring visit comes with the advantage of long days.

In July and August, the main Minoan sights and towns on the north coast come close to overflowing with tourists.

Take care, special care to avoid such places as Mallia and Limin Hersonissos, hideously developed towns where bars and pizzerias fill up with heavy-drinking northern Europeans on summertime package tours.

Even in the height of summer, though, you can enjoy many parts of the west and the southern coast without feeling too oppressed by crowds.

Crete can also be a pleasure in winter, when you can visit the museums and archaeological sites and enjoy the island's delightful towns and cities without the crush of crowds.

Remember, though, that rainfall can be heavy in January and February.

Remember that some hotels and restaurants close from November through mid-April.

8

Updated
by Stephen
Brewer

MOUNTAINS, SPLIT WITH DEEP GORGES and honeycombed with caves, rise in sheer walls from the sea. Snowcapped peaks loom behind sandy shoreline, vineyards, and olive groves. Miles of beaches, some with a wealth of amenities and others isolated and unspoiled, fringe the coast. But spectacular scenery is just the start of Crete's appeal: vestiges of Minoan civilization, which flourished on Crete some 3,000 to 4,000 years ago and is one of the most brilliant and amazing cultures the world has ever known, abound at Knossos, Phaistos, and many other archaeological sites around the island. Other invaders and occupiers—Roman colonists, the Byzantines, Arab invaders, Venetian colonists, and Ottoman pashas—have all left their mark on Heraklion, Hania, Rethymnon, and other towns and villages throughout the island.

Today Crete welcomes outsiders. Openly inviting to guests who want to experience the real Greece, Cretans remain family oriented and rooted in tradition. One of the greatest pleasures on Crete is immersing yourself in the island's lifestyle.

EASTERN CRETE ΑΝΑΤΟΛΙΚΗ ΚΡΗΤΗ

Eastern Crete includes the towns and cities of Heraklion, Ayios Nikolaos, Siteia, and Ierapetra, as well as the archaeological sites of Knossos and Gournia. Natural wonders lie amid these man-made places, including the palm-fringed beach at Vai and the Lasithi plateau, and other inland plains and highlands are studded with villages where life goes on untouched by the hedonism of the coastal resorts. You may well make first landfall in Heraklion, the island's major port. You'll want to spend time here to visit the excellent Archaeological Museum and Knossos, but you're likely to have a more relaxing Cretan experience in Ayios Nikolaos, a charming and animated port town; in the resorts on the stunning Elounda peninsula; or on the beautiful and undeveloped eastern end of the island, around Palaikastro.

HERAKLION ΗΡΑΚΛΕΙΟ

175 km (109 mi) south of Piraeus, 69 km (43 mi) west of Ayios Nikolaos, 78 km (49 mi) east of Rethymnon.

Crete's largest city—the fourth-largest city in Greece—is not immediately appealing: it's a sprawling and untidy collection of apartment blocks and busy roadways. Many travelers looking for Crete's more-rugged pleasures bypass the island's capital altogether, but the city's renowned Archaeological Museum and the nearby Palace of Knossos make Heraklion a mandatory stop for anyone even remotely interested in ancient civilizations. Besides, at closer look, Heraklion is not without its charms. The narrow, crowded alleys of the older city and the thick stone ramparts recall the days when soldiers and merchants clung to the safety of a fortified port. In Minoan times, this was a harbor for Knossos, the largest palace and effective power center of prehistoric Crete. (But the Bronze Age remains were built over long ago, and now

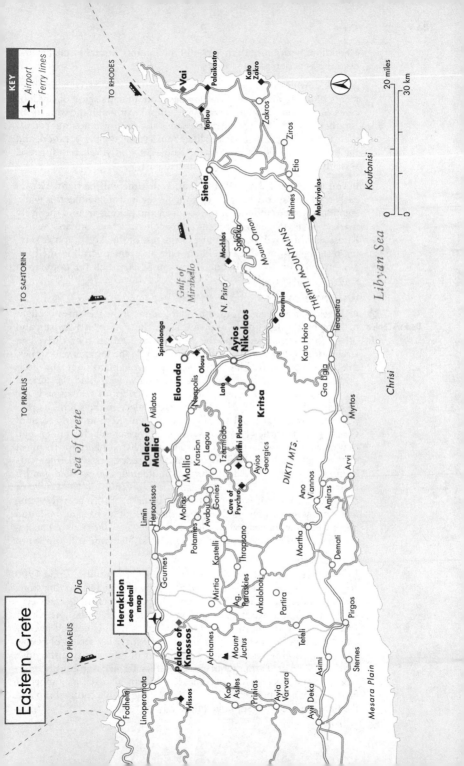

Heraklion, with more than 120,000 inhabitants, stretches far beyond even the Venetian walls.)

A walk down Dedalou and the other pedestrians-only streets provides plenty of amusements, and the city has more than its share of outdoor cafés where you can sit and watch life unfold. Although the waterfront is rather derelict, the seaside promenades and narrow lanes that run off them are slowly coming back to life, thanks to ongoing restoration, and the inner harbor dominated by the Koules, a sturdy Venetian fortress, is richly evocative of the island's storied past.

If you have just a day in Heraklion, your time will be tight. Get an early start and spend a couple of hours in the morning doing this walk, stepping into the churches if they're open and poking around the lively market. Save your energy for the Archaeological Museum and nearby Knossos, which will occupy most of the rest of the day. If you're staying overnight in or near Heraklion, take an evening stroll in the busy area around Ta Leontaria and Kornarou Square; half the population seems to converge here.

WHAT TO SEE

6 **Archaeological Museum.** Housed here are many of the treasures brought
Fodor's Choice to light by the legendary excavations at the Palace of Knossos and
★ other great monuments of the Minoan civilization that thrived in Crete some 3,000 years ago. Holdings include the famous seal stones, many inscribed with Linear B script and brought to light and deciphered by British archaeologist Sir Arthur Evans around the turn of the 20th century. The most stunning and mysterious seal stone is the so-called Phaistos Disk, found at Phaistos Palace in the south, its purpose unknown. (Linear B script is now recognized as an early form of Greek, but the earlier Linear A script that appears on clay tablets and that of the Phaistos Disk have yet to be deciphered.) Perhaps the most arresting treasures are the sophisticated frescoes, restored fragments found in Knossos. They depict broad-shouldered, slim-waisted youths, their large eyes fixed with an enigmatic expression on the Prince of the Lilies; ritual processions and scenes from the bullring, with young men and women somersaulting over the back of a charging bull; and groups of court ladies, whose flounced skirts led a French archaeologist to exclaim in surprise, "*Des Parisiennes!*," a name still applied to this striking fresco.

Even before great palaces with frescoes were being built around 1900 BC, the prehistoric Cretans excelled at metalworking and carving stone vases, and they were also skilled at producing pottery, such as the egg-shell-thin Kamaresware decorated in delicate abstract designs. Other specialties were miniature work such as the superbly crafted jewelry and the colored seal stones that are carved with lively scenes of people and animals. Though naturalism and an air of informality distinguish much Minoan art from that of contemporary Bronze Age cultures elsewhere in the eastern Mediterranean, you can also see a number of heavy, rococo set pieces, such as the fruit stand with a toothed rim and the punch bowl with appliquéd flowers.

Heraklion

The Minoans' talents at modeling in stone, ivory, and a kind of glass paste known as faience peaked in the later palace period (1700 BC–1450 BC). A famous rhyton, a vase for pouring libations, carved from dark serpentine in the shape of a bull's head, has eyes made of red jasper and clear rock crystal with horns of gilded wood. An ivory acrobat—perhaps a bull-leaper—and two bare-breasted faience goddesses in flounced skirts holding wriggling snakes were among a group of treasures hidden beneath the floor of a storeroom at Knossos. (Bull-leaping, whether a religious rite or a favorite sport, inspired some memorable Minoan art.) Three vases, probably originally covered in gold leaf, from Ayia Triada are carved with scenes of Minoan life thought to be rendered by artists from Knossos: boxing matches, a harvest-home ceremony, and a Minoan official taking delivery of a consignment of hides. The most stunning rhyton of all, from Zakro, is made of rock crystal. It's best to visit the museum first thing in the morning, before the tour buses arrive. Note that, at this writing, the collection is being shown in a one-room annex while the museum undergoes extensive renovation, which is scheduled to be completed in late 2008. ✉ *Eleftherias Sq.* ☎ *2810/224630* ⊕ *www.culture.gr* ⚲ *€4; combined ticket for museum and Palace of Knossos €10* ⊙ *Apr.–mid-Oct., daily 8–7:30; mid-Oct.–Mar., daily 8–5.*

10 Ayia Aikaterina. Nestled in the shadow of the Ayios Minas cathedral is one of Crete's most attractive small churches, Ayia Aikaterina, built in 1555. The church now contains a museum of icons by Cretan artists, who traveled to Venice to study with Italian Renaissance painters. Look for six icons (Nos. 2, 5, 8, 9, 12, and 15) by Michael Damaskinos, who worked in both Byzantine and Renaissance styles during the 16th century. ✉*Kyrillou Loukareos* ☎*No phone* ✇*€2* ⊙*Mon. and Wed. 9:30–1, Thurs. and Sat. 9–1 and 5–7, Fri. 9–1.*

2 Ayios Markos. This 13th-century church (now an exhibition space) is named for Venice's patron saint, but, with its modern portico and narrow interior, it bears little resemblance to its grand namesake in Venice. Hours are irregular; the church is open only for exhibitions. ✉*Eleftheriou Venizelou Sq.* ☎*No phone.*

9 Ayios Minas. This is a huge, lofty, but ultimately unprepossessing 1895 cathedral that can hold up to 8,000 worshippers. ✉*Kyrillou Loukareos.*

4 Ayios Titos. A chapel to the left of the entrance contains St. Tito's skull, set in a silver-and-gilt reliquary. He is credited with converting the islanders to Christianity in the 1st century AD on the instructions of St. Paul. ✉*Set back from 25 Avgoustou.*

Historical Museum of Crete. An imposing mansion houses a varied collection of early Christian and Byzantine sculptures, Venetian and Ottoman stonework, artifacts of war, and rustic folklife items. The museum provides a wonderful introduction to Cretan culture. Look out for the *Lion of St. Mark* sculpture, with an inscription that says in Latin I PROTECT THE KINGDOM OF CRETE. Left of the entrance is a room stuffed with memorabilia from Crete's bloody revolutionary past: weapons, portraits of mustachioed warrior chieftains, and the flag of the short-lived independent Cretan state set up in 1898. The 19th-century banner in front of the staircase sums up the spirit of Cretan rebellion against the Turks: ELEFTHERIA O THANATOS (Freedom or Death). Upstairs, look in on a room arranged as the study of Crete's most famous writer, Nikos Kazantzakis (1883–1957), the author of *Zorba the Greek* and an epic poem, *The Odyssey, a Modern Sequel*; he was born in Heraklion and is buried here, just inside the section of the walls known as the Martinengo. The top floor contains a stunning collection of Cretan textiles, including the brilliant scarlet weavings typical of the island's traditional handwork, and another room arranged as a domestic interior of the early 1900s. ✉*Kalokorinou, in a warren of little lanes near the seafront* ☎*2810/283219* ⊕*www. historical-museum.gr* ✇*€5* ⊙*Apr.–Oct., Mon.–Sat. 9–5; Nov.–Mar., Mon.–Tues. and Thurs.–Sat. 9–3, Wed. 9–3 and 6–9.*

5 Koules. Heraklion's inner harbor, where fishing boats land their catch and yachts are moored, is dominated by the Turkish-named fortress. Koules was built by the Venetians in the 16th century and decorated with three stone lions of St. Mark, symbol of Venetian imperialism. On the east side of the fortress are the vaulted arsenal; here Venetian galleys were repaired and refitted, and timber, cheeses, and sweet malmsey wine were loaded for the three-week voyage to Venice. The view from the battlements takes in the inner as well as the outer harbor, where freighters and passenger ferries drop anchor, and the sprawling labyrinth of concrete apartment blocks that is modern Heraklion. To the south rises Mt. Iuktas and, to the west, the pointed peak of Mt. Stromboli. ⊠*North end of 25 Avgoustou* ☎*2810/288484* ⌁*€4* ☉*Daily 9–1 and 4–7.*

③ Loggia. A gathering place for the island's Venetian nobility, this loggia was built in the early 17th century by Francesco Basilicata, an Italian architect. Now restored to its original Palladian elegance, it adjoins the old Venetian Armory, now the City Hall. ⊠*25 Avgoustou.*

NEED A BREAK?

Stop in at Kir-Kor, a venerable old *bougatsa* shop (⊠ *Eleftheriou Venizelou Sq.*), for an envelope of flaky pastry that's either filled with a sweet, creamy filling and dusted with cinnamon and sugar, or stuffed with soft white cheese. A double portion served warm with Greek coffee is a nice treat. Thick Cretan yogurt and ice cream are other indulgences on offer.

Martinengo Bastion. Six bastions shaped like arrowheads jut out from the well-preserved Venetian walls. Martinengo is the largest, designed by Micheli Sanmicheli in the 16th century to keep out Barbary pirates and Turkish invaders. When the Turks overran Crete in 1648, the garrison at Heraklion held out for another 21 years in one of the longest sieges in European history. General Francesco Morosini finally surrendered the city to the Turkish Grand Vizier in September 1669. He was allowed to sail home to Venice with the city's archives and such precious relics as the skull of Ayios Titos—which was not returned until 1966. Literary pilgrims come to the Martinengo to visit the **burial place of writer Nikos Kazantzakis.** The grave is a plain stone slab marked by a weathered wooden cross. The inscription, from his writings, says: I FEAR NOTHING, I HOPE FOR NOTHING, I AM FREE. ⊠*South of Kyrillou Loukareos on N. G. Mousourou.*

⑦ Eleftherias Square. The city's biggest square is paved in marble and dotted with fountains. The Archaeological Museum is off the north end of the square; at the west side is the beginning of Daidalou, the city's main street, which follows the line of an early fortification wall and is now a pedestrian walkway lined with tavernas, boutiques, jewelers, and souvenir shops. ⊠*Southeast end of Daidalou.*

⑧ Kornarou Square. This square is graced with a Venetian fountain and an elegant Turkish stone kiosk. Odos 1866, which runs north from the square, houses Heraklion's lively open-air market, where fruit and vegetable stalls and souvenir stands alternate with butchers' displays of whole lambs and pigs' feet. ⊠*At Odos 1866, south of Ta Leontaria.*

St. Peter's. Only a shell remains of this medieval church, which was heavily damaged during World War II in the bombing before the German invasion in 1941. ⊠ *West of harbor along seashore road.*

① Ta Leontaria. "The Lions," a stately marble Renaissance fountain, remains a beloved town landmark. It's the heart of Heraklion's town

8

center—Eleftheriou Venizelou Square, a triangular pedestrian zone filled with cafés and named after the Cretan statesman who united the island with Greece in 1913. This was the center of the colony founded in the 13th century, when Venice bought Crete, and Heraklion became an important port of call on the trade routes to the Middle East. The city, and often the whole island (known then as Candia), was ruled by the Duke of Crete, a Venetian administrator. ⊠ *Eleftheriou Venizelou Sq.*

WHERE TO STAY & EAT

¢–$$ ✕ **Erganos.** One of Heraklion's most traditional restaurants—just outside the old city walls south of Eleftherias Square—takes its name from one of the cities of ancient Crete and serves authentic local fare, including mouthwatering little pies (*pitarakia*) filled with cheese and honey, wild herbs from the mountains, and ground meats. Lunch and dinner both are often accompanied by Cretan music, often provided by a fellow patron. ⊠*Georgiadi 5* ☏*2810/285629* ☰*MC, V.*

¢–$ ✕ **Pantheon.** The liveliest restaurant in Heraklion's covered meat market has grilled and spit-roasted meats, as well as deftly prepared versions of moussaka and other traditional dishes. The surroundings are simple, but that doesn't stop locals from pouring in at all hours for a meal, which is nicely accompanied by salads made from the freshest Cretan produce. ⊠*Market off Kornarou Sq.* ☏*2810/241652* ☰*No credit cards.*

$$$–$$$$ 🛏 **Megaron.** A 1930s office building that for decades stood derelict ★ above the harbor now houses an unusually luxurious and restful hotel—the best one in town. Handsome public spaces include a welcoming library/lounge, a rooftop restaurant with stunning views of the city and sea, and a top-floor terrace where a swimming pool is perched dramatically at the edge of the roof. The large and sumptuous guest rooms bring together a tasteful combination of rich fabrics, marble, and woods, and the teak-floored baths are lavish. Special Internet rates are often lower than those at other hotels in this class, making the Megaron a relatively affordable indulgence. ⊠*Doukos Bofor 9, 71202* ☏*2810/305300* 🖷*2810/305400* ⊕*www.gdmmegaron.gr* ↩*38 rooms, 8 suites* ⚷*In-room: refrigerator, Wi-Fi. In-hotel: 2 restaurants, bar, pool, public Wi-Fi* ☰*MC, V* ⑂*CP.*

$$$ 🛏 **Astoria Capsis.** This sleek hotel opposite the Archaeological Museum in the most animated part of the city is attractive and welcoming, with contemporary rooms decorated in cool shades and furnished with blond wood. All rooms have balconies and all of the modern baths are equipped with bathtubs. Retreat to the rooftop swimming pool from June to August, when bar service is provided, or have coffee at the ground-floor bar, open 24 hours. Rates include a buffet breakfast that is nothing short of lavish. ⊠*Eleftherias Sq., 71201* ☏*2810/343080* 🖷*2810/229078* ⊕*www.astoriacapsis.gr* ↩*117 rooms, 14 suites* ⚷*In-room: refrigerator, Wi-Fi. In-hotel: restaurant, bar, pool* ☰*AE, DC, MC, V* ⑂*BP.*

$ 🛏 **El Greco.** At this basic-but-comfortable hotel smack dab in the city center, ask for a garden-facing room for a quieter night, or request a street-side balcony to watch the action around Ta Leontaria fountain, just steps away. The carpeted rooms are simply but pleasantly furnished with wood beds and a desk. Rates include a full breakfast, but air-conditioning costs €7 a day extra. Even so, the word is out about what a bargain this is, so it's best to reserve far in advance. ✉4 Odos 1821, 71202 ☎2810/281071 🖷2810/281072 ⊕www.elgreco-hotel.gr ➶90 rooms ⚠In-room: no a/c (some) ⊟DC, MC, V ⟍OⓁBP.

Ⅽ 🖭**Dedalos.** You'd have to look hard to find a more fairly priced accommodation in the city center. On pedestrians-only Daidalou, this place is an easy walk to the Archaeological Museum and other sights. Rooms are modest and not a lot of care goes into the decor, but they're comfortable and all have balconies. Be sure to ask for one that faces the sea and not the street, which is loud with merrymakers into the wee hours. Breakfast is available for €6. ✉Daidalou 15, 71202 ☎2810/244812 🖷2810/244391 ➶58 rooms ⊟MC, V.

THE MINOANS

They flourished on Crete from around 2700 BC to 1450 BC, and their palaces and cities at Knossos, Phaistos, and Gournia were centers of political power and luxury—they traded in tin, saffron, gold, and spices as far afield as Spain—when the rest of Europe was a place of primitive barbarity. They loved art, farmed bees, and worshipped many goddesses. But what brought about their demise? Some say political upheaval, but others point to an eruption on Thera (Santorini), about 100 km (60 mi) north in the Aegean, which caused tsunamis and earthquakes that brought about the end of this sophisticated civilization.

THE OUTDOORS

Ⓒ **Acquaplus Waterpark** (✉Hersonissos ☎28970/24950 ⊕www.acquaplus.gr 🖾€18 ⊙May–mid-Oct, daily 9 AM–sunset) is not the place to go if you've come to Crete in search of unspoiled scenery and traditional ways. But this 50-acre water park next to the Crete Golf Club has dozens of slides, pools, and game arcades—a nice reward for little ones who've been letting you drag them through museums and ruins.

PALACE OF KNOSSOS ΑΝΑΚΤΟΡΟ ΚΝΩΣΟΥ

FodorśChoice *5 km (3 mi) south of Heraklion.*
★

This most amazing of archaeological sites once lay hidden beneath a huge mound hemmed in by low hills. Heinrich Schliemann, father of archaeology and discoverer of Troy, knew it was here, but Turkish obstruction prevented him from exploring his last discovery. Cretan independence from the Ottoman Turks made it possible for Sir Arthur Evans, a British archaeologist, to start excavations in 1899. A forgotten and sublime civilization thus came again to light with the uncovering of the great Palace of Knossos.

The site was occupied from Neolithic times, and the population spread to the surrounding land. Around 1900 BC, the hilltop was leveled and the first palace constructed; around 1700 BC, after an earthquake destroyed the original structure, the later palace was built, surrounded by houses and other buildings. Around 1450 BC, another widespread

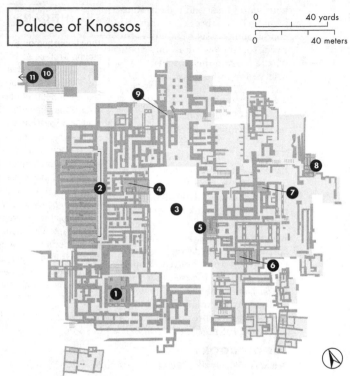

Palace of Knossos

disaster occurred, perhaps an invasion: palaces and country villas were razed by fire and abandoned, but Knossos remained inhabited even though the palace suffered some damage. But around 1380 BC the palace and its outlying buildings were destroyed by fire, and at the end of the Bronze Age the site was abandoned. Still later, Knossos became a Greek city-state.

You enter the palace from the west, passing a bust of Sir Arthur Evans, who excavated at Knossos on and off for more than 20 years. A path leads you around to the monumental **south gateway**. The **west wing** encases lines of long, narrow storerooms where the true wealth of Knossos was kept in tall clay jars: oil, wine, grains, and honey. The **central court** is about 164 feet by 82 feet long. The cool, dark **throne-**

THE REAL THING?

Although excavations at Knossos have revealed houses with mosaic floors, statuary, and a wealth of information about the Minoan civilization, colorful—and controversial—concrete reconstructions form much of the site. Opinions vary, but these restorations and fresco copies do impart a sense of what Knossos must have once looked like. Without the re-creation it would be impossible to experience a full Minoan palace—long, pillared halls; narrow corridors; deep stairways and light wells; and curious reverse-tapering columns.

room complex has a griffin fresco and a tall, wavy-back gypsum throne, the oldest in Europe. The most spectacular piece of palace architecture is the **grand staircase,** on the east side of the court, leading to the domestic apartments. Four flights of shallow gypsum stairs survive, lighted by a deep light well. Here you get a sense of how noble Minoans lived; rooms were divided by sets of double doors, giving privacy and warmth when closed, coolness and communication when open. The **queen's megaron** (apartment or hall) is decorated with a colorful dolphin fresco and furnished with stone benches. Beside it is a bathroom, complete with a clay tub, and next door a toilet, whose drainage system permitted flushing into a channel flowing into the Kairatos stream far below. The east side of the palace also contained **workshops.** Beside the staircase leading down to the **east bastion** is a stone water channel made up of parabolic curves and settling basins: a Minoan storm drain. Northwest of the east bastion is the **north entrance,** guarded by a relief fresco of a charging bull. Beyond is the **theatrical area,** shaded by pines and overlooking a shallow flight of steps, which lead down to the **royal road.** This, perhaps, was the ceremonial entrance to the palace.

For a complete education in Minoan architecture and civilization, consider touring Knossos and, of course, the Archaeological Museum in Heraklion (where many of the treasures from the palace are on view), then traveling south to the Palace of Phaistos, another great Minoan site, which has not been reconstructed. To reach Knossos by bus, take No. 2 (departing every 15 minutes) from Odos Evans, close to the market, in Heraklion. ☎*2810/231940* ⊕*www.culture.gr* ✉*€6; combined ticket for Knossos and Archaeological Museum in Heraklion €10* ⏲ *Apr.–Oct., daily 8–7:30; Nov.–Mar., daily 8–5.*

OFF THE BEATEN PATH

Archanes. If you continue south from Knossos, after about 3 km (2 mi) you'll come to a well-marked road to Archanes, about 5 km (3 mi) beyond the turnoff. After the town received EU funds to do a makeover, streets were repaved with cobblestones, houses were restored and painted in bold shades of ocher and pastels, many fine neoclassic stone structures were spruced up, and new trees and flowers were planted everywhere in town. Archanes now looks a bit like a stage set, but it's lovely, and the handsome squares and surrounding streets are well equipped with places for a snack or a meal—accompany either with a glass of wine from the vineyards that cover the slopes around town.

PALACE OF MALLIA ΑΝΑΚΤΟΡΟ ΜΑΛΙΩΝ

★ *37 km (23 mi) east of Heraklion.*

In its effort to serve mass tourism, the town of Mallia has submerged whatever character it might once have had. The sandy beach, overlooked by the brooding Lasithi mountains, is backed by a solid line of hotels and vacation apartments. The town itself may not be worth a visit, but the Minoan Palace of Mallia on its outskirts definitely is. Like the palaces of Knossos and Phaistos, it was built around 1900 BC; it was less sophisticated both in architecture and decoration, but the layout is similar. The palace appears to have been destroyed by an earthquake around 1700 BC, and rebuilt 50 years later. Across the west court, along one of the paved raised walkways, is a double row of **round granaries** sunk into the ground, which were almost certainly roofed. East of the granaries is the **south doorway,** beyond which is the large, circular limestone table, or *kernos* (on which were placed offerings to a Minoan deity), with a large hollow at its center and 34 smaller ones around the edge. The **central court** has a shallow pit at its center, perhaps the location of an altar. To the west of the central court are the remains of an imposing staircase leading up to a second floor, and a terrace, most likely used for religious ceremonies; behind is a long corridor with **storerooms** to the side. In the north wing is a large

> ## MINOS AND THE MINOTAUR
>
> As you tour Knossos, you are stepping into the pages of Greek mythology. It was here, allegedly, that King Minos imprisoned the Minotaur, a monster who was half man and half bull, in a labyrinth designed by Dedalus. As myth has it, Minos coveted the Minoan throne and prayed to Poseidon to send a white bull he would sacrifice in thanksgiving. His wife became smitten and, seducing the animal, gave birth to the Minotaur, for whom Minos ordered the architect Dedalus to build a labyrinthlike prison. The Minotaur was ultimately killed by Theseus.

pillared hall, part of a set of public rooms. The **domestic apartments** appear to have been in the northwest corner of the palace, entered through a narrow dogleg passage. They are connected by a smaller **northern court,** through which you can leave the palace by the **north entrance,** passing two giant old *pithoi* (large earthenware jars for storage of wine or oil). Excavation at the site continues, which is revealing a sizable town surrounding the palace. ⚓*3 km (2 mi) northeast of Mallia town* ☎*28970/31597* ⊕*www.culture.gr* 🎫*€4* ⊙*Nov.–June, Tues.–Sun. 8:30–3; July–Oct., Tues.–Sun. 8–7:30.*

AYIOS NIKOLAOS ΆΓΙΟΣ ΝΙΚΟΛΑΟΣ

★ *32 km (20 mi) southeast of Mallia, 69 km (43 mi) east of Heraklion.*

Ayios Nikolaos is clustered on a peninsula alongside the Gulf of Mirabello, a dramatic composition of bare mountains, islets, and deep blue sea. Behind the crowded harbor lies a natural curiosity, tiny Lake Voulismeni, linked to the sea by a narrow channel. Hilly, with narrow, steep streets that provide sea views, the town is a welcoming and animated place, far more pleasant than Mallia and the other resort centers in this part of Crete: you can stroll miles of waterside promenades, cafés line the lakeshore, and many streets are open only to pedestrians. Though many visitors bypass Ayios Nikolaos in favor of the nearby Elounda peninsula, the town makes an excellent base for exploring Eastern Crete.

The **Archaeological Museum** at Ayios Nikolaos displays some interesting artifacts, such as the *Goddess of Myrtos*, a statue circa 2500 BC (actually, the entire object is a rhyton, or vessel) of a woman cradling a large jug (the spout) in her spindly arms. There are also examples of late Minoan pottery in the naturalist marine style, with lively octopus and shell designs. ⊠ *Odos Palaiologou 74* ☎ *28410/24943* ▧*€3* ⊙ *Tues.–Sun. 8–5.*

The excellent **Folk Museum** showcases exquisite weavings, along with walking sticks, tools, and other artifacts from everyday rural life in Crete. ⊠ *Odos Palaiologou 2* ☎ *28410/24943* ▧*€3* ⊙ *Sun.–Fri. 11–3.*

BEACHES
You can dip into the clean waters that surround Ayios Nikolaos from several good beaches right in town. **Kitroplatia** and **Ammos** are both only about a 5- to 10-minute walk from the center. You can rent lounges and umbrellas at both.

WHERE TO STAY & EAT

$$-$$$ ✗**Migomis.** Dress well (no shorts), try to nab a seat by the windows, and partake of an excellent meal accompanied by stunning views of the town and the sea. At one of the best restaurants in town, the menu embraces both Greece and Italy, with some excellent pastas and Tuscan steaks and the freshest fish and seafood. Reservations are essential in summer. ⊠ *Plasira near 28th October* ☎ *28410/24353* ▭ *AE, MC, V.*

$-$$ ✗**Pelagos.** An enchanting garden and the high-ceilinged parlors of an
★ elegant mansion are the setting for what many locals consider to be the best seafood tavern in Ayios Nikolaos. Simple is the key word here: fresh catches from the fleet bobbing in the harbor just beyond are grilled and accompanied by local vegetables and Cretan wines. Reservations are recommended. ⊠ *Katehaki 10* ☎ *28410/25737* ▭ *MC, V.*

¢-$ ✗**Itanos Restaurant.** This old-fashioned taverna is a much better value than most of the seafront establishments and offers a very palatable house wine from a row of barrels in the kitchen. The *tzoutzoukakia* (oven-cooked meatballs) are tender and spicy, and vegetable dishes, such as braised artichokes or green beans with tomato, are full of flavor. ⊠ *Iroon Sq.* ☎ *28410/25340* ▭ *No credit cards.*

¢ ✗**Sarris.** Irini Sarris shows off her deft culinary skill best in traditional dishes, such as *stifado* (a rich stew made with lamb or sometimes with hare), and in the many *mezedes* (small dishes). The delightful, shady arbor set with tables overlooks an old church. ⊠ *Kyprou 15* ☎ *28410/28059* ▭ *No credit cards* ⊙ *Closed Nov.–Feb.*

$ ✗▦**Hotel Du Lac.** The handsomely appointed dining room with lakeside terrace ($-$$$) is one of the best places in town for a meal. Attentive and polished servers present house specialties such as steaks, other grilled meats, and seafood that's always fresh. The rooms upstairs are airy, spacious, and nicely done with simple, contemporary furnishings; studios, with kitchens and large baths, are enormous and an especially good value. Views from all rooms and their balconies are pleasant, but ask for a room overlooking the lake. ⊠ *28th October 17, 72100* ☎ *28410/22711* ▤ *28410/27211* ⊕ *www.dulachotel.gr* ⊷ *18 rooms, 6 studios* ⚴ *In-room: refrigerator* ▭ *AE, MC, V.*

¢ ▦**Hotel Kastro.** At this charming little inn at the end of a quiet street, on top of a hill just above the city center, watch the goings-on at the port

8

from your private balcony. In the pleasant and plain rooms, which cling to the hillside below the main entrance, arches form the doorways and beds are tucked into alcoves. Although rooms have cooking facilities, a homemade breakfast is served in the morning. ✉*Lathenous 23, 72100* ☎*28410/24918* 📠*28410/25827* ⊕*www.meraki.gr* 📍*12 rooms* ⚭*In-room: kitchen, no TV. In-hotel: no elevator* ▭*MC, V* ❚○❚*BP.*

SHOPPING

An appealing array of beads, quartz and silver jewelry, woven table-cloths and scarves, and carved bowls and other handicrafts fills **Chez Sonia** (✉*28th October* ☎*28410/28475*). You can get a very nice taste of the island to take home with you at **Elixir** (✉*Koundourou 15* ☎*28410/82593*) and **Melissa** (✉*Koundourou 18* ☎*28410/24628*), just across the street, both of which are well stocked with Cretan olive oils and wines and locally harvested honey and spices, as well as hand-made olive oil soaps.

ELOUNDA ΕΛΟΥΝΤΑ

11 km (7 mi) north of Ayios Nikolaos, 80 km (50 mi) east of Heraklion.

Traversing a steep hillside, a narrow road with spectacular sea views runs north from Ayios Nikolaos around the Gulf of Mirabello to the village of Elounda and the stark peninsula that surrounds it. The beaches tend to be narrow and pebbly, but the water is crystal clear and sheltered from the *meltemi* (the fierce north wind that blows in July and August). Elounda village is becoming a full-scale resort destination: dozens of villas and hotels dot the surrounding hillsides, and the shore of the gulf south of Elounda is crowded with some of the most luxurious hotels in Crete. Don't come here in search of the authentic Greece; expect to meet fellow international travelers.

Olous (✛*3 km [2 mi] east of Elounda*) is a sunken, ancient city visible beneath the turquoise waters off a causeway that leads to the Spinalonga peninsula (not to be confused with the island of the same name), an undeveloped headland. The combination of warm waters and the promise of seeing the outlines of a Roman settlement on the seabed are alluring to snorkelers and swimmers. A few scant remains, including a mosaic floor, can be seen on dry land (fenced and marked with a sign).

OFF THE BEATEN PATH

Spinalonga. The Venetians built a huge, forbidding fortress on this small, narrow island in the center of the Gulf of Mirabello in the 17th century. In the early 1900s the island became a leper colony, serving this purpose with cruelly primitive conditions for more than 50 years. Travel agents in Ayios Nikolaos and Elounda can arrange boat excursions to the island, some complete with a midday beach barbecue and a swim on a deserted islet; you can also just sign up with any of the many outfitters that leave from the docks in both towns (expect to pay about €10). The real treat is cruising on these azure waters, and as you sail past the islet of Ayioi Pantes, a goat reserve, you're likely to see the *agrimi* (Cretan wild goat), with its impressive curling horns (✉€2 ⊙ *Daily 8–7*).

WHERE TO STAY & EAT

$-$$ ✕**Marilena.** In good weather, meals are served in the large rear garden, or you can choose a table on a sidewalk terrace facing the harbor. The kitchen prepares an excellent fresh, grilled fish and a rich fish soup; any meal here should begin with a platter of assorted appetizers. ✉*Harborside, main square* 📠28410/41322 ▤*MC, V* ⊙*Closed late Oct.–early Mar.*

¢–$ ✕**Pefko.** Despite the presence of an enormous new resort at the edge of town, Plaka remains a delightful fishing village and Pefko (the Pine Tree) a pleasant place to take in village life and sea views. The menu offers a nice assortment of appetizers, salads, and such basics as moussaka and lamb, to be enjoyed on a shady terrace or in a cozy dining room where music is played some evenings. ✉*Near beach in center of town, Plaka* 📠28410/12510 ▤*No credit cards.*

$$$$ ▥**Elounda Beach.** One of Greece's most renowned resort hotels, on 40 acres of gardens next to the Gulf of Mirabello, Elounda Beach has inspired dozens of imitators. The architecture reflects Cretan tradition: whitewashed walls, shady porches, and cool flagstone floors. You can have a room in the central block or a bungalow at the edge of the sea; 25 of the suites have their own swimming pools. Two sandy beaches are the jumping-off point for numerous water sports, including scuba diving. ✉*3 km (2 mi) south of village, 72053* 📠*28410/41412* 📠*28410/41373* ⊕*www.eloundabeach.gr* ⇌*215 rooms, 28 suites* ⌂*In-room: refrigerator, Wi-Fi. In-hotel: 6 restaurants, bars, pool, water sports* ▤*AE, DC, MC, V* ⊙*Closed Nov.–Mar.* ⊙|*BP.*

$$$$ ▥**Elounda Mare.** If you plan to stay at one luxurious resort in Crete, make it this extraordinary Relais & Châteaux property on the Gulf of Mirabello, one of the finest hotels in Greece. More than half of the rooms, all bathed in cool marble and stunningly decorated in a soothing blend of traditional and contemporary furnishings, are in villas set in their own gardens with private pools. Verdant gardens line the shore above a sandy beach and terraced waterside lounging areas, a stone's throw from the large pool. ✉*3 km (2 mi) south of village, Elounda, 72053* 📠*28410/41102 or 28410/41103* 📠*28410/41307* ⊕*www. eloundamare.gr* ⇌*38 rooms, 44 bungalows* ⌂*In-room: refrigerator, Wi-Fi. In-hotel: 3 restaurants, pool, water sports* ▤*AE, DC, MC, V* ⊙*Closed Nov.–mid-Apr.* ⊙|*BP.*

Fodor'sChoice

★

$ ▥**Akti Olous.** This friendly, unassuming hotel on the edge of the Gulf of Mirabello outside Elounda and near the sunken city of Olus is a step away from a strip of sandy beach and provides sweeping views of the sea and peninsula. The rooftop pool and terrace are especially pleasant at sunset, and there is a waterside taverna and bar. The bright rooms, decorated in a handsome, modern neoclassic style, all have balconies overlooking the sea. Count on a sea breeze to keep you cool, because use of the air-conditioning costs €6 per day. ✉*Waterfront road, 72053* 📠*28410/41270* 📠*28410/41425* ⊕*www.greekhotels.net/aktiolous* ⇌*70 rooms* ⌂*In-room: refrigerator. In-hotel: restaurant, bar, pool* ▤*MC, V* ⊙*Closed Nov.–mid-Apr.* ⊙|*BP.*

8

KRITSA ΚΡΙΤΣΑ

20 km (12½ mi) south of Elounda, 80 km (50 mi) southeast of Heraklion.

The mountain village of Kritsa, 9 km (5½ mi) west of Ayios Nikolaos, is renowned for its weaving tradition and surrounds a large, shady town square filled with café tables that afford views down the green valleys to the sea.

The lovely Byzantine church here, the whitewashed **Panayia Kera,** has an unusual shape, with three naves supported by heavy triangular buttresses. Built in the early years of Venetian occupation, it contains some of the liveliest and best-preserved medieval frescoes on the island, painted in the 13th century. ⊠ *On main road before town* 🎟€1 ⊘ *Sat.–Thurs. 9–3.*

Lato, about 4 km (2½ mi) north of Kritsa, is an ancient city built by the Doric Greeks in a dip between two rocky peaks. Lato was named for the mother of Artemis and Apollo and her image appears on coins found at the site. Make your way over the expanse of ancient masonry to the far end of the site for one of the best views in Crete: on a clear day you can see the island of Santorini, 100 km (60 mi) across the Cretan Sea, as well as inland across a seemingly endless panorama of mountains and valleys. ⊠ *Follow marked road from Kritsa* 🎟€2 ⊘ *Tues.–Sun. 8:30–3; gate is often open and unattended at other times.*

SITEIA ΣΗΤΕΙΑ

55 km (32 mi) east of Kritsa, 143 km (87 mi) east of Heraklion.

Like Ierapetra, Siteia is an unpretentious town where agriculture is more important than tourism: raisins and, increasingly, bananas are the main crops. Even so, Siteia is a pleasant place to wander, and the whitewashed town with shady lanes behind the harbor seems almost Arabian. Siteia's waterfront, lined with cafés and tavernas, is lively from June through August, and a long, sandy beach that stretches to the east of the waterfront is the town's other principal gathering spot. From Siteia you can fly to Rhodes or take a ferry there via the small islands of Kassos and Karpathos. In July and August, there are usually weekly ferries between Siteia and Piraeus. Siteia is a good choice for an overnight while making the circuit of far eastern Crete.

An old Venetian fort, the **Kazarma,** overlooks Siteia from a height in the west. There's not much to see in the vast enclosed space, used to stage plays and concerts on summer evenings, but the view across the bay is spectacular. ⊠ *Follow signs up hill from waterfront.*

Siteia's **Archaeological Museum,** in addition to other artifacts, contains a rare treasure: a Minoan ivory and gold statuette of a young man, found on the east coast at Palaikastro. The figure dates from around 1500 BC and, though incomplete, is a masterpiece of Minoan carving. ⊠ *Siteia–Ierapetra road, outskirts of town* 🕿 *28430/23917* ⊕ *www.culture.gr* 🎟€2 ⊘ *Tues.–Sun. 8:30–3.*

WHERE TO STAY & EAT

$–$$ ✕**The Balcony.** A bit more stylish than you'd expect to find on the back-
★ streets of Siteia, this handsome dining room in an old house focuses
on local ingredients and, though a few dishes show an Asian influence,
excels at such traditional dishes as lamb cooked in lemon and rabbit
stew. An excellent selection of Cretan wines is available. Reservations
are recommended. ⊠*Fountalido 19* ☎*28430/25084* ☐*MC, V* ☺*No
lunch Sun.*

$ ▦**Hotel Flisvos.** Small and stylish, this waterfront hotel puts you within
steps of the beach and seaside promenades, and is right in the city center. The pleasant rooms all have balconies that overlook the sea or a
pretty garden behind the hotel. ⊠*Karamanli 4, 72300* ☎*28430/27135*
⇩*21 rooms* ⚲*In room: refrigerator. In hotel: bar* ☐*MC, V* ❍❘*CP.*

¢ ▦**Hotel El Greco.** This friendly establishment on a narrow street several blocks above the waterfront is perfectly comfortable and not
without charm. Many of the simple rooms have balconies overlooking the old town and the sea. ⊠*G. Arkadiou, 72300* ☎*28430/23133*
📠*28430/26391* ⇩*15 rooms* ⚲*In-room: refrigerator. In-hotel: bar*
☐*MC, V* ☺*Closed Nov.–Apr.* ❍❘*CP.*

▮ The fierce north wind that sweeps this region has twisted the few trees
EN   on hillsides surrounding the fortified monastery at **Toplou,** 13 km (8 mi)
ROUTE east of Siteia off the road to Vai, into strange shapes. Only a few monks
live here now, and the monastery is slowly being renovated. Inside the
tall loggia gate, built in the 16th century and from the top of which
monks once defended themselves against invading Turks and pirates,
the cells are arranged around a cobbled courtyard with a 14th-century
church at its center. Each of 61 scenes in its famous icon was inspired
by a phrase from the Orthodox liturgy. ⊠*Off road to Vai* ☎*No phone*
💶*€3* ☺*Daily 9–6.*

VAI ΒΑΪ

27 km (17 mi) east of Siteia, 170 km (104 mi) east of Heraklion.

Unique in Europe, the palm grove of the renowned beach at Vai existed
in classical Greek times. The sandy stretch with nearby islets in clear
turquoise water is one of the most attractive in Crete, but in July and
August, it gets very crowded. The appeal of the surrounding, fertile
coastal plain was not lost on the ancient Minoans, who left behind
some of Crete's most enchanting ruins. Modern towns that surround
the old Minoan settlements of Palaikastro, Ano Zakros, and Kato Zakros, are well endowed with tavernas and rooms to rent.

Palaikastro is a sprawling, once densely populated Minoan town,
currently being excavated by British and American archaeologists.
Although this site, once a working agricultural center, does not have
the drama of Knossos or Phaistos, you get a strong sense of everyday
life here amid the stony ruins of streets, squares, dwellings, and shops.
Follow a narrow track from the site through olive groves to a sandy
beach at Hiona. It's rarely crowded, and service is welcoming at the
waterside tavernas. ⊕*9 km (5½ mi) south of Vai, outside modern vil-*

lage of Palaikastro ⊕*www.culture.gr* ☞*Free* ⊙*Daily 8:30–3, often later (sight is usually unattended and unlocked).*

The ruins of the **Palace of Kato Zakros,** 20 km (12½ mi) south of Palai-kastro, are smaller than those of the other Minoan palaces on the island. You can drive down to the site by a circuitous but spectacular route, or stop at Ano Zakro (Upper Zakro) and follow a path that leads down through a deep ravine (known as the Gorge of the Dead) past caves used for early Minoan burials to the Minoan palace. The walk down and back up is steep but not overly arduous, and takes about two hours. The site includes the ruins of a small palace and a surrounding town that from 1650 BC to 1450 BC may have served as a port for trade with Egypt and the Middle East. The ruins, entered from the harbor through a gate and up a ramp, are surrounded by a terraced seaside village, Kato Zakros, which has narrow cobbled streets. On the fine beach is a cluster of tavernas with a few rooms to rent. ⊹*38 km (25 mi) south of Vai, ascend paved Minoan road from Kato Zak-ros harbor through gateway to northeast court down stepped ramp* ☏*28410/22462* ☞*€3* ⊙*Daily 8–3.*

WHERE TO STAY & EAT

¢ ✕⌂ **Hotel Hellas.** Sparkling clean and comfortable, each of the simple rooms here overlooks the town, the surrounding plains, and the sea from a balcony. The ground-floor restaurant (¢) spills into the square and serves excellent traditional Cretan fare, using fresh produce from the fields that run right up to the edge of town. ⊠*Main square, Palai-kastro, 72300* ☏*28430/61240* ⊕*www.palaikastro.com/hotelhellas* ⤶*17 rooms* ⚒*In room: refrigerator. In hotel: restaurant* ⊟*No credit cards.* ⏀*CP.*

WESTERN CRETE ΔΥΤΙΚΗ ΚΡΗΤΗ

Much of Western Crete's landscape—soaring mountains, deep gorges, and rolling green lowlands—remains largely untouched by mass tour-ism; in fact, only the north coast is developed. There is a wealth of interesting byways to be explored. This region is abundant in Minoan sites—including the palace at Phaistos—as well as Byzantine churches and Venetian monasteries. Two of Greece's more-appealing cities are here: Hania and Rethymnon, both crammed with the houses, narrow lanes, and minarets that hark back to Venetian and Turkish occupa-tion. Friendly villages dot the uplands, and there are some outstanding beaches on the ruggedly beautiful and remote west and south coasts. Immediately southwest of Heraklion lies the traditional agricultural heartland of Crete: long, narrow valleys where olive groves alternate with vineyards of sultana grapes for export.

PALACE OF PHAISTOS ΑΝΑΚΤΟΡΟ ΦΑΙΣΤΟΥ

Fodor's Choice ★ *11 km (7 mi) west of Ayii Deka, 50 km (31 mi) southwest of Heraklion.*

On a steep hill overlooking olive groves and the sea on one side, and high mountain peaks on the other, Phaistos is the site of one of the greatest Minoan palaces. Unlike Knossos, Phaistos has not been reconstructed, though the copious ruins are richly evocative. The palace was built around 1900 BC and rebuilt after a disastrous earthquake around 1650 BC. It was burned and abandoned in the wave of destruction that swept across the island around 1450 BC, though Greeks continued to inhabit the city until the 2nd century BC, when it was eclipsed by Gortyna.

You enter the site by descending a flight of steps leading into the west court, then climb a grand staircase. From here you pass through the **Propylon porch** into a light well and descend a narrow staircase into the **central court**. Much of the southern and eastern sections of the palace have eroded away. But there are large pithoi still in place in the old **storerooms**. On the north side of the court the recesses of an elaborate doorway bear a rare trace: red paint in a diamond pattern on a white ground. A passage from the doorway leads to the **north court** and the **northern domestic apartments,** now roofed and fenced off. The **Phaistos Disk** was found in 1903 in a chest made of mud brick at the northeast edge of the site and is now on display at the Archaeological Museum in Heraklion. East of the central court are the **palace workshops**, with a metalworking furnace fenced off. South of the workshops lie the **southern domestic apartments,** including a clay bath. From there, you have a memorable view across the Messara plain. ✛*Follow signs and ascend hill off Ayii Deka–Mires–Timbaki road* ☎*28920/42315* ⊕*www.culture.gr* 🎫*€4; combined ticket with Ayia Triada €6* ⊗*Apr.–Oct., daily 8–7:30; Nov.–Mar., daily 8–5.*

Ayia Triada was destroyed at the same time as Phaistos, which is only a few miles away on the other side of the same hill. It was once thought to have been a summer palace for the rulers of Phaistos but is now believed to have consisted of group of villas for nobility and a warehouse complex. Rooms in the villas were once paneled with gypsum slabs and decorated with frescoes: the two now hanging in the Archaeological Museum in Heraklion show a woman in a garden and a cat hunting a pheasant. Several other lovely pieces, including finely crafted vases, also come from Ayia Triada and are now also on display in Heraklion. Though the complex was at one time just above the sea, the view now looks across the extensive Messara plain to the Lybian Sea in the distance. ✛*Follow signs 3 km (2 mi) west from Phaistos* ☎*28920/91360* ⊕*www.culture.gr* 🎫*€4; combined ticket with Phaistos €6* ⊗*May–Sept., daily 10–7:30; Oct.–Apr., daily 8:30–3.*

EN ROUTE

The quickest route from Phaistos, Matala, and other places on the Messara plain to the north coast is the Heraklion road, a small section of which is even four lanes these days. But a very pleasant alternative leads northwest through Ayia Galini (the largest resort on this part of

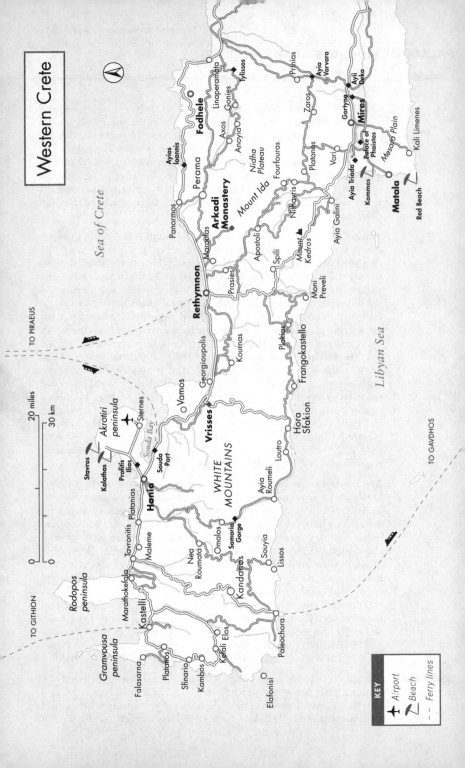

the southern coast) and the mountain town of Spili to Rethymnon. The route shows off the beauty of rural Crete as it traverses deep valleys and gorges and climbs the flanks of the interior mountain ranges. Just beyond Spili, follow signs to Moni Preveli (☎€2.50 ☉ *Daily 8–7*), a stunningly situated monastery perched high above the sea. A monument honors the monks here who sheltered Allied soldiers after the Battle of Crete and helped them escape the Nazi-occupied island via submarine. Below the monastery is lovely Palm Beach, where golden sands are shaded by a palm grove watered by a mountain stream. However, avoid this patch of paradise at midday during high season, when it is packed with day-trippers who arrive by tour boat from Ayia Galini.

FODHELE ΦΟΔΕΛΕ

13 km (8 mi) west of Heraklion, 10 km (6 mi) northwest of Tylissos.

If you are driving west on the north coast from Heraklion toward Rethymnon, a good place to break up the trip is the straggling, sleepy village of Fodhele, said to be the birthplace of Domenico Theotokopoulos, the 16th-century Cretan painter known as El Greco. The claim is disputed by some scholars; nonetheless, a stop in Fodhele allows you to sit in the shady square (where a plaque honors the alleged native son) and enjoy a look at rural Cretan life. Fodhele's **church of the Panayia,** at the edge of town, is a beautiful Byzantine structure with fine 14th-century frescoes. The church is sometimes open for prayer, though it is usually locked, in which case you'll have to look around for a guardian to let you in.

ARKADI MONASTERY ΜΟΝΗ ΑΡΚΑΔΙΟΥ

★ *18 km (11 mi) southwest of Fodhele, 30 km (19 mi) southwest of Heraklion.*

As you approach Arkadi through the rolling lands at the base of Mt. Ida (one of the contenders in the dispute over the alleged Cretan birthplace of Zeus), you'll follow a gorge inland before emerging onto the flat pastureland that is part of the monastery's holdings. Arkadi is a place of pilgrimage for Cretans, a shrine to heroes in the fight against the Turks for independence, and one of the most stunning pieces of Renaissance architecture on the island. The ornate facade, decorated with Corinthian columns and an elegant belfry above, was built in the 16th century of a local, honey-color stone. In 1866 the monastery came under siege during a major rebellion against the Turks, and Abbot Gabriel and several hundred rebels, together with their wives and children, refused to surrender. When the Turkish forces broke through the gate, the defenders set the gunpowder store afire, killing themselves together with hundreds of Turks. The monastery was again a center of resistance when Nazis occupied Crete during World War II. ✉*South of old Heraklion–Hania road* ☎€2 ☉ *Daily 8–8.*

8

RETHYMNON ΡΕΘΥΜΝΟ

★ *25 km (15 mi) west of Arkadi Monastery, 78 km (48½ mi) west of Heraklion.*

Rethymnon is Crete's third-largest town, after Heraklion and Hania. The population (about 30,000) steadily increases as the town expands—a new quarter follows the coast to the east of the old town, where the beachfront has been tastelessly developed with large hotels and other resort facilities catering to tourists on package vacations. However, much of Rethymnon's charm perseveres in the old Venetian quarter, which is crowded onto a compact peninsula dominated by the huge, fortified Venetian castle known as the Fortessa. Wandering through the narrow alleyways, you come across handsome carved-stone Renaissance doorways belonging to vanished mansions, fountains, archways, and wooden Turkish houses with latticework screens on the balconies to protect the women of the house from prying eyes.

The most visible sign of the Turkish occupation of Rethymnon is the graceful minaret, one the few to survive in Greece, that rises above the **Neratze,** a mosque–turned–concert hall at the center of town. You can climb its 120 steps for a panoramic view, though access is possible only when a performance takes place. ✉ *Odos Verna and Odos Ethnikis Adistaseos.*

A restored Venetian palazzo almost in the shadow of the minaret houses the delightful **Historical and Folk Art Museum.** Rustic furnishings, tools, and exquisite weavings provide a charming and vivid picture of what life on Crete was like until well into the 20th century. ✉ *Vernadou 28* ☎ *28310/29975* 💶*€3* ⊙ *Daily 9:30–2.*

The carefully restored **Venetian loggia** was once the clubhouse of the local nobility. It is now enclosed in glass and houses the Archaeological Museum's shop. ✉ *Arkadiou, near town center.*

Just down the street, at the end of Platanos square, is one of the town's most welcoming sights, the so-called **Rimondi Fountain,** installed by the Venetians and spilling refreshing streams from several lions' heads. You'll come upon several other fountains as you wander through the labyrinth of narrow streets.

Rethymnon's small **Venetian harbor,** with its restored 13th-century lighthouse, comes to life in warm weather, when restaurant tables clutter the quayside. Fishing craft and pleasure boats are crammed chockablock into the minute space, while the outer harbor, protected by a massive breakwater, acts as the port for the ferries that run between Rethymnon and Piraeus. ✉ *Waterfront.*

The west side of the peninsula is taken up almost entirely with the **Fortessa,** strategically surrounded by the sea and thick ramparts. Climbing up to the fortress is a bit of a letdown, because the high, well-preserved walls enclose not much more than a vast empty space occupied by a few scattered buildings—and filled with wildflowers in spring. Forced laborers from the town and surrounding villages built the fortress from 1573 to 1583. It didn't fulfill its purpose of keeping out the Turks: Rethymnon surrendered after a three-week siege in 1646. ⊠ *West end of town* ⚏€3 ⊙*Sat.–Thurs. 8:30–7.*

The **Archaeological Museum,** just outside the entrance to the Fortessa will impress you again with just how long Crete has cradled civilizations: a collection of bone tools is from a Neolithic site at Yerani (west of Rethymnon); Minoan pottery is on display; and an unfinished statue of Aphrodite, the goddess of love, is from the Roman occupation (look for the ancient chisel marks). The museum building used to be a Turkish guardhouse and prison. ⊠ *West end of town, next to entrance of Fortessa* ☎28310/54668 ⚏€3 ⊙*Tues.–Sun. 8:30–3.*

VENETIANS & TURKS

By the 16th century, when the Venetians built the Fortessa in Rethymnon, they had controlled Crete for almost 300 years. Crete was ceded to them by the Crusaders who disbursed the holdings of the Byzantine Empire. Possessing Crete gave Venice control of the very rich trade routes across the southern Mediterranean but Venetians were defeated by Ottoman Turks who overran the island in 1645. They ruled until 1898 when they, in turn, were expelled. Cretan independence fighter Eleftherios Venizelos became premier of Greece in 1910, and under his leadership, Crete became part of the Greek nation in 1913.

WHERE TO STAY & EAT

$$–$$$$ ★ ✕**Avli.** A stone, barrel-vaulted dining room and a multitiered garden are the attractive settings for creative interpretations of Cretan cuisine, made only from grass-fed lamb, fresh-caught fish, garden vegetables, and other organic and natural ingredients. Even a simple *horiatiki* (Greek salad) and grilled lamb chop can be transporting here, as is the excellent selection of the island's finest wines. Reservations are a good idea in summer. ⊠*Paleologou 22* ☎28310/26213 ▤*MC, V.*

$–$$ ✕**Cavo D'Oro.** This is the most stylish of the handful of fish restaurants around the tiny Venetian harbor. Lobster and fish dishes are always served fresh. The high-ceiling, wood-panel dining room was once a medieval storeroom; diners also sit on the old cobbled waterfront. ⊠*Nearchou 42–43* ☎28310/24446 ▤*DC, MC, V.*

¢–$ ✕**Kyria Maria.** At this simple, family-run taverna in the center of the old town, good home cooking is served from a small menu of traditional Greek specialties. Neighborhood life buzzes around the tables set beneath an arbor in a narrow lane. This place is open for breakfast daily. ⊠*Moschovitou* ☎28310/29078 ▤*MC, V.*

$$$$ ★ ▥**Palazzino di Corina.** Rethymnon has several hotels occupying old palaces; Corina is the most luxurious and provides stylish surroundings that include a courtyard with wood chaises, topiary planters, and statuary surrounding a small pool. Guest rooms, with exposed-stone walls and wooden beams, are furnished with a mix of antiques and contemporary pieces. ⊠*Damvergi and Diakou, 74100* ☎28310/21205 📠28310/21204 ⊕*www.corina.gr* ⇌*21 suites* ⌁*In-room: refrigerator, Ethernet. In-hotel: restaurant, pool, no elevator* ▤*MC, V* ⊖*BP.*

8

$$–$$$
Fodor'sChoice
★
Vetera Suites. A Venetian-Ottoman house evokes the rich ambience of old Rethymnon, with delightfully atmospheric and comfortable rooms and two-level suites—the most distinctive lodgings in town. All rooms display exposed beams, chimneys, stonework, and other original details, and are furnished with exquisite antiques. Modern comforts abound, too, such as compact stylish bathrooms and kitchenettes that are tucked into alcoves. A delicious breakfast is €10 extra. ✉ *Kastrinoyannaki 39, 74100* 📞 *28310/23844* ⊕ *www.vetera.gr* 🛏 *2 rooms, 2 suites* ⚐ *In-room: kitchen* 🖃 *MC, V* ⍟ *CP.*

$
★
Hotel Fortezza. Only steps from the fortress, the old town, and the beach, you can enjoy many of the advantages of the larger hotels on Rethymnon's charmless beach strip. The tile-floor rooms, with handsome traditional wood furnishings, are built around a marble atrium and sunny courtyard that has a pool; many rooms have balconies. A buffet breakfast is served. ✉ *Melisinou 16, 74100* 📞 *28310/55551* 📠 *28310/54073* ⊕ *www.fortezza.gr* 🛏 *54 rooms* ⚐ *In-hotel: restaurant, bars, pool* 🖃 *AE, DC, MC, V* ⍟ *BP.*

> ### HIKING CRETE
>
> Crete is excellent hiking terrain, and many trails crisscross the mountains and gorges, especially in the southwest. The Greek National Tourism Organization (GNTO or EOT) is a source of information. **Alpine Travel** (✉ *Bonaili 11, Hania* 📞 *28210/50939* ⊕ *www.alpine.gr*) offers many hiking tours throughout western Crete, while the **Greek Federation of Mountaineering Associations** (📞 *28210/44647 in the White Mountains, 2810/289440 on Mt. Ida, 2810/227609 in Heraklion*) operates overnight refuges in the White Mountains and on Mt. Ida.

SPORTS & THE OUTDOORS

★ **Dream Adventure Trips** (✉ *Beachfront, Almirida* 📞 *6944/357383*) operates highly enjoyable boat excursions off the Vamos peninsula into Almiros Bay (west of Rethymnon), with stops to snorkel, swim, and explore a seaside cave. The two-hour trips cost €20.

The **Happy Walker** (✉ *Tombazi 56* 📞 *28310/52920* ⊕ *www.happy-walker.com* ⊙ *July 1–Sept. 15*) arranges easy hiking tours in the surrounding mountains and gorges, adding a welcome stop for a village lunch to each walk. Each walk costs €30.

SHOPPING

★ The **Archaeological Museum Shop** (✉ *Paleologou* 📞 *28310/54668*), handsomely housed in a Venetian loggia, has an excellent selection of books, as well as reproductions of artifacts from its collections and from other sites in Crete and throughout Greece. **Avli** (✉ *Xanthoudidou 22* 📞 *28310/58250*) sells many of the herbs, spices, oils, and other ingredients that flavor the cuisine at the eponymous restaurant around the corner, as well as fine Greek wines. For a souvenir that will be light to carry, stop in at **Kalymnos** (✉ *Arampatzouglou 26* 📞 *28310/50802*), filled to the rafters with sponges harvested off the eponymous island and in other Greek waters.

EN ROUTE

One of the shortest routes to the remote southwestern coast is the road that climbs mountains and drops through gorges for some 20 km (12 mi) south from Vrisses to Hora Sfakion. Tucked between the sea and the arms of sheltering mountains, Hora has an end-of-the-road atmosphere to it and is a transit hub for the south coast. By car or bus you can make the steep, 12-km (7½-mi) drive up to the charming, unspoiled farming village of Anapoli, on an upland plain near the end of the hiking path through the Aradhena gorge. Or head 14 km (8½ mi) east to Frangokastello, where the romantic-looking shell of a 14th-century castle overlooks a beautiful beach. On foot you can follow the segment of the E4 European hiking path that links Hora with Loutro, a charmingly sleepy seaside village reachable only on foot or by sea. By ferry from Hora you can cruise to Paleochora, Ayia Roumeli, and other ports along the south coast and continue on to Gavdhos Island, 50 km (30 mi) south in the middle of the Lybian Sea.

VRISSES ΒΡΥΣΕΣ

26 km (14 mi) west of Rethymnon, 105 km (65 mi) west of Heraklion.

This appealing old village is famous throughout Crete for its thick, creamy yogurt—best eaten with a large spoonful of honey on top—that is served in the cafés beneath the plane trees at the center of town. Georgioupolis, on the coast about 7 km (4½ mi) due west, is another shady, lovely old town, where the Almiros River flows into the sea. The coast here is being rather unattractively developed, but inland walks—including one through a eucalyptus-scented valley that links Vrisses and Georgioupolis—make it easy to get away from the fray.

8

HANIA ΧΑΝΙΑ

Fodor$Choice
★

52 km (33 mi) west of Vrisses, 78 km (48 mi) west of Rethymnon.

Hania surrendered its role of capital of Crete to Heraklion in 1971, but this elegant city of eucalyptus-lined avenues, miles of waterfront promenades, and shady, cobbled alleyways lined with Venetian and Ottoman houses is still close to the heart of all Cretans. It was here that the Greek flag was raised in 1913 to mark Crete's unification with Greece, and the place is simply one of the most beautiful of all Greek cities.

The sizable old town is strung along the harbor (divided by a centuries-old seawall into outer and inner harbors), where tall Venetian houses face a pedestrians-only, taverna-lined waterside walkway, and fishing boats moor beside a long stretch of Venetian arsenals and warehouses. Well-preserved Venetian and Turkish quarters surround the harbors and a covered food and spice market, a remnant of Venetian trade and Turkish bazaars that's set amid a maze of narrow streets.

Kastelli hill, where the Venetians first settled, rises above the east end of the harbor. The hill became the quarter of the local nobility, but it had been occupied much earlier: parts of what may be a Minoan palace have been excavated at its base. ⊠*Above harbor.*

Kastelli hill creates a backdrop to the **Janissaries Mosque,** built at the water's edge when Turks captured the town in 1645 after a two-month siege. You can only enter the building when the town uses it to host temporary art and trade exhibitions, but the presence of the domed structure at the edge of the shimmering sea lends Hania an exotic air. Hours vary from show to show; the place is most often closed. ⊠*East side of inner harbor.*

As you follow the harbor front east from the mosque, you come to a long line of **Venetian Arsenali** from the 16th and 17th centuries, used to store wares and repair craft. The seawalls swing around to enclose the harbor and end at the **old lighthouse** that stands at the east side of the harbor entrance; from here you get a magnificent view of the town, with the imposing White Mountains looming beyond and the animated harbor below.

Just across the narrow channel from the lighthouse and marking the west entrance to the harbor is the **Firka,** the old Turkish prison, which is now the naval museum. Exhibits, more riveting than might be expected, trace the island's seafaring history from the time of the Venetians. Look for the photos and mementos from the World War II Battle of Crete, when Allied forces moved across the island and, with the help of Cretans, ousted the German occupiers. Much of the fighting centered around Hania, and great swaths of the city were destroyed during the war. Almost worth the price of admission alone is the opportunity to walk along the Firka's ramparts for bracing views of the city, sea, and mountains. ⊠*Waterfront at far west end of port* ☎*28210/91875* ⊠*€2.50* ☉*Daily 9–4.*

You'll get some insight into the Venetian occupation *and* the Christian centuries that preceded it at the **Byzantine and Post-Byzantine Collection,** housed in the charming 15th-century church of San Salvadore alongside the city walls just behind the Firka. Mosaics, icons, coins, and other artifacts bring to life Cretan civilization as it was after the Roman Empire colonized the island. ⊠*Theotokopoulou 82* ☎*28210/96046* ⊠*€2; combined ticket with Archaeological Museum €3* ☉*Tues.–Sun. 8:30–3.*

The **Etz Hayyim Synagogue** is tucked away in what was once the Jewish ghetto, a warren of narrow lanes known as Evraki, just off the harbor south of the Firka. The building was formerly the Venetian church of St. Catherine; it became a synagogue in the 17th century. It was stripped of all religious objects by the Nazis; the church was restored in 1999. Hania's once sizable Jewish population was obliterated during World War II; many residents drowned when a British torpedo sunk the ship carrying them toward Auschwitz in 1944. The building contains Venetian Gothic arches, a *mikveh* (ritual bath), and the tombs of three rabbis. ⊠*Parodos Kondylaki* ☎*28210/86286* ⊕*www.etz-hayyim-hania.org* ⊠*Free* ☉*May–mid-Oct., weekdays 10–6; mid-Oct.–Apr., weekdays 9:30–2 (hrs may vary).*

Two of the city's museums are at the edge of the old city, amid a busy shopping district in the shadow of the Venetian walls. Artifacts on display at the **Archaeological Museum** come from all over western Crete: the painted Minoan clay coffins and elegant late Minoan pottery indicate that the region was as wealthy as the center of the island in the Bronze Age, though no palace has yet been located. The museum occupies the former Venetian church of St. Francis. ⊠ *Chalidron* ☎ *28210/90334* ✉ *€2; combined admission with Byzantine and Post-Byzantine Collection €3* ⊙ *Tues.–Sun. 8:30–3.*

A folklife museum, the **Cretan House** is bursting at the seams with farm equipment, tools, household items, wedding garb, and a wealth of other material reflecting the island's traditional heritage. Packed to the rafters as the stuffy house is, the collection is not nearly as extensive or of the same high quality as those in folk and history museums in Heraklion, Vori, and Rethymnon. ⊠ *Off courtyard at Chalidron 46, near Archaeological Museum* ☎ *28210/90816* ✉ *€1.50* ⊙ *Mon.–Sat. 9–3 and 6–9.*

★ The shop at **Ayia Triada** has some of the island's finest olive oils. Lands at the northeast corner of the Akrotiri peninsula, which extends into the sea from the east side of Hania, are the holdings of several monasteries. The olive groves that surround and finance the monasteries yield excellent oils. ⊕ *16 km (10 mi) north of Hania, follow road from Chordaki* ☎ *No phone* ⊙ *Daily 9–3.*

★ From the monastery at **Goubermetou,** on the north end of the Akrotiri peninsula, a path leads down the flanks of a seaside ravine past several caves used as hermitages and churches. A 20-minute walk brings you to the remote monastery of St. John the Hermit; follow the path along a riverbank for another 20 minutes or so to a delightful cove that is the perfect place for a refreshing dip. The return walk requires a steep uphill climb. ⊕ *19 km (12 mi) north of Hania, follow road north from Chordaki* ☎ *No phone* ✉ *Free* ⊙ *Daily 9–3.*

OFF THE BEATEN PATH

Samaria Gorge. South of Hania a deep, verdant crevice extends 10 km (6 mi) from near the village of Xyloskalo to the Libyan Sea. The landscape—of forest, sheer rock faces, and running streams—is magnificent. The Samaria is the most traveled of the dozens of gorges that cut through Crete's mountains and emerge at the sea, but the walk through it is thrilling nonetheless. Buses depart the central bus station in Hania at 7:30 and 8:30 AM for Xyloskalo. Boats leave in the afternoon from the mouth of the gorge (most people don't hike back up) at Ayia Roumeli for Hora Sfakion, from where buses return to Hania. Travel agents also arrange day trips to the gorge. ⊠ *25 km (15 mi) south of Hania, Omalos.*

BEACHES

A string of beaches extend west from the city center, and you can easily reach them on foot by following the sea past the old olive-oil factory just west of the walls and the Byzantine Museum. They are not idyllic, but the water is clean. Locals who want to spend a day at the beach often head out to the end of the Akrotiri peninsula, which extends

8

north from the city's eastern suburbs, where **Kalathas** and **Stavros,** both about 15 km (9 mi) north of Hania, have excellent sand beaches. Part of *Zorba the Greek* was filmed at Stavros.

★ **Western Beaches.**Drive west from Hania to the magnificent beaches on the far coast, such as **Falasarna,** near Crete's northwestern tip, and **Elafonisi,** on the southwestern tip of the island. These are rarely crowded even in summer, perhaps because they are a bit off the beaten path. Elafonisi islet has white-sand beaches and black rocks in a turquoise sea (to get there you wade across a narrow channel). You can also head south from Hania across the craggy White Mountains to explore the isolated Libyan Sea villages of Paleochora, the area's main resort, and Souyia.

WHERE TO STAY & EAT

$-$$ ✕**Apostolis.** What is reputed to be the freshest and best-prepared fish in town is served on a lively terrace toward the east end of the old harbor, near the Venetian arsenals. Choose your fish from the bed of ice and decide how you would like it prepared, or opt for the rich fish soup. ⊠*Akti Enoseos* ☎*28210/41767* ▭*MC, V.*

¢–$ ✕**Faka.** Much to the delight of the many neighborhood residents who dine here regularly, Faka concentrates on traditional Cretan cooking. House specialties include *boureki,* a delicious casserole of zucchini, potato, and cheese; and *papoutsakia,* a baked dish with ground lamb, eggplant, and béchamel sauce. The generous meze platter is a meal in itself. ⊠*Off Archoleon, behind Venetian arsenals* ☎*28210/42341* ▭*MC, V.*

¢–$ ✕**Tamam.** An ancient Turkish bath has been converted to one of the most atmospheric restaurants in Hania's old town. Specialties served up in the tiled dining room, and on the narrow lane outside, include peppers with grilled feta cheese and eggplant stuffed with chicken. ⊠*Zambeliou 49* ☎*28210/96080* ▭*No credit cards.*

¢–$ ✕**Well of the Turk.** It's an adventure just finding this restaurant: ask passersby for help, because everyone in the neighborhood knows the place. Behind the Venetian warehouses on the harbor, it stands in a narrow alley near the minaret in the old Arab quarter. The food ranges from simple Greek fare (a prerequisite is the wonderful, large appetizer platter) to some Continental dishes, such as sautéed chicken in a wine sauce. ⊠*Kalinikou Sarpaki 1–3, Splantiza* ☎*28210/54547* ▭*No credit cards* ⊗*Closed Mon. year-round. Closed Tues. Nov.–Mar.*

$$$$ ⌂**Casa Delfino.** In the 1880s this Venetian Renaissance palace was
★   the home of Pedro Delfino, an Italian merchant; today it belongs to two of his descendants. The dramatically decorated guest rooms, four of which are housed in an adjoining building of the same era, are entered through graceful stone archways surrounding a courtyard paved in pebble mosaic. Most have upscale, contemporary wood furniture and rich fabrics, and distinctive architectural details—some occupy two levels, some have enormous marble baths, some have private terraces. ⊠*Theofanous 9, Palio Limani, 73100* ☎*28210/87400* ⊟*28210/96500* ⊕*www.casadelfino.com* ⇆*22 suites* ⌂*In-room: refrigerator, Ethernet. In-hotel: bar* ▭*AE, DC, MC, V* ⏀*BP.*

$$$$ ⛺**Villa Andromeda.** The German high command occupied this seaside villa during World War II (Rommel supposedly enjoyed the old swimming pool that is still next to a larger one in the garden). The yellow, neoclassic mansion contains large suites—some on two levels with sleeping areas upstairs—that overlook the garden or face the sea. Ornate painted ceilings, marble floors, and tapestry rugs add to the elegance of the communal spaces. ✉*Eleftheriou Venizelou Sq. 150, 73100* ☎*28210/28300 or 28210/28301* 🖷*28210/28303* ⊕*www.villandromeda.gr* ➾*8 suites* ♿*In-room: refrigerator. In-hotel: bar, pool, no elevator* ═*DC, MC, V* �*CP.*

$$$ ⛺**Doma.** Feel at home for a night in a 19th-century seaside mansion on
★ the eastern edge of town; it stands about a 20-minute walk along the water from the Venetian harbor. The simple guest rooms face either the luxuriant garden or the sea and have elegant, Cretan-style dark-wood furnishings. Carved-wood sofas and local and family photos fill the sitting room, and an exquisite collection of headdresses from around the world is displayed off the wicker-filled garden room. Breakfast, a lavish spread, includes fresh breads, homemade jams, and yogurt with a Turkish topping: a delicious mix of spices, quince preserves, and honey. On request the owners will prepare a traditional Cretan dinner for guests or nonguests and serve it in an airy upstairs dining room. ✉*Eleftheriou Venizelou Sq. 124, 73100* ☎*28210/51772 or 28210/51773* 🖷*28210/41578* ⊕*www.hotel-doma.gr* ➾*22 rooms, 4 suites* ♿*In-room: refrigerator. In-hotel: bar* ═*DC, MC, V* ☾*Closed Nov.–Mar.* 101*BP.*

$$–$$$ ⛺**Casa Leone.** A Venetian courtyard with a fountain, and a salon and balcony that hang over the harbor are among the dramatic flourishes at this 600-year-old mansion in the old town. The large and comfortable bedrooms are enhanced with modern baths and such details as curved walls, paneled ceilings, sleeping lofts, and private terraces. ✉*Theotokopoulou 18, 73100* ☎🖷*28210/76762* ⊕*www.casa-leone.com* ➾*5 rooms* ♿*In-room: refrigerator. In-hotel: bar, no elevator* ═*MC, V* 101*CP.*

$$ ⛺**Porto del Colombo.** This renovated Venetian town house, once the home of Greek prime minister Eleftherios Venizelos, is full of architectural surprises: wood ceilings and floors; small, deep-set windows; and two-story suites with lofts. The wood furnishings throughout are traditional Cretan. Weather permitting, breakfast is served on the narrow, old-town street out front. ✉*Theofanous and Moshon, 73100* ☎🖷*28210/70945* ⊕*www.ellada.net/colombo* ➾*8 rooms, 2 suites* ♿*In-room: refrigerator. In-hotel: bar, no elevator* ═*MC, V* 101*CP.*

$–$$ ⛺**Hotel Amphora.** Relax on the rooftop terrace and gaze out at views of the harbor, town, and mountains. This comfortable, well-run, and character-filled hotel is in a 14th-century Venetian mansion on a lane above the inner harbor. Rooms are large and many have sea views, as well as such extras as beamed ceilings, fireplaces, private balconies, and kitchenettes. The hotel offers a lavish buffet breakfast for €10, and the dining room, which is on the harbor-front promenade, serves excellent, basic Greek fare and good wines at a discount. ✉*Parodos Theotokopoulou, 73100* ☎*28210/93224* 🖷*28210/93226* ⊕*www.amphora.*

8

gr ⇆*20 rooms* ⌂*In-room: kitchen (some). In-hotel: restaurant, no elevator* ⊟*AE, MC, V.*

SHOPPING

One or two souvenir stores on the waterfront sell English-language books and newspapers. The most exotic shopping experience in town is a stroll through Hania's covered market to see local merchants selling rounds of Cretan cheese, jars of golden honey, lengths of salami, salt fish, lentils, and herbs.

★ The silver jewelry and ceramics at **Carmela** (⊠*Odos Anghelou 7* ☏*28210/90487*) are striking. The store represents contemporary jewelers and other craftspeople from Crete and throughout Greece, as well as the work of owner Carmela Iatropoulou.

★ **Top Hanas** (⊠*Odos Anghelou 3* ☏*28210/98571*) sells a good selection of antique blankets and rugs, most of them made for dowries from homespun wool and natural dyes.

CRETE ESSENTIALS

TRANSPORTATION

BY AIR

Olympic Airways connects Athens, and other islands, with Heraklion, Hania, and Siteia. Aegean Airlines flies between Athens and Heraklion and Hania. Airfares have risen substantially in the past few years, and summertime flights from Athens to Crete are expensive—expect to pay at least twice as much (if not much, much more) than you would to make the trip by boat. Fares come down in winter, when special offers are also often available.

Carriers Aegean Airlines (☏*801/112000 reservations within Greece [toll free], 28210/63366 in Hania, 2810/330475 in Heraklion* ⊕*www.aegeanairlines. gr*). **Olympic Airways** (☏*801/114444 reservations within Greece [toll free], 2810/244802 in Heraklion, 28210/57702 in Hania, 28430/24666 in Siteia* ⊕*www. olympicairlines.com*).

AIRPORTS The principal arrival point on Crete is Heraklion Airport, where up to 16 flights daily arrive from Athens, daily flights arrive from Rhodes and Thessaloniki, and two weekly flights arrive from Mykonos. Heraklion is also serviced directly by charter flights from other European cities. There are several daily flights from Athens to Hania Airport, and several a week from Athens to Siteia, which is also connected to Rhodes with a few weekly flights in summer. In summer, Hania is also served by flights to and from other European cities, mostly charters.

Information Hania Airport (⊠*15 km [9 mi] northeast of Hania, off road to Sterne, Souda Bay* ☏*28210/63264*). **Heraklion Airport** (⊠*5 km [3 mi] east of town, off road to Gournes, Heraklion* ☏*2810/245644*). **Siteia Airport** (⊠*1 km [½ mi] northwest of town, off main coast road, Siteia* ☏*28430/24424*).

AIRPORT
TRANSFERS
A municipal bus just outside Heraklion Airport can take you to Eleftheriou Square in the Heraklion town center. Tickets are sold from a kiosk next to the bus stop; the fare is €0.80. From Hania Airport, Olympic Airlines buses take you to the airline office in the center for €2. Cabs line up outside all airports to meet flights; the fare into the respective towns is about €5 for Heraklion, €7 for Hania, and €4 for Siteia.

BY BIKE & MOPED

Be cautious: motorbike accidents account for numerous injuries among tourists every year. Reliable rentals can be arranged through Blue Sea Rentals in Heraklion, and you'll find rentals in just about any town on the tourist trail. Expect to pay about €20 a day for a 50cc moped, for which you will need to present only a valid driver's license; law requires a motorcycle license to rent larger bikes. Fees usually cover insurance, but only for repairs to the bike, and usually with a deductible of at least €500. The law, and common sense, mandate that you wear a helmet, but few riders do.

Contact Blue Sea Rentals (✉ *Kosmo Zoutou 5–7, Heraklion* ☎ *2810/241097* ⊕ *www.bluesearentals.com).*

BY BOAT & FERRY

Heraklion and Souda Bay (5 km [3 mi] east of Hania) are the island's main ports, and there is regular service as well to Rethymnon, Ayios Nikolaos, and Siteia. The most frequent service is on overnight crossings from these ports to and from Piraeus, though note that Hellenic Seaways runs high-speed, four-hour service between Piraeus and Hania in summer. Ferries also connect Crete with other islands, mostly those in the Cyclades and Dodecanese. Service includes Minoan Lines catamarans between Santorini and Heraklion (cutting travel time to just under two hours) and a ferry linking Siteia with the Dodecanese islands of Kassos, Karpathos, and Rhodes. There is also weekly service from Kalamata and Gythion in the Peloponnese to Kissamos (Kastelli) in the far west of the island. Ships also sail from Heraklion to Limassol, in Cyprus; to Haifa, Israel; and to Venice.

On the overnight runs, you can book either a berth or an airplane-style seat, and there are usually cafeterias, dining rooms, shops, and other services on board. The most economical berth accommodations are in four-berth cabins, which are relatively spacious and comfortable and are equipped with bathrooms. A one-way fare from Piraeus to Heraklion, Rethymnon, or Hania without accommodation costs about €22, and from about €50 with accommodation. A small discount is given for round-trip tickets. Car fares are about €70 each way, depending on vehicle size.

In July and August, a boat service around the Samaria gorge operates along the southwest coast from Hora Sfakion to Loutro, Ayia Roumeli, Souyia, Lissos, and Paleochora, the main resort on the southwest coast. Ferries also sail from Paleochora to Ghavdos, an island south of Crete, and from Ierapetra to Krissi, an island also to the south.

8

Most travel agencies sell tickets for all ferries and hydrofoils; make reservations several days in advance during the July to August high season.

Contacts Anek (Piraeus to Heraklion, Rethymnon, and Hania) (⊠ *Karamanlis, Hania* ☎ *28210/24163* ⊕ *www.anek.gr*). **Anen (Peloponnese to Kissamos)** (⊠ *Port, Kissamos* ☎ *28210/20345* ⊕ *www.anen.gr*). **Hellenic Seaways (Piraeus to Hania via high-speed catamaran)** (⊠ *25 Avgoustou, Heraklion* ☎ *2810/346185* ⊕ *www.hellenicseaways.gr*). **Lane (Piraeus to Ayios Nikolaos and Siteia)** (⊕ *www.lanesealines.gr*). **Minoan Lines (Piraeus to Heraklion)** (⊠ *25 Avgoustou, Heraklion* ☎ *2810/346185* ⊕ *www.ferries.gr/minoan*).

BY BUS

You can find schedules and book seats in advance at bus stations, and tourist offices are well equipped with schedules and information about service. As efficient as the bus network is, you might have a hard time getting out of Heraklion, what with its confusing multitude of stations: the bus station for western Crete is opposite the port; the station for the south is outside the Hania Gate to the right of the archaeological museum; and the station for the east is at the traffic circle at the end of Leoforos D. Bofor, close to the old harbor. Ask someone at the tourist information office to tell you exactly where to find your bus and to show you the spot on a map.

Information KTEL (☎ *28410/22234 in Ayios Nikolaos, 28210/93052 in Hania, 2810/245020 in Heraklion, 28310/22785 in Rethymnon* ⊕ *www.ktel.org*).

BY CAR

Roads on Crete are not too congested, yet the accident rate is high compared to other parts of Europe. Driving in the main towns can be nerve-racking, to say the least. Most road signs are in Greek and English, though signage is often nonexistent or inadequate. Be sure to carry a road map at all times, and to stop and ask directions when the need arises—otherwise, you may drive miles out of your way. Gas stations are not plentiful outside the big towns, and gasoline is more expensive in Crete than it is in the United States—expect to pay about €1 a liter (about €4 a gallon).

Drive defensively wherever you are, as Cretan drivers are aggressive and liable to ignore the rules of the road. Sheep and goats frequently stray onto the roads, with or without their shepherd or sheepdog. In July and August, tourists on motor scooters can be a hazard. Night driving is not advisable.

CAR RENTALS   You can arrange beforehand with a major agency in the United States or in Athens to pick up a car on arrival in Crete, or work through one of the many local car-rental agencies that have offices in the airports and in the cities, as well as in some resort villages. For the most part, these local agencies are extremely reliable, provide excellent service, and charge very low rates. Many, such as the excellent Crete Car Rental, will meet your ship or plane and drop you off again at no extra charge. Even without advance reservations, expect to pay about €40 or less a day in high season for a medium-size car with unlimited mileage.

Weekly prices are negotiable, but with unlimited mileage rentals start at about €200 in summer.

Contacts Avis (⊕ *www.avis.com* ✉ *Hania Airport* ☎ *28210/63080* ✉ *Heraklion Airport* ☎ *2810/229402*). **Crete Car Rental** (☎ *28250/32690* ⊕ *www.crete-car-rental.com*). **Hertz** (⊕ *www.hertz.com* ✉ *Heraklion Airport* ☎ *2810/330452*). **Sixt** (✉ *Akti Konudourou 28, Ayios Nikolaos* ☎ *28410/82055* ⊕ *www.sixt.com* ✉ *Hania Airport* ☎ *28210/20905* ✉ *Heraklion Airport* ☎ *2810/280915* ✉ *Ikariou 93, Heraklion* ☎ *2810/280915*).

CONTACTS & RESOURCES

EMERGENCIES
Your hotel can help you call an English-speaking doctor. Pharmacies stay open late by turns, and a list of those open late is displayed in their windows.

Emergency Services Ambulance (☎ *166*). **Police (emergency)** (☎ *100*). **Hospitals** (☎ *28410/66000 in Ayios Nikolaos, 28210/22000 in Hania, 2810/368000 in Heraklion, 28310/87100 in Rethymnon*). **Tourist Police** (☎ *171 central operator, 28410/26900 in Ayios Nikolaos, 28210/5332 in Hania, 2810/289614 in Heraklion, 28310/28156 in Rethymnon*).

MEDIA
English-language books, magazines, and newspapers are available in the major towns and resorts, but difficult to find once you get off the well-beaten tourist path. In some of the larger hotels you may find CNN, Star News, or other English-language television broadcasts from the United States and the United Kingdom.

English-Language Bookstores Astrakianakis (✉ *Eleftheriou Venizelou Sq., Heraklion* ☎ *2810/284248*). **International Press Bookshop** (✉ *Eleftheriou Venizelou Sq. 26, Rethymnon*). **Kouvidis-Manouras** (✉ *Daidalou 6, Heraklion* ☎ *2810/220135*).

MAIL & SHIPPING
Post offices are generally open weekdays 7:30–2. You can often buy stamps at magazine kiosks.

Contacts Post offices (✉ *Tzanakaki 3, Hania* ✉ *Daskaloyianni Sq., Heraklion* ✉ *Koundourioti, Rethymnon*).

TOUR OPTIONS
Resort hotels and large agents, such as Canea Travel, organize guided tours in air-conditioned buses to the main Minoan sites; excursions to spectacular beaches such as Vai in the northeast and Elafonisi in the southwest; and trips to Santorini and to closer islands such as Spinalonga, a former leper colony off Ayios Nikolaos. El Greco Tours organizes hikes through the Samaria gorge and other local excursions. The Crete Travel Web site is an excellent one-stop source for tour information, with insights on many of the island's more-worthwhile sights and tours including hiking excursions and visits to out-of-the-way monasteries, as well as car rental and distinctive accommodation information.

8

A tour of Knossos and the Archaeological Museum in Heraklion costs about €40; a tour of Phaistos and Gortyna plus a swim at Matala costs about €20; a trip to the Samaria gorge costs about €25. Travel agents can also arrange for personal guides, whose fees are negotiable.

Contacts **Canea Travel** (✉ *Bonaili 12–13, Hania* ☎ *28210/52301*). **Crete Travel** (✉ *Monaho, Armenoi Chanion* ☎ *28250/32690* ⊕ *www.cretetravel.com*). **El Greco Tours** (✉ *Theotokopoulou 50, Hania* ☎ *28210/86018* ⊕ *www.elgrecotours.com*).

VISITOR INFORMATION

Tourist offices are more plentiful, and more helpful, on Crete than they are in many other parts of Greece. Offices of the Greek National Tourism Organization (GNTO or EOT), in the major towns, are open daily 8–2 and 3–8:30. The municipalities of Ayios Nikolaos, Siteia, and Ierapetra operate their own tourist offices, and these provide a wealth of information on the towns and surrounding regions, as well as helping with accommodation and local tours; most keep long summer hours, open daily 8:30 AM–9 PM.

Contacts **Ayios Nikolaos** (✉ *Koundourou 21A* ☎ *28410/22357*). **Greek National Tourism Organization** (✉ *Xanthoudidou 1, Heraklion* ☎ *2810/246106* ⊕ *www. gnto.gr* ✉ *Odos Kriari 40, Hania* ☎ *28210/92624* ✉ *Sofokli Venizelou, Rethymnon* ☎ *28310/56350*). **Siteia** (✉ *Port* ☎ *28300/23775*).

Rhodes & the Dodecanese

KOS, SYMI & PATMOS

Karpathos

WORD OF MOUTH

"Water parks, discos, nightclubs, crowded resorts? Yes, they exist but we didn't go looking for them. We spent a perfectly pleasant week on Rhodes with plenty to explore, good beaches to relax on, and good food, too—it is still possible to find all the things that attracted people to the island in the first place. Kos town was well worth a visit—for anyone who enjoys wandering around ruins, there were plenty, from 2,000-year-old Greek and Roman remains, to a huge Crusader castle."

—Maria_H

WELCOME TO RHODES & THE DODECANESE

TOP REASONS TO GO

★ **Medieval Might:** As much as sun and sand, the monuments the Knights of St. John built some 700 years ago are what draw visitors to Rhodes—no more so than its walled-in Old Town, a remarkably well-preserved and photogenic testimony to the Crusader past.

★ **Healing Hippocrates:** Kos's site of ancient healing, the Asklepieion, was the renowned medical school founded by Hippocrates, father of Western medicine.

★ **Natural Wonders:** The terrain yields butterflies (Rhodes), hot sea springs (Kos), countless coves (Patmos), and mountain paths (Symi).

★ **St. John's Patmos:** Called the "Jerusalem of the Aegean," Patmos is as peaceful as it was when the Apostle John glimpsed the Apocalypse in his cave here—the spiritual mystique of this little island is still strong.

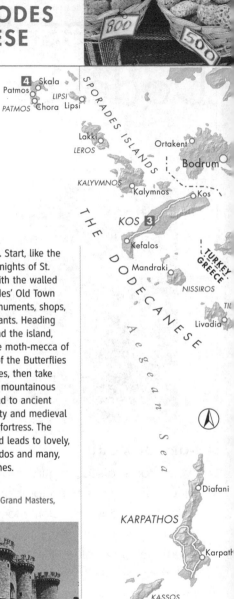

1 Rhodes. Start, like the crusading Knights of St. John did, with the walled city of Rhodes' Old Town with its monuments, shops, and restaurants. Heading south around the island, discover the moth-mecca of the Valley of the Butterflies in Petaloudes, then take the island's mountainous western road to ancient Kameiros city and medieval Monolithos fortress. The eastern road leads to lovely, car-free Lindos and many, many beaches.

Palace of the Grand Masters, Rhodes town

Sponges, a special souvenir from Rhodes (left); The Bay of Grikos on Patmos Island (right).

TURKEY

Datca

Yialos
2 Symi Chorio

SYMI **Palaiachora**

KHALKI

Ialyssos ○ Rhodes

Kameiros ○ Petaloudes

○ Epta Piges

Siana
1
Monolithos

○ Lindos

○ Gennadi

RHODES

0 ———— 20 mi

0 ———— 20 km

2 **Symi.** "Picturesque" is the word for both Yialos harbor, with its restaurants and shops, and Chorio located just above it. The inner island is populated mainly by small churches. The impressive Panormitis Monastery is a popular site, serviced by boats.

3 **Kos.** The port town is a funny blend of ancient stones and Northern European partying teens. A short drive out of town, Asklepieion was once the greatest healing site of the ancient era. Large swaths of coast are perfect for swimming.

4 **Patmos.** Make your pilgrimage to Chora to see the cave and the surrounding Monastery of the Apocalypse, hallowed by the presence of St. John. Towering over Chora's skyline is the imposing, fortified Monastery of St. John the Theologian, Skala, a pleasant—if modest—harbor.

GETTING ORIENTED

The Dodecanese (Twelve Islands), wrapped enticingly around the shores of Turkey and Asia Minor, are the easternmost holdings of Greece. Here, classic, Byzantine, and Ottoman architectures deliciously blend and multiculturalism is an old idea. Large, varied Rhodes is the vital linchpin, where Romans, Crusaders, Turks, and Venetians have all left their marks. Heading out, the traveler can discover the cypress-clad hillsides of Patmos, the craggy shoreline of Symi, and the holiday vibe (and lush fields) of Kos.

9

Agios Stefanos on Kos island

RHODES & THE DODECANESE PLANNER

When to Go

To avoid crowds, just before and after peak seasons (May–June and September) are good seasons to visit.

From October to May, though most archaeological places remain open, most hotels, restaurants, and shops are closed.

On the off-season, resorts go dead and boat travel is limited by the weather's whims. Patmos is packed at Easter.

Getting There

Though you can get to the hubs of Rhodes or Kos in under 10 hours nowadays on the faster boats, if there is limited time, it's best to fly to the airports on these two islands.

Make sure, however, for good rates and an assured spot that you book as far as possible (at least two weeks) in advance.

The big, 15-hours-plus boat rides from the mainland offer both romance and duress.

Remember that deck class passengers claim key spots on the floor, in the lounge areas, and even—in peak season—on the metal deck under the stars.

Pick a Beach, Any Beach

In the Dodecanese it's never hard to find a beautiful beach, or at least a rock from which to swim. Most islands have a beach for every mood. Although many beaches on Rhodes and Kos have been developed to the last grain of sand, on Rhodes the sheltered southeastern coast has long, exquisite, and undeveloped stretches of fine sand. The Gulf of Kefalos on Kos is a haven for those wishing to escape the tourist fray—broad, sandy, scenically magnificent, and for much of its length devoid of development, curving around an enchanting bay. One of the pleasures of being on Patmos is to seek out yet another perfect beach every day: in the morning, caïques make regular runs from Skala to several of the beaches; some can be reached by car or bus, and many delightfully empty strands are the reward for a short trek on foot. The rocky shores of Symi provide many a cove for superb swimming. When you ask your hotel or restaurant for the best beach, include information about what exactly you are seeking—crowds or isolation, shallow water or depths, sand or pebbles. Beach umbrellas and deck chairs are usually rented out (€8–€10), but spread out your towel on the beach instead if you prefer.

Finding a Place to Stay

Except for Athens, Rhodes has more hotels per capita than anywhere else in Greece. Most of them are resort or tourist hotels, with sea views and easy access to beaches. High season can prove extremely crowded and you may have difficulty finding a room in Rhodes if you don't book well in advance. However, there is such a plethora of resort hotels that some remain part-empty, even at the summer's peak. Mass tourist accommodations are also plentiful on Kos but, as in Rhodes, most lodging isn't especially Greek in style. Symi has more small hotels with charm, since the island never encouraged the development of mammoth caravansaries. Similarly, Patmos has attractive, high-quality lodgings that tend to be both more elegant and traditional than its resort-magnet neighbors. It also has a lot of rented rooms—and it is standard practice to check them out before booking.

Proceed with Caution

Unfortunately, because Rhodes and Kos attract so many thousands of tourists, it is easy to sometimes be treated as a number and get ripped off. You can avoid this by avoiding touristy cafés or restaurants, by confirming prices (especially taxis, boats, and sports-equipment rental) in advance, and having the tourist police number handy—and dialing it on the spot if need be.

Dining and Drinking, Dodecanese Style

Throughout the Dodecanese, especially on Rhodes, you can find sophisticated restaurants, as well as simple tavernas serving excellent food. It is sometimes best to wait until after 9 PM to see where the Greeks are eating. Fish, of course, is readily available on all islands. Tiny, tender Symi shrimp, found only in the waters around this island, have such soft shells they can be easily popped in the mouth whole. They are used in dozens of local dishes. Wherever you dine, ask about the specialty of the day, and check the food on display in the kitchen of tavernas. Large fish goes by the kilo, so confirm the exact amount you'd like when ordering. Finally, it is safest to order wine or beer instead of cocktails, as unscrupulous places often serve impure alcohol.

Dining & Lodging Prices in Euros

	¢	$	$$	$$$	$$$$
Restaurants	under €8	€8–€11	€11–€15	€15–€20	over €20
Hotels	under €60	€60–€90	€90–€120	€120–€160	over €160

Restaurant prices are for one main course at dinner, or for two mezedes (small dishes). Hotel prices are for a standard double room in high season, including taxes. Hotels operate on the European Plan (EP, with no meal provided) unless we note that they use the Continental Plan (CP, with Continental breakfast); Breakfast Plan (BP, with a full breakfast); Modified American Plan (MAP, with breakfast and dinner); or the Full American Plan (FAP, with all meals). Inquire when booking if these meal plans (which can entail higher rates) are mandatory. Guest rooms have air-conditioning, room phones, and TVs unless otherwise noted.

Getting Around

Renting a car (for €30–€40 a day) is very useful for exploring Rhodes or Kos, or to hop between Patmos's many beaches. (Make sure it's unlimited mileage, and that the engine has the power for hills!) In Symi, with its one road, a car is of little use and you should opt for the adorable van that serves as the island bus.

The bigger islands and Patmos have regular (if morning-oriented) bus service to sites and beaches. Radio taxis can be slow in coming. It's possible to travel to some spots by boat on Symi and Patmos (be sure to check prices in advance).

If you island-hop through the Dodecanese islands for the day, confirm the return boat schedule, as smaller islands have limited boats.

Feeling Festive?

In Greece, culture shifts to the islands in the summer. On Rhodes, the free international Ecofilms festival of environmental film takes place in late June.

A rich schedule of music and theater is featured at Kos's Ippokratia festival (July–September) and the Symi Festival (June–September).

Patmos's high-profile Festival of Sacred Music brings Byzantine and classical music to the amphitheater outside the Apocalypse Monastery (September).

9

Updated
by Angelike
Contis

LYING AT THE EASTERN EDGE of the Aegean Sea, wrapped enticingly around the shores of Turkey and Asia Minor, is the southernmost group of Greek islands, the Dodecanese (Twelve Islands), sometimes known as the Southern Sporades. The archipelago has long shared a common history: Romans, Crusaders, Turks, and Venetians left their mark with temples, castles, and fortresses in exotic towns of shady lanes and tall houses. Of the 12 islands, 4 are highlighted here: strategically located Rhodes has played by far the most important role in history and was for many years one of the most popular vacation spots in the Mediterranean. Kos comes in second in popularity and has vestiges of antiquity; the Sanctuary of Asklepios, a center of healing, drew people from all over the ancient world. Symi is a virtual museum of 19th-century neoclassical architecture almost untouched by modern development, and Patmos, where St. John wrote his *Revelation,* became a renowned monastic center during the Byzantine period and continues as a significant focal point of the Greek Orthodox faith. Symi and Patmos both have a peace and quiet that in large part has been lost on overdeveloped Rhodes and Kos. But despite the invasion of sunseekers, there are still delightful pockets of local color throughout the Dodecanese.

EXPLORING RHODES & THE DODECANESE

Rhodes and Kos unfold in fertile splendor, creased with streams and dotted with large stretches of green; their major towns sit next to the sea on almost flat land, embracing exceptionally large and well-protected harbors facing the mainland of Asia Minor. Both islands are worth visiting for a couple of days each. Patmos and Symi, however, resemble in some ways more the Cycladic islands: rugged hills and mountains are almost devoid of vegetation, with villages and towns clinging in lovely disarray to craggy landscapes. Symi is the closest island to Rhodes, an easy 50-minute hydrofoil ride away.

RHODES ΡΟΔΟΣ

Rhodes (1,400 square km [540 square mi]) is the fourth-largest Greek island and, along with Sicily and Cyprus, one of the great islands of the Mediterranean. It lies almost exactly halfway between Piraeus and Cyprus, 18 km (11 mi) off the coast of Asia Minor, and it was long considered a bridge between Europe and the East. Geologically similar to the Turkish mainland, it was probably once a part of it, separated by one of the frequent volcanic upheavals this volatile region has experienced.

Rhodes saw successive waves of settlement, including the arrival of the Dorian Greeks from Argos and Laconia early in the 1st millennium BC. From the 8th to the 6th century BC Rhodian cities established settlements in Italy, France, Spain, and Egypt and actively traded with mainland Greece, exporting pottery, oil, wine, and figs. Independence and expansion came to a halt when the Persians took over the island at the end of the 6th century BC and forced Rhodians to provide ships

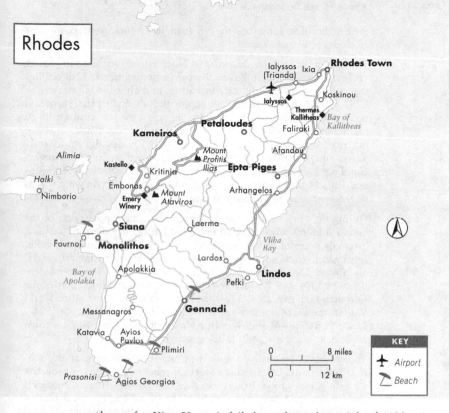

Rhodes

and men for King Xerxes's failed attack on the mainland (480 BC). A league of city-states rose under Athenian leadership. In 408 BC the united city of Rhodes was created on the site of the modern town; much of the populace moved there, and the history of the island and the town became synonymous. As the new city grew and flourished, its political organization became the model for the city of Alexandria in Egypt.

In 42 BC, Rhodes came under the hegemony of Rome, and through the years of the empire it was fabled as a beautiful city where straight roads were lined with porticoes, houses, and gardens. According to Pliny, who described the city in the 1st century AD, the town possessed some 2,000 statues, at least 100 of them of colossal scale. One of the most famous examples of the island's sculptural school is the *Laocöon*—probably executed in the 1st century BC—which showed the priest who warned the Trojans to beware of Greeks bearing gifts (it stands in the Vatican today). The ancient glory of Rhodes has few visible remnants. The city was ravaged by Arab invaders in AD 654 and 807, and only with the expulsion of the Arabs, and the reconquest of Crete by the Byzantine emperors, did the city begin to revive. Rhodes was a crucial stop on the road to the Holy Land during the Crusades. It came briefly under Venetian influence, then Byzantine, then Genoese. In 1309, when the Knights of St. John took the city from its Genoese masters, its most glorious modern era began.

The Knights of St. John, an order of Hospitalers, organized to protect and care for Christian pilgrims. By the beginning of the 12th century the order had become military in nature, and after the fall of Acre in 1291, the Knights fled from Palestine, withdrawing first to Cyprus and then to Rhodes. In 1312 the Knights inherited the immense wealth of the Templars (another religious military order, which had just been outlawed by the pope) and used it to fortify Rhodes. But for all their power and the strength of their walls, moats, and artillery, the Knights could not hold back the Turks. In 1522 the Ottomans, with 300 ships and 100,000 men under Süleyman the Magnificent, began what was to be the final siege, taking the city after six months.

During the Turkish occupation, Rhodes became a possession of the Grand Admiral, who collected taxes but left the Rhodians to pursue a generally peaceful and prosperous existence. They continued to build ships and to trade with Greece, Constantinople (later Istanbul), Syria, and Egypt. The Greek mainland was liberated by the War of Independence in 1821, but Rhodes and the Dodecanese remained part of the Ottoman Empire until 1912, when the Italians took over. After World War II, the Dodecanese were formally united with Greece in 1947. In the years post–World War II, tourism became king, Rhodes town expanded, and the island's farming activities shrank.

Today Rhodes retains its role as the center of Dodecanese trade, politics, and culture. Its diversity ensures it remains a polestar of tourism as well: Rhodes town brings together fascinating artifacts, medieval architecture, and an active nightlife. The island's east coast is blessed with white-sand beaches and dotted with copses of trees, interspersed with fertile valleys full of figs and olives. And though some of the shore is beset by vast resort hotels and holiday villages, there are still some wonderfully unsullied sections of beach to be found all around the island; if you look for it, you'll even find a taste of rural life.

RHODES TOWN ΡΟΔΟΣ (ΠΟΛΗ)

Fodor'sChoice *463 km (287 mi) east of Piraeus.*
★

Early travelers described Rhodes as a town of two parts: a castle or high town (Collachium) and a lower city. Today Rhodes town is still a city of two parts: the Old Town, a UNESCO World Heritage site that incorporates the high town and lower city, contains Orthodox and Catholic churches, Turkish structures, and houses, some of which follow the ancient orthogonal plan. Public buildings are all similar in style: staircases are on the outside, either on the facade or in the court; the facades are elegantly constructed of well-cut limestone from Lindos; windows and doors are often outlined with strongly profiled moldings and surmounted by arched casements. Careful reconstruction in recent years has enhanced the harmonious effect. Spreading away from the walls that encircle the Old Town is the modern metropolis, or new town.

In the castle area, a city within a city, the Knights of St. John built most of their monuments. The **Palace of the Grand Masters,** at the highest spot of the medieval city, is the best place to begin a tour of Rhodes; here you can get oriented before wandering through the labyrinthine Old Town. Of great help is the permanent exhibition downstairs, with extensive displays, maps, and plans showing the layout of the city. The palace building withstood unscathed the Turkish siege, but in 1856, an explosion of ammunition stored nearby in the cellars of the Church of St. John devastated it; the present structures are 20th-century Italian reconstructions. Note the Hellenistic and Roman mosaic floors throughout, which came from the Italian excavations in Kos. ⊠ *Ippoton, Old Town* ☎ 22410/25500 ☉ €6 ☉ *May–Oct., Mon. 12:30–7, Tues.–Sun. 8–7:30; Nov.–Apr., Tues.–Sun. 8–3.*

Before the court of the Palace of the Grand Masters is the **Loggia of St. John,** on the site where the Knights of St. John were buried in an early church. From the loggia, the **Street of the Knights** *(Ippoton)* descends toward the **Commercial Port,** bordered on both sides by the **Inns of the Tongues,** where the Knights supped and held their meetings.

The **Inn of France** was the largest of the Knights' gathering spots and is now the French Consulate. The facade is carved with flowers and heraldic patterns and bears an inscription that dates the building between 1492 and 1509. ⊠ *About halfway down St. of the Knights from Loggia of St. John.*

The hospital, the largest of the Knights' public buildings, was completed in 1489. The imposing facade opens into a courtyard, where cannonballs remain from the siege of 1522. Today it contains the **Archaeological Museum.** On the main floor there's a collection of ancient pottery and sculpture, including two well-known representations of Aphrodite: the *Aphrodite of Rhodes,* who, while bathing, pushes aside her hair as if she's listening; and a standing figure, known as *Aphrodite Thalassia,* or "of the sea," as she was discovered in the water off the northern city beach. Other important works include a 6th-century BC *kouros* (a statue of an idealized male youth, usually nude) that was found in Kameiros, and the beautiful 5th-century BC funerary stela of Timarista bidding farewell to her mother, Crito. ⊠ *Mouseou Sq.* ☎ 22410/25500 ☉ €3 ☉ *Tues.–Sun. 8:30–2:40.*

The **Byzantine Museum** collection of icons is displayed within the 11th-century Lady of the Castle church. ⊠ *Off Mouseou Sq.* ☎ 22410/25500 ☉ €2 ☉ *Tues.–Sun. 8:30–2:40.*

The **Museum of Decorative Arts** exhibits finely made ceramics, crafts, and artifacts from around the Dodecanese. ⊠ *Argyrokastrou Sq.* ☎ 22410/25500 ☉ €2 ☉ *Tues.–Sun. 8:30–2:40.*

The **Mosque of Süleyman,** (⊠ *At top of Sokratous* ☎ 22410/24918 ☉ *Free*) was built circa 1522 and rebuilt in 1808. At this writing, the restored building was open primarily to groups, by appointment only.

The **Turkish Library** dates to the late 18th century. Striking reminders of the Ottoman presence, the library and the mosque are still used by those members of Rhodes's Turkish community who stayed behind after the 1923 population exchange, a mass repatriation of Greek and Turkish migrants after their countries' second war. ⊠ *Sokratous, opposite Mosque of Süleyman* ☎ *22410/74090* ☲ *Free* ⊘ *Mon.–Sat. 9:30–4.*

> **SEE MORE AND SAVE**
>
> Plan on hitting all the old-town attractions? Purchase a multi-sight ticket (€10) which gets you admission to the Palace of the Grand Masters, Archaeological Museum, Museum of Decorative Arts, and Byzantine Museum.

The **walls** of Rhodes in themselves are one of the great medieval monuments in the Mediterranean. Wonderfully restored, they illustrate the engineering capabilities as well as the financial and human resources available to the Knights. (The 20th-century Italian rulers erased much of the Ottoman influence, preferring to emphasize the Knights' past when restoring architecture.) For 200 years the Knights strengthened the walls by thickening them, up to 40 feet in places, and curving them so as to deflect cannonballs. The moat between the inner and outer walls never contained water; it was a device to prevent invaders from constructing siege towers. Part of the road that runs the 4 km (2½ mi) along the top of the walls is usually accessible through municipal **guided tours** (⊠ *Tours depart from Palace of the Grand Masters entrance in Ippoton, Old Town* ☎ *22410/23359*); however, at the time of this writing, the walls were closed temporarily. You can get a sense of the enclosed city's massive scale by walking inside the moat. ⊠ *Old Town; moat entrances include gate near sound-and-light show* ☲ *Moat free.*

The soaring vaults of the ruins of **Our Lady of the Bourg,** once a magnificent Gothic church, are a startling reminder of Rhodes's Frankish past. ⊠ *Inside remains of walls, access through Panagias Gate.*

NEED A BREAK?

Partake in an Ottoman-era ritual by visiting **Rhodes's Hammam** ⊠ *Arionos Sq.* ☎ *22410/27739* ☲ *€1.50* ⊘ *Weekdays 10–5, Sat. 8–5)* , built in 1515 and open all year long for steam therapy. Locals visit the traditional Turkish-style public baths (with separate male and female facilities) to soothe arthritis, circulation problems, and muscle aches. Walk-in bathers start in a warm room, then pass into a hotter room, where they "steam" for hours before cooling off with a shower and a massage (€5). A wood-stoked fire heats the stone building, which is very stark apart from the carved stars in the domed shower area. ⚠ Check with your doctor before visiting, as the temperatures get very high.

The **commercial harbor,** at the "mouth" of the Old Town, is Rhodes's largest. The port authority and customs offices are here. ⊠ *Near St. Catherine's Gate.*

The medieval Old Town of Rhodes is now completely surrounded by the **new town.** The city first spread outside town walls during Otto-

Continued on page 410

NECTAR OF THE GODS

The roots of Greek wine run deep: Naughty Dionysus partied his way through mythology as the God of Wine and became a symbol for celebration in Greece. During the ancient festivities called Dionysia, husbands and wives alike let loose and drank themselves to a heady joy. Now that you're in the land of the god, be sure to enjoy some liquid Dionysian delights. Greece's wine is flavorful and original, so much so that some of the wines here you won't find anywhere else.

This is one reason why few can resist taking some bottles home (a bottle of excellent Greek wine will cost at least €15 to €20, but good varieties can be found for around €10). Remember to ask the clerk to pad them with bubble wrap so they won't break in your suitcase on the journey back. Following are some tips about vintners who are leading the new Greek renaissance of wine making, along with a rundown of the grape varietals that Grecian wineries specialize in.

THE GREEK WINES TO LOOK FOR

WHITES

Assyrtiko. One of Greece's finest white wines and found mainly in Santorini, Attica, and Macedonia, it is rich and dry with honeysuckle and citrus aromas and an earthy aftertaste. Pair with grilled fish, poultry, or pork and feta.

Athiri. One of the oldest Greek varieties and found mainly in Santorini, Macedonia, Attica, and Rhodes, it is vibrant and fruity with tropical fruit and honey tones. Pair with poultry or pork, pasta, grilled fish, or white cheeses.

Moschofilero. Originating in the Peloponnese, it is vivid and has rich fruity and floral aromas. Pair with poultry, pasta, and seafood.

Roditis. Popular in Attica, Macedonia, Thessaly, and Peloponnese, it is light and has vibrant scents of pineapple, pear, melon, and jasmine. Pair with poultry, fish, and mild cheeses.

Rombola. Grown in the Ionian island of Cephalonia, it is scented with citrus and peach and has a lemony aftertaste. Pair with fish or poultry.

Savatiano. Cultivated in Attica, it is full-bodied with fruity tones of apple, pear, and peach. Pair with poultry, pork, or fish as well as soft white cheeses.

White Muscat. Cultivated on the Aegean island of Samos and in the northern Peloponnese city of Patras, it is sweet and intense. Pair with desserts and ice cream.

REDS

Aghiorgitiko. The name means St. George and it's mainly found in the Nemea region of the Peloponnese. Richly colored and scented, with scents of sour cherries and pomegranate, it goes well with red meat and yellow soft cheeses.

Kotsifali. Grown mainly in Crete, it is rich and aromatic, with hints of raisins, prunes, and sage. Pair with red meat, light red sauces, and yellow cheeses.

Mantelaria. Mainly cultivated in Rhodes and Crete, it is rich and intense, with hints of pomegranate. Pair with grilled and stewed meats with spicy sauces and mild cheeses.

Mavrodaphne. Found in the Peloponnese regions of Achaia and Ilia and the Ionian Islands, it is a lovely dessert wine. Drink alone or with a light dessert.

Xinomavro. Found in Macedonia, it is rich, acidic, and bursting with aromas such as gooseberry with hints of olives and spices. Pair with grilled meats, casseroles, and yellow spicy cheeses.

WHEN IN RHODES...

Today, Rhodes has become a vibrant wine culture center. While its viticultural history goes back to the ancient Phoenicians, its vintages have become newly popular, thanks to its two delicious grape varieties, the Mandilaria and the aromatic Athiri, and the good showing of the native sweet Muscats. The Cair cooperative produces most of the island's wine, including first-rate Mandilaria and Athiri, as well as reds such as Xinomavro, Cabernet, Grenache, and Syrah. The most prominent winemaking force on the island is the Triantafyllou family, who opened the groundbreaking boutique Emery winery in the village of Embonas (www.emery.gr; see Siana in this chapter). The family has received notice for its Granrose made from Dimitina, a type of Mandelaria. Other top Emery wines include Athiri Vounouplagias, Rodofili, and Zacosta.

PICK OF THE VINE

Wherever you head in Greece, winemakers are perfecting the millennia-old traditions of Greek wine, with high-class estates such as Gaia, Boutari, and Porto Carras leading the way. These wineries can all be visited by appointment. A good introductory Web site is www.allaboutgreekwine.com.

Crete, Nikolaos Douloufakis. He is gaining attention with his Vilana 2000, with its spicy aromas and hints of banana and clementine. He comes from an established winemaking family in Dafnes (www.cretanwines.gr), near the major city of Heraklion in Crete. (His grandfather, Dimitris Douloufakis, used to transport his wine in goatskin when he began in the 1930s.)

Cyclades, Haridimos Hatzidakis. On Santorini, his winery (www.hatzidakiswines.gr) near Pyrgos Kallistis is comprised of a celebrated set of organic vineyards. One of his top organic wines is the Aidani Assyritiko, a dry fruity white.

Macedonia, Yiannis Boutaris. Up north, in Naoussa, Imathia wine lovers make a beeline to Yiannis's Ktima Kir-Yianni winery (www.kiryianni.gr). He split from his family's estate ten years ago to concentrate on producing standout dry reds.

The Great Colossus

At the end of the 4th century BC the Rhodians commissioned the sculptor Chares, from Lindos, to create the famous Colossus, a huge bronze statue of the sun god, Helios, and one of the Seven Wonders of the Ancient World. Two bronze deer statues mark the spot where legend says the Colossus once straddled the Mandraki harbor entrance. The 110-foot-high statue only stood for half a century. In 227 BC, when an earthquake razed the city and toppled the Colossus, help poured in from all quarters of the eastern Mediterranean. After the calamity the Delphic oracle advised the Rhodians to let the great Colossus remain where it had fallen. So there it rested for some eight centuries, until AD 654 when it was sold as scrap metal and carted off to Syria allegedly by a caravan of 900 camels. After that, nothing is known of its fate.

man domination. Today, there are many circa 1950s–1970s buildings that resemble those in Athens, though they have fewer stories overall. ⊠ *North of Old Town walls, bordering Mandraki harbor.*

The city's municipal buildings, an open-air bazaar, and the main shopping areas are along **Mandraki harbor.** The Governor's Palace is constructed in an arcaded Venetian Gothic style.

The town's cathedral, **Evangelismos Church,** which is modeled after the destroyed Church of St. John in the Collachium, dominates the waterfront. ⊠ *New town* ☎ *22410/77916* ⊙ *Church daily 7–noon and 5–7:30.*

Mt. Smith rises about 2 km (1 mi) to the west of the town center. Villas and gardens dot its slopes, but many more of them have been torn down to make way for modern apartment buildings. For a dramatic view, walk to the westernmost edge of Mt. Smith, which drops via a sharp and almost inaccessible cliff to the shore below, now lined with enormous hotels.

Atop Mt. Smith are the freely accessible ruins of the **acropolis.** These include a heavily restored **theater,** a **stadium,** the three restored columns of the **Temple of Apollo Pythios,** and the scrappy remains of the **Temple of Athena Polias.** ⊠ *Mt. Smith* ☎ *No phone.*

As you travel south along the east coast, a strange sight meets you: the buildings of the **Thermes Kallitheas** (⊠ *10 km [6 mi] south of Rhodes town*) look as if they have been transplanted from Morocco. In fact, this mosaic-tile bath complex was built in 1929 by the Italians. As far back as the early 2nd century BC, area mineral springs were prized; the great physician Hippocrates of Kos extolled the springs for alleviating liver, kidney, and rheumatic ailments. Though the baths are no longer in use, you can visit the restored ornate **rotunda** (☎ *22410/65691* ⊕ *www.kalithea.gr* ⊠ *€2.50* ⊙ *Apr. –Oct., daily 8–8, Nov. –Mar., daily 8–3*), which houses exhibits. You can also swim on the nearby beach.

BEACHES

The beach at **Elli** (✉ *North of Old Town, near Rhodes Yacht Club*) has fine sand; an easy slope; chairs, umbrellas, and pedal boats for rent; showers; and plenty of sunbathing tourists. All of the coast around Rhodes town is developed, so you can reach some of the best beaches only through the hotels that occupy them.

WHERE TO STAY & EAT

$$$$ ★ ✗**Ta Kioupia.** In a group of humble farm buildings, Ta Kioupia is anything but modest. The white-stucco rooms with exposed ceiling beams exude rustic elegance: antique farm tools are on display, and linen tablecloths, fine china, and crystal set the tables. In summer you dine in an enclosed garden. Food is presented on large platters and you select what you fancy: pine-nut salad, *tiropita* (four-cheese pie), an eggplant dip that regulars say can't be beat, cheese-and-nut *bourekakia* (stuffed phyllo pastries), *kokorosouvlaki* (rooster kebab) ... the list goes on; the food is extraordinary in its variety and quality. ✉ *7 km (4½ mi) west of Rhodes town, Tris* ☎ *22410/91824* ⌂ *Reservations essential* ▭ *AE, DC, MC, V* ⊘ *Closed Sun. No lunch.*

$$$–$$$$ ★ ✗**Dinoris.** The great hall that holds Dinoris was built in AD 310 as a hospital and then converted into a stable for the Knights in 1530. The fish specialties and the spacious, classy setting lure appreciative and demanding clients, from the mayor to hotel owners and visiting VIPs. For appetizers, try the variety platter, which includes *psarokeftedakia* (fish balls made from a secret recipe) as well as mussels, shrimp, and lobster. Other special dishes are sea urchin salad and grilled calamari stuffed with cheese. In warm months, cool sea air drifts through the outdoor garden area enclosed by part of the city's walls. ✉ *Mouseou Sq. 14a* ☎ *22410/25824* ⌂ *Reservations essential* ▭ *AE, MC, V* ⊘ *Closed Jan.*

$$–$$$ ★ ✗**Alexis.** Continuing the tradition begun by his father in 1957, Yiannis Katsimprakis serves the very best seafood and speaks passionately of eating fish as though it's a lost art. Don't bother with the menu; just ask for suggestions and then savor every bite, whether you choose caviar, mussels in wine, smoked eel, or sea urchins. He even cooks up *porphyra*, the mollusk yielding the famous purple dye of the Byzantine emperors. A side dish might be sautéed squash with wild *glistrida* (purslane). If you visit during the off-season, try Katsimprakis's other restaurant, Alexis 4 Seasons (✉ *Aristotelous 33* ☎ *22410/70522 or 22410/70523*), open year-round. ✉ *Sokratous 18* ☎ *22410/29347* ▭ *AE, MC, V* ⊘ *Closed Nov.–Apr. No lunch.*

$$ ✗**Palia Istoria.** An old house with high ceilings and genteel murals gets a shot of youth with the innovative cooking of Chef Mihalis Boukouris. Tantalizing entrées include shrimp ouzo with orange juice, pork tenderloin in garlic-and-wine sauce, marinated anchovies (which Boukouris calls "Greek sushi"), and spearmint-spice *keftedes* (meatballs). Cleopatra's Salad, with arugula and dried fig, reigns over the extensive salad choices. With 100 Greek wines, a drink may be harder to select. Luckily the flambéed banana dessert wrapped in phyllo and topped with a portlike Komantaria liqueur means you never have to choose between dessert and digestif. Palia Istoria is a bit out of the way, in the

9

new town—about €3 by taxi from the Old Town. ⊠ *Odos Mitropoleos 108, Ayios Dimitrios* ☎22410/32421 ☱*MC, V* ☉*Closed Dec.–Apr. No lunch.*

$$$$ ⊡ **Rodos Park Suites.** Nestled in a green corner of the new town, Rhodes's most luxurious hotel is also one of its quietest retreats, with more staff than guests. The hotel's welcoming common spaces include a warm cigar-cognac lounge, a tranquil landscaped pool area, and a wood-and-stone spa. The guest rooms' large, square headboards are the signature pieces in minimalist rooms with carpet or wood floors and plasma TV screens. Suites have the added luxury of hot tubs. Stunning views sweep the Old Town, which is a few minutes' walk away. ⊠ *Odos Riga Fereous 12, 85100* ☎22410/89700 ⊕*www.rodospark.gr* ⬚*30 rooms, 30 suites* ♿*In-room: refrigerator. In-hotel: restaurant, bar, pool, spa* ☱*AE, DC, MC, V* ☜*BP.*

$$$ ⊡ **Marco Polo Mansion.** Entering this renovated 15th-century Ottoman
★ mansion is like stepping into another world. The trip begins in the maze of the Old Town's colorful Turkish section, which gives a flavor of what's to come inside. Individually styled rooms are painted in deep, warm colors, with Oriental rugs adorning the pitch-pine floors and soft embroidered cushions beckoning from low sofas. Most of the Eastern furnishings are unusual antiques, including the large beds draped with translucent canopies. It's no wonder this truly beautiful hotel has been featured in dozens of glossy magazines. Homemade marmalades and cakes are served at breakfast. ⊠ *Aghiou Fanouriou 40–42, 85100* ☎22410/25562 ⊕*www.marcopolomansion.gr* ⬚*10 rooms* ♿*In-room: no a/c (some), no phone, no TV, Wi-Fi. In hotel: restaurant, no elevator* ☱*AE, MC, V* ☉*Closed Nov.—Feb.* ☜*CP.*

$$$ ⊡ **S. Nikolis Hotel.** A charming old-town accommodation occupies
★ a restored house on the site of an ancient agora. The small but tidy rooms are enlivened by arches and other architectural details, and many have balconies overlooking a lovely large garden. Excellent service, including laundry, is provided by Sotiris and Marianne Nikolis with care. Breakfast is served on the roof terrace, which affords a view of a long stretch of the city walls. ⊠ *Odos Ippodamou 61, 85100* ☎22410/34561 ☷22410/32034 ⊕*www.s-nikolis.gr* ⬚*10 rooms, 4 suites* ♿*In-room: kitchen (some), refrigerator. In-hotel: bar, no elevator, public Wi-Fi* ☱*AE, MC, V* ☜*CP.*

$ ⊡ **Hotel Andreas.** The owners of this old-town pension, set in a rather ramshackle 15th-century house, say it once belonged to a Turkish vizier and that most of the rooms were bedrooms for his wives. You can guess what the status was of each occupant—some rooms are lovely and have sea views, others are tiny with unconnected (though still private) bathrooms. All are decorated individually with soft washes of color on stucco walls, romantic bed canopies, international folk art, and tapestry bedspreads. Breakfast is €6–€8. You eat on the huge, plant-filled terrace with a magical view of the Old Town. ⊠ *Omirou 28D, 85100* ☎22410/34156 ☷22410/74285 ⊕*www.hotelandreas.com* ⬚*11 rooms* ♿*In-room: no a/c (some), no TV (some). In-hotel: no elevator, airport shuttle* ☱*AE, MC, V.*

¢ ☷**Pension Sofia.**The Old Town is full of rooms to rent, but budget-priced Sofia's is bright, pleasant, and framed by trailing jasmine; each room has a little bath. ✉*Aristofanous 27, 85100* ☎*22410/36181 or 22410/75166* ⊕*www.sofia-pension.gr* ⇔*9 rooms* ⚏*In-room: no phone, kitchen (some). In-hotel: no elevator* ▭*No credit cards.*

NIGHTLIFE & THE ARTS

BARS &
DISCOS

Sophisticated Greeks have created a stylish nightlife using the medieval buildings and flower-filled courtyards of the Old Town. Some bars and cafés here are open all day for drinks, and many—often those with beautiful medieval interiors—stay open most of the year. Nighttime-only spots in the Old Town open up around 10 PM and close around 3 or 4 AM. The action centers around narrow, pebble-paved Miltiadou street, where seats spill out from trendy bars set in stone buildings. Another hot spot is Arionos Square. Those wanting to venture to the new town's throbbing discos should head to Orfanidou street, where bronzed, scantily clad tourists gyrate 'til dawn at massive clubs.

Bar-café **Baduz** (✉*Arionos Sq.* ☎69366/74466) plays a range of international music and is decorated with old marble basins. *Rembetika* (acoustic music, with blueslike lyrics, played on the bouzouki) fans head to tiny **Cafe Chantant** (✉*Dimokritou 3* ☎22410/32277) for live music. The biggest area disco is the three-stage complex **Colorado** (✉*Orfanidou and Akti Miaouli, new town* ☎22410/75120) with live rock, as well as dance hits and R&B.

Hammam (✉*Aischylou 26* ☎22410/33242), in a 14th-century bath-house, hosts live Greek bands. Mellow **Selini** (✉*Evripidou 4B* ☎*No phone*) has frescoes of the moon, art exhibits, cushioned outdoor benches, and jazz. The candlelit **Theatro** (✉*Miltiadou 2* ☎22410/76973) plays funk and electronic music and even hosts live theater events in the off-season.

ENTERTAINMENT

You must show your passport to get into Rhodes's **casino** (✉*Hotel Grande Albergo Delle Rose, Papanikolaou 4, new town* ☎22410/97500 ⊕*www.casinorodos.gr*). The entry fee is €15 but drinks are free. They're open 24 hours a day, every day, and you have to be at least 23 years old to play.

PERFORMANCES

The **Nelly Dimoglou Folk Dance Theatre** (✉*Andronikou 7, behind Turkish baths, Old Town* ☎22410/20157) has kept alive the tradition of Greek dance since 1971, with strict adherence to authentic detail in costume and performance. From June until October, performances (€12) are held Monday, Wednesday, and Friday at 9:20 PM. The theater also gives dance lessons.

☾ From May through October the **sound-and-light** show (✉*Grounds of Palace of the Grand Masters in Ippoton, Old Town* ☎22410/21922 ⊕*www.hellenicfestival.gr*) tells the story of the Turkish siege. English-language performances are Monday, Wednesday, and Friday at 9:15 PM; Tuesday, Thursday, and Saturday at 11:15 PM. In September and October, performances start one hour earlier; the cost is €7; free for children up to 10 years old.

SPORTS & THE OUTDOORS

For €50 **Dive Med College** (✉ *Lissavonas 33, Rodini* ☎*22410/61115* ⊕*www.divemedcollege.com*) takes you by boat to Thermes Kallithea and after a 45-minute theory lesson and practice in shallow water, you descend for a 20-minute dive. They also have dives at Ladiko, 15 km (9 mi) south of Rhodes town.

You can rent bicycles, including mountain bikes and racing bikes, as well as ATVs and motor scooters, from **Margaritis Rent a Moto** (✉*Iannou Kazouli 23* ☎*22410/37420*).

SHOPPING

In Rhodes town you can buy good copies of Lindos ware, a delicate pottery decorated with green and red floral motifs. The Old Town's shopping area, on Sokratous, is lined with boutiques selling furs, jewelry, and other high-ticket items. The owner of **Astero Antiques** (✉*Ayiou Fanouriou 4, off Sokratous* ☎*22410/34753*) travels throughout Greece each winter to fill his shop.

EPTA PIGES ΕΠΤΑ ΠΗΓΕΣ

30 km (19 mi) south of Rhodes town.

Seven Springs, or Epta Piges, is a deeply shaded glen watered by mountain springs. In the woods around the springs, imported peacocks flaunt their plumage. The waters are channeled through a 164-yard-long tunnel, which you can walk through, emerging at the edge of a cascading dam and a small man-made lake where you can swim. Here an enterprising local shepherd began serving simple fare in 1945, and his sideline turned into the busy taverna and tourist site of today. Despite its many visitors, Seven Springs' beauty remains unspoiled. To get here, turn right on the inland road near Kolymbia and follow signs.

WHERE TO EAT

$ ╳**Epta Piges.** The family-run taverna spreads out below the plane and pine trees, directly overlooking the springs. There's always charcoal-grill lamb or fish on the menu, and starters include dishes like *pitaroudia* (fried potato balls) or thin fried zucchini and eggplant. ☎*22410/56259* ▤*AE, DC, MC, V* ⊘*Closed Nov.–Mar.*

LINDOS ΛΙΝΔΟΣ

19 km (12 mi) southwest of Epta Piges, 48 km (30 mi) southwest of Rhodes town.

Lindos, cradled between two harbors, had a particular importance in antiquity. Before the existence of Rhodes town, it was the island's principal maritime center. Lindos possessed a revered sanctuary, consecrated to Athena, whose cult probably succeeded that of a pre-Hellenic divinity named Lindia; the sanctuary was dedicated to Athena Lindia. By the 6th century BC, an impressive temple dominated the settlement, and after the foundation of Rhodes, the Lindians set up a *propylaia* (monumental entrance gate) on the model of that in Athens. In the mid-4th century BC, the temple was destroyed by fire and almost immediately rebuilt, with a new wooden statue of the goddess covered by gold leaf, and with arms, head, and legs of marble or ivory. Lindos prospered into Roman times, during the Middle Ages, and under the Knights of St. John. Only at the beginning of the 19th century did the age-old shipping activity cease.

> **EASY AS 1-2-3**
>
> Most of Lindos's mazelike streets don't have conventional names or addresses; instead, buildings are numbered, from 1 through about 500. Lower numbers are on the north side of town, higher numbers on the south.

Lindos is remarkably well preserved, and many 15th-century houses are still in use. Everywhere are examples of the Crusader architecture you saw in Rhodes town: substantial houses of finely cut Lindos limestone, with windows crowned by elaborate arches. Many floors are paved with black-and-white pebble mosaics. Intermixed with these Crusader buildings are whitewashed, Geometric, Cycladic-style houses with square, blue-shuttered windows.

Like Rhodes town, Lindos is enchanting off-season but can get unbearably crowded otherwise, since pilgrims make the trek from Rhodes town daily. The main street is lined with shops selling clothes and trinkets, and since the streets are medieval in their narrowness and twisting course, the passage slows to a snail's pace. Spend a night in Lindos to enjoy its beauties after the day-trippers leave. Only pedestrians and donkeys are allowed in Lindos because the town's narrow alleys are not wide enough for vehicles. If you're arriving by car, park in the lot above town and walk the 10 minutes down (about 1,200 feet) to Lindos.

The **Church of the Panayia** is a graceful building with a beautiful bell tower. The body of the church probably antedates the Knights, although the bell tower bears their arms with the dates 1484–90. The interior has frescoes painted in 1779 by Gregory of Symi. ⊠ *Off main square* ☎ *No phone* ⊘ *May–Oct., daily 9–2 and 5–9; Nov.–Mar., call the number posted on the church to have the door unlocked.*

Fodor's Choice ★ For about €5, you can hire a donkey for the 15-minute climb from the modern town up to the **Acropolis of Lindos.** The winding path leads past a gauntlet of Lindian women who spread out their lace and embroidery like fresh laundry over the rocks. The final approach ascends a steep flight of stairs, past a marvelous 2nd-century BC **relief** of the prow of a Lindian ship, carved into the rock.

The entrance to the Acropolis takes you through the **medieval castle,** with the Byzantine **Chapel of St. John** on the next level above. On the **upper terraces** are the remains of the elaborate **porticoes** and **stoas.** As is the case with Sounion, on the mainland southeast of Athens, the site and temple command an immense sweep of sea, making a powerful statement on behalf of the deity and city to which they belonged; the lofty white columns on the summit must have presented a magnificent picture. The main portico had 42 Doric columns, at the center of which an opening led to the staircase up to the **propylaia.** The temple at the very top is surprisingly modest, given the drama of the approach. As was common in the 4th century BC, both the front and the rear are flanked by four Doric columns. Numerous inscribed statue bases were found all over the summit, attesting in many cases to the work of Lindian sculptors, who were clearly second to none. ⊠ *Above new town* ☎ *22440/31258* 🖅 *€6* ⊘ *May–Oct., Tues.–Sun. 8:30–7, Mon. 12:30–7; Nov.–Apr., Tues.–Sun. 8:30–2:40.*

Escape the crowds by trekking to the **Tomb of Kleoboulos,** which archaeologists say is incorrectly named after Lindos's early tyrant Kleoboulos; it's actually the final resting place of a wealthy family of the 1st to 2nd century BC. After about 3 km (2 mi), a 30-minute scenic walk, you encounter the small, rounded stone tomb. You can peer inside and see the candle marks, which testify to its later use as the church of St. Emilianos. ⊠ *Look for sign at parking lot above main square. Follow dirt path along hill on opposite side of bay from Acropolis* ☎ *No phone.*

WHERE TO STAY & EAT

In Lindos it's possible through travel agents to rent **rooms** in many of the traditional homes that have mosaic courtyards, gardens, and sea views; an entire house may even be for rent. *Savaidis Travel* ☎ *22440/31347* ⊕ *www.savaidis-travel.gr.; Lindos Sun Tours* ☎ *22440/31333* ⊕ *www.lindosuntours.gr.*

$$–$$$ ✗**Mavrikos.** The secret of this longtime favorite is an elegant, perfect simplicity. Seemingly straightforward dishes, such as sea-urchin salad, fried *manouri* cheese with basil and pine nuts, swordfish in caper sauce, and lobster risotto, become transcendent with the magic touch of third-generation chef Dimitris Mavrikos. He combines the freshest ingredients with classical training and an abiding love for the best of Greek village cuisine. ⊠ *Main square* ☎ *22440/31232* ⊟ *MC, V* ⊘ *Closed Nov.–Mar.*

$$$$ ✗🏨**Melenos Hotel.** Michalis Melenos worked for years to make this
★   12-room stone villa overlooking Lindos bay into a truly special boutique hotel. Each room has a built-in, traditional Lindian village bed with hand-carved woodwork and antique furnishings brought from throughout Greece and Turkey. Colorful Turkish fountains splash throughout the grounds. A tranquil terrace, bathed by lamplight in evening, is the stage for the restaurant's($$$–$$$$) inspired Mediterranean cuisine. Entrées include fish with citrus or herbs, and filet mignon in wine sauce. Parents, take note: a fee of €65 per night applies to children ages 2 to 12 staying in the hotel. If you didn't bring along your computer, laptops are available upon request. ⊠ *At edge of Lindos, on path to Acropolis, 85107* ☎ *22440/32222* 🖅 *22440/31720* ⊕ *www.melenoslindos.com* ⊄ *12 suites* ⌂ *In-room: refrigerator, Ethernet. In-hotel: restaurant, no elevator, public Wi-Fi* ⊟ *AE, MC, V* ⫪⊡*BP.*

¢   🏨**Pension Electra.** Linger on the spacious terrace or down in the blossoming garden of this decades-old pension with high ceilings and several levels. Many rooms have sea views, and you can whip up your own breakfasts in one of two large kitchens. ⊠ *No. 66, 85107*

☎22440/31266 or 69735/15609 📞7 rooms, 1 with bath in the hall ☉In-room: no phone, refrigerator, no TV. In hotel: no elevator ▭No credit cards.

NIGHTLIFE

Most of Lindos's bars cater to a young, hard-drinking crowd; few are without a television showing soccer. Many are open year-round to serve the locals. The **Captain's House** (✉Akropoleos 243 ☎22440/31235), set, naturally, in an old captain's house with a courtyard, plays lounge, ethnic, and Greek music. **Gelo Blu** (✉Near Theotokou Church ☎22440/31761), run by the owners of Mavrikos, serves homemade ice cream by day and drinks day and night in its cool, blue-cushioned interior and pebbled courtyard, and on its rooftop terrace. Relaxed **Rainbird** (✉On road to Pallas beach ☎22440/32169) is open for coffee and drinks all day and has a romantic sea-view terrace.

GENNADI & THE SOUTH COAST ΓΕΝΝΑΔΙ & ΝΟΤΙΑ ΠΑΡΑΛΙΑ

20 km (12½ mi) south of Lindos, 68 km (42 mi) south of Rhodes town.

The area south of Lindos, with fewer beaches and less-fertile soil, is less traveled than the stretch to its north. Though development is increasing, the still-pretty and inexpensive coastal village of Gennadi has pensions, rooms for rent, and a handful of tavernas, nightclubs, and DJ-hosted beach parties.

BEACHES

Lachania beach begins a mile north of Gennadi and stretches uninterrupted for several miles; drive alongside until you come to a secluded spot. Past Lachania is a quiet beach, **Plimiri** (✉10 km [6 mi] south of Gennadi), which is reached by following a sign for Taverna Plimiri from the main road. If you're on a quest for the perfect strand and are armed with four-wheel-drive and a good map, aim for the pristine, cedar-lined beach at **Ayios Georgios**—though it will take some doing. (Rental-car companies discourage you from taking regular cars on the poor road.) If you dare, here's how to get there: About 4 km (2½ mi) past Plimiri, you can see the abandoned monastery of Ayios Pavlos. Just before the monastery, turn left down the cypress-lined dirt road. Follow the route about 8 km (5 mi) to a church, where the road forks. Keep going straight to reach Ayios Georgios, one of Rhodes's loveliest secret spots.

MONOLITHOS TO KAMEIROS ΜΟΝΟΛΙΘΟΣ & ΚΑΜΕΙΡΟΣ

28 km (17 mi) northwest of Gennadi, 74 km (46 mi) southwest of Rhodes town.

Rhodes's west coast is more forested, with fewer good beaches than its east coast, but if you're looking to get away from the hordes, it sylvan scenery, august ruins, and vineyards make it worth the trips.

The medieval fortress of **Monolithos**—so named for the jutting, 750-foot monolith on which it is built—rises above a fairy-tale landscape of deep-green forests and sharp cliffs plunging into the sea. Inside the fortress there is a chapel, and the ramparts provide magnificent views of Rhodes's emerald inland and the island of Halki. ✉ *Take western road from middle of Monolithos village; near hairpin turn there's a short path up to fortress* ☎ *No phone* 💲 *Free.*

Siana (✉ *5 km [3 mi] northeast of Monolithos*) perches above a vast, fertile valley and sits in the shadow of a rock outcropping crowned with the ruin of a castle. The small town is known for souma (which resembles a grape-flavored schnapps); look for roadside stands selling the intoxicant.

For another taste of the town, don't pass through without a stop at **Manos** (✉ *Past town church, on main road* ☎ *22460/61209* 🕐 *Feb.– Nov. 15, 7 AM–10 PM*) or one of several other shops along the street that sell Siana's renowned honey and walnuts.

The **Kastello,** a fortress built by the Knights in the late 15th century, is an impressive ruin, situated high above the sea with good views in every direction. ✉ *13 km (8 mi) northeast of Siana* ☎ *No phone* 💲 *Free.*

EN ROUTE Beyond Siana, the road continues on a high ridge through thick pine forests, which carpet the precipitous slopes dropping toward the sea. To the east looms the bare, stony massif of Mt. Ataviros, Rhodes's highest peak, at 3,986 feet. If you follow the road inland rather than continue north along the coast toward Kritinia, you climb the flanks of the mountains to the traditional, arbor-filled village of Embonas, in Rhodes's richest wine country.

The well-respected **Emery Winery** makes many good wines, and occasionally, a few outstanding ones. Tastings are free. ✉ *Embonas* ☎ *22460/41208* 🌐 *www.emery.gr* 🕐 *Weekdays 8–4:30.*

As you continue east you come into the landscape that, in medieval times, earned Rhodes the moniker "emerald of the Mediterranean." The exquisite drive up Mt. Profitis Ilias, overlooking dark-green trees carpeting mountains that plunge into the sea, is one of the loveliest passages of scenery in Greece. Near the 2,200-foot-high summit is the small Church of Profitis Ilias. From the church, you can follow the well-trodden path down to the village of Salakos. It's about a 45-minute walk through the woods.

The site of classical **Kameiros** (23 km [14 mi] northeast of Siana) is one of the three ancient cities of Rhodes. The apparently unfortified ruins, excavated by the Italians in 1929, lie on a slope above the sea. Most of what is visible today dates to the classical period and later, including impressive remains of the early-Hellenistic period. The guards say that the hill hides many more ruins. ✉ *Off main Rhodes road, turn at sign for Ancient Kameiros* ☎ *22410/40037* 🌐 *www.culture.gr* 💲 *€4* 🕐 *Tues.–Sun. 8:30–2:40.*

PETALOUDES & IALYSSOS ΠΕΤΑΛΟΥΔΕΣ & ΙΑΛΥΣΟΣ

★ *22 km (14 mi) east of Kameiros, 25 km (16 mi) southwest of Rhodes town.*

The Valley of the Butterflies, Petaloudes, lives up to its name, especially in July and August. In summer the *callimorpha quadripunctaria,* actually a moth species, cluster by the thousands around the low bushes of the pungent storax plant, which grows all over the area. Through the years their number has diminished, partly owing to busloads of tourists clapping hands to see them fly up in dense clouds. Don't agitate the butterflies. Access to the valley is through a main road and admission booth and involves a walk up an idyllic trail by a stream in the woods. ✉*Turn off the coastal road south and follow signs leading to the site with its own parking lot* ☎*22410/81801* ✈*€5* ☉*Late Apr.–Oct., daily 8–7.*

SYMI ΣΥΜΗ

The island of Symi, 45 km (27 mi) north of Rhodes, is an enchanting place, with its star attraction being Chorio, a 19th-century town of neoclassical mansions. The island has few beaches and almost no flat land, so it is not attractive to developers. As a result, quiet Symi provides a peaceful retreat for travelers, who tend to fall in love with the island on their first visit and return year after year.

Nireus, the ancient king of Symi, who sailed with three vessels to assist the Greeks at Troy, is mentioned in Homer. Symi was later part of the Dorian Hexapolis dominated by Rhodes, and it remained under Rhodian dominance throughout the Roman and Byzantine periods. The island has good natural harbors, and the nearby coast of Asia Minor provided plentiful timber for the Symiotes, who were shipbuilders, fearless seafarers and sponge divers, and rich and successful merchants. Under the Ottomans their harbor was proclaimed a free port and attracted the trade of the entire region. Witness to their prosperity are the neoclassical mansions that line the harbor and towns. The Symiotes' continuous travel and trade and their frequent contact with Europe led them to incorporate foreign elements in their furnishings, clothes, and cultural life. At first they lived in Chorio, high on the hillside above the port, and in the second half of the 19th century spread down to the seaside at Yialos. There were some 20,000 inhabitants at this acme, but under the Italian occupation at the end of the Italo-Turkish war in 1912, the island declined; the Symiotes lost their holdings in Asia Minor and were unable to convert their fleets to steam. Many emigrated to work elsewhere, and now there are just a few thousand inhabitants in Chorio and Yialos. Symi is an hour ride by hydrofoil from Rhodes town.

9

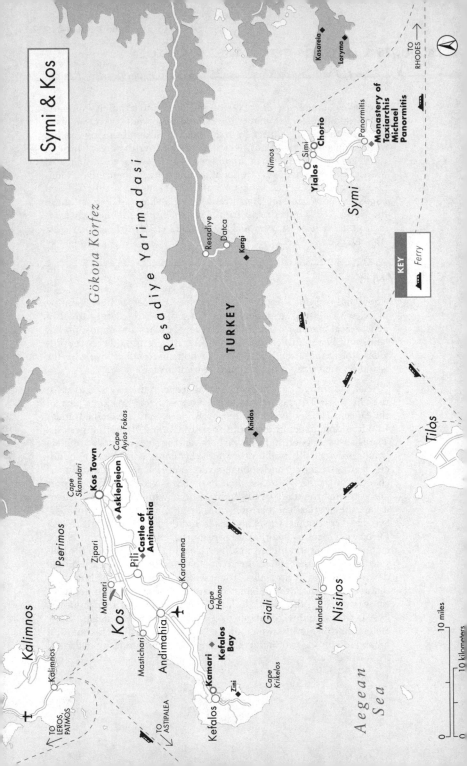

Symi & Kos

Gökova Körfez

Resadiye Yarimadasi

TURKEY

Resadiye
Datca
Kargi

Knidos

Kasarela
Loryma

TO
RHODES →

Nimos

Simi
Yialos
Chorio

Panormitis
**Monastery of
Taxiarchis
Michael
Panormitis**

Symi

KEY
Ferry

Tilos

Kalimnos

Pserimos

Cape
Skansdari

Kos Town
Asklepieion
Zipari

Pili
**Castle of
Antimachia**

Cape
Ayios Fokas

Marmari

Kardamena

Mastichari

Kos

Andimahia

Cape
Helona

Giali

Kamari
Zini
**Kefalos
Bay**

Cape
Krikelos

Kefalos

Cape

Mandraki

Nisiros

*Aegean
Sea*

TO
LEROS,
PATMOS

TO
ASTIPALEA

10 miles
10 kilometers
0
0

YIALOS ΓΙΑΛΟΣ

45 km (27 mi) north of Rhodes.

As the boat from Rhodes to Symi rounds the last of many rocky barren spurs, the port of Yialos, at the back of a deep, narrow harbor, comes into view. The shore is lined with mansions whose ground floors have been converted to cafés with waterside terraces perfect for whiling away lazy hours.

The **Church of Ayhios Ioannis** (⊠*Near center of Yialos village*), built in 1838, incorporates in its walls fragments of ancient blocks from a temple that apparently stood on this site and is surrounded by a plaza paved in an intricate mosaic, fashioned from inlaid pebbles.

Sponge-diving tools, model ships, 19th-century navigation tools, and anchors fill the teeny **Symi Naval Museum.** It's hard to miss the ornamental blue-and-yellow building. The sea memorabilia within gives a good taste of life in Symi in the 19th and early 20th centuries. ⊠*Yialos waterfront* 🖅€2 ⊙*Tues.–Sun. 10–2.*

WHERE TO STAY & EAT

$$$–$$$$ ✕**Mylopetra.** A delightfully converted old flour mill, Mylopetra is a feast
★ for the eyes: decorations include an ancient tomb embedded in glass beneath the floor. German couple Hans and Eva Sworoski painstakingly oversaw the transition of this extraordinary restaurant and tend to the excellent cooking and gracious service. The menu changes daily, but expect inventive sauces, homemade pasta married with anything from spinach to rabbit to salmon, and abundant seafood and meat (often game) options. ⊠*Behind church on the backstreet* 🖀22460/72333 ♨*Reservations essential* ▤*MC, V* ⊙*Closed mid-Oct.–Apr.*

¢–$ ✕**Trawlers.** Anna Kanli's home cooking is behind one of Yialos's most-successful, inexpensive tavernas. She prepares traditional meat and fish dishes, not to mention vegetarian moussaka. Weather permitting, you can also dine in a pretty square a few steps from the port. ⊠*Economou Sq., harbor front* 🖀22460/71411 ▤*MC, V* ⊙*Closed Nov.–Apr.*

$$$ 🏨**Aliki Hotel.** A three-story, 1895 mansion on the waterfront houses
★ this attractive hotel. Each of the rooms is different, but all are furnished with a tasteful mix of antiques and newer pieces. The best rooms, of course, are those that face the water. The hotel's lobby has a high, colorful ceiling and its rooftop, an enviable port view. In good weather breakfast is served on a waterside terrace that doubles as a bar in the evening. ⊠*Yialos waterfront, 85600* 🖀22460/71665 🖷22460/71655 ⊕*www.hotelaliki.gr* ➾*13 rooms, 2 suites, 2 apartments (in separate building behind hotel)* ♿*In-room: no TV. In-hotel: bar, no elevator* ▤*AE, DC, MC, V* ⊙*BP.*

BEACHES

One reason Symi's beaches are so pristine is that almost none are reachable by car. From the main harbor at Yialos, boats leave every half hour between 10:30 AM and 12:30 PM to the beautiful beaches of **Aghia Marina, Aghios Nikolas, Aghios Giorgos,** and **Nanou** bay. Return trips run

4–6 PM. The round-trips cost €5–€10. In summer, there are also small boats for hire from the clock tower.

For a swim near Yialos, you can go to the little strip of beach beyond the **Yialos** harbor—follow the road past the bell tower and the Aliki Hotel and you come to a seaside taverna that rents umbrellas and beach chairs. If you continue walking on the same road for about 3 km (2 mi), you come to the pine-shaded beach at **Niborios** bay, where there is another taverna.

FESTIVAL

The **Symi Festival** brings free dance, music, theater performances, and cinema screenings to the island every year from July through September. Most events take place in the main harbor square in Yialos, but some are scheduled in other places around the island. A schedule of events is posted at the square, and programs can be found at local shops, travel agents, and the town hall.

CHORIO ΧΩΡΙΟ

Fodor'sChoice
★

1 km (½ mi) east of Yialos.

It's a 10-minute walk from the main harbor of Yialos up to the hilltop town of Chorio, along a staircase of some 400 steps, known as Kali Strata. There is also a road that can be traveled in one of the island's few taxis or by bus, which makes a circuit with stops at the harbor in Yialos, Chorio, and the seaside community of Pedi. The Kali Strata is flanked by elegant neoclassical houses with elaborate stonework, lavish pediments, and intricate wrought-iron balconies. Just before the top of the stairs (and the welcome little Kali Strata bar), a line of windmills crowns the hill of **Noulia.** Most of Chorio's many churches date to the 18th and 19th centuries, and many are ornamented with richly decorated iconostases and ornate bell towers. Donkeys are often used to carry materials through the narrow streets for the town's steady construction and renovation work.

The collection at the **Archaeological Museum** displays Hellenistic and Roman sculptures and inscriptions as well as more-recent carvings, icons, costumes, and handicrafts. ⊠*Follow signs from central square to Lieni neighborhood* ☎22460/71114 ☜€2 ⊗*Tues.–Sun. 8–2:30.*

The **kastro** (*castle* ⊠*At top of town, in ancient acropolis*) incorporates fragments of Symi's history in its walls. A church and several teeny chapels dominate the area with only a few remnants of the castle walls. The view from here takes in the village of Pedi as well as both Chorio and Yialos.

WHERE TO STAY & EAT

$–$$ ✗**Georgio and Maria's Taverna.** Meals at this simple Chorio taverna, which is as popular with locals as it is with tourists, are served in a high-ceilinged, whitewashed dining room or on a terrace that is partially shaded by a grape arbor and affords wonderful views over the sea and surrounding hills. Fish is a specialty, and simply prepared *mezedes* (small dishes), such as roasted peppers topped with feta cheese and fried zucchini, can constitute a delicious meal in themselves. If you're lucky, one of the neighbors will stroll in with instrument in hand to provide an impromptu serenade. ⊠*Off main square* ☎*22460/71984* ⊟*AE, MC, V.*

$ 🖭**Hotel Fiona.** This bright, cheerful hotel is perched on the hillside in ★ Chorio, with splendid views. Just about all of the large rooms, with spotless white-tile floors and attractive blue-painted furnishings and pastel fabrics, have a sea-facing balcony. Breakfast, with yogurt and marmalade, is served in the breezy, attractive lobby lounge or on a cozy balcony. ⊠*Near main square* ☎*22460/72088* ⤙*14 rooms, 3 studios* ⚲*In-room: no TV. In-hotel: bar, no elevator* ⊟*No credit cards* ☺*Closed Nov.–Apr.* ⭕*CP.*

$ 🖭**Village Hotel.** Grand architecture meets quaint surroundings in this traditional neoclassical mansion on a small lane. The hotel has good views in all directions ... and requires a steep climb home after a morning coffee in the port. All the rooms open onto a balcony or terrace and surround an attractive garden. ⊠*Off main square* ☎*22460/71800* 🖷*22460/71802* ⤙*17 rooms* ⚲*In-room: refrigerator, no TV. In-hotel: bar, no elevator, parking (no fee)* ⊟*MC, V* ☺*Closed Nov.–Apr.* ⭕*CP.*

MONASTERY OF TAXIARCHIS MICHAEL PANORMITIS
ΜΟΝΗ ΤΑΞΙΑΡΧΗ ΜΙΧΑΗΛ ΠΑΝΟΡΜΙΤΗ

7 km (4½ mi) south of Chorio.

Fodor$Choice The main reason to venture to the atypically green, pine-covered hills ★ surrounding the little gulf of Panormitis is to visit the Monastery of Taxiarchis Michael Panormitis, dedicated to Symi's patron saint, the protector of sailors. The site's entrance is surmounted by an elaborate **bell tower,** of the multilevel wedding-cake variety on display in Yialos and Chorio. In the **courtyard,** which is surrounded by a vaulted stoa, a black-and-white pebble mosaic adorns the floor. The interior of the **church,** entirely frescoed in the 18th century, contains a marvelously ornate wooden iconostasis, flanked by a heroic-size 18th-century representation of Michael, all but his face covered with silver. There are two small **museums** devoted to Byzantine and folk art. The Byzantine includes a collection of votive offerings, including ship models, gifts, and bottles with notes containing wishes and money in them, which, according to local lore, travel to Symi on their own after having been thrown into the sea. A trip to the monastery can be accompanied by a refreshing swim at the designated edges of the deep-blue harbor. There's bus service twice a day from Yialos, which passes through Chorio, and boats from Yialos and Rhodes daily.

If a day trip isn't enough for you, the monastery, which no longer has monks but does have two clergy people, along with a supermarket, bakery, and more, rents 60 spartan rooms (☎22460/72414) with kitchens and private baths for about €20. Though the price doesn't include a towel or air-conditioning and there are insects (some rather

9

large), the spiritual aspect makes for an enriching experience. ⊠ *Symi's south side, at harbor* ☎ *22460/71581* ⊕ *www.impsymis.gr* ⊠ *Monastery free; museums €1.50* ⊙ *Monastery: daily 7–8; museums: Apr. –Oct. 8:30–1 and 3–4, Nov. –Apr. by appointment.*

KOS ΚΩΣ

The island of Kos, the third largest in the Dodecanese, is certainly one of the most beautiful, with verdant fields and tree-clad mountains, surrounded by miles of sandy beach. Its highest peak, part of a small mountain range in the northeast, is less than 2,800 feet. All this beauty has not gone unnoticed, of course, and Kos undeniably suffers from the effects of mass tourism: its beaches are often crowded, most of its seaside towns have been recklessly overdeveloped, and the main town is noisy and busy between June and September.

In Mycenaean times and during the Archaic period, the island prospered. In the 6th century BC it was conquered by the Persians but later joined the Delian League, supporting Athens against Sparta in the Peloponnesian War. Kos was invaded and destroyed by the Spartan fleet, ruled by Alexander and various of his successors, and has twice been devastated by earthquakes. Nevertheless, the city and the economy flourished, as did the arts and sciences. The painter Apelles, the Michelangelo of his time, came from Kos, as did Hippocrates, father of modern medicine. Under the Roman Empire, the island's Asklepieion and its renowned healing center drew emperors and ordinary citizens alike. The Knights of St. John arrived in 1315 and ruled for the next two centuries, until they were replaced by the Ottomans. In 1912 the Italians took over, and in 1947 the island was united with Greece.

KOS TOWN ΚΩΣ (ΠΟΛΗ)

92 km (57 mi) north of Rhodes.

The modern town lies on a flat plain encircling a spacious harbor called Mandraki and is a pleasant assemblage of low-lying buildings and shady lanes. The fortress, which crowns its west side, where Hippocrates is supposed to have taught in the shade of a large plane tree, is a good place to begin your exploration of Kos town. On one side of little Platanou Square, named after the tree, stands the graceful loggia, actually a mosque, built in 1786.

The **Castle of the Knights,** built mostly in the 15th century and full of ancient blocks from its Greek and Roman predecessors, is a repository of fragments of ancient inscriptions, funerary monuments, and other sculptural material. A walk around the walls affords good views over the town, whose flat skyline is pierced by a few remaining minarets and many palm trees. ⊠ *Over bridge from Platanou Sq.* ☎ *22420/27927* ⊠ *€3* ⊙ *Tues.–Sun. 8:30–2:30.*

Excavations by Italian and Greek archaeologists have revealed ancient **agora and harbor ruins** (⊠ *Over bridge from Platanou Sq., behind Castle* *of the Knights*) that date from the 4th century BC through Roman times. Remnants include parts of the walls of the old city, of a Hellenistic stoa, and of temples dedicated to Aphrodite and Hercules. The ruins, which are not fenced, blend charmingly into the fabric of the modern city; they are a shortcut for people on their way to work, a place to sit and chat, and an outdoor playroom for children. In spring the site is covered with brightly colored flowers, which nicely frame the ancient gray-and-white marble blocks tumbled in every direction.

★ The **Archaeological Museum** contains extremely important examples of Hellenistic and Roman sculpture by Koan artists. Among the treasures are a renowned statue of Hippocrates; a group of sculptures from various Roman phases, all discovered in the House of the Europa Mosaic; and a remarkable series of Hellenistic draped female statues mainly from the Sanctuary of Demeter at Kyparissi and the Odeon. ⊠*Eleftherias Sq., west of agora through gate leading to Platanou Sq.* ☎*22420/28326* ⊡*€3* ۩*Tues.–Sun. 8–6, Nov.–Mar., and April–late Oct. 8–2:30.*

The **west excavations** (⊠*Southwest of agora and harbor ruins*) have uncovered a portion of one of the main Roman streets with many houses, including the **House of the Europa Mosaic.** Part of the **Roman baths** (near main Roman street), it has been converted into a basilica. The **gymnasium,** distinguished by its partly reconstructed colonnade, and the so-called **Nymphaion,** a lavish public latrine that has been restored, are also of interest. These excavations are always open, with free access.

BEACHES

If you must get wet but can't leave Kos town, try the narrow pebble strip of beach immediately south of the main harbor. **Tingaki** (⊠*On north coast, 13 km [8 mi] west of Kos town*) has pretty, sandy, but heavily developed resort beaches. At **Mastichari** (⊠*On north coast, 32 km [20 mi] west of Kos town*) there's a wide sand beach, tavernas, rooms for rent, and a pier where boats sail on day trips to the uncrowded islet of Pserimos.

WHERE TO STAY & EAT

$$–$$$ ✕ **Petrino.** Greek-Canadian brothers Mike and George Gerovasilis have created a calm oasis a few streets in from the hustle and bustle of Kos harbor. A 150-year-old stone house provides cozy dining in cool months, and in summer, tables pepper a garden full of private nooks, fountains, and gentle music. The enormous menu lists Greek recipes, like zucchini pancakes and liver with oregano, side-by-side with European classics like chateaubriand. Servings are generous; the sauces, rich. Actor Tom Hanks has been among the VIP guests. ⊠*Ioannou Theologou Sq.* ☎*22420/27251* ▭*AE, DC, MC, V.*

$$–$$$ ✕ **To Limanaki.** Buttery Symi shrimp, tender calamari, and lightly fried *atherines* (tiny smelt fish) stand out among the many seafood choices. If fish isn't your thing, the menu also has all the Greek basics. The family-run taverna is even open for bacon and eggs in the morning. On one side of the restaurant is a buzzing street; on the other, silent

ruins and the chapel of St. Ann. ⊠ *Odos Megalou Alexandrou 11*
☎ *22420/21153* ⊟ *AE, D, DC, MC, V.*

$$$$ 🏨 **Grecotel Kos Imperial.** On a gentle slope over the Aegean, this spa
★ resort has a private beach as well as seawater and freshwater pools
and artificial rivers and lagoons. Indoors, there are glimmering glass-
tile hydrotherapy pools, dozens of spa treatments, and many guest
rooms with private hot tubs and pools. Grecotel's signature style of
simple but beautifully designed luxury is everywhere in evidence, as in
the airy rooms with bamboo furniture, sheer white linen, and sweeping blue sea views. ⊠ *4 km (2½ mi) east of Kos town, 85300Psalidi*
☎ *22420/58000* 🖶 *22420/25192* ⊕ *www.grecotel.com* ➴ *177 rooms,*
207 bungalows (including 55 suites) ♿ *In-room: refrigerator. In-hotel:*
4 restaurants, pools, spa, public Wi-Fi ⊟ *AE, DC, MC, V* ⊚⏐*BP.*

¢ 🏨 **Hotel Afendoulis.** Simple and friendly, the plain, whitewashed rooms
with dark-wood furniture are spotless and of far better quality than
most in this price range; they're also far enough off the main road, so
it stays quiet at night. You can walk to most places in Kos town
from here. Enjoy breakfast, which is extra, in the open marble lobby.
⊠ *Evripilou 1, 85300* ☎ *22420/25321* 🖶 *22420/25797* ➴ *20 rooms*
♿ *In-hotel: bar, public Wi-Fi* ⊟ *MC, V.*

NIGHTLIFE

Things start cooking before 7 PM and in many cases roar on past 7 AM
on Akti Koundourioti and in the nearby Exarhia area, which includes
rowdy Nafklirou and Plessa streets. Competing bars try to lure in bar-
hoppers with ads for cheap beer and neon-color drinks.

Fashion (⊠ *Odos Kanari 2* ☎ *22420/22592*), a massive club off of Delphinia Square, has an outdoor bar, happy hour, and a throbbing indoor
dance floor. Guest DJs seek to provide young, international tourists the
kind of club music they'd hear back home. The loungey seaside club **H20**
(⊠ *Aktis Art Hotel, beachfront, Vasileos Georgiou 7* ☎ *22420/47207*)
has a small, sleek interior as well as outdoor seating.

FESTIVAL

Every summer from July through mid-September Kos hosts the **Hip-**
pocrates Festival (☎ *22420/28665* ✍ *pkkos@internet.gr*). Music, dance,
movie screenings, and theater performances enliven venues such as the
Castle of the Knights and the Odeon. The festival also includes exhibits
around town and activities for children.

THE OUTDOORS

The island of Kos, particularly the area around the town, is good for
bicycle riding. Ride to the Asklepieion for a picnic, or visit the Castle
of Antimacheia. Note: be aware of hazards such as cistern openings;
very few have security fences around them. You can rent bicycles everywhere—in Kos town and at the more-popular resorts. Try the many
shops along Eleftheriou Venizelou street in town. Renting a bike costs
about €6 per day.

ASKLEPIEION ΑΣΚΛΗΠΙΕΙΟΝ

4 km (2½ mi) west of Kos town.

One of the great healing centers of antiquity, the Asklepieion is framed by a thick grove of cypress trees and is laid out on several **broad terraces** connected by a monumental staircase. The lower terrace probably held the Asklepieion Festivals. On the middle terrace is an **Ionic temple,** once decorated with paintings by Apelles, including the renowned depiction of Aphrodite often written about in antiquity and eventually removed to Rome by the emperor Augustus. On the uppermost terrace is the **Doric Temple of Asklepios,** once surrounded by colonnaded porticoes. ✉ *Asklepieion* ☎ *22420/28763* 🎟 *€4* 🕙 *Apr.–Oct., Tues.—Sun. 8:30–7; Nov.–Feb., Tues.–Sun. 8:30–2:30.*

OFF THE BEATEN PATH

Mountain villages. Leaving the main road southwest of the Asklepieion (turnoff is at Zipari, 9 km [5½ mi] southwest of Kos town), you can explore an enchanting landscape of cypress and pine trees on a route that climbs to a handful of lovely, whitewashed rural villages that cling to the craggy slopes of the island's central mountains, including Asfendiou, Zia, and Lagoudi. The busiest of them is Zia, with an appealing smattering of churches; crafts shops selling local honey, weavings, and handmade soaps; and open-air tavernas where you can enjoy the views over the surrounding forests and fields toward the sea.

WHERE TO EAT

¢–$ ★ **✗ Asklipios.** The town is noted for its Muslim minority, and you can have a memorable Turkish-inspired meal at the little restaurant called "Ali." Sit in the shade of an ancient laurel tree and try the selection of exquisite mezedes: *imam bayaldi* (baked eggplant), bourekakia, and home-prepared *dolmadakia* (small stuffed grape leaves). An array of kebabs includes excellent *soutzoukakia* (elongated meatballs); even the boiled cauliflower is perfect. ✉ *3 km (2 mi) west of Kos town, on main square, 85300 Platani* ☎ *22420/25264* 🖃 *MC, V.*

¢ **Fodor's Choice** ★ **✗ Taverna Ampavris.** The surroundings and the food are both delightful at this charming, rustic taverna, outside Kos town on a lane leading to the village of Platani. Meals are served in the courtyard of an old farmhouse, and the kitchen's emphasis is on local country food—including wonderful stews and grilled meats, accompanied by vegetables from nearby gardens. The owners wait on you, steering you toward meals, like zucchini blossoms stuffed with rice, or offering detailed advice on sightseeing. ✉ *Ampavris, on the way from Rhodes to Platani* ☎ *22420/25696* 🖃 *No credit cards.*

CASTLE OF ANTIMACHEIA ΚΑΣΤΡΟ ΑΝΤΙΜΑΧΕΙΑΣ

21 km (13 mi) southwest of Asklepieion, 25 km (15 mi) southwest of Kos town.

The thick, well-preserved walls of this medieval fortress look out over the sweeping Aegean and Kos's green interior. Around the fortress, which has a coat of arms from the Knights of the Order of St. John of Rhodes, are

9

the remains of a ruined settlement. ⊠ *On main road from Kos, turn left 3 km (2 mi) before village of Antimacheia, following signs to castle.*

KAMARI ΚΑΜΑΡΙ

10 km (6 mi) south of the Castle of Antimacheia, 35 km (22 mi) southwest of Kos town.

On Kefalos Bay, the little beach community of Kamari is pleasant and less frantic than the island's other seaside resorts. On a summit above is the lovely old town of Kefalos, a pleasant place to wander for its views and quintessential Greekness. Close offshore is a little rock formation holding a chapel to St. Nicholas. Opposite are the ruins of a magnificent 5th-century Christian basilica.

BEACHES

A chunk of the **Ayios Stefanos beach**, just north of Kamari, is now occupied by a Club Med; the rest belongs to beach clubs renting umbrellas and chairs and offering activities that include waterskiing and jet-skiing. Nearby **Paradise beach** (⊠ *3 km [2mi] north of Kamari*) has plenty of parking, and thus crowds, but the broad, sandy beach is magnificent and gives its name to a long stretch of sand that curves around the enchanting Gulf of Kefalos and, at its northern end, is undeveloped, almost deserted (and popular with nude bathers).

WHERE TO STAY & EAT

¢–$ ✕ **Faros.** It's not surprising that fish rules the menu at this seaside taverna at the very end of the beach in Kamari. In fact, some patrons arrive by dinghies from their yachts anchored offshore. The friendly staff will take you into the kitchen and show you the fresh catch of the day; then they'll grill or bake it to your liking. ⊠ *Beachfront, Kamari* 🕾 *22420/71240* 🖃 *MC, V.*

¢   🏨 **Hotel Kokalakis Beach.** The proprietors of this affordable hotel located on Kamari's beach road say they value quiet, and they're not just paying lip service. Many guests return annually for the peaceful proximity to pebble and sand beaches. The hotel is also walking distance from Kamari's strip of restaurants and cafés. Rooms are whitewashed, with ceramic tile floors, and six include cooking facilities. ⊠ *Waterfront, 85301 Kamari* 🕾 *22420/71496* 🛏 *32 rooms* ⚐ *In-room: refrigerator. In-hotel: pool, bar, no elevator, public Internet* 🖃 *No credit cards* ⊙ *Closed May–Oct.*

PATMOS ΠΑΤΜΟΣ

Rocky and barren, the small, 34-square-km (21-square-mi) island of Patmos lies beyond the islands of Kalymnos and Leros, northwest of Kos. Here on a hillside is the Monastery of the Apocalypse, which enshrines the cave where St. John received the Revelation in AD 95. Scattered evidence of Mycenaean presence remains on Patmos, and walls of the classical period indicate the existence of a town near Skala. Most of the island's approximately 2,800 people live in three villages:

Skala, medieval Chora, and the small rural settlement of Kambos. The island is popular among the faithful making pilgrimages to the monastery as well as with vacationing Athenians and a wealthy international set who have bought homes in Chora. Administrators have carefully contained development, and as a result, Patmos retains its charm and natural beauty—even in the busy month of August.

SKALA ΣΚΑΛΑ

161 km (100 mi) north of Kos.

Skala, the island's small but sophisticated main town, is where almost all the hotels and restaurants are located. It's a popular port of call for cruise ships, and in summer the huge liners often loom over the chic shops and restaurants. There's not much to see in the town, but it is lively and very attractive, and, since strict building codes have been enforced, even new buildings have traditional architectural detail. The medieval town of Chora, only 5 km (3 mi) above Skala, and the island's legendary monasteries are nearby.

Take a 20-minute hike up to **Kastelli**, on a hill overlooking Skala, to see the stone remains of the city's 6th- to 4th-century BC town and acropolis.

BEACHES

The small island is endowed with at least 24 beaches. Although most of them, which tend to be coarse shingle, are accessible by land, sun worshippers can sail to a few (as well as to the nearby islet cluster of **Arkoi**) on the caïques that make regular runs from Skala, leaving in the morning. Prices vary with the number of people making the trip (or with the boat); transport to and from a beach for a family for a day may cost around €35. The beach at **Melloi**, a 2-km (1-mi) taxi ride north of Skala or a quick caïque ride, is a sand-and-pebble strip with a taverna nearby. The beach at **Kambos** (✉ *6 km [4 mi] from Skala*) bay is the most popular on the island. It has mostly fine pebbles and sand, nearby tavernas, windsurfing, waterskiing, and pedal boats for rent.

OFF THE BEATEN PATH

Psili Amos, a sand beach located 15 km (9 mi) from Skala, on the south shore, is worth the extra effort to reach; it's arguably the most beautiful of the island. Getting there requires a 45-minute caïque ride (€10) or a 20-minute walk on a footpath from Diakofti, the narrowest point on the island, where visitors can park their cars by the taverna. Nude bathers sometimes line the edges of the beach.

WHERE TO STAY & EAT

$-$$ ✕ **Benetos.** A native Patmian, Benetos Matthaiou, and his American
★ wife, Susan, operate this lovely restaurant abutting a seaside garden that supplies the kitchen with fresh herbs and vegetables. Homegrown ingredients, including aromatic cherry tomatoes, find their way into a selection of Mediterranean-style dishes that include phyllo parcels stuffed with spinach and cheese, the island's freshest Greek salad, and a juicy grilled swordfish. Accompany your meal with a selection from the eclectic Greek wine list. Service is gracious and friendly, if a

9

bit slow. ✉ *On harborside road between Skala and Grikos, Sapsila* ☎ *22470/33089* ▭ *MC, V* ⊘ *Closed Mon. and mid-Oct.–May.*

¢–$ ✕**Ostria.** After a long day of swimming or boating, locals gravitate to this frill-free fish taverna on the harbor. Basic wooden furniture, plastic tablecloths, and bare lightbulbs are the only decor in the tented summer eating area. But this is the perfect place for watching Skala's human traffic pass by while sipping an ouzo and tackling an overflowing fried seafood *pikilia* (appetizer sampler). ✉ *Waterfront* ☎ *69794/38275* ▭ *No credit cards* ⊘ *Closed mid-Oct–May.*

$$$ ⌂**Porto Scoutari.** It seems only fitting that Patmos should have a hotel
★   that reflects the architectural beauty of the island while providing luxurious accommodations. Guest rooms are enormous and have sitting and sleeping areas, in addition to large terraces that face the sea and a verdant garden with a swimming pool. Furnishings differ from room to room and include brass beds and reproduction Greek antiques; the lobby and breakfast rooms are also exquisitely decorated with traditional pieces. Owner Elina Scoutari, who lived in Washington, D.C., for many years, is on hand to see to your needs. A short walk takes you to Melloi beach. ✉ *1 km (½ mi) northeast of Skala center, 85500* ☎ *22470/33123* 🖷 *22470/33175* ⊕ *www.portoscoutari.com* ⋙ *30 rooms, 4 suites* ⌕ *In-room: kitchen, dial-up. In-hotel: bar, pool, no elevator, public Wi-Fi* ▭ *MC, V* ⊘ *Closed Nov.–late Feb.* ⦿*BP.*

$ ⌂**Captain's House.** One of the very special places to stay in Patmos,
★   largely because the owners are so pleasant, this small pink hotel with green shutters faces the sea at the edge of Skala. Stone arches accent the multilevel lobby, re-creating the feel of old Patmos. The wood-furnished, plain rooms are pleasantly breezy, and all have balconies that face either the harbor or the pool area. The TV in the lounge gets satellite stations. ✉ *Inland, south of main street, 85500* ☎ *22470/31793* 🖷 *22470/34077* ⊕ *www.captains-house.gr* ⋙ *19 rooms* ⌕ *In-hotel: bar, pool, no elevator* ▭ *MC, V* ⊘ *Closed mid-Oct.–Mar.* ⦿*CP.*

SHOPPING

Patmos has some elegant boutiques selling jewelry and crafts, including antiques, mainly from the island. **Katoi** (✉ *Skala–Chora road* ☎ *22470/31487 or 22470/34107*) has a wide selection of ceramics, icons, and silver jewelry of traditional design. **Parousia** (✉ *Past square at beginning of road to Chora* ☎ *22470/32549*) is a good place to purchase Byzantine-style icons, wooden children's toys, and small religious items.

Whether made of ceramic, glass, silver, or wood, each work—by one of 40 different Greek artists—at **Selene** (✉ *Skala harbor* ☎ *22470/31742*) is unique.

CHORA ΧΩΡΑ

5 km (3 mi) south, above Skala.

Atop a hill due south of Skala, the village of Chora, clustered around the walls of the Monastery of St. John the Theologian, has become a preserve of international wealth. Though the short distance from Skala may make walking seem attractive, a steep incline can make this challenging. A taxi ride is not expensive, about €6, and there is frequent bus service (€1) from Skala and other points on the island.

In AD 95, during the emperor Domitian's persecution of Christians, St. John the Theologian was banished to Patmos, where he lived until his reprieve two years later. He writes that it was on Patmos that he "heard ... a great voice, as of a trumpet," commanding him to write a book and "send it unto the seven churches." According to tradition, St. John wrote the text of *Revelation* in the little cave, the Sacred
★ Grotto, now built into the **Monastery of the Apocalypse.** The voice of God spoke through a threefold crack in

> ### MMMMM...
>
> The best goods on the island might be of the baked variety. Be sure to sample specialities like *poogies* (confectioners' sugar-coated cookies stuffed with almond and walnut chunks) and soufflé-like cheese pies. Two places with grin-inducing treats are:
>
> The baker is up long before the roosters at **Fegaros Bakery** (✉ *Dimarxou Ioanni Fegaros, toward central square* ☎ 22470/31394) nestled in Chora's central whitewashed artery.
>
> **Koumanis Bakery** (✉ *Off central square* ☎ 22470/32894) is located near the chic shops.

the rock, and the saint dictated to his follower Prochorus. A slope in the wall is pointed to as the desk where Prochorus wrote, and a silver halo is set on the stone that was the apostle's pillow. The grotto is decorated with wall paintings of the 12th century and icons from the 16th. The monastery, which is accessible via several flights of outdoor stairs, was constructed in the 17th century from architectural fragments of earlier buildings, and further embellished in later years; it also contains chapels to St. Artemios and St. Nicholas. In late August or early September, the monastery hosts the **Festival of Sacred Music of Patmos,** with world-class Byzantine and ecclesiastical music performances in an outdoor performance space. ✉ *2 km (1 mi) south on Skala–Chora road* ☎ 22470/31234 *monastery,* 22470/29363 *festival* 🖃 *Free* ⊙ *Mon., Wed., Fri., and Sat. 8–1:30; Tues., Thurs., and Sun. 8–1:30 and 4–6.*

Fodor's Choice The **Monastery of St. John the Theologian,** on its high perch, is one of the
★ finest extant examples of a fortified medieval monastic complex. Hosios Christodoulos, a man of education, energy, devotion, and vision who built the Theotokos Monastery in Kos, came to Patmos in 1088 to set up the island's now-famous monastery. From its inception, it attracted monks of education and social standing, who made sure that it was ornamented with the best sculpture, carvings, and paintings. It was an intellectual center, with a rich library and a tradition of teaching, and by the end of the 12th century it owned land on Leros, Limnos, Crete, and Asia Minor, as well as ships, which carried on trade exempt from taxes. A broad staircase leads to the entrance, which was fortified by towers and buttresses. The complex consists of buildings from a number of periods: in front of the entrance is the 17th-century **Chapel of the Holy Apostles;** the **main church** dates from the time of Christodoulos

(whose skull, along with that of Apostle Thomas, is encased in a silver sarcophagus here); the **Chapel of the Virgin** is 12th century.

The **treasury** contains relics, icons, silver, and vestments, most dating from 1600 to 1800. Many of the objects are votives dedicated by the clerics, nobles, and wealthy individuals; one of the most beautiful is an 11th-century icon of St. Nicholas, executed in the finest mosaic work, in an exquisitely chased silver frame. Another treasure is an El Greco icon. On display, too, are some of the library's oldest codices, dating to the late 5th and the 8th century, such as pages from the Gospel of St. Mark and the Book of Job. The more than 600 vestments are of luxurious fabrics, elaborately embroidered with gold, silver, and multicolor silks. Though not open to the public, the **library** contains extensive treasures: illuminated manuscripts, approximately 1,000 codices, and more than 3,000 printed volumes. The collection was first cataloged in 1200; of the 267 works of that time, the library still has 111. The archives preserve a near-continuous record, down to the present, of the history of the monastery as well as the political and economic history of the region. ⊠ *3 km (2 mi) south of Monastery of the Apocalypse* ☎*22470/20800* ⊕*www.monipatmou.gr* ☒*Church and chapels free, treasury €6* ☉*Daily 8–1:30 (also 4–6 on Sun., Tues., and Thurs.); Dec.–Mar. call to arrange a treasury visit, as hrs are irregular.*

WHERE TO EAT

¢–$ ✕ **Vangelis.** At this pleasant taverna, you can choose between a table
Fodor'sChoice on the main square (perfect for people-watching) or in the Paradise
★ Garden out back, where a raised terrace has stunning views of the sea. Fresh grilled fish and lemon-and-oregano-flavored goat are the specialties, and simple dishes such as mint-flavored *dolmades* (stuffed grape leaves) and *tzatziki* (yogurt and cucumber dip) are excellent. Want traditional lodging to go with that meal? The management is happy to help find rooms in private homes in Chora. ⊠*Main square, 85500* ☎*22470/31967* ▬*No credit cards.*

RHODES & THE DODECANESE ESSENTIALS

TRANSPORTATION

BY AIR

CARRIERS There are more than eight flights per day to Rhodes from Athens on Olympic Airlines or Aegean Airlines, and extra flights are added during high season. The 45-minute flight costs about €115 one way. Olympic flies to Rhodes from Heraklion (1 hour, €100) at least three times per day and several times a week from Thessaloniki (1¼ hours, €117). It is possible to fly directly to Rhodes from a number of European capitals, especially on charters.

To Kos, Olympic Airlines runs three daily flights from Athens, and three flights a week from Rhodes. Schedules are reduced in winter. Neither Patmos nor Symi have airports.

Contacts Aegean Airlines (✉ *Rhodes Airport, Rhodes town* ☎ *22410/98345, 210/626–1000 in Athens* ⊕ *www.aegeanair.gr*). **Olympic Airlines** (✉ *Ierou Lochou 9, Rhodes town, Rhodes* ☎ *22410/24555, 210/966–6666 in Athens* 🖷 *210/966–6111* ✉ *Vasileos Pavlou 22, Kos town, Kos* ☎ *22420/28331 or 22420/28332* ⊕ *www.olympicairlines.com*).

AIRPORTS   Rhodes Airport is about 20 minutes from Rhodes town, and it's best to take a taxi (about €15). Though private vehicles must have permits to enter the Old Town, a taxi may enter if carrying luggage, no matter what a reluctant driver tells you. Kos airport is located 26 km (16 mi) southwest of Kos town. There is bus and taxi service from there to Kos town.

Information Kos Airport (☎ *22420/51229*). **Rhodes Airport** (☎ *22410/88700*).

BY BOAT & FERRY

When traveling from Piraeus to Rhodes by ferry (12–18 hours, €35–€90), you first make several stops, including at Patmos (6–10 hours, €25–€81) and Kos (10–16 hours, €30–€80). Bringing a car aboard can quadruple costs. Of the several ferry lines serving the Dodecanese, Blue Star Ferries and G&A Ferries have the largest boats and the most frequent service, both sailing several times a week out of Piraeus. The Athens–Dodecanese ferry schedule changes seasonally, so contact ferry lines, the Piraeus Port Authority, the Greek National Tourism Organization (GNTO or EOT) in Athens, or a travel agency for details.

BETWEEN THE   The easiest way to travel among the Dodecanese islands is by hydrofoil
ISLANDS   or catamaran. ANES has hydrofoils and catamarans running in the summer between Symi and Rhodes and other islands.

Contacts ANES (✉ *Harbor front, Yialos, Symi* ☎ *22460/71444* ⊕ *www.anes.gr*).

Piraeus Port Authority (🖷 *1442*). **Rhodes Port Authority** (🖷 *22410/22220*).

BY BUS

There is a decent bus network on all the islands, though there are more-infrequent routes on smaller islands. Buses from Rhodes town leave from two different points on Averoff street for the island's east and west sides. Symi's and Patmos's bus stations are located on the harbor. Kos has a city bus and KTEL island buses; locations of both stations are expected to change by 2009, so call if you can't find the relevant stop.

Information Kos KTEL bus station (✉ *Cleopatras, Kos town, Kos* ☎ *22420/22292*). **Kos town bus station** (✉ *Akti Koundouriotou [main harbor], Kos town, Kos* ☎ *22420/26276*). **Rhodes east-side buses** (✉ *Averoff near end of Rimini Sq., Rhodes town, Rhodes* ☎ *22410/27706*). **Rhodes west-side buses** (✉ *Averoff next to market, Rhodes town, Rhodes* ☎ *22410/26300*).

BY CAR

You may take a car to the Dodecanese on one of the large ferries that sail daily from Piraeus to Rhodes and less frequently to the smaller islands. On Rhodes, the roads are good, there are not many of them, and good maps are available. It is possible to tour the island in one day if you rent a car. Traffic is likely to be heavy only from Rhodes town to Lindos.

In Kos, a car is advisable only if you are interested in seeing points outside Kos town, and even then it's not necessary. In Patmos, a car or motorbike makes it easy to tour the island, though most other sights and outlying restaurants are easily reached by bus or taxi, and a few beaches can be reached by either bus or boat. Symi, which has only one road suitable for cars, is best explored on foot or by boat.

Rental Agencies **Budget Drive Rent-a-Car** (⊠ *Km 1 mark on Tsairi–airport road, Rhodes town, Rhodes* ☎ *22410/68243* ⊕ *www.driverentacar.gr* ⊠ *Airport, Rhodes* ☎ *22410/81011*). **Holiday Autos** (⊠ *Karaiskaki 9, Kos town, Kos* ☎ *22420/22997* 🖨 *22420/27608*).

Local Rental Agencies **Autoway** (⊠ *Vasileos Georgiou 18, Rhodes, Rhodes* ☎ *22420/25326* ⊕ *www.autowaykos.gr*). **Tassos** (⊠ *Skala, Patmos* ☎ *22470/31753* 🖨 *22470/32210*).

BY TAXI

Taxis are available throughout the island of Rhodes, including at most resorts. All taxi stands in Rhodes have a sign listing set fares to destinations around the island. Expect a delay when calling radio taxis in high season. ⚠ **Patmos taxi drivers move at breakneck speed on twisty roads. Fortunately, most journeys are short.**

Contacts **Taxis** (⊠ *Agious Apostolous, Rhodes town, Rhodes* ☎ *22410/64712 or 22410/64756*). **Taxis** (⊠ *Skala, Patmos* ☎ *22470/31225*).

CONTACTS & RESOURCES

EMERGENCIES

As elsewhere in Greece, pharmacies in the Dodecanese post in their windows a list showing which locations are open 24 hours and on which days.

Information **Hospital** (⊠ *Agion Apostolon, Rhodes town, Rhodes* ☎ *22410/80000* ⊠ *Ippokratous 34, Kos town, Kos* ☎ *22420/22300* ⊠ *Ippokratous 34, Skala, Patmos* ☎ *22470/31211* ⊠ *1 mi on the Skala—Chora road, Skala,Patmos* ☎ *22470/31211*). **Medical Clinic** (⊠ *Yialos, Symi* ☎ *22460/71290 [Yialos] and 22460/71316 [Chorio]*). **Emergency** (☎ *166 in Rhodes and Kos*). **Police** (⊠ *Ethelondon Dodekanissou 45, Rhodes town, Rhodes* ☎ *100 in Rhodes and Kos, 22470/31303 in Patmos, 22460/71111 in Symi*). **Tourist police** (⊠ *Odos Karpathou 1, Rhodes town, Rhodes* ☎ *22410/27423* ⊠ *Akti Miaouli 2, Kos town, Kos* ☎ *22863, 26666*).

INTERNET, MAIL & SHIPPING

Internet Internet Cafés are not hard to spot in the main port towns. They range from organized operations with scanners and printers, to cafés, bars, or pool halls with one or two computers in the back. Most have high speed connections. ¡**Arena** (⊠ *Navarinou 4, Kos town, Kos* ☎ *22420/25333*). **Blue Bay Hotel** (⊠ *South edge of Skala Harbor, Patmos* ☎ *22470/31165* ⊕ *www.bluebaypatmos.gr*). **Control Café** (⊠ *Alexandrou Diakou 44, Rhodes town, Rhodes* ☎ *22410/24564* ⊕ *www.controlcafe.gr*). **Del Mare** (⊠ *Alexander the Great 4a, Kos town, Kos* ☎ *22420/24244* ⊕ *www.cybercafe.gr*). **Kantirimi Café** (⊠ *Yialos Central Sq, Yialos, Symi* ☎ *22460/71381*). **Lindianet Internet Café** (⊠ *Next to*

Chinese restaurant and Pallas Travel, 85107 Lindos Rhodes ☎*22440/ 32142* ⊕*www.lindianet.gr*).

Mail Post Office (✉*Eleftherias Sq 1, Rhodes town, Rhodes* ☎*22410/35560* ✉*Vas. Pavlou 12, Kos town, Kos* ☎*22420/22250* ✉*Near clock tower and next to police station, Yialos, Symi* ☎*22460/71315* ✉*Harbour, Skala, Patmos* ☎*22470/31316*).

Shipping Rhodes has a host of international couriers. There are also big courier offices in Kos, and fewer in Patmos. There is courier service on Symi, but ask locals for help in finding local companies doing the shipments as these can change from year to year. **DHL** (✉*Kapodistriou 1, Rhodes town, Rhodes* ☎*22410/76215* ⊕*www.dhl.gr* ✉*Bouboulinas 23, Kos town, Kos* ☎*22420/21368*). **Speedex** (✉*Ethniki Antistaseos 39, Rhodes town, Rhodes* ☎*22410/70999* ⊕*www.speedex. gr* ✉*Mandilara 56, Kos town, Kos* ☎*22420/22493* ✉*Skala harbour, Skala, Patmos* ☎*22470/33000*).

MEDIA

The region's only English-language newspaper is found on Symi. The *Symi Visitor*, available at tourist spots, is full of information on events, news, and activities, plus has an overview of the sites, and bus and ferry schedules. The Web site also has weather updates and information on finding accommodations on Symi.

Contact Symi Visitor (✉*Yialos harbor front, near bus station, Yialos, Symi* ☎*22460/ 72755* ⊕*www.symivisitor.com*).

TOUR OPTIONS

From April to October, local island boat tours take you to area sights and may include a picnic on a remote beach or even a visit to the shores of Turkey. For example, Triton Holidays of Rhodes organizes a visit to Lindos by boat; a caïque leaves Mandraki harbor in Rhodes town in the morning, deposits you in Lindos for a day of sightseeing and beachgoing, and returns you in the evening for €20. You can also take their boat trip to Marmaris, Turkey (€35, plus €14 Turkish port tax), which includes a free guided tour of the city. On Symi, Kalodoukas Tours runs boat trips to the Monastery of Panormitis, as well as to secluded beaches and islets, which include swimming and a barbecue lunch. Aeolos Travel in Kos organizes one-day cruises to other islands. A1 Yacht Trade Consortium organizes sailing tours around the Greek islands near the Turkish coast. Many island agencies, such as Symi Tours, on Symi, and Astoria Travel, on Patmos, offer help with yacht-docking paperwork.

If you're not renting a car on Rhodes, it can be worth it to take a bus tour to its southern points and interior. Triton Holidays has, among other trips, a guided bus tour to Thermes Kallitheas, Epta Piges, and Lindos (€30); a bus tour to Kameiros, Filerimos, and Petaloudes (€30); and a full-day trip through several points in the interior and south (€35). Astoria Travel provides day bus trips to Patmos's St. John the Theologian Monastery and the Monastery of the Apocalypse (€20).

On Symi, George Kalodoukas of Kalodoukas Tours leads wonderful guided hiking tours around the island and does an excursion to his

Marathoudas beach–area organic farm. The company sells a short book by Frances Noble (€7) that outlines 25 walks around the island. On Rhodes, you can pick up a book with 18 walks from the Rhodes town EOT office (⇨ *Visitor Information*).

Contacts **A1 Yacht Trade Consortium** (⊠ *Vyronas 1, at Canada, Rhodes town, Rhodes* ☎ *22410/22927* ⊕ *www.a1yachting.com*). **Aeolos Travel** (⊠ *Navarinou 55, Kos town, Kos* ☎ *22420/26203* ⊕ *www.tritondmc.gr*). **Astoria Travel** (⊠ *Skala harbor, Patmos* ☎ *22470/31205* ⊕ *www.astoriatravel.com*). **Kalodoukas Tours** (⊠ *Behind Trawler's taverna, Yialos, Symi* ☎ *22460/71077* ⊕ *www.symi-greece. com*). **Symi Tours** (⊠ *Symi harbor, Yialos, Symi* ☎ *22460/71307* ☐ *22460/70011*). **Triton Holidays** (⊠ *Plastira 9, Rhodes town, Rhodes* ☎ *22410/21690* ⊕ *www. tritondmc.gr*).

VISITOR INFORMATION

In Rhodes, the Greek National Tourism Organization (GNTO or EOT), close to the medieval walls in the new town, has brochures and schedules for buses and boats. It's open June–September, weekdays 9–9 (8–3 the rest of the year). The central Rhodes Municipal Tourism Office, near the bus station, is open May–October, daily 7:30—11 PM. The city of Rhodes maintains a helpful English Web site.

Contacts **Greek National Tourism Organization (GNTO or EOT)** (⊠ *Archbishop Makarios and Papagou, Rhodes town, Rhodes* ☎ *22410/44335 or 22410/44336* ⊕ *www.ando.gr/eot*). **Lindos Tourist Information** (⊠ *Central Sq, Lindos, Rhodes* ☎ *22440/31900* ⊗ *Apr.—Oct., 9—9*). **Rhodes official Web site** (⊕ *www.rhodes. gr*). **Rhodes Municipal Tourism Office** (⊠ *Averoff 3, Rhodes town, Rhodes* ☎ *22410/35945*).

Kos Municipal Tourism Office (⊠ *Vasileos Georgiou 1, Kos town, Kos* ☎ *22420/24460*). **Patmos Municipal Tourism Office** (⊠ *Near ferry dock, Skala, Patmos* ☎ *22470/31666*). **Municipality of Southern Rhodes** (⊠ *Gennadi* ☎ *22440/43243* ⊕ *www.southrhodes.gr*).

The Northern Aegean Islands

LESBOS, CHIOS & SAMOS

St. John the Apostle

WORD OF MOUTH

"If you are looking for someplace a little off the beaten path, and don't care about trendy nightlife, you might want to look at the Northern Aegean islands such as Lesbos and Chios. Both are gorgeous, and very pleasant and relaxing places to spend time. Both have incredibly beautiful beaches. The food in this region of Greece, and particularly the seafood, is wonderful."

—eleni

WELCOME TO THE NORTHERN AEGEAN ISLANDS

TOP REASONS TO GO

★ **Samos Block Party:** Pythagoras, Epicurus, and the fabulous Aesop were just a few of this island's brightest stars, and their spirits probably still haunt the ancient Heraion temple.

★ **Mesmerizing Mastic Villages:** Pirgi in Chios is known for the resin it produces, but with its Genoese houses patterned in black and white, it's the Escher-like landscape that's likely to stick with you.

★ **Sappho's Island:** If it's beauty you seek, head to one of Lesbos's oldest towns, Molyvos—a haven for artists and an aesthete's dream.

★ **Sailing to Byzantium:** Colorful Byzantine mosaics make Chios's 11th-century Nea Moni monastery an important piece of history—and a marvel to behold.

★ **Dizzyingly Good Ouzo:** Though you can get this potent potable anywhere in Greece, Lesbos's is reputedly the best—enjoy it with famed salt-baked Kalloni sardines.

Monks at monastery, Lesbos.

1 Lesbos. Birthplace of the erotic songs of poet Sappho (6th century BC), this huge island still reveres women—rarely will you see so many statues of female leaders—and you could easily spend a glorious week exploring its beaches, villages, petrified forests, and rocky mountains. Mytilini has good museums but is in short supply of charm. For that, head to marvelous Molyvos: artists flock here to paint its cobblestone streets and red roofs (mandated by law). Other destinations include Agiassos, the prettiest hill town, and Skala Eressou, birthplace of Sappho.

2 Chios. The island depends on the sea and its mastic production, not tourism, so you'll find the real Greece here. But you'll have to look beyond the chaotic, architecturally unappealing main town to explore the isle's allurements, including black pebble beaches, lush countryside, and quaint

village squares. Chios is the "mastic island," producing the highly beneficial resin that is used in cakes, chewing gum, alcoholic drinks, and cosmetic products; the most noted mastic village is Pirgi, famed for the geometric patterns on its house facades. In addition, the 11th century monastery of Nea Moni is celebrated for its Byzantine court art.

3 Samos. Apart from its serene azure-water beaches and verdant landscapes, Samos's cuisine blends the flavors of Asia Minor with those of Greece in a most enticing way. At the top of any sightseer's list are the island's fabled ancient sites, such as the Temple at Heraion—once four times larger than the Parthenon—and the Roman baths and underground aqueduct at Pythagorio. With its close proximity to Turkey, Samos makes for a great stopover in a Greece-Turkey trip.

One of Samos's many churches.

GETTING ORIENTED

About the only thing the islands of Samos, Chios, and Lesbos share is their proximity to Turkey: from their shores, reaching from Macedonia down to the Dodecanese along the coast of Asia Minor, you can see the very fields of Greece's age-old rival. No matter that these three islands may be a long haul from Athens: Few parts of the Aegean have greater variety and beauty of landscape—a stunning blend of pristine shores and craggy (Homer's word) mountains.

10

tilini's harbor, Lesbos (left).

THE NORTHERN AEGEAN ISLANDS PLANNER

Getting Around

The public (KTEL) bus system on the Northern Aegean islands is reliable, cheap (a few euros one way), and obliging.

Buses run from Chios town to other villages to the north, west, northwest and south, from three to six times per day (usually from 7 AM to 4:30 PM, depending on the part of the island).

Buses depart from Mytilene town chiefly to Petra and Molyvos, and schedules depend largely on the time of year and day of the week, usually leaving at 11 AM and 1:15 PM and taking around two hours each way.

Buses on Samos are, as in Chios, more numbered and regular throughout the summer months, heading to the majority of towns and villages around the island.

Particularly in the case of Lesbos, where bus services leave something to be desired, but also on Chios and Samos, it is worth renting a car or motorbike to really explore the island.

An international driving license is a definite requirement, and fully insured cars will usually cost between 30–50 euros during the high season.

Making the Most of Your Time

If you have time to visit two islands over a 5–14 day period, start by exploring Mytilini, the capital of Lesbos, a bustling center of commerce and learning, with its grand old mansions overlooking the harbour. From there, head to the countryside, to the northern destinations: Molyvos, a medieval town sprawling under the impressive Molyvos castle; Skala Eressou with its fine beach and bars; and the hilltop Agiassos, immersed in verdant forests. For your second stop, take a ferry to Chios, where you can enjoy the nightlife in the main town, and don't miss the old quarter. Travel via Lithi—derived from Alithis limin, meaning "true haven," which is rather apt for this beautiful fishing village—to enjoy a good fish lunch. Next, go to the peaceful and unspoilt Vessa, Pirgi (famous for its unique mosaics), and Mesta, part of the "masticohoria" or mastic villages, world renowned for their cultivation of mastic trees, which preserve a Greece of centuries past. Alternatively, take the ferry from Piraeus directly to Samos, a fine scenario if you can just visit one island. Circle the island, stopping at its lovely beaches and at Pythagorio, the ancient capital, or the temple at Heraion, one of the Wonders of the Ancient World. Consider visiting the traditional fishing village of Kokkari, which has managed to keep its architectural authenticity, then to the beaches Tsamadou and Lemonaki, where the green pine slopes meet the heavenly blue waters of the Mediterranean. If you're drawn to the shores of Turkey, Samos makes a convenient stopover, as there's a daily ferry service.

Top Spots to Stay

On Lesbos, stay on Mytilini if you like a busy, citylike ambiance, on Molyvos for its dramatic medieval beauty or Skala Eressou for its laid-back beach style. On Chios avoid staying in the main town (Chios town) unless you're just stopping over briefly, as it lacks in beauty and style, and opt to stay in the picturesque mastic village of Mesta instead. Vathi (Samos town), the main town, is a good central option in Samos, but even more ideal is the atmospheric and naturally abundant Pythagorio.

Dining à la Lesbos, Chios & Samos

Hospitality and good, fresh food abound on the Northern Islands. Fish is relatively expensive; lobster (crayfish to Americans) is popular and pricey, and sweet fresh shrimp comes from Lesbos's Kalloni gulf. Kakavia, a dish found on many fish tavern menus around the Greek islands, is fisherman's soup made with small fish, seafood, tomatoes, and onions.

Lesbos, especially, is known for its good food: try the keskek (a special meat mixed with wheat, served most often at festivals) and Kalloni bay sardines, the fleshiest in the Mediterranean, which are salted for a few hours and eaten, with a texture reminiscent of succulent sushi. Octopus, simmered in wine or grilled, goes perfectly with the famous island ouzo, of which there are several dozen brands.

Fresh figs, almonds, and raisins are delicious; a Lesbos dessert incorporating one of those native treats is baleze (almond pudding).

Besides being recognized for its mastic products, Chios is known for tangerines. Preserved in syrup, they are served as a gliko koutaliou, or spoon sweet, meaning you spoon them into water or another beverage, or eat them with a spoon. Thyme-scented honey, yiorti (the local version of keskek), and revithokeftedes (chickpea patties), are Samos's edible claims to fame. In Chios you'll find a great variety of mastic-flavor sweets as well as savory foods, while in Samos the cuisine is flavored with interesting Turkish influences.

Dining & Lodging Prices in Euros

	¢	$	$$	$$$	$$$$
Restaurants	under €8	€8–€11	€11–€15	€15–€20	over €20
Hotels	under €60	€60–€90	€90–€120	€120–€160	over €160

Restaurant prices are for one main course at dinner, or for two mezedes (small dishes). Hotel prices are for a standard double room in high season, including taxes. Hotels operate on the European Plan (EP, with no meal provided) unless we note that they use the Continental Plan (CP, with Continental breakfast); Breakfast Plan (BP, with a full breakfast); Modified American Plan (MAP, with breakfast and dinner); or the Full American Plan (FAP, with all meals). Inquire when booking if these meal plans (which can entail higher rates) are mandatory. Guest rooms have air-conditioning, room phones, and TVs unless otherwise noted.

When to Go

Like everywhere else in the world, Greece is affected by the climate change phenomenon, which guarantees unpredictable weather; sometimes periods which are expected to be sizzling hot will be classified by rainfall and wind and vice versa.

However, as changes are not yet completely drastic, one can basically rely on the knowledge that from early May to early June, the weather is sunny and warm and the sea is still a bit chilly for swimming in.

From mid-June until the end of August, the weather goes through quite a sweeping change and can become very hot, although the waters of the Aegean can prove sufficiently refreshing.

In September the weather begins to mellow considerably, and by mid-October is usually at its warmth limit for swimming, although sunshine can continue throughout the year on and off.

Between November and March these islands can make for an enjoyable trip, and although unlike the smaller islands there are enough restaurants, museums, and sites open to visitors, the cold weather can make ferries unreliable.

10

Updated by
Adrian Vrettos

QUIRKY, SEDUCTIVE, FERTILE, SENSUAL, FADED, sunny, worldly, ravishing, long-suffering, hedonistic, luscious, mysterious, legendary—these adjectives only begin to describe the islands of the northeastern Aegean. This startling and rather arbitrary archipelago includes a number of islands, such as Ikaria, Samothraki, and Thassos; in this book we focus on the three largest—Lesbos, Chios, and Samos. Closer to Turkey's coast than to Greece's, and quite separate from one another, these islands are hilly, sometimes mountainous, with dramatic coastlines and uncrowded beaches, brilliant architecture, and unforgettable historic sites. Lesbos, Greece's third-largest island and birthplace of legendary artists and writers, is dense with gnarled olive groves and dappled with mineral springs. Chios, though ravaged by fire, retains an eerie beauty and has fortified villages, old mansions, Byzantine monasteries, and stenciled-wall houses. Samos, the lush, mountainous land of wine and honey, whispers of the classical wonders of antiquity.

Despite the Northern Islands' proximity to Asia Minor, they are the essence of Greece, the result of 4,000 years of Hellenic influence. Lesbos, Chios, and Samos prospered gloriously in the ancient world as important commercial and religious centers, though their significance waned under the Ottoman Empire. They also were cultural hothouses, producing such geniuses as Pythagoras, Sappho, and probably Homer.

These are not strictly sun-and-fun islands with the extent of tourist infrastructure of, say, the Cyclades. Many young backpackers and party seekers seem to bypass the northern Aegean. You can still carve out plenty of beach time by day and wander into lively restaurants and bars at night, but these islands reveal a deeper character, tracing histories that date back to ancient, Byzantine, and post-Byzantine times, and offering landscapes that are both serene and unspoiled. Visitors to the Northern Islands should expect to find history, culture, beauty, and hospitality. These islands offer commodities that are valued ever more highly by travelers—a sense of discovery and the chance to interact with rich, enduring cultures.

EXPLORING THE NORTHERN ISLANDS

The island of Lesbos is carved by two large, sandy bays, the gulfs of Kalloni and Yera. Undulating hills and cultivated valleys, pine-clad mountains, beaches, springs, desert, and even a petrified forest are also part of the Lesbos terrain. Deep green valleys and rolling hills punctuated by mastic villages characterize Chios. Samos, bathed in green, is filled with pine forests, olive groves, citrus trees, and grape vines, as well as soft hills that fall into the breathtaking Aegean Sea.

LESBOS ΛΕΣΒΟΣ

The Turks called Lesbos the "garden of the empire" for its fertility: in the east and center of the island, about 12 million olive trees line the hills in seemingly endless undulating groves. The western landscape is filled with oak trees, sheep pastures, rocky outcrops, and mountains. Wildflowers and grain cover the valleys, and the higher peaks are wreathed in dark green pines. This third-largest island in Greece is filled with beauty, but its real treasures are the creative artists and thinkers it has produced and inspired through the ages.

Lesbos was once a major cultural center, known for its Philosophical Academy, where Epicurus and Aristotle taught. It was also the birthplace of the philosopher Theophrastus, who presided over the Academy in Athens; of the great lyric poet Sappho; of Terpander, the "father of Greek music"; and of Arion, who influenced the later playwrights Sophocles and Alcaeus, inventors of the dithyramb (a short poem with an erratic strain). Even in modernity, artists have emerged from Lesbos: Theophilos, a poor villager who earned his ouzo by painting some of the finest naive modern art Greece has produced; novelists Stratis Myrivilis and Argyris Eftaliotis; and the 1979 Nobel Prize–winning poet Odysseus Elytis.

The island's history stretches back to the 6th century BC, when its two mightiest cities, Mytilini and Mythimna (now Molyvos), settled their squabbles under the tyrant Pittacus, considered one of Greece's Seven Sages. Thus began the creative era, but later times brought forth the same pillaging and conquest that overturned other Greek islands. In 527 BC the Persians conquered Lesbos, and the Athenians, Romans, Byzantines, Venetians, Genoese, and Turks took their turns adding their influences. After the Turkish conquest, from 1462 to 1912, much of the population was sent to Turkey, and traces of past civilizations that weren't already destroyed by earthquakes were wiped out by the conquerors. Greece gained sovereignty over the island in 1923. This led to the breaking of trade ties with Asia Minor, diminishing the island's wealth, and limiting the economy to agriculture.

Lesbos has more inhabitants than either Corfu or Rhodes, with only a fraction of the tourists, so here you can get a good idea of real island life in Greece. Many Byzantine and post-Byzantine sites dot the island's landscape, including castles and archaeological monuments, churches, and monasteries. The traditional architecture of stone and wood, inspired by Asia Minor, adorns the mansions, tower houses, and other homes of the villages. Beach composition varies throughout the island from pebble to sand. Some of the most spectacular sandy beaches and coves are in the southwest.

10

MYTILINI ΜΥΤΙΛΗΝΗ

350 km (217 mi) northeast of Piraeus. 218 km (135 mi) southeast of Thessaloniki.

Set on the ruins of an ancient city, Mytilini (so important through history that many call Lesbos by the port's name alone) is, like Lesbos, sculpted by two bays, making its coast resemble a jigsaw-puzzle piece. This busy main town and port, with stretches of grand waterfront mansions and a busy old bazaar area, were once the scene of a dramatic

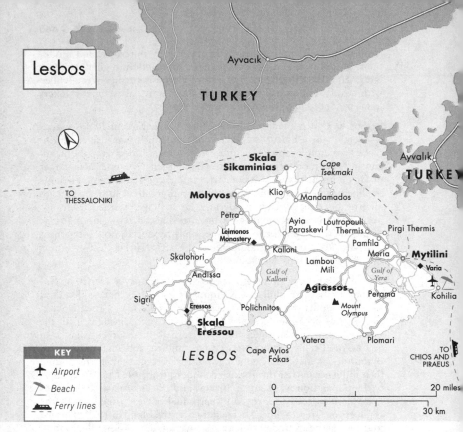

Lesbos

TURKEY

Ayvacık

TO
THESSALONIKI

Skala
Sikaminias

Cape
Tsekmaki

Ayvalık

TURKEY

Molyvos

Klio

Mandamados

Petra

Ayia
Paraskevi

Loutropouli
Thermis

Pirgi Thermis

Leimonos
Monastery

Kalloni

Pamfila

Skalohori

Gulf of
Kalloni

Lambou
Mili

Moria

Mytilini

Andissa

Gulf of
Yera

Varia

Sigri

Eressos

Polichnitos

Agiassos

Perama

Kohilia

Skala
Eressou

Mount
Olympus

Vatera

Plomari

TO
CHIOS AND
PIRAEUS

LESBOS

Cape Ayios
Fokas

KEY

Airport

Beach

Ferry lines

0   20 miles

0   30 km

moment in Greek history. Early in the Peloponnesian War, Mytilini revolted against Athens but surrendered in 428 BC. As punishment, the Athens assembly decided to kill all men in Lesbos and enslave all women and children, and a boat was dispatched to carry out the order. The next day a less-vengeful mood prevailed; the assembly repealed its decision and sent a second ship after the first. The second ship pulled into the harbor just as the commander of the first finished reading the death sentence. Just in time, Mytilini was saved. The bustling waterfront just south of the headland between the town's two bays is where most of the town's sights are clustered.

Stroll the main bazaar street, **Ermou,** which goes from port to port. Walk past the fish market on the southern end, where men haul in their sardines, mullet, and octopuses. Narrow lanes are filled with antiques shops and grand old mansions.

The elegant seaside suburb of Varia was home to the modern "naive" artist Theophilos; Tériade, publisher of modern art journals; and poet Odysseus Elytis.

The pine-covered headland between the bays—a nice spot for a picnic—supports a **kastro,** a stone fortress with intact walls that seem to protect the town even today. Built by the Byzantines on a 600 BC temple of Apollo, it was repaired with available material (note the ancient pillars crammed between the stones) by Francesco Gateluzzi of the famous Genoese family. Look above the gates for the two-headed eagle of the Palaiologos emperors, the horseshoe arms of the Gateluzzi family, and inscriptions made by Turks, who enlarged it; today it is a **military bastion.** Inside the castle there's only a crumbling **prison** and a **Roman cistern,** but you should make the visit for the fine view. ⊠*On pine-covered hill* ☎*22510/27297* 🎫*€2* ⊙*Tues.–Sun. 8–2:30.*

The only vestige of ancient Mytilini is the freely accessible ruin of an **ancient theater,** one of the largest in ancient Greece, from the Hellenistic period. Pompey admired it so much that he copied it for his theater in Rome. Though the marbles are gone, the shape, carved out of the mountain, remains beautifully intact. ⊠*In pine forest northeast of town.*

The enormous post-Baroque church of **Ayios Therapon,** built in the 19th century, is reminiscent of some styles in Italy. It has an ornate interior, a frescoed dome, and, in its courtyard, a **Vizantino Mouseio,** or Byzantine Museum, filled with icons. ⊠*Southern waterfront* ☎*22510/28916* 🎫*Church and museum €2* ⊙*Mon.–Sat. 9–1.*

In front of the cathedral of Ayios Athanasios there is a **traditional Lesbos house,** restored and furnished in 19th-century style. Call owner Marika Vlachou to arrange a visit. ⊠*Mitropoleos 6* ☎*22510/28550* 🎫*Free* ⊙*By appointment only.*

The **Archaeological Museum of Mytilene,** in a 1912 neoclassic mansion, displays finds from the Neolithic through the Roman eras, a period of 5,000 years. A garden in the back displays the famous 6th-century Aeolian capitals from the columns of Klopedi's temples. The museum's modern "wing," in a separate building, contains finds from prehistoric Thermi, mosaics from Hellenistic houses, reliefs of comic scenes from the 3rd-century Roman house of Menander, and temporary exhibits. ⊠*Mansion: Argiri Eftaliotis 7, behind ferry dock; modern wing: corner of Noemvriou and Melinas Merkouri* ☎*22510/28032* ⊕*www.culture.gr* 🎫*€3 for both* ⊙*Mansion Tues.–Sun. 8:30–3, modern wing Tues.–Sun. 8–7:30.*

Crammed to the ceiling in the **Museum of Theophilos** are 86 of the eponymous artist's naive, precise works detailing the everyday life of local folk such as fishermen and farmers, and fantasies of another age. Theophilos lived in poverty but painted airplanes and cities he had never seen. He painted in bakeries for bread, and in cafés for ouzo, and walked around in ancient dress. ⊠*4 km (2½ mi) southeast of Mytilini, Varia* ☎*22510/41644* 🎫*€2* ⊙*Tues.–Sun. 10–4.*

The **Musée–Bibliothèque Tériade** was the home of Stratis Eleftheriadis, better known by his French name, Tériade. His Paris publications *Minotaure* and *Verve* helped promote modern art. Among the works on display are lithographs done for him by Picasso, Matisse, Chagall, Rouault, Giacometti, and Miró. The museum is set among the olive trees of Varia, near the Museum of Theophilos. ⊠*4 km (2½ mi) southeast of Mytilini, Varia* ☎*22510/23372* 🎫*€2* ⊙*Tues.–Sun. 9–2 and 5–8.*

10

WHERE TO STAY & EAT

$ ✗**Polytechnos.** Locals and visiting Athenians pack the outdoor tables—a solid indication this restaurant has earned its reputation. Some folks choose from the impressive fish selection; others order simple, traditional Greek dishes like souvlaki or succulent pork medallions, and get a small salad of tomatoes and cucumbers to go with it. This casual restaurant lies across from the municipal building on the waterfront, and is the first along the quay. ✉*Fanari quay* 📞*22510/44128* 🚫*No credit cards.*

¢–$ ✗**O Stratos.** This no-nonsense, no-decoration restaurant serves the best fish in Mytilini. No surprise, then, that waterfront tables are hard to come by, so plan to come early if you want to sit outside. Ask the genial staff for the catch of the day, or go into the kitchen to take a look at the *sargoi* (sea bream), *tsipoures* (dorado), or *barbounia* (red mullet) before making your pick. If fish is not what you're in the mood for, the barbecue chicken is a worthy substitute. Consider an accompanying wine from the island of Limnos. ✉*Fanari quay* 📞*22510/21739* 🚫*MC, V.*

¢ ✗**Hermes.** Founded in 1790 in a building 100 years older, this *ouzeri* (ouzo bar, though the sign calls it a *kafeneion,* or coffeehouse) is where local and visiting artists, poets, and politicians prefer to sip their ouzo on a vine-shaded terrace, with marble-top tables. You might try octopus in wine sauce, long-cooked chickpeas, or homemade sausages. The interior, a popular gathering spot in winter, provides a glimpse of traditional Lesbos design with old wood and mirrors. The longstanding hangout has similarly long hours: from 6 in the morning until the last person leaves at night. ✉*Kornarou 2, near end of Ermou* 📞*22510/26232* 🚫*No credit cards.*

$$$$ 🏨**Loriet Hotel.** The most-exclusive digs in the area may be in the Loriet's ★ 1880 stone mansion, where high frescoed ceilings, friezes, and antique furniture set the mood—and where visiting dignitaries often stay. Rooms here are called "suites" and start at €550 in high season. These are considerably more enticing than the utilitarian rooms and studios in the hotel's modern section, which is separated from the mansion by a beautiful pool and a grove of tall pines. An on-site restaurant is open July and August. The hotel lies across from the beach and is a five-minute drive from town and the airport. ✉*2 km (1 mi) south of Mytilini, 81100 Varia* 📞*22510/43111* 🌐*www.loriet-hotel.com* 🛏*35 rooms* ⚒*In-room: no a/c (some), kitchen (some), refrigerator. In-hotel: restaurant, bar, pool, no elevator* 🚫*AE, MC, V.*

$$–$$$ 📷**Pyrgos of Mytilene.** A restored 1916 mansion in the ornate Second Empire style fuses modern-day amenities and 19th-century nostalgia. The guest rooms are lavish, with period furniture, chandeliers, and stucco moldings, and each has its own style and color scheme, ranging from pistachio green to Venetian red. Particularly charming are the round rooms in the towers. The reception rooms are inviting, elegant, and spacious. On nice mornings, repair to the veranda for the breakfast of local breads, fruits, preserves, and other products. ✉*Eleftherios Venizelou 49, 81100* 📞*22510/27977 or 22510/25069* ⊕*www.pyrgoshotel.gr* ⇨*12 rooms* &*In-room: refrigerator. In-hotel: bar, no elevator* ▭*MC, AE, V* ⦿*CP.*

$ 📷**Porto Lesvos I.** If you want to stay in the center of Mytilini, this old, carefully renovated building a block inland from the harbor is a solid moderately priced choice. You can feel the Papadakis family touch in the furnishings and service. The rooms all have exposed stonework and some have sea views; the breakfast room is nicely done in wood and stone. ✉*Komninaki 21, 81100* 📞*22510/41771* ⊕*www.portolesvos.gr* ⇨*12 rooms* &*In-room: refrigerator. In-hotel: bar, no elevator* ▭*MC, V* ⦿*CP.*

NIGHTLIFE

The cafés along the harbor turn into bars after midnight, generally closing at 3 AM. For a relaxed Caribbean-style start to your night, start with a cocktail at **Hacienda** (✉*East end of port* 📞*22510/46850*). You need transportation to reach **Kohilia** (✉*7 km [4½ mi] south of Mytilini, on beach opposite airport* 📞*No phone*), an outdoor beach bar with an upscale, artistic vibe.

SHOPPING

Much of the best shopping is along the Ermou street bazaar. Here you can buy a little of everything, from food (especially olive oil and ouzo) to pottery, wood carvings, and embroidery. Lesbos produces 50 brands of ouzo, and George Spentzas's shop, **Veto** (✉*J. Arisarchi 1* 📞*22510/24660*), right on the main harbor, has made its own varieties on the premises since 1948. It also sells local foods.

10

SKALA SIKAMINIAS ΣΚΑΛΑ ΣΥΚΑΜΙΝΙΑΣ

★ *35 km (22 mi) northwest of Mytilini.*

At the northernmost point of Lesbos, past Pelopi, is the exceptionally lovely fishing port of Skala Sikaminias, a miniature gem—serene and real, with several good fish tavernas on the edge of the dock. The novelist Stratis Myrivilis used the village as the setting for his *Mermaid Madonna.* Those who have read the book will recognize the tiny chapel at the base of the jetty. The author's birthplace and childhood home are in Sikaminia, the village overlooking Skala Sikaminias—and the Turkish coast—from its perch high above the sea.

WHERE TO EAT

¢–$ ✗**Skamnia.** Sit at a table of Skala Sikaminias's oldest taverna, under the same spreading mulberry tree where Myrivilis wrote, to sip a glass of ouzo and watch the fishing boats bob. Stuffed zucchini blossoms or cucumbers and tomatoes tossed with local olive oil are food for thought: light, tasty, and ideal for picking at. Other tempting dishes on the creative menu include fresh shrimp with garlic and parsley, and chicken in grape leaves. ⊠ *On waterfront* ☎ *22530/55319* ▭ *AE, MC, V.*

WORD OF MOUTH

"I highly recommend Molyvos as a base—stunning town with lots of reasonably priced car, scooter and bicycle rental places. I even managed to rent an automatic car for 35 euros one day!"   —murphy89

MOLYVOS ΜΟΛΥΒΟΣ

Fodor'sChoice *17 km (10½ mi) southwest of Skala Sikaminias, 61 km (38 mi) west*
★ *of Mytilini.*

Molyvos, also known by its ancient name, Mythimna, is a place that has attracted people since antiquity. Legend says that Achilles besieged the town until the king's daughter fell for him and opened the gates; then Achilles killed her. Before 1923 the Turks made up about a third of the population, living in many of the best stone houses. Today these balconied buildings with center staircases are weighed down by roses and geraniums; the red-tile roofs and cobblestone streets are required by law. Attracted by the town's charms, many artists live here. Don't miss a walk down to the picture-perfect harbor front.

Come before high season and walk or drive up to the **kastro,** a Byzantine-Genoese fortified castle, for a hypnotic view down the tiers of red-tile roofs to the glittering sea. At dawn the sky begins to light up from behind the mountains of Asia Minor, casting silver streaks through the placid water as weary night fishermen come in. Purple wisteria vines shelter the lanes that descend from the castle and pass numerous Turkish fountains, some still in use. ⊠ *Above town* ☎ *22530/71803* ▭ *€3* ⊙ *Tues.–Sat. 8–2:30.*

★ The stunning 16th-century **Leimonos Monastery** houses 40 chapels and an impressive collection of precious objects. Founded by St. Ignatios Agalianos on the ruins of an older Byzantine monastery, it earned its name from the "flowering meadow of souls" surrounding it. The intimate St. Ignatios church is filled with colorful frescoes and is patrolled by peacocks. A **folk-art museum** with historic and religious works is accompanied by a **treasury** of 450 Byzantine manuscripts. Women are not allowed inside the main church. ⊠ *Up a marked road 5 km (3 mi) northwest of Kalloni, 15 km (9 mi) southwest of Molyvos* ▭ *Museum and treasury €1.50* ⊙ *Daily 9–1 and 5–7:30.*

Island Celebrations

Festivals provide a wonderful view into age-old traditions—and lots of fun. Mixing folk traditions with myth and legend, the three-week-long Greek Carnival (Apokreas) is celebrated to varying degrees throughout the islands, including those beyond the northern Aegean. Other festivals, honoring patron saints, history, or the local culture, are unique.

Chios has some notable pre-Lenten events. Greek Carnival, which begins in February and shifts according to the start of Lent, reaches a climax in Thimiana, south of Chios town, where islanders reenact the expulsion of the Berber pirates in the Festival of Mostras. There on the last Friday of Carnival, youths masquerade and wear old men's and women's clothes. Three days later in villages across the island Clean Monday is celebrated with the custom of *Agas,* when an "Aga" is chosen to judge and sentence the people who are present in a humorous, recreational affair. On the evening before Easter the effigy of Judas is burned in Mesta. In Pirgi on August 15 and August 23, villagers perform the local dance, the *pyrgoussikos,* to commemorate the death of the Virgin Mary.

On Lesbos, Clean Monday brings Carnival to a close with lavish costume parades and theater performances at Agiassos.

Molyvos Theater Festival
(☎ *22530/71323 tickets*), the best known of the festivals held on these islands, is in July and August. With Molyvos castle as backdrop, artists from Greece and elsewhere in Europe stage entertainments that range from a Dario Fo play to contemporary music concerts.

On August 15 the islanders of Lesbos again flock to Agiassos to celebrate the Feast of the Dormition of the Virgin with dancing, drinking, and eating. Samos has many celebrations: a wine festival in late summer to early fall pleases with Panhellenic dances in Samos town. In high summer, a fisherman's festival centers on the harbor at Pythagorio. Swimming races in Pythagorio commemorate the battle of Cavo Fonias on August 6, a day of celebration for the entire island. On September 14, the Timiou Stavrou monastery celebrates its feast day with a service followed by a *paniyiri* (feast), with music, firecrackers, coconut candy, and *loukoumades* (honey-soaked dumplings).

10

WHERE TO STAY & EAT

$-$$ ✕ **Captain's Table.** At the end of a quay, this wonderful taverna serves
★ seafood caught on its own trawler, moored opposite. The best way to go is to mix and match a series of small dishes, or *mezedes:* maybe try *aujuka* (spicy eggplant slices), smoked mackerel with olives, vegetarian souvlaki, or grilled veggies and rice. Fresh fish may include red snapper, sea bream, lobster, and gilt. Owners Melinda and Theo, who are wonderful resources for visitors, also rent rooms in a house that's a 10-minute walk from the restaurant. Grab a seat at the Table early, as it tends to get busy quickly. ⊠ *Molyvos harbor across from Ayios Nikolaos chapel* ☎ *22530/71241* ▭ *MC, V* ☉ *Closed mid-Oct.–mid-Apr. No lunch.*

$-$$ ✕ **Gatos.** Gaze over the island and harbor from the veranda of this yellow-and-green-dressed charmer, or sit inside and watch the cooks chop and grind in the open kitchen: Gatos is known for its grilled meats. The beef fillet is tender, the lamb chops nicely spiced, and the salads fresh. You might also consider ordering the *kokkinisto* (beef in tomato sauce) with garlic and savory onion. ⊠ *Center of old market* ☎ *22530/71661* ☐ *V.*

¢–$ ✕ **Panorama.** High over the town, this terraced restaurant cooks terrific Greek food and, as the name suggests, it has a spectacular view. It's worth coming here just for a sunset drink, to see the sun illumine the red roofs of Molyvos and the sea beyond. Good appetizers include spicy cheese salad, and fried stuffed peppers; among the main courses are meat on the grill and fresh fish. It is also open for breakfast. ⊠ *Under kastro* ☎ *22530/71848* ☐ *No credit cards.*

$ 🏨 **Aeolis.** A little away from the buzz of Molyvos, this cluster of traditional red-roof buildings offers ample chance to relax, with deep-seated sofas in the light, airy lounge, a swimming pool (hard to find in Molyvos proper), and a nearby, if mediocre, beach. The beachside rooms have two or three low-to-the-ground beds, bathrooms with showers or baths, and French doors opening onto a veranda. The view from the veranda takes in the sea and Molyvos castle. A hotel shuttle service runs up to town, as does the local bus. ⊠ *On road to Eftalou, 81108* ☎ *22530/71772* ⊕ *www.aeolishotel.gr* ⇆ *71 rooms* ⚬ *In-room: kitchen (some), refrigerator. In-hotel: restaurant, bars, pool, no elevator* ☐ *MC, V* ⊙ *Closed Nov.–Mar.* ⦿ *BP.*

$ 🏨 **Sea Horse Hotel.** This delightful stone-front hotel on Molyvos harbor
★ overlooks the eateries on the photogenic quay; the lobby even extends into a waterfront café. Twelve of the rooms—simply decorated but perfectly charming with painted wood furniture—have full sea views, an additional three have partial sea views, and one room has a village view. ⊠ *Molyvos quay, 81108* ☎ *22530/71320 or 22530/71630* ⊕ *www.seahorse-hotel.com* ⇆ *16 rooms* ⚬ *In-room: refrigerator. In-hotel: restaurant, bar, no elevator* ☐ *MC, V* ⊙ *Closed mid-Oct.–mid-Apr.* ⦿ *CP.*

NIGHTLIFE & THE ARTS

The best-known celebration on the islands is the **Molyvos Theater Festival** (☎ *22530/71323 tickets*) in July and August. With the castle as backdrop, artists from Greece and elsewhere in Europe stage entertainments that range from a Dario Fo play to contemporary music concerts.

Molly's Bar (⊠ *On street above harbor* ☎ *22530/71209*) has relaxed music in an environment that's ideal for quiet conversations. **Music Cafe Del Mar** (⊠ *Harbor front* ☎ *22530/71588*) hosts live acoustic bouzouki music and has a cocktail terrace with a sea view.

SHOPPING

The **Earth Collection** (⊠ *Molyvos quay* ☎ *22530/72094*) sells organic clothes made exclusively of natural products. **Evelyn** (⊠ *Kyriakou Sq.* ☎ *22530/72197*) stocks a wide variety of local goods, including ceramics, pastas, olive oil, wines, ouzo, sauces, and marmalades.

SKALA ERESSOU ΣΚΑΛΑ ΕΡΕΣΟΥ

★ *40 km (25 mi) southwest of Molyvos, 89 km (55 mi) west of Mytilini.*

The poet Sappho, according to unreliable late biographies, was born here circa 612 BC. Dubbed the Tenth Muse by Plato because of her skill and sensitivity, she perhaps presided over a finishing school for marriageable young women. She was married herself and had a daughter. Some of her songs erotically praise these girls and celebrate their marriages. Sappho's works, proper and popular in their time, were burned by Christians, so that mostly fragments survive; one is "and I yearn, and I desire." Sapphic meter was in great favor in Roman and medieval times; both Catullus and Gregory the Great used it, and in the 19th century, Tennyson did, too. Today, many gay women come to Skala Eressou to celebrate Sappho (the word "lesbian" derives from Lesbos), although the welcoming town is also filled with heterosexual couples.

On the **acropolis** of ancient Eressos overlooking the coastal area and beach are **remains of pre-Hellenistic walls, castle ruins,** and the AD 5th-century church, **Ayios Andreas.** The church has a mosaic floor and a tiny adjacent **museum** housing local finds from tombs in the ancient cemetery. ⊠*1 km (½ mi) north of Skala Eressou* ☎*22530/53332* ⊠*Free* ☉*Tues.–Sun. 7:30–3:30.*

The old village of **Eressos** (⊠*11 km [7 mi] inland, north of Skala Eressou*), separated from the coast by a large plain, was developed to protect its inhabitants from pirate raids. Along the mulberry tree–lined road leading from the beach you might encounter a villager wearing a traditional head scarf (*mandila*), plodding by on her donkey. This village of two-story, 19th-century stone and shingle houses is filled with superb architectural details. Note the huge wooden doors decorated with nails and elaborate door knockers, loophole windows in thick stone walls, elegant pediments topping imposing mansions, and fountains spilling under Gothic arches.

BEACH

Some of the island's best beaches are in this area, which has been built up very rapidly—and not always tastefully. Especially popular is the 4-km-long (2½-mi-long) town beach at **Skala Eressou,** where the wide stretch of dark sand is lined with tamarisk trees. A small island is within swimming distance, and northerly winds lure windsurfers as well as swimmers and sunbathers. There are many rooms to rent within walking distance of the beach.

WHERE TO EAT

$–$$ ✕ **Soulatso.** The enormous anchor outside is a sign that you're in for some seriously good seafood. On a wooden deck, tables are set just a skipping-stone's throw from the break of the waves. Owner Sarandos Tzinieris serves, and his mother cooks. Fresh grilled squid is mellifluous, and the fish are carefully chosen every morning. ⊠*At beach center* ☎*22530/52078* ⊟*No credit cards.*

¢–$ ✕ **Parasol.** Totem poles, colored coconut lamps, and other knickknacks from exotic travels make this beach bar endearing. The owner and his wife serve omelets, fruits, yogurt, and sweet Greek coffee for breakfast, and simple dishes like pizzas, veggie spring rolls, and cheese platters the rest of the day. But the most obvious reason to come here is to relax after sundown with one of the bar's creative drinks, such as the signature green cocktail, the Wooloomooloo Wonder, made with vodka and fresh melon. The music might be characterized as sophisticated lounge; the owner calls it "intellectual." ⊠*Beachfront* ☏*No phone* ▤*No credit cards* ⊘*Closed Nov.–Apr.*

AGIASSOS ΑΓΙΑΣΟΣ

★ *87 km (53 mi) northwest of Skala Eressou, 28 km (17½ mi) southwest of Mytilini.*

Agiassos village, the prettiest hill town on Lesbos, sits in an isolated valley amid thousands of olive trees, near the foot of Mt. Olympus, the highest peak. (In case you're confused, 19 mountains in the Mediterranean are named Olympus, almost all of them peaks sacred to the local sky god, who eventually became associated with Zeus.) Exempted from taxes by the Turks, the town thrived. The age-old charm of Agiassos can be seen in its gray stone houses, cobblestone lanes, medieval castle, and local handicrafts, particularly pottery and woodwork.

The church of **Panayia Vrefokratousa** *(Madonna Holding the Infant)* was founded in the 12th century to house an icon of the Virgin Mary, believed to be the work of St. Luke, and remains a popular place of pilgrimage. Built into its foundation are shops whose revenues support the church, as they have through the ages. The **church museum** has a little Bible from AD 500, with legible, elegant calligraphy. ▨€0.50 ⊘*Daily 8–1 and 5:30–8:30.*

▌**NEED A BREAK?**   Stop at one of several cafés in the winding streets of the old bazaar area past the church of Panayia Vrefokratousa. On weekend afternoons you can listen to a *santoúri* band (hammered dulcimer, accompanied by clarinet, drum, and violin). As the locals dance, rather haphazardly, on the cobblestones, you might be tempted to join in the merriment.

WHERE TO EAT

¢ ✕**Dagielles.** If nothing else, you must stop here for a coffee made by owner Stavritsa and served by her no-nonsense staff. You might also try the *kolokitholouloudia* (stuffed squash blossoms) and the dishes that entice throughout winter: *kritharaki* (orzo pasta) and *varkoules* ("little boats" of eggplant slices with minced meat). For a few short weeks in spring the air is laden with the scent of overhanging wisteria. ⊠*Near bus stop* ☏*22520/22241* ▤*No credit cards.*

SHOPPING

For handmade, hand-painted pottery, have a look in **Ceramic Workshop Antonia Gavve** (⊠*On main street* ☏*22520/93350*), where you can watch the artist paint.

For woodwork inspired by Byzantine art and Hellenism, stop by the functioning workshop of **D. Kamaros & Son** (⊠ *Next to church* ☎*22213/22520*); the store is opposite the shop. Dimitris Kamaros exports his woodwork throughout the Orthodox world. Although specializing in walnut furniture (the trees are local), the store also sells small pieces such as chessboards, backgammon tables, carved religious pieces, and jewelry boxes.

CHIOS ΧΙΟΣ

"Craggy Chios" is what local boy Homer, its first publicist, so to speak, called this starkly beautiful island, which almost touches Turkey's coast and shares its topography. The island may not appear overly charming when you first see its principal city and capital, Chios town, but consider its misfortunes: the bloody Turkish massacre of 1822 during the fight for Greek independence; major earthquakes, including one in 1881 that killed almost 6,000 Chiotes; severe fires, which in the 1980s burned two-thirds of its pine trees; and, through the ages, the steady stripping of forests to ax-wielding boatbuilders. Yet despite these disadvantages, the island remains a wonderful destination, with friendly inhabitants, and villages so rare and captivating that even having just one of them on this island would make it a gem.

The name Chios comes from the Phoenician word for "mastic," the resin of the *Pistacia lentisca,* evergreen shrubs that with few exceptions thrive only here, in the southern part of the island. Every August, incisions are made in the bark of the shrubs; the sap leaks out, permeating the air with a sweet fragrance, and in September it is harvested. This aromatic resin, which brought huge revenues until the introduction of petroleum products, is still used in cosmetics and chewing gum sold on the island today. Pirgi, Mesta, and other villages where the mastic is grown and processed are quite enchanting. In these towns you can wind your way through narrow, labyrinth-like Byzantine streets protected by medieval gates and peered over by homes that date back half a millennium.

Chios is also home to the elite families that control Greece's private shipping empires: Livanos, Karas, Chandris; even Onassis came here from Smyrna. The island has never seemed to need tourists, nor to draw them. Yet Chios intrigues, with its deep valleys, uncrowded sand and black-pebble beaches, fields of wild tulips, Byzantine monasteries, and haunting villages—all remnants of a poignant history.

10

CHIOS TOWN ΧΙΟΣ (ΠΟΛΗ)

285 km (177 mi) northeast of Piraeus. 55 km (34 mi) south of Mytilini.

The main port and capital, Chios town, or Chora (which means "town"), is a busy commercial settlement on the east coast, across from Turkey. This is the best base from which to explore the island, and you don't need to venture far from the port to discover the beauti-

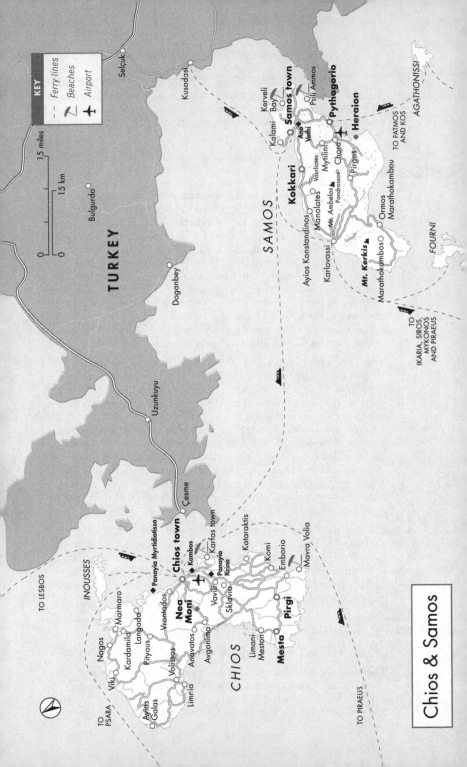

Chios & Samos

ful mansions of Kambos or the captivating orange groves just south of town. The daytime charm of the port area is limited, in part because no buildings predate the 1881 earthquake, in part because it needs a face-lift. But in the evening when the lights twinkle on the water and the scene is softened by a mingling of blues, the many cafés begin to overflow with ouzo and good cheer, and locals proudly promenade along the bayside.

The capital is crowded with half the island's population, but its fascinating heart is the sprawling **bazaar district.** Merchants hawk everything from local mastic gum and fresh dark bread to kitchen utensils in the morning but typically close in the afternoon. ⊠ *South and east of Vounakiou Sq. (the main square).*

The **old quarter** is inside the **kastro** (castle) fortifications, built in the 10th century by the Byzantines and enlarged in the 14th century by the Genoese Giustiniani family. Under Turkish rule, the Greeks lived outside the wall; the gate was closed daily at sundown. A deep dry moat remains on the western side. Note the old wood-and-plaster houses on the narrow backstreets, typically decorated with latticework and jutting balconies. An air of mystery pervades this old Muslim and Jewish neighborhood, full of decaying monuments, fountains, baths, and mosques. ⊠ *In northern highlands.*

The **Giustiniani Museum,** inside a 15th-century building that may have acted as the headquarters of the Genoese, exhibits Byzantine murals and sculptures, post-Byzantine icons, and other small Genoese and Byzantine works of art. ⊠ *Just inside old quarter* ☎ *22710/22819* ✉ *€3* ⊙ *Tues.–Sun. 9–2:30.*

In **Frouriou Square** (⊠ *At fort, old quarter*), look for the Turkish cemetery and the large **marble tomb** (with the fringed hat) of Kara Ali, chief of the Turkish flagship in 1822.

Along the **main street** are the elegant **Ayios Georgios** church (closed most of the time), which has icons from Asia Minor; houses from the Genoese period; and the **remains of Turkish baths** (north corner of fort).

In 1822, in the tiny **prison,** 75 leading Chiotes were jailed as hostages before they were hanged by the Turks, part of the worst massacre committed during the War of Independence. The Turks drove out the Genoese in 1566, and Chios, spurred by Samians who had fled to the island, joined the rest of Greece in rebellion in the early 19th century. The revolt failed, and the sultan retaliated: the Turks killed 30,000 Chiotes and enslaved 45,000, an event written about by Victor Hugo and depicted by Eugène Delacroix in *The Massacre of Chios.* The painting, now in the Louvre, shocked Western Europe and increased support for Greek independence. Copies of *The Massacre of Chios* hang in many places on Chios. ⊠ *Inside main gate of castle, near Giustiniani Museum.*

The only intact mosque in this part of the Aegean, complete with a slender minaret, houses the **Byzantine Museum,** which at this writing is closed indefinitely for renovation. It holds a *tugra* (the swirling

10

monogram of the sultan that indicated royal possession), rarely seen outside Istanbul; its presence indicated the favor Chios once enjoyed under the sultan. Housed inside are the Jewish, Turkish, and Armenian gravestones leaning with age in the courtyard. ⊠ *Vounakiou Sq.* ☏ *22710/26866.*

The **Chios Maritime Museum** celebrates the sea-based heritage of the island with exquisite ship models and portraits of vessels that have belonged to Chios owners over time. One exhibit highlights the Liberty ships and others constructed

> ### BEDROCK OF EDUCATION
>
> **Daskalopetra** *(Teacher's Rock)* where Homer is said to have taught his pupils, stands just above the port of Vrontados, 4 km (2½ mi) north of Chios town. Archaeologists think this rocky outcrop above the sea is part of an ancient altar to Cybele; you can sit on it and muse about how the blind storyteller might have spoken here of the fall of Troy in The *Iliad.*

during World War II that contributed to the beginning of Greece's postwar shipping industry. ⊠ *Stefanou Tsouri 20* ☏ *22710/44139* ⊕ *www. nauticalmuseum.com* ⊠ *Free* ⊗ *Mon.–Sat. 10–1.*

The **Chios Archaeological Museum** has a collection that ranges from proto-Helladic pottery dug up in Emborio to a letter, on stone, from Alexander the Great addressed to the Chiotes and dated 332 BC. It also displays beautiful Ionian sculptures crafted by Chiotes. ⊠ *Michalon 10, 82100* ☏ *22710/44239* ⊠ *€2* ⊗ *Tues.–Sun. 8:30–1.*

The **Philip Argenti Museum** houses a historic and folkloric collection, and sits on the second floor above the **Korais Library,** Greece's third largest. The museum displays meticulously designed costumes, embroidery, pastoral wood carvings, and furniture of a village home. ⊠ *Korais 2, near cathedral* ☏ *22710/28256* ⊠ *€1.50* ⊗ *Weekdays 8–4.*

Mastodon bones were found in the **Kambos district,** a fertile plain of tangerine, lemon, and orange groves just south of Chios town. In medieval times and later, wealthy Genoese and Greek merchants built ornate, earth-color, three-story mansions here. Behind forbidding stone walls adorned with coats of arms, each is a world of its own, with multicolor sandstone patterns, arched doorways, and pebble-mosaic courtyards. Some houses have crumbled and some still stand, reminders of the wealth, power, and eventual downfall of an earlier time. These suburbs of Chios town are exceptional, but the unmarked lanes can be confusing, so leave time to get lost and to peek behind the walls into another world. ⊠ *4 km (2½ mi) south of Chios town.*

BEACHES

Karfas beach (⊠ *8 km [5 mi] south of Chios town*) fronts a shallow sandy bay. Tavernas are in the area, and in summer there is transportation to town. Farther south, Komi has a fine, sandy beach.

WHERE TO STAY & EAT

$–$$ ✕**Bella Vista.** On the coastal road toward the airport, just outside the port, Bella Vista serves the island's best Italian food. Selections include salads with fresh mozzarella, thick crisp pizzas, and numerous pastas, such as spaghetti with fresh, juicy lobster—accompanied by fresh-baked bread. The delicious shrimp "terminator" is a dish of large shrimp smothered with mushrooms, peppers, and cream. The dining room has a mesmerizing tropical aquarium; street noise can disturb the tranquillity of the outdoor veranda. ⊠*South of center, Livanou 2* ☎22710/41022 ▤*MC, V.*

$–$$ ✕**Pyrgos.** Attentive service, fine food, and pretty surroundings characterize a meal at the poolside garden restaurant of the Grecian Castle hotel. Beef carpaccio and spinach salad are excellent starters, followed by beef *pagiar,* a fillet stuffed with *mastello* (the local goat cheese), sun-dried tomatoes, and pesto-olive sauce. Or try the pork with prunes, mushrooms, and *vin santo* (a sweet wine) sauce. The extensive menu also includes crepes, pastas, and seafood. Mastic ice cream with rose syrup closes a meal on a richly local note. ⊠*Chios harbor* ☎22710/44740 ▤*AE, D, MC, V.*

¢–$ ✕**Taverna tou Tassou.** Dependably delicious traditional food is why so 🕲 many locals eat here in a garden courtyard beneath a canopy of trees. ★ Fresh fish and seafood, lamb chops and other meats, stuffed peppers and cooked greens—you can't go wrong. Expect Greek owner Dimitrius Doulos and his son, the chef, to warmly welcome you. The taverna is at the south edge of town toward the airport, and there's a playground nearby for kids. ⊠*Livanou 8, south toward airport* ☎22710/27542 ▤*DC, MC, V* ⊙*Closed Nov.*

$$$–$$$$ ▦**Chios Chandris.** Only a few minutes' walk from the village center, Chios Chandris has the best location of any hotel in Chios town: it looks out at both the sea and the harbor, and has an inviting pool with panoramic views of both. Balconies have views of the mountains or of the ferries and fishing boats plying the harbor. Although the outside looks a bit worn, comfortable rooms are brightly decorated in shades of Aegean blue and yellow. ⊠*Between port and beach, 82100 Prokymea* ☎22710/44401 through 22710/44410 ⊕*www.chandris.gr* ⤴*129 rooms, 10 suites* 🔑*In-room: kitchen (some), refrigerator. In-hotel: restaurant, bar, pool, public Wi-Fi* ▤*AE, MC, V* ⦿*BP.*

$$ ▦**Grecian Castle.** With spacious (and a few not-so-spacious) rooms fur- ★ nished in warm, neutral tones; a pretty pool; and carefully landscaped grounds, this sophisticated hotel sets a high standard for Chios. A stone exterior of the main building, originally a pasta factory, was influenced by Chios's medieval castle; it's complemented by the elegant wood furnishings of the lobby and breakfast room. The hotel is near the sea, toward the airport. ⊠*Leoforos Enosseos, 1 km (½ mi) south toward airport, 82100* ☎22710/44740 ⊕*www.greciancastle.gr* ⤴*51 rooms,*

10

4 suites ♿ *In-room: refrigerator. In-hotel: restaurant, bars, pool* ☰*AE, D, MC, V.*

$$ **📷Perleas Mansion.** More than a thousand trees, mostly citrus, grow
FodorsChoice   on the beautiful grounds of this stunning estate. Owners Vangelis
★   and Claire Xydas have painstakingly restored the main stone house,
from 1640, and two smaller buildings. Guest rooms, which look out
to the orchards, are filled with antique furnishings and the fragrance
of jasmine. Common rooms have books and board games, and there
are wonderful spots for walking, reading, and relaxing. The service
here makes you feel like an aristocrat from a previous era. Should you
wish to retain that illusion for dinner, the hostess prepares meals three
nights a week upon request: delectable and healthy organic fare fresh
from the farm is served on the patio under the stars. ⊠ *Vitiadou, Kam-
bos district, 4 km (2½ mi) south of center, 82100* ☎*22710/32217 or
22710/32962* ⊕*www.perleas.gr* ⬅*7 rooms* ♿*In-room: no TV, refrig-
erator. In hotel: no elevator* ☰*MC, V* ❶*BP.*

$ **📷Kyma.** Begun in 1917 for a shipping magnate, this neoclassic villa
★   on the waterfront was completed in 1922, when it served as Colonel
Plastiras's headquarters after the Greek defeat in Asia Minor (Plastiras
went on to become a general and prime minister of Greece). Now the
villa is the prettiest hotel in town, run by the friendliest staff, under
Theo Spordilis. Many of Kyma's rooms have balconies with sea views,
and some are equipped with hot tubs. A large breakfast, including
fruits, juices, eggs, jams, yogurt, and honey, is served under frescoed
ceilings in the breakfast room. ⊠*Chandris 1, 82100* ☎*22710/44500*
⬜*kyma@chi.forthnet.gr* ⬅*59 rooms* ♿*In-room: refrigerator* ☰*No
credit cards* ❶*CP.*

NIGHTLIFE

Stylish nightspots along the harbor are more sophisticated than those
on most of the other northern Aegean islands, and many of the clubs
are filled with well-off young tourists and locals. You can just walk
along, listen to the music, and size up the crowd; most clubs are
open to the harbor and dramatically lighted. **Cosmo** (⊠*Aigeou 100*
☎*22710/81695*) stands out as an inviting cocktail lounge playing
international and Greek music.

SHOPPING

The resinous gum made from the sap of the mastic tree is a best
buy in Chios, and makes a fun souvenir and conversation piece;
the brand is Elma. You can also find mastic liquor called *mastíha,*
and *gliko koutaliou,* sugar-preserved fruit added to water. Stores
are typically closed Sunday, and open mornings only on Monday
through Wednesday.

At the elegant shop of **Mastic Spa** (⊠*Aigeou 12, on waterfront a block
from dock* ☎*22710/40223*), all the beauty and health products contain
the local balm. **Moitafiz** (⊠ *Venizelou 7* ☎*22710/25330*) sells mastíha,
fruit preserves, and other sweets and spirits. **Yiorgos Varias** (⊠ *Venizelou
2* ☎*22710/22368*) has a passion for pickles. His tiny store is crammed
with 36 varieties, including melon, chestnut, and fig. **Zaharoplasteion
Avgoustakis** (⊠*Psychari 4* ☎*22710/44480*) is a traditional candy

store where you can buy *masourakia* (crispy rolled pastries dripping in syrup and nuts) and *rodinia* (melt-in-your-mouth cookies stuffed with almond cream).

NEA MONI NEA MONH

Fodor'sChoice
★

17 km (10½ mi) west of Chios town.

Almost hidden among the olive groves, the island's most important monastery—with one of the finest examples of mosaic art anywhere—is the 11th-century Nea Moni. Emperor Constantine IX Monomachos ("the Dueler") ordered the monastery built where three monks found an icon of the Virgin in a myrtle bush. The octagonal *katholikon* (medieval church) is the only surviving example of 11th-century court art—none survives in Constantinople. The church has been renovated a number of times: the dome was completely rebuilt following an earthquake in 1881, and a great deal of effort has gone into the restoration and preservation of the mosaics over the years. The distinctive three-part vaulted sanctuary has a double narthex, with no buttresses supporting the dome. This design, a single square space covered by a dome, is rarely seen in Greece. Blazing with color, the church's interior gleams with marble slabs and mosaics of Christ's life, austere yet sumptuous, with azure blue, ruby red, velvet green, and skillful applications of gold. The saints' expressiveness comes from their vigorous poses and severe gazes, with heavy shadows under the eyes. On the iconostasis hangs the icon—a small Virgin and Child facing left. Also inside the grounds are an **ancient refectory, a vaulted cistern, a chapel** filled with victims' bones from the massacre at Chios, and a large **clock** still keeping Byzantine time, with the sunrise reckoned as 12 o'clock. ⊠*In mountains west of Chios town* ☎22710/79.391 ✉*Donations accepted* ☉*Tues.–Sun. 8–1 and 4–7.*

PIRGI ΠΥΡΓΙ

★ *25 km (15½ mi) south of Nea Moni. 20 km (12½ mi) south of Chios town.*

Beginning in the 14th century, the Genoese founded 20 or so fortified inland villages in southern Chios. These villages shared a defensive design with double-thick walls, a maze of narrow streets, and a square tower, or *pirgos,* in the middle—a last resort to hold the residents in case of pirate attack. The villages prospered on the sales of mastic gum and were spared by the Turks because of the industry. Today they depend on citrus, apricots, olives—and tourists.

Pirgi is the largest of these mastic villages, and in many ways the most wondrous. It could be a graphic designer's model or a set from a mad moviemaker or a town from another planet. Many of the buildings along the tiny arched streets are adorned with *xysta* (like Italian sgraffito); they are coated with a mix of cement and volcanic sand from nearby beaches, then whitewashed and stenciled, often top to bottom, in traditional patterns of animals, flowers, and geometric designs. The

10

effect is both delicate and dazzling. This exuberant village has more than 50 churches (people afraid of attack tend to pray for a continuation of life).

Look for especially lavish xysta on buildings near the main square, including the **Kimisis tis Theotokou church** *(Dormition of the Virgin church)*, built in 1694. ⊠ *Off main square* ⊘ *Daily 9–1 and 4–8.*

DID A GREEK
DISCOVER AMERICA?

About 50 people named Kolomvos live in Pirgi, claiming kinship with Christopher Columbus, known to have been from Genoa, the power that built the town. Some renegade historians claim Columbus, like Homer, was really born on Chios.

Check out the fresco-embellished 12th-century church **Agii Apostoli** *(Holy Apostles)*, a very small replica of the katholikon at the Nea Moni Monastery. The 17th-century frescoes that completely cover the interior, the work of a Cretan artist, have a distinct folk-art leaning. ⊠ *Northwest of main square* ⊘ *Tues.–Sun. 8:30–3.*

In the small mastic village of **Armolia,** 5 km (3 mi) north of Pirgi, pottery is a specialty. In fact, the Greek word *armolousis* ("man from Armolia") is synonymous with potter.

Earthal Art sells hand-painted pottery and handicrafts, as well as quality, inexpensive oil paintings of the Greek islands. ⊠ *Pirgi–Armolia road* ☎ 22710/72693.

BEACH

From Pirgi it's 8 km (5 mi) southeast to the glittering black volcanic beach near Emborio, known by locals as **Mavra Volia** *(Black Pebbles).* The cove is backed by jutting volcanic cliffs, the calm water's dark-blue color created by the deeply tinted seabed. Here perhaps was an inspiration for the "wine-dark sea" that Homer wrote about.

MESTA ΜΕΣΤΑ

Fodor's Choice
★   *11 km (7 mi) west of Pirgi, 30 km (18½ mi) southwest of Chios town.*

Pirgi may be the most unusual of the mastic villages, but Mesta is the island's best preserved: a labyrinth of twisting vaulted streets link two-story stone-and-mortar houses that are supported by buttresses against earthquakes. The enchanted village sits inside a system of three-foot-thick walls, and the outer row of houses also doubles as protection. In fact, the village homes were built next to each other to form a castle, reinforced with towers. Most of the narrow streets, free of cars and motorbikes, lead to blind alleys; the rest lead to the six gates. The one in the northeast retains an iron grate.

One of the largest and wealthiest churches in Greece, the 18th-century church of **Megas Taxiarchis** *(Great Archangel)* commands the main square; its vernacular baroque is combined with the late-folk-art style of Chios. The church was built on the ruins of the central refuge tower.

Ask at the main square for Elias, the gentle old man in the village who is the keeper of the keys.

BEACHES

Escape to the string of secluded coves, between Elatas and Trahiliou bays, for good swimming. The **nudist beach** (⊠*2 km [1 mi] north of Lithi*) has fine white pebbles.

WHERE TO STAY & EAT

¢–$ ✕**Restaurant Café Mesconas.** A traditional Greek kitchen turns out the
★ delicious food served on outdoor tables in the small village square, adjacent to Megas Taxiarchis. You dine surrounded by medieval homes and magical lights at night, but the setting is lovely even for a daytime coffee and relaxed conversation. The best dishes include rabbit *stifado* (stew), made with shallots, tomatoes, and olive oil; and *pastitsio,* a meat pie with macaroni and béchamel sauce. All of the recipes use local ingredients, with herbs and spices gathered from the region. *Souma* is the local equivalent of ouzo but made from figs—it can be blindingly strong, up to 70% alcohol. ⊠*Main square* 📞22710/76050 ▤*MC, V.*

¢ ✕**Limani Meston.** The fishing boats bobbing in the water only a few feet away supply Limani Meston with a rich daily fish selection. The friendly, gracious owner may well persuade you to munch on some of his smaller catches, such as sardines served with onions and pita, accompanied by calamari and cheese balls. Meats served at the simple taverna include homemade sausage, and lamb or beef on the spit. You can sit outside among the ivy and blossoms, where Mesta's working harbor unfolds before you. On colder days, enjoy the fireplace with the locals. The owner rents studio apartments within walking distance. ⊠*Mesta harbor, 3 km (2 mi) north of Mesta village* 📞22710/76389 ▤*No credit cards.*

¢ 🏠**Anna Floradi.** The charming Floradi family has remodeled a medieval
★ home into a guesthouse with four studio rooms and a two-bedroom apartment. All have rustic furnishings and cooking facilities—not bad for Byzantine accommodations smack in the center of a mastic village. Ask for one of the rooms upstairs; they open out onto an alfresco den built around an old wood oven, and one has a balcony. Anna Floradi leaves breakfast items (bread, honey, yogurt, or cheese pie) for guests to prepare on their own. ⊠*Village center, 82102* 📞22710/28891 📠22710/76455 ✉*floradis@internet.gr* 📶*4 rooms, 1 apartment* ⚒*In-room: kitchen. In hotel: no elevator* ▤*MC, V* 🍴*CP.*

NIGHTLIFE

Karnayio (⊠*Leoforos Stenoseos, outside town on road to airport* 📞*No phone*) is a popular spot for dancing.

SPORTS & THE OUTDOORS

Masticulture leads walking tours to mastic tree groves, where farmers show you how they gather mastic through grooves carved into the trees' bark. There are three daily tours, at 11, 5:30, and 7:30, that include a stop to pick fresh produce from the farm's organic vegetable gardens, to be nibbled during the tour. ⊠*Main square* 📞22710/76084 🌐*www.masticulture.com* 💶*€15.*

SHOPPING

Artists and craftspeople are attracted to this ancient area. **Agnitha** (⊠ *Delfon 34* ☎ *22710/76031*) is a magical shop selling handwoven textiles, silver jewelry, and local art. **Ilias Likourinas** (⊠ *Workshop: Delfon*) is an icon artist who will paint to order. The shop of **Sergias Patentas** (⊠ *Mesta–Limenas harbor road, 3 km [2 mi] north of Mesta*) sells sculptural fantasies he creates based on mythology and history.

SAMOS ΣΑΜΟΣ

The southernmost of this group of three north Aegean islands, Samos lies the closest to Turkey of any Greek island, separated by only 3 km (2 mi). It was, in fact, a part of Asia Minor until it split off during the Ice Age. Samos means "high" in Phoenician, and its abrupt volcanic mountains soaring dramatically like huge hunched shoulders from the rock surface of the island are among the tallest in the Aegean, geologically part of the great spur that runs across western Turkey. As you approach from the west, Mt. Kerkis seems to spin out of the sea, and in the distance Mt. Ambelos guards the terraced vineyards that produce the famous Samian wine. The felicitous landscape has surprising twists, with lacy coasts and mountain villages perched on ravines carpeted in pink oleander, red poppy, and purple sage.

When Athens was young, in the 7th century BC, Samos was already a political, economic, and naval power. In the next century, during Polycrates's reign, it was noted for its arts and sciences and was the expanded site of the vast Temple of Hera, one of the Seven Wonders of the Ancient World. The Persian Wars led to the decline of Samos, however, which fell first under Persian rule, and then became subordinate to the expanding power of Athens. Samos was defeated by Pericles in 439 BC and forced to pay tribute to Athens.

Pirates controlled this deserted island after the fall of the Byzantine empire, but in 1562 an Ottoman admiral repopulated Samos with expatriates and Orthodox believers. It languished under the sun for hundreds of years until tobacco and shipping revived the economy in the 19th century.

Small though it may be, Samos has a formidable list of great Samians stretching through the ages. The fabled Aesop, the philosopher Epicurus, and Aristarchos (first in history to place the sun at the center of the solar system) all lived on Samos. The mathematician Pythagoras was born in Samos's ancient capital in 580 BC; in his honor, it was renamed Pythagorio in AD 1955 (it only took a couple of millennia). Plutarch wrote that in Roman times Anthony and Cleopatra took a long holiday on Samos, "giving themselves over to the feasting," and that artists came from afar to entertain them.

In the last decade Samos has become packed with other holiday travelers—European charter tourists—in July and August. Thankfully the curving terrain allows you to escape the crowds easily and feel as if you are still in an undiscovered Eden.

SAMOS TOWN ΣΑΜΟΣ (ΠΟΛΗ)

278 km (174 mi) east of Piraeus. 111 km (69 mi) southeast of Mytilini.

On the northeast coast at the head of a sharply deep bay is the capital, Samos town, also known as Vathi (which actually refers to the old settlement just above the port). Red-tile roofs sweep around the arc of the bay and reach toward the top of red-earth hills. In the morning at the sheltered port, fishermen still grapple with their nets, spreading them to dry in the sun, and in the early afternoon everything shuts down. Slow summer sunsets over the sparkling harbor match the relaxed pace of locals. Tourism has not altered this centuries-old schedule.

★ The stepped streets ascend from the shopping thoroughfare, which meanders from the port to the city park next to the **Archaeological Museum,** the town's most important sight. The newest wing holds the impressive **kouros from Heraion,** a statue of a nude male youth, built as an offering to the goddess Hera and the largest freestanding sculpture surviving from ancient Greece, dating from 580 BC. This colossal statue, the work of a Samian artist, is made of the typical Samian gray-and-white-band marble. Pieces of the kouros were discovered in various peculiar locations: its thigh was being used as part of a Hellenistic house wall, and its left forearm was being used as a step for a Roman cistern. The statue is so large (16½ feet tall) that the wing had to be rebuilt specifically to house it. The museum's older section has a collection of pottery and cast-bronze griffin heads (the symbol of Samos). Samian sculptures from past millennia were considered among the best in Greece, and examples here show why. An exceptional collection of tributary gifts from ancient cities far and wide, including bronzes and ivory miniatures, affirms the importance of the shrine to Hera. ⊠ *Dimarhiou Sq.* ☎ 22730/27469 ⊠ €3 ⊗ *Tues.–Sun. 8:30–3.*

In the quaint 17th-century enclave of **Ano Vathi** (⊠ *Southern edge of Samos town, beyond museum, to the right*), wood-and-plaster houses with pastel facades and red-tile roofs are jammed together, their balconies protruding into cobbled paths so narrow that the water channel takes up most of the space. From here you have a view of the gulf.

10

OFF THE BEATEN PATH

Turkey. From Samos town (and Pythagorio), you can easily ferry to Turkey. Once you're there, it's a 13-km (8-mi) drive from the Kuşadası Kud on the Turkish coast, where the boats dock, to Ephesus, one of the great archaeological sites and a major city of the ancient world. (Note that the Temple of Artemis in Ephesus is a copy of the Temple of Hera in Heraion, which is now in ruins.) Many travel agencies have guided round-trip full-day tours to the site (€100), although you can take an unguided ferry trip for €35 with same-day return. You leave your passport with the agency, and it is returned when you come back from Turkey.

BEACHES

One of the island's best beaches is **Psili Ammos** (⊠ *Southeast of Samos town, near Mesokambos*), a pristine, sandy beach protected from the wind by cliffs. There are two tavernas here. The beach at **Kerveli bay**

(⊠*On the coast east of Samos town*) has an enticing pebbly beach with calm, turquoise waters.

WHERE TO STAY & EAT

$–$$ ✕ **The Steps.** Climb the steps and enter a softly lighted, airy terrace draped with ivy and overlooking the harbor. One of the chef's specialties is the mixed plate, which gives you a chance to try the lamb, chicken, beef fillet, and beef steak. He also serves *exohiko,* swordfish grilled with lemon-oil sauce. ⊠*Off Samos waterfront, behind Catholic church* ☎22730/28649 ⚒*Reservations essential* ▤*MC, V* ◷*Closed Nov.–Apr. No lunch.*

WORD OF MOUTH

"The Ino Village Hotel . . . is about five minutes' drive from the hustle of Samos town and is located in a nice treed and peaceful area, high on a hill with lovely sea views. The hotel has a good restaurant located on an outdoor terrace with a view to kill for. There are two to three tavernas within 10 minutes' walk. Staff are friendly. Make sure you ask for an air-conditioned room with a sea view."

—hambo

$ ✕ **Karavi.** From the shape of one of Samos town's oldest port-side tav-
★ ernas it's easy to see that *karavi* in Greek means "boat." To your benefit—and to the frustration of neighboring restaurants—the owner here has arranged for most local fish to be delivered to him. Fish soup, made the local way with vegetables and Aegean fish, tastes like a first-rate bouillabaisse. Other outstanding choices include the fresh grilled calamari, scampi, crawfish spaghetti, and lobster. When you're finished, stop for a cocktail at the stylish adjacent beach bar. ⊠*Kefalopoulou 3–5* ☎22730/24293 ⚒*Reservations essential* ▤*AE, DC, MC, V.*

¢–$ ✕ **Ostrako.** Greeks come here, amid colored lights, seashell-covered
� walls, and flowering trees, to devour octopus snacks, steaming hot mussels, shrimp *saganaki* (baked in a tomato sauce with cheese), stuffed calamari, and sea bream. As with other local favorites, Ostrako is a place to order and share mezedes. Meat lovers can choose from among 20 dishes, including lamb chops and grilled tenderloin. Fruit or Samian doughnuts topped with honey and cinnamon end dinner on a sweet note. All the action takes place on the restaurant's back garden patio, which has a small playground next to it. ⊠*Them. Soufouli 141, east side of port* ☎22730/27070 ▤*No credit cards.*

$ ▥ **Hotel Samos.** In this value-seeker's paradise, sleek modern rooms come equipped with amenities uncommon in this price range, like soundproof windows, hair dryers, and wireless Internet. There's also a roof garden, rooftop pool, and hot tub. A small marble lobby connects to a chic, street-level café along the town's waterfront, a perfect place for people-watching. ⊠*Them. Soufouli 11, 83100* ☎22730/28377 ⊕*www.samoshotel.gr* ⇆*98 rooms, 2 suites* ⚑*In-room: refrigerator, Wi-Fi. In-hotel: bar, pool* ▤*AE, DC, MC, V.*

$ ▥ **Ino Village Hotel.** North of the port on a sloping hill in residential Kalami, these sand-color stucco buildings draped with fuchsia bougainvillea surround a luminous pool, in a setting of tranquillity you're unlikely to find in Samos town. All rooms have balconies, dark-wood furnishings, and some black-and-white etchings of ancient Samos. Superior rooms include TVs, small refrigerators, and air-conditioning.

Request those in the 800 block for a spectacular view of Samos bay and the mountains beyond. The 15-minute walk to Samos town is downhill (you can call the hotel to arrange for transport back up). ⊠*1 km (½ mi) north of Samos town center, 83100Kalami* ☎*22730/23241* ⊕*www.inovillagehotel.com* ➷*65 rooms* ⚹*In-room: no a/c (some), refrigerator (some), no TV (some). In-hotel: restaurant, bar, pool, no elevator* ⊟*AE, D, DC, MC, V.*

NIGHTLIFE

Bars generally are open May to September from about 8 or 10 PM to 3 AM. Begin your evening at **Escape** (⊠*Past port police station, on main road out of town, near hospital* ☎*22730/28095*), a popular gathering place, with a sunset cocktail on the spacious seaside patio (drinks are half price from 8 to 10 PM daily). The music in this hip spot picks up later, and so does the dancing. Friday is theme night (rock, reggae, or funk, for example) and there are full-moon parties.

Next to Karavi restaurant, **Selini** (⊠*Kefalopoulou 3–5* ☎*22730/24293*) is a stylish beachfront cocktail bar designed in Cycladic white. A fashionable Greek and international crowd mixes outside, as blue lights reflect off the sea below. Lounge and dance music is played.

PYTHAGORIO ΠΥΘΑΓΟΡΕΙΟ

14 km (8½ mi) southwest of Samos town.

Samos was a democratic state until 535 BC, when the town now called Pythagorio (formerly Tigani, or "frying pan") fell to the tyrant Polycrates (540–22 BC). Polycrates used his fleet of 100 ships to make profitable raids around the Aegean, until he was caught by the Persians and crucified in 522 BC. His rule produced what Herodotus described as "three of the greatest building and engineering feats in the Greek world." One is the Heraion, west of Pythagorio, the largest temple ever built in Greece and one of the Seven Wonders of the Ancient World. Another is the ancient mole protecting the harbor on the southeast coast, on which the present 1,400-foot jetty rests. The third is the Efpalinio tunnel, built to guarantee that water flowing from mountain streams would be available even to besieged Samians. Pythagorio remains a picturesque little port, with red-tile-roof houses and a curving harbor filled with fishing boats, but it is popular with tourists. There are more trendy restaurants and cafés here than elsewhere on the island.

The underground aqueduct, the **To Efpalinio Hydragogeio**, or Efpalinio tunnel, which Herodotus considered the world's Eighth Wonder, was completed in 524 BC with primitive tools and without measuring instruments. Polycrates, not a man who liked to leave himself vulnerable, ordered the construction of the tunnel to ensure that Samos's water supply could never be cut off during an attack. Efpalinos of Megara, a hydraulics engineer, set perhaps 1,000 slaves into two teams, one digging on each side of Mt. Kastri. Fifteen years later, they met in the middle with just a tiny difference in the elevation between the two halves.

10

The tunnel is about 3,340 feet long, and it remained in use as an aqueduct for almost 1,000 years. More than a mile of (long-gone) ceramic water pipe once filled the space, which was also used as a hiding place during pirate raids in the 7th century. Today the tunnel is exclusively a tourist site, and though some spaces are tight and slippery, you can walk the first 1,000 feet. ⊠ *Just north of town* ☎ *22730/61400* 🕙*€4* ⊙ *Tues.–Sun. 8:45–2:45.*

Among acres of excavations, little remains from the **archaia polis** (*ancient city* ⊠ *Bordering small harbor and hill*) except a few pieces of the **Polycrates wall** and the **ancient theater** a few hundred yards above the tunnel.

Pythagorio's quiet cobblestone streets are lined with mansions and filled with fragrant orange blossoms. At the east corner sits the crumbling ruins of the **kastro** *(castle, or fortress)*, probably built on top of the ruins of the acropolis. Revolutionary hero Lykourgou Logotheti built this 19th-century edifice; his statue is next door, in the **courtyard** of the church built to honor the victory. He held back the Turks on Transfiguration Day, and a sign on the church announces in Greek: CHRIST SAVED SAMOS 6 AUGUST, 1824. On some nights the villagers light votive candles in the church cemetery, a moving sight with the ghostly silhouette of the fortress and the moonlit sea in the background.

The tiny but impressive **Samos Pythagorio Museum** contains local finds, including headless statues, grave markers with epigrams to the dead, human and animal figurines, and beautiful portraits of the Roman emperors Claudius, Caesar, and Augustus. Hours are approximate. ⊠ *Pythagora Sq., in municipal bldg.* ☎ *22730/61400* 🕙 *Free* ⊙ *Tues.– Sun. 8:30–3.*

WHERE TO STAY & EAT

¢–$ ✕**Maritsa.** A regular Pythagorio clientele frequents Maritsa, a simple fish taverna in a garden courtyard on a quiet, tree-lined side street. You might try shrimp souvlaki, red mullet, octopus, or squid garnished with garlicky *skordalia* (a thick lemony sauce with pureed potatoes, vinegar, and parsley). The usual appetizers include a sharp *tzatziki* (tangy garlic-yogurt dip with cucumber) and a large *horiatiki* ("village" or "country" salad) piled high with tomatoes, olives, onion, and feta cheese. Additional recommendations include lamb on the spit, the mixed grill, and stuffed tomatoes. ⊠ *Off Lykourgou Logotheti, 1 block from waterfront* ☎ *22730/61957* 〓*MC, V.*

$$$$ 🏨**Doryssa Bay Hotel-Village.** Guests here choose between beachfront accommodations in the plush main hotel building with a view of the sea or in the painstakingly created "village," with its winding cobblestone streets, colorful town-house facades, and rustic main square, complete with shops. Either choice provides elegant contemporary furnishings and gives you access to a well-trained professional staff and a wealth of resort facilities, including an on-site folklore museum. The hotel is popular with Greek and international travelers and receives many tour groups in summer. ⊠ *Pythagorio beach, near road to airport 83103* ☎ *22730/88300 or 22730/88400* ⊕ *www.doryssa-bay.gr*

↩172 rooms, 125 bungalows, 5 suites ⚭ In-room: refrigerator, Wi-Fi. In-hotel: 2 restaurants, bars, pool, spa, public Internet, some pets allowed ⊟ AE, DC, MC, V ⊘ Closed Nov.–Mar.

$$$$ 🏨 **Proteas Bay.** Standing on the sweeping terrace of the hotel restaurant,
☾ or on the balcony of one of the luxurious bungalows that cascade down
★ the steep hillside, is like being on the bridge of a ship: all you see are the blue sea and sky and the mountains of Turkey rising up from the water. The hotel is notably quiet. It's designed in a clean, contemporary style with large, airy spaces, gardens planted with local flowers, an Olympic-size pool, and a beautiful secluded-cove beach. ⊠ *Samos town, Pythagorio road, 83103* ☎ *22730/62144 or 22730/62146* ⊕ *www. proteasbay.gr* ↩ *20 rooms, 72 suites* ⚭ *In-room: refrigerator, dial-up. In-hotel: 2 restaurants, bars, pools, spa, public Internet* ⊟ *AE, DC, MC, V* ⊘ *Closed Oct.–May.*

$ 🏨 **Fito Bay Bungalows.** A knowledgeable, warm staff makes you feel
☾ at home at this relaxed, economical, and family-friendly place just steps from Pythagorio beach. Individual white bungalows with terra cotta roofs wrap neatly around a sparkling long pool, and paths wind between beds of roses and lavender on the beautifully kept grounds. Rooms are spare (even mini-fridges aren't standard fixtures, though they can be requested), but this is not a place to linger indoors: take breakfast on the vine-covered terrace, relax in a lounge chair on the beach, or have a meal in the excellent taverna. ⊠ *Pythagorio beach, on road to airport, 83103* ☎ *22730/61314* ⊕ *www.fitobay.gr* ↩ *87 rooms, 1 suite* ⚭ *In-room: no TV. In-hotel: restaurant, bar, pool, public Internet, no elevator* ⊟ *AE, MC, V* ⊘ *Closed Oct.–Apr.*

SPORTS & THE OUTDOORS

Sun Yachting (⊠ *Poseidonos 21, Kalamaki* ☎ *210/983–7312 and 210/983–7313* ⊕ *www.sunyachting.gr*) in Athens specializes in charter rentals to Samos; you can pick up the boat in Piraeus or Pythagorio for one- and two-week rentals.

HERAION ΗΡΑΙΟΝ

10

★ 6 km (4 mi) southwest of Pythagorio, 20 km (12½ southwest of Samos town.

The early Samians worshipped the goddess Hera, believing she was born here beneath a bush near the stream Imbrassos and that there she also lay with Zeus. Several temples were subsequently built on the site in her honor, the earliest dating back to the 8th century BC. Polycrates rebuilt the Iraio, or Temple of Hera, around 540 BC, making it four times larger than the Parthenon and the largest Greek temple ever conceived, with two rows of columns (155 in all). The temple was damaged by fire in 525 BC and never completed, owing to Polycrates's untimely death. In the intervening years, masons recycled the stones to create other buildings, including a basilica (foundations remain at the site) to the Virgin Mary. Today you can only imagine the Iraio's massive glory; of its forest of columns only one remains standing, slightly askew and only half its original height, amid acres of marble remnants in marshy ground thick with poppies.

At the ancient celebrations to honor Hera, the faithful approached from the sea along the **Sacred road,** which is still visible at the site's northeast corner. Nearby are replicas of a 6th-century BC sculpture depicting an aristocratic family; its chiseled signature reads "Genelaos made me." The kouros from Heraion was found here, and now is in the Archaeological Museum in Samos town. Hours may be shortened in winter. ⊠ *Near Imvisos river* ☎ *22730/95277* ⊕ *www.culture.gr* 🎫 *€3* ⊙ *Apr.–Oct., daily 8:30–3.*

KOKKARI KOKKAPI

 ★ *8 km (5 mi) northeast of Manolates, 5 km (3 mi) southwest of Samos town.*

Beyond the popular beaches of Tsabou, Tsamadou, and Lemonakia, the spectacular stretch of coast road lined with olive groves and vineyards ends in the fishing village of Kokkari, one of the most appealing spots on the island. Until 1980, not much was here except for a few dozen houses between two headlands, and tracts of onion fields, which gave the town its name. Though now there are a score of hotels, and many European tourists, you can still traipse along the rocky, windswept beach and spy fishermen mending trawling nets on the paved quay. Cross the spit to the eastern side of the headland and watch the moon rise over the lights of Vathi (Samos town) in the next bay. East of Kokkari you pass by Malagari, the winery where farmers hawk their harvested grapes every September.

BEACHES

Acclaimed coves of the north coast with small pebbly beaches and gorgeous blue-green waters include **Lemonakia, Tsamadou,** and **Tsabou;** all are just a few minutes from one another, and they're to be avoided when the *meltemi* (northern winds) blow, unless you're a professional windsurfer.

WHERE TO STAY & EAT

$ ✕ **Akrogiali Tavern.** Although this small beach shack is not nearly as stylish as some other restaurants up the beach, Akrogiali Tavern serves the town's tastiest fish. Sold by the kilo, the daily selections vary but are always extensive, with red mullet, swordfish, mackerel, salmon, and squid among the possible catches. The menu clearly indicates what's fresh and what's frozen, and Samos olive oil is used in the cooking. For more local flavor, try the native white wine, made from muscat grapes, with your meal. ⊠ *Kokkari promenade* ☎ *22730/92423* ▭ *No credit cards* ⊙ *Closed Nov.–Mar.*

¢–$ ✕ **Ammos Plaz.** Ammos Plaz serves what many locals consider the best traditional Greek food in Kokkari, and in an ideal location—smack on the beach. Expect the dishes to change daily, but you may find choices like lamb fricassee and rabbit stifado. The owner's father is a fisherman, and he brings his haul to the restaurant daily. Octopus in a sweet white wine sauce and grilled lobster are two favorites, but considerably more expensive than many selections on the menu. ⊠*Kokkari promenade* ☎*22730/92463* ⊟*AE, MC, V* ⊘*Closed Nov.–Mar.*

$ ⚟ **Olympia Beach/Olympia Village.** Flowery Samian ceramics decorate the spare, immaculate rooms with balconies overlooking the sea at the bright-white Olympic Beach hotel. The Olympic Village has apartments with a bedroom, a living room, two baths, and a kitchen. From here you can walk to Tsamadou cove, favored for its shallow water, pine trees, and seclusion. ⊠*Northwest beach road, 83100* ☎*22730/92324 or 02730/92353* ⊕*www.olympiabeach.gr* ⤙*12 rooms, 22 apartments* ⚏*In-room: kitchen (some), refrigerator. In-hotel: restaurant, bar, no elevator* ⊟*MC, V* ⊘*Closed Nov.–Apr.* ¶⊙*CP.*

¢ ⚟ **Galini.** Galini means "tranquillity," and this quiet pension deserves the name. Markela Moshous is a wonderfully hospitable host; she serves breakfast in either the garden or the charming breakfast room. Rooms have simple wood furnishings and impressive marble floors, and they come with balconies or terraces facing the town or sea (and access to a refrigerator). ⊠*Panayotis Moshous, 83100* ☎*22730/92331, 22730/92365, or 22730/28039* ⤙*9 rooms* ⚏*In-room: no a/c, no TV. In-hotel: bar* ⊟*No credit cards* ⊘*Closed Nov.–Apr.* ¶⊙*CP.*

SPORTS & THE OUTDOORS

☾ In summer **Kokkari Surf and Bike Center** (⊠*On road to Lemonakia* ☎*22730/92102* ⊕*www.samoswindsurfing.gr*) rents windsurfing equipment, motorboats, sea kayaks, and mountain bikes. They also provide windsurfing instruction and run treks for hikers and mountain bikers.

NORTHERN ISLANDS ESSENTIALS

TRANSPORTATION

BY AIR

CARRIERS Even if they have the time, many people avoid the 10- to 12-hour ferry ride from Athens and start their island-hopping trip by taking air flights to all three islands; they take less than an hour. Olympic Airlines has at least a dozen flights a week from Athens to Lesbos and Chios in summer; fewer to Samos. Aegean Airlines flies daily from Athens to Chios. There are several Olympic Airlines flights a week from Chios to Lesbos, Limnos, Rhodes, and Thessaloniki; and several a week from Lesbos to Chios, Limnos, and Thessaloniki. From Samos there are several weekly Olympic flights to Limnos, Rhodes, and Thessaloniki; there are few flights (usually only one per week) between Samos and the other Northern Islands.

Be aware that overbooking happens; if you have a reservation, you should be entitled to a free flight if you get bumped.

Contacts Aegean Airlines (⊠*Koundouriotou 87, Mytilini, Lesbos* ☎*22510/37355 and at Odysseas Elitis airport 22510/61120, 22510/61059 and 22510/61889; Chios airport 22710/81051-3; Samos airport 22730/62790* ⊕*www.aegeanair.gr*).

10

Olympic Airlines (☎ *80111/44444, 210/626–1000 in Athens* ⊕ *www.olympicair lines.com* ✉ *Egeou, Chios town, Chios* ☎ *22710/44727* ✉ *Kavetsou 44, Mytilini, Lesbos* ☎ *22510/28660* ✉ *Kanari 5, Samos town, Samos* ☎ *22730/27237 or 22730/61219).*

AIRPORTS Lesbos Airport is 7 km (4½ mi) south of Mytilini. Chios Airport is 4½ km (3 mi) south of Chios town. The busiest airport in the region is on Samos, 17 km (10½ mi) southwest of Samos town. More than 40 international charters arrive every week in midsummer.

Contacts Chios Airport (☎ *22710/81400)*. **Lesbos Airport** (☎ *22510/38700).* **Samos Airport** (☎ *22730/87800).*

BY BOAT & FERRY

Expect ferries between any of the Northern Islands and Piraeus, Athens's port, to take 10 to 12 hours. There are at least four boats per week from Piraeus and three per week from Thessaloniki to Lesbos. Boats arrive daily to Chios from Piraeus. Ferries arrive on Samos at ports in Samos town and Karlovassi (28 km [17 mi] northwest of Samos town) four to nine times per week from Piraeus, stopping at Paros and Naxos; and most of the year two or three ferries weekly serve Pythagorio from Kos and Patmos. Ferries and hydrofoils to Kuşadası, on the Turkish coast, leave from Samos town. Owing to sudden changes, no advance ferry schedule can be trusted. Port authority offices have the most recent ferry schedule information and the Greek Travel Pages Web site is helpful.

BETWEEN THE ISLANDS There is daily service between Lesbos and Chios. The regular ferry takes 3½ hours; the fast ferry 1½ hours. There can be as few as one ferry per week between Lesbos or Chios and Samos (both 3-hour trips). The only other way to reach Samos from Lesbos or Chios is to fly via Athens (an expensive alternative), on Olympic Airlines.

Contacts Chios Port Authority (☎ *22710/44433, 22710/44434 in Chios town).* **Greek Travel Pages** (⊕ *www.gtp.gr)*. **Lesbos Port Authority** (☎ *22510/47888 in Mytilini).* **Piraeus Port Authority** (☎ *210/422–6000)*. **Samos Port Authority** (☎ *22730/27318 in Samos town, 22730/30888 in Karlovassi, 22730/61225 in Pythagorio).*

BY BUS

Lesbos's buses are infrequent, though there are several a day from Mytilini to Molyvos via Kalloni. Buses leave the town of Chios several times per day for Mesta and Pirgi. Samos has excellent bus service, with frequent trips between Pythagorio, Samos town, and Kokkari.

Contacts Chios Blue and Green Bus System (✉ *Vlatarias 13, Chios town, Chios* ☎ *22710/23086 or 22710/24257).* **Lesbos Bus Station** (✉ *Konstantinopoleos Sq., Mytilini, Lesbos* ☎ *22510/28873).* **Samos Bus Station** (✉ *Ioannou Lekati and Kanari, Samos town, Samos* ☎ *22730/27262).*

BY CAR

Lesbos and Chios are large, so a car is useful. You might also want to rent a car on Samos, where mountain roads are steep; motorbikes are a popular mode of transport along the coast. Expect to spend about

€35–€50 per day for a compact car with insurance and unlimited mileage. Note that you must have an international driver's license to rent a car on Chios. Though a national license may be sufficient to rent a car at some agencies on other islands, if you are stopped by the police or get into an accident and cannot produce an international or EU license, you may find the rental companies' stance isn't an official one.

Budget, at Lesbos Airport, has newer cars and is cheaper than other agencies. Vassilakis on Chios has reliable, well-priced vehicles. Aramis Rent-a-Car, part of Sixt, has fair rates and reliable service on Samos.

Agencies Aramis Rent-A-Car (✉ *Directly across from port, Samos town, Samos* ☎ *22730/23253* 🖷 *22730/23620* ✉ *On main street near National Bank, Pythagorio, Samos* ☎ *22730/62267* ✉ *Town center, opposite Commercial Bank, Kokkari, Samos* ☎ *22730/92385*). **Budget** (✉ *Airport, Mytilini, Lesbos* ☎ *22510/61665* ⊕ *www.budget.com*). **Vassilakis** (✉ *Chandris 3, Chios town, Chios* ☎ *22710/29300* 🖷 *22710/23205* ⊕ *www.rentacar-chios.com*).

BY TAXI

Often there are taxi phones at the port or main bus stops. Due to the small number of cabs, prices are high: expect to shell out around double what you'd pay in Athens, but always check the rates in advance. If you do spring for a ride, it's a good idea to ask for a card with the driver's number in case you need a lift later in your trip.

CONTACTS & RESOURCES

EMERGENCIES
Contacts Ambulance (☎ *166*). **Fire** (☎ *199*). **Police** (☎ *100*).

INTERNET, MAIL & SHIPPING
Contacts Diamonds (✉ *87 Koundouriotou St., Mytilini, Lesbos* ☎ *22510/43366*). **In Spot Mytilini** (✉ *44 Christougennon St., Mytilini, Lesbos* ☎ *22510/45760*). **In Spot Chios** (✉ *86 Aigaiou Ave., Chios town, Chios* ☎ *22710/23438* ✉ *98 Aigaiou Ave., Chios town, Chios* ☎ *22710/41058*). **Internet Café** (✉ *Themistokli Sofouli St., Samos town, Samos* ☎ *22730/22469*). **Post Office** (✉ *2 Vournazou St., Mytilini, Lesbos* ☎ *22510/28823*). **Post Office** (✉ *Omirou & Rodoukanaki Sts., Chios town, Chios* ☎ *22710/44276*). **Post Office** (✉ *105 Sofouli St., Mytilini, Lesbos* ☎ *22510/45760*).

TOUR OPTIONS
Aeolic Cruises on Lesbos runs several island tours. In Molyvos, Panatella Holidays has two tours that take in villages, monasteries, and other sights. Petra Tours, located in Petra, just south of Molyvos, plans bird-watching, botanical, walking, and scuba-diving excursions. Chios Tours organizes land excursions to the south, central, and northern regions of that island, as well as day trips to Izmir in Turkey. Samina Tours, on Samos, runs an island tour, a one-day boat trip to Patmos island, and a picnic cruise.

Contacts Aeolic Cruises (✉ *Prokymea, Mytilini, Lesbos* ☎ *22510/23960 or 22510/23266* 🖷 *22510/43694*). **Chios Tours** (✉ *Aigeou, waterfront, Chios town, Chios* ☎ *22710/29444 or 22710/29555* ⊕ *www.chiostours.gr*). **Panatella Holidays**

10

(✉ *Possidonion, at town entrance, Molyvos, Lesbos* ☎ *22530/71520, 22530/71643, or 22530/71644* ⊕ *www.panatella-holidays.com*). **Petra Tours** (✉ *Petra, Lesbos* ☎ *22530/41390 or 22530/42011* ⊕ *www.petratours-lesvos.com*). **Samina Tours** (✉ *Them. Sofouli 67, Samos town, Samos* ☎ *22730/22425* ⊕ *www.samina.gr*).

VISITOR INFORMATION

Contacts **Chios Municipal Tourist Office** (✉ *Kanari 18, Chios town, Chios* ☎ *22710/44389 or 22710/44344* ⊕ *www.chios.gr*). **Greek National Tourism Organization** (*GNTO or EOT*) ⊕ *www.gnto.gr*). **Lesbos Municipal Tourist Office** (✉ *Harbor front, Mytilini, Lesbos* ☎ *22510/44165* ⊕ *www.lesvos.gr*). **Mesta's Tourist Information Office** (✉ *Main square, Chios town, Chios* ☎ *22710/76319*). **Samos Municipal Tourist Office** (✉ *Ikosipemptis Martiou 4, Samos town, Samos* ☎ *22730/81031* ⊕ *www.samos.gr*). **Tourist police** (✉ *Harbor front, Mytilini, Lesbos* ☎ *22510/22776* ✉ *Neoriou 37, Chios town, Chios* ☎ *22710/81539* ✉ *Harbor front, Samos town, Samos* ☎ *22730/81000*).

GREEK VOCABULARY

THE GREEK ABC'S

The proper names in this book are transliterated versions of the Greek name, so when you come upon signs written in the Greek alphabet, use this list to decipher them.

Greek	Roman	Greek	Roman
A, α	a	N, ν	n
B, β	v	Ξ, ξ	x or ks
Γ, γ	g or y	O, o	o
Δ, δ	th, dh, or d	Π, π	p
E, ε	e	P, ρ	r
Z, ζ	z	Σ, σ, ς	s
H, η	i	T, τ	t
Θ, θ	th	Y, υ	i
I, ι	i	Φ, φ	f
K, κ	k	X, χ	h or ch
Λ, λ	l	Ψ, ψ	ps
M, μ	m	Ω, ω	o

BASICS

The phonetic spelling used in English differs somewhat from the internationalized form of Greek place names. There are no long and short vowels in Greek; the pronunciation never changes. Note, also, that the accent is a stress mark, showing where the stress is placed in pronunciation.

Do you speak English?	Miláte angliká?
Yes, no	Málista or Né, óchi
Impossible	Adínato
Good morning, Good day	Kaliméra
Good evening, Good night	Kalispéra, Kaliníchta
Goodbye	Yá sas
Mister, Madam, Miss	Kírie, kiría, despiní
Please	Parakaló
Excuse me	Me sinchórite or signómi
How are you?	Ti kánete or pós íste
How do you do (Pleased to meet you)	Chéro polí
I don't understand.	Dén katalavéno.
To your health!	Giá sas!
Thank you	Efcharistó

NUMBERS

one	éna
two	dío
three	tría
four	téssera
five	pénde
six	éxi
seven	eptá
eight	októ
nine	enéa
ten	déka
twenty	íkossi
thirty	triánda
forty	saránda
fifty	penínda
sixty	exínda
seventy	evdomínda
eighty	ogdónda
ninety	enenínda
one hundred	ekató
two hundred	diakóssia
three hundred	triakóssia
one thousand	hília
two thousand	dió hiliádes
three thousand	trís hiliádes

DAYS OF THE WEEK

Monday	Deftéra
Tuesday	Tríti
Wednesday	Tetárti
Thursday	Pémpti
Friday	Paraskeví
Saturday	Sávato
Sunday	Kyriakí

MONTHS

January	Ianouários
February	Fevrouários
March	Mártios
April	Aprílios
May	Maíos

June	Ióunios
July	Ióulios
August	Ávgoustos
September	Septémvrios
October	Októvrios
November	Noémvrios
December	Dekémvrios

TRAVELING

I am traveling by car . . .	Taxidévo mé aftokínito . . . me
train . . . plane . . . boat.	tréno . . . me aeropláno . . . me vapóri.
Taxi, to the station . . .	Taxí, stó stathmó . . .
harbor . . . airport	limáni . . . aerodrómio
Porter, take the luggage.	Akthofóre, pare aftá tá prámata.
Where is the filling station?	Pou íne tó vensinádiko?
When does the train leave for . . . ?	Tí óra thá fíyi to tréno ya . . . ?
Which is the train for . . . ?	Pío íne to tréno gía . . . ?
Which is the road to . . . ?	Piós íne o drómos giá . . . ?
A first-class ticket	Éna isitírio prótis táxis
Smoking is forbidden.	Apagorévete to kápnisma.
Where is the toilet?	Póu íne í toaléta?
Ladies, men	Ginekón, andrón
Where? When?	Póu? Póte?
Sleeping car, dining car	Wagonlí, wagonrestorán
Compartment	Vagóni
Entrance, exit	Íssodos, éxodos
Nothing to declare	Den écho típota na dilósso
I am coming for my vacation.	Érchome giá tis diakopés mou.
Nothing	Típota
Personal use	Prossopikí chríssi
How much?	Pósso?
I want to eat, to drink, to sleep.	Thélo na fáo, na pió, na kimithó.
Sunrise, sunset	Anatolí, díssi
Sun, moon	Ílios, fengári
Day, night	Méra, níchta
Morning, afternoon	Proí, mesiméri, or apóyevma
The weather is good, bad.	Ó kerós íne kalós, kakós.

ON THE ROAD

Straight ahead	Kat efthían
To the right, to the left	Dexiá, aristerá
Show me the way to . . .	Díxte mou to drómo . . .
please.	parakaló.
Where is . . . ?	Pou íne . . . ?
Crossroad	Diastávrosi
Danger	Kíndinos

IN TOWN

Will you lead me? take me?	Thélete na me odigíste? Me pérnete mazí sas?
Street, square	Drómos, platía
Where is the bank?	Pou íne i trápeza?
Far	Makriá
Police station	Astinomikó tmíma
Consulate (American, British)	Proxenío (Amerikániko, Anglikó)
Theater, cinema	Théatro, cinemá
At what time does the film start?	Tí óra archízi ee tenía?
Where is the travel office?	Pou íne to touristikó grafío?
Where are the tourist police?	Pou íne i touristikí astinomía?

SHOPPING

I would like to buy	Tha íthela na agorásso
Show me, please.	Díxte mou, parakaló.
May I look around?	Boró na ríxo miá matyá?
How much is it?	Pósso káni? (or kostízi)
It is too expensive.	Íne polí akrivó.
Have you any sandals?	Échete pédila?
Have you foreign newspapers?	Échete xénes efimerídes?
Show me that blouse, please.	Díxte mou aftí tí blouza.
Show me that suitcase.	Díxte mou aftí tí valítza.
Envelopes, writing paper	Fakélous, hartí íli
Roll of film	Film
Map of the city	Hárti tis póleos
Something handmade	Hiropíito
Wrap it up, please.	Tilixteto, parakaló.
Cigarettes, matches, please.	Tsigára, spírta, parakaló.
Ham	Zambón
Sausage, salami	Loukániko, salámi
Sugar, salt, pepper	Záchari, aláti, pipéri

Grapes, cherries	Stafília, kerássia
Apple, pear, orange	Mílo, achládi, portokáli
Bread, butter	Psomí, voútiro
Peach, figs	Rodákino, síka

AT THE HOTEL

A good hotel	Éna kaló xenodochío
Have you a room?	Échete domátio?
Where can I find a furnished room?	Pou boró na vró epiploméno domátio?
A single room, double room	Éna monóklino, éna díklino
With bathroom	Me bánio
How much is it per day?	Pósso kostízi tin iméra?
A room overlooking the sea	Éna domátio prós ti thálassa
For one day, for two days	Giá miá méra, giá dió méres
For a week	Giá miá evdomáda
My name is. . . .	Onomázome. . . .
My passport	Tó diavatirió mou
What is the number of my room?	Piós íne o arithmós tou domatíou mou?
The key, please.	To klidí, parakaló.
Breakfast, lunch, supper	Proinó, messimergianó, vradinó
The bill, please.	To logariasmó, parakaló.
I am leaving tomorrow.	Févgo ávrio.

AT THE RESTAURANT

Waiter	Garsón
Where is the restaurant?	Pou íne to estiatório?
I would like to eat.	Tha íthela na fáo.
The menu, please.	To katálogo, parakaló.
Fixed-price menu	Menú
Soup	Soúpa
Bread	Psomí
Hors d'oeuvre	Mezédes, orektiká
Ham omelet	Omelétta zambón
Chicken	Kotópoulo
Roast pork	Psitó hirinó
Beef	Moschári
Potatoes (fried)	Patátes (tiganités)
Tomato salad	Domatosaláta
Vegetables	Lachaniká
Watermelon, melon	Karpoúzi, pepóni

Desserts, pastry	Gliká or pástes
Fruit, cheese, ice cream	Fróuta, tirí, pagotó
Fish, eggs	Psári, avgá
Serve me on the terrace.	Na mou servírete sti tarátza.
Where can I wash my hands?	Pou boró na plíno ta héria mou?
Red wine, white wine	Kokivó krasí, áspro krasí
Unresinated wine	Krasí aretsínato
Beer, soda water, water, milk	Bíra, sóda, neró, gála
Greek (formerly Turkish) coffee	Ellenikó kafé
Coffee with milk, without sugar, medium, sweet	Kafé gallikó me, gála skéto, métrio, glikó

AT THE BANK, AT THE POST OFFICE

Where is the bank? . . .	Pou íne i trápeza? . . .
post office?	to tachidromío?
I would like to cash a check.	Thélo ná xargiróso mía epitagí.
Stamps	Grammatóssima
By airmail	Aëroporikós
Postcard, letter	Kárta, grámma
Letterbox	Tachidromikó koutí
I would like to telephone.	Thélo na tilephonísso.

AT THE GARAGE

Garage, gas (petrol)	Garáz, venzíni
Oil	Ládi
Change the oil.	Aláksete to ládi.
Look at the tires.	Rixte mia matiá sta lástika.
Wash the car.	Plínete to aftokínito.
Breakdown	Vlávi
Tow the car.	Rimúlkiste tó aftokínito.
Spark plugs	Buzí
Brakes	Fréna
Gearbox	Kivótio tachitíton
Carburetor	Karbiratér
Headlight	Provoléfs
Starter	Míza
Axle	Áksonas
Shock absorber	Amortisér
Spare part	Antalaktikó

Greek Islands Essentials

PLANNING TOOLS, EXPERT INSIGHT,
GREAT CONTACTS

There are planners and there are those who,
excuse the pun, fly by the seat of their pants.
We happily place ourselves among the planners. Our writers and editors try to anticipate all
the issues you may face before and during any
journey, and then they do their research. This
section is the product of their efforts. Use it to
get excited about your trip to Greek Islands, to
inform your travel planning, or to guide you on
the road should the seat of your pants start to feel
threadbare.

GETTING STARTED

We're really proud of our Web site: Fodors.com is a great place to begin any journey. Scan Travel Wire for suggested itineraries, travel deals, restaurant and hotel openings, and other up-to-the-minute info. Check out Booking to research prices and book plane tickets, hotel rooms, rental cars, and vacation packages. Head to Talk for on-the-ground pointers from travelers who frequent our message boards. You can also link to loads of other travel-related resources.

▎RESOURCES

ONLINE TRAVEL TOOLS
While the brunt of the Web sites listed in this book have English translations (look for the American or British flag), there are a few that don't, or that aren't fully translated. If you hit upon a site that's Greek to you, try AltaVista's Babel Fish Translation site (www.babelfish.altavista.com), which converts Greek text and some Web sites to English: just paste in a block of text or the site's URL, select "Greek to English" and hit "Translate." The translations can be amusingly literal but are often sufficient for finding out information like opening hours and prices.

ALL ABOUT GREECE
The U.S. Web site of the Greek National Tourism Organization, ⊕*www.greek-tourism.com*, is well laid out and packed with information and pictures; it has different content from the GNTO's broader site, ⊕*www.gnto.gr*. You can also check out the official Web site of Athens (⊕*www.cityofathens.gr*); the site of the Hellenic Ministry of Culture (⊕*www.culture.gr*), has basic information about museums, monuments, and archaeological sites. Packed with info about traveling by ferry are ⊕*www.greekferries.gr* and ⊕*www.ferries.gr*, which let you book online. Another source for ferry schedules is ⊕*www.gtp.gr*.

SPECIAL INTEREST
The Hellenic Festival site, ⊕*www.hellenicfestival.gr*, lists summer programs for the Athens Festival and the Festival of Epidauros. The site of the Athens Concert Hall, ⊕*www.megaron.gr*, describes all the activities at this venue. A good resource guide to ancient Greece is ⊕*www.ancientgreece.com*. The Foundation for Environmental Education awards the Blue Flag designation to beaches, including those in Greece, that are clean, safe, and environmentally aware; ⊕*www.blueflag.org* has details.

Currency Conversion Google (⊕www.google.com) does currency conversion. Just type in the amount you want to convert and an explanation of how you want it converted (e.g., "14 Swiss francs in dollars"), and then voilà. **Oanda.com** (⊕www.oanda.com) allows you to print out a handy table with the current day's conversion rates. **XE.com** (⊕www.xe.com) is a good currency conversion Web site.

Safety Transportation Security Administration (TSA) ⊕www.tsa.gov).

Other Resources CIA World Factbook (⊕www.odci.gov/cia/publications/factbook/index.html) has profiles of every country in the world. It's a good source if you need some quick facts and figures.

VISITOR INFORMATION
Tourist police, stationed near the most popular tourist sites, can answer questions in English about transportation, steer you to an open pharmacy or doctor, and locate phone numbers of hotels, rooms, and restaurants. Also helpful are the municipal tourism offices. You can

contact the Greek National Tourism Organization (GNTO; EOT in Greece), as well, which has offices throughout the world.

The very complete *Hellenic Traveling Pages,* a monthly publication available at most Greek bookstores, lists travel agencies; yacht brokers; bus, boat, and airplane schedules; and museum hours.

EOT in Greece EOT (✉ Tsochas 7, Ambelokipi, Athens 📞 210/870-7000 ⊕ www.gnto. gr. ✉ Athens International Airport, Spata 📞 210/353-0445 or 210/354-5101 ✉ Georikis Scholis 46, Thessaloniki 📞 2310/471027 ✉ Thessaloniki International Airport, Thessaloniki 📞 2310/471170 ✉ Filopimenos 26, Patras 📞 2610/620353).

In the U.S. Greek National Tourism Organization (✉ Olympic Tower, 645 5th Ave., New York, NY10022 📞 212/421-5777 📠 212/826-6940 ⊕ www.greektourism.com).

Guide Hellenic Traveling Pages (✉ Info Publications, Pironos 51, 16341Athens 📞 210/994-0109 or 210/993-7551).

▌ THINGS TO CONSIDER

PASSPORTS & VISAS

All citizens (even infants) of the United States, Canada, Australia, and New Zealand, need only a valid passport to enter Greece for stays of up to 90 days. If you leave after 90 days and don't have a visa extension, you will be fined anywhere from €130 to €590 (depending on how long you overstay) by Greek airport officials, who are not flexible on this issue. Worse, you must provide *hartosima* (revenue stamps) for the documents, which you don't want to have to run around and find as your flight is boarding.

PASSPORTS

U.S. passports are valid for 10 years. You must apply in person if you're getting a passport for the first time; if your previous passport was lost, stolen, or damaged; or if your previous passport has expired and was issued more than 15 years ago

or when you were under 16. All children under 18 must appear in person to apply for or renew a passport. Both parents must accompany any child under 14 (or send a notarized statement with their permission) and provide proof of their relationship to the child.

▌TIP➔ Before your trip, make two copies of your passport's data page (one for someone at home and another for you to carry separately). Or scan the page and e-mail it to someone at home and/or yourself.

There are 13 regional passport offices, as well as 7,000 passport acceptance facilities in post offices, public libraries, and other governmental offices. If you're renewing a passport, you can do so by mail. Forms are available at passport acceptance facilities and online.

The cost to apply for a new passport is $97 for adults, $82 for children under 16; renewals are $67. Allow six weeks for processing, both for first-time passports and renewals. For an expediting fee of $60 you can reduce this time to about two weeks. If your trip is less than two weeks away, you can get a passport even more rapidly by going to a passport office with the necessary documentation. Private expediters can get things done in as little as 48 hours, but charge hefty fees for their services.

VISAS

A visa is essentially formal permission to enter a country. Visas allow countries to keep track of you and other visitors—and generate revenue (from application fees). You *always* need a visa to enter a foreign country; however, many countries routinely issue tourist visas on arrival, particularly to U.S. citizens. When your passport is stamped or scanned in the immigration line, you're actually being issued a visa. Sometimes you have to stand in a separate line and pay a small fee to get your stamp before going through immigration, but you can still do this at the airport on arrival.

Most visas limit you to a single trip—basically during the actual dates of your planned vacation. Other visas allow you to visit as many times as you wish for a specific period of time. Remember that requirements change, sometimes at the drop of a hat, and the burden is on you to make sure that you have the appropriate visas. Otherwise, you'll be turned away at the airport or, worse, deported after you arrive in the country. No company or travel insurer gives refunds if your travel plans are disrupted because you didn't have the correct visa.

U.S. Passport Information U.S. Department of State (☎877/487–2778 ⊕travel.state.gov/passport).

U.S. Passport & Visa Expediters

A. Briggs Passport & Visa Expeditors (☎800/806–0581 or 202/338–0111 ⊕www.abriggs.com). **American Passport Express** (☎800/455–5166 or 800/841–6778 ⊕www.americanpassport.com). **Passport Express** (☎800/362–8196 ⊕www.passportexpress.com). **Travel Document Systems** (☎800/874–5100 or 202/638–3800 ⊕www.traveldocs.com). **Travel the World Visas** (☎866/886–8472 or 301/495–7700 ⊕www.world-visa.com).

BOOKING YOUR TRIP

Unless your cousin is a travel agent, you're probably among the millions of people who make most of their travel arrangements online.

But have you ever wondered just what the differences are between an online travel agent (a Web site through which you make reservations instead of going directly to the airline, hotel, or car-rental company), a discounter (a firm that does a high volume of business with a hotel chain or airline and accordingly gets good prices), a wholesaler (one that makes cheap reservations in bulk and then resells them to people like you), and an aggregator (one that compares all the offerings so you don't have to)?

Is it truly better to book directly on an airline or hotel Web site? And when does a real live travel agent come in handy?

ONLINE

You really have to shop around. A travel wholesaler such as Hotels.com or Hotel-Club.net can be a source of good rates, as can discounters such as Hotwire or Priceline, particularly if you can bid for your hotel room or airfare. Indeed, such sites sometimes have deals that are unavailable elsewhere. They do, however, tend to work only with hotel chains (which makes them just plain useless for getting hotel reservations outside major cities) or big airlines (so that often leaves out upstarts like jetBlue and some foreign carriers like Air India).

Also, with discounters and wholesalers you must generally prepay, and everything is nonrefundable. Before you fork over the dough, be sure to check the terms and conditions, so you know what a given company will do for you if there's a problem and what you'll have to deal with on your own.

■ TIP→ To be absolutely sure everything was processed correctly, confirm reservations made through online travel agents, discounters, and wholesalers directly with your hotel before leaving home.

Booking engines like Expedia, Travelocity, and Orbitz are actually travel agents, albeit high-volume, online ones. And airline travel packagers like American Airlines Vacations and Virgin Vacations—well, they're travel agents, too. But they may still not work with all the world's hotels.

An aggregator site, like Kayak, will search many sites and pull the best prices for airfares, hotels, and rental cars from them. Most aggregators compare the major travel-booking sites such as Expedia, Travelocity, and Orbitz; some also look at airline Web sites, though rarely the sites of smaller budget airlines. Some aggregators also compare other travel products, including complex packages—a good thing, as you can sometimes get the best overall deal by booking an air-and-hotel package.

Sometimes you can even bypass the middle man: airlines like Aegean (⇨ By Air in Transportation, below) and ferry companies like Hellenic Seaways (⇨ By Boat in Transportation, below) offer online booking and discounted fares for booking two or more weeks in advance. Even smaller Greek hotels frequently have Web sites with information about accommodations and rates, and though you can't always book online, you can often e-mail, phone, or fax the hotel directly to do so. When reviewing hotel sites, however, it's advisable to read with a critical eye.

WITH A TRAVEL AGENT

If you use an agent—brick-and-mortar or virtual—you'll pay a fee for the service. And know that the service you get from some online agents isn't comprehensive. For example Expedia and Travelocity don't search for prices on budget airlines like jetBlue, Southwest, or small foreign carriers. That said, some agents (online or not) *do* have access to fares that are difficult to find otherwise, and the savings can more than make up for any surcharge.

A knowledgeable brick-and-mortar travel agent can be a godsend if you're booking a cruise, a package trip that's not available to you directly, an air pass, or a complicated itinerary including several overseas flights. What's more, travel agents that specialize in a destination may have exclusive access to certain deals and insider information on things such as charter flights. Agents who specialize in types of travelers (senior citizens, gays and lesbians, naturists) or types of trips (cruises, luxury travel, safaris) can also be invaluable.

■ **TIP→** Remember that Expedia, Traveloc-ity, and Orbitz are travel agents, not just booking engines. To resolve any problems with a reservation made through these companies, contact them first.

A top-notch agent planning your trip will make sure you get the correct visa application and complete it on time; the one booking your cruise may get you a cabin upgrade or arrange to have bottle of champagne chilling in your cabin when you embark. And complain about the surcharges all you like, but when things don't work out the way you'd hoped, it's nice to have an agent to put things right.

For travel in Greece, a good agent is especially useful when you're traveling in high season, and can be invaluable for dealing with oft-frustrating ferry schedules, particularly if boats are canceled due to inclement weather (one phone call to your travel agent can set a seemingly doomed itinerary to rights again). Look for a local agent or one who specializes in Greece.

Agent Resources American Society of Travel Agents (☎703/739–2782 ⊕www.

travelsense.org). **Hellenic Association of Travel & Tourist Agencies** (⊕www.hatta.gr).

Greece Travel Agents Dolphin Hellas (☎210/922–7772 through 210/922–7775 ⊕www.dolphin-hellas.gr). **Fantasy Travel** (☎210/331–0530 through 210/331–0532, 210/322–8410 ⊕www.fantasy.gr). **Horizon** (☎210/947–0700 ⊕www.horizon.gr).

■ ACCOMMODATIONS

Accommodations vary from luxury island resorts to traditional settlements that incorporate local architecture to inexpensive rented rooms peddled at the harbor. Family-run pensions and guesthouses outside Athens and Thessaloniki are often charming and comfortable; they also let you get better acquainted with the locals. Apartments with kitchens are available as well in most resort areas.

Although lodging is less expensive in Greece than in most of the EU and the United States, the quality tends to be lower. However, many hotels in Athens underwent massive renovations before the 2004 Olympics; a number of new hotels were built in the city, and prices have risen dramatically. Often you can reduce the price by eliminating breakfast, by bargaining when it's off-season, or by going through a local travel agency for the larger hotels on major islands and in Athens and Thessaloniki. If you stay longer, the manager or owner will usually give you a better daily rate. An 8% government tax (6% outside the major cities) and 2% municipality tax are added to all hotel bills, though usually the rate quoted includes the tax; be sure to ask. If your room rate covers meals, another 2% tax may be added. Accommodations may be hard to find in smaller resort towns in winter and at the beginning of spring. Remember that the plumbing in rooms and most low-end hotels (and restaurants, shops, and other public places) is delicate enough to require that toilet paper and other detritus be put in the wastebasket and not flushed.

Online Booking Resources

AGGREGATORS

Kayak	www.kayak.com	also looks at cruises and vacation packages.
Mobissimo	www.mobissimo.com	also looks at car rental rates and activities.
Qixo	www.qixo.com	also compares cruises, vacation packages, and even travel insurance.
Sidestep	www.sidestep.com	also compares vacation packages and lists travel deals.
Travelgrove	www.travelgrove.com	also compares cruises and packages.

BOOKING ENGINES

Cheap Tickets	www.cheaptickets.com	a discounter.
Expedia	www.expedia.com	a large online agency that charges a booking fee for airline tickets.
Hotwire	www.hotwire.com	a discounter.
lastminute.com	www.lastminute.com	specializes in last-minute travel; the main site is for the U.K., but it has a link to a U.S. site.
Luxury Link	www.luxurylink.com	has auctions (surprisingly good deals) as well as offers on the high-end side of travel.
Onetravel.com	www.onetravel.com	a discounter for hotels, car rentals, airfares, and packages.
Orbitz	www.orbitz.com	charges a booking fee for airline tickets, but gives a clear breakdown of fees and taxes before you book.
Priceline.com	www.priceline.com	a discounter that also allows bidding.
Travel.com	www.travel.com	allows you to compare its rates with those of other booking engines.
Travelocity	www.travelocity.com	charges a booking fee for airline tickets, but promises good problem resolution.

ONLINE ACCOMMODATIONS

Hotelbook.com	www.hotelbook.com	focuses on independent hotels worldwide.
Hotel Club	www.hotelclub.net	good for major cities worldwide.
Hotels.com	www.hotels.com	a big Expedia-owned wholesaler that offers rooms in hotels all over the world.
Quikbook	www.quikbook.com	offers "pay when you stay" reservations that let you settle your bill at checkout, not when you book.

OTHER RESOURCES

Bidding For Travel	www.biddingfortravel.com	a good place to figure out what you can get and for how much before you start bidding on, say, Priceline.

The lodgings we list are the cream of the crop in each price category. We always list the facilities that are available—but we don't generally specify whether they cost extra. When pricing accommodations, always ask what's included and what's not. Common items that may add to your basic room rate are breakfast, parking facilities, and, at some places, air-conditioning.

Note that some resort hotels also offer half- and full-board arrangements for part of the year. And all-inclusive resorts are mushrooming. Inquire about your options when booking.

Most hotels and other lodgings require you to give your credit-card details before they will confirm your reservation. If you don't feel comfortable e-mailing this information, ask if you can fax it (some places even prefer faxes). However you book, get confirmation in writing and have a copy of it handy when you check in.

Be sure you understand the hotel's cancellation policy. Some places allow you to cancel without any kind of penalty—even if you prepaid to secure a discounted rate—if you cancel at least 24 hours in advance. Others require you to cancel a week in advance or penalize you the cost of one night. Small inns and B&Bs are most likely to require you to cancel far in advance. Most hotels allow children under a certain age to stay in their parents' room at no extra charge, but others charge for them as extra adults; find out the cutoff age for discounts.

■ TIP➜ Assume that hotels operate on the European Plan (EP, no meals) unless we specify that they use the Breakfast Plan (BP, with full breakfast), Continental Plan (CP, Continental breakfast), Full American Plan (FAP, all meals), Modified American Plan (MAP, breakfast and dinner) or are all-inclusive (AI, all meals and most activities).

HOTELS

The EOT authorizes the construction and classification of hotels throughout Greece. It classifies them into six categories: L (stands for deluxe) and A–E, which govern the rates that can be charged, though don't expect hotels to have the same amenities as their U.S. and northern European counterparts. Ratings are based on considerations such as room size, hotel services, and amenities including the furnishing of the room. Within each category, quality varies greatly, but prices don't. Still, you may come across an A-category hotel that charges less than a B-class, depending on facilities. The classifications can be misleading—a hotel rated C in one town might qualify as a B in another. For the categories L, A, and B, you can expect something along the lines of a chain hotel or motel in the United States, although the room will probably be somewhat smaller. A room in a C hotel can be perfectly acceptable; with a D the bathroom may or may not be shared. Ask to see the room before checking in. You can sometimes find a bargain if a hotel has just renovated but has not yet been reclassified. A great hotel may never move up to a better category just because its lobby isn't the required size.

Official prices are posted in each room, usually on the back of the door or inside the wardrobe. The room charge varies over the course of the year, peaking in the high season when breakfast or half-board (at hotel complexes) may also be obligatory.

A hotel may ask you for a deposit of the first night's stay or up to 25% of the room rate. If you cancel your reservations at least 21 days in advance, you are entitled to a full refund of your deposit.

Unless otherwise noted, in this guide, hotels have air-conditioning (*climatismo*), room TVs, and private bathrooms (*banio*). Bathrooms mostly contain showers, though some older or more luxurious hotels may have tubs.

Beds are usually twins (*diklina*). If you want a double bed, ask for a *diplo krevati*. In upper-end hotels, the mattresses are full- or queen-size. This guide lists amenities that are available but doesn't always specify if there is a surcharge. When pricing accommodations, always ask what costs extra (TV, air-conditioning, private bathroom).

Use the following as a guide to making accommodation inquiries: to reserve a double room, *thelo na kleiso ena diklino*; with a bath, *me banio*; without a bath, *horis banio*; or a room with a view, *domatio me thea*. If you need a quiet room (*isiho domatio*), get one with double-glazed windows and air-conditioning, away from the elevator and public areas, as high up (*psila*) as possible, and off the street.

Information Hellenic Chamber of Hotels (✉ Stadiou 24, 10564 Athens ☎ 210/331–0022 through 210/331–0026 📠 210/322–5449); open weekdays 8–2.

RENTAL ROOMS

Most areas have pensions—usually clean, bright, and recently built. On islands in summer, owners wait for tourists at the harbor, and signs in English throughout villages indicate rooms available. The quality of rental rooms has improved enormously in recent years, with many featuring air-conditioning, a small TV set, or a small refrigerator—or all of these. Studios with a small kitchenette and separate living space are good choices for families. Around August 15 (an important religious holiday of the Greek Orthodox Church, commemorating the Assumption of the Virgin Mary), when it seems all Greeks go on vacation, even the most-basic rooms are hard to locate, although you can query the tourist police or the municipal tourist office. On some islands, the local rental room owners' association sets up an information booth. Room touts may show up at the dock when boats arrive; sometimes, they're a good way to find accommodations, but ask to view the

rooms before agreeing to a booking. Few rooms are available in winter and early spring. Check the rooms first, for quality and location.

▮ RENTAL CARS

When you reserve a car, ask about cancellation penalties, taxes, drop-off charges (if you're planning to pick up the car in one city and leave it in another), and surcharges (for being under or over a certain age, for additional drivers, or for driving across state or country borders or beyond a specific distance from your point of rental). All these things can add substantially to your costs. Request car seats and extras such as GPS when you book.

Rates are sometimes—but not always—better if you book in advance or reserve through a rental agency's Web site. There are other reasons to book ahead, though: for popular destinations, during busy times of the year, or to ensure that you get certain types of cars (vans, SUVs, exotic sports cars).

▮ **TIP→** Make sure that a confirmed reservation guarantees you a car. Agencies sometimes overbook, particularly for busy weekends and holiday periods.

Because driving in Greece can be harrowing, car rental prices are higher than in the United States, and transporting a car by ferry hikes up the fare substantially, think twice before deciding on a car rental. It's much easier to take public transportation or taxis, which are among the cheapest in Europe. The exception is on large islands where the distance between towns is greater and taxi fares are higher; you may want to rent a car or a moped for the day for concentrated bouts of sightseeing.

In summer, renting a small car with standard transmission will cost you about €275 to €400 for a week's rental (including tax, insurance, and unlimited mileage). Four-wheel-drives can cost you anywhere from €80 to €97 a day, depending on availability and the season. Luxury cars are available at some agencies, such as Europcar, but renting a BMW can fetch a hefty price—anywhere from €98 per day in low season to €120 a day in high season. This does not include the 19% V.A.T. (13% on the eastern Aegean islands). Convertibles ("open" cars) and minibuses are also available. Probably the most difficult car to rent, unless you reserve from abroad, is an automatic (which usually goes for €5 more a day). Note that car rental fees really follow laws of supply/demand so there can be huge fluctuations and, in low season, lots of room for bargaining. Off-season, rental agencies are often closed on islands and in less-populated areas.

If you're considering moped or motorcycle rental, which is cheaper than a car, especially for getting around on the islands, try Motorent or Easy Moto Rent, both in Athens. On the islands, independent moped rentals are available through local agents.

You can usually reduce prices by reserving a car through a major rental agency before you leave. Or opt for a midsize Greek agency and bargain for a price; you should discuss when kilometers become free. These agencies provide good service, and prices are at the owner's discretion. It helps if you have shopped around and can mention another agency's offer. If you're visiting several islands or destinations, larger agencies may be able to negotiate a better total package through their local offices or franchises. Some hotels may also have partner agencies that offer discounts to guests.

Official rates in Greece during high season (July–September) are much cheaper if you rent through local agents rather than the large international companies. For example, a small car, such as the Fiat Seicento, will cost you about €290 for a week's rental (including tax, insurance, and unlimited mileage) as opposed to at least €385 if you go through an international chain. Outside high season you can get some good deals with local agents; a car may cost you about €38 per day, all inclusive. Rates are cheaper if you book for three or more days. On the islands, you can often get a lower price by renting for a half day–between the time when a client drops off a car and the next booked rental.

In Greece your own driver's license is not acceptable unless you are a citizen of the European Union. For non-EU citizens an international driver's permit (IDP) is necessary (⇨ By Car in Transportation, below). To rent, you must have had your driver's license for one year and be at least 21 years old if you use a credit card (sometimes you must be 23 if you pay cash); for some car categories, you must be 25. You need the agency's permission to ferry the car or cross the border (Europcar does not allow across-the-border rentals). A valid driver's license is usually acceptable for renting a moped, but you will need a motorcycle driver's license if you want to rent a larger bike.

TRAIN PASSES

Greece is one of 18 countries in which you can use Eurail passes, which provide unlimited first-class rail travel, in all of the participating countries, for the duration of the pass. If you plan to rack up the miles in several countries, get a standard pass. These are available for 15 days ($673), 21 days ($875), one month ($1,086), two months ($1,533), and three months ($1,891).

In addition to standard Eurail passes, ask about special rail-pass plans. Among these are the Eurail Pass Youth (for those under age 26), the Eurail Saverpass (which gives a discount for two or more people traveling together), the Eurail Flexipass (which allows a certain number of travel days within a set period), and the Pass 'n Drive (which combines travel by train and rental car). Among those passes you might want to consider: the Greece Pass allows first-class rail travel throughout Greece; the standard 3 days' unlimited travel in a month costs $131, and the rate rises per day of travel added. The Greece-Italy Pass gives you 4 days' travel time over a span of two months; the cost is $343 for first class, $274 for second. The Balkan Flexipass covers train travel through Greece as well as Bulgaria, Romania, the Former Yugoslav Republic of Macedonia (FYROM), Turkey, and Yugoslavia (including Serbia and Montenegro); there are passes for 5, 10, or 15 travel days in a one-month period for about $248, $433, and $521, respectively (first class). Youths pay about 50% less, senior citizens over 60 20% less.

Whichever pass you choose, remember that you must purchase your pass before you leave for Europe. *For more information about train travel, see By Train in Transportation, below.*

Information & Passes Rail Europe (✉500 Mamaroneck Ave., Harrison, NY10528 ☎877/257–2887 or 914/682–5172 🖷800/432–1329 ✉2087 Dundas E, Suite 106, Mississauga, Ontario, CanadaL4X 1M2 ☎800/361–7245 🖷905/602–4198 ⊕www. raileurope.com).

▍GUIDED TOURS

Guided tours are a good option when you don't want to do it all yourself. You travel along with a group (sometimes large, sometimes small), stay in prebooked hotels, eat with your fellow travelers (the cost of meals sometimes included in the price of your tour, sometimes not), and follow a schedule.

But not all guided tours are an if-it's-Tuesday-this-must-be-Belgium experience. A knowledgeable guide can take you places that you might never discover on your own, and you may be pushed to see more than you would have otherwise. Tours aren't for everyone, but they can be just the thing for trips to places where making travel arrangements is difficult or time-consuming (particularly when you don't speak the language).

Whenever you book a guided tour, find out what's included and what isn't. A "land-only" tour includes all your travel (by bus, in most cases) in the destination, but not necessarily your flights to and from or even within it. Also, in most cases prices in tour brochures don't include fees and taxes. And remember that you'll be expected to tip your guide (in cash) at the end of the tour.

In Greece, True North organizes group and individual tours tailored to travelers' interests, from culinary or hiking tours to wellness retreats, on island and mainland destinations. The company also offers an "alternative" tour of Athens developed to give you an insider's feel for the city—the guide will even follow *your* itinerary. More localized is Culinary Sanctuaries, based in Crete and run by Nikki Rose, who puts together fascinating customized tours with an emphasis on traditional Mediterranean cuisine. In addition, the Skyros Center on the isle of Skyros runs the Atsitsa Retreat, which organizes local island tours as part of a broader program of yoga, writing, and other life-enhancing activities.

Recommended Company True North (✉Irodotou 13, Maroussi, 15122Athens ☎210/612–1537 ⊕www.truenorthroutes. com). **Crete's Culinary Sanctuaries** (✍info@ cookingincrete.com ⊕www.cookingincrete. com). **Skyros Center** (✉Skyros Holidays, 9 Eastcliff Rd., Shanklin, Isle of Wight, England, PO376AA ☎01983/865566 ⊕www.skyros. co.uk).

TRANSPORTATION

To make finding your way around as easy as possible, it's wise to learn to recognize letters in the Greek alphabet. Most areas have few road signs in English, and even those that *are* in English don't necessarily follow the official standardized transliteration code, resulting in odd spellings of foreign names. Sometimes there are several spelling variations in English for the same place: Agios, Aghios, or Ayios; Georgios or Yiorgos. Also, the English version may be quite different from the Greek, or even what locals use informally: Corfu is known as Kerkyra; island capitals are often just called Chora (town), no matter what their formal title; and Panepistimiou, a main Athens boulevard, is officially named Eleftheriou Venizelou, but if you ask for that name, no one will know what you're talking about. A long street may change names several times, and a city may have more than one street by the same name, so know the district you're headed for, or a major landmark nearby, especially if you're taking a taxi. In this guide, street numbers appear after the street name. Finally, there are odd- and even-numbered sides of the streets, but No. 124 could be several blocks away from No. 125.

■TIP→ Ask the local tourist board about local transportation and hotel packages that include tickets to major museum exhibits or other special events.

▮ BY AIR

Flying time to Athens is 3½ hours from London, 9½ hours from New York, 12 hours from Chicago, 16½ hours from Los Angeles, and 19 hours from Sydney.

Always find out your carrier's check-in policy. Plan to arrive at the airport about 2 hours before your scheduled departure time for flights within the United States and 2½ to 3 hours before international flights from the United States. You may need to arrive earlier if you're flying from one of the busier airports or during peak air-traffic times. Any sharp objects, such as nail files or scissors, may be removed if you take them through airport security. Pack such items in luggage you plan to check.

In Greece, you need to show identification for both domestic and international flights. For domestic flights in Greece, arrive no later than 1 hour before departure time; for flights to the rest of Europe, 1½ hours; and for other international flights, 2 hours. If you get bumped because of overbooking, international carriers try to find an alternative route on another airline, but Olympic Airlines usually puts you on its next available flight, which might not be until the next day. (Under European Union law, you are entitled to receive up to €250 compensation for overbooking on flights of 1,500 km (930 mi) or shorter, €400 on flights between 1,500 km and 3,500 km (2,170 mi), and up to €600 for longer flights. In the past, Olympic Airlines staff and traffic controllers have gone on strike for several hours a day; keep attuned to the local news. Check-in is straightforward and easy at Greece's larger airports, but on small islands, it sometimes gets confusing, since several airlines may use the same check-in counter, indicated by garbled announcements. Watch for movement en masse by the crowd.

If you have been wait-listed on an Olympic flight in Greece, remember that this list does not apply on the day of departure. A new waiting list goes into effect at the airport two hours prior to takeoff for domestic flights and three hours before international flights; you must be there to get a place.

You do not need to reconfirm flights within Greece. Athens International Airport (Eleftherios Venizelos) posts real-time flight information on its Web site (⊕*www.aia.gr*). It also has customer information desks throughout the airport that operate on a 24-hour basis, as well as more than a dozen courtesy phones that put you through to the customer call center. You can contact the Hellenic Civil Aviation Authority or the Quality Management Department, both at the airport, if you have complaints or concerns.

DOMESTIC FLIGHTS

The frequency of flights varies according to the time of year (with an increase between Greek Easter and November), and it is essential to book well in advance for summer or for festivals and holidays, especially on three-day weekends. Domestic flights are a good deal for many destinations. In summer 2007 the one-way economy Athens–Rhodes fare offered by Olympic was €87, excluding taxes; to Corfu, €100; to Santorini, €79; and to Heraklion, €58. Unless the flight is part of an international journey, the baggage allowance is only 33 pounds (15 kilograms) per passenger.

Scheduled (i.e., nonchartered) domestic air travel in Greece is provided predominantly by Olympic Airlines, which operates out of Athens International Airport in Spata. There is service from Athens to Alexandroupolis, Ioannina, Kastoria, Kavala, Kozani, Preveza, and Thessaloniki, all on the mainland; Kalamata in the Peloponnese; the Aegean islands: Astypalaia, Karpathos, Kassos, Kythira, Crete (Hania, Heraklion, and Siteia), Chios, Ikaria, Kos, Lesbos (listed as Mytilini in Greek), Limnos, Leros, Milos, Mykonos, Naxos, Paros, Rhodes, Samos, Skiathos, Syros, Skyros, Kastellorizo (only via Rhodes), and Santorini; Corfu (called Kerkyra in Greek), Kefalonia, and Zakynthos in the Ionian Sea. Flights also depart from Thessaloniki for Chios, Corfu, Hania, Heraklion, Ioannina, Limnos, Lesbos, Mykonos, Rhodes, Samos, and Santorini. You can also fly from Kozani to Kastoria on the mainland. Interisland

flights, depending on the season, include the following: from Chios to Lesbos; from Karpathos to Kassos; from Santorini to Rhodes and Heraklion; from Rhodes to Karpathos, Kassos, Kastellorizo, and Mykonos, as well as Kos (summer only); between Kefalonia and Zakynthos (winter); and from Lesbos to Chios, Limnos, and Samos (winter).

For those traveling to Thessaloniki, a good alternative is Aegean Airlines, which has regular scheduled flights and sometimes even cheaper prices than Olympic. It also flies from Athens to Alexandroupolis, Chios, Corfu, Hania, Heraklion, Ioannina, Kavala, Kos, Lesbos, Rhodes, Santorini, and Thessaloniki. Planes depart Thessaloniki for Alexandroupolis, Chios, Corfu, Heraklion, Ioannina, Kavala, Kos, Lesbos, Mykonos, Rhodes, and Santorini. In summer, LTU International Airways operates several flights between points in Greece such as Rhodes and Kos or Athens and Samos.

Airlines & Airports Airline and Airport Links.com (⊕www.airlineandairportlinks.com) has links to many of the world's airlines and airports.

Airline Security Issues Transportation Security Administration (⊕www.tsa.gov) has answers for almost every question that might come up.

Air Travel Resources in Greece Hellenic Civil Aviation Authority (✉Level 3, Room 607, main terminal bldg. ☎210/353–4157 weekdays 9–5, 210/353–4147 at other times). **Quality Management Department** (☎210/353–7240).

AIRPORTS

Athens International Airport at Spata, 33 km (20 mi) southeast of the city center, opened in 2001 as the country's main airport. Officially named Eleftherios Venizelos, after Greece's first prime minister, the airport is user-friendly and high-tech. The main terminal building has two levels: upper for departures, ground level for arrivals. Unless you plan to avoid Athens altogether or to fly via charter directly to the islands, the Athens airport is the most convenient because you can easily switch from international to domestic flights or get to Greece's main harbor, Piraeus, about a 50-minute drive south of the airport. Thessaloniki's airport has modern airport facilities for international travelers, and the airport in Rhodes is being expanded.

Five major airports in Greece, listed below, service international flights. Airports on some smaller islands (Santorini, Syros, Mykonos, and Paros among them) take international charter flights during the busier summer months. Locals will sometimes refer to the airports with their secondary names, so these names—along with the three-letter airport codes—are also given. Information about airports other than Athens is given on the Olympic Airlines Web site (⊕ *www.olympic-airlines.com*) and on the Civil Aviation Authority Web site (⊕ *www.hcaa.gr*).

Airport Information **Athens International Airport–Eleftherios Venizelos (ATH)** (⊠ Spata ☎ 210/353–0000 flight information and customer service, 210/353–0445 tourist information, 210/353–0515 lost and found ⊕ www.aia.gr). **Heraklion International Airport–Nikos Kazantzakis (HER)** (⊠ Heraklion, Crete ☎ 2810/397129). **Kerkyra (Corfu) Airport–Ioannis Kapodistrias (CFU)** (⊠ Corfu town ☎ 26610/89600). **Rhodes International Airport (RHO)** (⊠ Rhodes town ☎ 22410/83200). **Thessaloniki International Airport–Makedonia (SKG)** (⊠ Mikras ☎ 2310/985000).

GROUND TRANSPORTATION

See Athens Essentials in Chapter 3 for information on transfers between the airport and Athens and Piraeus. In Thessaloniki, municipal Bus 078 (€0.50) picks up travelers about every 40 minutes until 11:15 PM for the 45-minute ride (up to 90 minutes if there is traffic) into town; its final stop is the train station. The EOT office in the airport arrivals terminal has information. At other airports throughout Greece, especially on the islands, public transportation is infrequent or nonexistent; ask your hotel to make arrangements or take a taxi; rates are usually set to fixed destinations.

FLIGHTS

When flying internationally, you must usually choose between a domestic carrier, the national flag carrier of the country you are visiting, and a foreign carrier from a third country. You may, for example, choose to fly Olympic Airlines to Greece. National flag carriers have the greatest number of nonstops. Domestic carriers may have better connections to your home town and serve a greater number of gateway cities. Third-party carriers may have a price advantage.

In Greece, when faced with a boat journey of six hours or more, consider flying. Olympic Airlines has dominated the domestic market, with flights to more than 30 cities and islands. Alternative airlines providing cheaper fares (at times) and better service include Aegean Airlines.

Olympic Airlines, the state-owned Greek carrier, has incurred criticism over the years for its on-time record, indifferent service, and aging aircraft. Three privatization attempts have failed since 2001, and there have been schedule cutbacks. The airline has a fleet of more than 44 aircraft, including A340-300 airbuses. Improved service and fewer cancellations, especially since the opening of Athens International Airport, have left more passengers pleasantly surprised. Olympic is rated among the top three carriers worldwide for safety.

Many European national airlines fly to Athens from the United States and Canada via their home country's major cities. Remember that these are often connecting flights that include at least one stop and may require a change of planes. Air France, British Airways, Delta, KLM, and Lufthansa all now operate code-share flights within Greece; British Airways has some direct flights to Crete.

To & From Greece Air Canada (☎800/712–7786 ⊕www.aircanada.com). **Air France** (☎800/237–2747 ⊕www.airfrance.net). **Alitalia** (☎800/223–5730 ⊕www.alitalia.it). **British Airways** (☎800/247–9297 ⊕www.britishairways.com). **Continental Airlines** (☎800/523–3273 for U.S. and Mexico reservations, 800/231–0856 for international reservations, 210/353–4312 Athens airport ⊕www.continental.com). **Delta Airlines** (☎800/221–1212 for U.S. reservations, 800/241–4141 for international reservations, 210/353–0116 Athens airport ⊕www.delta.com). **easyJet** (☎0870/600–0000 ⊕www.easyjet.com). **Iberia Airlines** (☎800/772–4642, 210/353–7600 in Athens ⊕www.iberia.com). **KLM Royal Dutch Airlines** (☎800/447–4747 ⊕www.klm.com). **LOT Polish Airlines** (☎212/869–1074, 210/323–7762 in Athens ⊕www.lot.com). **Lufthansa** (☎800/645–3880 ⊕www.lufthansa.com). **Olympic Airlines** (☎800/223–1226 outside New York, 212/735–0200 ⊕www.olympicairlines.com). **Swiss International Airlines** (☎800/221–4750, 210/617–5320 in Athens ⊕www.swiss.com).

Within Greece Aegean Airlines (✉V;ltanioti 3, Kifissia, Athens ☎801/112–0000 ⊕www.aegeanair.com). **Air France** (☎801/111–0065). **British Airways** (☎801/115–6000). **KLM Royal Dutch Airlines** (☎210/911–0000). **LTU International Airways** (☎801/113–0320 ⊕www.ltu.com). **Lufthansa** (☎210/617–5200). **Olympic Airlines** (Main Athens ticket office and for prepaid tickets, ✉Filellinon 15, near Syntagma Sq. ☎801/114–4444 or 210/966–6666 reservations, 210/356–9111 airport arrival and departure information ⊕www.olympicairlines.com).

▌ BY BOAT

Ferries, catamarans, and hydrofoils make up an essential part of the national transport system of Greece. With so many private companies operating, so many islands to choose from, and complicated

timetables with departures changing not just by season but also by day of the week, the most sensible way to arrange island hopping is to select the islands you would like to see, then visit a travel agent to ask how your journey can be put together.

Greece's largest and busiest port is Piraeus, which lies 10 km (6 mi) south of downtown Athens. Every day dozens of vessels depart for the Saronic Gulf islands, the Cyclades, the Dodecanese, and Crete. In fact, the only island groups that are not served by Piraeus are the Ionian islands and the Sporades. Athens's second port is Rafina, with regular daily ferry crossings to Evia (Euboea) and the Cycladic islands Andros, Tinos, and Mykonos. The smaller port of Lavrion, close to Sounion, serves the less-visited Cyclades Kea and Kythnos.

Patras, on the Peloponnese, is the main port for ferries to Italy and the Ionian islands Corfu and Kefalonia. A short distance south of Patras, Killini has ferries to Kefalonia and Zakynthos, also in the Ionian chain. Igoumenitsa, on Greece's northwest coast, has ships to Italy, plus a local ferry to Corfu, which runs several times daily in each direction.

Boats for the Sporades islands depart from Agios Konstantinos and Volos on the central mainland, from Thessaloniki in northern Greece, and from Kimi on the east coast of Evia. The island of Skyros is only served by ferries from Kimi.

In the northeast Aegean, the islands of Limnos, Samothrace (Samothraki), and Thassos are more easily reached from the northern mainland towns of Kavala and Alexandroupolis.

When choosing a ferry, take into account the number of stops and the estimated arrival time. Sometimes a ferry that leaves an hour later gets you there faster. High-speed ferries are more expensive, with airplanelike seating, including fare classes and numbered seats. They'll get you where you're going more quickly but lack the flavor of the older ferries with the open decks. Note that real fast ferries can pitch like crazy (and often don't travel in high seas)—if you're prone to seasickness, chose a boat with an open deck as the breeze keeps queasiness in check.

From Piraeus port, the quickest way to get into Athens, if you are traveling light, is to walk to the metro station and take a 20-minute ride on the electric train to Monastiraki, Omonia, or Syntagma (the latter two involve a train change at Monastiraki). Alternatively, you can take a taxi, though this will undoubtedly take longer because of traffic and will cost around €12, plus baggage and port surcharges. Often, drivers wait until they fill their taxi with debarking passengers headed in roughly the same direction, which leads to a longer, more circuitous route to accommodate everyone's destination. It's faster to walk to the main street and hail a passing cab.

Be aware that Piraeus port is so vast that you may need to walk some distance, or even take a port minibus (gratis) from the port entrance, to your gate (quay) of departure. So be sure to arrive with plenty of time to spare. Confusingly, the gates of departure are occasionally changed at the last moment.

To get to Attica's second port, Rafina, take a KTEL bus, which leaves every half hour 5:30 AM to 9:30 PM from Aigyptou Square near Pedion Areos park in Athens (close to Viktoria metro station). The bus takes about an hour to get to Rafina; the port is slightly downhill from the bus station.

Timetables change in winter and summer, and special sailings are often added around holiday weekends in summer when demand is high. For the Cycladic, Dodecanese, and Ionian islands, small ferry companies operate local routes that are not published nationally; passage can be booked through travel agents on the islands served. Boats may be delayed by weather conditions, especially when the northern wind called *meltemi* hit in August, so stay flexible—one advantage of not buying a ticket in advance. You usually can get on a boat at the last minute. However, it is better to buy your ticket two or three days ahead if you are traveling between July 15 and August 30, when most Greeks vacation, if you need a cabin (good for long trips) or if you are taking a car. If possible, don't travel by boat around August 15, when most ferries are so crowded, the situation becomes comically desperate—although things have improved since strict enforcement of capacity limits. First-class tickets are almost as expensive as flying.

If the boat journey will be more than a couple of hours, it's a good idea to take along water and snacks. Greek fast-food franchises operate on most ferries, and on longer trips boats have both cafeteria-style and full-service restaurants.

If your ship's departure is delayed for any reason (with the exception of force majeure) you have the right to stay on board in the class indicated on your ticket or, in case of prolonged delay, to cancel your ticket for a full refund. If you miss your ship, you forfeit your ticket; if you cancel in advance, you receive a partial or full refund, depending on how far in advance you cancel.

You can buy tickets from a travel agency representing the shipping line you need, from the local shipping agency office, online through travel Web sites (the most reliable is www.greekferries.gr), or direct from ferry companies. Generally you can pay by either credit card or cash, though the latter is often preferred. For schedules, any travel agent can call the port to check information for you, although they may not be as helpful about a shipping line for which they don't sell tickets. On islands the local office of each shipping line posts a board with departure times, or you can contact the port authority (*limenarchio*), where some English is usually spoken. Schedules are also posted online by the Merchant Marine Ministry (www.yen.gr). The English edition of *Kathimerini*, published as an insert to the *International Herald Tribune*, lists daily departures from the capital. Or you can call for a recording, in Greek, of the day's domestic departures from major ports. At 1 PM, a new recording lists boats leaving the following morning.

Information Agios Konstantinos Port Authority (☎22350/31759). **Ferry departures** (☎1440). **Igoumenitsa Port Authority** (☎26650/22240 or 26650/22235). **Kimi Port Authority** (☎22220/22606) **KTEL bus to Rafina** (☎210/821-0872 ⊕www.ktel.org [in Greek only]). **Lavrion Port Authority** (☎22920/24125). **Patras Port Authority** (☎2610/341002 or 2610/341024). **Piraeus Port Authority** (☎210/412-4585 or 210/459-3000). **Rafina Port Authority** (☎22940/22300). **Thessaloniki Port Authority** (☎2310/531503 or 2310/531504). **Volos Port Authority** (☎24210/28888).

CATAMARANS & HYDROFOILS

Catamarans and hydrofoils, known as *iptamena delphinia* (flying dolphins), carry passengers from Piraeus to the Saronic islands (Aegina, Hydra, Poros, and Spetses) and the eastern Peloponnesian ports of Hermioni and Porto Heli. Separate services run from Piraeus to the Cycladic islands (Amorgos, Folegandros, Ios, Milos, Mykonos, Naxos, Paros, Santorini, Serifos, Sifnos, Syros, and Tinos), and from Rafina to the Cycladic islands (Mykonos, Naxos, Paros, and Tinos). You can also take hydrofoils from Agios Konstantinos or Volos to the Sporades islands Alonissos, Skiathos, and Skopelos). Through summer only, there is a service from Heraklion (on Crete) to the Cycladic islands Ios, Mykonos, Paros, and Santorini.

These boats are somewhat pricey, and the limited number of seats means that you should reserve (especially in summer), but they cut travel time in half. The catamarans are larger, with more space to move

around, although on both boats passengers are not allowed outside when the boat is not docked. If the sea is choppy, these boats often cannot travel, and cancellations are common. Tickets can be purchased through authorized agents or one hour before departure. Book your return upon arrival if you are pressed for time.

Information Hellenic Seaways (✉Syngrou 98–100, 11745 Athens ☎210/419-9000 ⊕www.hellenicseaways.gr).

HYDROPLANES

A limited hydroplane service began operating in the Ionian islands in 2005, offering daily flights between Corfu and Paxos. Although the company had initial teething problems, by August 2007 it was operating between Corfu and Paxos, and Corfu and Lefkas. It also began service to the Aegean, with hydroplanes for Mykonos, Santorini, Paros, Ios, Kalymnos, and Kos departing from Lavrion. Prices are lower than regular airfare and higher than boat passage, about €45 one way from Corfu to Paxos.

Information AirSea Lines (✉Possidonos 18, 17674 Kallithea, Athens ☎210/940-2880 and 210/940-2012 ⊕www.airsealines.com).

INTERNATIONAL FERRIES

You can cross to Turkey from the northeast Aegean islands. The Aegean Shipping Company sails between Rhodes and Marmaris, while Miniotis Lines sails between Chios and Ceşme. In addition, other routes have included Lesbos to Dikeli and from Samos to Kuşadası. Note that British passport holders must have €10 with them to purchase a visa on landing in Turkey, Australian citizens need $20 (American dollars) and U.S. citizens need $100; New Zealanders don't need a visa. Note that rates are due to go up in 2008 or '09. But it is best to purchase the visa beforehand, paying euros, at the Turkish Consulate in Athens (visa hours are weekdays 9 to 1).

There are also frequent sails between Italy and Greece, with stops at Ancona, Bari, Brindisi, and Venice. Note that there are no longer connections from Trieste. The shipping lines covering these routes are Agoudimos/G.A. Ferries (Bari to Igoumenitsa and Patras; Bari to Kefalonia; and Brindisi to Corfu and Igoumenitsa), Anek Lines (Ancona to Igoumenitsa and Patras; and Venice to Igoumenitsa, Corfu, and Patras), Minoan Lines (Venice to Igoumenitsa, Corfu, and Patras; and Ancona to Igoumenitsa and Patras), Ventouris Ferries (Bari to Corfu and Igoumenitsa), and Superfast Ferries (Ancona to Igoumenitsa and Patras; and Bari to Igoumenitsa, Corfu, and Patras).

The most respected (but no longer necessarily the most expensive) company is Superfast Ferries. Its modern, well-maintained vessels are outfitted with bars, a self-service restaurant, a pool, two cinemas, a casino, and shops. The trip from Patras to Ancona takes 19 hours (21 if the ship stops at Igoumenitsa en route), from Patras to Bari 15 hours 30 minutes, and from Igoumenitsa to Bari 9 hours 30 minutes.

Prices range widely, depending on the season and the way you choose to travel (deck, air seat, or cabin). Traveling on Superfast from Patras to Ancona during high season 2007 cost €74 for a one-way ticket on deck; €103 for a one-way ticket with seating; €168 for a one-way ticket with overnight accommodation in an inside cabin with four beds; and €380 for a one-way ticket with overnight accommodation in a deluxe outside cabin with two beds. Taking a car aboard from Patras to Ancona during high season on the same line cost €118. High season runs from late July to early September; prices drop considerably in low season. Some companies offer special family or group discounts, while others charge extra for pets or offer deep discounts on return tickets, so comparing rates does pay off. When booking, also consider when you will be traveling; an overnight trip can be offset against hotel costs, and you will spend more on incidentals like food and drink when traveling during the day.

Contacts Aegean Shipping Company (⊠ Grigoriou Lampraki 46, 85100Rhodes ☎22410/76535 ⊕ www.seadreams.gr). **Agoudimos/G.A. Ferries** (⊠ Kapodistriou 2, 18531Piraeus ☎210/414–1300 ⊕ www. agoudimos-lines.com). **Anek Lines** (⊠ Amalias 54, Syntagma Sq., 10558Athens ☎210/323–3481 or 210/323–3819, 210/419–7430 international reservations ⊕ www.anek. gr). **Miniotis Lines** (⊠ Neorion 21, Chios, 82100 ☎22710/24670 ⊕ www.miniotis.gr). **Minoan Lines** (⊠ Syngrou 100, 11745Athens ☎210/920–0020 ⊕ www.minoan.gr). **Superfast Ferries** (⊠ Amalias 30, 10558Athens ☎210/891–9130 ⊕ www.superfast. com). **Ventouris Ferries** (⊠ Gr. Lampraki 17, 18533Piraeus ☎210/482–8001 through 210/482–8004 ⊕ www.ventouris.gr).

Information Turkish Consulate (⊠ Vasilissis Pavlou 22, Paleo Psyhiko, Athens ☎210/671–4828 ⏃210/677–6430).

▌ BY BUS

Organized bus tours can be booked together with hotel reservations by your travel agent. Many tour operators have offices in and around Syntagma and Omonia squares in Athens. Bus tours often depart from Syntagma or adjacent streets. Most chapters in this guide have information about guided tours.

It is easy to get around Greece on buses, which travel to even the most far-flung villages. The price of public transportation in Greece has risen steeply since the 2004 Olympic year, but it is still cheaper than in other western European cities. Greece has an extensive, inexpensive, and reliable regional bus system (KTEL) made up of local operators. Each city has connections to towns and villages in its vicinity; visit the local KTEL office to check routes or use the fairly comprehensive Web site (⊕ *www.ktel.org*, which, as of this writing, was in Greek only) to plan your trip in advance. Buses from Athens, however, travel throughout the country. The buses, which are punctual, span the range from slightly dilapidated and rattly to air-conditioned with upholstered seats. There is just one class of ticket. Board early, because Greeks have a very loose attitude about assigned seating, and ownership is nine-tenths' possession. Taking the bus from Athens to Corinth costs €6.60 and takes about 75 minutes; to Nafplion, €9.70, 2½ hours; to Patras, €13.90, 3 hours 10 minutes; and to Thessaloniki, €30, 7½ hours.

Although smoking is forbidden on KTEL buses, the driver stops every two hours or so at a roadside establishment; smokers can light up then. Drivers are exempt from the no-smoking rule; don't sit near the front seat if smoking bothers you.

In Athens, KTEL's Terminal A is the arrival and departure point for bus lines to northern Greece, including Thessaloniki, and to the Peloponnese destinations of Epidauros, Mycenae, Nafplion, and Corinth. Terminal B serves Evia, most of Thrace, and central Greece, including Delphi. To get into the city center, take Bus 051 from Terminal A (terminus at Zinonos and Menandrou off Omonia Square) or Bus 024 from Terminal B (downtown stop in front of the National Gardens on Amalias). Most KTEL buses to the east Attica coast—including those for Sounion, Marathon, and the ports of Lavrion and Rafina—leave from the downtown KTEL terminal near Pedion Areos park.

In Athens and Thessaloniki avoid riding city buses during rush hour. Buses and trolleys do not automatically stop at every station; you must hold out your hand to summon the vehicle you want. Upon boarding, validate your ticket in the canceling machines at the front and back of buses (this goes for the trolleys and the subway train platforms, too). If you're too far from the machine and the bus is crowded, don't be shy: pass your ticket forward with the appropriate ingratiating gestures, and it will eventually return, properly punched. Keep your ticket until you reach your destination, as inspectors who occasionally board are strict about fining offenders; a fine may cost you up to 40 times the fare. On intracity buses, an inspector also boards to check your ticket, so keep it handy.

The KTEL buses provide a comprehensive network of coverage within the country. That said, the buses are fairly basic in remoter villages and on some of the islands—no toilets or refreshments. However, main intercity lines have preassigned seating and a better standard of vehicle.

See our Athens chapter Planner section for information on the city's convenient multiday transportation passes (good for buses, trolleys, and the metro). In large cities, you can buy individual tickets for urban buses at terminal booths, convenience stores, or at selected *periptera* (street kiosks). KTEL tickets must be purchased at the KTEL station. On islands, in smaller towns, and on the KTEL buses that leave from Aigyptou Square in Athens, you buy tickets from the driver's assistant once seated; try not to pay with anything more than a €5 bill to avoid commotion. Athens bus stops now have signs diagramming each route. It still helps if you can read some Greek, since most stops are only labeled in Greek. The Organization for Urban Public Transportation, north of the National Archaeological Museum, gives Athens route information and distributes maps (weekdays 7:30–3), but the best source for non-Greek speakers is the EOT, which distributes information on Athens and KTEL bus schedules, including prices for each destination and the essential phone numbers for the regional ticket desks.

Throughout Greece, you must pay cash for local and regional bus tickets. For bus tours, a travel agency usually lets you pay by credit card or traveler's checks.

For KTEL, you can make reservations for many destinations free by phone; each destination has a different phone number. Reservations are unnecessary on most routes, especially those with several round-trips a day. Book your seat a few days in advance, however, if you are traveling on holiday weekends, especially if you are headed out of Athens. Because reservations sometimes get jumbled in the holiday exodus, it's best to go to the station and buy your ticket beforehand.

Athens Public Transportation Organization for Urban Public Transportation (✉ Metsovou 15, Athens ☎ 185 ⊕ www.oasa.gr).

Regional Bus Service Downtown KTEL terminal (✉ Aigyptou Sq., Mavromateon and Leoforos Alexandras, near Pedion Areos park ☎ 210/823–0179 for Sounion, Rafina, and Lavrion; 210/821–0872 for Marathon ⊕ www. ktel.org). **Terminal A** (✉ Kifissou 100, Athens ☎ 210/512–4910 or 210/512–4911). **Terminal B** (✉ Liossion 260, Athens ☎ 210/831–7153).

▌ BY CAR

Road conditions in Greece have improved dramatically in the last decade, yet driving in Greece still presents certain challenges. In Athens, traffic is mind-boggling most of the time and parking is scarce, although the situation has improved somewhat; public transportation or taxis are a much better choice than a rented car. If you are traveling quite a bit by boat, taking along a car increases ticket costs substantially and limits your ease in hopping on any ferry. On islands, you can always rent a taxi or a car for the day if you want to see something distant, and intradestination flights are fairly cheap. The only real reason to drive is if it's your passion, you are a large party with many suitcases and many out-of-the-way places to see, or you need the freedom to change routes and make unexpected stops not permitted on public transportation.

International driving permits (IDPs), required for drivers who are not citizens of an EU country, are available from the American, Australian, Canadian, and New Zealand automobile associations. These international permits, valid only in conjunction with your regular driver's license, are universally recognized; having one may save you a problem with local authorities.

Regular registration papers and insurance contracted in any EU country or a green card are required, in addition to a driver's license (EU or international). EU members can travel freely without paying any additional taxes. *If you are a non-EU member (or are considering bringing your car from the United Kingdom), see Importing Your Car, below.* Cars with foreign plates are exempt from the rule that allows only alternate-day driving in Athens's center depending on whether the license plate is odd or even.

The expansion and upgrading of Greece's two main highways, the Athens–Corinth and Athens–Thessaloniki highways (*ethniki odoi*) and construction of an Athens beltway, the Attiki Odos, has made leaving Athens much easier. These highways (and the new Egnatia Odos, which goes east to west across northern Greece), along with the secondary roads, cover most of the mainland, but on islands, some areas (beaches, for example) are accessible via dirt or gravel paths. With the exception of main highways and a few flat areas like the Thessalian plain, you will average about 60 km (37 mi) an hour: expect some badly paved or disintegrating roads, stray flocks of goats, slowpoke farm vehicles, detours, curves, and near Athens and Thessaloniki, traffic jams. At the Athens city limits, signs in English mark the way to Syntagma and Omonia squares in the center. When you exit Athens, signs are well marked for the National Road, usually naming Lamia for the north and Corinth or Patras for the southwest.

AUTO CLUB

The Automobile Touring Club of Greece, known as ELPA, operates a special phone line for tourist information that works throughout the country; the club also has several branch offices. If you don't belong to an auto club at home, you can join ELPA for €115, which gives you free emergency road service, though you must pay for spare parts. Membership lasts for a year and is good on discounts for emergency calls throughout the EU. Visit your local auto association before you leave for Greece; they can help you plan your trip and provide you with maps. They also can issue you an international driver's permit good for one year. Your local membership may qualify you for cheaper emergency service in Greece and abroad.

In Greece Automobile Touring Club of Greece (ELPA ⊠ Mesogeion 395, Agia Paraskevi, Athens ☎ 210/606-8800 or 210/606-8838 ⊕ www.elpa.gr ⊠ Patroon-Athinon 18, Patras ☎🖷 2610/426416 or 2610/425411 ⊠ Papanastasiou 66, Heraklion, Crete ☎🖷 2810/210581 or 2810/210654 ⊠ Vas. Olgas 230 and Aegeou, Thessaloniki ☎ 2310/426319 or 2310/426320 🖷 2310/412413). **Tourist Information Line** (☎ 174).

GASOLINE

Gas pumps and service stations are everywhere, and lead-free gas is widely available. However, away from the main towns, especially at night, open gas stations can be very far apart (⇨ *Hours of Operation in On the Ground, below*). Don't let your gas supply drop to less than a quarter tank when driving through rural areas. Gas costs about €1.10 a liter for unleaded ("ah-*mo*-leev-dee"), €0.95 a liter for diesel ("*dee*-zel"). Prices may vary by as much as €0.10 per liter from one region to another. You aren't usually allowed to pump your own gas, though you are expected to do everything else yourself. If you ask the attendant to give you extra service (check oil and water or clean the windows), leave a small tip.

Want a receipt? The word is *apodiksi*. International chains (BP, Mobil, Shell, and Texaco) usually accept credit cards; Greek-owned stations (Elinoil, EKO, Avin, and Revoil) usually do not unless they are in tourist areas.

Customs Stamps Directorate for the Supervision and Control of Cars (DIPEAK) (⊠ Akti Kondili 32, 1st fl., 18545 Piraeus ☎ 210/462-7325 🖷 210/462-5182).

INSURANCE

In general, auto insurance is not as expensive as in other countries. You must have third-party car insurance to drive in Greece. If possible, get an insurance "green card" valid for Greece from your insurance company before arriving. You can also buy a policy with local companies; keep the papers in a plastic pocket on the inside right front windshield. To get more information, or to locate a local representative for your insurance company, call the Hellenic Union of Insurance Firms/Motor Insurance Bureau.

Insurance Bureau Hellenic Union of Insurance Firms/Motor Insurance Bureau (⊠ Xenofontos 10, 10557 Athens ☎ 210/323-6733 🖷 210/333-4149).

PARKING

The scarcity of parking spaces in Athens is one good reason not to drive in the city. Although a number of car parks operate in the city center and near suburban metro stations, these aren't enough to accommodate demand. They can also be quite expensive, with prices of up to €5 an hour. Pedestrians are often frustrated by cars parked on pavements, although police have become stricter about ticketing. "Controlled parking" zones in some downtown districts like Kolonaki have introduced some order to the chaotic system; a one-hour card costs €1, with a maximum of three hours permitted. Buy a parking card from the kiosk or meter and display inside your windshield.

Outside Athens, the situation is slightly better. Many towns and islands have designated free parking areas just outside the center where you can leave your car.

ROAD CONDITIONS

Driving defensively is the key to safety in Greece, one of the most hazardous European countries for motorists. In the cities and on the highways, the streets can be riddled with potholes; motorcyclists seem to come out of nowhere, often passing on the right; and cars may even go the wrong way down a one-way street. In the countryside and on islands, you must watch for livestock crossing the road, as well as for tourists shakily learning to use rented motorcycles.

The many motorcycles and scooters weaving through traffic and the aggressive attitude of fellow motorists can make driving in Greece's large cities unpleasant—and the life of a pedestrian dangerous. Greeks often run red lights or ignore stop signs on side streets, or round corners without stopping. It's a good idea at night at city intersections and at any time on curvy country lanes to beep your horn to warn errant drivers.

In cities, you will find pedestrians have no qualms about standing in the middle of a busy boulevard, waiting to dart between cars. Make eye contact so you can both determine who's going to slow. Rush hour in the cities runs from 7 to 10 AM and 2:30 to 3:30 PM on weekdays, plus 8 to 9 PM on Tuesday, Thursday, and Friday. Saturday mornings bring bumper-to-bumper traffic in shopping districts, and weekend nights guarantee crowding around nightlife hubs. In Athens, the only time you won't find traffic is very early morning and most of Sunday (unless you're foolish enough to stay at a local beach until evening in summer, which means heavy end-of-weekend traffic when you return). Finally, perhaps because they are untrained, drivers seldom pull over for wailing ambulances; the most they'll do

is slow down and slightly move over in different directions.

Highways are color-coded: green for the new, toll roads and blue for old, National Roads. Tolls are usually €2. The older routes are slower and somewhat longer, but they follow more scenic routes, so driving is more enjoyable. The National Road can be very slick in places when wet—avoid driving in rain and on the days preceding or following major holidays, when traffic is at its worst as urban dwellers leave for villages.

ROADSIDE EMERGENCIES

You must put out a triangular danger sign if you have a breakdown. Roving repair trucks, manned by skilled ELPA mechanics, patrol the major highways, except the Attiki Odos, which has its own contracted road assistance company. They assist tourists with breakdowns for free if they belong to an auto club such as AAA or ELPA; otherwise, there is a charge. The Greek National Tourism Organization, in cooperation with ELPA, the tourist police, and Greek scouts, provides an emergency telephone line for those who spot a dead or wounded animal on the National Road.

Emergency Services Automobile Touring Club of Greece (ELPA ☎10400 for breakdowns, 171 for a dead or hurt animal, 210/606–8800 outside Athens).

RULES OF THE ROAD

International road signs are in use throughout Greece. You drive on the right, pass on the left, and yield right-of-way to all vehicles approaching from the right (except on posted main highways). Cars may not make a right turn on a red light. The speed limits are 120 kph (74 mph) on the National Road, 90 kph (56 mph) outside urban areas, and 50 kph (31 mph) in cities, unless lower limits are posted. The presence of traffic police on the highways has increased, and they are now much more diligent in enforcing speed limits or any other rules. However, limits are often not posted, and signs indicating a lower limit may not always be visible, so if you see Greek drivers slowing down, take the cue to avoid speed traps in rural areas.

In central Athens there is an odd-even rule to avoid traffic congestion. This rule is strictly adhered to and applies weekdays; license plates ending in odd or even numbers can drive into central Athens according to whether the date is odd or even. (The *daktylios,* as this inner ring is called, is marked by signs with a large yellow triangle.) This rule does not apply to rental cars, provided the renter and driver has a foreign passport. If you are renting a car, ask the rental agency about any special parking or circulation regulations in force. Although sidewalk parking is illegal, it is common. And although it's tempting as a visitor to ignore parking tickets, keep in mind that if you've surrendered your ID to the rental agency, you won't get it back until you clear up the matter. You can pay your ticket at the rental agency or local police station. Under a new driving code aimed at cracking down on violations, fines start at €150 (for illegal parking) and can go as high as €300, if your car is towed; fines for running a red light or speeding are now €350, plus you risk having your license revoked for two weeks.

If you are involved in an accident, don't drive away. Accidents must be reported (something Greek motorists often fail to do) before the insurance companies consider claims. Try to get the other driver's details as soon as possible; hit-and-run is all too common in Greece. If the police take you in (they can hold you for 24 hours if there is a fatality, regardless of fault), you have the right to call your local embassy or consulate for help getting a lawyer.

The use of seat belts and motorcycle helmets is compulsory, though Greeks tend to ignore these rules, or comply with them by "wearing" the helmet on their elbows.

▌ BY TAXI

In Greece, as everywhere, unscrupulous taxi drivers sometimes try to take advantage of out-of-towners, using such tricks as rigging meters or tacking on a few zeros to the metered price. All taxis must display the rate card; it's usually on the dashboard, though taxis outside the big cities don't bother. Ask your hotel concierge or owner before engaging a taxi what the fare to your destination ought to be. It should cost between €25 and €40 from the airport (depending on the traffic) to the Athens city center (this includes tolls) and about €15 from Piraeus port to the center. It does not matter how many are in your party (the driver isn't supposed to squeeze in more than four); the metered price remains the same. Taxis must give passengers a receipt (*apodiksi*) if requested.

Make sure that the driver turns on the meter to Tarifa 1 (€0.30), unless it's between midnight and 5 AM, when Tarifa 2 (€0.60) applies. Remember that the meter starts at €1 and the minimum is €2.65. A surcharge applies when taking a taxi to and from the airport (€3) and from (but not to) ports, bus and train stations (€0.80). There is also a surcharge during holiday periods, about €0.30, and a comparable charge for each item of baggage that's over 10 kilograms (22 pounds). If you suspect a driver is overcharging, demand to be taken to the police station; this usually brings them around. Complaints about service or overcharging should be directed to the tourist police; at the Athens airport, contact the Taxi Syndicate information desk. When calling to complain, be sure to report the driver's license number.

Taxi rates are inexpensive compared to fares in most other European countries, mainly because they operate on the jitney system, indicating willingness to pick up others by blinking their headlights or slowing down. Would-be passengers shout their destination as the driver cruises past. Don't be alarmed if your driver picks up other passengers (although he should ask your permission first). Drivers rarely pick up additional passengers if you are a woman traveling alone at night. Each new party pays full fare for the distance he or she has traveled.

A taxi is available when a sign (ELEFTHERO) is up or the light is on at night. Once the driver indicates he is free, he cannot refuse your destination, so get in the taxi before you give an address. He also must wait for you up to 15 minutes, if requested, although most drivers would be unhappy with such a demand. Drivers are familiar with the major hotels, but it's good to know a landmark near your hotel and to have the address and phone number written in Greek. If all else fails, the driver can call the hotel from his mobile phone or a kiosk.

On islands and in the countryside, the meter may often be on Tarifa 2 (outside city limits). Do not assume taxis will be waiting at smaller island airports when your flight lands; often, they have all been booked by arriving locals. If you get stuck, try to join a passenger going in your direction, or call your hotel to arrange transportation.

When you're taking an early-morning flight, it's a good idea to reserve a radio taxi the night before (€2.50 surcharge, €1.50 for immediate response). These taxis are usually quite reliable and punctual; if you're not staying in a hotel, the local tourist police can give you some phone numbers for companies.

Complaints in Athens Taxi Syndicate (☎210/353–0575). **Tourist police** (☎171).

❚ BY TRAIN

Fares are reasonable, and trains offer a good, though slow, alternative to long drives, bus rides, or even flights. One of the most impressive stretches is the rack-and-pinion line between Kalavrita and Diakofto, which travels up a pine-crested gorge in the Peloponnese mountains. In fact, the leisurely Peloponnesian train is one of the more-pleasant ways to see southern Greece. In central and northern Greece, the Pelion and Nestos routes cross breathtaking landscapes.

The main line running north from Athens divides into three lines at Thessaloniki, continuing on to Skopje and Belgrade; the Turkish border and Istanbul; and Sofia, Bucharest, and Budapest. The Peloponnese in the south is served by a narrow-gauge line dividing at Corinth into the Tripoli–Kalamata and Patras–Kalamata routes. Two sample fares: Athens–Corinth, €6 and Athens–Volos, €20.70.

The Greek Railway Organization (OSE) has two stations in Athens, side by side, off Diliyianni street west of Omonia Square: Stathmos Larissis and Stathmos Peloponnisou (⇨ Athens Essentials in Chapter 3 for more information). OSE buses for Albania, Bulgaria, and Turkey also leave from the Peloponnese station. The Proastiakos light-rail line (⊕ www. proastiakos.gr) linking the airport to Stathmos Larissis in Athens has been extended past Corinth to Kiato; fares are €6 from Athens to Corinth and €8 from the airport to Corinth.

InterCity Express service from Athens to Thessaloniki is fast and reliable. The IC costs €45.20 (versus €14.10 for a regular train) but cuts the time by 90 minutes to about 4½ hours. The Athens–Patras IC train (3½ hours) costs €10 (compared to €5.30 and about 4 hours for a regular train). If you order your IC tickets no later than three days in advance, you can have them delivered to you in Athens by courier for a small fee.

If you're planning to make the Athens–Thessaloniki trip several times, buy an Intercity 6+1, which gives you seven trips for the price of six ($203 first class), and a discount on the next card when you return the old one. You can combine this with a Rail 'n Drive package offered by Hertz (⇨ *Rental Cars in Booking Your Trip, above*). They will have a rental car waiting for you at any of the IC stations—Athens, Larissa, Thessaloniki, Volos—at lower prices.

Trains are generally on time. At smaller stations, allow about 10–15 minutes for changing trains; on some routes, connecting routes are coordinated with the main line.

All trains have both first- and second-class seating. On any train, it is best during high season, around holidays, or for long distances to travel first-class, with a reserved seat, as the difference between the first- and second-class coaches can be vast: the cars are cleaner, the seats are wider and plusher, and, most important, the cars are emptier. Without a reservation, in second class you sometimes end up standing among the baggage. The assigned seating of first class (*proti thesi*) is a good idea in July and August, for example, when the Patras–Athens leg is packed with tourists arriving from Italy. First class costs about 20% more than second class (*defteri thesi*).

Many travelers assume that rail passes guarantee them seats on the trains they wish to ride. Not so. You need to book seats ahead even if you are using a rail pass *(for information on Eurail passes, see Train Passes in Booking Your Trip, above)*; seat reservations are required on some European trains, particularly high-speed trains, and are a good idea on trains that may be crowded—particularly in summer on popular routes. You also need a reservation if you purchase sleeping accommodations. On high-speed (IC) trains, you pay a surcharge.

You can pay for all train tickets purchased in Greece with cash (euros) or with credit cards (Visa and MasterCard only). Note that any ticket issued on the train costs 50% more. The best, most efficient contact is OSE's general-information switchboard for timetables and prices. You can get train schedules and fares from EOT and from OSE offices. The Thomas Cook European Timetable is useful, too.

Train Information Greek Railway Organization (OSF) (✉ Karolou 1, near Omonia Sq., Athens ☎ 210/529–7006 or 210/529–7007 ✉ Sina 6, Athens ☎ 210/529–8910 ⊕ www.ose.gr). **InterCity Express** (☎ 210/529–7313); open Monday Saturday 8–2.30 **OSE general information switchboard** (☎ 11100); open daily 7 AM–9 PM.

Train Timetables Thomas Cook, Timetable Publishing Office (✉ Box 36, Thorpe Wood, Peterborough, Cambridgeshire PE3 6SB ⊕ www.thomascookpublishing.com).

ON THE GROUND

■ COMMUNICATIONS

INTERNET

Greece may lag behind other European countries in Internet home penetration, but the country is wired. Major hotels have high-speed Internet connections in rooms and most smaller ones have at least a terminal in the lounge for guests' use. Telecom privatization has helped Greece close the Internet gap with other European countries and, especially on touristed islands, you'll find at least one Internet café with high-speed connections. On the mainland, several villages have created public wireless networks—a trend that seems to be growing.

Although major companies such as Toshiba, Canon, and Hewlett-Packard have representatives in Greece, computer parts, batteries, and adaptors are expensive in Greece and may not be in stock when you need them, so carry spares for your laptop. Your best bets are the national Plaisio and Germanos chains, although some camera shops carry computer equipment, too. Also note that many upscale hotels will rent you a laptop.

If you want to access your e-mail, you can visit one of the Internet cafés that have sprung up throughout Greece. Athens has more than 50, several of which are open 24 hours, and you're sure to find at least one on most islands (⇨ *Essentials at the end of most chapters*). Besides coffee, they offer a range of computer services and charge about €3 per hour; most do not accept credit cards. A few establishments, including Athens Airport and Starbucks, have Wi-Fi service. The City of Athens offers free wireless access in Syntagma Square, and a number of rural towns also have free wireless in public areas. If your cell phone works in Greece and you have a connection kit for your laptop, then you can buy a mobile connect card to get online.

Contacts Cybercafes (⊕ www.cybercafes. com) lists more than 4,000 Internet cafés worldwide.

PHONES

Greece's phone system has improved markedly. You can direct dial in most better hotels, but there is usually a huge surcharge, so use your calling card or a card telephone in the lobby or on the street. You can make calls from most large establishments, kiosks, card phones (which are everywhere), and from the local office of the Greek telephone company, known as OTE ("oh-*teh*").

Establishments may have several phone numbers rather than a central switchboard. Also, many now use mobile phones, indicated by an area code that begins with 69.

Doing business over the phone in Greece can be frustrating—the lines always seem to be busy, and English-speaking operators and clerks are few. You may also find people too busy to address your problem—the independent-minded Greeks are *not* very service-conscious. It is far better to develop a relationship with someone, for example a travel agent, to get information about train schedules and the like, or to go in person and ask for information face-to-face. Though OTE has updated its phone system in recent years, it may still take you several attempts to get through when calling from an island or the countryside.

The country code for Greece is 30. When dialing Greece from the United States, Canada, or Australia, you would first dial 011, then 30, the country code, before punching in the area code and local number. From continental Europe, the United Kingdom, or New Zealand, start with 0030.

CALLING WITHIN GREECE

For Greek directory information, dial 11888; many operators speak English. In most cases you must give the surname of the shop or restaurant proprietor to be able to get the phone number of the establishment; tourist police are more helpful for tracking down the numbers of such establishments. For operator-assisted calls and international directory information in English, dial the International Exchange at ☎161. In most cases, there is a three-minute minimum charge for operator-assisted station-to-station and person-to-person connections.

Pronunciations for the numbers in Greek are: one ("*eh*-na"); two ("*dhee*-oh"); three ("*tree*-a"); four ("*tess*-chr-a"); five ("*pen*-de"); six ("*eh*-ksee"); seven ("*ef-ta*"); eight ("och-*toh*"); nine ("ch-*nay*-ah"); ten ("*dheh*-ka").

All telephone numbers in Greece have 10 digits. Area codes now have to be dialed even when you are dialing locally. For cell phones, dial both the cell prefix (a four-digit number beginning with 69) and the telephone number from anywhere in Greece.

You can make local calls from the public OTE phones using phone cards, not coins, or from kiosks, which have metered telephones and allow you to make local or international calls. The dial ring will be familiar to English speakers: two beats, the second much longer than the first.

OTE has card phones virtually everywhere, though some may not be in working order. If you want more privacy—the card phones tend to be on busy street corners and other people waiting to make calls may try to hurry you—use a card phone in a hotel lobby or OTE offices, though these tend to have limited hours. You can also use a kiosk phone. If you don't get a dial tone at first, you should ask the kiosk owner to set the meter to zero. (Bo-*ree*-te na to mee-the-*nee*-ste?)

CALLING OUTSIDE GREECE

To place an international call from Greece, dial 00 to connect to an international network, then dial the country code (for the United States and Canada, it's 1), and then the area code and number. If you need assistance, call 134 to be connected to an international operator. You can use AT&T, Sprint, and MCI services from public phones as well as from hotels.

Long-Distance Carriers AT&T (☎800/225–5288). MCI (☎800/888-8000 or 800/444–3333). Sprint (☎800/877–7746).

Access Codes AT&T Direct (☎00/800–1311, 800/435–0812 in the U.S.). MCI WorldPhone (☎00/800–1211, 800/444–4141 in the U.S.). Sprint International Access (☎00/800–1411, 800/877–4646 in the U.S.).

CALLING CARDS

Phone cards worth €3, €6, €12, or €24 can be purchased at kiosks, convenience stores, or the local OTE office and are the easiest way to make calls from anywhere in Greece. These phone cards can be used for domestic and international calls. Once you insert the phone card, the number of units on the card will appear; as you begin talking, the units will go down. Once all the units have been used, the card does not get recharged—you must purchase another.

MOBILE PHONES

If you have a multiband phone (some countries use different frequencies than what's used in the United States) and your service provider uses the world-standard GSM network (as do T-Mobile, Cingular, and Verizon), you can probably use your phone abroad. Roaming fees can be steep, however: 99¢ a minute is considered reasonable. And overseas you normally pay the toll charges for incoming calls. It's almost always cheaper to send a text message than to make a call, since text messages have a very low set fee (often less than 5¢).

CUSTOMS OF THE COUNTRY

■ Greeks are friendly and openly affectionate. It is not uncommon, for example, to see women strolling arm in arm, or men kissing and hugging each other. Displays of anger are also quite common. You may see a man at a traffic light get out to verbally harangue an offending driver behind him, or a customer berating a civil servant and vice versa, but these encounters rarely become physical. To the person who doesn't understand Greek, the loud, intense conversations may all sound angry—but they're not.

■ But there's a negative side to Greeks' outgoing nature. Eager to engage in conversation over any topic, they won't shy away from launching into political discussions about foreign policy (best politely avoided) or asking personal questions like how much money you earn. The latter isn't considered rude in Greece, but don't feel like you need to respond. Visitors are sometimes taken aback by Greeks' gestures or the ease in which they touch the person they're speaking with—take it all in stride. If a pat on the hand becomes a bit too intimate, just shift politely and the other person will take a hint. On the other hand, kissing someone you've just met good-bye on the cheek is quite acceptable—even between men.

■ A woman who makes long eye contact with a man is interpreted as being interested in romance, but in most cases, Greeks openly stare at anything that interests them, so don't be offended if you are the center of attention wherever you go.

■ In some areas it still doesn't do to over-compliment a baby or a child, thought to provoke others' jealousy and thus bring on the evil eye. You will often see Greeks mock spitting, saying "ftou-ftou-ftou" to ward off harm, as an American might knock on wood after a threatening thought. (At baptisms, the godparent mock-spits three times to discourage Satan.)

■ Respect is shown toward elders; they are seldom addressed by their first name but called "Kiria" (Mrs./Ms.) and "Kirie" (Mr.) So-and-So. In country churches, and at all monasteries and nunneries, shorts are not allowed for either sex, and women may not wear pants. Usually, there is a stack of frumpy skirts that both men and women can don to cover their legs. In very strict places—the Patmos monastery, for example—women cannot reveal bare shoulders or too much cleavage. It's a good idea to carry large scarves for such occasions.

■ Jokes about Greek time abound—and with reason. Although relatively punctual when it comes to professional meetings, many have a more-relaxed attitude about keeping personal appointments, so don't be surprised if someone shows up 20 or 30 minutes late, especially if they know you're waiting at a café or bar or with company. When arranging to meet, pin Greeks down to a specific time, as you may find your definition of morning (before noon) may be quite different from theirs (anytime before 3 PM). If you're invited to someone's home, never turn up early—10 or 15 minutes after the agreed time is acceptable.

■ Globalization has forced Greeks to assimilate new business hours, in offices and shops, and one of the first casualties has been the midday siesta. But some habits are hard to break, and many simply shift their afternoon nap to late evening—especially on weekends, holidays, and during vacations. Still, unless you know someone is at work or doesn't nap, it's considered impolite to phone between 2 and 5 PM.

■ If you make such a mistake, however, it's unlikely Greeks will think you offensive. They're used to foreigners, don't expect you to know all the rules, and will probably chalk up the impropriety to *your* culture's strange dictates.

GREETINGS & GESTURES
■ When you meet someone for the first time, it is customary to shake hands, but with acquaintances the usual is a two-cheek kiss hello and good-bye. One thing that may disconcert foreigners is that when they run into a Greek with another person, he or she usually doesn't introduce the other party, even if there is a long verbal exchange. If you can't stand it anymore, just introduce yourself.

■ Greeks tend to stand closer to people than North Americans and northern Europeans, and they rely more on gestures when communicating. One gesture you should never use is the open palm, fingers slightly spread, shoved toward someone's face. The *moutza* is a serious insult. Another gesture you should remember, especially if trying to catch a taxi, is the Greek "no," which looks like "yes": a slight or exaggerated (depending on the sentiment) tipping back of the head, sometimes with the eyes closed and eyebrows raised. When you wave with your palm toward people, they may interpret it as "come here" instead of "good-bye"; and Greeks often wave good-bye with the palm facing them, which looks like "come here" to English speakers.

GETTING AROUND
■ Greeks can be quite impatient, and queues are nonexistent except in banks and supermarkets. People will push ahead to get on buses, catamarans, and planes—even though the latter have numbered seats.

OUT ON THE TOWN
■ Greeks often eat out of communal serving plates, so it's considered normal in informal settings to spear your tomato out of the salad bowl rather than securing an individual portion. Sometimes in tavernas you don't even get your own plate. Note that it is considered *tsigounia*, stinginess, to run separate tabs, especially because much of the meal is Chinese-style. Greeks either divide the bill equally among the party, no matter who ate

what, or one person magnanimously treats. A good host insists that you eat or drink more, and only when you have refused a number of times will you get a reprieve; be charmingly persistent in your "no." Greeks have a loose sense of time. They may be punctual if meeting you to go to a movie, but if they say they'll come round your hotel at 7 PM, they may show up at 8 PM.

LANGUAGE
■ Though it's a byword for incomprehensible ("It was all Greek to me," says Casca in Shakespeare's *Julius Caesar*), much of the difficulty of the Greek language lies in its different alphabet. Not all the 24 Greek letters have precise English equivalents, and there is usually more than one way to spell a Greek word in English. For instance, the letter delta sounds like the English letters "dh," and the sound of the letter gamma may be transliterated as a "g," "gh," or "y." Because of this the Greek for Holy Trinity might appear in English as Agia Triada, Aghia Triada, or Ayia Triada.

■ In most cities and tourist areas, all Greeks know at least one foreign language. It's best to use close-ended queries, however if you ask, "Where is Galissas?" a possible answer will be "Down a ways to the left and then you turn right by the baker's house, his child lives in Chicago, where did you say you went to school?"

■ If you only have 15 minutes to learn Greek, memorize the following: *yiá sou* (hello/good-bye, informal for one person); *yiá sas* (hello/good-bye, formal for one person and used for a group); *miláte angliká?* (do you speak English?); *den katalavéno* (I don't understand); *parakaló* (please/you're welcome); *signómi* (excuse me); *efharistó* (thank you); *ne* (yes); *óhee* (no); *pósso?* (how much?); *pou eéne ...?* (where is...?), *... ee twaléta?* (... the toilet?), *... to tahidromío?* (... the post office?), *... to stathmó?* (... the station?); *kali méra* (good morning), *kali spéra* (good evening); *kali níchta* (good night).

If you just want to make local calls, consider buying a new SIM card (note that your provider may have to unlock your phone for you to use a different SIM card) and a prepaid service plan in the destination. You'll then have a local number and can make local calls at local rates. If your trip is extensive, you could also simply buy a new cell phone in your destination, as the initial cost will be offset over time.

TIP→If you travel internationally frequently, save one of your old mobile phones or buy a cheap one on the Internet; ask your cell phone company to unlock it for you, and take it with you as a travel phone, buying a new SIM card with pay-as-you-go service in each destination.

If you take your cell phone with you, call your provider in advance and ask if it has a connection agreement with a Greek mobile carrier. If so, manually switch your phone to that network's settings as soon as you arrive. To do this, go to the Settings menu, then look for the Network settings and add.

If you're traveling with a companion or group of friends and plan to use your cell phones to communicate with each other, buying a local prepaid connection kit is far cheaper for voice calls or sending text messages than using your regular provider. The most popular local prepaid connection kits are Cosmote's What's Up, Vodafone's A La Carte and CU, or Wind's F2G or For All—these carriers all have branded stores, but you can also buy cell phones and cell phone packages from the Germanos and Plaisio chain stores as well as large supermarkets like Carrefour.

Contacts Cellular Abroad (☎800/287–5072 ⊕www.cellularabroad.com) rents and sells GMS phones and sells SIM cards that work in many countries. **Mobal** (☎888/888–9162 ⊕www.mobalrental.com) rents mobiles and sells GSM phones (starting at $49) that will operate in 140 countries. Per-call rates vary throughout the world. **Planet Fone**

(☎888/988–4777 ⊕www.planetfone.com) rents cell phones, but the per-minute rates are expensive.

▮ CUSTOMS & DUTIES

You're always allowed to bring goods of a certain value back home without having to pay any duty or import tax. But there's a limit on the amount of tobacco and liquor you can bring back duty-free, and some countries have separate limits for perfumes; for exact figures, check with your customs department. The values of so-called duty-free goods are included in these amounts. When you shop abroad, save all your receipts, as customs inspectors may ask to see them as well as the items you purchased. If the total value of your goods is more than the duty-free limit, you'll have to pay a tax (most often a flat percentage) on the value of everything beyond that limit.

You may bring into Greece duty-free: food and beverages up to 22 pounds (10 kilos); 200 cigarettes, 100 cigarillos, or 50 cigars; 1 liter of alcoholic spirits or 2 liters of wine; and gift articles up to a total of €175. For non-EU citizens, foreign banknotes amounting to more than $2,500 must be declared for re-export, but there are no restrictions on traveler's checks.

Only one per person of such expensive portable items as cameras, camcorders, computers, and the like is permitted into Greece. You should register these with Greek Customs upon arrival to avoid any problems when taking them out of the country again. Sports equipment, such as bicycles and skis, is also limited to one (or one pair) per person.

To bring in a dog or a cat, you need a health certificate issued by a veterinary authority and validated by the Greek Consulate and the appropriate medical authority (in the United States, the Department of Agriculture). It must state that your pet doesn't carry any infectious diseases and that it received a rabies inoculation not more than 12 months prior (for cats, six months) and no fewer than six days before arrival. Dogs must also have a veterinary certificate that indicates they have been wormed against echinococcus. For more information on Greek Customs, check with your local Greek Consulate or the Ministry of Foreign Affairs in Athens, which has more-detailed information on customs and import/export regulations.

Information in Greece Ministry of Foreign Affairs (⊠Akadimias 3, Stoa Davaki, Athens ☎210/368–2700 Athens ⊕www.mfa.gr).

U.S. Information U.S. Customs and Border Protection (⊕www.cbp.gov).

■ ELECTRICITY

The electrical current in Greece is 220 volts, 50 cycles AC. Wall outlets take Continental-type plugs with two round oversize prongs. If your appliances are dual-voltage, you'll need only an adapter; if not, you'll also need a step-down converter/transformer (United States and Canada).

Consider making a small investment in a universal adapter, which has several types of plugs in one lightweight, compact unit. Most laptops and mobile phone chargers are dual voltage (i.e., they operate equally well on 110 and 220 volts), so require only an adapter. These days the same is true of small appliances such as hair dryers. Always check labels and manufacturer instructions to be sure. Don't use 110-volt outlets marked FOR SHAVERS ONLY for high-wattage appliances such as hair dryers.

Contacts Steve Kropla's Help for World Travelers (⊕www.kropla.com) has information on electrical and telephone plugs around the world. **Walkabout Travel Gear** (⊕www.walkabouttravelgear.com) has a good coverage of electricity under "adapters."

■ EMERGENCIES

Regrettably, vacations are sometimes marred by emergencies, so it's good to know where you should turn for help. In Athens and other cities, hospitals treat emergencies on a rotating basis; an ambulance driver will know where to take you. Or, since waving down a taxi can be faster than waiting for an ambulance, ask a cab driver to take you to the closest "e-phee-me-*re*-von" (duty) hospital. Large islands and rural towns have small medical centers (*iatrikó kéntro*) that can treat minor illnesses or arrange for transport to another facility.

Medications are only sold at pharmacies, which are by law staffed by licensed pharmacists who can treat minor cuts, take blood pressure, and recommend cold medication. Pharmacies are marked with a green-and-white cross and there's one every few city blocks. Outside standard trading hours, there are duty pharmacies offering 24-hour coverage. These are posted in the window of every pharmacy. The *Athens News* and *Kathimerini* (the latter is inserted in the *International Herald Tribune*) have listings for pharmacies that are open late on a particular day. And if you speak Greek, you can call for a recorded message listing the off-hours pharmacies. In cases of emergencies, locals are fairly helpful and will come to your aid. The tourist police throughout Greece (numbers are given in each chapter) can provide general information and help in emergencies and can mediate in disputes.

Foreign Embassy United States (⊠Vasilissis Sofias 91, Mavili Sq., Athens ☎210/721–2951 through 210/721–2959 ⊕www.usembassy.gr).

General Emergency Contacts Coast Guard (☎108). **Duty hospitals and pharmacies** (☎1434). **Fire** (☎199). **Forest Service** (☎191 in case of fire). **National Ambulance Service (EKAV)** (☎166). **Off-hours pharmacies** (☎107 in Athens, 102 outside Athens). **Police** (☎100). **Road assistance**

(☎104–ELPA). **S.O.S. Doctors** (☎1016), a 24-hour private medical service. **Tourist police** (✉Dimitrakopoulou 77, Athens ☎171 in Athens, 210/171 from outside Athens).

▌HEALTH

Greece's strong summer sun and low humidity can lead to sunburn or sunstroke if you're not careful. A hat, long-sleeve shirt, and long pants or a sarong are advised for spending a day at the beach or visiting archaeological sites. Sunglasses, a hat, and sunblock are necessities, and be sure to drink plenty of water. Most beaches present few dangers, but keep a lookout for the occasional jellyfish and, on rocky coves, sea urchins. Should you step on one, don't break off the embedded spines, which may lead to infection, but instead remove them with heated olive oil and a needle. Food is seldom a problem, but the liberal amounts of olive oil used in Greek cooking may be indigestible for some. Tap water in Greece is fine, and bottled spring water is readily available. For minor ailments, go to a local pharmacy first, where the licensed staff can make recommendations for over-the-counter drugs. Most pharmacies are closed in the evenings and on weekends, but each posts the name of the nearest pharmacy open off-hours (⇨Emergencies, above). Most state hospitals and rural clinics won't charge you for tending to minor ailments, even if you're not an EU citizen; at most, you'll pay a minimal fee. Hotels will usually call a doctor for you, though in Athens, you can locate a doctor by calling S.O.S. Doctors (⇨Emergencies, above). For a dentist, check with your hotel, embassy, or the tourist police. Do not fly within 24 hours of scuba diving. In greener, wetter areas, mosquitoes may be a problem. In addition to wearing insect repellent, you can burn coils ("spee-rahl") to discourage them or buy plug-in devices that burn medicated tabs ("pah-steel-ya"). Hotels usually provide these. The only poison-ous snakes in Greece are the adder and the sand viper, which are brown or red, with dark zigzags. The adder has a V or X behind its head, and the sand viper sports a small horn on its nose. When hiking, wear high tops and don't put your feet or hands in crevices without looking first. If bitten, try to slow the spread of the venom until a doctor comes. Lie still with the affected limb lower than the rest of your body. Apply a tourniquet, releasing it every few minutes, and cut the wound a bit in case the venom can bleed out. Do NOT suck on the bite. Whereas snakes like to lie in the sun, the scorpion (rare) likes cool, wet places, in wood piles, and under stones. Apply Benadryl or Phenergan to minor stings, but if you have nausea or fever, see a doctor at once.

▌HOURS OF OPERATION

A new law passed in 2005 set uniform business hours (weekdays 9–9, Saturday 9–6) for retailers across Greece, although establishments in tourist resorts may remain open longer. For certain categories such as pharmacies, banks, and government offices, hours have always been standardized. Many small businesses and shops close for at least a week around mid-August, and most tourist establishments, including hotels, shut down on the islands and northern Greece from November until mid-spring. Restaurants, especially tavernas, often stay open on holidays; some close in summer or move to cooler locations. Christmas, New Year's, Orthodox Easter, and August 15 are the days everything shuts down, although, for example, bars work full force on Christmas Eve, since it's a very social occasion and not particularly family-oriented. Orthodox Easter changes dates every year, so check your calendar. On Orthodox Good Friday, shops open after church services, around 1 PM.

Banks are normally open Monday–Thursday 8–2, Friday 8–1:30, but select branches of Alpha and Eurobank are open until 8 PM weekdays and on Saturday mornings. Hotels also cash traveler's checks on weekends, and the banks at the Athens airport have longer hours.

Government offices are open weekdays from 8 to 2. For commercial offices, the hours depend on the business: large companies have adopted the 9–5 schedule, but some small businesses stick to the Mediterranean 8–2 workday.

The days and hours for public museums and archaeological sites are set by the Ministry of Culture; they are usually open Tuesday–Sunday 8:30 to 3, and as late as 7:30 in summer. (Summer hours are generally published on the ministry's Web site, www.culture.gr, in April or May.) Throughout the year arrive at least 30 minutes before closing time to ensure a ticket. Archaeological sites and museums close on January 1, March 25, the morning of Orthodox Good Friday, Orthodox Easter, May 1, and December 25–26. Sunday visiting hours apply to museums on Epiphany; Ash Monday, Good Saturday, Easter Monday, and Whitsunday (Orthodox dates, which change every year); August 15; and October 28. Museums close early (around 12:30) on January 2, the last Saturday of Carnival, Orthodox Good Thursday, Christmas Eve, and New Year's Eve. Throughout the guide, the hours of sights and attractions are denoted by the clock icon, ☉.

All gas stations are open daily 7–7 (some close Sunday), and some pump all night in the major cities and along the National Road and Attica Highway. They do not close for lunch.

Department stores, shops, and supermarkets may stay open until 9 PM on weekdays and 8 PM on Saturday, but some merchants are sticking to the old business hours and continue to close on Monday, Wednesday, and Saturday afternoons. There are no Sunday trading hours, except for the last Sunday of the year and in tourist areas like Plaka in Athens and island or mainland resorts.

Pharmacies are open Monday, Wednesday, and Friday from about 8:30 to 3 and Tuesday, Thursday, and Friday from 8:30 to 2 and 5 until 8 or 8:30 at night. The pharmacy at Athens International Airport operates 24 hours. According to a rotation system, there is always at least one pharmacy open in any area (⇨ *Emergencies, above*).

If it's late in the evening and you need an aspirin, a soft drink, cigarettes, a newspaper, or a pen, look for the nearest open kiosk, called a *periptero*; these kiosks on street corners everywhere brim with all kinds of necessities. Owners stagger their hours, and many towns have at least one kiosk that stays open late, occasionally through the night. Neighborhood mini-markets also stay open late.

HOLIDAYS

January 1 (New Year's Day); January 6 (Epiphany); Clean Monday (first day of Lent); March 25 (Feast of the Annunciation and Independence Day); Good Friday; Greek Easter Sunday; Greek Easter Monday; May 1 (Labor Day); Pentecost; August 15 (Assumption of the Holy Virgin); October 28 (Ochi Day); December 25–26 (Christmas Day and Boxing Day).

Only on Orthodox Easter and August 15 do you find that just about *everything* shuts down. It's harder getting a room at the last minute on Easter and August 15 (especially the latter), and traveling requires stamina, if you want to survive on the ferries and the highways. On the other hand, the local rituals and rites associated with these two celebrations are interesting and occasionally moving (like the Epitaphios procession on Good Friday).

▌ MAIL

Letters and postcards take about a week to 10 days to reach the United States. That's airmail. It takes even longer in August, when postal staff is reduced; and during Christmas and Easter holidays. If what you're mailing is important, send it registered, which costs about €2.65 in Greece. For about €2.60, depending on the weight, you can send your letter "express"; this earns you a red sticker and faster local delivery. The post office also operates a courier service, EMS Express. Delivery to the continental United States takes about two to three days and costs €26.40. If you're planning on writing several letters, prepaid envelopes are convenient and cost €4.25 for five.

Post offices are open weekdays 7:30–2, although in city centers they may stay open in the evenings and on weekends. The main post offices in Athens and Piraeus are open weekdays 7:30 AM–9 PM, Saturday 7:30–2, and Sunday 9–1:30. The post offices at Athens International Airport and the Acropolis are open weekends, too. Throughout the country, mailboxes are yellow and sometimes divided into domestic and international containers; express boxes are red.

At this writing, airmail letters and postcards to destinations other than Europe and weighing up to 20 grams cost €0.65, and €1.15 for 50 grams (€0.65 and €1, respectively, to other European countries, including the United Kingdom).

Contact American Express (⊠Ermou 7, 10563Athens ☎210/322–3380 ⊕www.americanexpress.com).

▌ MEALS & MEALTIMES

Greeks don't really eat breakfast and with the exception of hotel dining rooms, few places serve that meal. You can pick up a cheese pie and rolls at a bakery or a sesame-coated bread ring called a *koulouri* sold by city vendors; order a *tost*

("toast"), a sort of dry grilled sandwich, usually with cheese or paper-thin ham slices, at a café; or dig into a plate of yogurt with honey. Local bakeries may offer fresh doughnuts in the morning. On islands in summer, cafés serve breakfast, from Continental to combinations that might include Spanish omelets and French coffee. Caffeine junkies can get a cup of coffee practically anywhere, but decaf is available only in bigger hotels.

Greeks eat their main meal at either lunch or dinner, so the offerings are the same. For lunch, heavyweight meat-and-potato dishes can be had, but you might prefer a real Greek salad (no lettuce, a slice of feta with a pinch of oregano, and ripe tomatoes) or souvlaki or grilled chicken from a taverna. For a light bite you can also try one of the popular Greek chain eateries such as Everest or Grigori's, found fairly easily throughout the country, for grilled sandwiches or spanakopita and *tiropita* (cheese pie); or Goody's, the local equivalent of McDonald's, where you'll find good-quality burgers.

Coffee and pastries are eaten in the afternoon, usually at a café or *zaharoplastio* (pastry shop). The hour or so before restaurants open for dinner—around 7—is a pleasant time to have an ouzo or glass of wine and try Greek hors d'oeuvres, called *mezedes,* in a bar, ouzeri, or *mezedopoleio* (Greek tapas place). Dinner is often the main meal of the day, and there's plenty of food. Starters include dips such as *taramosalata* (made from fish roe), *melitzanosalata* (made from smoked eggplant, lemon, oil, and garlic), and the well-known yogurt, cucumber, and garlic *tzatziki*. A typical dinner for a couple might be two to three appetizers, an entrée, a salad, and wine. Diners can order as little or as much as they like, except at very expensive establishments. If a Greek eats dessert at all, it will be fruit or a modest wedge of a syrup-drenched cake like *revani* or semolina halvah, often shared between two or three diners. Only in fancier restaurants can diners order a tiramisu with an espresso. One option for those who want a lighter meal is the mezedopoleio.

In most places, the menu is broken down into appetizers (*orektika*) and entrées (*kiria piata*), with additional headings for salads (this includes dips like tzatziki) and vegetable side plates. However, this doesn't mean there is any sense of a first or second "course," as in France. Often the food arrives all at the same time, or as it becomes ready.

Breakfast is available until 10 at hotels and until early afternoon in beach cafés. Lunch is between 1:30 and 3:30 (and on weekends as late as 5), and dinner is served from about 8:30 to midnight, later in the big cities and resort islands. Most Greeks dine very late, around 10 or 11 PM. Unless otherwise noted, the restaurants listed in this guide are open daily for lunch and dinner.

▌ MONEY

Although costs have risen astronomically since Greece switched to the euro currency in 2002, the country will seem reasonably priced to travelers from the United States and Great Britain. Popular tourist resorts (including some of the islands) and the larger cities are markedly more expensive than the countryside. Though the price of eating in a restaurant has increased, you can still get a bargain. Hotels are generally moderately priced outside the major cities, and the extra cost of accommodations in a luxury hotel, compared to in an average hotel, often seems unwarranted.

Other typical costs: authentic Greek sponge: €8; soft drink: (can) €1.50, in a café €2; spinach pie: €1.50; souvlaki: €1.90; local bus: €0.50; foreign newspaper: €2.50–€3.90.

Prices throughout this guide are given for adults. Substantially reduced fees are

almost always available for children, students, and senior citizens.

ITEM	AVERAGE COST
Cup of Coffee	€2.60–€5 (in a central-city café; Greek coffee is a bit cheaper)
Glass of Wine	€3–€8
Glass of Beer	€2.80; €2.60–€6.50 in a bar
Sandwich	€2.60
1-mile Taxi Ride in Capital City	€2.50
Archaeological Site Admission	€3–€6; free on Sunday from November to March

▌**TIP→** Banks never have every foreign currency on hand, and it may take as long as a week to order. If you're planning to exchange funds before leaving home, don't wait 'til the last minute.

ATMS & BANKS
Your own bank will probably charge a fee for using ATMs abroad; the foreign bank you use may also charge a fee. Nevertheless, you'll usually get a better rate of exchange at an ATM than you will at a currency-exchange office or even when changing money in a bank. And extracting funds as you need them is a safer option than carrying around a large amount of cash.

▌**TIP→** PIN numbers with more than four digits are not recognized at ATMs in many countries. If yours has five or more, remember to change it before you leave.

ATMs are widely available throughout the country. Virtually all banks, including the National Bank of Greece (known as Ethniki), have machines that dispense money to Cirrus or Plus cardholders. You may find bank-sponsored ATMs at harbors and in airports as well. Other systems accepted include Visa, MasterCard, American Express, Diners Club, and Eurocard, but exchange and withdrawal rates vary, so shop around and check fees with your bank before leaving home. For use in Greece, your PIN must be four digits long. The word for PIN is pronounced "peen," and ATMs are called *alpha taf mi,* after the letters, or just *to mihanima,* "the machine." Machines usually let you complete the transaction in English, French, or German and seldom create problems, except Sunday night, when they sometimes run out of cash. For most machines, the minimum amount dispensed is €40. Sometimes an ATM may refuse to "read" your card. Don't panic; it's probably the machine. Try another bank.

■TIP➔ At some ATMs in Greece you may not have a choice of drawing from a specific account. If you have linked savings and checking accounts, make sure there's money in both before you depart.

CREDIT CARDS

Throughout this guide, the following abbreviations are used: **AE,** American Express; **D,** Discover; **DC,** Diners Club; **MC,** MasterCard; and **V,** Visa.

It's a good idea to inform your credit-card company before you travel, especially if you're going abroad and don't travel internationally very often. Otherwise, the credit-card company might put a hold on your card owing to unusual activity—not a good thing halfway through your trip. Record all your credit-card numbers—as well as the phone numbers to call if your cards are lost or stolen—in a safe place, so you're prepared should something go wrong. Both MasterCard and Visa have general numbers you can call (collect if you're abroad) if your card is lost, but you're better off calling the number of your issuing bank, since MasterCard and Visa usually just transfer you to your bank; your bank's number is usually printed on your card.

If you plan to use your credit card for cash advances, you'll need to apply for a PIN at least two weeks before your trip. Although it's usually cheaper (and safer) to use a credit card abroad for large purchases (so you can cancel payments or be reimbursed if there's a problem), note that some credit-card companies *and* the banks that issue them add substantial percentages to all foreign transactions, whether they're in a foreign currency or not. Check on these fees before leaving home, so there won't be any surprises when you get the bill.

■TIP➔ Before you charge something, ask the merchant whether or not he or she plans to do a dynamic currency conversion (DCC). In such a transaction the credit-card *processor* (shop, restaurant, or hotel, not Visa or MasterCard) converts the currency and charges you in dollars. In most cases you'll pay the merchant a 3% fee for this service in addition to any credit-card company and issuing-bank foreign-transaction surcharges.

Dynamic currency conversion programs are becoming increasingly widespread. Merchants who participate in them are supposed to ask whether you want to be charged in dollars or the local currency, but they don't always do so. And even if they do offer you a choice, they may well avoid mentioning the additional surcharges. The good news is that you *do* have a choice. And if this practice really gets your goat, you can avoid it entirely thanks to American Express; with its cards, DCC simply isn't an option.

Should you use a credit card or a debit card when traveling? Both have benefits. A credit card allows you to delay payment and gives you certain rights as a consumer. A debit card, also known as a check card, deducts funds directly from your checking account and helps you stay within your budget. When you want to rent a car, though, you may still need an old-fashioned credit card.

Both types of plastic get you cash advances at ATMs worldwide if your card is properly programmed with your personal identification number (PIN). Both offer excellent, wholesale exchange rates. And both protect you against unauthorized use if the card is lost or stolen. Your liability is limited to $50, as long as you report the card missing. However, shop owners often give you a lower price if you pay with cash rather than credit, because they want to avoid the credit-card bank fees. Note that the Discover card is not widely accepted in Greece. The local Citibank, which issues Diners Club and MasterCard, can't cancel your cards but will pass on the message to the head offices of those cards.

Reporting Lost Cards American Express (☎800/528–4800 in the U.S., 336/393–1111 collect from abroad ⊕www.americanexpress.com). **Diners Club** (☎800/234–6377 in the U.S., 303/799–1504 collect from abroad ⊕www.dinersclub.com). **Discover** (☎800/347–2683 in the U.S., 801/902–3100 collect from abroad ⊕www.discovercard.com). **MasterCard** (☎800/627–8372 in the U.S., 636/722–7111 collect from abroad ⊕www.mastercard.com). **Visa** (☎800/847–2911 in the U.S., 410/581–9994 collect from abroad ⊕www.visa.com).

CURRENCY & EXCHANGE
Greece's former national currency, the drachma, was replaced by the currency of the European Union, the euro (€), in 2002. Under the euro system, there are eight coins: 1 and 2 euros, plus 1, 2, 5, 10, 20, and 50 euro cents. Euros are pronounced "evros" in Greek; cents are known as "lepta." All coins have the euro value on one side; the other side has each country's unique national symbol. Greece's range from images of triremes to a depiction of the mythological Europa being abducted by Zeus transformed as a bull. Bills (banknotes) come in seven denominations: 5, 10, 20, 50, 100, 200, and 500 euros. Bills are the same for all EU countries.

Off Syntagma Square in Athens, the National Bank of Greece, Citibank, Alpha Bank, Commercial Bank, Eurobank, and Pireos Bank have automated machines that change your foreign currency into euros. When you shop, remember that it's always easier to bargain on prices when paying in cash instead of by credit card.

If you do use an exchange service, good options are American Express and Eurochange. Watch daily fluctuations and shop around. Daily exchange rates are prominently displayed in banks and listed in the *International Herald Tribune*. In Athens, around Syntagma Square is the best place to look. Those that operate after business hours have lower rates and a higher commission. You can also change money at post offices in even the most remote parts of Greece; commissions are lower than at banks, starting at about €2 for amounts up to €300. To avoid lines at airport exchange booths, get a bit of local currency before you leave home. At this writing the average exchange rate for the euro was €1.47 to the U.S. dollar, €1.47 to the Canadian dollar, €0.71 to the pound sterling, €1.67 to the Australian dollar, and €1.71 to the New Zealand dollar.

■TIP➔ Even if a currency-exchange booth has a sign promising no commission, rest assured that there's some kind of huge, hidden fee. (Oh … that's right. The sign didn't say no *fee*.) And as for rates, you're almost always better off getting foreign currency at an ATM or exchanging money at a bank.

Athens Exchange Services American Express Travel Related Services (✉Ermou 7, Syntagma Sq. ☎210/322–3380 ⊙Weekdays 8:30–4, Sat. 8:30–1:30). **Eurochange** (✉Karageorgi Servias 2, Syntagma Sq. ☎210/331–2462 ⊙Daily 8 AM–11 PM ✉Omonias 10, Omonia Sq. ☎210/523–4816 ⊙Daily 8 AM–10 PM). **National Bank of Greece** (✉Karageorgi Servias 2, Syntagma Sq. ☎210/334–8015 ⊙Mon.–Thurs. 8–2 and 3:15–5:15, Fri. 2:45–5:15, Sat. 9–3, Sun. 9–1); extended foreign exchange.

TRAVELER'S CHECKS
Some consider this the currency of the caveman, and it's true that fewer establishments accept traveler's checks these days. Nevertheless, they're a cheap and

secure way to carry extra money, particularly on trips to urban areas. Both Citibank (under the Visa brand) and American Express issue traveler's checks in the United States, but Amex is better known and more widely accepted; you can also avoid hefty surcharges by cashing Amex checks at Amex offices. Whatever you do, keep track of all the serial numbers in case the checks are lost or stolen.

Traveler's checks are a good way to carry your money into Greece, keeping your funds safe until you change them into euros. But it's important to remember that Greece is still a cash society, so plan accordingly. If you're going to rural areas and small towns, go with cash; traveler's checks are best used in cities, though even in Athens most tavernas won't take them. Lost or stolen checks can usually be replaced within 24 hours. To ensure a speedy refund, buy your own traveler's checks—don't let someone else pay for them: irregularities like this can cause delays. The person who bought the checks should make the call to request a refund.

Contact American Express (☎888/412–6945 in the U.S., 801/945–9450 collect outside the U.S. to add value or speak to customer service ⊕www.americanexpress.com).

▌ TAXES

Taxes are always included in the stated price, unless otherwise noted. The Greek airport tax (€12 for travel within the EU and €22 outside the EU) is included in your ticket (as are a further €12.15 terminal facility charge and a €5 security charge), and the 8%–12% hotel tax rate is usually included in the quoted price.

Value-added tax, 4.5% for books and about 19% (6%–13% on the Aegean islands) for almost everything else, called FPA (pronounced "fee-pee-ah") by Greeks, is included in the cost of most consumer goods and services, except groceries. If you are a citizen of a non-EU country, you may get a V.A.T. refund on products (except alcohol, cigarettes, or toiletries) worth €117 or more bought in Greece from licensed stores that usually display a Tax-Free Shopping sticker in their window. Ask the shop to complete a refund form called a Tax-Free Check for you, which you show at Greek Customs.

Have the form stamped like any customs form by customs officials when you leave the country or, if you're visiting several European Union countries, when you leave the EU. Be ready to show customs officials what you've bought (pack purchases together, in your carry-on luggage); budget extra time for this. After you're through passport control, take the form to a refund-service counter for an on-the-spot refund, or mail it back in the pre-addressed envelope given to you at the store. You receive the total refund stated on the form, but the processing time can be long, especially if you request a credit-card adjustment.

A refund service can save you some hassle, for a fee. Global Refund is a Europe-wide service with 225,000 affiliated stores and more than 700 refund counters at major airports and border crossings. The service issues refunds in the form of cash, check, or credit-card adjustment, minus a processing fee. If you don't have time to wait at the refund counter, you can mail in the form instead.

V.A.T. Refunds Global Refund (☎800/566–9828 ⊕www.globalrefund.com).

▌TIME

Greek time is Greenwich Mean Time (GMT) plus 2 hours. To estimate the time back home, subtract 7 hours from the local time for New York and Washington, 8 hours for Chicago, 9 for Denver, and 10 for Los Angeles. Londoners subtract 2 hours. Those living in Sydney or Melbourne, add 8 hours. Greek Daylight Saving Time starts on the last Sunday in March and ends the last Sunday in October. Stay alert—newspapers barely publicize the change.

▌TIPPING

How much to tip in Greece, especially at restaurants, is confusing.

On cruises, cabin and dining-room stewards get about €2 a day; guides receive about the same.

TIPPING GUIDELINES FOR GREECE	
Bartender	10% minimum
Bellhop	€1 per bag
Hotel Concierge	€3–€10, if he or she performs a service for you
Hotel Doorman	€1–€2 if he helps you get a cab
Hotel Maid	€1 per night
Hotel Room-Service Waiter	€1 per delivery, even if a service charge has been added
Porter at Airport or Train Station	€1 per bag
Skycap at Airport	€1–€3 per bag checked
Taxi Driver	Round up the fare to the nearest €0.50 or €1; during holidays, drivers legally receive a mandatory "gift"; the amount is posted in the cab during applicable days.
Tour Guide	15%–20%
Waiter	By law a 13% service charge is figured into the price of a meal. However, it is customary to leave an 8%–10% tip if the service was satisfactory. During the Christmas and Greek Easter holiday periods, restaurants tack on an obligatory 18% holiday bonus to your bill for the waiters.
Others	For rest room attendants €0.50 is appropriate. People dispensing programs at cinemas get €0.40.

INDEX

PHOTO CREDITS

fotostock. 80 (bottom left and 80 bottom right), *Visual Arts Library (London)/Alamy.* 81 (top left), *Mary Evans Picture Library/Alamy.* 81 (top right), *Picture History/Newscom.* 81 (bottom), *Popperfoto/Alamy.* 84, *Juha-Pekka Kervinen/Shutterstock.* 86, *Miguel Ángel Muñoz/age fotostock.* 105, *Warner Bros/Everett Collection.* 106 (top right), *Walter Bibikow/age fotostock.* 106 (bottom right), *Eliott Slater/age fotostock.* 107 (left), *Terence Waeland/Alamy.* 107 (top right), *Giulio Andreini/age fotostock.* 107 (bottom right), *Image Asset Management/age fotostock.* 108 (top left), *ACE Stock Limited/Alamy.* 108 (right), *Rene Mattes/age fotostock.* 109 (top left), *Warner Bros/Everett Collection.* 109 (center), *Peter Horree/Alamy.* 109 (bottom), *Keith Binns/iStockphoto.* 109 (right), *Peter Horree/Alamy.* 110 (top left), *Image Asset Management/age fotostock.* 110 (right), *T. Papageorgiou/age fotostock.* 111 (top left), *Aliki Sapountzi/Aliki Image Library/Alamy.* 111 (bottom left), *Terry Harris/Just Greece Photo Library/Alamy.* 122 (top), *LOOK Die Bildagentur der Fotografen GmbH/Alamy.* 122 (bottom), *Franco Pizzochero/age fotostock.* 123 (top), *Alvaro Leiva/age fotostock.* 123 (bottom), *Ingolf Pompe/Aurora Photos.* 124 (top), *foodfolio/Alamy.* 124 (2nd from top), *Liv Friis-Larsen/Shutterstock.* 124 (center), *imagebroker/Alamy.* 124 (4th from top), *SIME s.a.s/eStock Photo.* 124 (bottom), *IML Image Group Ltd/Alamy.* 125 (left), *Roberto Meazza/IML Image Group/Aurora Photos.* 125 (top right), *Christopher Leggett/age fotostock.* 125 (center right), *IML Image Group Ltd/Alamy.* 125 (bottom right), *Ingolf Pompe/Aurora Photos.* **Chapter 4: The Saronic Gulf Islands:** 167, *Stefano Lunardi/age fotostock.* 168, *Terry Harris/Just Greece Photo Library/Alamy.* 169 (top), *IML Image Group Ltd/Alamy.* 169 (bottom), *Robert Morris/Alamy.* **Chapter 5: The Sporades:** 193, *SIME s.a.s/eStock Photo.* 194, *Johanna Huber/SIME/eStock Photo.* 195 (top), *Roger Cracknell 10/Pagan Festivals/Alamy.* 195 (bottom), *Terry Harris/Just Greece Photo Library/Alamy.* **Chapter 6: Corfu:** 227—28, *PCL/Alamy.* 229 (top and bottom), *Ljupco/Smokovski/Shutterstock.* **Chapter 7: The Cyclades:** 255, *Stefano Brozzi/age fotostock.* 256, *Hemis/Alamy.* 257, *Sylvain Grandadam/age fotostock.* 286, *Anthro/Shutterstock.* 290 (left), *Buena Vista Pictures/Everett Collection.* 290 (center), *Interfoto Pressebildagentur/Alamy.* 291, *Ian Fraser/Alamy.* 316—17, *G.V.P./age fotostock.* 318, *Wolfgang Amri/Shutterstock.* 319 (top), *The Print Collector/Alamy.* 319 (bottom), *Wojtek Buss/age fotostock.* **Chapter 8: Crete:** 359, *Alvaro Leiva/age fotostock.* 360 (top), *image broker/Alamy.* 360 (bottom), *Irina Korshunova/Shutterstock.* 361 (top), *Paul Cowan/Shutterstock.* 361 (bottom), *LOOK Die Bildagentur der Fotografen GmbH/Alamy.* **Chapter 9: Rhodes & the Dodecanese:** 397, *Giovanni Simeone/SIME/eStock Photo.* 398 (top), *Alvaro Leiva/age fotostock.* 398 (bottom), *Werner Otto/age fotostock.* 399 (top), *Franck Guiziou/hemis.fr/Aurora Photos.* 399 (bottom), *FAN travelstock/Alamy.* 407 (top), *SuperStock.* 407 (bottom), *Walter Bibikow/SuperStock.* 409 (bottles), *blickwinkel/Alamy.* 409 (inset), *San Rostro/SuperStock.* **Chapter 10: The Northern Aegean Islands:** 437, *Walter Bibikow/age fotostock.* 438 (top), *Fausto Giaccone/Marka/age fotostock.* 438 (bottom), *Greek National Tourist Organization.* 439, *Steve Bentley/Alamy.*

ABOUT OUR WRITERS

Alexia Amvrazi spent most of her childhood away from her native Greece but returned there to pursue a full-time career in journalism after her studies in the UK. She has been working in the English-language newspaper, magazine, Internet, and TV media for 11 years and for the past three has worked at the City of Athens multilingual radio station (where she hosts her own show). For this edition, she helped update our chapters on the Sporades and the Northern Aegean Islands.

Stephen Brewer is a New York–based writer and editor who travels to Crete and other European shores for various national magazines and guidebooks. While he also writes about such northern locales as Ireland, England, and Venice, he especially cherishes his experiences climbing hairpin bends on the roads between Knossos and Phaestos. For this edition, he updated the Crete chapter and wrote our new Experience Greece chapter and photo features on Greek design and history.

Jeffrey and Elizabeth Carson, native New Yorkers, have lived on Paros since 1970; they teach at the Aegean Center for the Fine Arts. Jeffrey, a poet, translator, and critic, has published many articles and books. Elizabeth is a photographer who has had numerous solo exhibitions, and has been published widely, including the book *The Church of 100 Doors*. For this edition, they updated and wrote new texts for the Cyclades chapter and its photo features on mythology and Atlantis.

Linda Coffman, Fodor's resident Cruise Diva and author of this edition's "Cruising the Greek Islands" chapter, is a freelance travel writer whose articles have ~~appeared~~ in *Consumers' Digest,* the *Chicago Times,* and *USA Today.* An avid ~~cruiser~~ the author of two recent ~~books~~: *The Complete Guide* ~~to Cruises~~ and *The Complete* ~~Guide to~~ *Cruises.*

Angelike Contis was raised in Vermont, but took her first baby steps while visiting her grandparents in Arcadia. She has lived in Greece for a decade, writing for publications including the *Athens News* and directing independent documentaries. She is currently writing a book on today's Greek cinema. For this edition, she updated our chapters on the Saronic Gulf Islands (along with Natasha Giannousi) and Rhodes and the Dodecanese.

Joanna Kakissis was born in Athens but, raised in the prairies of the American Midwest, spent her childhood craving mountains, beaches, and loud people who gesticulate wildly while talking. A freelance writer and journalist, she relocated to Greece in 2004 and now revels in hiking, swimming and flailing her arms around during even the most mundane conversations. For this edition, she updated our Athens chapter and wrote the photo features on the Acropolis, Greek food, and the wines of Greece.

Diane Shugart was lured back to her mother's homeland more than a decade ago by the laid-back lifestyle and the stark, yet stunning, landscape. A journalist and translator, she makes her home in Athens—a city's whose cultural and history she has explored in the book *Athens by Neighborhood*. Diane updated our Greece Essentials and Corfu chapters for this edition.

Adrian Vrettos first traveled to Greece from London over a decade ago to work as a field archaeologist on prehistoric and classical excavations. All he managed to uncover, however, was the ancient inscription, "The laptop is mightier than the trowel" (loosely translated from Linear B). Thus he set to work decoding modern Greek life instead, and is now a freelance journalist and editor based in Athens. Adrian updated our Sporades and Northern Aegean Islands chapter for this edition.